P9-AGF-363

THE
DEATH
OF
INNOCENTS

THE
DEATH
OF
INNOCENTS

RICHARD FIRSTMAN
AND JAMIE TALAN

BANTAM BOOKS

NEW YORK TORONTO LONDON SYDNEY AUCKLAND

364.1523
F527d

THE DEATH OF INNOCENTS
A Bantam Book/October 1997

All rights reserved.
Copyright © 1997 by Richard Firstman and Jamie Talan.
Book design by Kathryn Parise.

The authors and publisher gratefully acknowledge permission for use of
the following material: Excerpts from *Pediatrics,* Volume 50, © 1972, and
Volume 52, © 1973, reproduced by permission of *Pediatrics.*
No part of this book may be reproduced or transmitted in any form or by any means, electronic or
mechanical, including photocopying, recording, or by any information storage and retrieval system,
without permission in writing from the publisher. For information address: Bantam Books.

LIBRARY OF CONGRESS CATALOGING-IN-PUBLICATION DATA:
Firstman, Richard.
The death of innocents / Richard Firstman and Jamie Talan.
p.   cm.
Published simultaneously in the United States and Canada.
Includes bibliographical references (p. 614) and index.
ISBN-0-553-10013-0
1. Filicide—United States—Case studies.   2. Van Der Sluys, Stephen.   3. Hoyt, Waneta, 1946–
4. Munchausen syndrome by proxy—United States—Case studies.   5. Sudden infant death syndrome.
6. Murder—United States—Investigation—Case studies.
I. Talan, Jamie.   II. Title.
HV6542.F57   1997
364.15'23'09747—dc21   97-3209
CIP

Published simultaneously in the United States and Canada

Bantam Books are published by Bantam Books, a division of Bantam Doubleday Dell Publishing Group,
Inc. Its trademark, consisting of the words "Bantam Books" and the portrayal of a rooster, is Registered in
U.S. Patent and Trademark Office and in other countries. Marca Registrada. Bantam Books, 1540
Broadway, New York, New York 10036.

Printed in the United States of America
BVG   10   9   8   7   6   5   4   3   2   1

9/98

A simple child,
That lightly draws its breath,
And feels its life in every limb,
What should it know of death?
—WILLIAM WORDSWORTH

In medicine one must pay attention not to plausible theorizing, but to experience and reason together.
—HIPPOCRATES, *PRECEPTS*

Contents

PART ONE

Burial Grounds

Discovery consists of seeing what
everybody has seen and
thinking what nobody has thought.
—ALBERT SZENT-GYÖRGYI

1

Years later, it seemed a perverse irony that the unearthing had begun with the conception of a baby.

It was on a spring day in 1994 that the saga and the first hints of its ramifications emerged from the burial ground of distant memory, but it could be said that the entire intricate affair had begun to percolate at one particular moment nearly a decade before: late on the afternoon of April 4, 1985, when Stephen Van Der Sluys came home to find two men in coats and ties talking to his wife at the front door.

In the upstate New York community of Canandaigua, deep in the Finger Lakes region between Rochester and Syracuse, Van Der Sluys lived with his wife and children, trying to outrun the darkness of his well-hidden past. The men at the door were not here about the past, however, but about a recent and much more easily grasped situation. This was a simple case of sexual impropriety, and the visit by a pair of New York State Police investigators came as no surprise to Van Der Sluys. He had set things in motion himself by walking over to the teenage girl's house and confessing his indiscretions to her father.

"Guess you're looking for me," Van Der Sluys called out as he walked up from the driveway. The investigators turned to see a small man, no more than five-five, five-six, who struck them as bearing a resemblance to—what was that actor's name? Robin Williams, that was it. They nodded their hellos and identified themselves for the record; Van Der Sluys asked how they were doing. One of the detectives, Bob Beswick, a mild man who had been out of uniform only a few months after twenty-two years of chasing speeders on the Thruway, found Van Der Sluys's casual good humor disarming. Long afterward, Beswick would remember glancing at Van Der Sluys's open-faced

3

wife, Jane, hearing the drone of the television occupying the couple's two small children inside, and wondering what it was about a guy like this. He would smile uncomfortably at the memory of how little he really knew about Van Der Sluys that day.

"Would you mind coming down for a talk?" Beswick asked. Sure, Van Der Sluys said, he'd talk to them. He told Jane he'd see her later. The investigators led the way to their standard-issue Chevrolet and showed Van Der Sluys to the rear seat. Beswick was set to back out the driveway for the fifteen-minute trip to troop headquarters when Van Der Sluys stopped him. "Why don't we just talk right here?" he suggested.

"All right, Steve," Beswick said, putting the car in park and switching off the ignition. "We can talk here." He turned to face Van Der Sluys. "You know why we're here."

"Uh-huh," Van Der Sluys said.

"Have you had sex with that girl?" Beswick asked.

"Yes."

"Did you get her pregnant?"

"Yeah, I did."

And then Van Der Sluys, with scant urging, told the detectives where and when and how many times and in what fashion, a tidy chronicle of statutory rape that they were later amazed to find matched up almost perfectly with the diary his sixteen-year-old mistress had been keeping. Having unburdened himself in the driveway, Van Der Sluys sat back for the brief ride to the booking room at the county jail. From the doorway, Jane Van Der Sluys watched somberly as the car pulled away. She was pregnant with their sixth child.

Bill Fitzpatrick, the chief assistant district attorney of Onondaga County, was swimming in work that spring. There were so many murders splashing across the Syracuse papers, sensational trials leading the local TV news, that the prosecutor might have thought he was back home in Brooklyn. Fitzpatrick had tried seven murder cases in 1984, his first full year as Dick Hennessy's top homicide man, and more were on the way. There were also the internal politics of the D.A.'s office to be aware of, and occasionally to worry about. With Hennessy, you had to watch your back, even if you were one of the golden boys—probably more so. And from the day he had walked into the office right out of Syracuse Law in the spring of 1976, Bill Fitzpatrick was definitely one of the golden boys.

So Fitzpatrick had a few things on his mind during those months in 1985. But when word came from Syracuse police headquarters a block away that

Stephen Van Der Sluys had turned up in a little town near Rochester, three counties and an hour's drive west, and was sitting in jail for getting a teenager pregnant, Fitzpatrick was instantly intrigued by the possibilities. A New York City police detective's son, he was at heart a gumshoe in a lawyer's suit, a prosecutor who sometimes found it difficult to let the sergeants do their jobs. This could have been trouble if not for the engaging way he got cops to think of him as one of them. He wanted solid police work, but he'd take half a case, a less-than-sure thing, if he believed in it. An old case, especially. Bring him the abandoned files in their dusty cardboard boxes. Cases without conclusion, cases that knocked around, unsolved, unavenged—these were Bill Fitzpatrick's kinds of cases.

Van Der Sluys, Stephen. It had been eight years since Syracuse police detective Frank Budzielek had opened a file on a hunch after a visit to the morgue one day. Budzielek had stayed with it, but had never managed to advance much beyond circumstantial suspicion. A year ago, closing in on retirement, he'd said what the hell, I'm out the door anyway, and finally persuaded his captain to let him bring what he had to Fitzpatrick, who loved it, wanted to run with it, only to have Hennessy shoot it down: *You guys have nothing; come back when you have something.* Now Budzielek was gone, a smart young detective named John Brennan was digging into the cardboard box he'd left behind, and Van Der Sluys was available for questioning. Maybe this was the spark Fitzpatrick had been waiting for.

For Syracuse detectives working in the Criminal Investigations Division in the 1970s, morgue detail meant stopping by the city medical examiner's office every so often to match up police reports in unusual death cases with the M.E.'s autopsy findings. Though the stated purpose was to make sure suspicious deaths didn't slip by without investigation, morgue detail rarely turned out to be anything more than routine administration: Pick up the incident reports at headquarters, look up the autopsy results, write the cause of death on the incident report, sign it, file it, move on.

Frank Budzielek was the rare investigator who regarded the assignment as something better than a chore. As far as he was concerned, there was no telling what you might find down there. An earnest man whose right arm featured a tattoo of a sailor beneath letters spelling FRANK, Budzielek had grown up in Syracuse, one of eleven children of Polish immigrants who had settled on the city's east side. He had put in four years in the navy and ten at Western Electric before taking a pay cut to join the police department in 1964. Moving up to Criminal Investigations a few years later, he turned out to be a conscientious street detective with uncommonly good instincts for the work.

Suspicious by nature, he possessed a gift for sensing when things were askew. He liked to tell people how he caught a liquor store gunman in his first ten minutes as a detective—he was "just lucky when it comes to shit like that." He once recognized a name on a routine burglary report and turned it into a year's work in a corner of the D.A.'s office. A dozen indictments for insurance fraud and conspiracy were the payoff.

Budzielek's fondness for morgue detail eventually earned him the sobriquet Doctor Death. Sometimes, he'd watch an autopsy being performed, "so if there's anything unusual," he'd explain to less intrepid detectives, "they can tell me right there and I don't have to wait for the report." It had been this way from the beginning. In fact, he could trace his affinity for the morgue to the day he first realized that hints of crime were sometimes hidden in the medical examiner's green file cabinets. It happened soon after his assignment to the morgue in the winter of 1977.

To get a feel for his new work, Budzielek had decided he ought to go through the previous months' reports, even the closed cases. If nothing else, he figured, he'd learn how to do the paperwork. Flipping through the files, he came upon the recent case of a three-month-old baby girl who had died suddenly in her crib one January night at the dinner hour. ". . . Brought outside by the parents . . . mouth-to-mouth administered . . . no avail . . . Eastern Ambulance . . . Community Hospital . . . pronounced dead 1845 hours. . . . Parents transported in Car 60 . . . notified by Dr. Kulfas about the death of their daughter." Turning the page, Budzielek saw a brief report by his predecessor on morgue detail. "Learned from Medical Examiner's Office that victim's death was attributed to SUDDEN INFANT DEATH SYNDROME," the detective had written a couple of weeks after the baby died. "Death Certificate signed by Dr. Martin Hilfinger. Natural, Case Cleared and Closed."

Sad, a little baby like that, Budzielek said to Victor Fisher, a morgue assistant tending to his own paperwork nearby.

It happens, said Fisher, not looking up. He'd worked at the morgue since 1959, and there was little he hadn't seen. For nearly twenty years it had been his job to drive to death scenes, pick up the bodies, prepare them for autopsy, strip them, weigh them, take the photos. It was a line of work he had become interested in after attending a cousin's funeral. Now he was more or less in charge of the day-to-day operations, and there wasn't much in the morgue that moved without his knowing about it.

"What's the name on that?" Fisher asked for no apparent reason.

Budzielek peered at the report, a cigar between his teeth. "Van Der Sluys. Heather Van Der Sluys. Three seventy-six Bryant Avenue."

Fisher looked up from his work.

"That's strange," he said. "There was another baby in here just a few months ago, same last name. Not really a baby, a little older. Must have been back sometime in the fall."

"Is that right?" Budzielek replied.

Back at police headquarters, he tracked down a report describing the death of Heath Van Der Sluys, a sixteen-month-old boy who had died, just as Fisher had recalled, in October. Different address. Same parents. The boy's father had told the police that he'd found the child unconscious, had shaken him, that a quarter had dropped out of his mouth. It was all right there in the police report, so the medical examiner had ruled the death an accident.

Frank Budzielek had problems with this. Two dead kids, one family, three months apart—what were the chances? He talked to the patrolmen who had responded to the emergency calls, found that the father was home alone with the kids both times. Budzielek began thinking that maybe morgue detail had yielded quick paydirt—the suggestion of a homicide, maybe two. But it was only a hunch, and proving a hunch was no easy thing in a case like this. A cop with a suspicion about a dead baby was up against two prevailing views: Medical examiners' rulings were gospel—did he think he knew more than the doctors? They say it's natural, it's natural. And, anyway, people didn't kill their own children—no, you could not go question the grieving parents. Not without some pretty goddamn good evidence. But sure, said Budzielek's captain, look into it if you want. In your spare time.

Budzielek did—for seven years. Along the way, half a dozen more people picked up paths of the trail: investigators in two other counties hundreds of miles apart, a funeral director who found himself in a strange place at the right time, a father-in-law who guarded his suspicions for his daughter's sake. But in all the years of poking around, building files, tracking, watching, wondering, all anybody had really done was to reach a perfectly logical conclusion without the benefit of any evidence that even a prosecutor as eager as Bill Fitzpatrick might serve up to the most submissive grand jury.

Now, in the middle of 1985, only months after Budzielek's retirement and with the impending births of two more babies fathered by Van Der Sluys, the investigators would take their shot at last. But it would be neither the final consequence of Budzielek's hunch, nor the most important one. Another decade later, when the rest of the story played out—an unlikely chain of events linking thirty years, two ill-fated families, and the power of one misconceived medical premise—those involved would see that these moments were not the climax. They were the genesis.

2

Jane Bowers met Stephen Van Der Sluys at an assembly of Jehovah's Witnesses in the spring of 1971, when he was nineteen and she was fifteen, though it wasn't until a year later, when Steve drove three hours from his home in Syracuse to see Jane, that her family realized she had a boyfriend, and that they did not like him.

It was not often that Jane's parents took a disliking to a fellow Witness, but they found themselves wondering whether Steve truly carried with him the word of God. They thought he was slick and insincere, and perhaps a little too elusive. Steve had graduated from Syracuse Central Technical High School, though it was not quite clear how he'd spent the two years since or in what direction he was headed. He told Jane he had turned down a college football scholarship, which struck her as curious. Steve was only five-foot-five. Still, for her there was no denying his charm. But where some people thought he was the life of the party—the shy and sheltered Jane among them—Jim Bowers judged his daughter's boyfriend a phony. "If he wanted to get on your good side," he recalled, "he would give you a compliment above and beyond what was required."

Jane had grown up in the countryside outside Mechanicville, a small industrial city not far from the state capital of Albany. With long dark hair and an innocent nature, she had always been what her parents considered the most agreeable child in the household. If she had a rebellious streak, it usually surfaced around her parents' uneasiness with the question of dating. When, barely eighteen, Jane announced that she and Steve were going to be married, the Bowerses scrambled to change her mind. With as much diplomacy as they could muster, they sat their daughter down and offered the opinion that perhaps she was too young to get married. When this failed, they came right out and said Steve was not the one for her, but this too was unavailing. With most of the congregation of three hundred in attendance, Jane and Steve were married on September 10, 1974, at the Kingdom Hall in Troy, the same room in which they had met three years earlier. Steve wore a white tuxedo with wide black lapels. Jane, who hoped to become a seamstress, made her own wedding gown, as well as the dresses for all her sisters and bridesmaids. Her father escorted her down the aisle, his grim face preserved by the wedding photographer. Later, at the reception at the firehouse, he sat alone and cried.

Heath Jason Van Der Sluys was born a few weeks short of nine months later in Syracuse, where his parents moved immediately after their wedding. A couple of months after Heath's birth, Steve's mother died of cancer, and the young family moved in with his father on South Salina Street, a forlorn residential section where the city's main thoroughfare ran out of steam. Steve was a young man with a taste for some of the big-ticket items of modern American life, flashy General Motors cars especially, but he seemed to have no particular game plan for acquiring the necessary means. Not infrequently, checks arrived from the Onondaga County Department of Social Services.

The summer following his mother's death, after which his father received a life insurance settlement, Steve decided his own family should be insured. He called a broker named Douglas Profitt, and on May 1, 1976, took out a $10,000 insurance policy on his son's life. He explained to Jane that it was the type of policy that could be cashed one day, so was a way to start saving for Heath's education. Three weeks later, Heath turned one. In accordance with the Jehovah's Witness prohibition against marking birthdays, the day came and went without fanfare.

When he began to walk, Heath made a production number of bedtime. He would climb the stairs a step at a time, turning with a big smile after each ascent, a journey that would take fifteen minutes and end with a round of applause for himself. The other thing Heath liked to do was to steal food from his grandfather's Pomeranians. He would sit on the floor, inch toward the dish, and grab a piece of dog chow when he thought the coast was clear.

Steve wrote a page of verse for his son: "A Poem About Heath Without Any Teeth." He taught his son how to make the dogs run out from their hiding place by squeezing a squeaky toy under the couch. On the other hand, he expressed a young father's lament, often complaining about how much attention his wife was giving the baby at his expense.

At 3:30 on the afternoon of October 8, 1976, a Syracuse police officer responded to a report of a Signal 78: A baby was choking at 3808 South Salina.

Arriving at the address, the officer, joined by two others, found sixteen-month-old Heath Van Der Sluys on a couch in the living room, unconscious. The child's father stood over him, distraught.

"He choked on a quarter," Stephen Van Der Sluys told the officers. "I found him in his crib, and he wasn't breathing." He was home alone with the baby; his wife was at an appointment with her obstetrician. She was in the ninth month of her second pregnancy.

The policemen took turns blowing air into Heath's mouth, trying to revive the child for nearly twenty minutes while waiting for an ambulance to arrive. Finally, paramedics ran into the house and whisked Heath's lifeless body to Community Hospital. A little while later, Victor Fisher arrived from the medical examiner's office to pick up the body.

Van Der Sluys explained to the police, and to Jane when she returned from her visit to the obstetrician, that he had put Heath down for a nap in his crib around noon. Ten minutes later, he went into the bedroom to put a quarter into a container on the dresser. It was one of those ceramic cubes with letters of the alphabet on the sides. If Steve's idea of a savings account was a life insurance policy, this was Jane's. After a while ... clink ... clink ... clink ... Heath would have a new pair of shoes.

"He was asleep, so I left the quarter on the diaper pail next to the crib so I wouldn't wake him," Steve said. "Then later when I went in to wake him ..."

At the medical examiner's office, Dr. Martin Hilfinger examined Heath's body and gave an immediate, if preliminary, finding to a detective who had been dispatched from the Criminal Investigations Division. "When the baby was examined at the medical examiner's office there were no signs of child abuse," the investigator wrote in his report. "The baby was very clean and there [were] no bruises or scratches. The child's home was also very clean and neat. . . . Closed pending results of autopsy."

But there would be no autopsy. Dr. Hilfinger felt no need to cut this child open. The quarter, it seemed, was the culprit. "Infant Dies; Chokes on Lodged Coin," the Syracuse *Herald-Journal* reported the next day in a three-paragraph item. Two days later, a large crowd of friends and relatives, nearly the size of Jane and Steve's wedding reception, assembled at the Onondaga Kingdom Hall for the funeral of their firstborn child. A hearse from the Butler Funeral Home, which, following tradition, did not charge the family for its services because of the age of the deceased, carried Heath's body to White Chapel Memorial Gardens Cemetery. Jane went home and swallowed Valium for a week. Twelve days later, on October 22, she gave birth to her second child. It was her husband's twenty-fifth birthday.

The baby was called Heather, a name Steve and Jane had picked before Heath's death. They liked the way the two names sounded together. And although they would never have the chance to collect their children by calling out *Heath! Heather!* they decided to stick to the original plan when Jane gave birth to a girl. Steve thought there was something poetic about it. He also saw the practicality of putting to immediate use the $10,000 check that arrived a week later from Springfield, Massachusetts, the home office of the Monarch Life Insurance Company. With cash, and an enthusiasm that Jane found disquieting, he went out and bought the car of his dreams, a brand-new Pontiac Trans Am, in black.

Soon, he and Jane had a new home as well. Not long after Heather was born, Steve's widowed father married Jane's sister Debbie, and asked his son and daughter-in-law if they wouldn't mind finding their own apartment. Just as well, Jane thought. A fresh start. Days before Christmas, she and Steve loaded up the Trans Am and moved into the second floor of a two-family house on Bryant Avenue, on the city's west side. It was a move up. The house was in a nice residential neighborhood, at the crest of a gentle hill near Burnet Park, which had a zoo and an arboretum. And Heather, unlike her brother, would have her own room, though it wasn't clear which of the three bedrooms it would be. The old house was drafty, and Jane took to moving Heather's bassinet from room to room in search of the warmest spot. Compared with Heath, she was a fussy baby, but at her six-week checkup, Dr. Robert Chavkin found her to be perfectly healthy. She smiled and cooed, recognized her mother, stared at objects, wriggled around while on her belly, did all the things a six-week-old baby was supposed to do.

In 1909, the New York State Legislature passed a section of law intended to prohibit a particularly wicked version of what had become known as "graveyard insurance." In its purest form, this was the practice, apparently rife in the Pennsylvania coal regions in the mid-nineteenth century, of shady insurance companies scouring the countryside for sick people on whom they could write policies and then sell them to equally shady customers who would, in effect, be placing bets on the deaths of the insured. By the turn of the century, there was evidence that the practice had evolved into an even more black-hearted routine, and in response the New York Legislature made it illegal for companies to sell insurance on the lives of children under one year of age—"to withdraw from unscrupulous parents," the attorney general explained in 1915, "the temptation of securing insurance upon their babies' lives and then compassing their death to obtain such insurance."

Though the law never left the books, the legislature loosened the regulations along the way, and by the 1970s, parents could insure their own children regardless of age, as long as the sum did not exceed twenty-five percent of the parents' own insurance. On December 1, 1976, two days before his daughter's six-week checkup, Stephen Van Der Sluys drove his new Trans Am to Doug Profitt's office and signed up for another $10,000 policy on his infant child's life.

Four weeks later, on the night of December 30, Jane was asleep, the beneficiary of her daughter's newfound ability to sleep through the night, when she awoke to find Steve standing over the bed, holding Heather and screaming. "Something's wrong with Heather! She's not breathing! Jane, wake up! The baby's not breathing!" Bolting from the fog of sleep, Jane grabbed Heather, who was limp and pale, her eyes open but unfocused. While Steve called for an ambulance, she began blowing into Heather's mouth, alternately jerking her abruptly in the darkness. She swept her finger across Heather's throat; there were no obstructions, but it caused the baby to vomit what seemed to be a mixture of milk and blood.

The ambulance workers came bounding up the stairs. They practically ripped Heather from her mother's arms and ran with her out into the cold, neglecting to wrap her in a blanket, which distressed Jane. She and Steve ran after them and got in the front seat of the ambulance as it sped off for Upstate Medical Center.

When Dr. Chavkin came to see her at the hospital the next day, Heather seemed fine. She was active and alert, just a little uncomfortable from a spinal tap she'd been given the night before to rule out meningitis. But Jane was not convinced Heather was perfectly fine. Steve had persuaded her that the baby must have a "condition," a breathing problem of some kind. She'd heard the nurses mention something called apnea. And during the four days she spent at the hospital while Heather was observed, tested, and given precautionary antibiotics, Jane had heard that an apparatus called an apnea monitor could be taken home if necessary. It sounded an alarm if a baby stopped breathing. She made a fight of it—"I've lost one, I don't want to lose another," she told one of the pediatric residents—but she could not persuade him or anyone else that home monitoring was necessary. The doctors concluded that something in the baby's throat—what, they couldn't say—had probably obstructed her breathing. When Jane brought Heather to Dr. Chavkin's office three days later for her regularly scheduled appointment, she was calmer. "Mom, she's okay," Jane told her mother over the phone, as if to reassure herself. "They did every test they could and found nothing wrong."

Still, it had been a terrible three months, to say the least. With Heather's birth coming so soon after Heath's death, Jane and Steve barely had time to mourn their loss. Perhaps, in a way, Jane thought, this was good. Heather kept her from dwelling on the tragedy. Her religious faith helped her—she would be reunited with Heath in an "earthly resurrection," she was sure—but the manner of his death left her with great conflict. Why had Steve left that coin there? She asked him this only once. "Well, you weren't home either," he'd said, desperately slinging the guilt back at her. And now they had Heather to worry about.

On Friday, Jane got her hair cut. When she got home, she hated the way it looked. Staring at the mirror, she decided what she needed was a curling iron. It was a cold, snowy afternoon in Syracuse, not quite the perfect time to be cruising the streets in search of beauty supplies. Jane debated the point aloud, finally deciding to go ahead with the mission with Steve's encouragement. Yes, the roads looked bad, but Steve's offer to stay home with the baby, who was sleeping anyway, pleased Jane. Aside from the hospital visits the previous week, she hadn't been out of the house much lately.

Supper was cooking, and Steve was talking about taking a shower when Jane went into the kitchen to check on Heather before going out. She touched the baby's back, rubbed it gently. This would usually wake her, or at least cause a reassuring move of an arm or leg. But now the baby was still. A horrible thought flashed through Jane's mind, and she grabbed Heather up instantly. And Heather woke up.

Jane left the house and headed over to her sister's. Debbie had a discount card for Karch's beauty supply store. Jane picked up the card, drove to Karch's, found the right curling iron, then headed home. The roads were icy, but Jane made the round trip in less than an hour.

Arriving home, she headed straight for the bathroom to try out the curling iron. Steve was shaving. "How's Heather?" he asked.

"I don't know," Jane said. "I didn't check her yet."

"I'm sure she's fine," Steve said when Jane made a move for the kitchen. "Finish your hair."

When she got to the kitchen, Jane glanced at the baby, still resting on her stomach, her usual position. She looked in on supper, then turned to the bassinet and picked Heather up. Her body was limp; this time, her eyes were closed.

"Not again! Not again!" Jane screamed, running toward the bathroom. She did not try to resuscitate her daughter. She knew she was dead. She just held her and paced as Steve followed her command to call the police. When two officers arrived at 376 Bryant Avenue, they found a pathetic tableau: a sorrowful young mother and father standing in front of a frame house at dusk, holding the lifeless body of their child.

The police report took note of the crisis the week before, then offered a preliminary conclusion: "Victim apparently died of natural causes, pending autopsy of Medical Examiner." The diagnosis was confirmed by Dr. William Alsever of the Onondaga County Medical Examiner's Office, whose autopsy report ran seven pages before reporting that no cause of death had been found. On the death certificate, Dr. Hilfinger, Alsever's boss, signed the case out under the common term for ambiguous circumstances like this one: Sudden Infant Death Syndrome, commonly known as SIDS.

Syracuse is the home not only of two major universities, with their respected schools of medicine, law, and communications, but also, since 1900, of one of the country's more prestigious institutions devoted to the study of funeral service. In the 1970s, a popular hangout for students from the Simmons School of Mortuary Science was the John G. Butler Funeral Home on South Salina Street, where an especially fortunate student might be offered the chance to live in one of the seven bedrooms in exchange for helping out around the funeral home. The unspoken payoff of the arrangement was the chance to serve an informal apprenticeship and learn the business from the inside.

One of these privileged students in 1977 was a young man named Bob Chase, an aspiring funeral director who was finishing up his studies at Simmons when the body of Heather Van Der Sluys arrived from the medical examiner's office the second Saturday in January. The baby was the second child in her family to be handled at Butler in less than three months, Chase learned from the manager, who assigned him the task of preparing the body for burial.

Extreme sadness was, of course, part of the permanent environment at an establishment such as Butler's, and one of the canons taught at Simmons was that funeral service could be an emotionally challenging pursuit that, like police or clergy work, required a certain professional distance. But Chase would not soon forget the grief that gripped the faces of the baby's young parents and their relatives, particularly the child's maternal grandfather, who once again made the three-hour trip from Mechanicville.

This time, however, there was more than grief enveloping Jim Bowers's mind. While Jane blamed the hospital for refusing to send Heather home with an apnea monitor, her father had other ideas about why his granddaughter had died. The circumstances of Heath's death had seemed strange to him, but he had kept his feelings to himself. Now, with Heather's death just three months later, he was inclined to believe the uneasy feeling welling in his gut, the feeling that his son-in-law, of whom he'd always been wary, was somehow responsible for the deaths of his grandchildren.

Jim shared his suspicions with his wife, offering the pointed observation that Steve had been alone with both children when they died. After twenty-four years, Anita Bowers was used to her husband's mistrustful nature. He was still convinced that one of Jane's younger sisters, who had died at birth—

drowned in her own amniotic fluid, the doctors said—had been the victim of a "sloppy delivery." One dynamic of the Bowerses marriage was that Anita would usually side with whomever Jim suspected of inappropriate or dishonest behavior. It was a kind of checks-and-balances system that Jim in fact appreciated. He felt it provided a helpful counterpoint to his penchant for distrust. On the mind-numbing question at hand, Anita remained true to form. "If there's anything wrong," she told Jim, "Janie would suspect it. And she would tell us." To which Jim replied: "Sometimes a wife is the last to know what's going on."

With only an uneasy feeling to go on, Jim decided that the best course of action was to try to persuade Jane to move back home to Mechanicville. He would set Steve up in his store-cleaning business. And he would keep an eye on him. If there were more children, he would watch over them. He would look after his daughter's interests. When he proposed the move to Jane, she said she would talk to Steve about it. A few phone calls later, she reported that he thought it sounded like a good idea. Steve got on the phone. "You really do love us," he told his father-in-law.

Perched on the banks of the narrowing Hudson River, twenty miles north of Albany in Saratoga County, Mechanicville was established at the turn of the twentieth century by Italian immigrants who made the site into an enterprising little settlement. But by the 1970s, the town's best days were long past. Most of the landmarks of local commerce—the freight terminal, the paper mill, the brickyards—were abandoned relics of another era, and the population, ten thousand at the close of World War II, had dropped nearly in half. People commuted to offices in Albany. Teenagers hung out at the McDonald's. Urban renewal turned a good chunk of the center of town into a parking lot for a Grand Union supermarket.

For many years, 411 Park Avenue was the home of Les Sibley, who had owned Mechanicville's Chevrolet dealership since the 1930s. Sibley's house was long considered one of the best in town, a formidable brick building with a hipped roof on the town's most prestigious residential block. But since the death of the Chevy dealer, it had become just another big old house cut up into apartments, the stately brick now covered by shingle. Jane and Steve Van Der Sluys's apartment was on the third floor. It had two bedrooms, a big living room that had once been the attic, and new flooring throughout. The current landlord sold linoleum for a living.

Jane's mother and father lived in the countryside outside town, an area of gentle hills known as Willow Glen. Jim Bowers was a Baltimore native who had been brought into the fold by a Witness who also taught him how to read.

He met and married a girl from northern New York while in the navy, and they settled in her home state. Bowers was a friendly, straightforward man, and his good reputation had helped him build a thriving industrial cleaning business. When his daughter and son-in-law moved to Mechanicville, Jim, as he had promised, taught Steve the ropes and gave him a floor-cleaning machine and a few of his accounts, including one of the big ones, the Grand Union in the town of Rotterdam. Steve, showing some promising initiative, traded in the Trans Am for a Ford Econoline van and eventually hired a helper. But he proved a poor businessman and an unpopular boss, working irregularly and often pressing his wife into service when his helpers quit in disgust. By late summer, however, Jane couldn't do much of anything. She was pregnant with her third child.

Within the family there was trepidation about the coming birth. The baby was unplanned, and Jane talked often about her conflicting feelings. She still wanted children, but her fear of losing another baby was unrelenting. She and Steve joined a local support group for couples who had lost their babies to the mystifying SIDS. The grieving parents gathered in a meeting room at Albany Medical Center to talk about their pain, their guilt, their apprehensions about having more children. In the lexicon, Jane and Steve were SIDS parents. Jim and Anita, meantime, had their own concerns, which they were not shy about making clear. Was their daughter really a SIDS mother—or something much worse? At one point during a discussion about their worry for the child on the way, Jim let it be known in Steve's presence that it had not escaped his notice that Steve was alone with both Heath and Heather when they died. "You'll see," Steve said, a bit flustered. "We'll have some children that will live."

Despite an unusual early-fall ice storm that sent her parents sliding off the road on the way to Saratoga Hospital, Vickie Lynn Van Der Sluys was safely delivered on the afternoon of October 14, 1977, nine months and one week after her sister's death. Jane snapped a picture of Steve in a hospital gown, cradling the baby, gazing lovingly at his tiny daughter. Five days later, the baby was taken directly to Albany Medical Center, where she spent forty-eight hours on an apnea monitor. A doctor examined her, pronounced her in excellent health, and sent her home.

Jim and Anita made the most of their proximity to Jane and the baby, the first grandchild they had had the chance to know well. They loved seeing Vickie, with her curly hair and big blue eyes, and spoiled her like any self-respecting grandparents. But, of course, there was something more. If there was one signal that Jim Bowers managed to get across to his daughter, without provoking an estrangement he knew would result if he made an explicit accusation, it was that he did not trust her husband and would do all he could to ensure that Steve was never alone with the baby. He would keep Jane close, but he would keep Steve closer. And so, the Bowers–Van Der Sluys clan became a strangely intimate family. They worked together, ate meals together, and worshipped together at the Kingdom Hall on Route 67.

In the baby's first months, Jane checked on her constantly as she slept. At nine months, Vickie Lynn was again put on an apnea monitor for a few hours at Albany Medical Center, just to confirm that she was as healthy as she looked. By Christmas 1978, Vickie was a walking, talking fifteen-month-old who had survived well beyond the high-risk period for SIDS. To all appearances, meanwhile, Steve was crazy about Vickie Lynn. The family photo album became filled with images of Daddy and Daddy's Little Girl: Steve sitting on the living room floor, propped against the sofa, scanning the TV listings, Vickie sitting on his outstretched leg, the comics spread before her. A sequence of snapshots of Steve feeding Vickie spaghetti in silly ways, the last few a series featuring father and daughter eating from opposite ends of a single strand, meeting in the middle with a kiss.

As the months passed, the family's trepidation waned. Jim, in fact, became so relaxed that when he needed help cleaning the Mechanicville Grand Union after a meeting at the Kingdom Hall one Thursday night in January and Jane volunteered, he thought nothing of Steve staying home alone with Vickie. Jane went home and changed into her workclothes, checked on Vickie, and headed for the stairs. Steve called out that he'd see her later.

The Grand Union was a two-hour job. Jim and his son Richie handled the machine, Jane mopped the edges. The store was just up the street and across the parking lot from Jane's apartment, but it was after midnight when they finished, so Jim dropped his daughter off. " 'Night, Dad," she said, walking up to the big old Sibley house.

This time, Jane did not even pick her daughter up. "I knew when I saw her that she was dead and so I left the room," she would later recount, stripping the memory of emotion. She didn't even remember screaming.

She called her father. Her mother answered the phone.

Anita Bowers listened in abject disbelief. "Jim, go down there and do something," she pleaded to her husband. "She *can't* be dead."

Jim took the phone. His daughter was crying. He asked no questions. He said he'd be right down. He called the Mechanicville police department. "This is Jim Bowers," he said. "I think my granddaughter might be dead."

An ambulance could be heard shrieking through the empty streets of Mechanicville. Then came a dispatcher's voice on the police radio: "We need a ten-fifty-two at four-eleven Park Avenue." It was a request for the coroner.

When Jim arrived at the house, Frank Kearney, the owner of Kearney's Garage, was driving up with a policeman. Kearney was the Saratoga County coroner. The three men climbed the stairs to the third floor.

The apartment was convulsed in activity. The rescue squad workers, the police, the coroner were crowded into Vickie's room, surrounding the crib. The parents were questioned at the kitchen table. The neighbors emerged to check on the commotion. In the midst of the turmoil, Steve was quiet; to some he seemed numb with shock, to others oddly calm, even aloof. Then he said, "Excuse me. I gotta go cry."

Jim Bowers turned to the coroner. "I hope there's an investigation here," he said.

As a politically elected coroner with no professional qualifications—he'd actually defeated a doctor for the job—Kearney could not pronounce death or make any medical rulings, but he could assign the county pathologist to perform an autopsy. He went into the kitchen, called the owner of the Dunn Funeral Home, and asked him to come five doors up the street and remove a child's body to the pathology lab at Saratoga Hospital. "It's the Van Der Sluys family," Kearney said. "They've lost a baby."

The funeral director dressed quickly, came up the street in his station wagon, and climbed the stairs to the third-floor apartment. He looked in at the people gathered in the kitchen. *I know everyone here,* he thought.

After graduating from the Simmons School of Mortuary Science and working awhile at the Butler Funeral Home, Bob Chase had left Syracuse, come home to Saratoga County with his wife, Pat, and taken over the Dunn Funeral Home, just down the street from the old Sibley house. Steve and Jane Van Der Sluys were his neighbors. Now he was in their apartment, about to carry away yet another of their dead children. "Something's not right here," he whispered to Ralph Peluso, one of the policemen. He wrapped the baby in her blanket and carefully lifted her into a small wooden box, then carried the box downstairs into the winter night. Half an hour later, Vickie's body arrived in the pathology lab in Saratoga Springs.

Jane and Steve spent the night at her parents' house, stopping first at the hospital emergency room where Jane was given a sedative. Not until the next day did Jane feel up to hearing Steve recount what had happened while she was cleaning the Grand Union. "She wanted a drink of water," he said. "She was acting real strange, she wasn't herself, she was making funny noises when she breathed. . . . I gave her the water . . . then she drank the water and she smiled at me and then I laid her back down."

Case 212 for the twelve-member Mechanicville police department began and ended with a one-page report that contained the account of the "complainant," James Bowers—minus his cryptic whispers—and a diagram of the apartment. Instead, the police deferred to the four words Dr. Jack Paston, the county pathologist, wrote at his desk in Saratoga Springs the day after Vickie's death. As far as he was concerned, the child had died suddenly, unexpectedly, and of a cause unknown, as thousands of babies did every year. Fifteen months was on the old side, but, Paston decided, it wasn't unheard of. Sudden Infant Death Syndrome, he wrote.

It is for reasons of public health, and not preservation, that the remains of the dead are embalmed. This was one of the first things Bob Chase learned in mortuary school. Several of the great plagues of history, in fact, were hatched in the water that ran down the hills of cemeteries, picking up the bacteria of the dead on its way to the drinking supplies of the small villages of Europe. But if preservation was only a side effect of the disinfecting process, it was the side effect Chase had in mind when he picked up Vickie Lynn Van Der Sluys's body from Paston's pathology lab and brought it to the embalming room.

Babies and very small children are often not embalmed in the conventional way because their blood vessels are too tiny. Instead, they might be "fume embalmed," exposed to disinfecting chemicals in a bag, or in the casket. This was how Chase had prepared Vickie's sister Heather in Syracuse. But he resolved to embalm Vickie, and to do an especially good job of it. Though he was not charging the family for his services, Chase also chose a casket, a Wilbert Cherub, which was made of space-age plastic. "I thought to myself," Chase later recalled, *"This body is coming back up someday."*

Vickie was buried in Hudson View Cemetery, next to her mother's baby sister, the one who had died at birth. Chase's work was not finished, however. A man in his position had to be extremely careful about a matter such as this, but the more he thought about it, the more he talked about it with his wife, the more he became persuaded that he ought to run it by one of the new acquaintances he'd made since moving back home.

Harvey LaBar, a big, lumbering man with a booming voice, was a true son of Mechanicville. He knew every inch of the town—even knew the spot, fifty miles north, where you could jump across the Hudson if you took a running start—and like many of those of his time and place, he'd worked in the brick-yard and the paper mill, then served in Korea. And for the past sixteen years, he had been a member of the New York State Police's Bureau of Criminal Investigation.

When LaBar came by the funeral home, Chase laid out his apprehensions with as much professional restraint as he could summon—the three deaths, the Syracuse connection, how he couldn't let it go. LaBar listened with interest; he remembered hearing the ambulance sirens that night, and the call for the coroner on the police radio he kept on top of his refrigerator. He took copious notes, then reported back to his BCI captain. "The funeral director thinks this guy killed his kids," LaBar summed up, slightly overstating. "And I believe him."

Arriving at Jim Bowers's house in Willow Glen, LaBar found a man who had a litany of complaints about his son-in-law and a fair amount of suspicion about the manner of his grandchildren's deaths, but who seemed to be struggling with himself to be fair-minded, if only to protect his daughter. Steve was a nice enough guy, Bowers told LaBar over coffee at the kitchen table, but the young man seemed to complain constantly about his rotten luck. He had trouble holding on to jobs and staying out of accidents, and seemed to live mostly on checks from the government and insurance companies.

LaBar asked Bowers about the children. "I have my suspicions," Jim said, "but it's nothing I can prove. And he's still my daughter's husband. I don't want to say anything that would make things worse for her than they already are."

LaBar went down to the bar in the back of Mechanicville's central firehouse to talk to the rescue squad members who responded to 411 Park the night of January 11. Several said they were suspicious of Van Der Sluys— thought he was "strange," and not particularly overcome by grief. But they hadn't passed these observations on to the coroner, because they were afraid they'd be told it wasn't their business. LaBar's next query was to the Syracuse police department. By phone, he reached a captain in the Criminal Investigations Division, who recognized the case immediately. Sure, he told LaBar, he'd be glad to send the police reports on the first two children. You know, he said, we have a guy here who's been suspicious of this from the beginning.

Few things in life stunned Frank Budzielek, but when he heard that a third Van Der Sluys child had died, all he wanted to do was jump in his car and head for Mechanicville, wherever the hell that was. This, however, was the sort of initiative that needed approval in triplicate. Approval was not forthcoming. Not our jurisdiction, said the captain. There was only one open case here, and it was in Saratoga County.

"I am sorry to learn of the death of your daughter and wish at this time to extend my most sincere sympathy," began a letter sent to Stephen and Jane Van Der Sluys on February 20, 1979. "We have received the claim papers which you have completed. Since your daughter died within the contestable period we are making our customary investigation. As soon as it has been completed we will advise you further."

The letter was signed by Nanette Pyrek, an assistant claims examiner for the Massachusetts Mutual Insurance Company. In October 1978, Van Der Sluys had called a life insurance broker named Chuck Mayberry and said he wanted to buy a policy for his family. You need a plan, Mayberry had said, and drew up a proposal that covered only Van Der Sluys and his wife. Van Der Sluys said he wanted to include their one-year-old daughter. On the application, there was a section on family history. Steve mentioned his two previous children, offering the vague suggestion that the doctors seemed to think they may have died of something hereditary. Mayberry expressed some fear for Vickie's health and volunteered that perhaps the couple ought to look into adopting next time. Nonetheless, when the final application was signed at Steve and Jane's kitchen table six weeks later, on December 6, Vickie Lynn was insured for $30,000—the maximum the law allowed, based on the $120,000 policy Steve had on his own life. At the bottom of the application, under Remarks, Mayberry wrote: QUICK ISSUE. A month later Vickie was dead. The day after her death, Van Der Sluys called Mayberry. "Chuck, I have a problem," he said.

When Nanette Pyrek wrote to Van Der Sluys in mid-February to say the insurance company was working on his claim, she did not mention that its "customary investigation" was in this instance not so customary, and that it had been going on for more than a month. A few days after Vickie died, claims investigator Dick McCormack called Coroner Frank Kearney, who told him about Dr. Paston's autopsy findings. McCormack called Paston. The final report wasn't finished, the pathologist told him, but, as McCormack later wrote in his file, "There was nothing on the deceased to indicate any foul play or cruel treatment on the part of the parents. To his knowledge this was a natural death due to a crib death."

McCormack tracked down the records from Vickie's two uneventful visits to Albany Medical Center. On the back of one of the forms, he found a notation about the deaths of her two siblings. He called Paston back.

"Were you aware of this?" he asked. The pathologist, getting the investigator's drift, said he had heard about it subsequent to the autopsy, but it didn't change anything. "He stated that even though there had been two previous infant deaths, there was the possibility that a crib death is a hereditary illness in a family," McCormack wrote in his log. "He stated this is being fully researched." Paston directed McCormack to a Dr. Susan Standfast, who ran a Sudden Infant Death Syndrome unit at the State Health Department in Albany. According to Paston, she was in charge of investigating all crib deaths in the state. Nanette Pyrek authorized three more hours of investigative time.

When McCormack reached Standfast, she told him he had it all wrong: The state didn't run investigations, at least not the kind he was interested in. She was doing scientific research on risk factors for SIDS. She was interested in the Van Der Sluys case, and had asked Paston for information from the autopsy because she wanted to explore the "very remote possibility" that two crib deaths could occur in one family. "Therefore," McCormack wrote in his report, missing the nuance of her implication, "she could add nothing." In Albany, Nanette Pyrek began processing the paperwork on the Van Der Sluys claim.

Paston's ruling was also a case-killer in the eyes of Harvey LaBar's boss, a man who liked to play the percentages and had a particular distaste for wild-goose chases. By early February, he was ready to cut LaBar off the Van Der Sluys case. How could you pursue a homicide investigation, he felt, when you have the county pathologist saying it's a natural death? But he saw that LaBar had put a good deal of time into the case and agreed to let him stay with it a little while longer.

In his office LaBar had a book that a retired county coroner had left him. It was a classic volume by Milton Helpern, the New York City medical examiner in the 1950s and 1960s, the man widely credited with popularizing modern forensic pathology. LaBar looked up the section on Sudden Infant Death Syndrome and learned Rule Number One about crib death: From the pathologist's point of view, it was indistinguishable from homicide. You could call the smothering of a baby one of those perfect crimes because it looked the same as SIDS at autopsy, which is to say it looked like nothing. In that regard, Paston's finding was technically correct. If Van Der Sluys had smothered Vickie, the last person to be able to confirm it would be a pathologist.

LaBar began casting about for someone who knew something about SIDS and ended up in Susan Standfast's office in Albany. She had first encountered the Van Der Sluys family, Standfast told LaBar, after Heather's death in Syracuse two years before. The Onondaga County medical examiner, like his counterparts in nineteen other upstate counties, was cooperating with a study of SIDS she was conducting with a federal grant. Following the protocols, Dr. Hilfinger had sent her slides of tissue sections and other autopsy material on Heather. Now she had Heather's sister, which raised all kinds of interesting questions. The important thing to know, Standfast told LaBar, was that contrary to what some people seemed to think, SIDS was not hereditary. Further, she pointed out, Vickie was much older than the typical SIDS victim.

"What are the probabilities of two or three children dying like this in the same family?" LaBar asked Standfast.

"Astronomical," she said.

Would she put this in writing? No, she said. Her field was medical research, not odds-making.

What McCormack and LaBar's cursory medical inquiries suggested was that Paston was not especially sensitive to the subtleties of what medical examiners like Milton Helpern called infanticide. Perhaps it was that although Paston was a perfectly competent hospital pathologist, he was not a *forensic* pathologist: He was not inclined, by training and practice, to probe for evidence of crime that was not plainly visible at autopsy. As he told both LaBar and McCormack, he had spent several hours carefully examining every inch of this child and had found nothing amiss. LaBar knew that it would have been out of character for Paston to do something so bold as to include the two previous deaths or any other circumstances in his diagnosis or to ask a lot of questions. Under Paston's interpretation of the coroner system, he had only one job and that was to examine the body on the table. The rest was for the police.

LaBar turned his attentions back to Van Der Sluys. It occurred to him that what he had here, basically, was an insurance thief. In the Mechanicville police files he found a burglary report in which Van Der Sluys had claimed that thousands of dollars' worth of stereo equipment and other possessions had been stolen. The police found everything in a garage behind his apartment, but for unclear reasons they didn't arrest him. "He seldom works but always seems to have money," LaBar wrote in his file. "On public assistance, workmen's compensation, claimed several disabilities as results of auto accidents and on-job injuries. He has made at least two fraudulent burglary insurance claims." This is the kind of guy, LaBar observed, who buys a disability policy, then—what a coincidence—has an accident a month later.

In March, LaBar noticed that Van Der Sluys had a new car. In fact, it was hard to miss this particular car on the streets of Mechanicville. It was another Trans Am—not just an off-the-floor model but the silver-and-gray Limited, featuring a leather interior, a T-roof, a $15,000 sticker price, and the assurance of General Motors that it was one of only fifteen hundred of its kind. Jane had wanted to save the $30,000 payment from Massachusetts Mutual, but Steve thought he had won the lottery. He proceeded to consume conspicuously. His new Hickey-Freeman suit, a belt with an onyx buckle, and two coats he bought for Jane—one leather, one rabbit—pleased him particularly. He was, however, most openly thrilled about the Trans Am, prompting Jane to scold finally, "You shouldn't be so happy."

Had he known she'd said even that, LaBar would have been surprised. He considered Jane Van Der Sluys an enigma. Did she know what was going on? Could she be as naïve as she seemed? LaBar concluded that she was just a very submissive, amazingly trusting wife, a young woman who seemed to have grown up in a house where the man was boss. It was also true that as a devoutly religious person, and as her parents' daughter, she, like them, valued the marriage commitment above most worldly things. She could overlook a lot.

In April, LaBar and his senior investigator, Bob Bryan, went to Ballston

Spa, the Saratoga county seat, to brief District Attorney David Wait on the Van Der Sluys case. Their ultimate goal was to persuade the prosecutor to open a grand jury investigation. LaBar had done the spadework; now he needed the legal backing for a deeper look.

"So," said Wait, "what do you need?"

"Well," said LaBar, "we'd like to exhume the body." Wait grimaced. He wasn't going down that road, not now, anyway. How about subpoenaing the life insurance records? LaBar had a pretty good idea where the money for the Trans Am came from, but a canvass of local life insurance brokers had failed to turn up anyone willing to look through his files without a court order. He had no idea Jack Paston had had several conversations with an investigator for Massachusetts Mutual. Wait agreed it all sounded suspicious. But no, he wouldn't give them the subpoena. For one thing, whom would he subpoena? Get back to me, the D.A. told the detectives, when you have something more.

What that might be, short of an eyewitness or a confession, LaBar had no clue. He and Bryan decided the time had come to knock on Van Der Sluys's door. They would ask him to come down to the station, and of course he'd say sure; they'd sit him down, do their good cop–bad cop routine. At 6 feet 3 inches, 230 pounds, with a voice that could explode without notice and a fondness for picking up his old Underwood typewriter with one hand and slamming it down on the big wooden interrogation table, LaBar was the bad cop.

They drove over to Park Avenue, climbed the stairs of the old Sibley house to the third floor, and rapped on the Van Der Sluyses' door. The apartment was empty. LaBar called the landlord. Van Der Sluys? They moved out. No forwarding address. LaBar called Jim Bowers. No, he didn't know where they were. Jane said they were heading south for a while.

3

Frank Budzielek had been hoping something would break in Mechanicville, which he referred to as "up north," even though it was due east of Syracuse. Kept at bay by his captain, refused permission to cross county lines, he'd had no reason to consult a map. From Syracuse he'd watched and waited for Harvey LaBar to make a case in Saratoga. When he heard from LaBar that Van Der Sluys was gone, he was not particularly troubled. *He'll be back,* Budzielek thought. *They always come back.*

It wasn't a reason to quit. He kept gathering scraps. Occasionally, something—a newspaper article about SIDS, or maybe just a mental itch—would reactivate his interest in the Van Der Sluys case. Every once in a while, he'd call and try some new approach with Dr. Hilfinger, the medical examiner who'd signed off on SIDS as Heather's cause of death. Hilfinger said he was sorry; he'd done the autopsy and nothing was going to change the findings. Budzielek began focusing on personal finances. From a friend, an ex-FBI man who did a lot of private insurance investigation, he learned that Van Der Sluys had collected insurance on all three of his children's deaths. Still, this was unofficial intelligence, not legally subpoenaed evidence. And even if this was a major discovery, there was still a slew of open questions. For instance: Where was Stephen Van Der Sluys?

In Mechanicville, Harvey LaBar would sit down at the computer every once in a while, log into the Department of Motor Vehicles, and punch in:

VAN DER SLUYS, STEPHEN
DOB 10/22/51

The first few times, 411 PARK AVE MECHANICVILLE NY came on the screen. After a while, LICENSE EXPIRED came up. But the computer checks became a part of his work routine. Maybe, eventually, Van Der Sluys would show up back in New York and get himself a new driver's license. On August 11, 1981, more than two years after he'd knocked on the door of the empty apartment on Park Avenue, LaBar logged on. He hadn't tried in a while. VAN DER SLUYS, STEPHEN, he typed. The computer answered: 6174 SILVER BIRCH ROAD VICTOR NY.

LaBar checked his map and found Victor in Ontario County, way over near Rochester, the other side of the state. He called the state police station in Canandaigua, a lakefront town a few miles from Victor and the headquarters of Troop E. An investigator named Bill Morshimer answered in the BCI office, and LaBar filled him in. Morshimer said he'd poke around. When he did, he learned something that worried LaBar: Jane Van Der Sluys had given birth to her fourth child that April, shortly after she and her husband had returned to New York. Morshimer went down to the Victor rescue squad and put a notice up on the bulletin board: The state police were to be informed immediately if a baby-in-distress call came from 6174 Silver Birch Road.

Soon after Vickie's death, Steve and Jane had moved to Oklahoma. Steve had decided he was tired of Mechanicville. He was tired of Jane's family. Jane had to admit, so was she. They needed a fresh start, and Steve had a plan. He would enroll in the Tulsa Welding School, where he would learn a special kind of aluminum welding. Then they'd head back north and he'd start a welding business with a friend from Rochester.

Shane Van Der Sluys was conceived in the swelter of a Tulsa summer, and in the months before his birth the following spring in a hospital on the edge of Lake Ontario, his mother began taking steps to ensure there would be no more ambulances and autopsies. For one thing, there would be no money on the life of their next child. It was not that Jane suspected Steve. Rather, she had reduced any possible cause-and-effect to superstition. She did not want to tempt fate with Shane's life and told Steve: No more insurance policies.

What she wanted was a baby monitor, the kind the doctors in Syracuse wouldn't send home with Heather after the frightening episode the week before her death. Sometime before Shane's birth, Jane called the local chapter of the National Sudden Infant Death Syndrome Foundation. The woman who answered directed her to a pediatric respiratory specialist at the best hospital in Rochester, Strong Memorial.

As he sat before this couple and listened to their tragic tale, Dr. John Brooks did not betray that he thought there was something askew. There seemed to be no medical pattern to the deaths of their three children. The second death sounded like a standard SIDS case, complete with the "near-miss," as such frightening episodes had come to be known, only days before she died. But the third one seemed too old, and the first was ostensibly a freak accident. There was also something a little strange about this couple, Brooks thought, the husband especially. He seemed a little jumpy, at times even hostile.

"Has this ever happened before?" Van Der Sluys asked the doctor. "Three in one family? Has that happened to other people?" Brooks said that it was rare but not unheard of.

"So it has happened."

"Yes," Brooks said. "It has happened." He would later recall wondering if a genetic metabolic problem had caused the deaths of the earlier children. On a gut level, he hoped this was the case.

Brooks concluded that the best course was to look forward, not back. The ambiguity of the case led him to a thought. His department was conducting research on the brain stems of newborns. It was related to the current leading theory of SIDS, which held that some babies had a subtle physiologic abnormality that caused them to stop breathing during sleep—apnea, it was called—and never start up again. Some people thought this anomaly could run in families, and many regarded "near-misses" as a warning sign. The theory had led many in the national SIDS community to believe that a new device called a home apnea monitor could be used to save these babies. Jane Van Der Sluys was now among them.

While all newborns stop breathing for a few seconds every so often, the monitors were designed to alert parents to prolonged and potentially dangerous pauses. Theoretically, a baby could be resuscitated before it was too late. Though clinical researchers had not yet established that the monitors actually accomplished this purpose—nor proven the apnea theory of SIDS, for that matter—a profitable industry was growing out of the fears of parents like Jane. The devices had still been considered fairly exotic when she tried to get one for Heather early in 1977, but four years later the popularity of the theory and aggressive marketing by the device's leading manufacturer—a company founded by a man who had lost his baby son to SIDS—were making home monitors ubiquitous. Doctors were prescribing them as much to allay the anxieties of mothers and fathers—especially those who had lost previous children—as to protect their babies. In fact, the whole collective theory of sleep apnea, familial SIDS, and home monitoring had been hatched by a leading SIDS researcher, Alfred Steinschneider, who had written a landmark paper in the early seventies about a family that had lost four babies and a toddler, the last two of whom had survived several near-misses before their eventual deaths. A decade later, hospitals everywhere were operating apnea programs within their pediatrics departments, and some were doing research in further pursuit of the theory. Strong Memorial's was run by John Brooks.

He asked Steve and Jane if they wanted to volunteer their baby for the brain-stem study. The test was simple and not invasive—just a couple of electrodes listening in on brain waves—and maybe it would reveal something. Brooks made it clear that the research was entirely speculative, but when Shane was born a few weeks later and his test came back slightly abnormal, it confirmed Jane's worst fears. Given the family history, Brooks concluded that putting the baby on a monitor was the safe thing to do. And the simplest: Jane made it plain that she wasn't going home without one.

Brooks referred Jane and Steve to a pediatrician named Saul Sokolow. When they went to see him, Sokolow, like Brooks, was wary of the deaths of the first three children, but to him, too, it was not much more than a feeling, and he was mindful of the results of Shane's brain-stem test. Sokolow prescribed the apnea monitor, schooled Jane and Steve in its use, and saw the baby regularly.

Both Brooks and Sokolow received visits from Investigator Bill Morshimer that summer. They told him the same thing: The circumstances of the three deaths made them uneasy, but there wasn't anything they could even begin to prove. Shane, meantime, was sleeping with the monitor and doing fine. Morshimer reported his findings to LaBar, who then called Frank Budzielek's captain in Syracuse. What they had here, they all decided, was just more suspicion—another dead end. They could bring Van Der Sluys in for questioning if they didn't mind going at him without any real evidence, but if they didn't leave with a confession, they'd be dead in the water. There was a good chance he'd see through the bluff, get himself a lawyer, and that would be that. The police would get only one shot at accusing a parent of killing his children. And when they did, they'd better be right. The Rochester doctors never heard from Morshimer again.

Instead of talking to the police, Van Der Sluys talked to a psychiatrist. Things were not going well for him, and he had filed an insurance claim for a mental disability that needed the validation of a professional. His grand plan to start a welding business hadn't panned out, he told the psychiatrist. The machinery made his hands hurt, and he had to go back to cleaning offices at night. He also had aches and pains from the car accident he and Jane had been in on the way to the hospital the day Vickie was born nearly four years before. That made him depressed. But none of this was the worst of it, he confided. The loss of his three children pained him no end; because he had been with them when they died, people looked at him suspiciously, pointed fingers. The psychiatrist sympathized. Losing three kids like that—how awful. He had an idea: Have another child, he advised Steve. It will be good therapy.

Jane gave birth to her fifth child, a girl named Jennifer, in March of 1983. She brought her in to Dr. Brooks, who looked her over and pronounced her perfectly healthy. But Brooks was reluctant to leave it at that. By now, Shane was nearly two and he hadn't had a moment's distress. Brooks wondered if the monitor he'd slept with his first year had something to do with his survival, and perhaps not in the way intended by the manufacturer. The state police investigator's visit had stayed with him. Much as he hated to cast suspicion on SIDS parents, he found himself considering the possibility that the device had performed as a criminal deterrent. He recommended that Jennifer go home with a monitor as well.

In Syracuse, Frank Budzielek realized there still was no special interest in this case within the police department, and that it was a prosecutor's support that he needed. He started quietly marketing the case to various Onondaga County A.D.A.s. He persuaded one of them to issue a subpoena for the insurance records, but the tactic advanced the case only marginally. He got no further than Harvey LaBar had gotten three years before with the Saratoga County district attorney. Then, in the fall of 1983, there came a personnel change in the district attorney's office that Budzielek regarded as extremely good news.

Budzielek had known Bill Fitzpatrick since the prosecutor's first days in the office back in 1976, when he was a freshly minted assistant district attorney trying to make his way up the ladder of the trial bureau. In the years since, Budzielek, like many in CID, had grown to regard him as their man in the D.A.'s office, a prosecutor who was comfortable on police turf. Fitzpatrick thought like a cop. It was in his blood. And now that Dick Hennessy had made Fitzpatrick his chief homicide prosecutor, a promotion certifying his rise, at age thirty-one, to the highest-profile job in the office, Budzielek persuaded his captain that this was the time to take their best shot. Budzielek was now in his early fifties, contemplating a policeman's retirement package and a pair of fully covered knee operations. He was out of leads on the Van Der Sluys case, if not flat out of gas.

"You've been working on this for *seven* years?" Fitzpatrick asked when Budzielek came to his office. Fitzpatrick studied the files: the police reports of the deaths, the autopsies, the insurance policies. He looked up from the file. "I'm in," he said. "Wait here."

Fitzpatrick walked back to Hennessy's office. He wanted the D.A.'s office to pick up the investigation, and for that he needed the boss's green light. Fitzpatrick came back a few minutes later. Budzielek knew immediately they'd been shot down. It was a great case, Fitzpatrick said, but it was a matter of priorities. Hennessy was interested, but he wanted more. The case would have to stay with the police department for a while. Keep going, he told Budzielek.

The next day, Fitzpatrick dashed off a memo to Hennessy, a crisp rundown of the case written in the ardent cadence of the present tense. By the time he got to the Van Der Sluyses third child, Fitzpatrick could barely contain his gathering indignation. "It is my opinion," he wrote, "that Mr. and Mrs. Van Der Sluys are mass murderers of the worst order." He was convinced Van Der Sluys could not have acted without his wife's knowledge. He said he wanted to head up a major investigation involving authorities in three counties.

Hennessy didn't change his mind, but he did send a copy of the memo to Saratoga County D.A. David Wait, saying he'd be in touch. But nothing was to happen anytime soon. So it was that when Frank Budzielek retired from the Syracuse Police Department on December 5, 1984, after a little more than twenty years of service, got his knees rebuilt, and became the director of security at the new Sheraton University Inn and Conference Center, his work on Stephen Van Der Sluys remained unfinished, the files and scraps left behind in a cardboard box in the Criminal Investigations Division.

Early in 1985, Fitzpatrick had the Van Der Sluys file assigned to one of the department's best homicide teams, Investigators John Brennan and Danny Boyle. While Fitzpatrick had respected Budzielek's instincts and diligence, he viewed him as perhaps not the most astute detective in the CID. By contrast, he considered Brennan, who was about his own age, one of the city's best young investigators and often requested his services on unsolved cases. Brennan was low-key, but in Fitzpatrick's view was an exceptionally smart, clearheaded, and determined detective—a strong interrogator.

Brennan and Boyle started with Budzielek's cardboard box. Sorting out an eight-year-old case was a task in itself, made no easier by Budzielek's less-than-exemplary recordkeeping skills. The detectives decided that once they got the files in order, they would begin interviewing people: the funeral director, the insurance people, the doctors, the neighbors. Eventually, they would knock on the man's door. First, of course, they would have to find him. It had been four years since the last call from Harvey LaBar.

"Paula Byron" was a teenager with troubles at home. Her father was physically abusive; she needed to get out of the house for a while. The Byron family lived in the same complex of apartments outside Canandaigua where Jane and Steve Van Der Sluys now lived. They told the county social services caseworker that the families belonged to the same church, and they would be happy to take Paula and her sister for a while. The day after Christmas, 1984, shortly after making the move, sixteen-year-old Paula began keeping a diary of her sexual encounters with her temporary foster father, a man twice her age. Paula was back home less than two months later, but the damage was done. One day in March, her father came home from work to find Van Der Sluys waiting to talk to him. He had gotten his daughter pregnant, Van Der Sluys said tearfully. He was sorry. Evidently he had taken his psychiatrist's advice very much to heart. His wife was newly pregnant too, due to deliver their sixth child the same month as Paula would give birth to her first.

It was on April 4, 1985, that Paula and her father appeared at the front desk of the state police station in Canandaigua, and Investigator Bob Beswick drove up to Mertensia Road with a fellow detective to question the suspected rapist. Taking the free-flowing admissions right in the accused's driveway, Beswick had no idea he was holding anyone other than a local jerk who was sexually involved with an underage female and who seemed to like talking about it.

A day before the Fourth of July holiday, Van Der Sluys pleaded guilty to thirty-six counts of statutory rape and sodomy. When a reporter for the Rochester *Democrat and Chronicle* called to ask him about the charges, Van Der Sluys talked about the emotional distresses of his life. He'd lost three children to crib death, he said, and though he and his wife had since had two who were fine, the earlier traumas had hounded him. This, he said, was why he had become involved with the teenager. "I still cry at night," he told the reporter. "I keep thinking there had to be something I overlooked, something I could have done to keep them from dying."

The next day, Investigator John Brennan got a call from Frank Budzielek. "Take a look at the paper," Budzielek told him. "Van Der Sluys is in Ontario County. They busted him for getting his foster daughter pregnant. He's crying about his dead kids. This is it, buddy. Go for it."

"Troop E, Investigator Beswick."

Brennan said he was calling from Syracuse about Stephen Van Der Sluys. "We've got an open homicide case," he said, getting right to the point. "We believe this guy killed his kids."

Beswick thought of the two children he'd seen at the duplex out on Mertensia Road, and the two babies to be born a week apart to two mothers. He filled Brennan in on the rape case: the girl's problems at home, the diary, how Van Der Sluys could hardly wait to confess.

"We're thinking about coming out there to talk to him," Brennan said.

"Well, he's lawyered up," Beswick said. "You'll have to wait until he's a sentenced prisoner. I'll tell you one thing, though. For some reason, I've got a good rapport with him. He's quite a talker."

In August, Van Der Sluys was sentenced to a year in the county jail. He was no longer represented by an attorney. Brennan called Budzielek at work the first week of September. "We're going to Canandaigua tomorrow," he said. "Want to come along? It's really your case."

Budzielek found his retirement job as a hotel security chief pretty dull work but he appreciated the weekends off. He liked the feeling of being a retired cop. "You go do it," he told Brennan. "And I'm telling you he's gonna give it up. He's a cherry. He's gonna give it up."

Brennan and Boyle's captain was unconvinced. He'd allowed them to go to Mechanicville in the intervening months to do some background work, but he was not persuaded they had much of a case. Even if Van Der Sluys did it, he wasn't going to be stupid enough to admit it. The captain figured the detectives would spend a few unfruitful minutes with Van Der Sluys and be done.

They arrived in Canandaigua at about ten the next morning. They collected Bob Beswick at Troop E headquarters and headed for the Ontario County Jail. Beswick, mindful of his encounter with Van Der Sluys five months earlier, had no doubts about the outcome. "If he did it," he told the Syracuse investigators along the way, "you're gonna know it today."

Van Der Sluys was brought down to a room in the booking section of the jail. "Steve," Beswick said, "these guys are detectives from Syracuse. They'd like to talk to you." Brennan was surprised by his first impression. *This is a wimpy little guy,* he thought.

They drove back to Troop E headquarters, a long brick building on the main road leading into Canandaigua, and brought Van Der Sluys into a small room. With much more anxiety than he had shown Beswick months before, Van Der Sluys began to lead the detectives through his recollections of the past decade: his marriage, the births of his children, their deaths. Twenty minutes in, they told him it didn't add up. Tell us the truth, Steve. C'mon, buddy. We know about the insurance. Tell us the truth. You'll feel better. Tell us what happened. Van Der Sluys would not budge about Heath's death, but when they got to Heather, Brennan and Boyle knew he was starting to slip. He acknowledged that he had put her into her crib facedown, on a pillow, and as he said this, tears came. But he seemed to make less sense the more he talked, his accounts a nervous, sobbing jumble of incomplete thoughts and clumsy rationalizations. He felt guilt because he had not saved his children, he said. Terrible things kept happening that were beyond his control. He wanted to be closer to his wife. The insurance was the idea of the insurance salesmen. He didn't even want to spend the money when the payments came.

He related Vickie's last moments: "She had real big blue eyes, you know, and ... she was just lookin' up at me, and I'll never forget that look, it was like Daddy, somethin's happenin' to me, you know, 'help me' type of thing." He began to sob. He contended that this scene occurred before he calmed her down and put her down to sleep. Brennan saw that Van Der Sluys's hands were shaking, his eyes damp. For the next two hours, he and Boyle worked him, challenged him, confronted him. Ultimately, they let him follow his own path. One moment it seemed he wanted it to come out, the next he would retreat into denial, as if still trying to talk his way out of it—to talk himself out of it. At 5:20, they left him in the room with a legal pad and a pen. He began writing a rambling composition about his "beloved, sweet, innocent firstborn son, Heath" and his "cute, cuddly little daughter, Heather," before Brennan came back into the room and pushed him to come back to the point. He reminded Van Der Sluys that he'd already admitted putting Heather and Vickie facedown in their cribs. He asked him to dictate the rest of his statement—the time-honored police technique of interrogation-room collaboration. Van Der Sluys talked. Brennan typed. Van Der Sluys signed. He began with a description of the night Heather died. "I went to check on Heather and noticed that she had difficulty breathing, and it seemed that her breathing was getting worse," he said. "At first I was indecisive and I had this intense feeling that she was going to die. I felt that there was nothing I could do and I felt that she should die. I had Heather in my arms and I took her and laid her facedown into the crib. I laid her face on something white, but I don't remember if it was a pillow or a bassinet. I watched her for a few minutes, and Heather was making noises like she couldn't breathe. Finally she stopped the noise, and I thought that she was dead. I went into the bathroom and took a shower." After a few more details, he said, "I felt that she had to die. I felt by not helping Heather I was doing her a favor."

Then, Brennan asked Van Der Sluys about the night in Mechanicville when Jane went to help her father clean the Grand Union, leaving him alone with their third child: "Shortly after Jane left the apartment, Vickie started screaming and crying loudly. I went to see what was wrong and Vickie was standing in her crib screaming. I picked her up and put her on the dressing table and she was still screaming. I then took my hand and put it over Vickie's mouth and kept it there about a minute, trying to get her to calm down. I picked her up, and she was still crying and I knew that Vickie was going to die. I put her head against my shoulder and held her head against my shoulder with her nose and mouth against my shoulder. I wanted her to stop crying and I held her like that for about five minutes until she stopped crying and then I felt her go limp. ... I then took Vickie and laid her facedown in her crib and put her face into the pillow, just like I had done to Heather. I stood there looking at Vickie and thinking, This is the way it had to be and that she was going to die anyway. I then went into the bedroom and laid there and waited for Jane to come home." Then, he added, "I would like to say that I did kill my daughters Heather and Vickie. I would like to say that I did not plan to kill them nor did I do it for the money. I think the reason I killed them was because I wanted someone, namely my wife, Jane, to love me more. . . ."

It was 9:30 P.M. Brennan called Fitzpatrick and gave him the news. They decided they wouldn't arrest Van Der Sluys just yet. He wasn't going anywhere. "I'll talk to Mitchell," Fitzpatrick said excitedly. Erik Mitchell was Onondaga County's new medical examiner. A couple of weeks later, word of the case leaked in a front-page story in the *Herald-Journal*.

DEATHS OF COUPLE'S THREE INFANT CHILDREN PROBED

Authorities in Onondaga County are investigating the mysterious deaths of three children of a former Syracuse couple. The youngsters died in 1976, 1977 and 1979.

Sources close to the investigation said the bodies may be exhumed by court order as part of the reexamination of cases that had been closed years ago. The cases were reopened, according to the sources, on the "hunch" of a retired Syracuse police officer who had investigated the death of the first child in 1976. . . .

Van Der Sluys was arrested the first week of October—nearly nine years since Frank Budzielek had pulled the morgue reports on Heath and Heather. It was amazing to Fitzpatrick that Van Der Sluys had managed to get away with so much for so long. He could have been taken down at so many points earlier, by any number of people. Vickie Lynn could have been saved, he realized. The case, in fact, had spanned such a length of time that had things gone differently, Van Der Sluys could have been Fitzpatrick's first case as chief homicide prosecutor. Not, as it would turn out—for he did not see the turn of events coming his way— his last.

4

The four dozen lawyers of the Onondaga County district attorney's office occupied half the twelfth floor of the Civic Center building in downtown Syracuse. Like any sizable prosecutor's office, it was a maze of cramped warrens that was scarcely big enough to contain all the ego and aggression of the people who worked within.

Certainly, the appeals bureau, the first stop through the door, was not going to contain Bill Fitzpatrick very long after he was hired as a rookie assistant district attorney in the spring of 1976. Actually, he had arrived as a law clerk while a third-year student at Syracuse University Law School. John Cirando, the senior assistant district attorney, who ran the appeals section, had gone there to judge the moot-court competition, and one of the professors had tipped him about Fitzpatrick: You've gotta see this kid argue the prosecution side. Cirando, like a baseball scout with a good eye, saw that the prospect had all the tools and signed him right up. Years later, an old mentor would remark, with amused admiration, that Fitzpatrick's parents were such wonderfully gentle people, "and out comes this goddamn guy who just wants to kick ass and take names."

He had been raised in New York City, in the Brooklyn neighborhood of Bay Ridge, a working-class enclave at the edge of the Narrows, the body of water separating Brooklyn from Staten Island. For most of Fitzpatrick's youth, his father, Bill Senior, was a detective working out of Brooklyn's 88th Precinct, though he was an immensely friendly and warmhearted man who sorely missed his days on uniformed foot patrol. "They were short on guys who could smack the typewriter" is how he explained his promotion.

Back in their father's patrol days, Billy and his older brother, Barry, who would grow up to be a brother in a Catholic order, loved the rare days when Officer Fitzpatrick came home in uniform rather than changing at the station house. Billy's favorite police story was how Dad, back in 1949, ran down a robbery suspect who had grabbed another cop's revolver right in the station house and escaped into the street, shooting all the way. "Well, out he came," his father would say, "and we chased him down the street. I shot him just as he hit the curb. He rolled over and shot back, and the bullet landed in another detective's belt. He got up and started to run and I shot him a second time, and then a third. Each time he's shooting back. A civilian gets hit in the butt getting out of the subway. And then I tackled him."

Billy Fitzpatrick's eyeglasses gave him a studious appearance, but his personality leaned toward the rambunctiously inquisitive. His father took him to the police academy when he was ten, and Billy brought home a fingerprint kit. He dusted the entire house for evidence. He wanted to grow up to be a real cop—if he couldn't play baseball, his first true love—but by high school he had begun to realize that his interests would lead him to a different place. American politics intrigued him, as well as Russian history. He prayed that Princeton would take him. Syracuse did. For a time he thought he might like to become a journalist, but when a professor recommended law school, Fitzpatrick felt a click of recognition. It wasn't long before he knew that he would be a prosecutor. If there was one thing he had not left home without, it was an innate desire to chase bad guys down the street, firing a second time, then a third. And then blowing them away on summation.

He figured he'd go home after graduation and work in one of New York City's mega-prosecutors' offices, where they were always hiring, criminal justice being one of his hometown's leading industries. But then John Cirando arranged a full-time job in Onondaga County, and Fitzpatrick withdrew his applications from Brooklyn and the Bronx. Having spent six years in Syracuse as a student, he had come to like the place. Onondaga was a medium-sized county of nearly half a million people, 150,000 of them within the Syracuse city limits. Downtown was in need of renewal, but the city had a buzzing political life (marked by a steady parade of scandal), the culture of the university, and not too far off, countryside rolling south toward the Finger Lakes, north to the Great Lakes. Fitzpatrick also realized that it would be a lot easier to make his mark in a more manageable place, in an office with thirty or forty lawyers as opposed to three or four hundred. And if he took the Thruway, he could stop at Cooperstown on the way home to Brooklyn.

So there he sat in the appeals bureau, opposite Kevin Mulroy, an equally brash young Syracuse Law graduate with big plans, looking up case law and writing briefs by day, drinking long and late, hitting golf balls with a seven iron down Harrison Street by night, then reporting, hung over, to the district attorney the next morning for cross-examination: "All right, what were you fuckers doing last night?" Dick Hennessy would demand. The two young prosecutors learned to deny everything. You work hard and you play hard— that was their credo. Sooner or later you'll be up there in the big courtrooms getting your name in the paper. They had it all figured out: who was good and who wasn't, who to learn from, who to step on, who to fear.

Fitzpatrick was a tall and lean young man with a serious, bespectacled face, lips that formed a tight wave, and a chin that tended to cave in when he talked. While he did not have Mulroy's smooth looks, he had presence, a prominent part of which was the verbal moxie of the New York Irishman, his glibness barely softened for Syracuse. Right from the start, he made it clear to Norman Mordue, the head of the trial unit and a man whose eye every young A.D.A. wanted to catch, that he would take any case, even the ones others "wouldn't go near with their good shoes," as the saying went. It was one of those cases that established Fitzpatrick, in Mordue's mind, as a serious hotshot.

A woman had been brutally beaten and apparently raped, but she couldn't remember a thing. The case was going nowhere when Fitzpatrick told Mordue he wanted to take a shot at it; he had an idea. Why not? Mordue thought. Let's see what the kid can do. What Fitzpatrick did was to hire a hypnotist. The woman remembered enough to give the twenty-five-year-old prosecutor his first major conviction. Later, the conviction was overturned; the appeals court found that Fitzpatrick's maneuver, while enterprising, had failed to produce properly admissible evidence. Eventually he got a second conviction and a small footnote in legal history: The case established what became known in New York State as the Hughes Hearing, named for Fitzpatrick's defendant, in which a judge could determine whether there was a proper basis for the use of hypnosis in a case before him.

"Hennessy liked guys that weren't afraid to go into court and tear somebody's balls off," Mulroy remembered. "And Billy and I just tried every case we could. There was a real fight for good trial files, and in the beginning you had to do all the crappy little burglaries, criminal mischief, the junk. But the guys who wanted to go out and tear somebody's throat out, they were homicide guys. You didn't get any uglier than that. That was the goal. Within the trial unit there was a hierarchy. Norm Mordue sat at the end of the office, and he had an office with a door on it. At the beginning he was the only one doing homicides, but as we had more murders in the city, other senior guys got in there. And eventually Billy rose even above them. He leapfrogged a lot of inbetween guys."

It wasn't just that he possessed the proper jungle instincts. From Mordue, Fitzpatrick learned the value of trial preparation and of working a jury. This struck a chord. When he was thirteen, Fitzpatrick read a book about the Lindbergh baby case, and what he never forgot was how intricately the prosecutor, David Wilentz, wrapped the circumstantial evidence around Bruno Richard Hauptmann's neck. He found it a virtuoso performance, like Don Larsen's perfect game or Willie Mays's spectacular over-the-head catch in the 1954 World Series. In fact, if there was one person Fitzpatrick always wanted to meet as much as Larsen or Mays, it was Wilentz.

From their early days working from facing desks in the lowly appeals bureau, Fitzpatrick and Mulroy each dreamed of one day running the whole office. As they rose through the ranks, they worried that the close friendship they'd developed would fall victim to a bloody clash of ambitions. But something told Mulroy that although he had the advantage of a local political pedigree—the building in which they worked was named for his father—the top job would probably not go to him, but to Fitzpatrick. To Mulroy, Fitzpatrick was living proof of the maxim that great trial lawyers are born, not made; he had the cockiness, the little something extra. Fitzpatrick was not just one of the golden boys in the D.A.'s office, Mulroy thought. He was *the* golden boy. *Someday, he'll be D.A.,* Mulroy thought, *and I won't.*

By the mid-1980s, Fitzpatrick had made himself a small legend around the marble corridors of the county courthouse, an ornate copper-domed building next door to the Civic Center. He had prosecuted most of the big murder cases in recent years with a courtroom style that was fast, loose, and right on the money. But for him, it wasn't always enough to prosecute a crime; there were times he wanted to go back and *solve* it. He kept a lookout for cases that puzzled the police. If they couldn't put it together, he was ready to pick up the pieces. Sometimes he even fantasized himself as a homicide detective, a preoccupation that did not always go over well with the homicide detectives. It was not unheard of for a police investigator to tell him, "You're too involved in this case. Let us do our job and you do your job." It was also not unheard of for Fitzpatrick to say, "I'll let you do your job, but you're not doing it right. So let me do it right."

One day he said to Kevin Mulroy, "Let's dig out that U-Haul thing and work on it." It was the unsolved case of a kid barely out of his teens who was shot to death while working the night shift at a U-Haul office. A couple of robbers had dragged him into a bathroom and shot him, apparently for the hell of it. Two years later, the case was all but dead. Fitzpatrick, though, felt it just needed some more work. He and Mulroy, who was more or less going along for the ride, retrieved a box of reports from storage, and when Mulroy moved on to other things, Fitzpatrick brought in his buddy Peter Tynan, his favorite police detective. Tynan worked Fitzpatrick's homicides for years, and played golf and drank with him. There was an understanding between them that if Fitzpatrick ever got elected district attorney, his first hire would be Tynan as chief investigator. They reinterviewed witnesses, found some new ones, got a fluky break on a ballistics match, and solved the case. Mulroy was astounded. "In my mind, this was the case that separated Fitzy from everybody else. It ate him up to see things not solved. So he took something that was nothing but a cardboard box, the files and photographs, and it represented a dead kid nobody cared about and two or three assholes who were out there free. And he took that dusty box and brought two people before the bar and sent them to prison for life."

In District Attorney Dick Hennessy's office, it was dangerous for a subordinate's star to shine too brightly. Eclipsing the boss in the public consciousness could be a fatal mistake, though one could never be sure where the line was or when it was about to be crossed. It was a hazard that came with the highly visible job of chief homicide prosecutor—especially if the holder of that position was known to have designs on the boss's job. In fact, Fitzpatrick had gotten his big promotion the day Hennessy apparently decided that Norm Mordue's face had been on TV once too often. Driving back from a suburban murder arraignment at which the cameras had turned not to him but to Mordue, Hennessy informed his deputy that he'd prosecuted his last homicide. "Fitz is taking your cases," he said. Mordue, who was commonly regarded as Hennessy's heir apparent, left the office soon after and ran for the county court bench. His first murder trial as a judge was a classic whodunit involving a millionaire roofer from the suburbs, his mistress, some missing money, and a fatal gunshot. It was prosecuted by his successor and former protégé, thirty-one-year-old Bill Fitzpatrick.

Fitzpatrick picked up where Mordue left off, and probably outdid his mentor on the tote board of press coverage. His dogged prosecution of the case of the murdered roofing magnate had everyone talking, and he was named one of the area's "movers and shakers" by the *Herald American*. Now it was Fitzpatrick people were talking about as the next district attorney.

Hennessy had been good to Fitzpatrick through the years, and Fitzpatrick had reciprocated with his loyalty. It was no secret that he fully intended to be the district attorney someday, but he promised publicly that he would never run against his boss. Then, in the fall of 1985, Fitzpatrick made the mistake of appearing for the People in the courtroom of Judge Mordue and successfully prosecuting an awful son-of-a-bitch named Hubert James Allen. The defendant stood accused of slaying his common-law wife, along with a witness who happened to be their six-year-old son, crimes that earned him the sobriquet Mad Dog, and this sheepish disclaimer by his court-appointed attorney at

summation: "I'm not here to argue to you that this man is one of life's innocents." The defense lawyer, Edward Menkin, was once a colleague of Fitzpatrick's in Mordue's trial unit in the district attorney's office, and when it
was over and Mad Dog was on his way to oblivion, Menkin, the only member
of the Syracuse bar with a doctorate in English, offered Fitzpatrick a "Nice
job, Willy," remarking to the nearby Syracuse *Post-Standard* columnist Dick
Case that this was "a gladiatorial courtesy."

Though Fitzpatrick didn't know it yet, he too was quickly approaching
the imaginary line. He was starting to work on the next big murder case, getting ready for grand jury and preparing the papers for an exhumation, when
Hennessy called him in and told him to turn over the case file. The district
attorney was going to personally try Stephen Van Der Sluys for murder.

Fitzpatrick was angry but not particularly surprised. He knew the district
attorney's office was a political position, and Hennessy could hardly be con-
demned for envisioning himself standing up in a courtroom and pointing an
accusatory finger at a man who had killed his own children. What concerned
Fitzpatrick more was what this might portend.

One afternoon a couple of months later, two sheriff's detectives came to
see Fitzpatrick about a case of arson. There had been a fire and two children
had died. Another assistant district attorney had gone to the scene and classified the fire as an accident, but the sheriff's detectives were convinced there
was more to it. The children's mother was involved with a woman who was a
known arsonist. There was evidence of a quarrel, possibly a lesbian lovers' tri-
angle. The detectives were hoping Fitzpatrick would see it their way. What
they didn't mention was that they'd already been to see the other A.D.A., who
had kicked the file up to Hennessy. Hennessy, in turn, had jotted a cryptic
note in the file: "There's always hope." It was Hennessy's way of saying he
wanted no action until the police brought in a confession.

Fitzpatrick read the file, then looked up at the detectives. "I'm gonna put
this in for a grand jury investigation," he said. "She's going down." The detectives practically high-fived their way out of the office.

When Hennessy found out the case was across the hall at the grand
jury, he was livid. "Goddammit, you've usurped my authority!" he told
Fitzpatrick. "Who do you think's in charge here?" He refused to sign the
indictment.

"You've got to sign it," Fitzpatrick told him, incredulous. "The grand jury
voted it." Hennessy did, but the struggle was not over. Fitzpatrick got a true
bill from the grand jury. From Hennessy, he got a Mordue Memo, as it
became known. Henceforth, he would do homicides only every other month.
The rest of his time he would be the liaison between the district attorney's
office and Family Court. For a prosecutor, Family Court basically meant

juvenile delinquency. It was a serious demotion. "No, it's not a demotion," Hennessy told the press. "It's an expansion of his duties."

Fitzpatrick had never seriously considered going out into private practice. That would mean actually defending criminals. But he also had no doubt that his relationship with Hennessy was suddenly at the point of no return.

On October 1, 1985, with Investigators John Brennan and Dan Boyle looking on, Dr. Erik Mitchell, the Onondaga County medical examiner, exhumed the bodies of Heath and Heather Van Der Sluys from the White Chapel Cemetery in Syracuse. Two days later, in Mechanicville, Harvey LaBar and Bob Chase were among a small group standing in silence as Vickie Lynn was brought up from Hudson View Cemetery.

The unembalmed bodies of the first two children were in no condition to offer much meaningful information to Mitchell. Bob Chase had prepared Heather's body for burial in Syracuse, but had seen no reason to preserve it especially well. But his work on fifteen-month-old Vickie two years later in Mechanicville was astounding. The child's body was in almost perfect condition. Those present at the exhumation thought she looked like a sleeping angel.

The gathering in the pathology lab at Albany Medical Center included Dr. Jack Paston, whose autopsy findings six years before had shielded Van Der Sluys from a more serious investigation. This time, however, Paston would be an observer. The re-autopsy would be performed by Dr. Jack N. P. Davies, a British-born pathologist who had worked for the New York State Police on a number of homicide cases. "Congratulations," he said to Chase when he first saw the body. "What a lovely job of embalming you've done."

Even before he opened the child's body, Davies knew that her age made Paston's SIDS diagnosis invalid. And when he looked inside, he observed what might have been another effect of her age: lung lesions that would not normally be found in a SIDS case. More likely, they were an indication of a toddler's struggle for breath. "The child certainly died of asphyxiation and with gross pulmonary edema and congestion," Davies wrote. "No natural causes of this were found, the condition was not SIDS and the appearances are more consistent with smothering."

Even without such a forthright finding on Heather, Erik Mitchell was able to testify to an Onondaga County grand jury that the circumstantial evidence indicated that a natural death was, under the circumstances, "not very likely." There was a certain want of conviction to Mitchell's testimony—a careful reading left the inference that he thought she was *probably* murdered, but that the absence of physical evidence from autopsy left him slightly equivocal. For a grand jury, though, it was enough to return an indictment. The jurors did not have to consider the thornier question of Heath's death: Absent an admission from Van Der Sluys, Hennessy had decided not to charge him with killing his firstborn child.

For the next nine months, the parallel murder cases, Heather's in Onondaga and Vickie's in Saratoga, simmered while Van Der Sluys's court-appointed lawyers began preparing their defenses. In Saratoga, Van Der Sluys was given a public defender. In Onondaga, Judge William Burke assigned the case to Ed Menkin. Menkin was thrilled that Hennessy would be trying the case himself. They'd had their ups and downs over the years; now he could hardly wait to go at him in court. He was going to "kick Hennessy's ass," Menkin would tell Fitzpatrick whenever he ran into him. "I'm gonna embarrass your boss," he'd razz. To which Fitzpatrick replied: "Man, you're lucky I'm not trying that case."

By summer, Fitzpatrick had made up his mind to quit the office over his falling-out with the boss. But it was a painful time for Hennessy; his wife was dying of cancer, and the effect on him was obvious. The Van Der Sluys case was scheduled for September, and there was a real question whether he was prepared. Fitzpatrick decided he would put off his departure for a while; in spite of their falling out, he still had some residual affection for Hennessy, whom he'd considered something of a surrogate father in Syracuse, and whose ego problems as a boss had come out only after a long and mutually prosperous tenure. As he later told people, "I worked for the guy for ten years, and nine of them were great."

One day in August, Hennessy called him in. "I'm giving Van Der Sluys back to you," he said. For a split second, Fitzpatrick considered revenge. *Menkin's geared up,* he thought, *and now I'm supposed to bail you out.* What he said was, "Okay, Dick. Give me a couple of weeks and I'll be ready. It's a great case." The trial was less than a month away.

5

Fitzpatrick had to scramble. Dave Wait was scheduled to take Stephen Van Der Sluys to trial in Saratoga County in early September, and as soon as there was a verdict in Vickie's death, the Onondaga County sheriff's department would haul the defendant back to Syracuse to stand trial for Heather's. From the moment Hennessy handed the case back to him, Fitzpatrick had found himself emotionally absorbed. He had seen a lot in his ten years as a prosecutor, but nothing like this. The victims were just babies.

He had gotten a chance to cross-examine Van Der Sluys during a pretrial hearing months earlier, when he stood in for Hennessy. Peering at the witness stand, the prosecutor was surprised to find a whimpering, self-absorbed, physically insignificant killer. He could not believe Van Der Sluys's self-pity. "He broke down and cried," he remembered. "Nothing to do with the deaths of his children. Just with the way he was treated: 'I was tricked, they put pressure on me, you don't know what it was like, the way you're putting pressure on me now.' And you just wanted to get up and grab him around the collar and give him a thorough pummeling. It was like his confession: 'Jane is my whole life, and then my sweet adorable cuddly little Vickie was born.' Like she was a doll, my sweet little Vickie, who by the way I snuffed out like a matchstick. Well, I give the cops a lot of credit, because I would have slugged him during the interrogation. I wouldn't have been able to control myself. And then the confession would have been worthless."

As the trial approached, Fitzpatrick knew he had to get a grip on his emotions. Time was running out in more ways than one. Van Der Sluys was to be his last case as an assistant district attorney—though he would wait until after the trial to tell Hennessy—and he wanted to go out a winner. This was no slam dunk. As he recalled: "We've got a confession. Great. And we've got a dead body. But we don't have a murder case. They've got a murder case in Saratoga County. But we don't have a murder case here." The problem was in corroborating Van Der Sluys's sometimes ambiguous confession—in proving that a crime had, in fact, been committed. A jury could not convict on the confession alone. Bob Chase and Dr. Davies, with their collaboration of mortuary science and forensic pathology, had taken care of that problem in Saratoga, but physical evidence was going to be a big problem in Syracuse.

"I can't tell you what this child died from," Erik Mitchell had told Fitzpatrick after the re-autopsy of Heather. Yes, a big problem. True, Mitchell could testify that SIDS was an all-purpose way of saying, "Who knows?" How smothering was, as he put it, "a great way to kill a child without leaving much in the way of evidence." He could even say, as he had to the grand jury, that the suspicious circumstances of the Van Der Sluys family history led him to believe that Heather was in all likelihood murdered. But there is no cross-examination by a defense attorney in a grand jury hearing. And when it came to the magic words *reasonable degree of medical certainty,* Ed Menkin was going to be jumping around the courtroom like a jackrabbit. Menkin knew from his own conversations with Mitchell that the medical examiner's hedging represented a hole in the prosecution's case the size of a medicine ball. He could do a lot of damage with Mitchell's incertitude. If he could no longer have the pleasure of kicking Hennessy's ass, Menkin could at least enjoy the gladiatorial redemption of kicking Fitzpatrick's.

Fitzpatrick recognized that the dilemma in prosecuting this particular form of child abuse was defining the line between infanticide and SIDS. One was a riddle of the contorted mind, the other an aberration of the undeveloped body. On the pathologist's table the two could be indistinguishable; in a court of law they could be either clarified or further obscured. From the prosecutor's perspective, Fitzpatrick was coming to conclude, the case of Heather Van Der Sluys boiled down to a fairly uncomplicated scenario: "I'm going to say, Dr. Mitchell, is the condition of this child on physical examination back in 1977 by Dr. Alsever consistent with the defendant's confession? 'Yes, it is.' Thank you, the People rest. The defense cross-examination: Could this child have died from SIDS? 'Yes.' The defense rests. Reasonable doubt. See you later."

For now, though, Fitzpatrick felt he had to stick with Mitchell. He had nobody else.

Beth Van Doren had joined the district attorney's office two years earlier, after a judicial clerkship and a stint working in a law office with Fitzpatrick's wife, Diane. It also did her no harm that her father, an obstetrician, had delivered Dick Hennessy's children. On the other hand, she wasn't expecting easy advancement.

The D.A.'s office was a severely male environment, a place where a smart, educated woman could not expect to be carried by merit alone. This was not news to Van Doren. In her brief life as a young, female defense attorney, she'd heard it all: "Defendants standing next to me, starting to cry, saying, 'Please tell me you're not my lawyer.' Clients calling my partner and saying, 'Don't ever send your secretary to court again.' Being kicked out of courtrooms: 'Honey, you've got to wait until your lawyer gets here.' "

She worked in an obscure nook of the D.A.'s office known as the legal research unit. Now Fitzpatrick wanted her to back him up on the Van Der Sluys case. "Here, Beth," he said one day late in the summer, handing her a pile of medical literature gathered by a law clerk. "We've got a real problem with the medical. Read through this stuff and see if there's anything in there we can use."

In the technical writings of physicians and researchers, Van Doren found herself confronting observations like this: "Petechial hemorrhages of the pleurae, epicardium, and thymus; epidural hemorrhage in the spinal canal; and pulmonary congestion and edema may or may not be found in various combinations with death by asphyxia or crib death." But if there was a message in the literature, it was that eyes were starting to open to something ghastly. The notion of SIDS as a camouflage for murder (and the closely related, fiercely debated question of whether there could be multiple SIDS deaths within families) was gaining considerable notice from the small corner of medicine where pathology, pediatrics, and forensics crossed paths.

One article in particular caught Van Doren's eye. Titled simply "Child Abuse," it had appeared three years earlier, in the June 1983 volume of a publication called *Clinics in Laboratory Medicine—Symposium on Forensic Pathology*. The author was a physician named Linda Norton, a forensic pathologist in Dallas who also described herself as a "medicolegal consultant." It was a trenchant twenty-two-page review that, as the author promised in her opening, explored "unrecognized or ignored" aspects of child abuse. Most of the paper dealt with traumatic physical abuse and neglect, illustrated by horrific photographs that made Van Doren recoil. But she pressed on and began to detect an iconoclastic, almost moralistic point of view. This seemed to be a doctor with no small scorn for those of her fellow physicians who could look at a set of facts that pointed directly at child abuse and come to a completely opposite and naïve conclusion. Historically, Norton noted, physicians had given far greater weight to the medical history given by a child's caretaker than to the ominous signs they saw themselves in the examining room.

"Discrepancies," she wrote, "were handled by either ignoring inconsistencies—making square pegs fit into round holes—or by proffering an 'isn't that curious' attitude and burying the issue entirely."

Four pages from the end, Van Doren found a section on infanticide, the murder of children under a year of age. This was where the square-pegs-in-round-holes problem was most subtle, Norton wrote, because smothering, the easiest way to kill a baby, could be virtually undetectable. She subtitled this section of her paper "Child Abuse and the Sudden Infant Death Syndrome":

> Unlike homicidally asphyxiated adults who, unless debilitated, will invariably have some other injury indicating a struggle, an infant will not. His small size relative to the adult precludes any struggle which would produce visible injury. Furthermore, it has been noted in studies on both human and monkey infants that blockage of the airway most often produces no active response in the awake state and that apnea produced in this fashion will sometimes persist even after the occlusion is removed, necessitating active resuscitation to save life. Airway occlusion in a sleeping infant rarely even disturbs his rest.
>
> Another interesting observation with SIDS is that in large studies there is no evidence of genetic transmission. Yet there are numerous reports in the literature of this phenomenon occurring up to five times in the same family. Simultaneous death in twins has even been reported and attributed to SIDS. Although this is possible, it is much more likely that these cases are actually homicidal smotherings. Unlike infant battering, where inconsistencies between injury and history are apparent, or at least should be apparent, it is impossible clinically to distinguish spontaneous apneic spells from those deliberately induced, and likewise impossible for the pathologist to distinguish between the two at autopsy. Thus, a case of infant smothering is usually discovered either as a result of a confession by the perpetrator or overwhelming circumstantial evidence. . . .
>
> Most cases of SIDS do not represent homicidal smothering, and the questioning of parents who have just lost a child to SIDS may appear to be insensitive and unnecessary. Certainly such interrogation should not be the norm. However, when there is a history of other deaths from SIDS in the same family, when other potential signs of abuse are present, or when circumstances surrounding the death are suspicious, then further investigation is warranted.

Van Doren read on as the article delved into the sleep apnea theory of SIDS, and its unique relationship to fatal child abuse. The theory, that SIDS was essentially a fatal pause in respiration, had swelled into a controversial medical movement in the past decade. It had spawned the profitable industry of home infant monitors on the basis of two of its central suppositions: that apnea-induced SIDS could run in families and that some babies developed "symptoms" that could be used to predict and prevent death—spells sometimes so severe that they were dubbed "near-miss SIDS." But Norton took a decidedly cynical view of the apnea theory. She described the case of a woman from Baltimore named Martha Woods, who was convicted of smothering an adopted baby in her care—one of seven infant deaths linked to Woods during her trial in 1972, the same year the apnea theory was conceived. The deaths spanned three decades, from the 1940s to the 1960s, and all of them, Norton noted, were preceded by supposed "near-misses" that were reported by the mother but unconfirmed by medical personnel. She continued:

> Although the case is probably the most dramatic known to date, it is certainly not isolated. In a pending case involving a 15-month-old child, eight apneic episodes preceded the child's death; at least one well-respected pediatrician considers this to be ample proof that the child suffered from "near-miss" SIDS, ultimately culminating in SIDS. However, the child was well past the age for a SIDS death and all the "near-misses" occurred when the mother was alone with him both in and out of the hospital. When interrogated, she admitted to "holding her hand over his nose and mouth until he stopped breathing."
>
> Ironically, the article which appears to have been most influential in propagating the sleep apnea hypothesis and the subsequent vigorous research and monitoring efforts is based on five infants who all probably belong in the same category as the child described above. The first two subjects, in particular, are noteworthy. Infant 1 was admitted to the study because of recurrent episodes of apnea and cyanosis. Her numerous hospital admissions were fairly uneventful. Profound apneic episodes, however, were frequent at home after hospital discharges. She died at home. Three siblings had succumbed at home following similar episodes.
>
> Infant 2 was born one year after the death of his sibling, infant 1, and was immediately monitored in the hospital for over one month. On the day following discharge he experienced a severe apneic episode resulting in another hospitalization of over another month. The morning after this discharge he was readmitted for alleged aspiration during a feeding. This hospitalization lasted six days. The morning after this final discharge he had another apneic episode and died. Thus, 78 days of this child's 81 days of life were spent in the hospital and only three at home. The catastrophic events in the child's life occurred during those three days.

This was all very interesting, but could any of it help convict Stephen Van Der Sluys? There were similarities between his case and those Norton cited, but what could you use in court? Van Doren moved on to the next article in the pile.

One afternoon a few days later, Fitzpatrick told her to put the research aside. They were going to Canandaigua to interview Jane Van Der Sluys.

Beth appreciated the invitation; she was glad to be included in the case beyond the task of reading scholarly articles that seemed to agree on little beyond what color babies turned when they became "cyanotic." Still, something she had read in Linda Norton's paper stayed with her. She had absorbed a number of articles since then, and while driving to Canandaigua with Fitzpatrick and John Brennan, it struck her that the Texas pathologist's paper had an important, perhaps pivotal, bottom line: Contrary to what seemed to be common belief, crib death did not run in families. According to this doctor, multiple unexplained infant deaths were in all likelihood homicides.

Jane Van Der Sluys didn't know what to make of the entourage from Syracuse that showed up at her door that late summer day. When John Brennan had called to set up the meeting, Jane told him she really didn't want to talk to them. Steve was still her husband. Did she have to talk to them? "Well," Brennan told her, "if you want to get at the truth, I would think you would want to tell what you know."

This pitch had resonance for Jane. The year since her husband's arrest had been a time of tormenting internal conflict. Steve could be so secretive, and his statement seemed to unlock so much. Yet, she could not bring herself to believe the worst of it. One weekend, her father drove to Canandaigua to try to persuade her to come home to Mechanicville. Come back to the family, he pleaded; we'll support you. Come home with the children. But Jane could not take that final step of abandonment. Outside her apartment, Jim Bowers sat at the wheel of his parked car and wept. His youngest child, thirteen-year-old Jake, sat beside him, frozen with fear and sadness.

Now, though, less than a month before the trial, Jane was softening. She was finally starting to look at things objectively. She told her family: I still can't believe it, but if he's convicted, I will accept it and I will come home.

She knew she was going to be in the uncomfortable position of testifying as a key prosecution witness. She was the only person who could establish that Steve was alone with the children when they died, and the only one who could offer an independent firsthand account of the night of Heather's death. That's all Fitzpatrick really wanted out of her—that, and her testimony about how Steve couldn't wait to spend the insurance money. He knew she was fighting hard to stand behind her husband, and he was careful not to try to persuade her of Steve's guilt. He had no interest in debating the point with her. If she was a compliant and dutiful wife, Fitzpatrick hoped, maybe she would also be a compliant and dutiful witness.

Van Doren, on the other hand, had come into the case wondering how Jane could not have been involved. At the least, how could she not have *known?* "And then I looked at her, and I thought, who knows?" she recalled. "You looked at this woman and you saw that she was living in a cloud, and if she wasn't she was doing a great job of acting. When we got there she seemed more concerned with the practical aspects, where will we sit, who's going to watch the children while we talk, instead of the magnitude of what we were there to talk about."

It was Beth who was going to watch the children. She played with five-year-old Shane and three-year-old Jennifer out in the yard. You couldn't have them listening to this. The baby, Corey, stayed inside with his mother. He had been born a few weeks after his father confessed to murdering his siblings, and five days after Paula Byron gave birth to his half-sister. Like Shane and Jennifer, both babies had slept with apnea monitors during their first months of life.

Corey played on the floor as Jane related to Fitzpatrick and Brennan the details of the night, nine years before, when she went out to get a curling iron and came home and found Heather dead. "He was very insistent that I go out even though it was snowing," she told them, and a wave of reality began to wash over her. When they left, she knew something was different. "Before they came, I was starting to question, but I still wanted to hear him say he didn't do it," she later said. "And when they left, I thought, *I better start thinking more.* Some of it didn't make sense. A lot of it didn't make sense. And soon after that I started to reason more, instead of feel."

Fitzpatrick sensed her transition. Before he left, he took Jane's hand and told her how bad he felt for her. "She's going to be a good witness," he told Van Doren and Brennan on the drive back to Syracuse. "When the jury sees her, they'll understand what was going on in that family. All she has to do is tell the truth and she'll bury him."

The conversation turned in the direction of the big blind curve of the upcoming trial: How were they going to medically corroborate Van Der Sluys's police statement? The insurance policies were good circumstantial evidence. Jane's testimony would help. But none of this would be enough. You had to have some forensic validation that this was a case of murder.

On this question, Van Doren had an idea. She felt comfortable offering it to Fitzpatrick. They had dated years before, and had remained friends through Diane. "I think we need an outside expert," she said. "I don't think we can stay with Erik Mitchell."

Fitzpatrick hadn't thought much about getting a second opinion. He wasn't big on bringing in a lot of experts to say whatever you wanted them to say—"whores," as the worst of them were known in the trial business.

"They'll say the sun's rising in the west tomorrow if you want, and do a convincing job of it for the jury" is how Fitzpatrick saw them. Erik Mitchell wasn't really the problem anyway, as far as he could tell. It was unlikely that another forensic pathologist could find what Mitchell couldn't.

Mitchell's good, Beth said, but this slice of pathology isn't his field. He knew no less than most medical examiners about the subtleties of infanticide, but no more. And there was a potentially thorny issue: How would Mitchell deal with having to say, in essence, that his predecessor had screwed up? Even if he did, there was the problem of perception: The medical examiner's office was often seen as an extension of the prosecutor's office. In a case like this, where the doctor would be offering an unusually subjective opinion, that could hurt.

"We need someone with no local ties," Van Doren said. "We need someone who can give some credibility to the medical evidence." She told Fitzpatrick about the article by the forensic pathologist from Texas, Linda Norton. Her physical findings wouldn't be different than Mitchell's, but her interpretations might be. She appeared to be someone with strong convictions, Van Doren noted. Definitely not a whore. "She looks like the only one who supports the theory that you can't have multiple SIDS in one family. I think we should get her in here."

"Don't they say that multiple deaths means you've got something hereditary?" Fitzpatrick asked.

"This Norton seems to say something else."

"Well, does she know what the hell she's talking about?"

"She seems to be an expert in child abuse."

"Is there anybody else out there we should be talking to?"

"Norton's the one," said Van Doren.

Linda Norton's voice on the phone had a southern drawl that sounded more southeast than southwest in origin. She talked the way she wrote, with style and conviction, straight to the point.

"Honey, you don't have SIDS," she told Van Doren after she heard only a brief rundown of the facts. "You've got yourself a homicide."

Van Doren couldn't decide which was more jarring: that Norton's judgment was so swift and certain, or that a professional woman she'd never met was calling her honey.

Norton started talking, asking questions, citing cases. Van Doren scribbled. *Any difference autopsy ... near "misses" ... nothing to distinguish ... Woods—Get it ... Steinoper—article—all smothered....*

Van Doren asked Norton if she was available to testify in court—was that

something she did? All the time, Norton said. She said she'd send a curriculum vitae and some other background material to Syracuse. Van Doren
said Fitzpatrick would probably call her. The trial was just a few weeks away.

When he got the envelope containing her c.v., some other medical articles
she'd written, and some written about her, Fitzpatrick saw that Norton was a
medical examiner after his own heart. Like many in his line of work, he
appreciated the value of a little macabre humor now and then; he could
always count on Erik Mitchell to lighten things up at death scenes. He noticed
that the doctor from Texas had a taste for the eccentric, which he thought was
to her credit. "Suicide by Snake Venom Injection" was the title of one paper
she'd coauthored. There was "The Norton Technique for Dental Identification" and "The Exhumation and Identification of Lee Harvey Oswald."
Norton had headed a team that exhumed the body of the presidential assassin
in 1981 at the request of his widow. Marina Oswald had spent a year in court
fighting for a second look after a British author persuaded her that a Russian
agent had been substituted for Oswald during his defection to the Soviet
Union and that it was the imposter who returned to the United States to
assassinate President Kennedy. "The remains in the grave marked as Lee
Harvey Oswald are indeed Lee Harvey Oswald," Norton's article in the
Journal of Forensic Science concluded wryly.

Norton had wandered into forensic pathology shortly after realizing,
while still at Duke Medical School, that she couldn't handle being a doctor to
live people. "I was going to be Florence Nightingale, the Great Healer," she
related one day in Dallas. "The day I realized I couldn't handle doctor-patient
contact was when the head of hematology-oncology allowed me, a piddling
little fourth-year medical student taking a rotation in hematology, to work up
a brand-new private patient of his from a distant part of the state. She was
fifty-three and she came in with her husband, her son, her daughter, her son-
in-law, her daughter-in-law, the whole family. And I worked her up, I did
the history and the physical and the blood smear and the bone marrow exam,
and I was so flattered that he would let me do this. She had a very rare, very
fascinating kind of leukemia that was also very rapidly fatal. Then it came
time to tell the family. So I went back to find the doctor because it's his
patient. And he had left. He had deliberately done that to me, I think to see
what I was made of, like, okay, you love this stuff, let's see if you can handle
this part of it. Well, I went in and started telling this family about this rare,
rapidly fatal leukemia and by the time we finished, I was crying harder than
anyone in the family and they were holding me and patting me and telling
me, 'Please don't cry, it's not your fault.' Yes, the patient is comforting the
doctor. And I thought: This is not going to work."

She didn't fare much better with people who were only a little sick. "I'd get so angry when they wouldn't do what you instructed them to do to get better, and then *they* would be angry at *you*. So I decided I needed a layer of doctor between me and the patient. It was either radiology or pathology and to me there's no question pathology is far more interesting. And then forensic pathology is like being a medical detective. It's fun. When I was at the chief medical examiner's office in North Carolina, we did a psychologic autopsy on Jeffrey MacDonald. Boy, there was no doubt what happened there. Oh, God, yes, he had done it. And then we dug up Oswald, which was really fun. Of course, I wouldn't have gotten myself involved in that if I thought there was going to be nobody in the grave. Can you imagine finding yourself all of a sudden involved in a true conspiracy? No, I didn't want to have to be put into a federal witness protection program for the rest of my life."

But these offbeat forensic adventures were mere diversions for a medical examiner whose work was propelled by a fierce moral resolve. Her interest in exposing the fatal mistreatment of children went all the way back to her introduction to forensic pathology itself, to 1974, the year she testified in her first child abuse case while serving a fellowship in North Carolina's central medical examiner's office. She knew then that the way to be a *doctor,* in the Great Healer sense, in a specialty that many physicians dismissed as pseudo-medicine, was to shed light on the methods and means of unnatural, unde-tected child death, an area of medicine and law that not many people wanted to talk about in those years, much less do something about. In the decade since, she had made not just a specialty but a virtual obsession of preventing even one case of child abuse—no matter what kind or whether the outcome was death or mere serious injury—from slipping by unnoticed.

This was what appealed most to Bill Fitzpatrick. If there was one fact that hooked him when he went over Norton's credentials, it was that she had per-formed virtually every pediatric autopsy in Dallas County in the five years she had spent as a medical examiner there. He could imagine how well her opening credits would play.

"Let me guess," Norton said when Fitzpatrick phoned her about the case of Stephen Van Der Sluys. "Dad was the only one around when the kids had these problems."

"Right. The one we're prosecuting him for, Heather, he said he found her having trouble breathing and they rushed her to the hospital. That was a week before she died."

"And when they died, Mom was never home."

"You got it."

"That's always the way. It's great that you're going after this case. I can't tell you how many prosecutors I've had to browbeat. They won't go without a gunshot wound or a stab wound or bruises all over the body to show the jury."

"Well, we've got his statement. And we've got the insurance policies."

"And you're lucky. It's very rare to get a confession, even when a child's been beaten to death and it's just obvious. What you usually get is the perpetrator tells you everything in exact detail about what happened that day, what they ate for breakfast, what the child ate, everything up until the time of the injury. Then they lie about the mechanism of the injury. And then they go straight back to the truth."

"This guy was all over the place. But it's a good statement."

"Well, you have the fact that there's three deaths. I mean, that just doesn't happen." She asked why Van Der Sluys wasn't being tried for all three.

"We're not charging him on the first one because he wouldn't confess to it," Fitzpatrick said. "I think he did that one too, but I think we'd have a real tough time proving it."

Norton was disappointed. "What was the story with that one?" she asked.

"Dad's story was that the child reached through the bars of his crib and grabbed a quarter and choked on it."

"Well, that's bullshit."

Fitzpatrick liked Norton's style. She wasn't some country coroner playing it safe. She knew her subject, and she was used to talking about it, spreading her indignation like gospel. Fitzpatrick could tell he wasn't her first audience. He felt as though he'd picked up the phone and been connected to a pulpit. In fact, Norton had been trying to get timid prosecutors to go after all kinds of child abusers since her first job as associate chief medical examiner of Chapel Hill in 1975. It was always the same story: Cases were usually circumstantial, and circumstantial wasn't enough for the local district attorney. Yes, this child has a fractured skull and massive intracranial bleeding, and yes, those children all died for no natural reason and only while in the care of their mother, but I'm not taking *that* into open court. Get me a witness; get me a confession. Get me manna from the morgue. There was a paradox in this: Here was a medical examiner, the one member of the criminal justice system to whom all the others looked for incontrovertible physical proof, and she was telling cops and lawyers that they should hang their cases on circumstance. On logic. And if they didn't listen? Well, there was the time she very nearly got into a fistfight with a detective in San Antonio who wouldn't so much as question a father who, after the death of his baby, called the morgue and said, "Have you checked for Bentenyl?" They hadn't, but when they did, they found a lethal dose. "I'm not wasting my time," said the detective. "The district attorney doesn't do child abuse."

Physical abuse—first labeled Battered Child Syndrome in the early 1960s—was widely recognized by now, but Norton had come to realize that there was another kind of child abuser, a furtive, sociopathic killer whose weapon was a pillow or a shoulder or a pair of soft, fleshy hands. This killer left no marks. That's why you had to look harder, look at other things, at the history, at the death scene—at the caretaker. Of course, the overwhelming majority of SIDS deaths were legitimate and heartbreaking. But if there was a pattern, you had to ask some hard questions and use your common sense. This had become Linda Norton's mission by the time Bill Fitzpatrick called her about the Van Der Sluys case: to educate police, prosecutors, pediatricians, social workers, SIDS volunteers, and anyone else in her line of fire about the idea of parents murdering their children and blaming a breathing problem.

She'd had enough of the apnea theory. Pediatricians might think it sounded reasonable, but Norton found it specious. At best, she thought, it was one more unproven theory of SIDS. And at worst? At worst, it could be a medical cover for murder—an alibi that could be used over and over because a companion to the apnea theory was the assumption that whatever mechanism caused prolonged, life-threatening pauses in respiration could very well be familial, if not in the genes themselves. Whereas it was Norton's conviction that the weight of SIDS research clearly showed no familial factor—that serial SIDS more than likely meant serial homicide. Could sudden infant death run in the family? Yes, she liked to say—if there happened to be a murderer in the family.

"I'm gonna need some things," Norton told Fitzpatrick. "All the autopsy reports. Medical records. His statements, the police reports. And I'm gonna need to look at the tissue slides from the autopsies."

"See you in a couple of weeks," Fitzpatrick said. "We're set for opening statements on the twenty-third."

He hung up and told Van Doren, "We're done. Don't look for anyone else." It might have been her best moment in the prosecutor's office. But she was slightly uneasy. *We've got two very strong personalities here,* she thought. *I hope they get along all right.* She also wondered how Erik Mitchell would take the news.

In Dallas, Norton had her assistant book a flight to upstate New York. For her, it was just another courtroom job, if a little farther away than usual. She'd fly up, give her testimony, and be home in twenty-four hours. She did not, at that moment, register the flash of recognition that would become so obvious just a few days later. She was simply going to Syracuse, New York, to testify against a parent who had killed his children.

6

On Tuesday, September 23, 1986, a flock of newspaper and television reporters gathered on the third floor of the Onondaga County Courthouse, an eighty-year-old Beaux Arts building faced with Indiana limestone and once labeled Syracuse's "Great Marble Palace of Justice." The courthouse was filled with elaborate arches and original turn-of-the-century lighting fixtures, with marble floors and a central staircase framed on the lower floors by allegorical murals of legendary episodes from local history.

Judge William Burke, a slight man with a crown of white hair, took his seat in front of the four wooden pillars that were the backdrop of his court. Before him sat the defendant, Stephen Van Der Sluys, accused of smothering his second child, Heather. Next to Van Der Sluys was his court-appointed lawyer, Ed Menkin. At the prosecution table, Bill Fitzpatrick sat alone with his files. The jury box was empty.

Weeks before the trial, Menkin had decided that his client could not afford the risk of being judged by a jury of his peers. Regardless of the rules of evidence, he believed that twelve citizens wouldn't take long to convict Stephen Van Der Sluys on his ramblings alone. A former English professor, Menkin was a trial attorney who made an art form of courtroom drama. But in this case he would go with the law. He would go with Judge Burke, a jurist he regarded as "the one judge in Syracuse who goes out of his way to respect and reward good lawyering"—a defense lawyer's way of saying: He's our guy. For what it was worth, Menkin was also sure he had a personal edge. Burke liked him, and the feeling was mutual.

The same could not be said of Fitzpatrick. Privately, he thought Burke was burned out, a judge who'd been around too long and tended to whine about his missed opportunities in local politics. And even publicly there had been some bad blood. The last time he'd tried a nonjury case before Burke, the judge had left his verdict in an envelope and gone to Long Island for the weekend. He was supposed to consider both murder and manslaughter, and Fitzpatrick was sure he had a winner on the lesser charge. But all the note inside the envelope said was "Not Guilty, Murder." Nothing about manslaughter. Fitzpatrick tried to control himself when the reporters called. "It's kind of ridiculous the way we got the verdict," he told them. Burke didn't speak to him for a year.

Fitzpatrick was approaching the opening of the trial with a renewed determination to win a murder conviction. In Saratoga County just weeks before, District Attorney Dave Wait had surprised him by making a deal with Van Der Sluys in the death of his third child. Fitzpatrick had thought the new autopsy on the perfectly preserved Vickie made Wait's case much stronger than his. He'd even envisioned the possibility of a guilty verdict in Saratoga and then a plea in Onondaga, canceling a trial. But Wait had a different perception. He didn't like the disjointed nature of Van Der Sluys's confession—"he did it, he didn't do it" was his reading. It was an old case, and Wait worried that the results of the new autopsy could be successfully disputed by a pathologist hired by the defense. Wait offered Manslaughter One, and Van Der Sluys took it. He'd get eight and a third to twenty-five years.

Fitzpatrick was annoyed by the plea bargain, but also invigorated: He resolved not to allow Van Der Sluys off without at least one murder conviction, and relished the arrival of his new star witness. Linda Norton, he realized, had given him a wonderful opportunity to sandbag the defense. Now he would use Erik Mitchell not as his key medical witness, but as a decoy. If Menkin was going with the law, Fitzpatrick was going right along with him. And it was going to be beautiful.

Shortly before 10:00, Fitzpatrick rose to deliver his opening statement. With no jury to play to, he offered a straightforward summary of the proof he intended to offer, then asked the judge to understand a few things about the issues at hand. He explained how easily a smothering could pass for Sudden Infant Death Syndrome, and asked Burke to disregard the words Dr. William Alsever, who had died the year before, had written on Heather's original death certificate. SIDS is a hollow term, Fitzpatrick explained. It is not a cause of death—in fact, it means the absence of a cause of death. Had Van Der Sluys made his statements to the police at the time of Heather's death, rather than eight years later, Fitzpatrick asserted, "there is no medical examiner in the world who would have signed that death certificate as SIDS."

Then, Fitzpatrick laid his trap. There would be testimony from Dr. Erik Mitchell, he told Burke. And Mitchell, "if allowed to look at the total picture," would offer his opinion of the death of Heather Van Der Sluys. It was an ostensible reference to the legal question of whether Burke would permit Mitchell to offer an opinion based on circumstance rather than on physical observation. But, in fact, the prosecutor himself had no intention of allowing Mitchell to look at "the total picture" or to give his opinion of the cause of death. He would ask him three or four innocuous questions and send him on his way. By that time, Linda Norton would have already testified that there was no doubt in the world that Heather had been smothered.

Menkin missed the ruse. He was so eager to rip into Mitchell that he heard Fitzpatrick's words in the context of his own plans to co-opt the medical examiner's testimony. Still, he knew he would have to deal with the doctor from Texas. She had come out of nowhere, a virtual mystery witness, and Menkin had tried without success to persuade Burke to exclude her on the grounds of unfair surprise: He'd only been informed of her existence forty-eight hours before trial. If there was only one thing he knew about Norton, it was that she wasn't coming fifteen hundred miles to say she was pretty sure Heather had been murdered.

Fitzpatrick began presenting his case. He entered his exhibits—the confession, the insurance policies. He called his witnesses. Dr. Robert Chavkin, the pediatrician, who testified that Heather was a fine little baby. The police officer who responded to the emergency call the night she died. The insurance brokers who'd sold policies on three babies. The detectives who recounted how Van Der Sluys had come to confess that day in September—and how, during another series of interviews a month later, they couldn't get him to stop talking. At one point, one investigator testified, Van Der Sluys had actually blocked the door of the holding cell to keep him from leaving.

And there was Jane Van Der Sluys. As Fitzpatrick expected, she proved to be an innocent, sympathetic figure. Her gentle manner helped underscore her victimization—and, he hoped, her husband's guilt.

"And, Jane, who lives with you?" Fitzpatrick asked early in her testimony.

"My son Heath . . . or, excuse me . . . I'm sorry."

"That's all right," Fitzpatrick said. He couldn't have scripted it better. "You take as much time as you want."

"My son Shane, my daughter Jennifer, and my baby Corey."

She recalled the incidental details of life the decade before; her testimony matter-of-fact, unaffected by any discernible attitude. Occasionally she would say something curious about her husband in passing. "He liked sleeping with a baby pillow," she said at one point, "versus a large standard-sized pillow." She steeled herself for the moment when she would have to go back to the night of January 7, 1977.

"What do you observe when you go to check on Heather?" Fitzpatrick asked.

"That she was laying on her stomach. And I picked her up because I wanted to see her face"—her voice broke and she dabbed her eyes—"so I picked her up and that's when I knew that she had died."

Finally, Fitzpatrick asked her about her three living children. "To clear up the matter: Is there any insurance on those three children?"

"Not that I know of," Jane said.

Cross-examination was where Ed Menkin hoped to win his case. The law said he was not obliged to call a single witness, and he intended to exercise that option. He had nobody strong, least of all the defendant himself. Instead, he would pound away at Fitzpatrick's twelve witnesses, attack the cops and the confession with both a sledgehammer and a chisel, and play for reasonable doubt. He hoped that Burke would insist on a high level of corroboration and conclude that the prosecution hadn't proven its case.

Menkin could play tough with the others but he had to be careful with Jane. He couldn't beat up on her.

"Do you recall how much rent you paid?" he asked her early in his questioning.

"A hundred fifty a month."

"Did that include utilities?"

"No, I don't think so."

From his seat in the gallery, Jim Bowers wondered where Menkin was going with this. He couldn't imagine what the rent had to do with his murdered grandchildren. Bowers was there not to judge Stephen Van Der Sluys, for he had done that long before. He was there on behalf of his daughter. He wanted his son-in-law to know it.

"Was there a thermostat in the apartment?" Menkin asked Jane.

"Yes, there was."

"What kind of heat was there?"

"I think it was gas."

"Forced air?"

"Uh-huh."

Menkin turned to the cleaning business. "Did you use ammonia?"

"Yeah."

"Did you use salicylic acid to take off rust?"

"I don't recall any."

"What about oxalic acid?"

"I don't know."

"And is it also a fact that after you moved into the flat on Bryant Avenue, you did some painting?"

"Yes."

"All right. Now, Mrs. Van Der Sluys, up till just a couple minutes ago, did anybody ever ask you about the presence of chemicals in your home?"

"I'll have to say no."

"Did anyone ever ask you about the paint that was used in your home?"

"No."

"I know this is difficult enough for you, but I hope you don't take this as too personal a question. . . . Did you have a permanent at that time?"

"No."

"You did not? You're sure about that?"

"Yes, I'm positive."

"So you didn't use any chemicals on your hair?"

The broad implication, of course, was that sudden infant death was so mysterious that who knew why it happened? And that the police hadn't checked into whether Heather could have been accidentally poisoned by chemicals wafting from the storage room or from Jane's hair into Heather's crib. Menkin kept at it. Was there a fireplace in the apartment? Didn't Heather have a lot of colds? Wasn't she born with her umbilical cord wrapped around her neck? Did you participate in a SIDS study? Were you a member of a SIDS support group? Didn't you have a lot of trouble rousing Heather from her nap an hour before she died? Do you recall falling down some stairs while she was in your arms? Didn't Dr. Brooks in Rochester have Shane on an apnea monitor?

"Mrs. Van Der Sluys, did you have any illnesses during your pregnancy?" Menkin asked.

"I know at the beginning of each pregnancy I would be nauseated," Jane answered innocently, trying to be cooperative. "I would have nausea, and I would also get a severe cold. Whenever I got a cold, it was severe. Now, I'm generalizing saying that because of the number of pregnancies I've had, that's held true with each one, so I would have to say yes, I had some sickness during my pregnancy."

Jim Bowers had to hand it to Menkin. The guy was trying everything. Every so often, Bowers looked at his son-in-law with a steely gaze. He hoped Steve noticed.

Linda Norton arrived in Syracuse late Wednesday afternoon. She strode briskly off the jetway at Syracuse-Hancock International Airport, a purposeful woman in her early forties with short, dark hair—almost a John Lennon cut—round-rimmed glasses, and a knowing, mischievous smile. She was quick, direct, divorced—a mother of two whose drolly effervescent manner was perhaps partly a result of spending her days with dead bodies and her nights with teenage girls.

Beth Van Doren met Norton at the gate and drove her into town. She got her checked into the Hotel Syracuse, then brought her up to the office to meet Fitzpatrick, who was just back from court. Dr. Chavkin had testified in the afternoon, and the reporters decided that the news of the day was that the pediatrician said he was "uncomfortable" with Heather's SIDS diagnosis because her brother had died "under circumstances that were somewhat unexplainable." For Fitzpatrick it was a perfect setup for Norton. She would lead off Thursday morning.

For now, though, she was hungry. "How about we eat, then get to work?" she suggested after a few pleasantries. She didn't work well on an empty stomach.

"Well, I'd prefer to work first and then eat, if that's okay," Fitzpatrick said. He didn't eat well on a trial stomach.

Uh-oh, Van Doren thought. Then, a compromise. They'd bring some sandwiches up from the cafeteria, hunker down, then go out for a late dinner. They moved into the conference room next to Hennessy's office. What unfolded there was a little dance that struck Van Doren as something like the sight of two cats staking out their territory. On one side there was Fitzpatrick, an abundantly confident prosecutor who knew what he wanted from his witness and how he intended to get it. On the other side was Norton, an expert with an unambiguous point of view who knew what she wanted to say and, one suspected, favored prosecutors who knew how to act the straight man.

Norton was a seasoned expert witness who testified in all kinds of cases, not all of which involved children. She had first become drawn to child abuse because she saw it as a stark clash of good and evil, but she found it necessary to step back from the fray at regular intervals. She knew that the only way she could specialize in murdered and assaulted children was to erect an emotional wall—"it's a kind of denial," she observed—and that if she did too many of these cases without the distraction of something "extraordinarily boring," the wall would begin to crumble and she would start to feel pain. At that point, it was time to take on a product liability case, or maybe an autopsy review for a family looking for a second opinion before they sued somebody for millions.

It was in the courtroom that Norton felt she did some of her most important work. While she made her professional judgments and diagnoses objectively, on the subject of child abuse Norton was in some sense testifying as an advocate. She viewed the relationship between trial attorney and expert witness as a delicate alliance. She didn't like prosecutors who brought her in and said, "Well, what should I ask you?" but it was also true that nothing disturbed her more than leaving the witness stand without getting her points across because the questioning was so poor. So she'd developed a few guidelines for the lawyers who hired her: "Don't keep me up there more than an hour. Get to the important stuff in the first thirty minutes—after that the jurors start thinking about what they're going to cook for dinner. Keep my qualifying credentials brief. Zip through 'em. And most important: Give me as much leeway as possible. Ask a very broad question and allow me to talk as if I were giving a lecture on child abuse for a bunch of DSS caseworkers."

Fitzpatrick liked the idea of stepping aside and allowing Norton to take Judge Burke into her realm, to educate him about the broad and subtle aspects of SIDS and smothering. He wanted it to build to what he regarded as the pivotal moment of the whole trial: when he would ask Norton for her medical opinion about the cause of Heather's death. All he needed was for Burke to allow himself to hear Norton's answer. Menkin had filed a brief arguing that, Norton's credentials notwithstanding, she had no way of knowing, based on a pile of papers and some tissue slides, how Heather had really died—in legal terms, that she was not competent to answer that particular question.

In Norton's view—and she considered this a basic tenet of her work, her personal catechism—she was not just a pathologist, but a "death investigator." As such, she based her judgments on every piece of evidence and information available, not just on what she saw on the autopsy table. "It's entirely appropriate, in fact I think it would be *in*appropriate to sit up there on the witness stand and say, 'I don't know what the cause of death is' because I'm going to pretend that I don't know any of the rest of the stuff. I'm sure you can find forensic pathologists who really do believe that their limited role is to crawl around in the morgue and sop up dead bodies and report on what they find. We call these 'chop shops.' If you're trained in a chop shop you might feel that's your role because you were stuck down in a morgue someplace and you processed bodies all day long and you were never asked to render an opinion about anything. You'd just report what you found in the body and move it on because you've got twelve more that you've got to process that day."

While all forensic pathologists are called upon to consider circumstances in investigating the typical violent homicide, generally these are physical circumstances—angles of knife wounds, gunshot characteristics, the presence of poison. With the smothering of a baby, medical examiners like Norton rely on factors that are much less tangible. Which is why with Norton, Fitzpatrick was on tricky legal ground. Burke was no pro-prosecution judge. If he ruled for the defense, Fitzpatrick thought, that could be the case.

They began the dance. Fitzpatrick told Norton that he wanted to focus on her expertise in pediatric pathology, and how she came to specialize in child abuse and SIDS. "I want the judge to know you did all the autopsies on the kids in Dallas," he said. "I'll ask you to talk about some basic principles and define some terms."

"Okay, now the important thing there is that SIDS is basically a wastebasket term," Norton said. "It's only appropriate when there's a complete autopsy and you can't find any anatomic cause of death. If you find viral pneumonia or meningitis or something, that's not SIDS. A lot of medical examiners, especially where you have a coroner system, instead of doing an autopsy, they'll just put down SIDS for basically any death of a child. I also want to make the point that I've had cases, not many, but a few cases that I signed out as SIDS and then later changed the death certificate when further investigation showed it was something else. Either another natural cause, or a homicide. I mean, death certificates are not carved in stone."

This was important, Fitzpatrick thought. He wanted to establish that Dr. Alsever had called Heather's death a SIDS only because he had nothing else to go on at the time. He didn't have Vickie's death, and he didn't have Van Der Sluys's statements. But it didn't mean he was right.

"Heather was a couple of months old, and that's right at the start of the high-risk period," Norton said. "With the fifteen-month-old, though, whoever called that SIDS was just out to lunch, but it's not like it hasn't happened before. I've seen a lot of people that don't use the standard cutoff of nine months. I've actually seen a death certificate where a four-year-old was put down as SIDS. But it's amazing that the doctors and the police let this happen. They really screwed up. It's just so obvious what was going on here with the insurance."

"Well, I'm not sure it's just that," Fitzpatrick said. "I think he did it to be alone with his wife."

"Nah, it's the insurance money, that's all."

"Whatever it is, this is one I'd go for the death penalty if we had it in this state. I'm not a big death penalty guy, but this is one I'd pull the switch myself."

"It's not usually so cold and simple as this one. A lot of these cases involve this really strange thing called Munchausen syndrome by proxy." Fitzpatrick asked what the hell that was. "It's when a parent deliberately makes a child sick to attract attention. Or kills. There are some cases in the literature of multiple SIDS deaths that I'm sure are actually homicides, and if you looked at them, you'd probably find this kind of behavior."

Fitzpatrick didn't want to bring up some psychiatric syndrome to explain Van Der Sluys's crime—beyond the insurance, his true motive didn't much matter to the prosecutor's case—but the concept of a parent causing breathing distress struck a chord. He could use it to address the incident with Heather the week before she died.

"Now, talking about multiple SIDS, are there a lot of cases? I mean, that's one of the big things I want to get into with you. And the defense attorney is going to bring this up too. Whether SIDS can be hereditary."

"It's not. If you have more than one in a family, I get uncomfortable. I mean, I get real antsy with that. And if it's more than two, to me that's pointing right at homicide. Now, a lot of people think there is a genetic factor, because of some so-called anecdotal evidence by a few people in medicine who don't know what they're looking at. But all the reliable studies show there's no genetic link. But you're right. He's going to bring it up. They always do."

"So you'll explain that it's not hereditary, and get into some of the theories about SIDS. The possible causes and so forth." He wanted the judge to see that Norton really knew what she was talking about—that the opinion she was about to give was informed. Fitzpatrick also knew Menkin would spend a lot of time in this area on cross-examination. If he was throwing out things like paint fumes and cleaning chemicals, he could imagine what Menkin would do with published theories of SIDS.

"Here's where you want to just let me give a lecture," Norton said. "I'll talk mostly about the apnea theory because this is what they're going to try to cram down your throat: that babies have these periodic cessations of breathing and sometimes if these periods become prolonged the child stops breathing altogether and dies. And a good part of the medical community accepts this theory, even though there's been no proof offered."

"You think this'll be their defense?"

"It's *the* defense in cases like this. It's apnea. It's SIDS. It runs in families. And here they have the supposed event the week before the baby died. But it's garbage. In fact, the paper that started this whole theory was actually a case of homicide that's always been called SIDS. I've cited this case for years. I talk about it whenever I give a talk to district attorneys or medical examiners. Because it's always being used by defense attorneys in cases like this. They'll say—"

Norton stopped herself abruptly. "Wait a second."

Fitzpatrick and Van Doren looked on blankly as Norton's face lit up in astonishment.

"My God," she said. "I can't believe this. The paper I'm talking about is by this guy named Steinschneider. And he's from right here in Syracuse. The guy they're gonna eat you with is from right in your own backyard. You think Van Der Sluys is bad? You think you guys fumbled the ball on this one? You should see what you did fifteen years ago."

Fitzpatrick and Van Doren were utterly perplexed. He was a college freshman fifteen years earlier. She was in junior high school.

"Well," Norton said, "you might have a serial killer right here in Syracuse."

Fitzpatrick's eyes widened.

"Okay. There's this paper by this Dr. Steinschneider at your university medical center here. I'm going back now to the early seventies. He's got two very young babies in his so-called study who are brother and sister. And they spend most of their lives in his lab in the hospital. The first baby keeps getting discharged and then rushed back with these supposed attacks of apnea. Finally, she dies—the day after she goes home. She's a few months old. And the exact same thing happens to that baby's later sibling. Dies the day after going home. And they have three other siblings who've also died. So that's five dead babies in this family."

"*Five* in one family?" Fitzpatrick said. Van Doren remembered reading something about this in Norton's "Child Abuse" article. It had also come up during their first phone conversation, though Norton hadn't said anything about Syracuse.

"Five," Norton repeated. "And Steinschneider writes this idiotic paper in *Pediatrics,* which is a very respected journal. And he says the two babies that he studied had spells of prolonged apnea before they died. And so therefore the implication is that apnea causes SIDS and SIDS is familial. He puts in all these charts and graphs that are just meaningless. It's always been clear to me that all these babies were smothered, probably by their mother because she seems to be the one reporting the incidents. But out of this came this big theory, and this whole huge business of apnea monitoring. He started it. Steinschneider was really the father of the notion that SIDS deaths can occur repeatedly in the same family, and in fact he's built an entire theory of Sudden Infant Death Syndrome on *homicides*. And that woman's from right here in Syracuse."

Fitzpatrick was gripped. "Did he give her name?" he asked.

"No, this was a research article," Norton said. "He used the babies' initials."

How could this be? Fitzpatrick wondered. How could a doctor pass off *five* homicides as natural deaths in a prestigious professional publication without people picking up on it? It just didn't make sense.

Norton brushed him off. "You'd be amazed. A lot of people are just ignorant and naïve. They believe what they want to believe. And they don't want to believe that a mother could possibly do something like this to her child." Norton suggested Fitzpatrick read the article for himself; he'd see what she meant. Fitzpatrick jotted some notes: *Steinschneider* . . . *Pediatrics* . . . *early seventies.*

Norton was surprised to see how electrified Fitzpatrick seemed by the possibilities. It wasn't her intention. She wasn't bringing this up because she expected him to do something about it. That didn't even occur to her. She wasn't here to report murder. This had always been an anonymous case from the literature, an object lesson, almost a prop in a crusade. Who these babies were, who their mother was, had never mattered to her as much as what they represented: not just a case of undiagnosed homicide, but the classic one— ground zero of the apnea theory, with all its misguided implications about recurring familial SIDS and the baby-monitoring industry that grew out of it. Now, suddenly, Norton found herself sitting less than a mile from the hospital where these babies lived their brief lives and across a conference table from a man who seemed to want to actually do something about it. Well, that was not going to happen, of course. Fitzpatrick might be excited now, but he'd get over it. He was just a nice young A.D.A. prosecuting some horrible bastard for murder.

I've got to stay focused, Fitzpatrick thought. *I've got a trial here. Is this woman still in Syracuse? I've got to win this case. Did she have more kids?* Tomorrow was getting close. The sun was long gone; the district attorney's office was all bright lights and empty desks.

"Your choice," Fitzpatrick said when the work was done.

"Italian," Norton said.

"What's open this late?" Fitzpatrick asked his research assistant.

"Grimaldi's," said Beth Van Doren.

7

All set, Judge?" Fitzpatrick said the next morning. "Call Linda Norton." She stepped confidently up to the witness stand, breezing by the defense table with barely a glance at Van Der Sluys.

Earlier that morning, Norton had left her room in the Hotel Syracuse and gone to the county morgue on West Onondaga Street, where Erik Mitchell kept twenty-five tissue slides made during Heather's autopsy nine years before. Norton found nothing surprising. Mitchell was courteous, if a little cool, and the slides were unrevealing. She had been confident the sections taken from the baby's organs would show nothing irregular; now she could say so in court.

"Ma'am, good morning," Fitzpatrick said. From his seat next to Van Der Sluys Ed Menkin regarded Norton carefully, trying to size her up. Fitzpatrick didn't make him wait long to see why she'd been flown all the way up from Texas. For twelve years, Norton testified, she'd specialized in child abuse and its occasional relationship to Sudden Infant Death Syndrome.

"And at any time as Dallas medical examiner," Fitzpatrick asked, "did you do all the autopsies on children?"

"Except on weekends when I was not on call and a child's body came in, then I did all the autopsies on the children," Norton replied.

"And as medical examiner, are you able to offer an opinion as to the cause and manner of death solely on an autopsy?"

"In some cases you could do it based solely on an autopsy; in some cases an autopsy is of very little benefit and you must rely on other data. There are many cases where an autopsy alone will simply not give you any hint as to the manner of death. . . ."

"Have you ever had occasion to alter or amend a death certificate that you had originally signed out as SIDS?"

"More than once," Norton said. "When new information came to light."

"And would you define SIDS for the Court, Dr. Norton?"

"Okay. SIDS. S-I-D-S . . . The death occurs in an infant from age one to nine months, with the most common age group being from two to six months. The child dies during sleep. The child is found after being put down. The child has been in all respects relatively healthy. There is no outcry. There is no evidence of struggle. And this is very important: When a complete autopsy is done, there is no anatomic cause of death found. Years ago, all these deaths used to be considered homicides and there would be a witch-hunt, and I think we have come to realize that most of these deaths are some form of a nonsuspicious and unfortunate, you know, type of death."

"And have there been occasions where other types of deaths are misdiagnosed as SIDS?"

"Many individuals simply sign out all dead children as SIDS. You don't have to do much in the way of investigation. You don't bother with a complete autopsy and you have something that you can put on a death certificate that seems to satisfy the powers that be, whoever they might be."

"Doctor, is there any evidence to suggest that there's a hereditary connection to SIDS?"

"There is not. Large-scale studies have shown no hereditary predisposition to SIDS. Therefore, if you happen to have a child who legitimately falls into the SIDS category, there is no reason for you to be any more concerned about your second or your third child than anyone else needs to be concerned about theirs."

Fitzpatrick moved on to a line of questioning he hoped would further the argument that this case didn't add up to natural death. He anticipated Menkin would make much of the incident the week before Heather died, when she was rushed to Upstate Medical Center in the middle of the night. He wanted to head him off. "Is there such a thing, Doctor, as near-miss SIDS?" Fitzpatrick asked. "And could you first define near-miss SIDS?"

"All right," Norton said. "To define 'near-miss SIDS' we have to define the term 'apnea' and to define that, we have to get into the theories of what actually causes SIDS."

"All right," Fitzpatrick replied. "Let's talk about that. Let's talk about the theories that have been proffered to explain SIDS."

"I'd be happy to. There are many things that have been pursued in trying to figure out why normal, healthy infants can be put down for a nap and wake up dead, as it were. The various things that have been investigated and have been discounted at this point are things like anaphylaxis to cow's milk, allergic reactions, overwhelming viral infections, things that are wrong with the conduction system of the heart, and exotic things like that. And my opinion is that every one of these theories is probably responsible for a certain percentage of what we call Sudden Infant Death Syndrome, but we are not able to differentiate at autopsy which of these causes are actually responsible.

"One theory that has gotten a fairly wide constituency behind it is one prepared by Dr. Steinschneider right here in Syracuse, and that is the sleep apnea theory. Normal infants when they sleep will have periodic cessations of breathing. They stop breathing for a period of time and then normal breathing mechanisms take back over. Dr. Steinschneider's theory is that if one of these periods of apnea becomes prolonged the child stops breathing altogether and death ensues, so the sleep apnea theory is one that's still widely held by a large proportion of the medical community.

"A certain very small percentage of Sudden Infant Death Syndrome deaths are probably homicides, and they're probably isolated cases where this particular infant is actually deliberately smothered by an adult. The problem is that, at autopsy, you cannot differentiate between an asphyxial death, regardless of which of the causes. The prolonged apneic episode that's proposed by Dr. Steinschneider cannot be differentiated from a smothering death, unless you have some sort of other injury. And of course an infant being so much smaller than an adult, it is very uncommon to find injuries due to smothering."

Fitzpatrick pulled Norton back to the concept of near-miss SIDS. They had discussed its relationship to child abuse the night before, and now they would try to indoctrinate Judge Burke. "Those who believe that such a thing exists," Norton explained, "believe that 'near-miss' refers to episodes where the child has a prolonged apnea spell . . . and by sheer luck and circumstance, the parents happen to walk into the room or be present when this occurs."

"Do you accept the existence of cases of near-miss SIDS?" Fitzpatrick asked.

"I am never going to say that anything is not possible. However, there is also a malady among some human beings where the deliberate induction of apneic episodes is performed so that the child can be rushed into the hospital and receive medical care, and the individual gets a benefit from having a sick child. And in my opinion, probably most of what are considered near-miss SIDS are apneic episodes that are deliberately induced by a parent." Without actually mentioning the term Munchausen syndrome by proxy, Norton explained that a person wishing to gain attention from a baby's distress— without making it fatal—can simply cut off the infant's breathing long enough to require resuscitation. "You don't have to keep your hand over the infant's nose and mouth for the full five minutes that it takes to kill."

Now, to the heart of the matter. Norton had been on the stand about an hour.

"Dr. Norton," Fitzpatrick said, "have you reviewed, prior to coming into court here today, any documents that I have provided you in connection with this particular case?"

"Yes, sir, I have." She listed them: transcripts of Van Der Sluys's various statements, the death certificates, the autopsy reports, and finally the record of Heather's visit to the emergency room of Upstate Medical Center on the night of December 30, 1976.

"And do you see any correlation between the information you gained in that document and the onset of SIDS in Heather?"

"No."

"Pardon me," Menkin said. "I object. I think the doctor is incompetent to answer that question. I think there's no foundation for it."

"No," Judge Burke said. "I'll let that answer stand."

"I think you also indicated, Dr. Norton," Fitzpatrick said, "that you reviewed at least three versions of the incident of December thirtieth that were proffered by the defendant, Stephen Van Der Sluys?"

"Yes."

"Are any, and I repeat, *any* of the three versions that you reviewed consistent with an onset of SIDS?"

"Objection," Menkin interrupted. "Incompetent." He glanced at Norton. "Nothing personal, Doctor."

"I'm going to let her answer it," Burke said.

"The answer is no, none of those three versions would fit the syndrome that we know as Sudden Infant Death Syndrome, where the parent basically puts the child down for a nap and comes back to discover the child dead. A child who displays breathing problems right around the time of death is, by definition, not a SIDS death."

"You also reviewed Dr. William Alsever's autopsy reports relative to Heather Van Der Sluys. And are Dr. Alsever's findings consistent with SIDS?"

"Yes. The autopsy findings are consistent with SIDS."

"Are they consistent with an intentional smothering of Heather Van Der Sluys?"

"Object as irrelevant," Menkin interjected. "Object on competence."

"No," Burke said. "I'm going to hear that answer."

"Yes. They're also consistent with a death due to deliberate smothering. The autopsy findings alone are consistent with either one."

"Doctor, answer this question yes or no, please: Do you have an opinion, with any reasonable degree of medical certainty, as to the cause of death of Heather Van Der Sluys?"

"Yes."

"And what is your opinion as to the cause of death of Heather Van Der Sluys?"

"Doctor, just before you answer that," Menkin interrupted. He reminded Burke of the brief he'd submitted. "I would object to the doctor, in this case, offering her opinion."

The whole trial came down to this, Fitzpatrick believed.

"Overruled."

Fitzpatrick looked at Norton expectantly.

"In my opinion," she said, "Heather was smothered to death."

Menkin's cross-examination was a fine, swift duel, a fight to the end that almost made Linda Norton miss her plane.

"Prior to coming in yesterday, had you reviewed any of the materials that you've alluded to as the basis of your opinion?"

"No, I had not."

"So the sum total of your knowledge of this case, apart from the preliminary contact with either Mr. Fitzpatrick or somebody else from the district attorney's office, stems from a knowledge of less than twenty-four hours, is that right?"

"That's correct."

"What is it that you base your opinion on with respect to suggesting that this was the result of an intentional act?"

"I'll be happy to do that. First, we have two deaths, and of course I know of a third, but—"

"Oh, you do?"

"Yes. But I will discount it for the moment. . . . If I were only to review the autopsy report of Heather, and I had no other information whatsoever—I did not know anything about the hospitalization, I had no knowledge of the death of her sibling, I had no knowledge that the respiratory episode, her death, and the death of the sibling all occurred when these children were alone with the same individual—and I only had an autopsy report on Heather, then I would be inclined to call this death a Sudden Infant Death Syndrome. But when you put the evidence together, the overwhelming conclusion is that this is not a natural death, that this is a deliberately inflicted death, and it's the individual who has been alone with these children each time something catastrophic happens to them."

"Do you want to know from the defendant more about the mechanics of Heather's death before you formulate an opinion?"

"No. I have no interest in talking to the defendant in order to formulate an opinion."

"Pardon me?"

"No interest in doing that. They tend to lie and so, therefore, talking to defendants has never gotten me anywhere in particular, and so I don't do it."

"There is such a thing as accidental smothering, is that right?"

"There is. When I mean accidental smothering, I use the term 'accidental smothering.'"

"I sort of had that feeling. . . . With respect to Heather being smothered, is that your medical opinion?"

"That is my *opinion* opinion. Keep in mind that I am a forensic pathologist and so my medical opinion encompasses opinions that other medical doctors may not feel competent to reach."

"Well, does the fact that you are a forensic professional qualify you to base an opinion on nonmedical facts?"

"Yes, absolutely."

"Now, you told us earlier this morning, in response to one of Mr. Fitzpatrick's questions, that gasping would not be a prelude to a SIDS death, is that right?"

"Gasping would not be a prelude to a SIDS death regardless of whether you [subscribe] to the sleep apnea theory or to the mechanical theories. Gasping would not be a prelude."

"How do you know that, Doctor? How do you know that? Let me make it easier. Is there one reported incident, as far as you know, of anybody personally witnessing the death of an infant as a result of SIDS?"

"No."

"So what actually happens to a child in the perhaps seconds or moments before death is theorized with great imagination and effort, but nobody has ever seen it happen. Isn't that so?"

"I would say that's correct. All of the theories, however, I would like to say they're based on a little more than imagination. . . . Gasping would not fit with any of the currently espoused theories of SIDS."

"Fine."

"With the exception of homicide."

"Is that right? Okay. Thank you for that clarification. . . . Doctor, I heard you say very carefully earlier this morning that there is no hereditary disposition toward SIDS."

"Correct."

"However, isn't it also true, Doctor, that there is a definite increased risk for SIDS in family members, whether it's tied to genetics or not. Isn't that true, statistically?"

"Statistically, quote, SIDS has been reported to occur more than once in a family. . . . Simultaneous death in twins, the same night, has been reported in the literature as due to SIDS. A careful review of cases where this is reported to have happened would tend to indicate that they represent that fairly small percentage of cases where the SIDS is due to homicidal smothering, and that is why it is recurring in the same family."

With that thought hanging in the air, Norton stepped down a few minutes later. She exchanged a glance with Fitzpatrick, and walked past Van Der Sluys, who had listened to her testimony with no visible reaction. She made her way into the hallway, where she was approached by the defendant's father-in-law. Listening to the testimony, Jim Bowers thought Norton was just about the smartest woman he'd ever heard.

"Doctor," he said, "my name is Jim Bowers. These were my grandchildren."

"I'm sorry," Norton said.

"I just wanted to ask you . . . Do you think he killed Heath also? He was the first child."

Norton paused. "Yes," she said. "I do."

Erik Mitchell was next, and Menkin could hardly wait to get to him. As the prosecution's final witness, he would support Norton's finding on direct examination, but then, on cross, he would qualify it to death. Menkin was going to turn the Onondaga County medical examiner, who in the normal course of events was virtually a member of the prosecution team, into a witness for the defense. He needed this. Menkin thought Norton had been a fabulous witness for the prosecution.

Fitzpatrick, of course, had something else planned. "I'm going to ask you about five questions, and it's going to drive him crazy," Fitzpatrick had told Mitchell gleefully. By avoiding anything of substance on direct examination, Fitzpatrick would cut off Menkin's cross-examination. The defense attorney could challenge Mitchell only on what he said on direct, and Fitzpatrick had no intention of asking Mitchell for his opinion of Heather's death. Mitchell thought this was brilliant. And he loved being the bait. He was glad to have the burden of the prosecution's case lifted off his shoulders.

"The last witness," Fitzpatrick told Judge Burke. "Dr. Erik Mitchell."

Fitzpatrick asked Mitchell a series of pro forma questions—where he'd gone to college, how long he'd been medical examiner, what his duties were—before bringing up the autopsy Dr. Alsever had performed on Heather.

"Have you reviewed the findings reached by Dr. Alsever back in 1977?"

"Yes, sir."

"What conclusion did he reach as to the cause of death of Heather Van Der Sluys?"

"He decided upon Sudden Infant Death Syndrome."

"And is that reflected in some death certificate, as far as you know?"

"Yes, sir."

"Okay. Thank you very much, Doctor."

Fitzpatrick returned to his seat.

"Is that it?" Menkin asked incredulously. "Really? Is that it?"

"Yes," Fitzpatrick said.

Menkin stood up, raised his arm, pointed an index finger in the air, as if to speak. He nodded silently a couple of times, and then his finger and head bobbed in conjunction. "Judge," he said finally, "I'd ask for a fifteen-minute adjournment."

"Sure," said Burke. "Fifteen minutes."

"I'd like to consult with myself."

Menkin knew he'd been had. Fitzpatrick struggled to keep a straight face.

The next morning, Menkin rested his case without having called a single witness, including the defendant. All he had was his summation.

"I'd like to publicly say that I have never seen a better job of prosecuting a case ... than the job that Bill Fitzpatrick did in this case," Menkin told the judge. "However, even Bill Fitzpatrick can't make a horse a cow, and I think that in order for you to find Stephen Van Der Sluys guilty as charged, that's what you're going to have to do.

"The prosecution relied upon the testimony of Dr. Linda Norton ... certainly a woman who had her mind made up and had pretty impressive credentials to go along with her opinion. However ... it is obvious she is a paid consultant, and I don't mean to denigrate her at all, but she comes in here, looks at a case on less than twenty-four hours' examination, and tells you, Judge, how this child died. . . . A forensic pathologist doesn't have any special license or ability to divine an event. It seems her opinion is not a medical opinion." He spent the next forty-five minutes declaring the various small victories of his cross-examinations, attacking the confession from all conceivable angles and tossing off various alternative scenarios. "I just don't think, Judge, that this case adds up to murder," he concluded. "I'd ask you to do some justice." He was hoping Burke would bring in a manslaughter verdict.

In his summation, Fitzpatrick countered with the insurance policies. "I'm telling you, and I submit to you, the evidence is crystal clear this is a killing for greed, and it's a killing because of inadequacy," he said. Van Der Sluys's oral confessions to the police, Fitzpatrick said, were more than enough evidence of guilt. "But then you add to that the expert testimony of Dr. Linda Norton, and I think you can describe her as a fair witness. . . . She came right out and said the witch-hunt days are over. She's not on any witch-hunt. She said a small percentage of SIDS deaths are actually homicides. And that doesn't sound to me like a witness who's going to come in here and lightly make a statement that 'from my review of these facts, in my expertise ... this child was smothered.' And a lot of people have waited a long time to hear those words said in court, what everyone knew and what we know now: that Heather Van Der Sluys was smothered."

Five days later, on the first of October, Judge Burke's secretary typed two copies of the verdict, put them in envelopes, and called the lawyers. Fitzpatrick hustled up to the judge's chambers with Brennan and Boyle. He opened the envelope, flipped to the verdict on the second page, smiled broadly, and gave a thumbs-up to the detectives, who broke into applause. Guilty of murder.

Menkin called Van Der Sluys at the jail and broke the news. He told the reporters he was not surprised by the verdict, though he was upset that Burke hadn't seen fit to deliver it in open court. "It's wrong," he said.

Three weeks later, Van Der Sluys appeared before Burke for sentencing. "Do what you will, say what you will," he told the judge, "I have always loved all my children. No one can or will take these treasures from me because my children love me."

For the murder of his second child, Burke sentenced the defendant to the maximum, twenty-five years to life. That sentence would follow the eight and a third to twenty-five years he would serve for the death of his third. "I've thought about what to say to you, Mr. Van Der Sluys," the judge said softly. "What I think of you is better left unsaid."

Fitzpatrick was not so reticent. "It totally made me nauseous to sit there and listen to that crap about how his children love him," he told the assembled reporters afterward. "His children don't even know him, and the only reason they're alive is his wife wouldn't let him take out any more insurance."

A few days later, Fitzpatrick called Jane Van Der Sluys to thank her for her cooperation, to offer his sympathy, and to wish her well. He wondered about her plans. Jane said she would move back to Mechanicville with her surviving children. Shane was now in kindergarten, and Jennifer would soon follow. Corey, a year old, had never seen his father. Fitzpatrick said Mechanicville sounded like a good idea; being near family would help her. "You might want to think about going back to your maiden name," he said. "It might make life a little easier for the kids."

That winter, Jane Bowers filed for divorce.

8

Diane Langenmayr had been one year out of law school, a defense attorney learning the ropes in one of the suburban justice courts ringing Syracuse, when a cocky young assistant district attorney swaggered over and asked, "Can I help you with your case or anything?" She looked at him oddly and said no thanks, but the A.D.A. was one of those persistent types. The next time he saw her, she was working on her first felony case, a stolen property situation, and he was covering Judge Cunningham's calendar call. He got her to go for a felony plea—"No state time," she insisted. "Deal," he said—and then orchestrated a less adversarial encounter at a Christmas party hosted by an obliging judge. A year and a half later, in the spring of 1981, the prosecutor and the defense attorney were married.

In the five years since, Bill and Diane Fitzpatrick had had their rougher moments, philosophically speaking. "I once won a rape trial against one of his coworkers, and Bill didn't know how to feel about it," Diane recalled. "I'm sure he thought my client was guilty." Eventually, as the discomfort level increased with Bill's ascension to the top ranks of the district attorney's office, Diane decided crime didn't pay and made her solo practice strictly civil.

Now, after a career of crime fighting, Bill was about to go to the other side. His resignation would be effective the last day of the year, which would give him a couple of months to wind down his affairs as chief assistant district attorney and start preparing for his new life as a private defense attorney. For Fitzpatrick, the Van Der Sluys trial had both relieved and intensified the anguish of having to leave a job he loved because of what he regarded as the betrayal of a father figure. Hennessy had brushed off Fitzpatrick's complaints about the Family Court assignment with one of his well-known "Ah, c'mon, big boy" dismissals, but Fitzpatrick, as always, saw things in black and white. He felt that Hennessy was forcing him to go to work for the bad guys. He refused even to set foot in Family Court. The only consolation—and it wasn't bad as consolations went—was that he felt confident he would be back. One day, he expected, the big twelfth-floor corner office would be his.

As he began to tie up the loose ends of his ten years as a prosecutor, there was only one case left that Fitzpatrick really cared about. A new case. A few days after the end of the Van Der Sluys trial, he drove the few blocks to the University Hospital complex, found his way to the medical school library, and asked the woman at the front desk where he could find back issues of the journal *Pediatrics*.

"How far back?" he was asked. The library had more than 100,000 bound volumes of medical journals. "October 1972," he said.

Fitzpatrick waited at the counter until the librarian emerged with the issue and made a photocopy of the nine pages in question. He peered at the title at the top of the first page:

PROLONGED APNEA AND THE SUDDEN INFANT DEATH SYNDROME: CLINICAL AND LABORATORY OBSERVATIONS

Alfred Steinschneider, M.D., Ph.D.

From the Department of Pediatrics, State University Hospital
of the Upstate Medical Center, Syracuse, New York

So this was the paper Linda Norton was talking about. Famous in the medical world. Camouflage, so she said, for a serial killer. To Fitzpatrick, it looked like heavy reading. He fingered through the pages, saw a lot of medical terminology and charts and graphs. He headed back to the office to dig into it.

In the formal tone and scholarly language appropriate to a prestigious medical journal such as *Pediatrics,* Dr. Alfred Steinschneider theorized in the fall of 1972 that the thousands of apparently well babies who died of SIDS each year were perhaps not well at all—that they were like time bombs. His data, he wrote in the abstract at the top of the paper, "support the hypothesis that prolonged apnea, a physiological component of sleep, is part of the final pathway resulting in sudden death. It is suggested also that infants at risk might be identified prior to the final tragic event."

Steinschneider described how he had studied five young babies, from three families, in something called the Children's Clinical Research Center. Fitzpatrick presumed this was part of the pediatrics department at Upstate

Medical Center, a highly regarded teaching hospital of the State University of New York whose name had since been changed to the SUNY Health Science Center at Syracuse.

There were two sets of siblings in Steinschneider's study—a sister and brother whose initials were M.H. and N.H., and a brother and sister identified as R.B. and L.B. The last baby, J.B., came from a third family. Three of the babies were referred to the research clinic at one month of age "because of cyanotic episodes of undetermined etiology." The other two babies were brought in days after their birth simply on the basis of family ties—they were siblings of two of the earlier babies. The infants were put on apnea monitors, and a record was kept of their breathing. What the doctor found that all five had in common were frequent periods of brief apnea, along with "a number of prolonged apneic and cyanotic episodes during sleep, some requiring vigorous resuscitative efforts. Two of the infants subsequently died of SIDS." He included fourteen graphs charting the babies' apnea spells.

Fitzpatrick skipped ahead to the Case Reports section. He wanted to read about the two who died.

Patient 1

M.H. was a 29-year-old [sic] Caucasian female first admitted to the Children's Clinical Research Center (CCRC) because of recurrent cyanotic episodes. She was born at term following an uneventful labor and delivery. She did well at home until the 8th or 9th day of life when she was found cyanotic and either apneic or "barely breathing" while asleep in her crib. A similar episode occurred five days later when she was given mouth-to-mouth resuscitation and admitted to a local hospital. She was discharged at the age of 25 days without diagnosis. M.H. was admitted to the CCRC following still another severe cyanotic episode.

Siblings: (1) Male; birth weight, 3.2 kg. He had been noted to develop recurrent cyanotic spells while asleep and died suddenly at 102 days of age. No autopsy was performed.

(2) Female; birth weight, 3.4 kg. At 48 days of age and during a bottle feeding she suddenly "seemed to choke," turned blue, and died. No autopsy was performed.

(3) Male; birth weight, 3.3 kg. Following breakfast, he called out and died suddenly; he was 28 months old at this time. An autopsy was performed and revealed congestion of the liver, kidneys, and brain. The adrenal glands were considered to be of small size.

My God, Fitzpatrick thought. *Norton may actually be right.* He'd been predisposed to believing her, simply because of who she was and how persuasive she could be, but he had also thought: *How could this be so?* How could someone write about five murders in a prestigious medical journal and convince a world of doctors that they were all natural deaths? Now, reading about the first three children in the H. family, he could only ask the question again. How could this doctor—and all the doctors who'd read this account since 1972—not have seen right through this? Fitzpatrick didn't have children, but his recent experience as a prosecutor had taught him a few things about babies. He knew by now that they didn't choke on their bottles and then just fall over and die in front of their mothers. He knew that two-and-a-half-year-olds didn't "call out and die suddenly," and that a child that age could not be considered a SIDS death. He knew the odds against such bad luck in one family had to be astronomical. And he hadn't even gotten to where Steinschneider described the deaths of the babies he studied. He continued reading about the baby known as M.H.

> Physical examination on admission to the CCRC was essentially unremarkable except for a grade II/VI blowing systolic murmur heard best at the 2-3 LICS. During this hospitalization, which lasted 52 days, she was observed continuously on an apnea monitor and had a total of 15 prolonged apneic spells. Two days following discharge she was readmitted because of frequent prolonged apneic episodes, some of which required stimulation (vigorous shaking). Physical examination at the time revealed rhinorrhea and a slight cough. She was discharged eleven days later and readmitted the following day because of two prolonged apneic and cyanotic episodes. Examination on this occasion revealed no abnormalities. This last hospitalization (15 days) was uneventful except for one prolonged apneic episode. She went home at 79 days of age.
>
> On the evening of her discharge M.H. appeared to be "coming down with a cold." From 6 A.M. to 8 A.M. the following day she had six prolonged apneic episodes. At 8:15 A.M., M.H. awoke, was disconnected from the alarm, bathed, and fed without difficulty. At this time she had slight rhinorrhea and a rectal temperature of 101°F. Mrs. H. placed her in the crib and left the room for "a minute to get something." When she returned M.H. was apneic and cyanotic. She was given mouth-to-mouth resuscitation without success. . . .

Number four, Fitzpatrick thought, his suspicion raised one more notch.

Patient 2

N.H. was born at term approximately one year after the death of his female sibling (patient 1). In view of the family history he was transferred to the CCRC for study at five days of age. Physical examination on admission was unremarkable. He was observed on an apnea monitor as well as in the laboratory and finally discharged 33 days following admission.

On the morning following discharge N.H. had a prolonged apneic and cyanotic episode. A similar episode occurred 15 to 20 minutes later for which he was given mouth-to-mouth resuscitation and brought to the unit. Examination revealed a nasopharyngitis. This period of hospitalization lasted 34 days. He was readmitted the day following discharge for a period of six days because of apparent aspiration during a feeding.

At about 8 A.M. on the morning following discharge and while asleep, N.H. had an apneic and cyanotic episode which failed to respond to resuscitative efforts. . . .

Number five. Fitzpatrick was astonished, not just at his conclusion but by how unambiguous it was. He hadn't expected so little to reveal so much—hadn't expected it to be so *obvious.* He had looked up the paper out of curiosity, anticipating a pretty substantial mystery: Maybe there would be a homicide case here, maybe not. But *this?* Fitzpatrick had no doubts that it was just as Norton had said. These babies were murdered.

Fitzpatrick read those paragraphs over again. How could Steinschneider have missed what was happening here? he thought. Did he think it made sense that M.H. and N.H. would live most of their lives in the hospital, a year apart, and in both cases die within twenty-four hours of going home? To Fitzpatrick, it was clear that Steinschneider was trying to make facts fit into his theory. Didn't he see the big picture? How could five children in one family die the way these five were reported to have died without questions being raised—or without this doctor who was studying SIDS realizing that what he had here didn't add up to SIDS? Maybe less was known about sudden infant death in 1972, but in 1986, it sure looked like sudden infant homicide.

Fitzpatrick called Norton. "I can't believe any doctor could be this naïve," he told her indignantly. "Steinschneider was practically encouraging the mother, instead of doing something about it. This should have been reported." He asked Norton why *she* had never reported it.

Report it? "Even where I had a lot more power, a lot more impact on D.A.s," Norton later reflected, "I still couldn't get them to prosecute cases that were fresh and were in my backyard where I was the medical examiner, and where the child was actually beaten to death. I was certainly not going to call from the state of Texas up to Syracuse, New York, and suggest that the police investigate this case." Norton could just imagine the conversation. Names? Well, they start with the letter "H." Bodies? They must be somewhere. Dates of death? Don't know exactly—two decades or so ago. And you are? Oh, I'm just a medical examiner from Texas who reads a lot of old journals.

Fitzpatrick asked Norton if she'd ever talked to Steinschneider.

"No," she said. "Pointless."

She had first read the paper in 1974, right at the beginning of her career, and then watched the theory it proposed sweep the SIDS world over the next decade. The repercussions went beyond research and treatment, crossing into her territory. Crib death had always been indistinguishable from smothering; the apnea theory's fundamental premise, that SIDS was an abrupt and fatal stoppage of respiration, blurred the distinction even further. It could be an effective cover for infanticide. Morever, Steinschneider's paper had led many people to conclude that SIDS could run in families, so it legitimized not only Mrs. H. but others like her who came later. It was their alibi. Norton believed there were more of them out there than people imagined.

Back in the seventies, she had begun talking about the case of the H. family at meetings, but realized very quickly that not a lot of people saw it her way, or cared to listen. It was paradoxical that during the same decades when physical child abuse was becoming a recognized medical and legal entity, other social forces were making it unacceptable to even consider the sugges-tion that parents could kill their own babies and blame SIDS. After eras when mothers of babies who died suddenly and without explanation were routinely and unfairly suspected—the "witch-hunt days," as Norton put it—the en-lightened view of the 1970s went the other way: It just didn't happen. Stein-schneider's theory, Norton thought, not only took advantage of this climate but did a great deal to propagate it.

The grip of the apnea theory was powerful. "When you read pediatric textbooks in those years," she remembered, "they would go through the various and sundry things that had been investigated to explain SIDS, and they'd stop with sleep apnea because that was the most widely accepted theory. And they would cite that paper. But your average pediatrician wouldn't go back to the article from which the idea originated and actually critically review the paper itself. You'd simply accept whatever conclusions were written in the textbook. And most people bought into it. And then I'd say—I'd always bring it up as part of my standard child abuse lecture—'Have you ever actually read the article?' Nobody could read that paper and not come to the conclusion that the very subjects who were being used as evidence of a sleep apnea theory were actually homicide victims. And the reaction would be about the same reaction you'd get if you went around the country talking about how we really have the wrong idea, we should all become Hindus. And the more pediatricians that were in the group, the worse it was. People want to be part of the majority. It's just the way human beings function."

Human nature was one thing. Criminal justice was quite another. If Fitz-patrick wanted to reach back in time and try to find a mother who had killed her children—and he left Norton with the clear impression that this was exactly what he wanted to do—she was all for it but she wasn't holding her breath. "I'd had prosecutors do the rant, the rave, 'My God, that's horrible, we're gonna do something about this,' and then find out later, well, that case went by the wayside because they got involved in something else. It's like their attention span is short. I had even sent this paper to people, D.A.s in other cases, to show what they were up against, and I don't think they even read it. So I thought it was wonderful that this guy had actually read it. He seemed to be really indignant about it."

Norton followed the call from Fitzpatrick with one of her own. She phoned her friend Vincent DiMaio, who was the medical examiner down the road in San Antonio. "Remember the Steinschneider paper?" she asked.

"Of course," DiMaio said. One of the nation's leading authorities on infanticide, he had first heard of the paper from Norton. She showed it to him soon after they met in 1976, and they'd talked about it over the years. Like Norton, DiMaio had always felt there was no question that the babies in Steinschneider's paper had been murdered.

"I told a D.A. in New York about it," Norton told him. "He actually wants to look into it."

"You're kidding," DiMaio said.

Diane was behind the wheel for the ride home from work that night. Bill sat next to her, and she could see that something was going on. He started talking about the extraordinary case of the five H. babies—how Linda Norton had told him about this article from 1972, how there might be a woman in Onondaga County who had killed her children in the sixties and early seventies. How he wanted to try to find her.

Diane thought it was a preposterous idea. "How on earth would you track this woman down?" she asked. "Twenty years, she could be anywhere. You don't even know her name." She was also wondering what difference it made all these years later. "She's probably not having any more children," she pointed out.

"What if she's a grandparent?" her husband replied. "What if she's working in a day-care center?" And, of course, there was, for him, the plain question of justice. Officially, after all, he was still the chief homicide prosecutor of Onondaga County. Diane pointed out that he could not even say that these alleged murders had occurred in Onondaga County. True, he said, but he had every intention of finding out.

The next day, Fitzpatrick called over to the former Upstate Medical Center and asked to be connected to the pediatrics department. "Do you have a Dr. Steinschneider?" he asked a nurse who answered the phone. "Dr. Alfred Steinschneider?"

"Dr. Steinschneider?" said the nurse. "Oh, he's no longer here. He's been gone for years."

"Well, is there some way to find some records of his work? I have this article from a pediatrics magazine. He did a paper back in the early seventies, he did some research at Upstate."

"I'm sorry. I really can't help you. I don't know anything about it. You'd have to talk to Dr. Steinschneider. I believe he went to Maryland. You could try the University of Maryland."

Fitzpatrick asked Mike Martinez, his primary homicide investigator, to hunt Steinschneider down. Don't talk to him, Fitzpatrick said, just find him. Martinez called the University of Maryland medical school in Baltimore, but found that Steinschneider had left there as well. He had run some sort of SIDS institute, but moved on sometime around 1983. Martinez went down to Erik Mitchell's office, and started leafing through his huge medical directories. He found a listing in the *Directory of Board Certified Medical Specialists:*

Steinschneider, Alfred. Cert Ped 68. b 29 Brooklyn NY. MD SUNY Syracuse 61. Int 61-62 Res Ped 62-64 (SUNY Upstate Med Ctr Syracuse). APA - APR - APS - SRCHD. Am Sudden Inf Dth Syn Inst 275 Carpenter Dr Atlanta, Ga. (404) 843-1030.

Martinez punched the eleven digits on his phone.

"American SIDS Institute," said a woman with a friendly Georgia drawl.

"Hello," he said. "Is there a Dr. Steinschneider at this number?"

"Yes, there is," she confirmed. "He's the president of the institute."

"Thank you. I'm just verifying that."

And that, for now, would be the extent of Fitzpatrick's investigation. He did not call Steinschneider. It seemed both too soon and too late; if timing was everything, Fitzpatrick felt his was all askew. His time in the D.A.'s office was running out. It was nearly December, and he had cases to finish. One of them was the investigation of a woman who, the previous summer, had repeatedly dropped her ten-week-old son on his head while drunk, killing him. With Erik Mitchell's help, one of Fitzpatrick's last acts as a prosecutor was to see the woman charged with manslaughter.

There was also his new life to tend to. He and Diane had just bought a house in the outer suburbs, a big, raised ranch on two acres, and they were talking about having kids. He had a law practice to get off the ground. He arranged to rent space in a building populated by lawyers, dentists, and real estate brokers. It wouldn't be fancy; it was one of those offices where the windows were painted shut. He'd have to sign up for the assigned counsel list to get started.

He hated to do it, he told Diane, but he had no choice: Along with everything else he was dumping on John Duncan and Richard Plochocki, the two homicide prosecutors he was leaving behind, he would have to hand off the mystery of the H. babies. He'd leave it with Duncan, because he was closer to him than to Plochocki, but he didn't expect much to come of such vague suspicions. "Look, here's what I've got, which is nothing," he told Duncan. "I've got this article, and I think these children were murdered." Duncan took the Steinschneider paper, a few pages from an old medical journal mixed in with a stack of real, live homicide cases. When Fitzpatrick asked him about it some months later, Duncan's vague response confirmed the presumption that any number of active cases were much higher priorities and that the case of the H. babies hadn't made much of an impression.

Fitzpatrick had two farewell parties—one from the D.A.'s office, and one from the cops, which was held at the Holiday Inn and ended only after the group drifted over to a lingerie show in another part of the hotel and Fitzpatrick took over as emcee. The farewell by the D.A.'s office featured the presentation of the traditional video lampoon, a rite of passage that was in this case based on fact. It concentrated on Fitzpatrick's penchant for being a hotshot prosecutor whose home kept getting burglarized.

There were, though, serious undercurrents to the farewell. Some thought Fitzpatrick's falling-out with Hennessy was not entirely the boss's fault. There had been two camps in the office in his final months. A few of his colleagues thought Fitzpatrick was disloyal and maybe a little too ambitious, that he was leaving in order to run against Hennessy the following fall. But few in the room, on either side of the divide, expected Fitzpatrick to be gone forever, least of all Fitzpatrick himself.

A few days later, he went into the office to pack up his files, the pictures of Diane, the souvenirs from big cases. There was a paperweight from a woman whose husband had been murdered, and a caricature of Mad Dog Allen drawn by a detective. *Pretty good for a cop,* Fitzpatrick thought. He hated to leave. He would remember the day vividly. "It was December 31, 1986. New Year's Eve. And I was just alone. And I packed up and literally walked out the door, put up a sign at my new office, and looked at the phone, hoping for it to ring."

9

On February 4, 1986, five months after Stephen Van Der Sluys was confronted by the Syracuse police, a pair of detectives in another city in upstate New York came to the home of a woman named Marybeth Tinning. Interrupting her favorite soap opera, *Days of Our Lives,* the detectives asked if she wouldn't mind answering some questions about the recent death of her four-month-old daughter, Tami Lynne. They asked her to come with them to the station, where they had their files. Tami Lynne was the ninth of Marybeth and Joe Tinning's children to die mysteriously.

Some six hours later, Tinning admitted to smothering three of her children, including Tami Lynne. Authorities in her hometown of Schenectady, just outside Albany and not far from Mechanicville, uncovered a pattern of probable infanticide that had begun with the deaths of Tinning's first three children—a four-year-old daughter, a two-year-old son, and an eight-day-old daughter—within a two-month period in the winter of 1972. It was the start of a fourteen-year chain of mysterious deaths that went uninvestigated, in part because a number of them had been attributed to the vaguely defined SIDS. Though whispers of suspicion had followed Tinning through the years, autopsies revealed nothing and there were never any signs of abuse. Moreover, this was the era when the medical community presumed that in some rare cases SIDS could run through a family like a plague—a supposition born largely of Alfred Steinschneider's landmark 1972 paper about the unfortunate H. family. It wasn't until the case of Stephen Van Der Sluys broke into public view thirteen years later that the police in Schenectady moved to investigate Tinning. Their suspicion, however, did not come in time to save Tami Lynne. She died on December 20, 1985—two months after Van Der Sluys's arrest. Her mother made her own confession a month and a half later.

The Schenectady authorities took some of their clues from the Van Der Sluys case, but they rejected Bill Fitzpatrick's urgings that they charge her with numerous murders. The Schenectady district attorney decided to focus on the clearest and most recent death—Tami Lynne's—and won a single murder conviction against Marybeth Tinning in the summer of 1987. She was sentenced to twenty years to life in New York State's maximum security prison for women in Bedford Hills.

On an October Saturday in Syracuse three years later, Fitzpatrick invited a hundred people to a party at the Tavern on the Square restaurant following the Syracuse-Rutgers football game. It was his thirty-eighth birthday—and the kickoff of his long-awaited campaign for district attorney of Onondaga County. The 1991 election was a year away, but after four years as a defense attorney Fitzpatrick was aching to come home. His plan was to start early, raise a lot of money, and scare off the competition. It was a good plan. A few months later, even the incumbent decided not to run.

The incumbent was not Dick Hennessy. Six weeks before the 1987 election, the Syracuse papers had run a series of stories in which Hennessy's chief investigator accused the district attorney of using him for personal business. The stories were fatal to Hennessy's career as D.A. He had won his previous reelection by 623 votes; this time he lost to a dark horse Democrat named Robert Wildridge.

Fitzpatrick was indignant about Wildridge's unexpected ascension to the job he considered his rightful inheritance. He briefly considered running for Congress, but decided to stay in private practice and bide his time when it soon became clear that the new D.A., a Harvard-educated lawyer elected as a breath of fresh air, was not long for the job. Wildridge's office lost three murder trials and a big bag of cocaine in his first year, and Fitzpatrick started thinking about the 1991 election.

As a defense lawyer facing his former colleagues, Fitzpatrick represented defendants accused of just about everything modern American crime had to offer: people who had bought and sold drugs, killed their girlfriends, molested their coworkers, robbed McDonald's, burned down apartment buildings, charged the elderly too much for cutting down trees. He found himself telling reporters things such as, "If this was such a horrendous, horrible case as everyone is making it out to be, why wasn't he charged with murder right away?" and pleading to jurors, "He's guilty of loving his sister, he's guilty of loving his girlfriend. He's guilty of nothing more." And to cops he knew who were offended by his new role, he'd simply say, "Hey, I got a mortgage just like you." He found he didn't talk about his work so much with his father anymore.

Fitzpatrick, a Democrat in his youth, accepted the Republican nomination for district attorney in June 1991. With Wildridge already having decided against a reelection bid and all the other contenders having fallen by the wayside, Fitzpatrick realized he was going to achieve his dream before his fortieth birthday, and without a fight. He began limbering up his tough prosecutor's voice. His prosecutors weren't going to be plea bargainers, he promised: "You'll never hear from an A.D.A. the expression, 'We wanted to save the victim the trauma of going to trial.' The only people going through trauma will be the defendants."

He had a few particular defendants in mind. Right after it became clear he was going to be the next district attorney, Fitzpatrick made his first personnel move. He called Peter Tynan and officially asked him to come over from the Syracuse Police Department to be the chief investigator for the D.A.'s office. Tynan, of course, accepted; this had been the plan for years. Professionally and personally, Tynan was Fitzpatrick's kind of guy—chummy, flippant, serious about his work but liked a good time. The two were even alike physically, both tall-framed men with sly grins and glasses, schoolboy haircuts, and impatient gaits. They were the same age, and each had put off having children until his late thirties. At least once a football season, they went out of town and made a weekend out of an SU road game.

One day after golf, as Fitzpatrick was preparing for his return to the D.A.'s office, the two men went over to Kennedy Station, the corner bar. They talked about how great it was going to be, how they'd go back into the cardboard boxes and open up some old, unsolved murders, as they had with the U-Haul robbery-murder case years before. They started throwing around names, figuring which cases were worth digging up, which ones weren't. There was the Kilborne case—an old woman in a run-down neighborhood raped and strangled in her apartment in 1983. It was a case nearly a decade old but one of the first hits tossed out by the new fingerprint-matching system they were using in Albany. And Hector Rivas, who killed his girlfriend, a nurse. Tynan wanted to do that one. Wildridge's people hadn't thought there was enough, but the guy should have been tried and convicted by now, as far as Tynan was concerned. The D.A.'s office was not just going to be a bunch of prosecutors showing up in court with police files. Fitzpatrick wanted Tynan to get rid of the investigators who were little more than subpoena servers who owed their jobs to political patronage. He wanted him to hire the best cops and head up an elite investigations bureau in the D.A.'s office, a professional operation that would be a sort of unsolved cases strike force. Fitzpatrick was full of do-gooder ideas for the office—applying some social policy to drug prosecutions, sending assistant district attorneys out to talk to classes of schoolchildren—but catching murderers who were walking free was what excited him the most.

"I'll tell you the one I want to go after right away," he said to Tynan. "The one I told you about. The mother who killed her five kids."

Tynan wasn't too interested. He thought this case, which wasn't even really a case—it didn't have a manila folder with a case number and a bullet-riddled body in Erik Mitchell's refrigerator—should go in the not-worth-the-time category. Fitzpatrick had first mentioned the mysterious Mrs. H. a few years before, and Tynan couldn't quite grasp it. He'd spent nearly twenty years in CID, and knew every open homicide case in Syracuse back to 1965, which was where the files stopped. Five child murders? This was something he would have remembered. That's the point, Fitzpatrick said. They never called it homicide. The lady got away with it. But it happened so long ago, Tynan argued. It wasn't like Tinning or Van Der Sluys, where the last deaths in the series triggered an investigation. Fitzpatrick was talking about *starting* an investigation twenty years after the last death. He also had to concede that he couldn't even say that he had jurisdiction. Upstate Medical Center drew patients from many counties. *Well then,* Tynan thought, *may as well start looking in Iowa.*

Fitzpatrick, of course, was unaffected. Not long before the election, he went to speak to a class at Nottingham High School. He loved to go out and talk to kids, give them a lesson in real life. He'd speak to children as young as eight or nine, "show 'em pictures of dead bodies, nothing too graphic, maybe a nice shooting or something—I get permission from teachers and everything, though some say it's too much. And I'll have them play detective: So here's a guy who's shot, what can you tell me about what happened?" Speaking that day in early fall to a class of seniors in Mr. Gaw's course in the American legal system, he couldn't stop himself. He gave his stump speech on murder, and just kept going. "You all think you know what killers look like," he said. "Some of you think it's someone with dark skin who hides in alleys. Some of you think it's a white guy. The fact is that killers come in all shapes and sizes, colors, and genders, and they kill for all kinds of different reasons. I prosecuted a man named Van Der Sluys who killed his own children. There was a lady named Marybeth Tinning who killed seven or eight of hers. And there's somebody out there who I believe killed five children twenty years ago and has never been brought to justice. And when I take office, I'm going to catch this person."

Fitzpatrick had been coming in to speak to Bob Gaw's classes for years; the prosecutor's jaunty style and all that talk of murder and mayhem had led the teacher to regard the visits as just about the liveliest forty-five minutes of the school year. But this was something new. *Fitz is going to get somebody,* Gaw thought. *Somebody's going to jail.* He wondered when he'd be hearing about this on the six o'clock news. He could tell Fitzpatrick knew a whole lot more than he was letting on.

The fact was, though, Fitzpatrick really didn't know a whole lot more.

Fitzpatrick's mother and father came up from Florida on election night, and hardly stopped smiling as politicians and friends came in and out of a suite at the Marriott Residence hotel near Carrier Circle. On New Year's Day 1992, the new D.A. returned to the twelfth floor of the Civic Center and took possession of the big corner office he'd coveted for a decade.

He filled the walls with his collection of baseball memorabilia, and in the corner he installed a vintage jukebox. Selection L4 was Bobby Fuller's "I Fought the Law and the Law Won," which the new prosecutor planned to crank up when the office won a big case. On the credenza behind his desk, he put his family photographs. In the five years since he had last worked here, Fitzpatrick had become a father. Daniel, his oldest, was two; Sarah was a baby. By the end of the year, he and Diane would have a third child.

With his experience of the past decade or so, Fitzpatrick was now a smoother operator—no more circumspect or less driven, yet a more refined version of his younger, impudent self. He fired and replaced several prosecutors and began administering an office of a hundred people, including forty-five assistant district attorneys and ten investigators. He commissioned a brochure describing the office's operations, with a cover featuring a wide-angle picture of the resolute-looking district attorney standing tall, right foot forward, shoulder out, a police car in the background. There was a buzz around the twelfth floor in those first weeks, as there always is when there's a change in a political office and people find themselves trying to reflect the personality and energy of the new boss. Fitzpatrick had more personality and energy than most. The Syracuse media made much of how he had finally achieved the job he was born to do.

One morning a few weeks after taking office, Fitzpatrick handed Pete Tynan a folder containing nine photocopied pages from a medical journal. He directed him to a paragraph on the fourth page:

> At about 8 A.M. on the morning following discharge and while asleep, N.H. had an apneic and cyanotic episode which failed to respond to resuscitative efforts. An autopsy (A-71-109) performed that same day at the State University Hospital (Syracuse) did not reveal the cause of death.

"See if you can get a name to go with that autopsy number," Fitzpatrick said. N.H. was Dr. Alfred Steinschneider's Patient 2, the last of the five H. children to die—at least as far as he knew. Fitzpatrick had decided not to consult with Steinschneider at this embryonic stage of his investigation, but he thought it good of him to include such a convenient clue.

Tynan didn't think the paper looked like very good reading, so he didn't go much beyond the paragraph with the autopsy number. He called one of the old hands down at the Medical Examiner's Office, Morris Lupia. "It's kind of a long shot, but we're trying to find an autopsy from the seventies, or the late sixties," he said, and gave Lupia the number.

Lupia put him on hold. Tynan looked out the window of his new office. He had a nice view of the city. Lupia came back. "Our numbers don't run like that," he said. "We don't have A-something. If you had a name . . ."

"We don't have a name, Mo," Tynan said. "That's what I'm looking for."

"You're sure it was a medical examiner's case?"

"Well, in this paper it says the autopsy was done at Upstate."

"Then you should call over there. If it was one of their autopsies, it wasn't a medical examiner's case. Call their pathology department."

Tynan did, and someone named John answered the phone. He sounded to Tynan like a young kid—probably some technician or something. He had an aim-to-please voice, but even so, Tynan started pouring on his own I-really-need-your-help manner. He did not want the guy to say, sure, get a subpoena and then you can come down here and spend a week looking through the books yourself. He didn't figure some overworked, underpaid state employee looking at slides all day was likely to drop everything to hunt down a name from twenty years ago. "I know this is unusual, but it's really important," Tynan said. "We really need to come up with a name for this number."

"No problem," John said. "I can look it up. But those are really old books. I'll have to call you back."

John Falitico was actually quite an important person in the pathology department of the medical center. Though he was not a physician himself (he had a mortuary background), it was his job, as the department's technical director, to teach second-year medical students how to remove organs and dissect them for autopsy. He also taught nursing students. He'd met his wife, he liked to say, "over a pair of lungs." His office was crammed with jars of floating anatomical components, microscopes, books of physiology, and macabre Gary Larson cartoons: *"Oh, don't be silly,"* a woman holding a brain tells a humpbacked man. *"No thanks needed. Just take the brain—but tell that doctor you work for not to be such a stranger."*

Falitico headed out of his second-floor office in the new wing of Weiskotten Hall and down the corridor to a bank of elevators. Pathology's dank, institutional passageways, autopsy labs, and storage rooms evoked an earlier time, when this was Upstate Medical Center, the name still used by people in a broad swath of New York State. Falitico descended two floors to the basement, walked down a wide corridor, and through a pair of automatic doors. He passed the anatomy department, turned a corner, and unlocked the door to Room 102, a subterranean chamber with unpainted cinder-block walls and the air of a place that saw few visitors. "Did you know that autopsy means 'see for oneself'?" Falitico remarked to a visitor sometime later, flicking on the light to the pathology department's records storage room.

It was filled with rows of green metal cabinets holding index-card-size drawers. These contained slides from organ tissue sections taken during every autopsy dating to 1959. There were sixty-six cabinets, each holding fifty drawers, and each drawer held two thousand slides, so that this room contained more than six million slides in all. In another part of the room, there were forty-nine bound books, each six inches thick, with dates marked by hand on the bindings.

Falitico pulled a book marked *1963–1972* from the lower left-hand shelf. It was a dirty, faded volume that appeared to have been unopened in the two decades since the last entry. He flipped the pages to the year 1971, then followed the numbers until his finger came to autopsy number A-71-109. He jotted down a name and date, then moved over to another book. Inside, he found a series of pages describing an autopsy of a baby boy performed on July 28, 1971, at 2:30 in the afternoon.

Falitico read an introductory paragraph summarizing the baby's life and death. It opened with the notation that "four previous siblings have died from crib death." *Uh-oh,* Falitico said to himself. *The district attorney wants this? Something's happening.* He replaced the book, turned out the lights, locked the door, and went back upstairs.

Back from lunch, Pete Tynan found a pink message slip on his desk. Call John Falitico.

Tynan felt a rush of anticipation. Since his earlier call to the pathology department, he had read the pertinent parts of Steinschneider's paper and now understood why Fitzpatrick was so anxious to pursue an investigation. The *Pediatrics* article struck a nerve in Tynan: For a number of years, he had taught a section about SIDS at the Syracuse police academy. It was a subject that police departments throughout the country had begun including in their training in the 1970s—a direct result of the work of national parents' groups whose objective was to replace suspicion with compassion. In fact, in many large cities, SIDS activists—often SIDS parents themselves—worked directly out of medical examiners' offices, in order to provide a layer of insulation between parents and public officials.

Tynan's view had always been that parents of SIDS victims had to be questioned with sensitivity and restraint, but questioned nonetheless. Teaching at the academy in the 1980s, he tried to play it down the middle with young police recruits: Treat the scene of a SIDS death like any other death scene, but know what a SIDS death looks and feels like and understand that the vast majority are legitimate. Once a year he'd check in with the central New York chapter of the National SIDS Foundation to see if there were any new research developments. They'd send over the latest pamphlet, which always had a section titled "How Can a Police Officer Help?" in which officers were urged to use "the greatest tact" when questioning parents about the circumstances of a baby's death. "Most unfortunate of all," it suggested, "is the SIDS family who, in a state of shock and sorrow, is treated with suspicion or is accused of abuse or neglect by those investigating the death."

To Tynan, Alfred Steinschneider's paper put this reasonable suggestion in a provocative new light. He called the number on the pink message slip. "Hey, John," he said. "Pete Tynan from the D.A.'s office."

"Hey, how ya doin'?" Falitico said brightly.

"I didn't expect to hear from you so soon."

"I got a name for you."

"Oh, that's great, John."

"Noah Hoyt."

"Noah Hoyt. Great. Spell that for me?"

"Okay, the first name is Noah, which is N-O-A-H. And then the last name is H-O-Y-T."

"Noah Hoyt. N.H. That's it. Did you find any information, anything about him? A cause of death?"

"The ledger book only gives the name and the date of the autopsy. That was July 28, 1971."

"What about the autopsy report?"

"That's all I can really give you. We can't give out the actual autopsy. We'd need a subpoena."

Hanging up, Falitico couldn't resist going back down to Room 102. He pulled the autopsy book and began reading the full report of the postmortem that had been performed upstairs on the afternoon of July 28, 1971.

Tynan headed for Fitzpatrick's office. "Noah Hoyt," he said.

The unraveling began with a simple sentence: *Please provide any and all medical records, including but not limited to autopsy reports of one Noah Hoyt, treated on or about the year 1971.*

An astonishing record arrived on Fitzpatrick's desk a day later. In addition to an eight-page autopsy report, the hospital's medical records department dug out 253 pages of notes, charts, and patient history—virtually an hour-by-hour account of Noah Hoyt's eighty days of life. Right there, under the introductory notes of May 13, 1971—"This is the 1st S.U.H. admission for this four-day-old white male who enters the hospital for observation because of infant deaths of four siblings"—the records revealed the names of Noah's brothers and sisters.

Eric. Julie. James. Molly. She was M.H., Steinschneider's Patient 1.

Fitzpatrick could hardly wait to pore through the records yielded by one of his first subpoenas as district attorney. He was tantalized by the secrets they might hold and where they might lead. But for the moment, he was after a simple piece of information. It would tell him whether he could lay claim to a case. If these children were murdered, he was praying that they had been murdered within the borders of Onondaga County. He looked for the names of the parents. What he needed was their address.

Near the top of the pile of documents was a copy of a hospital form:

STATE UNIVERSITY HOSPITAL
UPSTATE MEDICAL CENTER
AUTHORIZATION FOR POST MORTEM EXAMINATION

I, Waneta & Timothy Hoyt, bearing the relationship of Mother & Father to Noah Hoyt a deceased patient, do hereby authorize the authorities of this Hospital to perform a complete examination of the body of said patient with the object of ascertaining the correct cause of death. Further permission is granted for the removal of such tissues as may seem desirable for microscopic examination. Authority is also granted for the preservation and study of any and all tissues or parts which may be removed.

With Dr. Alfred Steinschneider and a nurse named Frances Tomeny signing as witnesses that July afternoon in 1971, Timothy A. Hoyt and Waneta E. Hoyt agreed to a thorough medical exploration of the death of their fifth child. They were the mother and father of N.H. and M.H., and of the three children who lived and died in the years preceding. Waneta Hoyt was Steinschneider's Mrs. H.

Fitzpatrick would have been ecstatic at the swiftness of his success in identifying her if not for what he found on Noah's inpatient admission record. The Hoyt family, it said, lived on RD #1, Newark Valley, New York. Fitzpatrick had no idea where that was, but he knew it was not in Onondaga County. He was crestfallen.

On a map, he and Tynan found Newark Valley two large counties south, in Tioga County, a rural region whose southern edge sat on the Pennsylvania border. It was seventy miles from Syracuse—close enough for a mother and father to have brought their babies up for special medical treatment, but not close enough for a prosecutor's jurisdiction. To Fitzpatrick, Newark Valley might just as well have been in Iowa. Steinschneider's paper indicated the last two babies died at home, and there wasn't much reason to believe otherwise for the first three. Still, he was not ready to rule out some circumstance, some legal contortion, that would allow him to keep the case. And even if it turned out that no crimes had been committed in Onondaga County and he had no choice but to turn the case over to another prosecutor, he wanted to do so with conviction and at least some notion of evidence. He was determined to take this as far as he could. The first thing to find out, of course, was whether the Hoyts were still alive, and whether they were still living in Tioga County. That was Tynan's task. Fitzpatrick, meanwhile, turned to the records.

He started with Noah's autopsy. A narrative description ran three pages, and four more were filled with the baby's medical history, the results of microscopic tissue studies, and finally, the pathologist's diagnoses. The record began with a curious introductory paragraph:

> This patient is an 80-day-old white male whose four previous siblings have all died from crib death before one year of age. The patient was first admitted to State University Hospital for observation because of high risk of crib death. During that hospitalization the patient was found to have several episodes of apnea. He was placed on an apnea monitor and sent home. Within 24 hours of having been released the patient has a long period of apnea at home which required re-hospitalization. During this second hospitalization he was also on an apnea monitor and had several episodes of apnea. One week prior to his demise the patient was again admitted to Upstate Hospital after having aspirated some of his feeding. The patient was then on an apnea monitor and found to have several periods of apnea. Twenty-four hours before his demise he was discharged from Upstate Hospital. The following morning he was found dead in his crib.

The paragraph was notable for the significant error appearing in the very first sentence. Not all of Noah Hoyt's siblings had died before their first birthday—the third Hoyt child was nearly two and a half years old. Ascribing crib death to the second child, who was reported to have choked during a bottle feeding, also seemed off the mark. But in some ways it was the theme running through the summary that was most remarkable. The pathologist who wrote it was plainly preoccupied with apnea at a point in the history of SIDS research before he would have reason to be. To infer a connection between apnea and sudden death in 1971, as the summary strongly implied, a pathologist would almost certainly have had to have heard about a theory that would not be published for another year. It was not hard to imagine Dr. Steinschneider's influence on the pathologist's perception of five deaths in a single family, or on his apparent failure to raise obvious questions.

Two pathologists were listed on the full report, suggesting that one was teaching the other. Dr. William Kleis was the "prosector" who actually cut and removed the baby's organs, dictated his observations, and offered a "provisional diagnosis." Dr. Bedros Markarian was listed as "witness." They described the remains of a normal, blue-eyed infant boy whose organs revealed nothing unusual. Their final diagnosis: "1. Pulmonary edema. 2. Cerebral edema."

Fitzpatrick had picked up enough medical knowledge in his years as a homicide prosecutor to know that edema, a swelling caused by an excessive accumulation of fluid in body tissue, was not a cause of death. Rather, it was an effect. What caused the edema? *That* was the question.

Pete Tynan pulled up to the computer next to his desk and punched the name *Hoyt* into an Involved Persons Search. This would bring up every Hoyt who had been involved in any way in any police report, whether as victim, suspect, or witness. He was hoping there would be something, somewhere, about a suspicious death. Nothing came up. He went into the Department of Motor Vehicles and brought up all the Hoyts in New York State with a driver's license. There were dozens. Tynan scrolled down through the alphabetized first names until he spotted a match:

HOYT, TIMOTHY A.
11202 RT 38
NEWARK VALLEY, NY
DOB 7/16/42 M

He scrolled down further, and found the other half:

HOYT, WANETA E.
11202 RT 38
NEWARK VALLEY, NY
DOB 5/13/46 F

There was not so much as a traffic ticket between them.

Fitzpatrick knew now that there was probably no way he could hold on to the case. It frustrated him no end. He had not been able to forget about this woman and these babies for nearly six years, and in a flash he had identified her and lost her. He would have to turn over his suspicions to some district attorney he didn't know, in a rural county that was little more to him than a rough square on a map. He knew there was a good chance this prosecutor, whoever it turned out to be, just might not get it. Even if he did, could he pull off the kind of investigation this case would require? Fitzpatrick kept trying to think of ways to hang on to jurisdiction. Maybe it would turn out to be akin to a kidnapping-murder scenario, where the victim is abducted in one jurisdiction, killed in another, and found in yet another. Any one of the three could claim the case. What if one of the babies, Molly or Noah, had been killed on the way home from Syracuse? Or could intent be a factor in jurisdiction? He assigned an assistant to research the matter and also to see if any of the death certificates turned up in Onondaga County's vital-statistics office. The search proved negative, and the assistant came back with the fatal citation from the black book of New York State's Criminal Procedure Law. Section 20.40 and years of case law told Fitzpatrick that he was grasping at straws. "It would be a real stretch," he acknowledged, "to argue that when she came from Tioga County to pick up Noah from the hospital that she intended to kill him the next day."

There was one more thing. He phoned his friend Jim Hayden, the district attorney in Chemung County, which was just to the west of Tioga, and asked him about the D.A. in the next county. "He's a stand-up guy," Hayden said. Tynan, meanwhile, called one of his cousins who was the chief investigator for the D.A.'s office in Broome County, which was adjacent to Tioga to the east. "Well, Tioga's a big county and it's very rural, mostly farmers," his cousin told him. "They just made the D.A. full-time a couple of years ago, and he's got, like, two or three part-time assistants. But he's a decent guy."

10

To someone just passing through, Tioga County might qualify as one of those boundless stretches of anonymous American countryside, an array of unprepossessing farming communities indistinguishable from a thousand others. Driving along New York State Route 17, perhaps to connect with the interstate and get on to Buffalo or Rochester, or climbing the two-lane Route 96 on the way to Ithaca and Cornell University, a traveler might not even notice the names of the towns—Nichols, Waverly, Candor, Richford, Newark Valley—dotting the gentle hills that fan out from the county seat of Owego.

Nestled in the Appalachian foothills in what is known as the Southern Tier of New York State, Tioga County is a 526-square-mile patchwork of dairy farms, country stores, and simple frame houses that appear in groups of varying size every five or ten miles. They are tiny, insular communities whose 50,000 inhabitants must cross into other counties for many of the essential frills of modern life. Their daily newspapers come from Binghamton, Elmira, and Ithaca, as do their television and radio signals. They leave the county to go to the movies, to the mall, to the hospital, and, if they are not still making their living from milk and cream, to work.

If the passerby were to pull off and stay awhile, he would find a county two centuries old locked in a continual struggle for economic improvement. Tobacco farming, and later IBM, brought some prosperity and helped create a small privileged class in Owego, but prosperity never reached the far corners of the county. In Newark Valley and Berkshire and Richford, the villages in the northern hills, trailers and humble farmhouses form a good part of the housing stock. In 1990, when the county legislature commissioned a comprehensive history for the Tioga bicentennial, sixteen pages were devoted to the county's proud record of looking after its poor.

The southern end of the county is dissected by 25 miles of the Susquehanna River, a brief section of the waterway's 444-mile journey from central New York to the Chesapeake Bay. A riverboater might identify Tioga County by the romanticized teardrop of land called Hiawatha Island that once housed a grand hotel served by steamboats, and, 3 miles upriver, by the Erector-set steel bridge that crosses the water and empties directly in front of the century-old Tioga County Courthouse, a memorable square brick building with four subtly mismatched towers at its corners. On one side of the courthouse there is a gazebo, and, facing in the direction of Newark Valley and the other northern villages, a turn-of-the-century statue surrounded by a fountain. It is the figure of an elaborately mustached fireman in blue coat and red hat; with one hand he carries a lantern, and with the other, he cradles a baby, rescued in its nightclothes.

Bob Simpson, the Tioga County district attorney, worked in the old county clerk's building across the street from the courthouse, next door to the county jail and the sheriff's department. At the moment, his office was a windowless storage room on the second floor, temporary quarters while the county built a small annex that would contain a modest suite for the first full-time district attorney in its history. Simpson, who was divorced and lived in a similarly cramped apartment above a dry cleaner and a secondhand shop on the humbler side of Main Street, found the storage room pretty well unbearable. He spent most of his time in the adjacent room the county had provided for his secretary, Pat Gray, who had been with him for twenty years. If he had a visitor, they would retire to the storage room, which is where Simpson kept the old oak conference table, with the inlaid burgundy leather top, that served as his desk. He didn't have much use for one of those big old lawyer desks. He'd rather spread his paperwork across the conference table, lean back in his wooden chair, and do the work of the big small-town lawyer, preferably on a day when he didn't have court and could pad around in a pair of slacks and a V-neck Izod sweater.

Simpson was methodical and not especially ambitious. Though the Tioga County district attorney traditionally moved up to be Tioga County judge, Simpson had no such aspirations. He'd started as a part-time assistant district attorney in 1970, soon after graduating from Albany Law School, and got himself elected D.A. eight years later, though it wasn't until 1990 that the county legislature decided that the crime rate had reached the point where it was necessary to have a full-time prosecutor. Now he was just where he wanted to be—at least he would be as soon as the annex was finished. Late in 1991, when his predecessor as district attorney, Andrew Siedlecki, was preparing to retire after a dozen years as the county judge, Simpson, whose father had been a prominent state judge in Ithaca, passed up almost certain election and let a Binghamton lawyer named Vincent Sgueglia have the job. Simpson hated family court—he felt it was filled with animus and hypocrisy—and he realized that it constituted more than half the work of the county judge. He had little need for power and prestige. Closing in on fifty, he was happy to follow the gentler rhythms of rural crime, prosecuting the burglaries and drug possessions and the occasional barroom homicide, and handling his share of the folksy village justice courts, where judges with day jobs and no formal legal training other than a few annual seminars presided over weekly menus of speeding tickets, dog licensing infractions, and missing-muffler charges. Simpson divided the justice courts equally with his three assistants. He covered Owego, Nichols, and Spencer, and did the work with the same diligence he applied to felony cases in the county courthouse.

With his gap-toothed smile and casual, deadpan disposition, Simpson was an easygoing presence around Owego. He'd spend a Wednesday morning in the Owego village court, a place where he could step outside to plea-bargain directly with a defendant, then go for lunch at the old Parkview Hotel, order a ham-and-cheese melt, and razz the waitress about the poor tip headed her way. To most people in Owego, he was just Bob. He fit well as the prosecutor in a sleepy county such as Tioga, though he could also be selectively aggressive. A hint of this side of his personality could be found in the way he spent his Monday nights. An inveterate ice hockey player, he was the oldest left wing in the Polar Cap Ice Rink league.

One day in the winter of 1992, Simpson got a call from the new district attorney of Onondaga County. Bill Fitzpatrick introduced himself and tried to sound friendly. "I know this is going to sound strange," he said after a few pleasantries, "but I think you have a woman living in your county who killed five of her children about a quarter of a century ago."

"Uh-huh," Simpson said, as if waiting for more. Fitzpatrick knew right away he was in for a tough sell. He gave Simpson the background, from Linda Norton's tip during the Van Der Sluys case six years before to how he'd identified the Hoyts and traced them to Tioga County. He told Simpson he'd fax the Steinschneider article, a copy of Noah's autopsy, and a cover sheet outlining everything he knew.

"I'll look into it," Simpson said in a manner Fitzpatrick took as ominously low-key. *He doesn't get it,* Fitzpatrick thought.

He was right. Simpson had no idea what to make of the pages that came over the fax, and he couldn't imagine what he was supposed to do with them. He read Steinschneider's article, but it didn't make any particular impression on him other than that some doctor in Syracuse thought there was a connection between something called apnea and something called SIDS. Simpson saw no link between the account of the five children's lives and deaths and murder. "I'm just a hick lawyer up here," he would later explain with characteristic, if slightly disingenuous, self-effacement, "who's all of a sudden being exposed to a new concept, with no background at all. I didn't even know what SIDS was, other than it had something to do with a child dying. Now I learn of this case where five people die and some doctor up in Syracuse has written an article where you would assume that everything is A-okay, that it's a natural thing, and now I'm supposed to make the jump down here in Owego that, 'Oh, yeah, these are homicides.' No, I don't make that jump." Everything about this was unfamiliar to him. "Every other crime I'd prosecuted, I had a sense of what had happened. You could see it or feel it or touch it or smell it. It happened today or last week. Here, there were no bodies with wounds on them. There weren't even bodies."

But if one thing did come through to Simpson during his conversation with Fitzpatrick it was that the guy on the other end of the phone was probably not easily sloughed off. He sounded like a man who seemed utterly convinced he was right, who probably had such feelings on a regular basis, and who was not accustomed to being ignored.

With his partner off on a three-week trip to Ireland, a warmup for his coming retirement, New York State Police investigator John Sherman was alone in the Owego barracks, the only member of the Bureau of Criminal Investigation in Tioga County. In the vernacular of the state police, Sherman was a veteran "pots-and-pans" investigator. He wasn't assigned specifically to homicides, narcotics, or other major crimes, though he could become involved in any one of them at any moment. Thefts, assaults, small drug cases—these were the usual fare—and they had a way of piling up. Sherman had a stack of cases on his desk when Bob Simpson called and said he had five homicides he wanted him to look into.

It was classic Simpson, and Sherman laughed. "That's pretty funny, Bob," he said. Simpson said he wasn't kidding.

"Okay," Sherman said, playing along, "when and where?"

"About twenty-five years ago," Simpson said.

"Twenty-five years ago," Sherman repeated.

"I got a call from a guy named Fitzpatrick who's the district attorney up in Onondaga County. He sent me some article in a medical journal about a family where five kids died that he thinks are homicides. They're from up in Newark Valley. It happened in the sixties and seventies."

"And we're supposed to do what?"

"Well, I'll give you what I have. The medical article and the autopsy for one of them. Let's first just check out the family up there. See if they're even still there. See if they had any more kids."

"I gotta tell you, Bob, this is pretty thin," Sherman said.

"I know. Just check around a little bit. But do it quietly. You ask the wrong person and these people know about it fifteen minutes later."

"Didn't anyone look into this twenty-five years ago?" Sherman wondered. "We had BCI people back then. Sheriff had detectives. I came on the job in '68, and I never heard anything about this."

"Yeah, I have the same questions. See if you can find anything on it. I'll see if there's anything over here."

"Where the hell is this coming from anyway, and why now, all of a sudden? After all these years. I mean, who's Fitzpatrick?"

"He says he heard about it from some doctor. Just do me a favor, John. Check around a little."

Trooper Bob Bleck manned the state police substation in Berkshire, a few miles north of Newark Valley on Route 38. It was a couple of rooms with desks and maps, housed in a horizontal one-story building that also contained the Berkshire Post Office. Bleck, who was known informally as Bubba, grew up in Berkshire and lived with his wife and teenage children in a house across the street from the substation. Although he was one of an army of men and women who wore the distinctive heavy gray shirt and slacks, purple tie, and gray Stetson of the New York State Troopers, in northern Tioga County he was for all practical purposes the town cop. Working out of the substation, he patrolled the state roads and responded to the run of police calls, a job that acquainted him with a good percentage of the population that he didn't already know from having lived among them most of his life.

Bleck was down at the Owego barracks to drop off some paperwork one day when John Sherman called after him. "Hey, Bubba," he said, "you know a family called the Hoyts?"

"Well, you've got Hoyts and you've got Holts," Bleck said. "Which ones do you want? They're both pretty large families."

"Waneta and Tim."

"Then that's the Hoyts."

"Right."

"I know them a little bit."

"What can you tell me?"

"Let's see, Tim's a decent guy. I think he's working security at Cornell now. They lived three or four different places up there before the house they're in now on Thirty-eight."

"What about Waneta?"

"She seems like a nice lady. Her health is kind of iffy, though. She looks a lot older than she is, and you hardly ever see her without Tim. I'll see him gassing up or getting the mail, and she's just about always with him."

"They have any kids?"

"A son. Jay. He's, what, fifteen, sixteen. I think he's adopted. The only reason I know about him is that some people down on Brown Road were complaining about some kid in a stock car that kept ripping down the road at night. So I stayed down there for a couple of evenings trying to catch him. I didn't catch him, but I found out it was Jay Hoyt, and I went and talked to his dad, and he took care of it. It was no problem after that. But he's really not a bad kid at all. He's a good kid. So what's up?"

"Oh, I got some papers that Simpson got from some D.A. up north, and the guy thinks this lady possibly killed her five babies."

"Geez," Bleck said. He thought instantly of the last time he had seen Waneta and Tim Hoyt. It was just recently. "I was outside the Newark Valley Bank when this kid came up to me who I arrested a few times," he said. "And he told me he'd cleaned up his act, and he's married, and his wife just had a kid. I was congratulating them. And then the Hoyts just happened to be standing there and they walked over, and Waneta says, 'You know, you have to be careful. You have to watch them, because I had five that died of SIDS.' And I was thinking, hmmm. Interesting."

Neither Sherman nor Simpson pursued the Hoyt matter with any urgency, certainly not with the kind of attention they would have devoted if they suspected five children had been murdered recently, or even five or ten years ago. Sherman added the Hoyt folder to the pile on the shelf next to his desk. There wasn't much he could do without alerting the family, but every once in a while, he'd come up with an idea. His wife was a nurse who worked for a pediatrician. He asked the doctor what he thought about five SIDS deaths in one family. "Well," said the pediatrician, "it seems awfully strange." But that was about all he could say without a lot more information.

Sherman found no record of an investigation of the Hoyts by the state police back in the sixties or seventies. He went over to the sheriff's department, across from the courthouse. Nothing. Meanwhile, Simpson had called Andy Siedlecki, the recently retired judge who had been the district attorney in the years of the babies' deaths. (Simpson himself had been a young part-time assistant D.A. in the years Molly and Noah Hoyt died.) Siedlecki had a marvelous memory, but when Simpson ran the case of the Hoyt babies by him, it rang no bells, nor did Simpson find the name when he checked the office's antiquated index-card file. Then one day he decided to go next door to the county clerk's office and fish through the coroner's records. Under Hoyt, he found one entry. It was a typed two-page report by Dr. John Scott, a locally well-known osteopath who was a county coroner in 1971.

Report of Coroner's Case

Deceased: Noah Timothy Hoyt   D.O.B. 5/9/71
        Davis Hollow Road   Father, Timothy Hoyt
        Newark Valley, New York   Mother, Waneta Hoyt

On the morning of July 28, 1971, shortly after 8:00 A.M., I was notified by the Tioga County Sheriff's Department that a tragedy was in progress involving this infant and that neither the parents nor the Sheriff's Department had been able to obtain any medical assistance. I was rushed to the scene by emergency vehicle of the Sheriff's Department.

On arrival at the trailer home, this two months infant was lying on the couch in the living room area. Glued to his chest wall was the receptor electrode complete with cable and jack such as supplied to persons connected to electric monitoring devices such as found in the acute care areas of hospitals. The child was not breathing when I entered. The usual signs of death were performed for confirmation. To examination the child appeared normal in every way.

From the father I learned that the child had been discharged from the hospital of the Upstate Medical Center in Syracuse on the afternoon of the day before. The child had been sent home with an apnea monitoring machine and that he had been under the care of Doctor Steinschneider of the Pediatric Department of the previously mentioned hospital.

Doctor Steinschneider was reached and he gave this history. The child was approximately 2½ months of age and had spent almost his entire time in a hospital. He had been born in the Tompkins County Hospital and was but a very few days at home after birth and was transferred to the hospital of the Upstate Medical Center. The child suffered apneic spells with very considerable frequency and for this reason he had been maintained in the nursery for a prolonged stay. Of great interest is the fact that Noah is the fifth child of these parents. All four of the previous children died of causes that are ill defined, but that clearly belong in the "crib death" problem. Two of the previous children died between the ages of one and three months, another died at approximately the age of one year, and the oldest lived to only age of two years. Several of these children were autopsied with findings that were not altogether sufficient to explain the death. This is a typical situation in the still perplexing problem that is best known as "crib death."

Because the patient had received so much care at the Upstate Medical Center, and because that is a teaching institution, and because of their extensive interest in this medical problem, Doctor Steinschneider requested that the autopsy I ordered be done at the Pathology Department at his institution. This was, of course, most agreeable, and the body was sent to the morgue at that institution for the postmortem examination.

The autopsy was performed by Doctor Markarian the hospital's pathologist. His findings were Bronchiolitis, Pulmonary Edema, Cerebral Edema, and Pulmonary Atelectasis. All of these are in actuality secondary to some causative situation. None such was found as was anticipated in the circumstances.

This is best described scientifically as "sudden unexplained death" but this has not been widely accepted as a cause of death for use on Death Certificates by registrars and by some people in the medical profession. Since it is currently more accepted to list the factors, the cause of death was stated to be:

Acute Bronchiolitis.

Although Simpson would not discern this until later, Scott's report did not reveal him to have been an especially careful coroner. It contained two errors about the Hoyt children's ages, significant given the importance of age in considering the SIDS diagnosis. In one instance, he blamed crib death for the demise of a two-year-old. Even in the early seventies, one year was commonly accepted as the cutoff. Why had he not grasped the incongruity? One clear possibility was that the coroner was deferring to what he considered a higher authority, and like the pathologists at Upstate, was taking his cues from the SIDS expert from Syracuse, Alfred Steinschneider.

For the moment, though, so was Bob Simpson. He did not yet grasp these nuances, and he found that this initial document did little to further a homicide investigation. But he did think a conversation with Dr. Scott was in order.

Scott was now in his early seventies and still practicing in Apalachin, a tiny hamlet in the southeastern corner of Tioga County that was most famous for having hosted the largest known gathering of mob bosses in history—a weekend meeting in the fall of 1957 at Joseph Barbara's stone house attended by some sixty Mafiosi in dark suits, followed by a score of New York State troopers in dark uniforms. Scott lived not far from the site of the infamous mob conclave, and just a few hundred yards from the Owego state police barracks. On Simpson's instruction, Sherman called Scott and asked if he wouldn't mind dropping by for a chat. The next day, the doctor was sitting in the chair beside Sherman's desk.

"Thanks for coming in," Sherman opened. "As I was saying on the phone, the reason I asked you to come down is that, well, the district attorney has asked me to talk to you in regards to some questions that have come up about the Hoyts up in Newark Valley. Do you remember the Hoyts?"

"Not very well," Scott said. "I believe I responded to an emergency up there, having to do with a child in distress. But it was many, many years ago."

"I know I'm asking you to go back a long way," Sherman said. "Can you tell me anything about the call?"

"I do remember going up there in a sheriff's car at a hundred and eight miles an hour," Scott said. "It's really the only reason I remember this at all. I remember looking at the speedometer, and I'd never been in a car going that fast, nor have I since." He explained that he had been summoned not as the coroner, but as a physician. An emergency call had come to the sheriff's department, and no other doctor was available, so a sheriff's deputy had raced him the ten miles up to Newark Valley. "Apparently the baby was alive when they called me," Scott said. "I certainly hope he was alive, for the deputy's life and mine, because I don't think it's necessary to drive at a hundred eight miles an hour to see somebody that's dead."

"Can you remember anything much about the family?"

"No, not really." Scott glanced down at Sherman's desk. He saw that the detective had a copy of the report he'd written twenty-one years before. "Just what it says there. I can't tell you anything more."

"Well, you know five children died in this family, right?" Sherman asked.

"That's what I was told."

"Did you think anything was strange about it at the time?"

"No, not at all. You know that SIDS tends to run in families."

Sherman didn't press him. The next day, he called Simpson and told him that Scott didn't have much to say. "Now what?" Sherman asked. He'd gone about as far as he could with what he had.

Now what indeed, Simpson thought. Was it a homicide case? Steinschneider said it wasn't. The pathologists at Upstate said it wasn't. Dr. Scott said it wasn't. Only Bill Fitzpatrick and some doctor from Texas said it was.

Fitzpatrick was getting fidgety. It was the midsummer of 1992, six months after he and Pete Tynan first identified Steinschneider's H. family and traced it to Tioga County. Bob Simpson was moving with all deliberate speed, much to Fitzpatrick's simmering frustration. In July, he dropped Simpson a note, hoping to nudge him forward without becoming too pushy. "I had not heard from you regarding the Hoyt children," he wrote. "I was wondering if you've made any progress. Again, without imposing, I'd be glad to commit my office's help in any way you'd like." Three weeks later, Simpson wrote back that a state police investigator was "doing some research on the matter." He promised to keep him posted on his progress.

Fitzpatrick thought it over a few days, then decided a phone call would not be out of line. He dialed Simpson's number and got him directly. Within seconds he knew, as he suspected, that the case had failed to intrigue the Tioga County prosecutor. He decided to give Simpson a little push, suggesting that the thing to do now was to find every document still in existence on each child—hospital records, birth and death certificates, autopsy reports. Simpson agreed that this was the right approach. He told Fitzpatrick he might take him up on his offer of help. A few days later, keeping things legally clean, he drew up a subpoena for his own copy of Noah Hoyt's Upstate records and sent it to Fitzpatrick to serve.

By now, Fitzpatrick had become well-acquainted with the eighty days of Noah's life. He had read through the two-inch-thick hospital record several times and found nothing to alter his suspicions that Noah, as well as Eric, James, Julie, and Molly, had been murdered. Indeed, the patient history section at the head of the records offered the outlines of an arresting story. Noah and his brothers and sisters had lived and died in succession over a seven-year period that began with Eric's birth on October 17, 1964, and ended with Noah's death on July 28, 1971. Two of the children—James, the twenty-eight-month-old, and Julie—had died within three weeks of each other in September 1968.

The history of the first three children, given by their parents upon Noah's admission to the hospital, offered the first hint of inconsistency that pointed to something more sinister than crib death. The summaries of Eric ("had recurrent cyanotic 'passing out' spells" ... "died suddenly on 1/26/65") and Julie ("turned blue and died during bottle feeding") essentially matched Steinschneider's description in *Pediatrics*. But the paragraph about James was significantly different. Steinschneider's paper reported that "following breakfast," the two-year-old "called out and died suddenly." The hospital record, however, put it this way: "Bled from nose and mouth and died suddenly."

Noah's records began on May 13, 1971, the first day of his nearly lifelong stay in the Children's Clinical Research Center. Steinschneider wrote that day:

NB [newborn] admitted to CCRC for study of possible apneic spells. Pt born into family in which 4 previous siblings died suddenly and without explanation.... Baby transferred here for study because of family history. ... Plan: 1. Study in Autonomic lab. 2. Apnea monitor.

What followed was page after page describing, in more than forty different hands, how Noah slept, breathed, ate, and performed his bodily functions. Fitzpatrick found some of it vaguely curious. "We are having trouble with the apnea alarm on the monitor," a nurse wrote two days after Noah's admission. "It keeps going off but the child is not apneic. No documented apneic spells. Plan: continue monitoring." Two months later, the false alarms were still annoying the nurses and perhaps raising questions about the legitimacy of the apnea problem. On June 13, a nurse's aide named Gail Dristle seemed to betray frustration when she wrote, "Monitor went off six different times within five-minute period. Noah was breathing at all times."

There did seem to be a subtle debate going on between the nurses who cared for Noah and the doctor who was studying him. "No apnea noted," the nurses wrote day after day. "No cyanosis noted." But in his fifth-floor lab, to which the tiny baby was shuttled from the pediatric ward on the fourth floor, Steinschneider seemed to be seeing a different story. "The peak incidence of apneic episodes occurred on the 11th day of life," he wrote in a "summary of results so far" on June 4, when Noah was four weeks old. "Since then there has been a progressive decrease in apneic spells. However the frequency of apneic spells still continues to be elevated. . . . Presently studying the effect of sleep position by recording continuously on ward."

Noah's stay at Upstate lasted seventy-five days, interrupted only briefly by two trips home, each lasting less than twenty-four hours. He would be discharged, only to be rushed back to Syracuse by his mother. On June 27, Steinschneider discharged Noah for the third and last time. At 6:30 that evening, a nurse named J. Manley wrote: "Mother fed pt. Playing with parents." At 7:30, she wrote: "Dressed and discharged to parents." That was the last notation in the records. It was followed by a page dated the next afternoon: the Authorization for Post Mortem Examination, signed by Waneta and Timothy Hoyt and witnessed by Alfred Steinschneider.

Poignant and suggestive as the records were to Fitzpatrick, Simpson found them not at all clarifying when he read his copy shortly after Labor Day. They were an extremely detailed running account of a baby under intense medical scrutiny, but without the benefit of the kind of background Fitzpatrick had acquired during the Van Der Sluys case, they led him to no particular interpretation. He didn't know if these records described a healthy baby about to be murdered, or a sick baby about to die of SIDS.

Still, if he found he could infer little from Noah's hospital record, least of all evidence of homicide, Simpson could at least use it to keep probing further. Despite his misgivings, he felt he had no choice but to continue collecting hospital records in an effort to piece together the medical story and see if it added up to anything. It would be a classic paper chase, each record telling where to look for the one that came before, like peeling an onion, so that when you laid it all out on the conference table you used as a desk, maybe you'd come to the heart of it.

In early fall Simpson subpoenaed Molly Hoyt's records from the hospital in Syracuse. They arrived the first week in October, ran 237 pages, just 16 fewer than Noah's, and described a course of events that was strikingly similar to those that would await her brother a year later. She was admitted to Upstate on April 15, 1970, four weeks after her birth in Tompkins County Hospital in Ithaca, and like Noah, spent most of her life under the care of doctors and nurses who studied and documented her breathing patterns and daily body functions but whose attentiveness could not save her. Like Noah, she had been repeatedly admitted to hospitals—first to Tompkins County, then to Upstate—only to be discharged and then quickly readmitted when her parents reported "apneic and cyanotic episodes." In all, she was brought in four times in her two and a half months of life. Finally, on June 4, 1970, at 7:00 P.M., a nurse named C. Dower wrote: "Mother & Father in. Baby dressed. Mother talked to Dr. Steinschneider on telephone. Discharged in a carriage. Condition good. No apnea noted." The next morning, at nearly the same hour as Noah, and after reaching almost exactly the same age, Molly died at home. She had lived two months, eighteen days. Noah would live two months, nineteen days.

Like Noah's, Molly's hospital records contained threads of inconsistency in the way her parents described the deaths of their first three children, and in the way Steinschneider reported them in his research paper. When they first brought her to Upstate, the Hoyts spoke to an intern named Wheeler who took down the details of the family's litany of tragedy, a numbered paragraph for each dead child. Here, the Hoyts reported that James had died after calling out "Mommy!" Again a careful reader could pick up a few significant variations of detail: Eric's death, the Hoyts told Wheeler, was accompanied by "bleeding from the nose," a factor that would not be mentioned when his death was noted in Noah's records a year later. Then, when Steinschneider followed Wheeler's intake notes with his own, he wrote that Eric, according to the parents, "didn't 'seem to breathe right' and bled from mouth"—not the nose. In any case, Steinschneider omitted any mention of blood when he reported Eric's death in *Pediatrics,* just as he had with James.

Like Upstate Medical Center, Tompkins County Hospital had changed its name since the early 1970s. It was now Tompkins Community Hospital, a private institution with an expanded bureaucracy, reflecting the changes in the hospital business over the years, and its staff now included a senior medical records analyst. His name was Ward Romer. On October 19, 1992, responding to a stack of subpoenas from the Tioga County district attorney's office, Romer certified and turned over "full, complete, true, and exact" copies of the birth and pediatric records of Eric Allen, James Avery, Julie Marie, Molly Marie, and Noah Timothy Hoyt. They had all been born at Tompkins County, delivered by the same obstetrician, Dr. Noah Kassman.

There were footprints of the newborns in the files; weight charts, authorizations for circumcisions, nursery records with Apgar ratings, and a few tid-bits about the parents—they were Protestant, their middle names were Ethel and Avery, and the father changed jobs often. He was a shipping clerk at National Cash Register when Eric was born in October 1964; worked for Endicott Forging at James's birth in May 1966; and was a laborer for con-struction companies when Julie, Molly, and Noah were born in the years that followed. Sprinkled amid the records were a few new details contributing to the chronology of brief life and sudden death in the Hoyt family.

The records opened with Eric's birth on Saturday, October 17, 1964—"6:06 P.M. Spont. del. by Dr. Kassman." Eric's file was thin and contained no evidence of illness during his three months of life. As an apparent response to his sudden death, the doctors at Tompkins County ordered an electrocardio-gram of the Hoyts' next child, James, born sixteen months later. The EKG was normal. Julie, born two years later, at a point when James was still alive, was not similarly tested. She died at forty-eight days, on September 5, 1968, twenty-one days before the death of James. He was the only child who did not die before the next one was born.

Four days after each of the first three births, the maternity nurses ended their notes with a standard phrase: "Discharged to mother in apparent good condition." But with Molly's birth in March 1970, the tone of the records changed. Unlike the routine birth notes in the files of her three siblings, Molly's early records were marked by indications of puzzlement and the first signs of alarm. There were several references to the Hoyts' string of anoma-lous infant deaths, along with records of tests and notes that included, liter-ally, a lot of question marks. In one inconspicuous notation on Molly's birth record, just under where her Apgar score was put down as a healthy 9, a delivery room nurse jotted these cryptic words as a kind of addendum to the birth process:

1 child died ? heart
1 child died ? thymus
1 child "choked on chicken bone"

The chicken bone apparently belonged to Julie. She, though, had "turned blue and died during a bottle feeding," according to what the Hoyts later told the doctors at Upstate. Here, it was a chicken bone, in an infant less than two months old.

When the newborn Molly moved on to the care of a pediatrician, the response was no more astute. A certain shrug of the shoulders seemed to come through in the notes of Dr. Roger Perry, who wrote at her birth: "3 siblings died sudden deaths. Cause? Will obtain chest X ray, check electrolytes before discharge."

All the tests came back normal, and Molly was discharged on schedule. When she was rushed back to the hospital two weeks later, Perry wrote an admission note that contained, almost as an aside, what appeared to be the first consideration of something amiss:

> 3 week old baby was found in bed after feeding this morning, not breathing. She had a similar episode last week. Both times responded to stimulation. Spell last week thought due to aspiration. Otherwise baby has done well. . . .
>
> 3 siblings have died sudden deaths following meals
>
> Eric January 1965   3 months
> James Sept 1968   2½ years
> Julie Sept 1968   7 weeks
>
> The remainder of the family history is unremarkable. Investigation by Social Service showed no evidence of foul play and I would believe this to be true.

For the first time, somebody had put on paper the possibility of homicide, even if dismissively and even if he left no elaboration of what had constituted an "investigation." A few days after he wrote the note, Perry referred the Hoyts to Dr. Alfred Steinschneider at Upstate Medical Center.

Simpson wrote to Fitzpatrick on October 20, 1992. He'd collected the Hoyt children's records from Tompkins County, he said, along with all those from the old Upstate Medical Center. He'd written to Albany for the birth and death certificates. "Once I have all the medical information available," he wrote, "I intend to employ an expert to review the records and render an opinion as to what direction, if any, the investigation should take." He asked Fitzpatrick if he could recommend anyone.

Simpson obtained the five death certificates soon after. They listed five different causes of death—from "strangulation, was eating rice cereal" for Julie to "acute bronchiolitis" for Noah. In these months Simpson also issued subpoenas to every hospital in the Southern Tier, on the chance that the babies had been brought in for emergency treatment that might help clarify their deaths. But reaching so far into the past was a difficult business. Half the hospitals had either been taken over, renamed, and reorganized by larger hospital groups, or gone out of business entirely. In some cases records this old had been destroyed, if they had ever existed. In all, the subpoenas turned up only one new record, but it was an important piece: In its pathology department, the Charles S. Wilson Memorial Hospital in Johnson City found the 1970 autopsy report and tissue slides for Molly Hoyt. The report listed three diagnoses: "acute interstitial pneumonitis, congenital heart disease, coarctation of aorta." Of the three autopsies that had been performed, only one report was missing now: the one for James, the two-and-a-half-year-old who, according to his parents, screamed out "Mommy!" and died on the spot.

Simpson thought Molly's autopsy made her sound like a sick child, but Fitzpatrick was confident there was more to it. "Glad to hear you are making progress," he wrote, and offered Simpson the names of three experts. "In a similar case several years ago I employed the services of Dr. Linda Norton of Dallas, Texas, who rendered an opinion that multiple SIDS deaths in a single family are not SIDS but homicide. I would also recommend Dr. Erik Mitchell, our local medical examiner. He would be significantly less expensive than Dr. Norton. Finally, the New York State Police Forensic Unit employs the services of Dr. Michael Baden, who is a nationally known expert on unexplained deaths. I am going to be at a seminar where he is lecturing on November 17. If you'd like, I'll run the case by him and see if he's interested. The cost might be picked up by the State. Let me know." A few weeks later, without having heard from Simpson, Fitzpatrick returned from the seminar and wrote him again. He'd talked to Baden about the case and Baden had said he'd be glad to help. "I assure you there is no one better," Fitzpatrick wrote, and gave Simpson three phone numbers for Baden. "Good luck and I'll wait to hear from you."

He waited quite a while. Fall turned to winter, winter to spring. Fitzpatrick hadn't heard a word and was losing patience. It had now been a year since he had sent the case to Tioga County. Finally, he called Simpson to see what was happening. Simpson said he had put the Hoyt case aside for a while. He wasn't quitting on it, but he had gotten busy with other things.

Chrissake, Fitzpatrick thought to himself. He started thinking again about whether there was any way to stretch his jurisdiction. Maybe, Diane suggested, he could get the governor to appoint him special prosecutor. No, Fitzpatrick decided, the children were murdered in Tioga County. It was Simpson's case. "If I were him," Fitzpatrick reflected later, "and someone like me tried to do what I was thinking, I'd be pissed as hell." But it was not in his character to sit down and shut up. With as much professional diplomacy as he could summon, he called his fellow prosecutor and urged him to get these records in front of someone who knew what they meant.

"Yeah, you're right," Simpson said. *Let's figure this damn thing out,* he told himself. This time, he meant it.

God, yes, Linda Norton told Simpson when he called her in Dallas. Five child deaths in a family is absolutely suspicious. In fact, it was almost certainly homicide. Simpson laid out the essentials and asked Norton how much it would cost to have her review a few pounds of records. She said her fee would be $1,500. Simpson said he'd get back to her.

He considered $1,500 too much for a fishing expedition. It was one thing to use the resources already at your disposal to investigate a case, or to pay experts for testifying at a trial. It was quite another to spend a lot of money on the preliminary investigation of a questionable case when your budget for the whole year, beyond salaries, was only $60,000. "We're Tioga County," Simpson explained. "I mean, you start talking dollars and I gotta start justifying."

Norton's fee was such a conversation stopper that Simpson never got around to saying that it was the *Steinschneider* case he was calling about. He told her he'd gotten her name from Bill Fitzpatrick, but didn't get much beyond that. Norton didn't make the connection; it had now been seven years since she'd tipped Fitzpatrick about the 1972 paper. So all she knew was that some prosecutor out there in the world wanted to consult on a case of multiple infant deaths. She got calls like this all the time, and in fact wouldn't even remember having this conversation years later. But had she known that Simpson was looking into the deaths of Alfred Steinschneider's H. babies, the cases he had used to launch the apnea theory, she would have told him to send the records down to Texas right away. She'd have read them for nothing. And if they actually made an arrest and put the mother on trial, all they'd have to do was send her a plane ticket. She'd take no fee for testifying. But the conversation never went that far, and Norton never heard from Simpson again.

He went to the next name on Fitzpatrick's list: Erik Mitchell. It so happened that Simpson had retained the Syracuse medical examiner on a homicide case a few years before and liked his work. Now he called him, asked if he wouldn't mind taking a look at some old medical records and clarifying a few things for a country prosecutor. Mitchell agreed that the deaths sounded awfully suspicious. He said he'd be happy to have a look.

Now we're making progress, Simpson told himself. Oblivious to the ironies, he packed up the records and sent them back to Syracuse.

11

Morale was terrible in Troop C of the State Police these months of 1993. The troop, which covered Tioga and six other mostly rural counties, was in the midst of an unfolding scandal involving the discovery that several of its BCI men had planted evidence in a number of criminal investigations, including a prominent murder case. The fiasco tainted the whole troop, if not the entire force of state police. It also had an indirect effect on the investigation of the deaths of the Hoyt children. Preoccupied by the scandal, trying to ride out an episode that carried Troop C to the pinnacle of disgrace—a lead segment on *60 Minutes*—the troop command was hardly of a mind to notice, much less elevate, something so remote as the Hoyt case. For many months, John Sherman was the only investigator in the Owego barracks. His boss, the nearest senior investigator, worked in the next county.

Eventually, the dust began to settle on the evidence-tampering affair, and there was a flurry of delayed reassignments, most of them unrelated to the scandal itself. One of these took effect the first week of July, when Robert Courtright, a taut man in his early fifties with a helmet of snow-white hair and nearly always a cigarette between his fingers, walked into the Owego station as the new senior investigator, responsible for the assignment and investigation of criminal cases in Tioga and parts of two other counties. Courtright's transfer to Tioga County was auspiciously timed; it coincided with Bob Simpson's newfound determination to resolve the Hoyt question. "Let's take care of this," he told Courtright his first week in Owego, handing over a fresh copy of the medical records.

Like Simpson, Courtright came in with no background that might help him sort out the medical complexities contained in the stack of documents occupying the center of his new desk. He'd spent the past ten years supervising narcotics investigations. But he did know the region. He'd been stationed in Owego years before and had worked on cases with Simpson for two decades. He had lived most of his life in Tioga County.

Courtright had quit Waverly High School to get married, became a father at seventeen, then spent a few years as a seagoing brig guard in the marine corps, a stint that put him offshore at the Bay of Pigs. He came home to Waverly and joined his hometown police department, a force of twelve he hoped would be a stepping-stone. In most parts of New York, the state troopers were the prestige police, and Courtright dreamed of becoming one of them. It took him three tries to pass the test, and he made it onto the job only after taking special measures to fulfill the height requirement. Troopers had to be at least five-nine; Courtright came in at five-eight and three-quarters. A doctor advised him to take the physical again, but to do it early in the day— "You're a quarter-inch taller in the morning because your spine compresses during the day," he said. Courtright got his trooper's uniform in the fall of 1968 and loved it. His shoes got a marine spit-shine every day. It wasn't long, though, before he had to give up the uniform in favor of the street garb of an undercover narcotics cop. He grew his dark hair long and sprouted a beard, learned to talk the talk of the early 1970s drug trade and to "act kind of nutty," as he would later put it. He worked at a filling station in Johnson City during daylight—actually pumped gas eight hours every day as his cover—then went around in a VW Beetle making drug buys at night. Anyone meeting him for the first time twenty years later would have a hard time envisioning the picture. With his solemn Joe Friday manner, his assiduously combed white hair and gleaming black shoes, his collection of perfectly pressed suits and ties with tie clips, the Mod Squad just didn't leap to mind.

Almost immediately after his arrival in Owego the summer of 1993, Courtright, by then a grandfather of three, became a devoted reader of the medical files of the Hoyt babies. The records sucked him in like a good mystery. The pages of often cryptic handwritten records, a few others from the carriage of a manual typewriter, were like a medical detective's buried treasure, and Courtright pored over them, yellow highlighter in hand.

It was the blood he noticed first—the blood mentioned by Waneta and Timothy Hoyt when they talked about the deaths of their children. To a detective, blood is a red flag. And there were all those stories that just didn't ring true and made Courtright wonder how the people who heard them twenty-five years ago could have thought they did. The one about James, obviously. "He's two and a half, he comes running, screams out, dies," Courtright said. "I just can't buy that, not one bit. And Julie. Choked on rice cereal.

I mean, if you're feeding a baby that's choking, you take care of it. It's the whole picture. Five in one family. Something's real wrong here."

Reading through the records, Courtright found it intriguing that the last two babies, Molly and Noah, died while under the intensive care of a prestigious teaching hospital, and that the doctor in charge was a specialist in SIDS. He could almost hear the voices of the nurses and doctors, and he wondered what they might have thought but not written. And then Courtright came upon a striking entry in Molly's record that reinforced his suspicion. It was a note one of the nurses wrote in the log just one day before the baby died:

> I discussed my concern for this baby with Dr. Steinschneider this AM. At times Molly will not respond to her surroundings at all—her head is turned to the left and she has a glassy stare.... She rarely smiles in response to another person. The interaction between mother and baby is almost nil in my opinion.

Courtright was exhilarated by the discovery. He highlighted the note in bright yellow, and wrote down the nurse's name: "T. Schneider."

These things leaped out at Courtright, but there was something else, too, that he sensed as he tried to school himself in the underlying medical question at hand: Did these children have apnea, or did they simply have apnea monitors that didn't work very well? When Simpson asked what he thought, Courtright told him: "I'm not a doctor, but to me they look like pretty normal, healthy kids."

While Courtright was not a doctor, Erik Mitchell was, and Simpson had high hopes that he would tell him if there was a medical foundation for a criminal prosecution. Simpson's thinking was turning a corner. With the informal opinions of Mitchell and Norton, and now Courtright, a detective he had known and respected for years, he felt for the first time that he had good reason to keep going. He waited for Mitchell's official finding.

Mitchell's assessment of the deaths of the Hoyt children would have been interesting, considering his diffidence about the case against Stephen Van Der Sluys. But months passed after Simpson sent the records to Syracuse, with no word from him. What Simpson didn't know, until Fitzpatrick told him, was that Mitchell was having some problems at the office. The New York State Health Department had been investigating how some of the corpses in Mitchell's lab had come to be acquired, and what had become of them. It seemed that in his zeal to make Syracuse a regional forensic lab, Mitchell had taken a few liberties with the concept of informed consent. Fitzpatrick, who was starting to think that he might wind up actually having to indict his old colleague if he didn't resign, felt that now was not the best time for Simpson to get involved with Erik Mitchell. The guy to go to, Fitzpatrick told Simpson again, was Mike Baden.

Once the chief medical examiner of New York City, Dr. Michael Baden was now the director of the New York State Police Forensic Sciences Unit. He had a national reputation, and spent half his time as an expensive private consultant, often on some of the highest profile deaths of the day: MIAs, airline crashes, serial killings, political mysteries, celebrity ODs. He'd consulted on the cases of John Belushi (for the prosecution) and Claus von Bulow (for the defense), exhumed Medgar Evers, and reviewed Elvis Presley's autopsy for an exposé by Geraldo Rivera. He loved to reminisce—even from the witness chair of a criminal courtroom, where he spent a good deal of his time—how, as a young New Yorker, he'd hear radio reports of killings in the city, then read in the next morning's *Daily News* how the medical examiners had instantly cracked the case. "Magic occurred," he regaled one jury while recounting his illustrious career. "The human body gave forth secrets. . . . " In 1989, he had written a well-received book about his adventures: *Unnatural Death: Confessions of a Medical Examiner.*

Though there were those who considered him a big man with a big ego, perhaps too enamored of the limelight, Baden was Fitzpatrick's kind of forensic pathologist: smart, scrappy, hard-charging like TV's Quincy, a shade eccentric. He was a medical examiner with backbone, who relished getting down in the muck when necessary. He was an expert in exhumation—not just the inspection and evaluation of the remains but the eerie process of reclaiming the remains from the earth. It was a delicate science, for which he brought along his own special bag of archaeological tools and his state police windbreaker. In the more conventional venue of his office, which occupied part of his brownstone house across the street from Gracie Mansion, the New York City mayoral residence, Baden surrounded himself with images of death that were bigger than life. The walls were covered by a huge double triptych of a repeated image of an electric chair, the backgrounds in varying shades of garishness. Among his more discreet mementos was a framed and numbered bullet, complete with certification and accompanying photographs, fired from "the most famous handgun in the world," Jack Ruby's .38.

To Fitzpatrick, who had consulted Baden during his time as a homicide prosecutor and private defense attorney, it was only natural that he become involved in the Hoyt case. Not only was he the chief forensic expert for the police agency that was investigating the matter—he wouldn't cost the taxpayers of Tioga County a nickel—but he was well-schooled in the issues. In fact, his very first consultation for the state police after he was hired to set up and run its state-of-the-art forensic sciences unit in 1986 was the investigation of Marybeth Tinning. "It is clearly my opinion beyond a reasonable medical certainty that the Tinning children died as the result of homicidal asphyxia,"

Baden wrote at the time, the last memo delivered to the state police investigators before they knocked on Tinning's front door.

When Simpson gave his assent to pass the itinerant Hoyt records on to Baden, Fitzpatrick was only too happy to make the arrangements. In fact, he had already set things in motion when he had mentioned the case to Baden the previous November. He'd also talked to him about it since then, at one point piquing his interest with a copy of Steinschneider's apnea paper. "I have a hunch we may be working on this case in the future," Fitzpatrick wrote. Now, he officially invited Baden into the Hoyt case. It made him feel as though he had not totally relinquished this investigation. "Once we hear from you," Fitzpatrick wrote to Baden in a cover letter with the records, "and if in your judgment Noah Hoyt (at least) was a homicide victim, then I think a meeting would be in order to discuss how best to approach the interrogation of Mrs. Hoyt." Meanwhile, he added, he was going to try to locate the doctor who started all this.

Though it was clear to all involved that Alfred Steinschneider played an intricate role in this case and needed to be approached carefully, Fitzpatrick thought now might be a good time to feel him out. He called Simpson. "He might have a smoking gun sitting in his files somewhere," he said. Simpson didn't object, but cautioned him. "You don't want him calling the Hoyts after he talks to you." Fitzpatrick assured him he'd be careful not to say too much.

On a summer afternoon in Manhattan, Baden opened a cardboard box and began reading through the five hundred pages of records left behind by the doctors and nurses and coroners who had touched the brief lives of the five children of Waneta and Timothy Hoyt. Baden had gotten off the phone with the clear impression that Fitzpatrick was hoping he would confirm his suspicions, and he wasted no time accommodating him. He called a few days later and said he thought that all the Hoyt children had been suffocated.

"There's no evidence that any of the babies died of the causes of death attributed to them," he said. "So the causes of death are wrong. That's number one. I see no evidence of natural disease. Number two is the pattern of deaths. The age of the two-and-a-half-year-old, who could not be a SIDS death, and the circumstances of the individual cases indicate they were suffocated."

It was Baden's opinion that the doctors and coroners who had performed the autopsies and signed the death certificates were reaching for medical explanations that amounted to space fillers. How, for instance, could Eric's death have been certified as having been caused by "congenital anomalies of the heart" when there had been neither clinical findings nor an autopsy?

Baden felt he knew why the doctors had taken this approach: They were conditioned to believe what patients told them. They didn't believe that parents killed their children. So they looked for something, anything, on which to pin the blame, even if it didn't really make sense. Whatever they came up with made more sense to them than the notion of a mother killing her children, one after another.

Studying the records of Molly and Noah, it was also Baden's view that the apnea issue, and the repetitive nature of the case as a whole, pointed to a case of Munchausen syndrome by proxy, the psychiatric concept that Linda Norton had mentioned to Fitzpatrick when they were planning her Van Der Sluys testimony in 1986. Munchausen by proxy wasn't recognized and named until 1977, five years after the last of the Hoyt babies died, but by the early 1990s it was well documented, if not well understood, that there were some mothers in the world who faked or caused illnesses in their children to gain attention for themselves, particularly from the medical establishment. It seemed to Baden that Waneta Hoyt was one of these mothers: She had pulled off an elaborate medical deception. All her reports of cyanosis, which Steinschneider and others had so easily taken as evidence of apnea and ultimately SIDS, were actually hints of something else—something no less obvious to Baden. SIDS babies don't turn blue, he told Fitzpatrick. Suffocated babies do.

Fitzpatrick was confident Baden's findings would have a major impact on the future of this case. He didn't have to wait long. Baden quickly made his opinion official in a memorandum to his captain, the head of special projects for the BCI at state police headquarters in Albany. "All of these babies," he wrote, "were born healthy and normal, were described by their mother as having suffered multiple episodes of otherwise unwitnessed breathing difficulties with development of cyanosis, and all died suddenly and unexpectedly in the presence of their mother. No explanations for the deaths were found at autopsy and the causes of death were certified in various forms of medical jargon to indicate crib death or Sudden Infant Death Syndrome." The doctor summed up in legal terms: "It is writer's opinion, beyond a reasonable degree of medical and scientific certainty, that the circumstances, the medical findings, the clustering of the deaths, and the autopsy results demonstrate that the five children did not die of natural causes. To the contrary, these findings are typical of deaths due to homicidal suffocation as occurs in the Munchausen-by-proxy syndrome."

The memo had the effect Fitzpatrick was hoping it would. It led instantly to a meeting between Simpson, Courtright, and Courtright's captain, Frank Pace, who had been transferred into the troop during the denouement of the evidence-tampering scandal. The Hoyt investigation had now moved up a notch in the chain of command, to a level populated by men who knew that a case of this magnitude carried double-edged implications. For the members of Troop C, the Hoyt case could bring redemption and reward. On the other hand, if they screwed up—say, by charging an innocent, grieving woman of shocking crimes she hadn't committed—it could plunge them into much deeper disgrace.

It wasn't a long meeting. Simpson said he wanted a second opinion, and nobody in the room disputed the wisdom of his judgment.

Fitzpatrick was pleased by the progress when Simpson called to tell him about the meeting that afternoon, but he was curious about the apparent lack of confidence in Baden. "He's the most famous pathologist in the world, as far as I'm concerned," he said. "He's done thousands of autopsies."

"Yeah," Simpson said. "Well, they're not too high on him in Troop C, and I'm not getting involved in that."

His international reputation notwithstanding, Baden had something of an image problem among some in the state police in these parts. On the Southern Tier, he was the fast-talking, fast-moving New Yorker, always off in a thousand directions, maybe a little too sure of his own infallibility. The perception was at least in part traceable to a case a few years before, when Baden found a knife wound on the exhumed body of a man who had been run over by a train outside Owego, and then buried for several years. A discovery like that was a hallmark of Baden's brand of modern forensic medicine, but the BCI men were skeptical of the dramatic finding and the case, Baden's last in Tioga County, was never prosecuted.

The case at hand, however, was not so easily dismissed. While Baden was the first forensic pathologist to review the raw materials documenting the Hoyt babies' deaths—the first to officially contradict Steinschneider and everyone else who had encountered the family a generation before—Simpson thought his memo was a bit facile, considering the enormity of the crimes being alleged and the volume of documents available. If he was even going to think about accusing someone of such crimes, Simpson felt strongly that he wanted more beneath his feet than what he saw here. Baden was undeniably a top man and his opinions were important, but his experience ran the gamut of unnatural and usually violent death. He was a generalist. Simpson wanted the next opinion to come from someone who was an authority on the gentle murder of babies. Whether the subject was life or death, he reasoned, a tricky medical case called for a specialist.

Trying to learn all he could about a brand of crime with which he had no experience—and hoping to come up with another expert to review the records—Bob Courtright started calling lawyers at the National Center for the Prosecution of Child Abuse and detectives in Florida, Texas, and New Jersey who had experience with infanticide cases. In Miami he found Dr. Marie Valdes-Dapena, a pediatric pathologist who was, in her seventies, the doyenne of SIDS research. However, though she could tell him all there was to know about SIDS, Valdes-Dapena was not a forensic pathologist with an expertise in the ways and means of infant murder.

Gathering literature on SIDS and fatal child abuse, Courtright began to understand that mothers who killed their babies often displayed the behavior Baden had mentioned in his report. It was in one of these articles about the role of Munchausen by proxy that he came across a case that sounded similar to the one he was working on. It mentioned a pediatrician and child abuse expert named Carolyn Levitt, who was the head of the Midwest Children's Resource Center, in St. Paul, Minnesota. Courtright gave the article to Simpson, who promptly called St. Paul and found himself talking to Carolyn Levitt's assistant, a nurse practitioner named Kim Martinez. He asked if the doctor, or anyone else at the center, might be in a position to render a new opinion on an old case. It was quite an unusual situation, he told her. It had to do with the deaths of five children in one family, many years ago. There were a lot of medical records that needed interpretation.

"Sure," Martinez said. "That's the kind of thing we do. Go ahead and send the records. You can send them to my attention."

Ten days later, Dr. Carolyn Levitt sat at her desk in downtown St. Paul. Engrossed, she was reading a six-page summary of the Hoyt case Martinez had prepared from the pile of records sent by Simpson. Finally, Levitt looked up. "I think Jan better get involved in this," she said to Martinez.

The Monday before Thanksgiving, Simpson called St. Paul again and got Levitt on the phone. She told him she'd referred the case to a colleague at Children's Hospital who was better qualified to handle something as extraordinary as this. She gave Simpson the phone number, and he punched it in as soon as he hung up.

"This is Jan Ophoven," came the next voice on his phone.

"Yes, hello. Doctor, my name's Bob Simpson and I'm the district attorney here in Tioga County, New York." He had no idea who she was or what her qualifications were, but when she said she was a pediatric forensic pathologist, that was good enough for him. Would she be willing to review the medical records?

Yes, Ophoven said. She quoted a fee Simpson thought extremely reasonable. "A hundred fifty dollars," he'd report later, with great satisfaction. "Now you're talking things I understand." Simpson had no idea how much of a bargain it was. Only later would he discover that he had stumbled upon a doctor who knew as much about the medical and legal intricacies of hidden child abuse and murder as anyone in America.

———

With her cheerfully blunt manner and moralistic view of the study of child-hood death, Dr. Janice Ophoven could be taken for an Upper Midwest version of Linda Norton. They were both part of the new breed in forensic medicine. Both were women who used their forensic perspectives to root out the victimization of children, and both saw themselves as medical detectives on a mission.

A Minnesotan in her late forties, Ophoven, like Norton, had taken her postgraduate medical training in the 1970s, just as medical examiners like Michael Baden and his counterpart in Los Angeles, Thomas Noguchi, were bringing the sepulchral world of forensic pathology into prominence. With a dash of showmanship, Baden's generation stood at the alluring intersection of medicine and mystery, where Hippocrates met Holmes. Ophoven had an appropriate admiration for Baden—though they'd never met, she remembered attending a symposium he once gave with some other prominent medical examiners on a subject she remembered as "Getting Screwed by the Media"—but she felt she and her contemporaries came at forensic pathology from a slightly more scholarly angle than those of his generation, whom she viewed as pioneers and mavericks. "They had to have courage and stamina to withstand the kind of cultural barriers put up by medicine, where the perception was that you had decided not to practice medicine," she observed. "You had decided to be a cop. So there used to be this show-and-tell mentality: 'I'll show you my most exciting and weird case and you show me yours.' And there was that flamboyance and autonomy, which came with the power of ultimately saying what killed Bill Holden and Natalie Wood."

Baden and his peers succeeded the generation that had been the icons of the field, forensic men like New York City's Milton Helpern, who was Baden's mentor, and Minnesota's John Coe, who reviewed the autopsy of President Kennedy as a member of the Warren Commission, and under whom Ophoven trained. But it wasn't until Ophoven's generation came into its own that forensic pathology started to become accepted as a part of mainstream medical education and public health. In pediatrics—where the expanding role of forensics was arguably most relevant, given the growing recognition of child abuse as a serious national problem—a milestone was reached in 1991, when a chapter on forensic pathology was included for the first time in a pediatric pathology textbook. This meant that medical students learning about fatal childhood disease would now also read about child abuse and murder. The chapter was written by Ophoven. "What that said to me," she said, "was that my peers in pediatric pathology had finally accepted that forensic thinking was an important part of pediatric medicine. That it's important to working on behalf of kids. That's where a lot of the narrow thinking comes in with child abuse, whatever its form—if you're not taught to think about the possibilities, then you won't *see* the possibilities. For instance, starved children usually don't die of starvation. They die of an infection. And for many years children who were starved to death were signed out as pneumonia. That's not good, especially if the parents are left in the same situation that made that possible in the first place. We're not getting anywhere with helping children until we include forensic medicine."

As a working pediatrician who became a forensic pathologist, Ophoven had a broad perspective and a rare combination of expertise. It was partly because the worlds of pediatrics and forensic pathology almost never intersected that so many child abuse cases had gone undetected in the past. Now her regular work included teaching doctors, detectives, and prosecutors how to spot the often subtle signs of child abuse—especially the peculiar manifestations of Munchausen by proxy, the most subtle of all. She'd consulted on cases throughout the United States, and with her colleagues in Minnesota had produced a primer on Munchausen behavior for the FBI. But like Linda Norton, with whom she shared a certain righteous indignation, Ophoven had her horror stories. She'd once had a case in an affluent Minneapolis suburb whose police chief, confronted with a dead baby covered by human bite marks and suggestions of smothering, looked her in the eye and said, "We ain't ever had a homicide here, Doc, and we ain't starting today." Medical knowledge and technical skill were essential to their work, yet to Ophoven and Norton, it was simple perspective that often mattered most.

The day before Thanksgiving, Bob Courtright, John Sherman, Captain Frank Pace, Bill Fitzpatrick, and Pete Tynan gathered in Bob Simpson's office in Owego. After twenty months of phone calls and letters and unspoken uneasy feelings, it was the first time Fitzpatrick and Simpson had met face-to-face. The occasion was a strategy session, featuring a conference call with Janice Ophoven. Though he was still pushing Baden, Fitzpatrick sensed that Simpson had decided he would rise or fall with the doctor from Minnesota. Fitzpatrick could live with that. He was relieved to see matters had advanced to this point, and glad to be invited to the meeting.

Simpson's entire suite on the second story of the new county clerk's annex was not much bigger than the reception area of Fitzpatrick's office on the twelfth floor of the Civic Center in Syracuse. By choice, he kept his desk essentials—his phone and diary—on the window ledge. Seated at the oak conference table, he opened the meeting by asking Fitzpatrick to tell the group how this whole thing got started, which Fitzpatrick did crisply. Courtright offered a brief rundown of what he'd done; his next move, he said, would be to start looking more deeply into the Hoyts' background. Now it was time to hear from the expert from the Midwest. Simpson called St. Paul and put Ophoven on the speakerphone. He asked her to talk some about her background. ("Better ask how many autopsies she's done," Courtright had told him.) Ophoven talked about her work on cases similar to this one. She said she'd personally performed some two thousand autopsies, participated in another thousand. Probably three-quarters of them were on children.

Simpson asked her what she thought of this case.

"Well, there are some things I'm going to need," she said. "I'll need the autopsy slides for Molly and Noah, and James if you can get them. And of course you'll need to do a classic police investigation. You'll need to interview the family and see if what they tell you changes anything. But based on the information you sent, I think there's a likelihood that these children died from foul play. A significant likelihood."

"Why do you think that?" Simpson asked.

"Well, based on what I consider to be striking inconsistencies with what we know about sudden death in children. Now, I do think it would be a good idea for the records for Molly and Noah to be reviewed by an infant apnea specialist. There's a pediatrician here named Stephen Boros, whom I've worked with on a couple of cases like this. Stephen and I have been working on a paper about Munchausen's by proxy and infant apnea. I seriously question whether these children were anything but completely normal, but since I'm not a practicing apnea specialist I'd like someone in today's world to evaluate whether these children had any apnea at all, or whether they would be worried about the possibility of some kind of inherited disease."

"So this would be considered a case of Munchausen syndrome?" Courtright asked. "Is that an accurate statement?"

"Forget Munchausen," Ophoven said quickly. "This is murder."

For the purposes of the people in Simpson's office, Ophoven knew, applying some exotic psychological label would only distract them—and perhaps ultimately give Hoyt an excuse before a jury. Ophoven wanted the investigators to focus on the criminal act of fatal child abuse. "You're still a ways from being definitive," she said. "But if I had those tissue slides, it would be possible to rule out natural disease and actually rewrite the death certificates. I'd also like to have the autopsy on the older child."

Like everyone else, Ophoven was most suspicious about the death of James. "To me, that's a huge flag," she said. "A two-year-old dying suddenly, and I'm sorry, but it's not an invisible fact about the blood. I mean, this is a recurring piece of information about blood from that boy's mouth. I can't put the retrospectoscope on, but it's pretty hard for me to go, 'That makes sense.' "

The records from Upstate reported that James's autopsy had yielded a finding of "acute adrenal insufficiency," while the death certificate offered "enlarged thymus," though "unknown and undecided as to cause" was also added. Neither an acute adrenal insufficiency nor an enlarged thymus explained the death, Ophoven told the group. A bloody nose or mouth in a sudden death of a two-year-old child with no prior medical history, and no findings at autopsy, pointed to the kind of trauma that leaves no marks: suffocation. But without actually seeing the autopsy report it would be difficult to completely rule out some other natural cause.

"We haven't been able to find that one," Courtright said.

"The histories say that he just called out and died," Ophoven said. "Well, that just doesn't happen. Something caused that kid to die."

On the way home to Syracuse, Fitzpatrick and Tynan decided to make a stop. From Owego, they drove up Route 38, through Newark Valley. They knew the Hoyts lived right on the main road, and tried to figure out which house it was, but before they realized it they found themselves in the next town, Berkshire. A few miles more, and they were in Richford. They made the left at the Richford traffic light, then found their way to a dirt road with a small sign that said HIGHLAND CEMETERY. According to the death certificates, this was where the five Hoyt children were buried.

It was a pretty spot set on a hilltop clearing between a pair of creeks feeding a tributary of the Susquehanna. The burial ground was shrouded by a gathering of Norway spruce trees whose branches drooped like canopies above a few hundred imperfectly arranged graves dating back to the late 1800s. Fitzpatrick and Tynan walked around in the crisp autumn air, checking headstones. Finally they came upon two small grave markers, almost flush to the ground.

ERIC HOYT   JAMES HOYT
1964–1965   1966–1968

They could find no markers for Julie, Molly, and Noah. "She couldn't spring for the other three?" Fitzpatrick said sardonically. Then he and Tynan stared at the ground in uncharacteristic silence. "These would have been five adults now," Fitzpatrick said.

"They'd be in their twenties," Tynan said. "Eric would be turning thirty this year."

"They never had a chance. Never went to the prom or drove a car or did anything." Fitzpatrick thought about how people in criminal cases tended to be so fascinated by defendants that they forgot about their victims. "Well, we're going to make their lives mean something," he said. They got back in their car and headed home for Thanksgiving.

Responding to a subpoena served by Tynan eight days later, John Falitico descended once more to the pathology storage room in the basement of the old Upstate Medical Center in Syracuse. He pulled a drawer containing two thousand of the six million organ tissue slides in the room, and removed the twenty-six that were marked HOYT, NOAH. Before the day was out, the slides were in an overnight express envelope bound for St. Paul, Minnesota. The next day, in Tioga County, Investigator John Sherman drove a few miles east of Owego to Wilson Memorial Hospital in Johnson City, and served a subpoena for the tissue slides taken during Molly's autopsy on June 5, 1970. They, too, were headed for Janice Ophoven's microscope.

Now Courtright turned up the heat. He was the catalyst, the organizer. Quietly resolute, extremely structured, his years in the marine corps still seemed to define his bearing. He was all over the Hoyt case now, and both Simpson and Fitzpatrick were coming to believe that it was Courtright's arrival in Owego, as much as the involvement of either Baden or Ophoven, that was turning this case into a viable investigation. If it led to an arrest, it would be largely because Courtright, in his unassuming way, had brought all the elements together. For his part, Courtright viewed the case as the challenge of his twenty-five-year career. He'd worked his share of homicides over the years, but he'd never been in charge of one.

With interviews of Waneta and Timothy Hoyt seeming increasingly likely, Courtright and Sherman went about the work of quietly excavating their lives. They wanted to learn everything they could without alerting them. If there was one thing that could stop this investigation in its tracks, they knew, it was a lawyer.

They managed to dig out a few things inconspicuously. From assorted records, they learned that Waneta Hoyt, who was now forty-seven, had neither graduated from high school nor been employed in the years since, while her husband, who was fifty-one, had graduated from Newark Valley High in 1961 and spent most of his adult life as a construction laborer. He was now working as a security guard at the Johnson Museum of Art at Cornell University, earning $8.04 an hour. The investigators determined that the Hoyts had married in January 1964, with Michael C. Harbac as best man and Janet L. Kuenzli as maid of honor; that they had twice filed for bankruptcy, in 1984 and again in 1991; that they rented a small house next to a big red barn on Route 38 whose electrical service was subsidized by the Tioga County Department of Social Services. With a subpoena, Courtright obtained medical records for the Hoyts and for their teenage son, Jay, who was adopted shortly after his birth on July 26, 1976, which was the same week as the fifth anniversary of the death of their last natural child. The records showed that Waneta went to doctors as often as some people went to the hairdresser.

Courtright's diligence gave the Hoyt case, finally, the feel of a major investigation. Memos were now going back and forth, and for the first time the highest levels of the New York State Police were aware that a case of multiple homicide was being investigated in Tioga County. On December 3, Captain Pace wrote to the assistant deputy superintendent for investigations in Albany and told him he was putting together a task force to help Courtright. In January, the task force would meet to plot the next step.

Courtright knew he was getting close to taking the case as far as he could without exposing it, but there was one thing he wanted to do in advance of the meeting. The death of James Hoyt nagged at him a little more than the others. He had a grandson about the same age, and he could not help imagining the last moments of that boy's life. Janice Ophoven's words rang true. She wanted the autopsy report, and Courtright had one more idea.

The man who signed James's death certificate—as he had for Eric and Julie—was a physician named Arthur Hartnagel, a beloved country doctor who practiced for decades from a big red house on Main Street in Berkshire and doubled as county coroner. But when he went looking, Courtright found only evidence of how hard it was going to be to corroborate such a long-overlooked case. Hartnagel had died years before, and so had his widow. Courtright tracked down their daughter in Florida, but it was another dead end. Marilyn Hartnagel said she was sorry, but she'd never heard her father talk about the Hoyts or their babies; she'd already moved away by then. Did she know where her father's records might be found? Oh, they were thrown out years ago, she said, not long after he retired and moved up to a house on Cayuga Lake, back in 1969.

12

Janice Ophoven flew to the Southern Tier of New York State from the heart of a Minnesota winter on January 14, 1994, and remarked how deadly cold it was. It was one of the things she and a number of others would remember about this pivotal day in the unearthing of the truth about the children of Waneta Hoyt.

Bill Fitzpatrick was too excited to notice the weather. He would recall driving down to Owego with Pete Tynan, walking into a meeting room of the best hotel in Tioga County, the fifty-eight-dollar-a-night Treadway Inn, surveying the assemblage of police investigators, prosecutors, and out-of-town forensic pathologists, and thinking how wonderful it was that all these people were gathered for the purpose of pursuing a case he'd thought about for seven years, and never stopped believing in.

There were sixteen people in all, which probably made this the largest and most momentous strategy session on the subject of crime in Tioga County since the infamous Apalachin Conference in 1957. Simpson brought in his three part-time assistant district attorneys. The senior assistant, George Mundt, a soft-spoken lawyer in his mid-fifties, happened to live and work in Newark Valley and knew the Hoyts. He had once drawn up a will for them, though they never came in to execute it. Mundt also had a memory of Tim Hoyt arriving at his house with a road crew after a prodigious snowstorm in the early eighties and drinking coffee on the porch after the work was done. The Hoyts seemed like nice people to Mundt, though he could not say he knew them well. He made no effort to conceal his shock and sadness about the accusations.

The police were there in force. Courtright called in John Sherman,

Sherman's new partner, Bill Standinger, and three more investigators, two men and a woman, recruited from other parts of Troop C for the expanding investigation. Sitting in for Captain Pace, who was spending these months in Massachusetts working on the widely publicized abduction and murder of a little girl named Sara Anne Wood, was one of the troop's BCI lieutenants, Larry Jackmin.

Hearing about this case in detail for the first time, some among the group found it unnerving. They had questions—a lot of questions. The answers would come from Janice Ophoven and Michael Baden, and how the doctors responded, in style as well as in substance, would go a long way toward determining where this case went from here. For Bob Simpson, it was the moment of truth. Ultimately it was his call. And he still had the same dilemma that had troubled him from the first: How could the doctors be so sure, with neither conventional physical evidence nor witnesses, that these children were murdered? How could they be sure they hadn't had some undetected genetic disease? Even if Baden and Ophoven felt the medical records indicated the children were normal and healthy before their deaths, why did that rule out SIDS? Wasn't that what SIDS was—the sudden, unanticipated death of a healthy baby? These doctors seemed to be making accusations by exclusion, a concept that made some people in this room uncomfortable. The investigators were trained to be suspicious by nature, but they were also trained to seek evidence that was positive and physical, not conceptual. For now, therefore, it was necessary for them to direct their skepticism not at the supposed perpetrator but at her accusers. One thing was clear: If it took all day, which it would, Simpson wanted the meeting at the Treadway to end in resolution. Either the group would buy homicide or the case was over. And if they did buy it, the next step would be an extraordinary one. There would be no turning back.

Four long tables were arranged in a square so that the participants could see one another. At the front of the room was a blackboard; a fireplace flickered in the background. Baden was late, which was not unusual for him, so Ophoven would be the first of the medical experts to speak. She came in knowing she had some persuading to do, but she was unworried. She understood the dynamics of the relationship between forensic science and criminal science. As she scanned the faces of the investigators and prosecutors in the room, she could almost read their minds. The look she saw was the kind she'd seen a hundred times before. It said: Prove it to us. Tell us why it would be a responsible thing to go up to this little town in the hills, look Mrs. Waneta Hoyt in the eyes, and ask if she is a mother who killed her babies all those years ago.

OPHOVEN: *It was really a police thing. It was like Simpson was chairing a committee that was going to decide whether or not there was anything here that would provide the critical mass to do this amazing investigation. They wanted to know what I thought, and I told them. Then they just started firing questions at me: "Are you telling me twenty-five years later that you could go into a court of law and testify that these people were murdered? On what basis?" For them it had to do with learning about apnea and about this thing where people kill their kids and pretend they have disease. And there was a lot of skepticism, either real or affected. The questions became quite pointed. And what I said was in my years of evaluating the deaths of children, there is one underlying concern that, when it presents itself, is very worrisome, and that is when there is a dead child and the story doesn't make sense. And that is as compelling for the diagnosis of foul play as if I were to find cancer cells. When the answers do not make medical sense then you would be making as serious a mistake not considering the possibility of foul play as it would be to say, "Oh, I just really don't want to call this cancer. Just think about how the family's gonna feel."*

Here, of course, were not one but five dead children, and in Ophoven's judgment the stories given for at least four of them made no medical sense. In the weeks before the meeting, she had performed the final tasks that confirmed her original diagnosis. She had peered into her microscope at sections of tissue taken from Noah's and Molly's organs—their hearts and lungs and kidneys, the thymus, thyroid and parathyroid, the trachea, aorta, spleen, liver, esophagus, appendix, large intestine, stomach, pancreas, adrenal glands, ureter, bladder, muscle, spinal cord, lymph nodes, bone marrow, and skin— and found no evidence of any lethal disease. Put together with the narratives of the autopsies found in the files at Upstate and Wilson Memorial hospitals, the tissue sections provided as accurate a look at the babies' bodies as if Ophoven herself were in the pathology labs on the afternoons of June 5, 1970, and July 28, 1971. A central precept of autopsy requires that the body and its organs be methodically, thoroughly, and neutrally described so that a hundred years later, it would be possible for a pathologist to make a diagnosis, even a diagnosis different from the original, based on that objective description. This was a point Ophoven, and later Baden, stressed: Taken with all the other circumstances, the autopsies, if competently described, could allow them to rule out natural causes.

As she said she would, Ophoven had also showed the voluminous Upstate records to an infant apnea specialist in Minnesota, Dr. Stephen Boros. He had found no evidence that either Noah or Molly had an apnea problem. What he saw was that for weeks on end, the nurses and doctors, including

Steinschneider, kept meticulous medical diaries of babies who were utterly normal.

OPHOVEN: *The histories for Molly and Noah reported very devastating episodes of apnea, precipitating emergency reactions, that were never validated in the hospital. Neither baby had episodes of anything that remotely resembles true apnea. And they both ended up dead. And then with the other three having no explanation, the probability is that all these children died for the same reason. One of the investigators said, "Well, how would you counter all these death certificates?" And I said, "They're not right. And you may want to think about revising the death certificates, because based on today's world, a couple of them, James and Julie, just don't make any sense at all. And you might want to revise Molly's and Noah's as well." Both of their autopsies had suggested there was something wrong with their lungs. This was based on the tissue sections, which did have descriptions around the lungs. But neither one of them described a fatal pulmonary disease. You could tell they were reaching when they filled out the death certificates. In those days it was not uncommon to just sort of pick the thing that was most wrong and call it that.*

What I wanted to get across was that this was a different set of dynamics and different kinds of folks than you find in the traditional chronically tortured or habitually abused child. This is just a much more complex, smarter kind of deal. It takes a pretty crafty individual to outsmart everyone—to understand and use the medical dynamics to get people to draw conclusions about your child when it goes against the actual facts. And it made sense when you read the charts. If you looked at the history as it was being given, it got increasingly sophisticated over the years. In the earlier years it was a little bit primitive, kind of simple explanations, and then by the time you got to Noah, the history seemed to be fairly full of complex things. You could take the point that she figured out what Steinschneider needed and gave it to him. Traditionally, the by-proxy form of child abuse is very sophisticated, very compelling, very believable. If you get into the Munchausen literature it's amazing the kind of stuff that people are willing to do to children. And the part that's so hard is we become an instrument of abuse. Oh, Lord, we put a child in a sterile environment, we stick needles in him, we test him, we do operations on him. I had a case where the child had been admitted to the hospital something like 220 times by the time he was eight years old, and he had literally dozens of operations on his head and his nose, and there was nothing wrong with him at all. It's an amazing dynamic. I told the police at this meeting about the tapes we had seen, surveillance tapes of children being suffocated by their parents while in the hospital. And the police were saying,

"Are you kidding? You've actually seen people do this in the hospital? You're not making this up?" I think until you see one of these tapes, it's really hard to believe. So that's why I thought they needed to know what kind of person she was. That was going to be an important piece. Is she of reasonable enough intelligence to have the capacity to pull this off?

Baden came into the room like a gust of wind, momentarily drawing attention away from Ophoven. Courtright had made a point of calling both medical examiners some weeks before to let them know the other was involved. But he hadn't made Ophoven's special credentials clear to Baden, or perhaps Baden, forever distracted, wasn't paying attention and only heard something vague about a doctor from Minnesota. So as she spoke, Ophoven sensed that Baden was a little edgy at first, looking at her as if skeptical of who she was and what qualified her to be here. "To the point," she recalled, "where I felt Simpson had to interrupt and kind of say, maybe we need to redo the introductions here: Dr. Ophoven is a forensic pediatric pathologist, trained with Dr. Coe in Minnesota. And then Baden kind of went, *Ohhhh.* I think he thought I was a pediatrician coming in and talking about pathology. He lightened up and pretty soon we were a team."

BADEN: *I drove up from the city, and I remember snow. It took me a long time to get up there. There was a very supportive feeling that Ophoven, from her perspective, and I from mine, had both independently reached the same conclusions. Second opinions are just as needed in forensic pathology as in surgery or internal medicine. I think I prefer that, especially if you have an expertise in that area. What sometimes happens is you get a dermatologist coming in as a friend of the family to see if the autopsy is done right. I was impressed with Ophoven, so I had no turf problems. I knew that before the district attorney was going to proceed he had to be satisfied in his own mind he really had a case, and that it was a provable case. I thought Ophoven gave a very good presentation and analysis of the whole thing. Simpson was listening—everybody was listening.*

FITZPATRICK: *I had kind of taken for granted that everyone was as convinced as I was, and I began to realize that this was not the case. And you're certainly not going to find a more favorable audience than a roomful of law enforcement people. Jan Ophoven did a magnificent job of very quietly, patiently explaining why these were murders. And I thought: Bob's come up with a real diamond in the rough here. She'll be very effective in front of a Tioga County jury. She's not Madison Avenue Mike Baden. Baden's like me, from New York City, and I just love listening to the guy talk. He always looks like he's just run a marathon. But you're talking about country folks, people who might know Waneta Hoyt, might even have known about the deaths of the babies. I mean, every time a waitress would come into the room, we'd be quiet. And you think, geez, it really is a small community. You don't know who the waitress might be related to.*

Baden and Ophoven each went through the lives and deaths of the five children, hoping to impart, as clearly and specifically as possible before moving on to the next point, why they thought each one had been murdered. They used the blackboard as a visual aid.

Eric: Dies suddenly at three months. Interviews with the parents during the care of Molly and Noah reflect conflicting stories: "no apnea" and "episodes of apnea," and died with blood coming from his nose. Death was attributed to congenital heart disease but this was never medically evaluated and no autopsy was performed. Viewed in the context of the other four, Eric's death is highly suspicious.

Julie: Dies suddenly at two months. Death attributed to "choking" on milk or rice cereal. This is not an adequate explanation for cause in an otherwise healthy infant—children don't die of strangulation from a bottle feeding. Rather, they would aspirate the food. No autopsy was performed.

James: Dies suddenly at two years after "calling out." Autopsy, though not available, reported in later records to have found no cause of death. This child is also reported to have blood coming from the nose and mouth, indicating trauma and likely suffocation. Age and circumstances—including its timing just three weeks after Julie died—make this death especially suspicious.

Molly: Dies suddenly at two months, the day after discharge from hospital. Death certificate lists "acute interstitial pneumonitis" and "coarctation of aorta," but examination of autopsy report and tissue slides refutes these conditions as causes of death and fails to provide any medical explanation for the death. Review of medical records does not confirm a life-threatening apnea problem and is more consistent with "factitious" apnea, or Munchausen syndrome by proxy. Reports of cyanosis, or turning blue, are not consistent with SIDS.

Noah: Dies suddenly at two months, also the day after discharge from hospital. As with his sister, there is no evidence of a life-threatening medical condition, nor would the hospital have sent either baby home with a serious infection. (Infections of the sort described on the death certificates, even if present, could not have killed so rapidly.) Autopsy does not provide a medical

explanation for the death. Once again, cyanosis is more consistent with suffocation than with SIDS.

There were a couple of other things both doctors wanted the police and
prosecutors to understand. If these deaths occurred now, the absence of
autopsies and/or full-scale investigations would preclude the SIDS diagnosis.
And finally, there was the big picture: The odds against five infant deaths in
one family in six years, with no suggestion of a genetic condition, were virtually incalculable.

OPHOVEN: *What they needed to do now was a competent death investigation. That was the missing piece. If I'm the medical examiner and I'm
looking at these cases, I need a death investigation and I need it now. You
need to ask clear and detailed questions about the health and well-being of
the kids, get details of their lives and details of the events and get the stories
from the parents. Because you need to know that I'm very worried that
without additional information the only plausible explanation is homicide.*

SIMPSON: *I was absolutely fascinated with Baden and Ophoven and what
they had to say. And we hammered away at the issue from all sides. There
was a lot of skepticism there: How do you know this? How do you prove it?
Why couldn't it be something else? We talked about all these things you don't
look at until somebody force-feeds it to you. We talked about SIDS, what it is
and what it isn't. And we talked a lot about apnea, and that apnea is normal.
If you read the medical record you say, My God, these kids had apnea, how
did they live so long? And once these doctors explain to you what these
medical records mean and don't mean, then you're looking at them and
saying, Why in the hell didn't somebody figure this out twenty-five years ago?
Well, probably the climate wasn't right for an investigation. Even when I got
into this, I'm thinking, who am I to question Dr. Steinschneider? Who was
Floyd Angel* [the county coroner who signed Molly's death certificate]
*to question Steinschneider? Hell, back in the seventies, just think about
what would have happened if somebody became really suspicious. Steinschneider would have taken care of them in a hurry.*

Steinschneider. He was the unseen but pervasive presence in this case, at
this meeting. Who was Alfred Steinschneider? What were his responsibilities? What were his motives? Did he know more than what he had put on
paper? All the key players on the Hoyt task force had seen the influential 1972
article—it had been included in everybody's package of records—and though
they were far more concerned with its subject than with its author, for some

the heart of the matter always came back to Steinschneider, and to the inevitable question of how two murders could have occurred virtually under his nose. Given what came later, did he benefit by failing to notice?

Fitzpatrick, for one, wasn't sure whom he reviled more, the mother or the doctor. Linda Norton's reading of the 1972 paper had always left her with the conviction that Steinschneider bore some responsibility for allowing the last child, probably the last *two,* to be killed—the casual "isn't that curious?" attitude taken to appalling extreme. Fitzpatrick embraced this view passionately. The language and methods of Steinschneider's study suggested he saw himself more as a research scientist than as a doctor with patients, and to Fitzpatrick this raised questions of basic medical obligation. "I always felt that M.H. and N.H. were the most egregious because now they are under the care of a doctor," he said. "And I'm a new father. And what's going through my mind as I'm reading the medical records is I want to reach back in time and save them. I had thought about Noah for a long time. I had every day of his life in front of me. He was the one who didn't have to die. Who shouldn't have died. Steinschneider may have thought he was doing great research, but his responsibility was to his patients. And his patients are dead."

From her first reading of the hospital records, Janice Ophoven also felt that Noah could have been saved. "The fact that Molly's case never validated these apnea episodes and she ended up dead left the devastating awareness— because I have these two cases sitting here—that Noah's death was clearly preventable. And that's made me sad." She tried to be charitable. She wondered if Steinschneider, intrigued by SIDS and confronted by a family with an arresting history, had gotten a little overexcited at the prospect of solving one of the great mysteries of medicine—of cracking the code. Perhaps he saw in the H. family not a cause for alarm but an opportunity for science—a regrettable but honest misjudgment.

But then Ophoven reminded herself that Steinschneider had gone on to become a classic name in SIDS. He now ran the American Sudden Infant Death Syndrome Institute, a clinical research center he founded in Atlanta in 1983. He knew what SIDS looked like. He had to have seen that the children in this family were dying in all kinds of strange ways. Was it a case of a zealous researcher's naïveté, or something more disturbing? Ophoven found troubling evidence in the comparison between Steinschneider's article and the hospital records. "The paper has a slightly different slant than you'd get from reading the medical records," she said. "We pride ourselves in giving a clinical history that's based on a neutral assessment of the facts. This paper just doesn't feel so unbiased. It's very biased toward these being very sick kids. And when you look at the cases, they just don't look like very sick kids."

Like Linda Norton, Ophoven found herself absorbed by the medical and scientific undercurrents of the Hoyt case. The apnea theory that Stein-schneider put forth in his paper had profoundly influenced the way the world viewed SIDS for two decades. The paper itself had been quoted nearly four hundred times in research and medical journals, and the thriving industry of home apnea monitoring had been conceived as a result. Now, a roomful of doctors, detectives, and prosecutors were discussing whether the babies who started it all actually stopped breathing more often than any other babies. It was science that the Nobel Prize–winning biochemist Albert Szent-Györgyi was thinking about when he remarked that "discovery con-sists of seeing what everybody has seen and thinking what nobody has thought." But his observation could be applied to crime as well as to science— and now to both at once. It was not the purpose of this investigation to probe the methods and consequences of medical discovery, but it was intriguing to consider the ramifications of the day, nearly twenty-four years before, when the research doctor and the young mother from the rural hills first crossed paths.

When the subject of Steinschneider came up, Fitzpatrick told the group about the phone call he'd made to Atlanta six months before. He had made a careful record of the conversation.

"This is Dr. Steinschneider."

"Doctor, I'm the district attorney here in Syracuse, your former home-town. I'm calling about a case that you may be able to help us with. Do you remember the Hoyt family?"

"I'm sorry. I can't discuss patients without their permission."

"Well, can you talk to me about the family you wrote about in your article in Pediatrics *in October of 1972? The H. family?"*

"I can't tell you the name of the family in the paper."

"Do you have any notes that you saved, relative to your interviews with the family?"

"No, that would be confidential. Who did you say you were?"

"I'm the district attorney of Onondaga County."

"This was thoroughly reviewed back then."

"I was just calling to see if you had any additional information."

"They were a very nice couple, very supportive of each other, as I remember. I think he worked in construction and she was a housewife. These were all very tragic occurrences."

"Well, didn't it seem a little peculiar to you, five children dying one by one?"

"First, let me say, there is a lot of evidence that SIDS recurs in families. All these cases were thoroughly reviewed, and the autopsies on the last two babies revealed no evidence of foul play. The last child had several life-

threatening episodes while under observation in the hospital. And after he died, I believe they went on to adopt a baby."

"Are you familiar with Munchausen syndrome by proxy?"

"Yes."

"And?"

"I'm familiar with it."

"Didn't it strike you as odd that all these things happened to all five of these children only when their mother was around? Don't you think somebody else would have seen episodes of breathing difficulty?"

"As I said, the babies I studied had life-threatening episodes in the hospital."

"Is that right? Well, didn't it seem strange that they all died in the presence of their mother?"

"There's only three possibilities. It would happen in the presence of the mother, or the father, or both."

Hearing Fitzpatrick describe Steinschneider's defensiveness, there were few doubts among those at the Treadway what role the doctor would and would not play in this case. Though in all likelihood he knew more than anyone except the Hoyts themselves, Steinschneider was probably the last person the investigators could count on for help. Then as now, it seemed, he had his interpretations—his agenda. For them, however, Steinschneider's attitude was beside the point. What mattered was that these cases were now indeed being "thoroughly reviewed." The momentum of the meeting was shifting. A hurdle had been cleared, a line crossed.

OPHOVEN: *There was a great deal of feeling in there about what they were getting ready to do, and concern for the family. It's not like they wanted to run in there and raise this question to a family that could have suffered five horrendous tragedies and had this very difficult life. I had the strong impression that they felt that, even though they had the authority to go in and ask questions any time they wanted to, if there was any way not to do it, that's what they wanted to come out of this. But by the end I think they had what they needed. It's interesting how the police do this. It's like they almost have two personalities in these cases involving parents and children. The first one is "I'm skeptical. Let's not accuse people of things we shouldn't." But once they believe that murder is likely, they move into a different way of thinking. It's a bit more peaceful, like they're getting ready to move. And near the end, Bob Simpson wanted to be absolutely sure and he said, "Let me get this straight one last time. Give me the cause and manner of death in each of these cases." And he would say each of the children's names and Mike and I would sort of say it together, in a very clear and dramatic way:*

Eric: Homicide.
James: Homicide.
Julie: Homicide.
Molly: Homicide.
Noah: Homicide.

SIMPSON: *I asked a few questions, but I didn't say a whole lot. I just listened. And what they had to say made so much sense to me when taken in conjunction with the medical records that I was convinced that Mrs. Hoyt had suffocated these children. And I decided by the end of that meeting that we were going to go ahead with the prosecution. I don't know how a big-city D.A. would look at it, but sometimes you make decisions that you just know are right. I think of it more in terms of what do I think of myself, not what the voters are going to think of me. I think the five kids deserved that.*

The meeting broke up into the bar at the Treadway, one of the cozier spots in Tioga County in this harsh winter of 1994. In the darkness beyond the windows at the far end of the bar, the headlights of the cars and pickups traveling Route 434 across the freezing Susquehanna River passed like searchlights in the pitch-black night. Fitzpatrick, Tynan, Ophoven, and some of the state police investigators had a few beers at the bar, and as they talked and drank, there was an undercurrent of relief and anticipation. Fitzpatrick felt a kinship with Ophoven. He liked the strength of her convictions. "Fascinating cases like this don't come along that often," he'd say later. "It's exciting, and that's what we do." Though the two of them had no small stake in what was to come, they also had the luxury of detachment. They neither lived nor worked in this county; in this case they were advisers, instigators. Ultimately, though Fitzpatrick wished it were otherwise, he was a spectator.

Bob Simpson and Bob Courtright, meanwhile, went home that frigid night and thought about what lay ahead. They lived here. Before the spring thaw, they knew, their actions were likely to change a good number of lives, in Tioga County and far beyond.

13

The Bureau of Criminal Investigations of Troop C was composed of forty-four men and one woman.

Susan Mulvey was thirty-eight, divorced, the mother of a three-year-old daughter. She had shoulder-length, light brown hair, merry eyes when she smiled, a certain hardness when she didn't, and an affability with her co-workers that served her well in an agency that didn't swear in its first woman until 1974, the year Mulvey graduated from high school. Her father, once a trooper himself, went on to become the sheriff of Broome County, just east of Tioga, and there were those in the Southern Tier's criminal justice culture who still knew Sue Mulvey as Sue Andrews, the sheriff's plucky daughter.

Mulvey liked the backroom world of the BCI, having long ago recognized the professional advantages of being the only woman around. If they needed a female to go undercover in narcotics, there she was, all blue jeans and attitude. If there was a child abuse case, that was hers. It was difficult but important work. When the lawyers who'd been hired by women troopers elsewhere in the state came around to ask if she wanted to join their big sex-discrimination lawsuit, she told them no thanks. She'd made sergeant and investigator right on track, she told them; she'd been treated like everyone else. Among her classmates at the police academy in 1979 had been Bobby Bleck, the uniformed trooper in Berkshire.

A couple of weeks before the Treadway meeting, Bob Courtright had begun gathering the investigative team that had been authorized by Captain Pace for the duration of the case. To the group of men who worked for him directly he added Sue Mulvey. She'd worked for Courtright ten years before, when she was a uniformed road trooper on assignment to undercover narcotics, and he liked her way with people. Courtright had a pretty good idea where Mulvey fit in when he asked that she be assigned, but he wanted to think about it awhile and kept it to himself. All she was told by her boss in Binghamton was that she was being put on the Hoyt case, that Bob Courtright was in charge, and that she should go to a meeting at the Owego Treadway Inn on January 14.

She had sat in the conference room and listened like everyone else as the doctors laid out their findings, and when the program turned to police strategies, she wondered what Courtright planned for her. She left the meeting invigorated, happy to be included in such a major case, then went back to Binghamton and waited to hear what would happen next. As far as she knew, she was just another member of the team.

It was to be a reverse investigation, of sorts. Talking to anyone in Newark Valley who might have something important to say would blow the secrecy that Courtright and Simpson had worked hard to preserve, so the "death investigation," as Jan Ophoven had put it, would have to start with an interview with Waneta and Timothy Hoyt, and then work backward. Anyone else who might know something about how the Hoyt children died—best friends and old neighbors, sisters and brothers, doctors, nurses, ambulance workers, and the undertaker—would have to be interviewed after the Hoyts, though not long after. Courtright felt the window of opportunity would be small, especially if Mrs. Hoyt claimed innocence and got herself a lawyer who would immediately tell her to keep her mouth shut and circle the wagons. That would be some infernal public spectacle, Courtright thought. He could just imagine the headlines in the Binghamton *Press*: NEWARK VALLEY MOM CLAIMS WITCH HUNT. Even if she did confess, the investigators would have to move fast. They would be in the odd position of making an arrest and then going out to investigate the case. Simpson could count on strong medical testimony, but it wouldn't be physical or eyewitness evidence. It was anybody's guess what they'd find once they started asking questions. So Courtright spent much of the winter planning what amounted to an invasion of Newark Valley by the state police, to be carried out in the hours and days after the Hoyts were questioned. But it was the interviews with the Hoyts that he was thinking about most.

He mulled the logistics: how the Hoyts would be approached and asked to cooperate, how they would be separated, where they would be questioned and by whom. He thought about the follow-up interviews. There was so much they didn't know about the Hoyts' world: who was alive and who wasn't, where people lived, even the names of some of the people who mattered.

Some of the information, no doubt, would come out of the interviews themselves. It occurred to Courtright that he might have to ask his captain for a few more people.

Unbeknownst to them, Waneta and Timothy Hoyt were the targets of an investigation so intense that it would be hard to imagine them being under greater scrutiny had they been a pair of international drug lords. Courtright and his superiors arranged a Postal Service "mail cover" that would allow the state police to check the outside of the Hoyts' mail, incoming and outgoing, and take down the names of their correspondents, people the investigators might want to talk with later on. The operation would go into effect the day of the interviews. They made plans to seek an order from Vincent Sgueglia, the county judge, authorizing the local phone company to install a device that would show whom the Hoyts called long distance. The names and numbers it yielded would be put on "lead sheets" for later interviews. (There was discussion of a wiretap, but the crimes being alleged had occurred so long ago that Simpson and Courtright agreed they couldn't justify it to the judge.) Plans were made to pick up the Hoyts' garbage the day after the interviews. Maybe they'd panic, Courtright thought, and throw out something incriminating. An old pillow, perhaps. The courts had ruled that once someone brings his garbage to the curbside, it's fair game.

On the other side of the Court Street Bridge, meanwhile, Simpson was contending with a difficult issue: whether to seek a court order to exhume the bodies. And if so, when? Instinctively, he hated the idea. But Baden was pushing it hard; he thought there was still a chance, if the bodies were reasonably preserved, to find evidence of suffocation or some previous child abuse. For that matter, he thought it conceivable, if unlikely, that he could find evidence of fatal disease. When the question came up at the Treadway meeting, he suggested Simpson have a court order ready to go, so that they could exhume the bodies at the same time they were questioning the parents.

Fitzpatrick also had some thoughts on the subject. He remembered how perfectly preserved Vickie Lynn Van Der Sluys had been, and how Dr. Davies, in his re-autopsy, found something that turned into testimony. Simpson's reluctance had been obvious at the January meeting, and afterward Fitzpatrick pulled him aside. "Bob," he said, "you really ought to exhume the bodies. I'm sure I have no idea what your political problems are, and yeah, they're gonna call you a grave robber and all this stuff, but you know, in the long run you've got to do it. Because if you don't, the defense is going to say, 'Okay, Dr. Ophoven, you say these children were smothered, but twenty-five years ago Dr. Jones saw the body in front of him, touched it, autopsied that body, and he says the child died of SIDS.' "

Simpson didn't like his options. He was unconvinced anything useful would be found all these years later. He knew one thing, though: If the bodies were going to be exhumed, it would not be until after the Hoyts were questioned.

On Tuesday, March 22, the task force regrouped at the Treadway. Bob Courtright stood before fifteen police investigators and prosecutors and stated for the record what everyone in the room already knew: "We're going to interview Waneta and Timothy Hoyt tomorrow."

There were no doctors in the room this time. This was a police thing. The task force had grown to eight BCI investigators, including a polygraph specialist. And there was now one uniformed trooper among them. Bobby Bleck, who had been invited to the January meeting but had opted for his road duties that day, drove down to Owego from Berkshire in his blue-and-yellow patrol car, walked into the meeting room, doffed his Stetson, and flashed his trademark friendly cop grin. This time, he had been ordered to attend.

In the days before, Courtright had come to some important decisions about how he wanted things to go. What he had in mind was a nice, clean, self-incriminating statement from Waneta Hoyt. Without a confession, he knew, this was going to be one tough case to prove to a jury of Tioga County citizens. That's if it got that far. Simpson hadn't said yet whether he planned to pursue an indictment if things didn't go their way in the interview room. Courtright's face was a sketch of stress. "Take the confession or take the blame," was how he viewed the situation.

He was determined to go in with more psychological edge than he'd ever taken into an interview. One day in early February, he and Sherman drove two hours east to Schenectady to talk to some of the people connected with the 1986 investigation of Marybeth Tinning. Among them was Bill Barnes, a state police senior investigator who had since been elected Schenectady County sheriff. Barnes had taken Tinning's confession, and he told Courtright and Sherman that he felt it was not an insignificant factor that he had known Marybeth since they were kids. Courtright made a mental note: *a familiar face.* He had questioned his share of murderers and other criminals, but a suspect's frame of mind was probably never more critical than it was now. So much rested on Waneta Hoyt's response to the situation.

She was, he imagined, an unassuming, unsophisticated woman, but who could know what lay underneath? Was she "crafty," as Jan Ophoven guessed, so crafty that people made the mistake of thinking she was simple? What kind of person, after all, could do what Waneta Hoyt was supposed to have done? He couldn't quite get his head around Munchausen syndrome. But whatever the motive turned out to be, Courtright would have to make Waneta feel safe, emotionally if not legally. That was Joel Dvoskin's advice.

He was the chief of forensic psychology for New York State's mental health agency, a man accustomed to guiding detectives through the vagaries of the criminal mind. "She needs to know that you're not going to judge her for what she did," Dvoskin told Courtright over the phone. "Be patient. Let her set the emotional tone. If there's a long pause when she's talking, let it continue. Don't use tricks—tricks will scare her, ice her up. Just be supportive, because it's not unlikely that at some level there might be a part of her that wants to tell you. She's held it in a long time."

Dvoskin hadn't told Courtright anything he didn't already know instinctively. He would get her guard down, and keep it there. Start her on the "negative" interview—the part where you just sit and let her tell her version of events before moving on to the "accusatory" phase—and keep her talking. Keep her focused. She would be questioned in the Owego station in a six-by-ten, windowless, paneled room. The copying machine that was usually there had already been removed, and a plain metal table, three-by-five, with three chairs, had been brought in. He knew where he wanted Waneta to sit. He knew where he would sit. And he knew whom he wanted in the third chair, the one closest to Waneta.

Two days before, he had called Sue Mulvey in Binghamton. "It's going to be me and you in there," he told her. "Are you up for it?"

Mulvey said, "Sure," and thought what she would later express as "Yikes." Courtright drove to Binghamton and spent parts of two days talking to her about how they were going to approach the interview, how they were going to gain their suspect's trust—two days of double-checking that Mulvey was the right choice. She was going to be the main interviewer. Courtright had decided that a woman, a mother, should lead the questioning, and Mulvey was the only one in the troop. It would be only her second interview of a homicide suspect, but Courtright did not doubt that she could pull it off. He just wanted to keep hearing it from her.

He wanted Bobby Bleck involved. He would be the familiar face—the local cop who was so much a part of life in northern Tioga County that he could recite the routines of any number of people. He could tell you, for instance, that the Hoyts came into the post office next to the trooper substation every morning to pick up their mail. Bubba was the guy people up there went to with their problems. There was the time, in fact, that Waneta Hoyt came up to him on the street and complained about a peeping Tom situation. She thought somebody was looking in at night, when Tim was on the night shift at Cornell. Matter of fact, Bleck remembered, she'd brought her complaint to him during that conversation in front of the bank, right after she told that young couple that they had to be careful with babies—she'd lost five.

"Here are your assignments," Courtright was saying now. With the exception of Bleck and George Mundt, nobody on this task force had ever seen so much as a picture of the woman they'd spent so much time investigating. They knew all kinds of disparate things about her, from the five-dollar balance in her checking account to the fact that her adopted sixth child had survived to become a strapping teenager with aspirations of becoming a race car driver. But they could only imagine how she might respond to the events about to be set in motion.

"Sue and I will do the interview with Waneta," Courtright told the group. "Hyman and Stroh, you'll be our backups. If we don't have a rapport with her, one of you or both of you will go in. You'll also be available to go out on anything that comes up during the interviews. Standinger and Sherman will interview Timothy Hoyt up in Ithaca, where he works. If he's not getting along with you, Mastronardi and Stark will be your backups. Daniels, you'll stand by here in Owego with the polygraph. I've also arranged to have a stenographer at the barracks."

He laid out the plan: Bleck and Mulvey would drive an unmarked BCI car up to Newark Valley, followed by Courtright in his. He would stay back while they knocked on the Hoyts' front door precisely at ten o'clock—the same time he'd arranged to have Tim Hoyt brought to the Cornell public safety office by the university police. "Bubba will introduce Sue to Mrs. Hoyt, and she will tell her that we would like to talk to her about the lives and deaths of her children, and would she agree to come down to the Owego barracks? I'll meet you back at the barracks. We'll Mirandize her there."

Mulvey interpreted Courtright's plan to mean: Tell her the truth, not all of it, but enough to get her to the barracks. Mulvey had one question: "What happens if she doesn't want to come with us?"

"Well, now she's going to know what we're there for," Courtright said, "so we're going to do the interview at the house. We'll do it right at the kitchen table if we have to. We'll probably just get the one shot. And if she doesn't want to talk to us, we'll just have to buckle down and really dig into this investigation. Same thing with Mr. Hoyt."

Timothy Hoyt's job guarding the Cornell art museum had led Courtright to call Scott Hamilton, the chief investigator for the university police, and they'd hatched a plan. "They had a theft of some artwork from the museum, and Scott wants to talk to him about it anyway," Courtright explained. "So Scott has arranged for him to come down to his office at ten o'clock. When we pick up Waneta, I'll call on the radio to go ahead and pick him up."

The importance of questioning the Hoyts separately needed no discussion. Isolation was a standard technique to maximize the chances of confession. Moreover, though the betting was that the children's father was probably not involved, he was still a potential suspect. The medical records indicated it was

Mrs. Hoyt who usually found the children in distress, or dead, and called for help. And when Courtright used a computer program to check the days of the week of the five deaths, he found a striking pattern: All had occurred on weekdays, during working hours. The first had died at 1:30 in the afternoon, all the others between 8:30 and 10:00 in the morning. Still, nobody could be sure who was there when the children died.

If the assumptions of the doctors and detectives were correct, Waneta Hoyt would be the far trickier interview. Courtright typed out a list of eighteen questions he wanted to ask her. The first one was "Was husband or anyone else home at time of the deaths?" Later, Courtright took Mulvey aside and went over the final details of how they were going to conduct the interview, and what language they would use. They would not say the word *murder,* Courtright told her. Too inflammatory. Or *smother.* Too specific. They would accuse her of "causing the death" of her children and let her fill in the details. He wanted the words to come out of her mouth. Courtright's plan was to be low-key but unrelenting. Yes, Mrs. Hoyt needed to feel "safe," but she also needed to feel caught. That was the paradox of interrogation, Courtright knew. Hard questions had to be softened by an illusion of trust. Mulvey could play a pretty good bad cop, but that routine wouldn't work here. Shouting at Waneta Hoyt would probably just shut her down.

With the showdown fast approaching, Courtright asked Simpson the question that was nagging him. "Bob," he said, "what if she doesn't confess?"

"We're still going with it," Simpson said. "We want her to make a statement, but if she doesn't, we're still going ahead. We'll go out and get more, and we'll take it to a grand jury, and we'll let a jury decide."

Courtright felt better, but not a lot better. He was relieved that Simpson wasn't about to give up after taking the case this far. But he knew that without a confession—or at the very least an inconsistent negative statement that could be used against her—even a grand jury might have reasonable doubts. Never mind a trial jury.

There was one person in the room at the Treadway who professed little hesitation about where this would fall in twenty-four hours. "She's gonna go for it," Fitzpatrick told Courtright. He could not contain his excitement. "I was sky-high," he later remembered. "I was literally on the edge of my seat." He came home and proceeded to tell Diane every detail he could remember of the meeting in Tioga County, down to the seating arrangements. He couldn't wait to go back in the morning.

He called Linda Norton in Dallas. "Remember Steinschneider?" he asked. "Remember the H. babies?"

"Yeah," Norton said. "I remember those." She hadn't talked to Fitzpatrick in a while.

"We're planning to go down and talk to their mother tomorrow. I think we're going to get a confession."

"Yeah," Norton said. "And pigs fly. These people don't confess."

Bob Courtright rose at 6:00 the next morning. He made himself a cup of coffee and opened his closet. He had eighteen suits. The night before, he'd reviewed the candidates, looking for something soft. The medium gray would do fine, he had decided. You look at this and you don't get all excited. With the gray-and-white striped tie.

It was a cool, sunny morning, this third day of spring. Bonnie Courtright kissed her husband good-bye, wished him luck, and was out the door. She worked for a dentist. Courtright got on the road by 7:30, and twenty minutes later he was in his office at the Owego barracks. A couple of uniformed troopers were getting ready to go out on the road. He told them, "Don't come back to the station today unless it's absolutely necessary. We're doing a very, very important interview today. I don't want a lot of people around." Especially people wearing uniforms. At the meeting the day before, he'd also arranged for the small crowd that was going to accumulate at the barracks—Simpson, the BCI lieutenants, Fitzpatrick and Tynan, Investigators Stroh, Hyman, Daniels, and the stenographer from Binghamton—to gather in a back section of the station before they brought Mrs. Hoyt in, and to stay out of view until the door to the interview room was closed.

Sue Mulvey arrived a few minutes after Courtright. She had slept fitfully, but now she was ready to go. She was dressed in a plain blue suit with a white blouse. Around her neck hung a locket bearing a baby picture of her daughter, Jackie. The child was now three, but in the tiny photograph she was six months old, dressed in the required maroon velvet dress with lace collar. Mulvey felt as if she'd heard a hundred suggestions fly at her during the meeting the day before, but she was listening to her own instincts. Find common ground. Draw Waneta in. Close the gap. Open the locket. Bring yourself down a notch. Ask for coffee if she does. Kick off your shoes. Make sure she notices.

Bobby Bleck left his house across the street from the Berkshire substation, drove down to the Owego barracks in his patrol car, then went out to the garage in back of the barracks to swap it for a plain gray criminal investigations vehicle. He was probably the least tense member of the team. He figured all he had to do was say, "Sue, this is Waneta Hoyt. Waneta, this is Sue Mulvey," then hit the road and catch some speeders on 79.

At a quarter of ten, Mulvey slid next to Bleck. "Good luck," Courtright said tensely. He lit a cigarette. The two cars crossed the river and began winding their way through the back roads of Owego leading to Route 38 and the fifteen-minute drive up to Newark Valley.

Bleck drove into the village, past the laundromat and the bank and the churches, the empty stores on Water Street, and the truck stop on the edge of town. A mile on, they sailed past Newark Valley High School, a rambling brick building constructed in 1971 on an expansive plain bordering Davis Hollow Road. It was the school from which the five Hoyt children would have graduated—classes of '82, '84, '86, '88, and '89—and where Jay Hoyt was now a senior, Class of '94.

Inexperienced in operations as delicate as this, Bleck silently practiced his lines one last time as he neared his destination. He slowed as he approached a small, oddly shaped house at the edge of a field on the right side of the road. There was a picnic table beside a row of lilac bushes on one side of the house, a white car on the other. Bleck's eyes narrowed as he took his foot off the gas pedal.

"Sue, this is not good," he said.

"What is it?" Mulvey asked tentatively.

"That white Oldsmobile. That's the car Tim drives."

"Keep going," Mulvey told him.

Bleck drove on a few hundred yards, and pulled off the road. Courtright rolled up next to them and lowered his window.

"Tim's car is there," Bleck said.

"Shit," Courtright muttered. "You're sure?"

"Well, that's the car he drives."

If Tim was home, they'd have to call it off for today. "Go back there and make sure," Courtright told Bleck, then dragged on a cigarette and waited, his car idling. A minute later, Bleck and Mulvey were back. Yes, it was definitely Tim's car. "Let's get out of here," Courtright said. "We'll go up to the Berkshire satellite. I'll call up to Ithaca and see if he's at work. See what the fuck's going on."

The two cars moved north a few miles into Berkshire, a hamlet even smaller than Newark Valley. Bleck pulled up to the state police satellite station he worked out of, parked in front, and headed for the door. Courtright drove up a few seconds later and parked off to the side. As he alighted from his car, he noticed Bleck exchanging pleasantries with a middle-aged woman who had just come out of the post office housed in the same building. She wore a shapeless shirt overhanging black pants, white socks with black shoes, no coat. Courtright might not have paid much attention if not for the woman's most striking physical feature: She was nearly bald on top. His mind did a double take. *I think that's her,* he thought.

She was just as Bleck had described: drab, paunchy, slow-moving—and you just didn't see many women with so little hair. She was forty-seven but looked a decade older. She seemed a pitiful figure as she made her way toward an old red pickup truck.

Mulvey walked over to Courtright.

"I think that's her," she whispered.

"Geez, I think so too," Courtright said.

Bleck came over, cocking his head in the woman's direction. "That's Waneta Hoyt," he muttered. Courtright was momentarily stunned. This wasn't part of the plan.

She was getting in the pickup now. "Go over and talk to her," Courtright told Bleck. "Try to find out where her husband is."

Bleck sidled up to her with his usual informality. "Hey, Waneta, weren't you sick last time I saw you?" he said, breaking the ice with his best mischievous smile. "Now, how come you don't have a hat on?"

"Oh, it's such a nice day out," Waneta Hoyt said, brightening slightly.

"Where's Tim at today?"

"He's at work. I just took him over to Cornell. I'll pick him up tonight and we'll go out for supper."

Bleck reported the news to Courtright and Mulvey.

"Okay," Courtright said. "Let's do it." He headed back to his car.

Bleck returned to the red pickup, a Ford made the year the last Hoyt child died, and leaned into the window. "Waneta, do you have a minute?" he said.

"Sure, Bobby," she said pleasantly.

"Could you come in here to the station?"

Inside, they found Mulvey standing in the back office, a small room with a large wall map of Tioga County, and a desk where Bleck did his paperwork.

"Waneta, I'd like you to meet Sue Mulvey," Bleck said. "Or should I say Sue Andrews? Sue went to the police academy with me, and now she's an investigator with the state police."

Bleck paused to let Mulvey smile and say hello. "Waneta," he continued, "what's happened is some doctors reviewed, you know, the unfortunate deaths, the lives and deaths of your babies, and Investigator Mulvey here would like to ask you some questions about that. Is that okay with you?"

"Sure," she said, and sat down.

"We heard about your children from a medical article written by Dr. Steinschneider from Syracuse," Mulvey opened. Waneta peered up at her blankly. "And we've talked to a doctor from Minnesota about it and looked at the medical records. But the information is a little sketchy to us, so we'd like to know a little bit more, and you're the best person to talk to because you were there. So I've been assigned to get as much information as possible, about how your babies lived and died, and the reason I'm doing it and not the doctors is that this isn't their area of expertise. This is what I do every day, talk to people. That's why they asked me to talk to you. So maybe we can prevent this from happening to other children. Would you be willing to talk with us?"

"If I can help anybody else . . ."

"Now, I don't have my paperwork right here with me. Would you mind coming down to the Owego barracks?"

"All right. But I've got to go home first and drop my son at school. He's got a late day today. Then I have to pick him up at four. So I'm free until then."

Mulvey loosened. There had been, up to now, no discernible trepidation in Waneta's voice or on her face, no suggestion of surprise or fear or even recognition that this was anything other than as good a way as any to spend a Wednesday morning in March. But then she took Bleck's hand. "Is it okay if Bobby comes with me?" she asked.

"Sure, that's fine," Mulvey said.

"Uh, sure," said Bleck, caught off guard. "How about you ride down with us, Waneta? You can drop your car off at home, and then we'll give you a ride down. Might as well use state police gas."

"All right," Waneta said. "There's something I want to get at home."

"Okay if I ride with you?" Mulvey asked her. She wanted to be with Waneta every second from this moment on—didn't want her to be alone with her thoughts and maybe decide she didn't want to talk to them after all.

"I don't mind. You know, if my husband was home, he could go with us because he knows more about what the doctors said. He knows all about the SIDS and he could explain it better."

Mulvey went outside to Courtright. "She's coming with us," she said. "We have to stop at her house first." Relieved, Courtright picked up his radio transmitter to call Ithaca, then headed back for the Owego barracks.

"They've got her," John Sherman told his partner.

"Let's go," Bill Standinger said. Walking his dog that morning, Standinger had rehearsed the coming moments in his mind. Best approach: Don't tell him what it's about until we get to the barracks. Unless he asks. Maybe he won't.

They got out of their car and went into the Cornell University public safety office. Inside they found Scott Hamilton sitting with a stern-faced man in the uniform of a Pinkerton guard. He was in his early fifties, with a head of gray-black hair combed straight back, and thick glasses.

"Mr. Hoyt, I'm Investigator Sherman and this is Investigator Standinger.

We're with the state police. We'd like to discuss some things with you, and we wonder if you might come with us to the Ithaca barracks."

"Okay," said Tim Hoyt.

Just out of the shower, Jay Hoyt was eating a bowl of cereal at the kitchen table when Bleck and Mulvey came into the house at his mother's invitation. He was a clean-cut seventeen-year-old in jeans and tee-shirt, with an adolescent's aspiring mustache.

"This lady's with the state police," his mother told him. "I'm going down to talk to them about your brothers and sisters."

Jay looked at Mulvey, then went back to his breakfast. He finished, started gathering his stuff for school, and asked his mother for lunch money.

She was rummaging around the living room. "I have a picture album. Is it all right if I bring it? It has pictures of the babies."

"That would be just fine," Mulvey said. *That would be more than just fine,* she thought. *That would be evidence.*

Waneta pulled out a worn spiral book from a cabinet. "It'll help me remember," she said.

"Is there any medication you ought to take with you?" Bleck asked. "I'm not sure how long this is going to last."

She said she had a couple of prescriptions, for hypertension and arthritis, but hadn't used them in a while.

"Better take 'em just in case. Tim would kick my butt if you got sick."

She retrieved two bottles of pills.

"Can we give you a lift to school?" Bleck asked Jay. He added quickly, "It's an unmarked car."

"Yeah, okay," Jay said.

He sat up front with Bleck. "You got your car all fixed up?" Bleck asked him, pulling out onto the road. He looked at the teenager and smiled. "I'd hate to think you'd be out on Brown Road." Jay chuckled sheepishly.

"Guess we're through with winter," Bleck commented, trying to keep a light mood. "And not a minute too soon. We had so much snow on the roof, the carport fell on the wife's Jeep."

"Oh, that's terrible," Waneta said. "One of my neighbors had their garage collapse."

"And to top that off," Bleck continued, "I was trying to be a nice guy one day, and I see the minister and Mr. Lawton over shoveling off the back of the church. So I go over and help them. And Mr. Lawton's there with a pipe in his mouth, and he grabs the top four inches of snow, gives it a heave just as I come up and he slashes me right across the side of my head. Six stitches."

"I guess I shouldn't tell you I was in Florida last week," Mulvey said. "I took my daughter to Disney World."

Bleck pulled in front of the high school. Jay got out, said, "See ya later, Mom," and disappeared through the doors.

"He seems like a real nice kid," Mulvey said, as Bleck, sitting alone in front now, taxicab style, guided the car back onto Route 38.

"He's been working up at the barns at Cornell after school," Waneta said. "He's talking about starting up my brother Archie's old farm. It's in pitiful bad shape. 'Course, what he really wants to be is a NASCAR driver. Racing season, he's always up to Thunder Mountain." She paused. "How old is your daughter?"

"She's three now," Mulvey said. "I have a picture of her when she was a baby." She opened the locket.

"She's beautiful," Waneta Hoyt said.

She peered out the window as the police car glided across the Newark Valley town line, down Route 38, out of her world. The small talk waning, she stared into the distance with unreadable eyes, her hands gripping the book of photographs of her long-dead daughters and sons.

PART TWO

Convergence

We see only what we know.

—GOETHE

14

Spring 1960

She peered out the window in studied silence as the school bus came barreling down Route 38. It was a good ten miles between her farmhouse in the hills of Richford and the Central School in Newark Valley, and it had become her ritual to commence staring at about mile eight, knowing that in a minute or two the bus would be pulling up to the Yetter farm for its last pickup.

At fourteen, Waneta Nixon was exceptionally slender, with a sharp, narrow nose, a slightly jutting jaw, and a head full of soft black curls. She wore teardrop-shaped glasses that accentuated her serious, detached disposition and shielded eyes that seemed to take in everything but reveal nothing. Sometimes there would be moments when you might catch something—a look, a pointed comment. Mostly, though, it seemed she was just *there*. That's the way her third-grade class mother would later put it. Off in her own world, that Waneta Nixon.

A few acres past mile eight, the bus pulled up to the Yetter farm, and Waneta watched the boy with the crew cut and the black-rimmed glasses climb aboard and plant himself up front. It was his usual spot: The seats were always taken by the time he came aboard. Waneta had noticed him the very first time the bus had made this extra stop. She leaned over conspiratorially to her friend Bonnie. "Someday I'm gonna marry him," she said. How bold this was, coming from Waneta. Neta, to those close.

She was born eight months after the end of the Second World War, the fifth of six children of Albert and Dorothy Nixon, if you didn't include two others who died. The Nixons had spent the wartime era growing their family, starting in 1939 with the birth of Albert Junior. A year later there was Archie, a year after that Ruth, a year after that Dorothy Joan. The next baby, Robert, born in 1944, died of spinal meningitis before his third birthday, just after Waneta's birth in 1946. She was followed by another baby who was stillborn, choked by his umbilical cord. The last child, Donna, came in 1948. Neta always felt closest to her younger sister, who was an especially warm and true person. Through the years it became interesting to some in the family how two sisters could be so close and yet so different.

Neta and her siblings came into the world right on the Nixon homestead, a small dairy farm passed down through generations of a family long established in one of the poorest regions of New York State. Richford was a hamlet of barely a thousand people tucked into the northeast corner of Tioga County, composed mostly of narrow valleys and gentle upland, and the highest hills around. From the Dalrymple farm on West Hill, you could see eight counties all the way to Pennsylvania. The Nixons lived in a small four-bedroom farmhouse that sat up on a more modest foothill overlooking Route 38, just north of the Richford crossroads and hard by Highland Cemetery, which had once been a part of their land.

Theirs was a spartan life. The kids shared their rooms, sometimes their beds, and fought over a single bicycle. They swam down at the creek, and while Albert Nixon took his sons out hunting, returning with a catch of rabbits for supper, the girls played house, picking weeds for food. Their assigned roles were unalterable: Ruth, the oldest, always got to play the mother. Joan was the father, Donna the child. Neta was the neighbor.

The Nixons were clannish, but in some ways they coexisted, bound more by proximity than open emotion. Dorothy Nixon was the dominant presence, and she was not an easy woman. She ruled the house, and Neta, especially, clung to her. Albert Nixon tended to defer to his wife's authority, never raised his voice, never even looked as though he might. He had inherited the homestead from his father, just as he inherited and perpetuated the Nixon family tradition of naming its first sons Albert or Archie, a succession that went Albert-Archie-Albert-Archie all the way back to the last century and resulted in a family tree so confusing that, other than the Nixons themselves, it could be mastered only by Clarence Lacey, who wound up burying them in Highland Cemetery. Lacey was not only caretaker and president of the cemetery association, and the Richford town historian, but Albert Nixon's friend, neighbor, and, because he owned the truck, employer. The New York State Department of Public Works paid them thirty-eight cents an hour in the early days before the war (plus a dollar a day to Clarence for use of the truck) to patch the major state roads, cut the brush, toss sand when it snowed. It wasn't unusual for the phone to ring in the Nixon house at two or three on a winter morning, Clarence Lacey calling from a hundred yards away to tell Albert it was time to go to work. The Nixons and the Laceys were neighbors in life and death. Their homes were adjacent, and so were their plots at Highland Cemetery.

Since Waneta's father took more to working the state road crew than to milking cows at daybreak, the local industry skipped a generation on the Nixon farm. By the time her brother Archie got old enough to try his hand at it, times were changing all over Tioga County. In the years before World War II, every town had a little Borden's milk plant, with ice to chill it cut from local ponds in January. A family could make a living with fifteen or twenty milking cows, a few acres of cash crops—corn, potatoes, oats, buckwheat—and a team of horses to do the plowing and cultivating. But by the 1950s, the smaller farms were starting to fall away. Some from up here began commuting to Owego to work at the huge new IBM installation, which made electronic components for the space program. With its long access roads, sleek buildings, and man-made lake, the IBM campus looked like something dropped from another planet. But harsh agricultural economics couldn't destroy a way of life. Even as top secret work went on at IBM, the route men from the creameries tooled around the county, picking up brimming ten-gallon cans early each morning at the farms that survived, dropping off equal numbers of empties for the next day's run.

It would be hard to distinguish the ebb and flow of Richford's hardscrabble life from that of the innumerable farming communities surrounding it, so it was paradoxical that one of the things these towns shared was their isolation from one another, their conviction that whatever went on down the road was down the road's business. When you asked someone from Richford about the ups and downs of the dairy industry, he'd tell you about the ups and downs of the Richford dairy industry, though it was no different from the Berkshire dairy industry or the Newark Valley dairy industry. There was almost a cultural imperative to remain apart from the outside world, and if you were from Richford, that could be Newark Valley. The outside world just wasn't that important.

There was the example of John D. Rockefeller and the ENTERING RICHFORD signs. John D., as he was sometimes known, was born in Richford on July 8, 1839, but the significance of this fact was debatable, as much the source of hard feelings as pride. He had stayed only four years, later going to school at the Owego Academy before moving on to Ohio. Not until he was in his eighties did Rockefeller return to his Richford roots. He arrived in town each July, directed his chauffeur to stop in front of Bert Rawley's store, stepped out of his fabulous automobile, and gave out shiny new dimes to the children who surrounded him. Decades later, when the town fathers voted to put up signs—RICHFORD EST. 1882 THE BIRTHPLACE OF JOHN D. ROCKEFELLER 1839–1937—on the two roads into town, a number of people thought it was a bad idea. If anyone's name deserved to be put on those signs, they thought, it was Bert Rawley's. He did a lot more for Richford than Rockefeller ever did: ran the biggest store in town, owned the printing press, served as town supervisor, directed plays at the Odd Fellows Hall. That was the kind of place Richford was—a village of nine hundred people where a person could immortalize himself by keeping real busy. In 1948, after a lifetime of service to his community, Rawley dropped dead at the annual meeting of the Highland Cemetery Association, of which he had been an active member.

One of Rawley's close friends was the eminent doctor Arthur Hartnagel, another of northern Tioga County's famous citizens. He came from Berkshire, but since he was a medical doctor, as well as county coroner, he enjoyed prominence and respect beyond the borders of his hometown. Whole generations of people grew up without ever finding out exactly what was in those purple pills Doc Hartnagel kept in a big glass jar on a shelf in his office and dispensed like aspirin, though nobody doubted their effectiveness for the general ailments of life. That was part of the country doctor–patient covenant: He's the doctor, only one we've got. Nobody's yet come up with a reason not to trust him with your life. Nearly everyone in town was familiar with the front door of Hartnagel's office, which occupied a corner of the first floor of his house on Berkshire's Main Street. The door was half glass, with gold-painted block lettering explaining the doctor's office hours and other pertinent information. The doctor himself was an appealing figure, a hefty man with a mustache that embellished his friendly smile. He would often appear on house calls dapper in a three-piece suit, his stethoscope hanging from his neck like a fashion accessory, his fedora carefully dipped. Back in the thirties and forties, he would sometimes be accompanied on his rounds by Bert Rawley, out for a drive in his own suit and a racing cap.

There was only one other doctor in Richford in this century. John Edwin Leonard, himself a local legend, had married a Richford woman and set up his practice in 1889. Over the next six decades he delivered more than a thousand babies in Tioga and Cortland counties, most of them in their homes. A lot of families paid the five- or ten-dollar fee in barter: crops, chickens, milk, honey. Doc Leonard was also known for his uncanny knack for accurately diagnosing cases on sight, an ability that led old-timers to nickname him "the human X ray." He died in 1956, leaving the medical field to Doc Hartnagel, a slightly younger physician of merely mortal abilities.

Waneta Nixon's first serious exposure to the outside world came when she began taking the long bus ride to the Newark Valley Central School at the beginning of seventh grade. She'd gone to the Richford schoolhouse, the "graded school," as it was called, for the first three grades; then, when it was closed, she went on to the Edward R. Eastman School, which was between Richford and Berkshire, for grades four through six. Eventually, she made it all the way down to Newark Valley, ten miles from home. Compared with Richford, Newark Valley was practically cosmopolitan. It had two intersecting streets of stores, Main Street and Water Street, which included Betty's snack bar, a popular after-school hangout for "townies," as kids from Newark Valley were known, and over on Watson Avenue an eight-lane bowling alley. Newark Valley even had some industry. There was a ladder factory that employed a hundred or so workers.

The Central School, a two-story brick building with busts of the major U.S. presidents in the front hallway, graduated classes of sixty or so students drawn from Newark Valley, Berkshire, Richford, Speedsville, Weltonville, Jenksville, Candor, Owego, Marathon, and Flemingville. Every spring there would be "moving up day," when each class would sit in its assigned seats in the auditorium, and then the principal, Nathan T. Hall, would instruct the seniors to rise from their seats front and center and come up on stage, at which point the juniors would move up to where the seniors had been, the sophomores to where the juniors had been, all the way back to the eighth grade. The Central School was the center of social life in Newark Valley. Saturday nights the auditorium was turned into a theater, with first-run movies flicking through a projector run by Bus Decker, the janitor, who was later promoted to manager of the bus routes. There was roller-skating in the gym on Friday nights. A truck would pull up outside and the driver would bring in long racks of roller skates, along with his own music and amplification system.

At the Central School, Neta found a rural caste system firmly in place. If you were from Newark Valley, a townie and not a farm kid, you were at the top of the heap. If you were a farm kid from Newark Valley, or an athlete, you had a chance. But if you came from a place like Richford, you started at a great disadvantage. You were from the boondocks. It would take some work, good looks, great personality, to get inside. It started with the shoes. Did you wear work shoes to school, or dress loafers? Did your dad milk cows or did he *go* to work, leave in the morning, come home at night in a decent car?

Neta might have been fine in Richford. She was a Nixon; her dad had a good job with the state. But in Newark Valley—"Nerk Valley," as most people pronounced it—she was just a shy, unremarkable teenager whose father worked on the road. The farther she got from home, the less comfortable she was. You could track the evolution in her class pictures. In second grade, in the Richford schoolhouse to which she walked each morning, she was right in the middle of the group when the photographer snapped the shutter: all smiles, her face sweet and open, eyes sparkling, hands folded contentedly. In the fourth grade, in Berkshire, the smile was replaced by a defensive, distancing posture; she threw the camera a sharp, wary look. By tenth grade, at the Central School, she was standing at the far edge of the second row, looking self-conscious and uneasy, as if she had been coaxed into the pic- ture a second before it was taken. It was an appropriate metaphor for a teenager who was always at the social fringes, an outsider who had no apparent interest in challenging the barriers set for her. She had certain understandings about how her life was supposed to play out.

Neta's mother worked in a factory for a while, sewing baby clothes. This kind of work was fitting, considering the values Dorothy Nixon imparted to her daughter, or at least the values that Neta interpreted and took to heart. She was placed on earth, she heard her mother say, to bear children and to be a good wife to her children's father. That's it. Neta felt exceptionally close to her mother and didn't question her wisdom, though she did allow herself to ruminate on the possibility of a career as a hairdresser. As a child she would spend hours in the kitchen cutting images of glamorous women from magazines, fashioning them into paper dolls. It made her mother angry.

Whether it was an effect of her mother's worldview or just a function of her general character and ability, Waneta did not apply herself in school, nor did she take part in after-school activities. Crowds, in fact, repelled her. She retreated to the attentions of her family, which was a small crowd itself. Each summer, Clarence Lacey watched the Nixons drive by, loaded to the gills in the camper they hooked up to their Chevy pickup, headed for one of the lakes north of Syracuse.

Midway through his forty-two years with the mighty Endicott Johnson shoe company, George Hoyt moved his wife and eight children from a respectable house in Endicott, just west of Binghamton in Broome County, to a dairy farm in Newark Valley. It was on Davis Hollow Road, half a mile off Route 38, and came with 129 acres, two big barns, thirty-five cows, a loose gathering of chickens and pigs, and a house with missing windows and no electricity or running water. Hoyt had grown up on a farm in Pennsylvania, and it was his plan to keep his job in the shoe factory while putting his sons to work milking cows at the crack of dawn, "sometimes before the crack even got there," remembered one of his five sons, Chuck, whose most vivid early memory of the move was an abrupt awakening one Saturday morning in 1947, when he was nine years old. "C'mon, get up!" his father was bellowing, standing over him. "We're goin' to the barn! Gotta milk cows!"

George Hoyt was a horrible drunk who left his sons and daughters plenty of painful memories. In a boozy rage one day like so many others, he threw a pitchfork at his son Donald. The boy ducked, and the pitchfork ricocheted off the side of the barn and landed squarely in his father's back. Chuck came running, pulled the pitchfork out, then ran to his mother, yelling in a panic, "Dad got stuck with the pitchfork! He's bleeding! He's gonna die!" To which Ella Hoyt matter-of-factly replied, "He's too mean to die."

Chuck was the second of five brothers. His oldest brother, George Junior, was a scrappy, cantankerous kid. The youngest, Timothy, was shy and bespectacled—his gentle nature earned him the nickname "Abigail"—though he was as physically strong as any of them. All the Hoyt boys learned to stay out of their father's way, especially on those occasions when he had a gun in his hand. Tim never forgot the day his dad shot at him with a rifle because he thought the boy had failed to milk the cows.

One by one, the boys managed to find ways to get away from their father. George Junior joined the Air Force, then Endicott Johnson, and finally moved to New Jersey and got a job in a brewery. Chuck found work as a mason; one of his jobs was at the sprawling stone house in Apalachin owned by the Canada Dry distributor and reputed mobster Joe Barbara. Tim decided he'd had enough of his father before his senior year of high school. He got himself a live-in job at Walter and Gladys Yetter's farm, right on Route 38 by the railroad tracks, and limited his time home to weekends.

The Yetters had about thirty head of cattle, and they paid $12.50 a week plus room and board. Tim would get up each morning, milk the cows and do his chores, then wait out on the road for the bus to school. It came from Richford, and he was the last stop, not part of the regular Newark Valley route. He'd ride up front, standing beside the driver, and through his black-rimmed glasses he could see a girl with curly black hair, maybe a ninth or tenth grader, eyeing him through her own eyeglasses from her window seat midway back. When Waneta told her friend Bonnie she intended to marry that boy, Bonnie told her not to get her hopes up. He's a lot older than you, she pointed out. He'll be off on his own after next year, and you've got four more years of school. "I'm going to marry him," Waneta assured her friend.

Tim Hoyt and Waneta Nixon were no doubt two of the quietest members of the student body of Newark Valley Central School, and it wasn't until they found themselves in the same classroom nearly a year later that words were actually exchanged. It was Student Control Day, when classes were turned over to seniors with the best grades. Tim's marks were high in health and world history, and among his students in those classes that day was the girl from the bus. They said their awkward hellos, and not long after, Tim opened a letter from a Waneta Nixon. She had admired him from afar, she wrote, and wondered if they might get to know each other better. Tim was surprised to learn she was Archie Nixon's younger sister. Archie was president of the Newark Valley chapter of the Future Farmers of America; Tim was vice president. He was also surprised to realize maybe she wasn't so shy after all.

Tim phoned Waneta's house on the pretext of discussing chickens with Archie. "And of course," Tim recalled years later, "the old man, her father, knew that the only chicken I was interested in, 'cause I hated chickens anyway, was her." They went out twice, taking the back road over the hill to the drive-in at the Broome County airport, and Neta confided that she believed they would be married someday. Tim, though flattered, did not take this too seriously. Appealing as she was, Neta was only fifteen, and he was about to graduate. It was the spring of 1961, and his mind was elsewhere. He'd grown up in a town where the phone company was in someone's house and everyone was on a party line. As the end of high school approached, Tim was thinking about what the world might be like beyond Newark Valley.

His brother George was living in East Orange, New Jersey. A few months after graduation, Tim packed a suitcase, hit the road in his beat-up 1951 Mercury, and drove down to Jersey. He moved in with George and found work as a machinist for an aircraft company. East Orange was a part of the world unlike anything he could have imagined. He counted a dozen murders during his eight months there, "and they were coming right down the street." That was enough for him. Next stop in the world: New Britain, Connecticut. A friend of George's got him a job washing dishes at a hospital. It was a start. When a groundskeeper's job came up, he applied. "I was a farm boy, and I could fix lawn mowers," Tim said. "But they went by me three times. I said the hell with you—I quit. So I got on a bus, and the damn bus had an accident, got smashed up, and then the bus that came to fix us broke down, and then I had a layover. Took me eighteen hours to get home. And I never want to see either one of those states again. I don't want anything to do with them. Damn right, I was glad to get home to Newark Valley."

Back home after his year abroad, Tim went to work making fiberglass boats at the Grumman plant in Cortland County. And after a while, feeling lonely, he decided to give Waneta Nixon a call. It was the summer of 1963, and Neta was about to start her senior year of high school. They hadn't seen each other in a couple of years, but Neta was thrilled when Tim called. They went out, and discovered something important: They could talk to each other. "She was honest," Tim remembered. "She wasn't trying to pull any wool over my eyes or anything. She was very pretty. She had really black hair. She didn't believe in getting painted up and powdered to try to make an impression. She was just Neta." There wasn't much more Tim needed to know. Four months later, just before Christmas, he proposed.

Saying yes caused Neta some problems. She and Tim set out from Newark Valley to break the news to her mother and father. They came back through Tim's door a while later. "So what happened?" Tim's mother asked.

"Well," Tim said, "she threw her out."

Dorothy Nixon may have regarded motherhood as her daughter's one true calling, but it was to be on a proper timetable. If Neta got married before finishing high school, her mother said, she would do it on her own. And don't bother inviting us to the wedding.

Neta's father's feelings about the marriage were not clear, and apparently not relevant. It was Dorothy Nixon who counted when it came to the children. Her husband never gave the impression he was particularly interested in them. An inconspicuous, aloof man, he seemed closer to his chums on the road crew. In any case, their mother's wrath was enough for two. In Neta's suddenly turbulent world, it was only the beginning.

The trouble started the day she came to school wearing Tim's shirt. Neta thought it was like having Tim around: a symbol. It was also just about the first thing she ever did that caused the world to take notice. In fact, it caused quite a stir. In the halls of Newark Valley Central School, there came the whispers: shy little Waneta Nixon, traipsing around school in her boyfriend's clothes. Maybe she's pregnant. "Hey, Annie," Tim's sister, who was in Neta's grade, would hear from her friends, "is it true that Neta's expecting?" Ann was a notorious no-nonsense type. "I haven't been watching," she'd snap. "You got a question, ask her."

In fact, Waneta was not pregnant, but that hardly seemed to matter. Hearing of the impending marriage, Principal Hall decreed that she would have to leave school if she went through with it. Whether or not she was expecting a child, he didn't want Neta coming to school talking about her sex life. She wouldn't be the first Newark Valley student to get married while still in school, nor the first to get pregnant. In fact, another member of the class had already gotten married, but when Hall threatened to throw her out of school, she took him on—right out in the hallway, in front of everybody. "You throw me out, I'm gonna raise a stink," she said to him. "I know a few things about you." The principal, as well as at least some of the onlookers, seemed to know what she meant by this. The girl never did miss a day of school.

Neta didn't have that kind of moxie. On the other hand, if anyone expected her to submit to authority, either at home or at school, they were surprised to see how willful she could be, especially in light of how devoted she was to her mother. Over the years, people saw the tug of their relationship. "She was so close to her mother, trying to please her, and yet her mother shoved her away," remembered one relative. "She tried and tried to get into her mother's good graces."

But in this instance, she found something she wanted more: the good graces of Tim Hoyt. When he asked if she wanted to put off the wedding until after she graduated, Neta said no. She didn't mind leaving school. She never liked the pressures of teenage culture. Given the choice between school and marriage, she knew exactly what she wanted, and in the end she got her way.

She moved in with the Hoyts, and for a month before the wedding shared a room with Ann. Tim had a new job in the warehouse at National Cash Register in Ithaca, working in shipping-receiving alongside his high school buddy Mike Harbac. Neta, meanwhile, spent her days waiting for him to get off work. She clung to him, sometimes to the point of jealousy. She did not react well when his attention wandered casually and innocently to someone else, particularly another girl, even if it was just an old family friend or one of his sisters-in-law. Well, the Hoyts supposed, maybe this was to be expected. She was, after all, only seventeen years old, with neither school nor work to divert her. She had what she wanted, and she wasn't letting go.

On January 11, 1964, Waneta Ethel Nixon married Timothy Avery Hoyt in the parsonage of the Faith Bible Church in Richford. Tim's sister Janet, married only two months herself, was the matron of honor and Mike Harbac served as Tim's best man. There was a reception in a room with a pool table at the local historical society building. The couple held hands and posed awkwardly behind a four-tiered wedding cake, which leaned like the Tower of Pisa atop a folding table decorated with pink crepe paper, and was topped by the requisite miniature bride and groom framed by the poignant plastic heart. Waneta and Tim fed each other cake, and then they kissed long and unselfconsciously for Ella Hoyt's camera. Waneta's parents stayed home.

There was no honeymoon. Neta and Tim moved into the front bedroom of the house on the Hoyt farm on Davis Hollow Road, and if you asked anybody who lived with them how the newlyweds were getting along, they might say, as one did many years later, "The lovebirds? Joined at the hip." When they walked, they held hands; when Tim sat down, Neta was apt to sit on his lap. This was fine as far as it went, but as Tim's extended family got to know Neta, some among them had the notion that she was a bit peculiar. They found it hard to pinpoint, but pressed for particulars, they'd say, well, she seemed to have an unusual need to be the center of attention. This struck them as quite odd, considering her introverted manner and how uncomfortable she seemed around people, at least at Hoyt family gatherings, which were a lot more frequent than Nixon get-togethers.

One day, Tim went with his brothers Don and Chuck to do some work on their brother-in-law Weldon Wait's farm at the corner of 38 and Brown Road. It was one of several owned by Weldon, who was one of the most successful dairy farmers in the region, and who was married to their oldest sister, Marion. Neta came along with Tim, which put him in something of an awkward position. Although he enjoyed Neta's attentiveness, he didn't want to appear chained to her. He prided himself in being an industrious worker.

"Let's go bale the hay," Weldon said when the Hoyt boys arrived, starting for the barn, his three brothers-in-law a step behind.

"No, Tim," Neta implored. "Stay here with me."

"I can't now," Tim said, walking with the others to the barn. "I'm here to work. I'll see you later."

"Tim," Neta implored.

He kept walking.

"Tim, I'm feeling faint," she called. The four men turned and looked at her. She dropped dramatically into the mud.

Tim had to decide what to do. He stopped for a moment, looked at her, looked at the boys. "Aw, let her lay there," Weldon said. "She'll wake up in a minute."

Tim took a deep breath of exasperation, turned his back on his teenage bride, and went in the barn to bale hay. Eventually, Neta picked herself up and left.

The incident turned into a piece of Hoyt family lore. If you wanted to know about Waneta, the consensus was, this pretty much summed it up. Tim tried to take his wife's need for attention in stride. Driving to work one morning, he remarked to Mike Harbac that Neta was nervous staying home alone. "She thinks someone's gonna come and rape her while I'm gone," he said. "She's been watching too many soap operas." He sensed it was a ploy to keep him home with her, but he felt bad just the same. She seemed to need him so much, and he hated to let her down.

Tim's father hanged himself that summer. He climbed up the silo, put a rope around his neck, tied the other end around one of the ladder rungs, and stepped out. To his children, it was a sad end to an unfortunate life.

It was only one event in an eventful year on Davis Hollow Road. In April, the Hoyts' neighbor Gary Wilcox reported that two Martians had landed in one of his fields. As he told the world's reporters, who beat a path to his barn and kept him talking for weeks, Wilcox got off his manure spreader (a device that was invented in Newark Valley), chatted with the aliens for a couple of hours about fertilizer and other agricultural matters, and promptly made himself famous in the chronicles of extraterrestrial encounters: It would become one of seventy incidents worldwide cited in the UFO section of the *Atlas of the Supernatural,* among other major volumes on the subject. Thirty years later, it wouldn't be hard to find people in Newark Valley who believed it had happened, or at least that it might have.

Up Davis Hollow just a hundred yards, meanwhile, Waneta and Tim Hoyt were preparing to start a family. Their first child was conceived within days of their wedding in January, and by spring even Tim's shirts couldn't hide the news. As her classmates were heading into the stretch run of high school, Waneta was graduating to motherhood. This time, she really was pregnant.

15

With nervous excitement and a day off, Tim Hoyt helped his wife to their 1958 Pontiac at 7:30 the morning of Saturday, October 17, 1964. They sped down Davis Hollow Road, heading for the maternity ward of Tompkins County Hospital in Ithaca, a three-story stucco-and-stone building erected originally as a tuberculosis hospital in the 1930s. It was built into rolling grounds at the edge of Cayuga Lake, one of the Finger Lakes, and was more evocative of an English country school than a municipal hospital. From some of the rooms, patients could take in a postcard view of the lake, with the venerable stone buildings of Cornell University nestled in the hills beyond.

Neta's pregnancy had been the usual thirty-eight-week mixture of happy anticipation and seemingly endless physical stress. Like many expectant mothers, she complained freely as time went on, eager to have it over with, and at 6:16 that Saturday evening, ten hours and forty minutes after the contractions began, she got her wish. Leaning in under the lights of the delivery room as Tim waited outside, Dr. Noah Kassman presented Neta with a boy weighing an even seven pounds, twenty and a half inches long, with a cap of blond hair and a solid 9 on the Apgar scale. A bracelet was wrapped around the baby's tiny wrist—"Hoyt, Baby Boy"—and when the nurse asked what name she had chosen, Neta said, "Eric Allen."

Dr. Roger Perry, a pediatrician recommended by Dr. Kassman, came for his first visit on Sunday morning. He looked the baby over, listened through his stethoscope, chatted a bit with Waneta. Then he picked up a clipboard and whipped off a single straight line through fourteen boxes where any abnormalities were to be noted. General appearance, eyes, thorax, heart, genitals, trunk and spine, extremities, reflexes—all were fine. On Tuesday morning, Neta was back in the Pontiac, her three-day-old baby in her lap.

She proved an exceptionally orderly mother, meticulous about feeding and clothing. Even Eric's bibs were clean; if someone happened to drop by and see a bit of spitup, she would apologize. She was conscientious about the minutiae of motherhood, the patting, the burping, the changing. She carried out these duties in a quiet, matter-of-fact way. Though the baby was by acclamation sweet-natured and full of young life, growing amazingly fast, his presence in his mother's life did not make her any more animated than usual. Tim, on the other hand, would hold Eric and beam, make silly faces to induce a smile for the camera. It came effortlessly. Neta was not that way. Her lips were naturally downturned and tight, her smiles often half-smiles. "She was sitting in my brown chair rocking the baby and talking to him, but she wasn't mushy over him or anything like that," Tim's sister Janet remembered many years later. "That just wasn't Neta." Janet thought a moment, then added, "God, she had the cleanest kids."

Neta was vigilant when it came to matters of health. In fact, her nurturing bordered on overprotection. Whether she had reason to be so chary was something her relatives couldn't quite decide. The baby's nose was stuffy; it appeared he had a cold. But somehow colds turned into something more, at least in the telling. By the time he was two months old, it seemed she had him to Dr. Hartnagel on a regular basis. He was checking the baby's heart, Neta informed the family. "Doc Hartnagel thought he had a heart problem," Tim would later say. "By listening through his stethoscope, and like that."

One day around Christmastime, Neta and Tim visited Janet with the baby. "We just got through taking Eric to the hospital," Neta said, stepping in from the cold. When Janet asked why, Neta said, "He's sick. We had to get an ambulance."

Janet thought: *Well, he must be pretty sick. My kids get sick, they give 'em something and send 'em home.*

Betty and Rodney Lane lived on Davis Hollow Road, across the street from the Hoyts. Rodney built homes up on the hill, inexpensive little houses that sold well in Newark Valley. Despite their proximity, the Lanes and the Hoyts were not close. In fact, the two families did not like each other very much. The animosity was of such long standing by the time Waneta moved in that it wasn't until the early afternoon of Tuesday, January 26, 1965, that she had any contact with the Lanes.

Betty was doing housework when she heard the screams. She went to the front door, and saw Waneta on the dirt driveway in front of the Hoyt farm-house. "Somebody help!" Waneta was calling.

Betty came out and asked what was wrong. "Something's the matter with my baby!" Waneta said, and turned back toward the house. Betty followed her inside. The baby was lying on a table, limp and lifeless. Betty had never seen the infant before, didn't even know if it was a boy or girl.

"Did you try to revive him?" she asked nervously.

"No," Waneta said. She stood a few feet away, shaken, Betty thought, but in control.

Betty picked up Eric, laid him back down on the table, and put her mouth to his. She noticed a white substance like thick cereal, with pinkish streaks, coming out of his mouth and nostrils. Wiping it away, she blew into his mouth, but after a few puffs without response, she told Waneta, "I think he's dead." She dashed out of the house, went across the street, and told her husband to phone the rescue squad. She never went back.

Margaret Horton's husband, Howard, was Newark Valley's part-time police chief, and she was the town's emergency dispatcher. The calls came to Margaret in her kitchen; then she'd call over to the firehouse, where bells would ring and anyone on the squad who heard them would hightail it over and jump into the ambulance. Margaret got the call from Rodney Lane that day, and a few minutes later, a pair of squad members pulled up to the Hoyt house. They repeated the mouth-to-mouth and felt for a pulse, but it was clear that the baby, three months and ten days old, was gone.

Chuck Hoyt was working at a gas station in town when he got the news. He realized he had to be the one to tell his kid brother. Tim was now working at Endicott Forging, just a half mile from Ideal Hospital, where the rescue workers were bringing the baby. Waneta rode with them, and Chuck followed most of the way.

He went up to the office at the forging works and asked the secretary to summon Tim from the shop. But when Chuck saw his brother, he couldn't say the words. "We've got to go to the hospital," was all he could manage.

"Tim," he said finally, a little later when they were in the hospital elevator, headed for the third floor, "Eric died."

Tim looked at his brother and burst into tears. Chuck put his arms around him and said nothing more. When the elevator doors opened at the third floor, Tim saw Waneta. She began to tremble. "I don't know what happened," she said. "He just turned blue . . . I went for help."

The death was certified by Dr. Hartnagel, acting as coroner. Waneta told him that Eric "wasn't breathing right," and then he had just stopped breathing altogether. Babies could die unexpectedly, Hartnagel knew, and he told the grieving young parents that it was an unexplainable act of God, that they should not blame themselves. Hartnagel considered the family history. Waneta had told him that one of her brothers had lost a two-month-old baby to "heart problems." On Eric's death certificate, Hartnagel wrote, in clear block letters, CONGENITAL ANOMALIES OF THE HEART.

That he could offer only supposition as the foundation for this opinion was probably not an issue for Hartnagel. "Congenital anomalies of the heart" sounded better than "crib death." It certainly sounded better than "unknown" or "unexplained." In cases such as this, it was not an uncommon practice to offer a plausible (if undemonstrated) cause of death that might satisfy both the bureaucratic requirements of the Office of Vital Records and the emotional requirements of the parents. Hartnagel saw no good reason for a pathologist to take a knife to the body of Eric Allen Hoyt. Babies died suddenly, and it was the considered opinion of the medical world, country doctors and prestigious authorities alike, that when they did, they left no clues behind.

The land that became Highland Cemetery was once farmed by Albert Nixon, Waneta's great-grandfather. In 1889, he sold the parcel to Wallace Pierce and Clarence Finch, who formed a cemetery association with half a dozen other men. At their first meeting, they voted to set the price of a square foot of prime cemetery space at fifteen cents, and that summer a team of horses dragging a metal scraper leveled the first section of the burial ground. Albert Nixon chose not to buy space in the cemetery, but his son Archie, Waneta's grandfather, became an active member of the association. Some years later his son Albert purchased a plot in the southwestern corner, next to Clarence Lacey's. So far, there was only one grave marker in Albert and Dorothy Nixon's plot, that of their young son who had died of meningitis just after Waneta's birth in 1946. The gravestone, flush to the ground, read simply BOBBY. The rest of the plot, beneath a tall Norway spruce tree, was wide open.

Neil MacPherson picked up Eric's body at Ideal Hospital and brought it back to Newark Valley in his Cadillac hearse. The MacPherson Funeral Home was on Whig Street, just up the street from the Central School. In consideration of the age of the deceased and the limited means of his parents, MacPherson decided to charge only fifty dollars for Eric's funeral, not including the cost of the gravestone, and accepted five dollars from Tim as a down payment, the balance to be paid on time. Two days after the baby's death, the family gathered for a brief service, and all eyes were on Neta. She stood beside the tiny casket and wept, and Tim comforted her. The relatives came by, one by one, and Neta accepted embraces from them all. From his view at the service, Chuck Hoyt sensed that for Neta, the pity was a salve. He didn't find this terribly surprising. His wife, Loretta, could not shake the chilling image of the tiny casket. The baby had come and gone so quickly. Born as the leaves were in full fall color, gone by the dead of winter. The mourners climbed into their cars for the ten-mile journey to Highland Cemetery, where Clarence Lacey had dug a fresh grave. An hour later, Eric's remains were buried a few feet from the grave of Bobby Nixon, in the earth their ancestors had once farmed.

A month later, Neta and Tim moved out of his mother's house. Eric's death was still in the air of the old farmhouse, and they wanted to make a fresh start. They bought a used trailer, forty-two feet long, with a living room, kitchen, bath, and two small bedrooms; set it next to his mother's house, and went down to Bern's Furniture in Owego and opened an account. Life would go on, Tim told Neta; they would have other children. He felt he had to be strong for her, and for him to dwell on the sadness would do her no good.

Soon, things were looking up. With Chuck's help, Tim got into the laborers' union, which boosted his pay from the $1.95 an hour he was getting running the big shears at Endicott Forging to the $3.33 he'd earn working on state road construction projects. Route 17—AMERICA'S MOST SCENIC ROAD 1964–65, said the signs—was coming west, and there would be plenty of work along the Southern Tier.

Neta was a project herself. By now, Tim knew that his wife needed more than the usual amount of attention, and it could not be entirely blamed on the tragedy that had befallen them. She complained routinely of generalized aches and pains, and visited doctors as a matter of course, moving from one to the next when none could find anything wrong. She was not shy about sharing her distress, whether it was over a card table with family gathered around, or during a visit to town. "If you had a cold, she had the flu; if your knee hurt, her knee, her elbow, and her neck hurt," remembered one acquaintance. She owned a medical dictionary and consulted it often. At a family get-together, Tim's sisters Ann, Janet, and Marion tired of merely rolling their eyes at her endless complaints and decided to have some fun. They concocted a fictitious illness, giving it an elaborate name. When Neta was in earshot, Marion waxed lamentable about her symptoms, ascribing the problem to the polysyllabic diagnosis. Sure enough, a week later, word made its way around the family that Neta had the bogus malady. It worked so well that the women made a regular game of it. Sometimes the news of Neta's latest illness came from Tim. It was Chuck's sense that his brother believed Neta and catered to her needs with unquestioning devotion. *Good thing the laborers' union has good medical coverage,* Chuck thought.

If Tim's father had been the black sheep of the family, his wife was the odd duck. Neta's personal relationships were strange at times, difficult in a way that people found hard to clarify. At various moments she could fit into many of the usual personality categories—pleasant, aloof, attentive, self-centered—and yet, taking her as a whole, none of these characterizations really fit. It was as though her responses to life were askew. She was capable of being affronted by the most innocuous remark, though the offender might not realize the transgression until days or weeks later, when Neta would serve up a biting rejoinder, leaving the recipient to figure out what had just happened. "You had to choose your words so carefully," Loretta Hoyt observed. "So we just backed off. We didn't want the retaliation."

Neta possessed an acerbic sense of humor and a willfulness that sometimes seemed out of kilter with her generally reserved disposition. People who knew her casually perceived her as solicitous and needy, while others considered her a study in control. Loretta experienced both sides. Years later, she would remember getting a number of calls from Tim while he was at work. Neta's talking about suicide again, Tim would say. Can you check on her? Loretta would walk over to the trailer, and find Neta in a reasonably chipper mood. Once, they wound up playing cards and laughing. Another time, they went for a pleasant drive. The encounters left Loretta more puzzled than unsettled. "What am I doing here?" she asked herself each time. For years afterward, Neta would take Loretta's hand and thank her for saving her life. And for years, Loretta urged Tim to get psychiatric help for Neta.

There was this joke among some in the family: If you saw Neta wearing a maternity dress, it meant she and Tim had had sex the night before. It was meant as both a commentary on Neta's imagination—she could dream up pregnancy as well as illness—and on the pleasure she derived from being pregnant. It wasn't the baby that seemed to be the payoff, so much as the attention she got from pregnancy itself. And she had little trouble getting her wish. If her imagination was fertile territory, so was her body. By the end of the summer following Eric's death, just seven months after his burial in Highland Cemetery, Neta was pregnant. She would try again to fulfill the destiny her mother had laid out for her.

Natalie and Art Hilliard were new to the neighborhood. A young couple with a baby son, they'd bought one of Rodney Lane's houses and moved to Davis Hollow Road shortly before Christmas 1964. One day a month or so later, a woman came to their door, welcomed Natalie to the neighborhood, and asked if she would like to make a contribution to the Hoyt family. Waneta and Tim had just lost their baby son, she said, and the neighbors were taking up a collection for flowers.

Natalie expressed her sorrow and went for her pocketbook. "Where do they live?" she asked her new neighbor.

"Right over there," the woman said, gesturing across the street and up maybe fifty yards. The Hoyts and the Hilliards were practically next-door neighbors.

Art Hilliard was a happy-go-lucky sort with a thousand-watt grin and a joyous cackle of a laugh. Natalie was ballast for Art's exuberance. She was quieter, her temperament more subtle. They'd gone together since they were both fourteen, Newark Valley townies who had each grown up within walking distance of the Central School. They were two years older than Tim, six ahead of Neta, and while they knew of the Hoyts by reputation, mainly through Tim's and Neta's older siblings, it wasn't until after they contributed to the collection following Eric's death that they actually met.

Whether it was that Waneta spared Natalie the behavior others found peculiar or that Natalie saw her way past it, the two women formed a friendship that belied their age disparity and some basic differences in their backgrounds. Natalie's father operated a successful business, the bowling alley in town. She had an associate's degree in nursery education and taught nursery school before her baby was born, a job she planned to return to one day. At eighteen, Waneta was a high school dropout with few interests. But to Natalie and Art, attentive and nonjudgmental people by nature, she was a nice young woman with a good heart and a sharp sense of humor, who'd been dealt a cruel blow and deserved their compassion and friendship. Their son Dana had been born just before Eric. They brought Waneta and Tim into their church, the United Methodist in Newark Valley, and introduced them to their pastor, Gary Kuhns.

Neta and Natalie spent hours on end, drinking coffee in each other's kitchens, chatting away the time. And time Waneta had. Soon after Eric's death, she had gotten a job at Endicott Johnson. It was the first job she'd ever had, but it didn't last long. She decided she couldn't handle what she would later describe as "the pressure" of working with so many people, and quit. Housewife was the only job she wanted.

Art and Tim were also becoming good friends. They were both avid hunters, and up on Davis Hollow you could just about walk out your door and start shooting. They managed to bag a deer apiece once a season, which was the quota. They'd skin and gut the deer, use their kitchen tables to cube the meat, and then can it for winter. One brutally cold day late in the season, the wind howling and the temperature well below zero, Tim and Art went out into the fields around their houses, looking for deer. Tim was on one side of the field, Art on the other, close enough to see each other but too far to hear. Not too long into it they realized it was colder than they'd imagined and started losing interest in anything other than going home to a hot cup of coffee. The only thing was, neither of them was willing to be the first one to surrender to the elements. They prowled the edge of the field for game, more often looking across the field at each other, sustaining the standoff. Finally, Tim saw Art waving his arms, motioning to pack it in. Thank God, Tim muttered to himself. Their bond was sealed.

In time, the Hoyts and the Hilliards became a rural version of all those recognizable urban TV neighbors: the Ricardos and the Mertzes, the Kramdens and the Nortons. It was Art Hilliard's nightly ritual to look out his front door until he saw Neta or Tim in their window across the road, and then he'd flick the porch light on and off, a signal that supper was over and it was time for cards. Pretty soon the Hoyts would come wandering down the hill for a night of canasta.

At 9:00 on the night of Memorial Day 1966, Waneta and Tim celebrated the birth of their second child in Tompkins County Hospital.

Dr. Kassman delivered James Avery Hoyt after Neta labored three hours and thirty-two minutes, a birth nearly identical to the one two years before. At his first full exam the next day, James, like his brother, received fourteen check marks signifying the absence of any significant problems. But this time, the pediatrician on hand, Dr. Thomas Mosher, went further. Given the "congenital anomalies of the heart" that had apparently killed the baby's older brother at three months of age, he ordered an electrocardiogram. The nurses struggled to attach the leads to the squirming newborn, but the EKG revealed nothing abnormal, and four days after his birth Waneta and Tim brought him home.

They called him Jimmy. He was an ebullient baby, blond and robust, healthier, it seemed, than his brother. The veins in Eric's head had bulged; nearly everyone in the family wondered if that was somehow related to his sudden death. Jimmy's head was perfectly smooth. As his face began to take shape, the definition favored his father's broad features. Tim was square-jawed and wide-eyed, and Jimmy seemed to come from the same mold.

The first three months of Jimmy's life were surrounded by an air of anxiety, but as summer passed and the baby advanced beyond the age at which Eric had died, life in the Hoyt trailer began to take on the pleasant routine of any young family. Tim went to work on the newest section of Route 17, and Neta stayed home with the baby, cleaned the house, and whiled away mornings with Natalie Hilliard and the other young mothers of Davis Hollow. She had a second chance at motherhood. Once again, she carried out the duties in her quiet, diligent way. Patting the baby was her favored form of interaction, and years later it would be this that one of her sisters-in-law would remember most vividly as evidence that Neta enjoyed being a mother—that she was a good mother. "She did a better job burping her babies than I ever did mine," Janet would say with evident admiration. Most in the family did not know that Neta had been physically abusive on at least one occasion. One of her sisters-in-law saw her slam Jimmy against a wall in anger. The baby, less than a year old, had soiled his diaper.

His first birthday was a cause for both celebration and relief in the Hoyt and Nixon families. He had lived a year, and the sharp pain of Eric's death, if not the memory itself, was beginning to fade. On Memorial Day there was a large gathering at the Hoyt farm, featuring a birthday cake with a resolute candle planted in the icing. Ella Hoyt snapped pictures, which she proudly displayed a few weeks later for the ladies she worked with at Endicott Johnson.

Tim's mother was developing an especially close relationship with Jimmy, and when he began to walk, and then to run, it was most often to grandma's house he headed. By the time he neared his second birthday, he was scooting across the field separating the trailer from the farmhouse, where his grandmother would scoop him up, take his hand, and lead him on an exploration of the acreage. Unlike his mother, Jimmy's grandmother didn't mind getting down on her hands and knees to look for bugs and snakes and go "rock hunting," as she called it. They'd take a paper sack and collect stones as if they were jewels. If they got dirty, they'd wash off in a mud puddle—that's what mud puddles were for, it seemed to Grandma Hoyt. If he fell and cried, she'd say, "Y'aren't bleeding, are ya?" Jimmy would pull up his pant leg and say, "No," through his tears. "All right then," she'd say, and they'd resume the hunt for the finest rocks on Davis Hollow Road.

Jimmy's first friend, aside from his grandmother, was Dana Hilliard, Natalie and Art's son. Dana was an only child and Jimmy, two years his junior, was the next best thing to a little brother. While their mothers drank coffee, Dana would take his two-year-old pal by the hand. "C'mon, Jimmy," he'd say, "this is what we're gonna do today." In the summer, they splashed in the plastic kiddie pool beside the trailer, the kind you brought home on the roof of your car.

Jimmy was a happy little kid and an early talker, and some in the family thought him remarkably independent considering the way Neta watched over him. At the first sniffle, she would have him to Doc Hartnagel's office. But it was a mystifying brand of vigilance. On one occasion when Jimmy took a spill and began to cry, Loretta picked him up and comforted him. She had never before held him—Neta had not allowed it—and Neta yanked him from her arms. "Leave him alone," she said curtly. "He fell, he'll be fine. He's got to learn for himself. Just don't touch him."

Health, though, was nothing like the issue it had been with Eric. Jimmy was fit and sturdy, much to his father's relief.

Tim was enthralled with his son. He took pictures of Jimmy at play, at family gatherings, with Neta on the couch. The three of them were in the kitchen one day when Tim asked his mother to snap a photo. He scooped Jimmy up and held him close with his right arm so that their heads were at the same level, Jimmy's feet dangling, as if standing on air. They smiled and waved. Neta stood next to them, slightly to the side, eating a piece of cake.

Jimmy adored his father. When Tim came home from work, his little boy would start walking like him. "What did you and grandma look at today?" Tim would ask, and Jimmy would show him his pockets full of rocks, then take his father by the hand and show him where each of the best ones had been discovered, where they'd seen a jackrabbit or spied a snake.

These were to be Waneta's and Tim's best days. They had a fine, healthy son and a new home. Working two construction jobs, Tim had saved enough money to buy a brand-new trailer for $7,200 cash, a fourteen-by-seventy-foot model that he and Waneta kept immaculate. The good fortune would continue. In the summer of 1968, shortly after Jimmy's second birthday, Neta was in the last stages of her third pregnancy. After two boys, she was hoping for a girl. In fact, she told her sister-in-law Janet, who had two girls herself and was also pregnant again, she was betting on it. Shortly before their due dates, the two women went belly-to-belly for the camera. Janet was considerably bigger. She figured Neta would have the smaller and better-looking baby. Neta's babies always came out just gorgeous, Janet thought.

Janet gave birth to her third daughter on July 17, and two days later, Dr. Kassman did the honors for Neta once again. Her third baby was a seven-pound girl her parents named Julie Marie. "See," Neta told Janet, "I got my girl."

Janet looked at the baby and melted. Her own baby was a whopper, nine pounds, five ounces, "and Neta had this little doll that was so beautiful." Julie's weight was average and her health perfectly fine, but her face was so tiny and her features so delicate that she seemed smaller and more fragile than usual.

"My God," Loretta said when she saw the baby, "I didn't know they made them that small."

16

Driving his garbage truck up Davis Hollow Road on Thursday morning, September 5, 1968, Dick Rinker saw a young woman running at him with a bundle in one arm, flagging him down with the other. "Something's wrong with my baby!" Waneta Hoyt trembled. Julie Hoyt was forty-eight days old, and she wasn't breathing.

Rinker, as it happened, was a member of the Newark Valley emergency squad. He ran inside, called for help, and a few minutes later, squad members Bob Vanek and Morris Lyons came racing up the hill in their station wagon ambulance, the siren blaring, and screeched to a halt in front of the Hoyt farm. They found Rinker working on the baby inside the trailer, as Waneta, terribly agitated, paced nearby and Jimmy sat quietly on a couch. Vanek took the baby, set her down, and began feeling for a pulse. He checked the baby's mouth, her ears, her nose. She was limp, drained of color. Vanek looked up.

"This child is deceased," he told Lyons. "Will you verify that?"

Lyons repeated the routine. "That's correct," he said quietly.

Tim Hoyt was working on a road project near Waverly when he saw a foreman striding up to him. There's some trouble at home, the foreman said. Racing home, Tim thought of Jimmy, and shuddered. A few weeks before, his son had taken a spill off the top of a blanket chest in his grandmother's house. Dr. Hartnagel said it was a badly bruised collarbone and put the child's arm in a sling, but it seemed to Tim that Jimmy was still missing a good deal of his get-up-and-go. Now, Tim was in a near panic.

When he arrived home, he learned that it was not Jimmy but Julie who was the cause of alarm. Hearing that his third child, like his first, was dead, he went straight for Neta, and held her close. He found it impossible to understand what powers might cause such mind-bending misfortune. "We had a dog," he remembered vividly many years later. "He was a basset, and we called him Zoomer. And he howled the night before. He just wailed and wailed. And then, Julie died. And shortly after that, the dog died. I thought he ate a bone that killed him, but I don't know. I couldn't afford to take him to a damn vet to find out how he died."

When Dr. Hartnagel asked Waneta what happened, she said she had been feeding Julie, and the baby had begun to choke. Then she had gone limp. That was when she called for help. "What were you feeding her?" Hartnagel wondered. "Rice cereal," Waneta said.

In the midst of their shock, some in the Hoyt family were baffled by the circumstances of Julie's death. Eric's death was tragic, but explained. A heart problem, Dr. Hartnagel said. But choking to death on a bottle? How could rice cereal have been thin enough to get through the nipple, yet thick enough to strangle the baby? Why hadn't Waneta, such a good burper, been able to simply pat the baby on her back or clear the obstruction with a finger?

Whatever his own thoughts about these questions, Hartnagel made quick work of his coroner duties. He returned to his office in Berkshire, pulled out a blank death certificate, and completed the record of Julie Hoyt's seven weeks of life. As the cause of death, he wrote: "STRANGULATION—WAS EATING RICE CEREAL." Again he saw no need for an autopsy, and released the body to Neil MacPherson.

"Oh, I'm so sorry," Clarence Lacey said when Waneta and Tim drove up to Richford and climbed the steps to his porch once again to say they were going to need another grave. He went up the hill with his shovel, and the next day the family gathered at the Nixon plot, where Julie's pine coffin was buried alongside that of her brother Eric.

On the morning of the funeral, Neta and Tim left Jimmy with the Hilliards. Natalie and Art found the anguish unimaginable. What would it be like to lose *two* babies? And what about Jimmy? What would the effect be on him? Would he remember Julie, or her death? He had been there when she died. "I told him to stay on the couch when I ran outside with the baby," Waneta later related. "And he was so good. I said, 'Stay here, Jimmy. Something's wrong with Julie. Mommy's got to go take care of her.' And he stayed right there on the couch. He was good as gold."

A few days after the funeral, Natalie went to the trailer and spent a while in the baby's room packing away her blankets and clothes. She folded them neatly and put them in boxes, while Neta sat alone in the front room.

Two weeks later, on the morning of September 26, Natalie was preparing to go out for a round of errands when she happened to look out the window in her front room and see something that just could not be. It was exactly three weeks after Julie's death, almost to the hour. The shock and sympathy, the immense, cumulative sadness among the Hoyts and the Nixons, their friends and neighbors, was still overwhelming them all. Now, incredibly, Waneta was coming down the hill with Jimmy in her arms. *No,* Natalie thought, *this just can't be.*

She dashed out the front door, and met Waneta in the road.

"Help me," Waneta said. "Jimmy's sick."

Natalie realized that he was not just sick, but unconscious, his face ashen. She saw that Waneta's blouse was completely unbuttoned, as if something had happened while she was getting dressed.

They rushed into Natalie's house and Waneta put Jimmy on the living room couch as Natalie ran for the kitchen phone. Standing amidst the sudden commotion, Dana looked on, perplexed, as his little friend lay motionless on the couch, cushioned by two throw pillows. "Jimmy's sick, honey," Natalie told him, pointing him away. "Please go to your room and play." She went into the kitchen, her mind swirling, and called Margaret Horton. "This is Natalie Hilliard on Davis Hollow Road," she said. "I have a very sick child here. His name is Jimmy Hoyt. He's unconscious. His mother is here. Hurry—please." She hung up the phone, and returned to Waneta, who was moving about aimlessly in the living room.

"What's Tim's number at work?" Natalie asked. He would be out on a job by now, but Waneta gave Natalie the office number in Waverly.

"Can I leave a message for him? It's urgent," Natalie was telling someone at Streeter Construction a few seconds later. "Please tell him that he's needed at home as soon as possible. Tell him his son is sick."

Waneta was crying softly now, sobbing and pacing, waiting for the rescue squad. There was not a sound from Jimmy, still lying motionless on the couch. In shock, Natalie was afraid to touch him.

"What *happened?*" she asked.

"I was getting dressed. . . . He came to me, he just collapsed in my arms. . . . He just collapsed. . . . Did you call Tim?"

"I just called over there," Natalie said, trying to stay calm herself. "They're getting a message to him."

"I wish they'd hurry up," Waneta said, peering out the window for the rescue squad.

"They'll be here any minute," Natalie assured her. She put her arm around Waneta's shoulder. "Better button up your blouse."

"Are you sure they're getting Tim?" Waneta asked again.

"I'm sure he's on his way." Natalie didn't know what to do. "Try to sit down," she said. "Let's wait in the kitchen."

Waneta wouldn't move from the front room. She kept looking out for the squad, and for Tim.

She was standing in the doorway when the station wagon ambulance pulled up and Hank Robson and Morris Lyons came toward the house. Robson worked the second shift at IBM and was available for morning emergency calls. He'd heard, of course, about the deaths of the two Hoyt babies, and now here was a strapping two-year-old, lying lifeless on the neighbors' couch as his mother beseeched, "Please *do* something!"

Robson knelt down and felt for a pulse. There was none. He began administering mouth-to-mouth resuscitation and CPR. "Nothing," Robson said. He looked at Lyons, then at Waneta.

"He's gone," he said softly.

"Can I use your phone?" Robson asked Natalie. She heard his muted voice in the kitchen but paid no attention to what he was saying. All she could think of was Jimmy. And Waneta. And Tim. She didn't believe what had just happened. It just could not be.

Robson and Lyons stayed with the body until they heard a car pull up and the door slam. "Hello, Doc," Robson said to Dr. Hartnagel.

Nineteen sixty-eight was a tumultuous year in America. Martin Luther King and Robert Kennedy were assassinated two months apart, battles from the jungles of Vietnam to the streets of Chicago raged on television screens, and as they campaigned for president that fall Richard Nixon and Hubert Humphrey vied for the soul of a country in agony. But to a good number of the citizens of a rural farming community in central New York State, none of it was as riveting, as mysterious and shocking and eerie, as what was going on in the trailer home of one of their neighbors up the hill.

The sudden deaths of Julie and Jimmy within twenty-one days of each other, together with Eric's death three and a half years before, caused a quiet uproar in Newark Valley. Bewilderment, incredulity, horror—these were some of the emotions twisting in the air that September. And suspicion. It all depended on how close one was to the events. Those closest, like the Hilliards, could be ripped apart by the whispers going around, so they sequestered themselves from the talk. They saw only devastating loss, felt only tremendous pain and sympathy. Those on the outskirts, meanwhile, heard the murmurings about the tragic couple up on Davis Hollow. Waneta Hoyt was only twenty-two, and already she had lost three children. Many people knew the essential facts, but not what to think, other than that it was probably the *strangest* thing they had ever heard. But there were some among them who had much more uneasy thoughts, and they wondered whether the right questions were being asked by the right people. Could Waneta Hoyt actually be *doing something* to her children?

Dr. Hartnagel was certainly one of the right people, and this time, he did not hesitate to order an autopsy. He sent Jimmy's body directly to the pathology lab at Tioga General Hospital, in Waverly. Then he called Howard Horton, Newark Valley's part-time police chief.

Later that day, there was a knock on the door of the trailer.

"Hello, Tim," Hartnagel said. He had come with Horton and a deputy county sheriff. "Can we come in?"

Tim, obviously distraught, glanced warily at the deputy.

"Waneta, Tim," Hartnagel began. "I'm sorry. We're going to have to check into this."

"Whenever there's more than one death in a family the law dictates we have to look into the possibility of foul play," Horton said, implying that they could look it up.

Tim could not believe what he was hearing. How could Doc Hartnagel actually suspect such a thing? He was Doc Hartnagel. If you called him at 3:00 in the morning, he'd be at your house at 3:10, in his pajamas. Maybe you'd get a bill, maybe not. And Howard Horton, the police chief they'd known since they were kids, who worked practically alongside Tim's mother at Endicott Johnson. How could he accuse them of something so horrible? "We got nothin' to hide," Tim said angrily. "My God, we wouldn't do something to our own children. We don't know what's wrong. We want to find out ourselves."

"Can you tell us what happened?" Hartnagel asked.

"I don't know what you're trying to say," Waneta said. She had been silent up to now. "We didn't do anything. The children were in trouble and I called for help, and now you're saying I did something."

"We just have to check into it," the deputy sheriff said. Waneta said she was getting dressed when she heard Jimmy running to her. And then he just collapsed in her arms. "Then I carried him across to Natalie Hilliard's house," she said. Asked again about Julie, Waneta told Hartnagel, as she had three weeks before, that the baby had choked on rice cereal.

The conversation was brief. Both Hartnagel and Horton were indeed out of their element, and Tim sensed that they were terribly uncomfortable about the situation in which they found themselves. Townspeople invariably regarded Horton as an affable amateur policeman, "a part-time Andy of Mayberry," in one person's memory, who, since before the war, had counted among his usual duties the keeping of order at the Memorial Day parade and the wagging of a finger at truant teenagers. Murder investigations were not part of the job. He left that sort of thing to the sheriff's department or the state police. And while death was part of Hartnagel's business, he was far more accustomed to fulfilling his coroner duties by saying, "Yes, this person is indeed dead," checking his watch, and signing his name, than to confronting so disquieting and strange a circumstance as the one before him now. He was, after all, a country doctor, not a medical examiner, and these were his patients. He had delivered Waneta twenty-two years before.

Still, a country doctor saw a lot of things in his life. Revered in these parts for his easygoing kindness, Hartnagel was now in his late sixties and thinking about retiring to a house up on Cayuga Lake. Having practiced since the Depression, he had once been known to see to patients by horse-drawn sleigh in harsh winters, and one time delivered a baby on a kitchen table, in a house with dirt floors and pigs and ducks at his feet. More than once, his daughter, Marilyn, saw her father go out on a house call to take care of a baby—and come home with the baby. "They said they couldn't take care of him," he'd explain, then try to find someone to adopt the child. He also saw some things that he knew were just not right. In a poor county like Tioga, child abuse was not uncommon, though nobody called it that. When he came upon a child he thought was in trouble, Hartnagel tried to do something about it. Twice he had shown Marilyn pictures of children with burn marks that he believed were inflicted by their parents. In each case he went to the county judge down at the courthouse in Owego, and each time the judge ruled against him. "My father was livid," Marilyn later remembered. "When he was coroner he had lots of cases that were suspicious and no one ever did anything. He grew disgruntled. It made him fed up with medicine."

The deputy sheriff told Tim and Waneta he would have to take some things with him. The cereal. The dish. Food from the refrigerator. The clothes Jimmy was wearing when he died. The diaper pail, with the diapers. A washcloth, and the box of Julie's blankets. Tim put up a perfunctory protest and gathered the items, as Waneta sat still. They wouldn't find anything, he promised the men as they headed for the door.

Howard Horton saw Chuck Hoyt in front of his mother's house. "Charlie, I need to talk to you," he said. He took him off to the side.

"Charlie, what's going on here?" he asked.

Chuck was stunned by the question; he stared right back at Horton. He was not among those whose first thoughts were the worst. He was still absorbing what had happened that morning, just trying to keep his brother from going over the edge. "What do you mean, what's going on?" he asked.

"Something's not right here," said Horton. "Look, Charlie, I gotta ask you this. Do you think Waneta is doing something to these kids?"

"What?" Chuck stammered. "No. *No!*"

"Well, you know we have to investigate this," Horton said.

By the time he got inside, Chuck was sobbing. "You're not gonna be-lieve what Howard Horton just asked me," he said to Loretta. "He thinks Neta's doing something to the kids." Loretta looked at him. Then she too broke down.

"The body is opened by a Y-shaped incision," dictated Dr. James Mitchell, the pathologist at Tioga General. "There is no external evidence of injury to the head or body . . . the pupils are dilated and equal . . . the lips appear somewhat cyanotic. . . ."

Mitchell began Jimmy's autopsy at 10:30 that same morning, one hour after his mother carried him to Natalie Hilliard's house. Standing over the little boy's body beneath a bright surgical lamp, the pathologist was on a hunt for signs of disease that might explain his strange death. He began removing and inspecting organs, dictating his observations into a tape recorder.

He started with the larynx, trachea, esophagus, and lungs. Finding nothing remarkable, he moved on to the cardiovascular system. "The valves show no vegetation or thickening," he said as he examined Jimmy's heart. "The coronary arteries are in their normal position and show no gross patho-logic changes. The great vessels are in their normal relationship. No con-genital abnormalities are noted."

Removing the liver, Mitchell took a section of the organ and noted that it was dark red. All livers are various shades of deep red but for some reason Mitchell thought Jimmy's showed evidence of congestion. A section of the kidney was also dark red. When he examined the child's head, Mitchell found no evidence of hemorrhage, though there was "some congestion of the subpial vessels," meaning the delicate wrapping around the blood vessels that cover the brain. But none of the supposed congestion could explain the death. If anything, it was an effect, not a cause.

Now, the organs of the endocrine system. Here Mitchell found something he thought interesting, perhaps revealing. The adrenal glands, he thought, were unusually small. They weighed just $2^1/_2$ grams, less than half what he expected. Looking further, he removed and weighed the thymus gland, and judged that it, too, was not the normal size for a child this age. He didn't think the gland was too small, however, but too large. A two-lobed organ at the root of the neck and above the heart, the thymus's function was ambiguous. (Medical researchers would later show the gland to be critical to the development of the immune system.) Unlike other organs that grow with the body to adulthood, the thymus is largest at birth and diminishes in size as a child matures, virtually disappearing after puberty. Jimmy's thymus weighed 40 grams when Mitchell put it on his organ scale. He thought it should have weighed no more than 25.

Perhaps the discrepancies Mitchell noted were valid, perhaps not. He may not have been especially familiar with children, living or dead. "It is the body of a well-nourished well-developed four-year-old child," he had dictated at the start of the autopsy. Jimmy, though big for his age, was just a few months past two. Mitchell hadn't verified Jimmy's age with a birth certificate or a phone call to Hartnagel or the family. He also did not pay too much attention to precision. Weighing the child's small organs on a standard pathology scale, instead of one fine enough for autopsies of small children, was not the most accurate method. In any event, the size of a child's thymus is variable, and it has nothing to do with life and death.

The autopsy left Mitchell fishing for a plausible cause of death. As his final anatomic diagnosis, he chose congestion of the liver, kidneys, and brain, and adrenal insufficiency. Under cause of death, he wrote: "Acute adrenal insufficiency." The child's supposedly undersized adrenal glands, he concluded, were lethally ineffective.

Hartnagel didn't buy this. Even if the adrenal glands were too small for a child Jimmy's *true* age, it wouldn't then follow that it was "acute adrenal insufficiency" that had killed him. Problems with the adrenals, two triangular glands atop the kidneys that produce crucial hormones, would have been evident long before he died. But in rejecting Mitchell's conclusion when he filled out Jimmy's death certificate two days later, Hartnagel could do no better. Going back into the pathologist's findings, Hartnagel pulled out the only thing that came within a hundred miles of a fatal diagnosis. "Enlarged thymus," he wrote under "immediate cause of death." Beneath that, where the form asked what the immediate cause was "due to or a consequence of," Hartnagel left two blank lines.

Though typically applied to infants as an explanation for crib death, the finding of "enlarged thymus" was an old chestnut for the sudden, unexplained death of young children. The archaic theory, first proposed in the 1700s, was that the oversized organ could interfere with the normal function of the heart and lungs. By the 1960s, it was a hopelessly anachronistic hypothesis—pathologists had known for decades that all children have "enlarged thymuses"—but after nearly two centuries, there were still physicians left who welcomed the convenient reasoning. And as Hartnagel demonstrated by implication if not in precise words, doctors were willing to attribute just about any sudden death of a child to the all-encompassing crib death, whether the child was young enough to sleep in a crib beneath a twirling mobile or old enough to run over to Grandma's house and fill his pockets with sticks and stones. Still, even Hartnagel seemed to acknowledge that the thymus finding was not much more than a space filler. Under "Conditions contributing to death but not related to cause given," Hartnagel wrote: "Unknown and undecided as to cause."

To many who heard about them, the autopsy results were a sea of ambiguities. On one hand, it was full of medical language that gave the impression that Jimmy was a very sick child indeed. *Congested liver and kidney, congested brain, adrenal insufficiency, enlarged thymus.* The interpretation that made its way around the family was that this enlarged thymus had choked Jimmy, and who was to say it didn't run in the family? This was the first autopsy. Perhaps Eric and Julie had had the same problems. Maybe an enlarged thymus had caused Eric's heart to stop and Julie to choke to death. Weren't some diseases genetic, striking family members again and again? Waneta, for one, suddenly started talking a lot about enlarged thymuses.

On the other hand, there were common logic and gut feelings. Jimmy was a healthy, energetic little boy. Wouldn't he have shown some signs of illness? And if his death made no sense, one had to then go back to the others and consider the pattern. Tim's oldest brother, George, never one to mince words, came right out and spoke his mind to Chuck. "I think she's killing these kids," he told him.

George had moved back to Newark Valley from New Jersey and was working in a Chevrolet dealer's garage when he got the call about Jimmy and raced home. George had always been a gruff, irascible character, full of over-wrought opinions, but he sometimes demonstrated a surprising insight and a penchant for forming conclusions from odd little pieces of experience. He thought of a time he was driving up Route 38 into Berkshire and saw Neta in her car, pulled off to the side of the road, staring straight at her steering wheel. He tooted his horn, but Neta never moved. To him it was part of the picture. He thought something bad was going on here. He'd seen Jimmy just a few days before, and he remarked to himself what a vigorous little kid he was. He couldn't have just died, not just three weeks after Julie. George's wife, Gloria, shared this opinion, as did his dairyman brother-in-law Weldon Wait. Weldon was well-known as one of the valley's more entertaining characters, and among the farmers he visited in his social rounds it became almost common knowledge that he openly regarded Waneta as his wife's crazy, child-murdering sister-in-law. He did not, however, feel moved to do anything about it. That was for the Hoyts to worry about.

The Hoyts did plenty of worrying, and yelling at each other, over what was going on. When they gathered for Jimmy's funeral that Sunday afternoon, there was an air of unreality hanging over them. In her head, Tim's sister Janet could still hear Jimmy yelling, "Grandma, Grandma, Grandma" as he ran happily across the field to Ella Hoyt. Jimmy was physically precocious; not yet two and a half, he was already learning to tie his shoes. Janet thought this was remarkable. She had collapsed on the sidewalk when she heard the news. Her mother was so traumatized that she blanked out the moment. She had come out of her house when she heard the ambulance, had screamed in abject horror when she saw Jimmy's body, and fainted. When she came to, she had no memory of what had happened in the moments before she dropped to the ground. The last thing she remembered was that Jimmy had been over early that morning, an hour before his death.

Even Neil MacPherson, the funeral director, was having a hard time. He was an old man, about to pass on the reins of the funeral home to a young associate, and he found the unfathomable tragedy of the Hoyt children almost unbearable. "You know," he remarked to Tim's brothers, "these little kids haven't had a chance. They should be just starting out on a long trip."

As family members and the Methodist minister Gary Kuhns mounted their second brief journey to Richford in three weeks, their shock was now compounded by a cloud of suspicion. Some found themselves focusing on Waneta. They watched how she comported herself, searched for a hint of inappropriate behavior. Loretta always looked into Neta's eyes, and it seemed to her that there was a certain hollowness that the rest of her behavior—that of the helpless, grieving mother, holding on to her stoic husband—could not completely mask. With Eric's funeral, and then Julie's, there was all that awful crying and carrying-on. This time, something else was in the air.

A lot of people in northern Tioga County shook their heads in disbelief and thanked God for sparing them such misfortune. But there were some who spent that fall waiting for the other shoe to drop. The questioning was con-tained and discreet. "Why aren't they looking into this?" Margaret Cornwell said to her husband after dinner one night. From her store on Water Street, the Valley Dress Shop, Margaret heard plenty of "sidewalk talk," as she termed the snippets of conversation she'd catch from people passing by. Many people in town knew the Hoyts, but not much about Waneta. They just knew that she'd married into the family, that she came from up in Richford, and that her children kept dying while Tim was at work. Some heard that the Sheriff's Department had "raided the Hoyt place," others that Doc Hartnagel was asking people what they thought. When Hartnagel asked Loretta during an appointment, "What do you make of these deaths?" she said she just didn't know. Few were so bold as George Hoyt and Weldon Wait. The notion of Waneta, or any mother, hurting her own children—much less killing them—was so horrendous that few could let themselves articulate it. If something was going on, people told one another, the authorities would find out.

The authorities, though, found nothing. Not long after their visit to the Hoyts, Horton and the sheriff's deputy returned the things they had taken—the diapers, the blankets and clothes, the cereal. Nothing unusual had been discovered, they told Waneta and Tim, and with the thymus finding of the autopsy, there seemed no reason for further investigation. They were just doing their duty, they said apologetically. Well, Tim said, you've got to do what you've got to do. "It would have been nice if they did the diapers," Tim said scornfully when he told Chuck about it later.

As much as anything, it was the autopsy that cooled the suspicion—that and the fact that to most, the Hoyts seemed like such a perfectly average couple. The police decided the right thing to do was to leave it alone. Horton's brief conversation with Chuck was the extent of their questioning, and they bothered Waneta and Tim no more. As cryptic and unfulfilling as the cause of death was, as skeptical as Hartnagel might have been, ultimately nothing he said or did dispelled the spreading notion that Jimmy, and therefore Eric and Julie, had died of some unknown but natural condition. It is impossible to know who first suggested the words, but it was the impression of many that the Hoyt babies were dying of the sudden, mysterious, and vaguely defined entity known as crib death.

This was the impression of nearly all two dozen members of the Newark Valley rescue squad. They were by nature and training disinclined to challenge the doctor's findings, and there was nothing about the Hoyts that seemed suspicious. They were nice people—Waneta made a point to send a note of thanks to the squad after each rescue effort. "The whistle blew, you'd run in—'What's going on?' 'Hoyt kid having trouble breathing again'—we thought nothing of it," Arthur Balzer would later recall. "You know, there are sick families with breathing problems. A lot of families have asthma."

But this response was not quite unanimous. Bob Vanek, for one, was skeptical. The squad met on the first Tuesday of each month to discuss business and practice its techniques, and Vanek was puzzled by the absence of suspicious talk about all those calls to the Hoyt farm on Davis Hollow Road. Vanek seemed to be alone in his feeling that Waneta's behavior was a bit too strange to discount. "When you got there she wouldn't talk to you or answer you," he'd recall. "She would stand away, in the doorway. She didn't cry or go into hysterics. I would say, 'The child is deceased' and glance at her. She'd be staring, like this. And Tim was never there." Of course, Vanek considered whether Waneta's demeanor meant she was in shock. But he could not shake the vague sensation that the circumstances might mean something else. He talked to his wife about it. "Three in a row, there's something funny about it," he told her. Let the police handle it, his wife advised. If there's a problem, they'll come to you.

Vanek waited. But they never came.

Though it was commonly perceived that Jimmy was closer to his father than to his mother, and that Tim seemed more emotionally bonded with the children generally, it was Waneta who expressed her pain more openly. In town, she appeared weary and drawn and accepted sympathy in a way that tended to engender even more pity. The mystery was part of what made it all so dreadful—as if God Himself were playing a cruel joke on this hapless woman. At home, Waneta would often tell Tim that the deaths of the children were the result of her inadequacy as a mother. If she had been more vigilant, she would say, gotten to them sooner, they would still be alive. Or maybe there was something wrong with her genes. Tim would have none of this. "It's not your fault," he'd insist. "It's nobody's fault." And they would not give up on the idea of having a family.

Holding his wife up, seeing to her needs, was the only response that gave Tim any sort of comfort. It was by now the central dynamic of their relationship. He didn't go to work for months after the deaths of Julie and Jimmy, and eventually his solicitude cost him his job. "I couldn't make myself leave her alone," he later recalled. More than once, when Tim dropped in on his brother Chuck he would say, "I gotta leave soon. Neta's talking about killing herself."

Art Hilliard tried to lessen the burden for Tim. "Every once in a while we might go hunting and not take our guns," Art said years later. "And he and I would just walk on the hill. It wasn't that we would go up and sit under a great big old maple tree and talk. That's not the way it happened. We'd walk up on the hill and talk about what we saw up there. We'd look at the woodchucks, the turkey, deer, squirrels, chipmunks, birds. And just shoot the bull. Maybe just look and see how the field was developing. What's the hay gonna be? The things us old hill people would talk about."

In early October, a young woman named Joyce Aman drove up to Newark Valley and knocked on the front door of the Hoyt trailer. "Good morning. Mrs. Hoyt?" she said when Waneta opened the door. "I'm with the Tioga County Public Health Nursing Service. I'm just here to pay a visit to see how you're doing with your baby."

In counties like Tioga, it was not uncommon for babies to be born to young or poor mothers. The county had started its public health nursing service with a staff of four in the summer of 1966, and Aman had joined them that December, soon after finishing nursing school. Among their key jobs was to visit new mothers, counsel them, see if they needed any help. Aman vividly remembered her first case, "a pregnant twelve-year-old who wanted to talk about hopscotch." After that, nothing shocked her—until that day in Newark Valley.

Weeks before, she had gotten a referral form from Tompkins County Hospital directing her to the home of Waneta and Timothy Hoyt, who had brought home a newborn baby girl during the summer. "Assess bonding skills, feeding, baby's reaction in home" was the assignment. She came several times, but found no one home. This time, Waneta answered the door. Quickly, she learned the dreadful news. Not only was the baby dead, but so was her two-year-old brother.

They sat at the kitchen table, and Waneta tearfully recounted the tragedies of her dead children. Aman, pregnant herself, was aghast. "It doesn't make sense," she said sympathetically, "one after another like that."

"It doesn't make sense to me either," Waneta said.

Aman suggested professional counseling to help cope with the grief, and Waneta liked the idea. Tioga County had recently opened a mental health clinic, and on October 17, three weeks after Jimmy died, she was sitting in the office of a psychiatrist named Waldo Burnett, explaining that all her children had died of enlarged thymuses. "It runs in the family," she reported. "It shuts off their air." She said that six other children in her extended family had also died of either unknown causes or enlarged thymuses.

Waneta told Burnett that she'd led a tortured life since Eric's death three years before. She slept fitfully and cried several times a day. "I tried to be consoling with her," the psychiatrist wrote in his notes that day. "I pointed out to her the possible gain which she might derive from active religious participation. She told me that she did think it caused her to feel somewhat better, coming to this clinic and talking about the unhappy events of the past." Burnett didn't detect any mental disorders: "It is true she is unhappy; however, her unhappiness seems to me to be a normal grief reaction. I would feel that just because she is grieving the loss of her children would not cause her to be considered mentally ill."

Waneta was feeling better when she came back eleven days later. She and Tim had gone out to the movies, and her minister was coming by once a week to visit. Reverend Kuhns had invited them over for supper the following week. "She says she goes grocery shopping with her husband, is doing her dishes and sweeping the floor in her mobile home and at times, makes the bed," Burnett summed up in his notes. "She said she did not cry today. Yesterday, she visited young children and cried briefly. She did not cry the day before that."

Waneta saw Waldo Burnett twice more, and by February, the psychiatrist was finding her to be "cheerful." Tim came along to her last appointment and agreed that she no longer needed counseling. Burnett told Waneta to call if she needed help in the future. She thanked him effusively for his help. She felt much better. "Final diagnosis," he wrote. "No mental disorder."

Joyce Aman, meanwhile, continued to drop in on Waneta and Tim, and she discussed the family with her supervisor, Grace Gurdin. At one point, Gurdin questioned the enlarged thymus finding that was listed as Jimmy's cause of death. She thought the little boy's death should probably have been called a "sudden infant death."

Gurdin's remark reflected the increased attention crib death was beginning to receive. Some people in the medical world were starting to use this more dignified name, with its implication to the uninformed that it was an actual, identifiable disease, not just some inexplicable consequence of being alive, and that like other diseases, it could strike older children as well as small babies, and run in families. Whatever was killing the Hoyt children, it was the consensus of nearly everyone who knew them that there could be no good reason to tempt fate again, so it was assumed that Waneta and Tim would take the appropriate measures to prevent the birth of any more doomed babies. It was with dismay, then, that people around them greeted the news in the spring of 1969, only six months after the September deaths of Julie and Jimmy, that Waneta was pregnant yet again.

17

Babies have always died suddenly and mysteriously. Indeed, the Old Testament recounts the world's first recorded case.

As the classic story goes, two harlots were sharing a bed with their newborn babies when one of them found hers lifeless beside her. Rising in the night, she placed the dead infant beside her bedmate and claimed the survivor as her own. The other woman discovered the ruse, and when both laid claim to the living baby, the dispute was brought to King Solomon. Brandishing a sword, he offered to split the baby in two so that each could have a piece of the living child. The true mother relinquished her claim to save her baby's life. Thus, the King knew who the rightful mother was and awarded her the child. In *The Judgment of Solomon,* a ceiling fresco by the Italian Renaissance painter Raphael, history's first recorded victim of crib death was depicted lying on the floor, lifeless and forgotten, as the surviving baby was held in the air by his legs and Solomon pondered his decision.

Solomonic wisdom aside, *why* babies die suddenly has long been an elusive question, with morality a perpetual presence in the background. Accidental suffocation—"overlaying," or smothering by sheets or bedclothes—was the presumed cause in the biblical story, but this has proven to be an uncertain element of sudden infant death throughout history. As the prime, if unsubstantiated, suspect for many centuries, overlaying—or stifling, as it was called in England and Italy in the 1600s—led Florentine craftsmen to develop a wood-and-iron device called an *arcuccio* ("little arch") that fit over a bed and prevented blankets and people from lying directly on a baby. "Every nurse in Florence is obliged to lay the child in it, under Pain of Excommunication," read an eighteenth-century British advertisement trying to bring the idea to

England. But it did not escape notice that even *arcuccios* did not always prevent babies from dying.

Through the ages, suspicious eyes have turned toward mothers, though accusation and punishment have generally been influenced more by the prevailing social politics of the day than by legal or medical reason. In the first century B.C., Egyptian mothers who were thought to have even inadvertently smothered their children in bed were forced to hug the dead baby for three days and nights. Because history is laden with the murder of children, with everything from poverty to insanity playing a role, and because accidental and intentional suffocation cannot be distinguished, infanticide has always been inseparable from the question of unexpected infant death. Indeed, it was in part a moral imperative to separate the accidental from the purposeful that led doctors, as far back as the 1600s, to ponder causes more subtle than overlaying.

Sudden infant death slowly evolved into a medical question with the development of pathological anatomy, first taught in the French medical schools in the late 1700s. For the first time, doctors began looking inside the bodies of babies who had died of presumed overlaying to see if any clues had been left behind. In these early autopsies, doctors noticed that babies who died mysteriously seemed to have large thymus glands. They theorized that the oversized organs interfered in some way with the body's cardiopulmonary functioning, cutting off the airway or perhaps the blood vessels supplying oxygen to the brain. The thymus hypothesis was both the first theory of sudden infant death and the first to be widely accepted without being proven. "Status thymico-lymphaticus," as it became known, remained a popular diagnosis well into the twentieth century. And because the gland's crucial role in the maturation of the immune system was not understood, it was thought to be expendable; so for a time in the 1930s it became fashionable for doctors to irradiate the thymus glands of some babies in the first attempt at preventing sudden infant death. It didn't save any lives, but it left its mark decades later, in the form of cancers of the nearby thyroid gland.

By the 1940s, as the thymus theory finally began to lose credibility, "unknown" and "unexplained" began to turn up on death certificates. Crib death emerged as one of the great, inscrutable mysteries of modern medicine.

Doctors were not short on theories. Perhaps a hypersensitivity to cow's milk sent some infants into fatal shock. Maybe they choked on regurgitated formula. Some pathologists pointed to low levels of gamma globulin, antibody proteins in the blood plasma; others to electrolyte disorders. Severe respiratory infection had a big following. But all these were little more than hunches, largely untested and little discussed beyond occasional mentions in medical journals. Thousands of otherwise healthy babies were dying each year, but the world's doctors did not come together for so much as a discussion of crib death until 1963, the year politics entered the picture.

Fred Dore was a veteran Washington state senator from Seattle when he and his wife, Mary, lost their baby daughter Christine Marie on September 8, 1961. The three-month-old, the couple's fourth child, had died, her parents were told, of "acute pneumonitis." The coroner told the Dores that he saw dozens of babies like theirs every year—infants who were completely healthy one minute and dead the next. He went on to admit to the Dores that their daughter didn't really have pneumonia. It was just simpler and neater than saying that the death was medically unexplained. The Dores left the conversation shaken and bewildered. They learned, though, that they weren't alone. The coroner himself had lost a baby to crib death.

In the mail a week after they buried their daughter, the Dores found a note of sympathy from a woman who had seen Christine's obituary. Her baby son had died, ostensibly of pneumonia, on the very same day. Mary Dore started combing the obituaries in Seattle and surrounding King County, and calling parents whose babies had died as suddenly and inexplicably as hers. There were more than she imagined. A decade later, in fact, an epidemiologist at the King County Health Department would find that the rates of sudden infant death were higher in the Pacific Northwest than in any other region of the country. Why that was so was as mysterious as the entity itself, but it would become the backdrop for Seattle's emerging reputation as America's crib death capital.

Mary Dore saw the value of mothers giving each other emotional support, but she also wanted to know why her daughter had died. If it wasn't pneumonia or an enlarged thymus, then what? She and her husband quickly discovered that very little was known about crib death, and that neither medicine nor government seemed to have much interest in studying it in any kind of serious, organized way. Washington's state medical association had a committee on sudden infant death, but it was largely dormant. The chairman of the committee, a physician they knew, told the Dores that nobody even had a handle on how common crib death was. "Some babies get autopsied," he said. "Some don't."

The Dores had some power in the state of Washington, and they decided to use it. They embarked on a campaign to change the state's autopsy laws, and to get money to the state university's new medical school for some basic research into crib death. Fred Dore introduced a bill, and recruited a Republican sponsor who had once worked in a coroner's office. "This was hard for a daddy to do," Mary Dore remembered. "Men don't express grief very well." Her husband found immediate resistance. "This doesn't happen very much," one legislator told Dore dismissively. He was a physician.

Across the country in Greenwich, Connecticut, a couple named Jedd and Louise Roe were living a parallel life. When their baby son Mark died suddenly during the summer of 1958, the local police listed it as a "suspected homicide." An officer asked Roe, "Did your wife love your son?" Only the assurance of the Roes' pediatrician persuaded the police that there was no reason to suspect the parents—that babies did, in fact, die for no apparent reason. The pain of the accusation, though, and the mystery of their baby's death, obsessed the Roes for the next several years. They, like the Dores, found that other parents had experienced the same trauma, isolation, and guilt, and began searching for some sort of research foundation to which they could contribute the proceeds of an insurance policy the baby's grandparents had bought in his name. Not only did they find no organized effort to study crib death, but their encounters with physicians left them with the unpleasant realization that there was more to overcome than the malady itself. "Laypersons," some doctors told them flatly, should stay out of scientific affairs.

The Roes were undeterred. In 1962, four years after their son's death, they incorporated the Mark Addison Roe Foundation. Among the trustees was a young Greenwich lawyer, Lowell Weicker Jr., a close friend of the family. The Roes also managed to attract an important medical figure, a Philadelphia pathologist named Marie Valdes-Dapena. If little was known about crib death, it was not because Valdes-Dapena wasn't trying. She had been studying the entity for several years and had quietly become the world's most eminent authority—if anyone could be an authority on the unknown.

Back in Seattle, the Dores continued to push their cause, and on March 11, 1963, the day before the birth of their fifth child, they witnessed the passage of the first state law in the United States requiring an autopsy of all children under three who died suddenly and "apparently in good health." The legislators directed the University of Washington School of Medicine to set up a program for performing the postmortems and studying the results, and gave the school $20,000 for the task. Some at the school chafed at the idea of politicians telling them what to do, but they didn't turn down the money. It did her cause no harm that, even before the bill was introduced, Mary Dore had swooped down on the medical school and lured two researchers into the mystery. When the bodies of crib death victims began arriving in the school's pathology lab, pediatric cardiologist Warren Guntheroth and epidemiologist Donald Peterson began searching the autopsy findings for some clues.

The Dores had also taken their case to the medical school's pediatrics chairman, Dr. Robert Aldrich. It turned out to be a shrewd and prescient move. Early in 1963, President Kennedy appointed Aldrich the first director of a new unit of the National Institutes of Health that would be devoted to the research of childhood health. Kennedy's sister Rosemary was severely retarded, and he created the National Institute of Child Health and Human Development primarily to study the condition. But it was crib death that Aldrich had on his mind when he arrived in Bethesda, Maryland, with Gerald LaVeck, another Seattle pediatrician, who would be his deputy. One of Aldrich's first official acts as chief of the NICHD was to award a contract to the University of Washington to stage the first international conference on sudden infant death. It would later be said that this gathering, the product of one couple's private grief, was the birth of the SIDS movement.

For two days in September 1963, five experts from the United States and three from England, along with thirty other pathologists, pediatricians, and health-care professionals with an interest in learning about crib death, met in Seattle to discuss collectively, for the first time, what they knew and what they didn't know. The latter far outweighed the former.

Pathologists described their frustrations at opening up infants only to find nothing amiss. An epidemiologist estimated that two of every thousand American infants was dying mysteriously, with no hint of disease, and that there was a disproportionately higher number of these deaths among the lower socioeconomic groups. There was a review of the various scientific theories and a searching discussion of the facts that were known: Sudden death occurred in children primarily under six months of age and was uncommon after the age of two; recurrence within families was rare; routine infections were often associated with these deaths. Like a homicide squad listing clues on a blackboard, the group of fledgling medical detectives tried to discern a pattern that might narrow the list of suspects.

The discussion was frank, the graphics at one point gruesome. Dr. Lester Adelson, the chief deputy coroner of Cleveland, told the gathering that he saw the bodies of about one hundred infants a year whose deaths he could not explain. His own two children were born after he had seen too many of these babies on his autopsy table, and he would often find himself peering into their cribs, listening for every breath, poking at their toes for reassurance.

A pediatrician in the audience asked Adelson what he told parents concerned about having another child after losing one to crib death. "This same type of tragedy is no more apt to happen to them than it is to happen to their neighbor," he replied. He had rarely seen sudden death more than once in a family, but parents often had to be disabused of the myths that had grown up around crib death. "By the time either one or both parents have come in to see us, they have been talked to by their neighbors, relatives, and that toothless old crone who lives next door who has brought up a dozen children and is certain that the child undoubtedly smothered in its bedclothes," Adelson told the group. "The first thing I tell parents is that the child did not die of smothering or suffocation. The parents, in most instances, are relieved. The next question is 'What did it die from?' I usually say the child died of an acute viral infection. The death is the result of natural causes and no one is to blame. Whether or not the death is actually the result of a viral infection is beside the point under these circumstances. What I am trying to do is give parents something that will furnish them with a reasonable answer to a very burning question. At the same time I am eradicating their great sense of guilt."

As a forensic pathologist, however, Adelson confessed to a dilemma: assuaging guilt while still investigating the remote possibility of foul play. "One cannot ignore the possibility that the child who looks unhurt externally may have severe or fatal injury on internal examination," he said. He flashed a slide showing a child with his scalp peeled away. On the skull, one could see a linear fracture that would have gone unnoticed without the complete autopsy. "This child is an example of the infant who is brought to the coroner's office with the monotonous story that he was found dead in his crib in the morning after being perfectly well the previous evening." The father later admitted that he'd had too much to drink and while playing with his son had accidentally tossed him into the crib. Adelson referred the group to "battered child syndrome," a term coined the year before by a team of doctors from the University of Colorado (one of whose key members, Dr. C. Henry Kempe, was in this audience), who had published a landmark paper with that title in the *Journal of the American Medical Association* in July, 1962.

Adelson did not explore intentional smothering, a more subtle form of child homicide that could masquerade as crib death, but this omission did not disturb the pediatricians in attendance. Despite the Colorado team's unprecedented paper, the group was highly skeptical of the notion that child abuse was a serious problem, and they were not particularly sympathetic to Adelson's problems as a coroner. They were here to discuss medicine, not murder. In that sense, they were slightly ahead of the times. In these years, it was not uncommon for people in authority, particularly in and around major cities with medical examiners' offices run by forensic pathologists, to think of homicide when confronted by a sudden and unexplained infant death. As had happened to the Roes, police officers would routinely question grieving parents, often coldly and without good reason, and especially those who were poor. Thus, the Seattle conference would become the genesis of a movement whose goal was not only to discover the cause and prevention of crib death, but to establish crib death as a legitimate medical entity, thereby shifting guilt, and certainly suspicion, away from the parents who were also victims, and placing the burden of discovery on medical science.

Perhaps nobody in the world was as dedicated to this goal as the physician the Roes had attracted to their cause, Dr. Marie Valdes-Dapena. She was a pediatric pathologist who was more familiar with crib death—at least what crib death was *not*—than anyone in the room. "There were more theories than pint-sized pickles," she recalled, and she had tested a good number of them. She had stumbled into this area of pathology while working at the Women's Medical College Hospital in Philadelphia in 1957. As a general pathologist with a developing interest in the deaths of children, she asked Philadelphia's medical examiner, Dr. Joseph Spelman, if she might come by two or three times a week to perform the autopsies of the youngest of the bodies that arrived in his morgue. Spelman eagerly agreed. His office was swamped with work. But Dapena became frustrated by the absence of findings in the majority of babies she saw and told Spelman she was quitting the arrangement. She wasn't learning anything, she said. Spelman turned her perspective around. Did she know that as many as 15,000 babies died without explanation every year in the United States? It was a wide-open field, Spelman told her. Hardly anyone was doing research.

By the Seattle conference half a decade later, everyone concerned about sudden infant death had heard of Molly Dapena. By then she was in her early forties, a deputy medical examiner and hospital pathologist with a specialty that could be viewed as both incongruous and fitting. As she explored the bodies of crib death victims during these years, she almost always seemed to be pregnant. She'd had ten children in sixteen years, and in fact was carrying her eleventh, to be her last, at this first SIDS meeting. Dapena and her pathologist husband, Antonio, lived with their brood in a twelve-bedroom castle built at the turn of the century in Wallingford, Pennsylvania, and got around in a Volkswagen minibus. She was a petite, gregarious woman who spoke in a clear, authoritative voice, and she brought a pioneering spirit to her work. She was also something of a maverick. Her early studies refuted the gamma globulin hypothesis, and she had hunted and killed viral theories for years. "I was considered a debunker for some time," she remarked years later. By the 1963 conference, she had seen enough "healthy dead babies" in her pathology lab in Philadelphia's St. Christopher's Hospital for Children to know that the hardest thing to find was anything at all.

Dapena had, in fact, come to the meeting in the midst of trying to solve the country's most perplexing mystery of crib death, that of a couple in suburban Philadelphia who were losing baby after baby—seven in all since 1950. One was stillborn, but the rest, she told her colleagues in Seattle, had died between one and eight months of age. Nothing conclusive had been found in any of the autopsies. Only two months before, the family's run of tragedy had been chronicled in a sorrowful story in *Life* magazine: "Worn almost to gauntness, and stung by sharp-eyed stares from her neighbors, Martha Moore spent several days in the hospital this spring in an effort to build up her health and spirit and restore some sense of equilibrium. . . . Her eighth baby will be born this month."

The story about the pseudonymous Moore family reported that the case confounded Dapena and everyone else involved, and noted that the local district attorney had investigated and found "nothing to indicate any criminality." The couple was questioned, as were their neighbors, doctors, and hospital personnel. "The house was clean and well-heated," said the police report. "The crib was clean and had a sheet on it." The case seemed to contradict Adelson's assertion that familial recurrence was not a characteristic of crib death. To the doctors gathered in Seattle, it was an extreme and particularly affecting example of how much work needed to be done.

Theories proposing to explain this mysterious, fatal malady burgeoned after Seattle. Epidemiologists found that babies who died came from homes where parents smoked more often than not. Some researchers suggested that because infants breathed through their noses, a common cold could be enough to block breathing and cause a baby to suffocate. Warren Guntheroth, one of the early researchers recruited by Mary Dore, wondered if the key lay in respiration, and some of his Seattle colleagues massaged their suspicion that a sudden airway blockage was part of the picture. Meanwhile, researchers pondered why there seemed to be more sudden infant deaths among mothers who were young as well as poor. To some it suggested that inadequate prenatal care might be a factor; others thought a vaguely defined notion of poor mothering could contribute to the death of a fragile newborn.

So many new hunches were tossed about in the years following the 1963 meeting that by 1969 a second international meeting was organized by doctors from Seattle and underwritten once again by the National Institute of Child Health and Human Development. By this point, state funds and private donations had made Seattle's Children's Orthopedic Hospital the home of the country's leading research project, and two doctors in particular—Abraham Bergman, a pediatrician, and J. Bruce Beckwith, a pediatric pathologist—had emerged as two of the most vigorous voices in the field. To Beckwith and Bergman, this was nothing short of a righteous battle, but one in desperate need of direction. That's why they had big plans for the second conference. If the work of the previous few years showed anything, it was that the disciplines involved—pediatrics, pathology, epidemiology, and virology—saw the unexplained deaths of babies from sharply different angles. They didn't even call it the same thing. Pediatricians tended to use Sudden Death Syndrome or the traditional crib death, while some virologists used Sudden Unexpected Death, or SUD. In Britain, cot death was preferred. This time, Beckwith and Bergman resolved, researchers would leave with a definition of sudden infant death that would allow medical examiners, pediatricians, and researchers throughout the world to start speaking the same language.

Beckwith was a pathologist who, like most people who became gripped by the mystery of crib death in these years, had entered this little room of medicine through the back door. A poised and earnest man, he was raised in a minuscule town in the foothills of the Montana Rocky Mountains where, he liked to say, he was part of the upper crust because the floors in his family's house were not made of dirt. He was the only member of his high school class to go to college, let alone medical school. He cherished the ancient medical scholars, and had learned Latin, German, and Italian in order to study their writings. The manuscript room of the British Museum was one of his favorite places on earth.

In the spring of 1958, during his last year of medical school in Seattle, Beckwith was asked to look after a pregnant American Indian woman whose first child had congenital heart disease. One night several months after her second baby was born, the woman called Beckwith saying the infant had a cold. It sounded like nothing serious, so he asked if she could wait until the next day to come in. Early the following morning, the woman called in tears. She had found her baby dead in his crib. "The coroner's office diagnosed interstitial pneumonitis," Beckwith remembered. "And of course, I felt horrible. I thought I had basically killed a baby by ignoring viral pneumonia. And then I looked at the microscope slides and I said, gee, there really isn't that much pneumonia. How does that kill? The coroner said, 'We see a lot of babies like this.' I didn't realize it until many years later—I felt so guilty about it that I just put it in my subconscious—but this was the point where my soul became part of the SIDS story."

His conscious involvement started two years after the death of that baby, during his residency at Children's Hospital in Los Angeles. A father of two, he was moonlighting nights and weekends in the L.A. County coroner's office and realized he was signing out two or three babies a week to interstitial pneumonitis. It was just part of the job, he was told by one of the assistant medical examiners, a young forensic pathologist named Thomas Noguchi who was teaching him how to do autopsies for criminal cases. "Once you've done one of these babies," said the pathologist, who would later join the ranks of the celebrity medical examiners, "you've done them all. They all look the same." Curious, Beckwith started going through the records. He found that the coroner's office was signing out three hundred dead infants a year and calling them, for lack of something better, victims of pneumonia. Almost every day a baby was dying mysteriously somewhere in Los Angeles County, yet despite this diagnosis, most had, if anything, only a hint of bacterial infection. What Beckwith did notice when he performed the autopsies was that many of these babies had tiny bleeding points called *petechiae,* which looked like spots of cayenne pepper, spread over the surface of the chest organs.

Beckwith wondered if the petechiae were produced when the baby tried to take deep breaths against some obstruction in the airway. But he couldn't find the obstruction.

One day in the lab, he happened to be holding the larynx of one of these babies, and noticed how small the air passageway was, how easy it was to close off, especially if the head was in the wrong position. He wondered if a sudden spasm of the larynx could cause the airway to close long enough for a baby to suffocate. "I got intrigued that maybe I had an answer to crib death. I guess everybody who gets involved probably has a theory and gets excited about it. I started calling parents because I needed to have a lot of information. And I discovered a couple of things. One, these babies were almost always on their tummies. Very few exceptions to that. And two, I realized how important it was to be calling these parents, because if I hadn't, there was nobody talking to them. I'd been doing this for about three years, doing my autopsies, filling out my death certificates, feeling pretty good about myself, and I realized I'd been completely insensitive to the fact that the real consumers of our diagnoses out there were these families. It was important for someone to tell them, 'We have three hundred babies a year dying this way. You're not alone. And your baby did die of something. We don't understand it, but it is a medical problem and it's not your fault.' "

Beckwith was hooked. In 1964, he moved back to Seattle to teach at the University of Washington Medical School and become the first pediatric pathologist on staff at Children's Orthopedic Hospital. The grant that Mary and Fred Dore had brought to the university helped Beckwith begin his own research. It also allowed him to do right by all those parents. In this, Beckwith was sometimes at odds with those of his fellow pathologists who were medical examiners—forensic pathologists like New York's Milton Helpern, who, in Beckwith's view, believed that real crib death only happened to doctors' babies, most of the rest being victims of either neglect or homicide. "We had a lively correspondence," Beckwith later remembered.

Abe Bergman was a Seattle native who had arrived at the university the same year as Beckwith after a decade-long tour of medical training that took him to Cleveland, Boston, London, and Syracuse, New York. Bergman was a teaching pediatrician who had begun practicing what he called "political medicine" in behalf of children, traveling regularly between Washington State and Washington, D.C., to instigate national legislation such as the Flammable Fabrics Act Amendments and the Poison Prevention Packaging Act. Thirty-seven years old, a father of two, Bergman had been drawn into the mystery of sudden infant death by the growing preoccupation of his Seattle colleagues.

Beckwith in particular guided Bergman's early interest in crib death, and by 1969, they and virologist C. George Ray were a prominent team looking at the problem from all the angles. Bergman's main research interest was the epidemiology—how many babies died, when they died, what they had in common. He found it remarkable that crib death did not claim the tiniest babies, but seemed to begin to strike around the third week of life, occurred most often between the second and fourth months, and then began to wane, rarely striking after six months. The more he thought about these facts, the more time he spent with the numbers, the less abstract they became. He, too, felt for the parents, very often people in their twenties who were especially ill-equipped to handle the devastation. He began to see them as a tragic, unseen subculture in America, and felt that his role should be in helping them cope, first with the powerful grief and then with the inevitable realization that nobody could tell them why their babies had died. He hoped that some day soon this would no longer be the case.

By 1969, having pieced together a patchwork of anguished families from across the country, Bergman was firmly established as a professional crib-death guru—the parents' advocate in the medical establishment. He found it deeply disturbing that the vast majority of babies who died before their first birthday fell into this black hole of sudden unexplained death, yet the government of the United States was committing almost no money to exploring it, much less conquering it. No wonder, he thought, so many of the parents he talked to were haunted by self-doubt: "Did I kill my baby? Did I do something wrong?" That kind of thinking had to go. No parent should be held responsible for a crib death, Bergman fervently believed. Much less criminally blamed.

He was forever grateful to the pioneering pathologists of the late 1940s and 1950s, such as Cleveland's Lester Adelson, whose early suggestions of infection as the cause of many crib deaths had largely dispelled widely held notions of suffocation and neglect, at least among doctors. There was a certain irony in this, for in the summer of 1961, Adelson had published a disturbing and much-discussed article in the *The New England Journal of Medicine* titled "Slaughter of the Innocents." It was a study of forty-six probable homicides of babies and small children, going back to 1944, that he had found in the files of the Cuyahoga County coroner's office.

It seemed likely to Bergman and his colleagues in Seattle that infection was only part of the picture, perhaps one of a series of triggers. But even if the early pathologists turned out to be wrong about infection, they had opened the market to new ideas. That was good, Bergman thought. He saw sudden infant death as, literally, political science; the way to attack the science was to first do the politics: to raise consciousness, and then money. Support had to come from the federal government, and the fires of inquisition had to be lit under some of the nation's better scientists. What crib death needed was what every legitimate scientific quest needed: an "organized search for knowledge involving repetitive, laborious work," as Bergman once described it, policed by the honest review of peers. That's what he, Beckwith, and Ray hoped would emerge from the 1969 meeting.

They planned the conclave for a remote place, an island in North Puget Sound, and put together an impressive list of twenty-seven pathologists, pediatricians, and epidemiologists from the United States, Canada, and Europe, along with some notable guests from the ranks of the growing parents' movement. Mary Dore would be there, as would Sylvia and Saul Goldberg, a couple from Maryland who had lost their baby daughter to crib death in 1963. Jedd and Louise Roe would not be present. Two years before, they had left their foundation in the custody of Ann and Arthur Siegal, SIDS parents in New York who owned an advertising agency and offered to run it from their offices. With the assent of the Roes, who never wanted to build a monument to their son, the Siegals changed the group's name to the National Foundation for Sudden Infant Death.

A light rain fell from the gray northwestern sky as Bergman and Beckwith welcomed the researchers and parents on a dock at Bellingham, Washington, twenty miles south of British Columbia. A captain from the Armed Forces Institute of Pathology was there, along with the deputy chief of the federal Neurological and Sensory Disease Control Program. A pediatrics professor from Czechoslovakia stood with the state pathologist of Belfast, Ireland. There was an immunochemist from Baltimore, a biostatistician from Seattle, and a virologist from Case Western Reserve named Frederick Robbins who was a Nobel laureate. The group boarded a small ferry that would bring them to Orcas Island, a venerable resort in the San Juan Islands housing little more than an ornate hotel, the Rosario, that had seen better days. The Second International Conference on Causes of Sudden Death in Infants was not going to be just another medical meeting.

"A good title for this entity should be short and euphonious," Bruce Beckwith declared in the opening minutes on Orcas Island, "sufficiently descriptive to prevent confusion with other types of sudden death, and readily comprehensible to laypersons." Sudden Death Syndrome, which the Seattle doctors had been using since 1963, was the first proposal. "Syndrome" signified the presence of a set of symptoms and characteristics, rather than a specific, identifiable disease process, though Beckwith noted that a name whose acronym was SDS might be a problem, since those initials "are at the present time popularly used for a militant student group." He suggested the word *infant* be inserted.

"I should, therefore, like to cast my vote for the term Sudden Infant Death Syndrome, or SIDS."

After several other proposals and a lengthy debate, the group agreed to accept Beckwith's idea, and hammered out the first official definition of SIDS: *The sudden death of any infant or young child, which is unexpected by history, and in which a thorough postmortem examination fails to demonstrate an adequate cause of death.*

At the very least, the new definition was precise in its imprecision. It would give medical examiners, coroners, and hospital pathologists something uniform to write on death records—and something to tell parents—when they found nothing else. Not pneumonia. Not unknown or unexplained. SIDS would be a way for doctors to rule out every possible medical explanation and still leave parents with the impression that their babies had died of *something*. It would become the proverbial wastebasket diagnosis.

Having settled on a name, the doctors shifted from style to substance. Molly Dapena stepped up to the podium and led the group on a tour of the research that had been conducted since the 1963 conference. All told, she reported, twelve researchers had proposed new hypotheses, or new versions of old ones, in the past six years: everything from electrolyte imbalances to parathyroid inadequacy, from nasal obstruction to a slew of new takes on bacterial infection. One researcher suggested stress as a cause, and another had an even more adventurous theory—one so repugnant that no one at the meeting dared explore it. A year before, Stuart Asch, a New York psychiatrist, had published a paper proposing that a specific version of infanticide—murder at the hands of mothers consumed by extreme cases of postpartum depression—was an unrecognized cause of some sudden infant deaths.

The inclusion of Asch's theory on Dapena's list wasn't the only time such a repellent thought was broached. Dapena herself took a passing glance at the issue of whether infanticide played a role in SIDS. It came as a coda to the discussion of epidemiology, when Bergman raised the possibility of a genetic predisposition to crib death. "When laypersons inquire about inheritance factors, I state that at the present time there is no evidence that SIDS runs in families," Bergman said. "They then frequently ask about the seven members of one family in Philadelphia who were alleged to die suddenly and unexpectedly. This case received a great deal of attention in the lay press; it was never reported in the scientific press."

"I'm familiar with that particular family," Dapena volunteered. All eyes turned to her. This was the story of "Martha Moore" published in *Life* shortly before the 1963 conference. In the six years since, the family had gone on to lose three more children, bringing the total to ten. Meanwhile, stories in newspapers and magazines had continued to present the bizarre string of deaths as a baffling phenomenon. The Philadelphia medical examiner had ruled out a number of possible causes—including "the notion that the children were in some way murdered," *Newsweek* reported a week after the tenth death, early in 1968. But Dapena had some startling news for her colleagues on Orcas Island: "Dr. Joseph Spelman, the chief medical examiner of the city of Philadelphia, has concluded that these children did *not* die of SIDS," she announced. "However, because of legal implications, we are not at liberty to report the results of his investigation."

It was perhaps the most provocative remark to be heard at the conference, but Dapena's revelation was met only by uncomfortable silence and two dozen blank stares. By this point, despite their statements to the press, Spelman and members of the Philadelphia police believed the "Moores" had in fact killed their children—for insurance payoffs. Now the authorities were privately battling over whether they could make a murder case without any physical evidence. But none of this information about the world's most famous case of familial crib death was revealed. Much to Dapena's relief, no questions were asked, and the agenda moved on to pathological anatomy.

Absorbing the speculations of the experts, one of the newcomers to the group recognized that, alas, nobody here really had a clue why babies died suddenly. Much as he loved statistics, he concluded the answer would not come from the epidemiologists, nor did the pathologists and virologists and immunologists seem to have any promising leads. It wasn't their fault, he thought, and it was laudable that they had the integrity to admit their ignorance. But after listening patiently for nearly two days, Alfred Steinschneider, a thirty-nine-year-old pediatric researcher who had flown across the country from Syracuse, New York, was anxious to let the group know what he thought. He was not a crib death researcher, but he had come with what he thought was a pretty good idea. He was the fifteenth of sixteen presenters.

"We need an explanation for SIDS," he said when his turn finally came at the podium late the second afternoon, a prelude to proffering his own theory. "There is little doubt in my own mind that an abnormally intense and persistent autonomic nervous system discharge, in an otherwise normal individual, can result in sudden death."

Hearing Steinschneider discuss the *otherwise normal* baby, Abe Bergman listened closely. This was precisely why he had invited Steinschneider to the conference. A pediatrician with a doctorate in psychology to go with his M.D., Steinschneider had gone to medical school and served his internship and pediatric residency at New York's Upstate Medical Center earlier in the decade. Bergman had spent a year there as a pediatric fellow and had come to

admire Steinschneider's research skills, especially his agility with statistics—
he'd never met anybody in medicine with a better head for numbers. Steinschneider had stayed in Syracuse after his residency and had become devoted
to the study of the infant nervous system, publishing papers at a ferocious pace
in the process—nearly two dozen by the time of this meeting. Bergman had
followed his work and thought his research might bear directly on the matter
at hand. If sudden infant death was caused by some unseen abnormality, who
better to explore the question than an expert in what was *normal*? And who
better to research the question on a large scale than a man who was just ter-
rific with numbers? Finally, there was the hotly debated question of whether
crib death actually had something to do with cribs. Steinschneider had made a
specialty of hooking up premature newborns to innovative laboratory monitors and recording their heart rates and respiration as they slept in their Isolettes. When Bergman invited Steinschneider to Orcas Island, he was hoping
to entice him to shift his focus slightly—to join the battle to unlock, and perhaps someday prevent, the mysterious baby killer that so absorbed him.

Steinschneider had a large, engrossed face darkened by the shadow of
heavy stubble, thick, jet-black hair with sideburns that dipped just below the
ears, and black-rimmed glasses. Though a few years younger and a few
pounds lighter, he bore a resemblance to the actor Michael Constantine, who
appeared on Wednesday nights as the put-upon but eternally patient high
school principal on the television show *Room 222*. The resemblance, however,
applied to physical bearing, not temperament. Steinschneider was animated,
jocular, and intensely opinionated. Back in Syracuse, many people found him
a compelling if sometimes overstrung presence.

Steinschneider was no expert in sudden infant death, but he did know as
much as anyone at the table how young babies lived and breathed. His specialty was the autonomic nervous system, a part of the central nervous system
that controls the most vital, involuntary body functions: breathing, digestion,
sweating, salivating, heartbeat. Steinschneider's studies had made him inti-
mately familiar with the periodic pauses in respiration—apnea—that all
young babies experienced as they adjusted to life outside the womb. He told
the group that it was this work in Syracuse that had led him to suspect that in
some infants, an "abnormally intense" nervous system could bring on severe
and possibly dangerous disturbances of heart, lung, and blood vessel function.

One premature baby in particular had gotten him to thinking this way. It
was a newborn boy with many periods of apnea who had spent much of his
first three months in the hospital. In his lab, Steinschneider found that the
baby's heart rate and respiratory function changed abruptly even during as
normal an activity as sucking on a bottle. These studies, he told the group, led
him to consider a stark possibility: Something as benign as a feeding "could

initiate in a predisposed infant cardiac and respiratory abnormalities of sufficient magnitude to threaten his very life."

Although Steinschneider's studies focused on premature babies—who
were known to experience more apnea than full-term infants—it was easy for
him to imagine a similar set of circumstances for the general population of
newborns. After a lengthy presentation, complete with charts and graphs
showing such things as respiration during defecation and heart rates during
hiccups, he told the group that his data, while "far from sufficient" to under-
write a theory of SIDS, suggested a link that ought to be looked at closely. "I
advocate a concentrated research effort," he said, exploring the possible relationship between sudden infant death and cardiopulmonary functioning.

Warren Guntheroth, for one, was delighted by Steinschneider's presentation. The pediatric cardiologist had first proposed a respiratory abnormality
back in 1963. He believed that the normal respiratory center, which slows
during sleep, might be pathologically depressed in some newborns, putting
them at risk for death. All babies had apnea; maybe some simply never
emerged from these episodes. He thought Steinschneider's experience advanced this line of thinking nicely.

"What could be done, if this were the case, in prevention or treatment?"
Guntheroth asked rhetorically during his own presentation a while later. "I
know that Dr. Bergman finds this a repellent thought"—he glanced at his
fellow Seattle pediatrician—"but a portable monitor would be very inexpensive, and a patient who is at risk and who had a respiratory infection, for
example, could have a small monitor. This may cause a great many neuroses,
but at least it is a possibility of doing something in terms of prevention."

As Guntheroth anticipated, Bergman found this suggestion disturbing.
Passing out monitors implied that parents could *do something* to prevent crib
death. There was, at the moment, no evidence that they could. The next
logical assumption was that if the baby did die, it was their fault. A great
many neuroses indeed. While Bergman thought there was merit in a theory
that respiratory abnormality was a factor in SIDS, a monitor took the idea
way beyond the available science, while setting parents up for more than the
usual guilt.

Another physician in the room was even more disconcerted. Listening to
Steinschneider and then Guntheroth, Dr. Dwain Walcher found the entire
line of thought troubling. A pediatrician who headed an institute on human
development at Penn State, he was one of the most influential people at the
meeting. He had recently left a ranking position at NICHD, where he had
spent six years trying to foster the country's crib death research despite the
absence of a specific budget for the purpose. The shortage of grant money,
and the fact that so much was unknown, made it a tough sell to the scientific

community. But Walcher had guided such research as there was with what Bergman judged a discerning scientific mind and a deft bureaucratic hand. He and Beckwith liked to refer to Walcher as "the godfather" of crib death investigation.

Walcher had no idea who Steinschneider was, but he was wary of what he was hearing. Connecting a bottle feeding to the threat of death seemed a flying leap, though this in itself was not what troubled him. Rather, it was Steinschneider's call for a "concentrated research effort" in pursuit of his theory. The research gatekeeper in Walcher found this arrogant. Whoever this man was, Walcher thought, he had obviously come to this meeting without much appreciation for the communal nature of the scientific process. Given that crib death research was so marginally funded, you just didn't commit an entire research strategy to a theory that had barely been considered, let alone tested. Moreover, Guntheroth's suggestion of monitors struck Walcher as a dangerous, even irresponsible, invitation to medical profiteers. When Guntheroth finished, Walcher's astringent voice filled the room.

"I would like to know from Dr. Steinschneider," he said, "if a baby displaying some of these cardiovascular irregularities you have recorded has actually gone on to die."

"The baby that I described did not go on to die," Steinschneider conceded. "What did happen was that these episodes decreased. He was in the hospital for an additional two weeks and did well. He was home, I think, for four or five days when the parents noted he was acting 'funny' and then suddenly stopped breathing. They resuscitated him and brought him back to the hospital. The father made a very interesting observation. He said that the only thing different about that weekend was that it was very hot. . . . Following up on that observation, we watched the baby asleep when we had the room temperature down to seventy-five degrees and also up to ninety degrees. For what it's worth, the baby showed periodic breathing only at the higher temperature. As to what the significance of this is, I really don't know. . . ."

Walcher listened with growing impatience as Steinschneider continued to elaborate on his work.

"Have you observed *any* infant with apneic spells," he persisted, "who subsequently died of the Sudden Infant Death Syndrome?"

"No," Steinschneider said uncomfortably.

Guntheroth tried to rescue him. "We have observed close calls in two prematures who had apneic spells at home and were resuscitated," he offered.

What troubled Walcher, and also Dr. Thomas James, a physician from the University of Alabama, was that Steinschneider and Guntheroth seemed to be ignoring an obvious point. "*All* babies have this instability," James reminded the group. "Some have it more markedly than others, but relative autonomic instability is a characteristic of the newborn in the first few months."

Still, a number of the researchers thought that these "near-misses," as some were calling episodes in which babies were resuscitated, might well have something to do with those who did go on to die. The chief medical examiner of Maryland, Dr. Russell Fisher, said he had seen two cases of babies brought into hospitals in Baltimore by frantic parents saying their children were not breathing. "After a relatively short period of appearing normal, the children were sent home," Fisher said. "Within a week, both were listed as crib deaths."

Bergman had seen the same thing in Seattle. "There is no reason why 'near-misses' should not exist," he said. "At present, however, we have no means of predicting or identifying such cases. The only certain cases exist on the autopsy table."

Listening to the proceedings on Orcas Island, Sylvia and Saul Goldberg were a long way from the simple surburban life they had once envisioned. They had married in 1952 and settled in Baltimore, where Saul joined a two-man ad agency and Sylvia went to work for a radiologist. Their first child, Ann, was born in 1959, Michele a year later, and Suzanne in the fall of 1963. Packing their gaggle of little girls into the backseat of their white Mercury Comet, the Goldbergs were the very image of an American family deep in the baby boom. One night when Suzanne was two months old, she woke her parents for a midnight feeding. The Goldbergs fed her, then played with her on their bed, taking a few pictures with their Instamatic before putting her back in her crib. Suzanne was wide-eyed when they kissed her good night. These were simple moments like a thousand others, but they would forever be fixed in time. The next afternoon, Sylvia put the baby in her carriage and rolled her out in the backyard for some air. She was on the telephone for a few minutes and returned to find her daughter limp and unconscious. She tried blowing air into her baby's mouth, then screamed for help.

A few hours later, at the hospital, the Goldbergs were told about a mystery called crib death. The doctors were sympathetic but helpless. Not long after, the Goldbergs chartered the Guild for Infant Survival, the first organized parent support group, and went to see medical examiner Russell Fisher. He set up a foundation to accept contributions and assured the Goldbergs that crib death would be a primary focus of his office. Eventually they helped him build and equip a wing of his building for research.

Even more than the Roes, more than the Dores, the Goldbergs became gripped by this cause. It was the activist 1960s, and this became their singular battle—to "conquer crib death," whatever it took. Death became their life, and other parents' pain their burden. For Saul Goldberg, a tall, studious-looking man with dark-rimmed glasses, it was a kind of holy war, with advertising. Looking on from Seattle, Mary Dore felt a worrisome clash of style: "Saul was going to sell this like Ivory soap. He was hell-bent on spreading the word, and he didn't care about the scientific method." When the Goldbergs invited Molly Dapena to Baltimore to give a talk to their group, and she mentioned that the epidemiology showed a higher rate of sudden infant death among the poor—she had made a map of Philadelphia showing more cases in the least affluent sections of town—the Goldbergs let her know they were deeply offended by her inference.

As newspaper and magazine stories about the Goldbergs' efforts spread, letters from grieving parents poured in. Anybody who called was asked to head a new chapter, and soon another group of Guild parents would be meeting in somebody's living room, talking about fund-raising, new research, and publicizing the cause. In 1968, Barbara Walters invited Sylvia to appear on the *Today* show. *Life* came out to take pictures. Over and over, the Goldbergs told their story. "What I will always hear is what the doctor said to me when I reached the hospital where the ambulance had taken Suzanne: 'Your baby is dead,'" Sylvia told the *Ladies' Home Journal*. By 1969, the Guild had affiliates all over the country. Chapters were starting up in Africa and India. The Goldbergs helped draw support for the second international conference. They made sure Fisher was on the list of invited guests and paid his way.

The meeting on Orcas Island was a milestone for the Goldbergs. From the beginning, they had campaigned for federal research money, and they were starting to engage in a pitched battle with the Department of Health, Education, and Welfare, whose inaction would come to frustrate and embitter them. But for now they were exhilarated to be mingling with the biggest names in crib death research and to listen to the serious discussion about where the hunt should go from here. Much of what they heard during this marathon of presentations was a haze of medical arcana. But the Goldbergs were there not so much to learn as to bear witness. They felt, in a real sense, that they represented what all this was really about: the parents. There seemed no doubt that progress was being made. The thing that killed their daughter six years ago now had an official name and a legion of scientists was on the case.

"In 1969," Bergman said optimistically at the end of the conference, "we can say that Sudden Infant Death Syndrome is a definable disease. It can no longer be called a mystery killer. It is a real disease every bit as much as cancer is a disease. We do not know the cause, but it can be readily diagnosed and the aura of mystery removed."

Brought together on this isolated island, the group had made its way through a thicket of theories, and conceived scientific, political, and personal relationships that would evolve for many years. Molly Dapena, the veteran,

thought Beckwith was smart, well-balanced, and thorough, a fellow pathologist with high standards. She thought Bergman was a bundle of energy, if a bit
impetuous. She thought the newcomer, Alfred Steinschneider, was a serious
researcher with some interesting ideas, along with plenty of passion. For the
first time, she felt the winds of progress at her back.

A brisk nor'wester buffeted the ferry as it made its way back to the main-
land, but the SIDS group was too ebullient to notice the storm. As Peter Froggatt, an epidemiologist from Belfast, would later remember, "The mood of
anticipation approached suppressed euphoria, or even unsuppressed euphoria
in some cases." Rocking their way across Puget Sound, the doctors and parents left the retreat energized by the possibility that someday soon, perhaps in
one of the two dozen laboratories to which the researchers were returning,
one of the new ideas would emerge as the breakthrough that might reveal the
answer to what everyone could now officially call SIDS.

18

Alfred Steinschneider flew home from Seattle astonished by what he had just heard. He had never realized that so many seemingly healthy babies were dying mysteriously. Most of his work to date, most of the research he had published, had been so focused on how the mechanisms of new life worked that he had not noticed how often they failed. For him, Orcas Island was an epiphany.

Steinschneider had some thoughts on the subject of sudden infant death, but he knew the ideas he'd presented at the meeting were only by-products of his work on the infant nervous system—as Dwain Walcher had demonstrated, swipes and hunches tossed up by a novice in the field. Now, returning to Syracuse, he was struck by the realization that SIDS was the place to be in pediatric research. Thousands of babies were dying every year. There had to be a way of saving them. Abe Bergman's plan had worked: Of all the participants at the 1969 meeting, it would be hard to find anyone on whom the proceedings had a more powerful impact than Al Steinschneider.

At this stage of his career, Steinschneider was virtually on his own in his research pursuits. His first mentor at Upstate Medical Center, Dr. Earle Lipton, had died in 1965, and Lipton's research partner, Dr. Julius Richmond, to whom Steinschneider was also close, was busy running the bustling pediatrics department and serving as dean of the medical faculty. Richmond was a nationally prominent academic pediatrician and health policy expert who, a few years later, would be appointed the nation's Surgeon General. In Syracuse he had created a flourishing, close-knit community in pediatric research, and few had taken better advantage of the creative climate, or benefited more from Richmond's intellectual largesse, than Steinschneider. Now, a fresh opportunity beckoned. Returning home from Orcas Island, he told Richmond that he wanted to close down the pediatric psychosomatic clinic he was running and devote himself to exploring Sudden Infant Death Syndrome. "When do you want to do this?" Richmond asked. "Monday," said Steinschneider. "Then do it," said Richmond.

Though trained as a pediatrician, Steinschneider had never aspired to be a clinical physician. Even as a teenager, he knew that his calling was research. "Alfred was a very determined child," his sister, Toby, remembered. "He was born determined. He always wanted his way. He was going to go to medical school, but he said, 'Don't expect me to carry a bag. I'm not going to be a doctor. I'm going to do research.' And when Alfred made up his mind, he made up his mind. You didn't push him."

Steinschneider and his two older siblings, Toby and their brother Max, grew up in a household like thousands of others in the ethnic pockets of prewar New York City. They watched their father, Charlie, a voracious reader who had come from Austria and settled in Brooklyn, spend nearly his whole life painting and papering the walls of apartments and row houses. Their mother, Molly, who was born in Poland, sat on a stool in their apartment placing tiny rubber tips on the wire ribs of umbrellas, tedious piecework that had helped the family survive the Depression. Like many of their time and place, the Steinschneiders pushed their children to achieve. Max later decided that one of the ways to do this was to change the family name to Stone. He made the arrangement for himself and went into the retail food business, but his younger brother took the suggestion as an affront. "I'm Alfred Steinschneider," he said.

Alfred Steinschneider's road to success would be a learning curve. Enrolling in New York University in the fall of 1947, he embarked on an academic journey that was to last the better part of two decades, financed by his father's sweat and fueled by his own overriding ambition to be not just Alfred Steinschneider, but Alfred Steinschneider, M.D. He graduated with a degree in psychology from NYU in 1950, expecting to move on immediately to medical school. But to his crushing disappointment, his applications were rejected. As he related it to his sister, he believed he was the victim of a quota system—prevalent at that time—limiting the number of openings available to Jewish applicants. He wrote letters to the admissions committees, but failed to change their minds.

Putting his ambition aside for the moment, Steinschneider married his first love, Roz Glassman, and applied to graduate school. Roz and Al had dazzled each other almost from the moment they met as students at Brooklyn's Abraham Lincoln High School. "He grew on me very quickly," Roz once said. "He had such goodness and integrity." Also a child of immigrants, she was gregarious, energetic, and completely infatuated with her husband, who returned the sentiment openly and often. Years later, she would say that the three things she could always count on were "death, taxes, and Al's love."

They went west to the University of Missouri for Al's master's degree, and then two years later—Roz having had enough of the Midwest—back east, to Ithaca and the doctoral program at Cornell University. Steinschneider settled into the world of experimental psychology, spending the next three years testing theories of human behavior with J. J. Gibson, a prominent psychologist noted for his research in depth perception. Exploring a subdiscipline known as experimental psychopathology, he studied the nuances of human drive and determination, and one of the things he learned from watching rats scurry around their cages was that too much focus could sometimes be blinding. He made it the subject of his doctoral dissertation. "Every member of the department wanted a copy," Roz later recalled, her pride undiminished by the years. She reveled in her husband's intellect and his burning ambition.

He still dreamed of becoming a doctor one day, but at twenty-five and a new father, Steinschneider concluded that he could not delay earning a living. He found a job right on the Cornell campus. General Electric had opened a kind of commercial think tank it called the Advanced Electronics Center, and it was Steinschneider's job to help engineers design user-friendly equipment, chiefly for the military. His job title was "human engineer." In some sense, he was like a lab rat. He would imagine himself a bomber pilot, for instance, and help the engineers design an instrument panel conducive to the tasks of the Cold War. There were meetings. "What's the hit rate?" someone would ask. And somebody else would answer, "Oh, you don't have to hit the plane. If you explode *near* the plane, you'll blind the pilot and he'll crash." Steinschneider hated the meetings. After three years, he resolved to try for medical school once more.

This time, he set his sights on two New York schools: the Albert Einstein Medical College in New York City and the state university medical school in Syracuse, about an hour's drive north of Ithaca. Einstein rejected him—they wanted younger students, he concluded—but Syracuse made him a very happy man. Charlie Steinschneider, the immigrant who worked hard with his hands all his life so his American children could work with their heads, rewarded his son's diligence by promising that he would pay for his medical education. Alfred Steinschneider was going to be a medical doctor at last.

The State University of New York's Upstate Medical School had once been part of Syracuse University, but in the early 1950s, when Governor Thomas Dewey decided his state needed more medical schools, rather than start up brand-new schools he had the state government buy three existing ones—in Brooklyn, Buffalo, and Syracuse—and made them, along with the hospitals they came with, part of the SUNY system. Arriving in the fall of 1957, Steinschneider was confident he had come to the right place. Syracuse was attracting major young talent to its medical faculty and gaining as a research center. He was undecided about a specialty, but psychiatry was the early, natural front-runner.

Steinschneider enrolled in a seminar for first-year students that was team-taught by members of the medical faculty from various departments. Among these were the pediatrics department's star research partners, the chairman Julius Richmond and his protégé Earle Lipton. A man of high accomplishment early in his career, Richmond was only thirty-seven when he was lured from the University of Illinois, and Lipton had followed him east. By the time Steinschneider arrived in Syracuse, the two men were a widely known team, publishing numerous papers in an area of pediatrics that they themselves were defining: the study of the newborn.

Steinschneider was stimulated by the seminars, and he found the pediatric professors especially engaging—more so than the professors of psychiatry. It seemed to him that Richmond and Lipton lived in a marvelous world of cerebral adventure, of questioning and discovery. In turn, Richmond and Lipton noticed Steinschneider, who was distinguished both by his age—at twenty-eight, he was five or six years older than most of his classmates, and only three years younger than Lipton—and by his background and personality. He not only had a doctorate in psychology with a grounding in research, but he was also clearly a young man with ambition. At the close of a seminar near the end of the academic year, Lipton asked Steinschneider if he'd be interested in a summer research position. He needed someone with a background in statistics and research design.

Steinschneider thrived on the lab life, fascinated by his mentors' ongoing exploration of the physiological differences in newborns. At the summer's end, with classes about to resume, Steinschneider asked Richmond if he could continue working in the lab part-time. Richmond agreed, and said he would pay him an hourly wage. A few weeks into the fall semester, as Steinschneider was racking up the hours, Richmond called him into his office. "It's not working," Richmond said. "Your primary commitment has to be to medical school, and if you have an exam coming up, you ought to be preparing for that, not stealing time to earn a living." Steinschneider explained that it wasn't just that he needed the money. He loved working in the lab. Richmond offered him a deal: He'd pay him every two weeks whether he had worked or not. He could make up the time on holidays and weekends. Richmond was the sort of administrator who tried to recognize and encourage talent, and Steinschneider felt lucky to be one of the chosen. He soon decided that pediatric research, not psychiatry, was his future. Richmond and Lipton were teaching him that within the bodies of newborn babies were many secrets waiting to be discovered, clues about the developing person that remained relevant throughout life.

By 1960, his third year, Steinschneider was a co-author on publications with the two senior researchers. The tools of their trade were not stethoscopes and tongue depressors so much as big, clumsy, homemade machines whose gauges, alarms, and polygraph paper measured and recorded the cardiorespiratory performance of their test subjects, primarily prematures and healthy newborns waiting for foster placement. With Lipton leading the way, Syracuse was a leader in this new technology, and the machines became central to the team's work. The first model, developed by Lipton and a technician named Leo Walsh in 1957, used a small, temperature-sensitive bead that could be placed either in the nose or at the mouth to check the respiration of premature infants, who were especially vulnerable to spells of apnea. The bead sensed exchanges of cool and warm air that were then recorded electronically, setting off an alarm when respiration failed to occur. The raucous alarm, reminiscent of a foghorn, had two purposes: to startle the infant and summon a nurse. With their innovative monitors, Richmond and Lipton were also among the first to come up with the important finding that heart rates were so variable in newborns that it could not be said that one baby's was normal and another's not. Steinschneider, still a medical student, found himself part of one of the hottest research teams in pediatrics, a trio that would virtually define the physiology of the normal newborn. Their series of eight papers titled "Autonomic Function and the Neonate" became a staple of research journals in the early sixties. A definitive work, "The Autonomic Nervous System in Early Life," was published in *The New England Journal of Medicine* in 1965.

It was in these crucial early years of his medical career that Steinschneider absorbed, primarily from Lipton, the importance not only of research and discovery, but of putting the work on paper. To Lipton, scientific investigation was almost moot without dissemination. Steinschneider not only liked sharing what he knew, he took Lipton's philosophy a step further—sometimes to Lipton's frustration. No matter how incremental or ambiguous the findings, Steinschneider came to believe that if it was worth knowing, it was worth publishing. His aggressiveness sometimes left Lipton annoyed and exhausted.

Though Lipton found Steinschneider a little brash for his taste, Richmond saw a lot of raw talent and admired his drive. Steinschneider, meanwhile, was discovering that the universe of medical research was vast, and that an investigator could go as far as his imagination and energy took him. At one point, he and Lipton began taking measurements of babies swaddled in blankets, an ancient practice still used in many parts of the world. In 1961, at the height of the Cold War, Lipton and Richmond traveled to the Soviet Union to learn more about swaddling practices there. (The Soviets agreed only after the American doctors promised not to reveal the names of anyone they talked to.) They didn't take Steinschneider, but upon their return the research partners, along with their junior member, published a forty-six-page supplement to the prestigious journal *Pediatrics* on the history and future of swaddling. As Steinschneider always suspected and was now seeing firsthand, a doctor doing research could make his mark on the world in a way a clinician could not.

He also learned some basic lessons about science and money. By the time of his residency, pediatric research at Syracuse virtually owed its existence to the grants the federal government awarded each year to Richmond's department. The chairman had set up a small but innovative program called the Children's Clinical Research Center, or CCRC, and the money was a big part of what made it innovative. Before the 1960s, medical centers conducting clinical research used patients already in the hospital as their test subjects, tacking on a day or two to the patients' stay and allowing insurance companies to pick up the tab. But such research was scattershot and secondary to the government's own work at the National Institutes of Health. Under the Kennedy and Johnson administrations, NIH began subcontracting much of the country's research to hospitals—and opened the vault to pay for it. Small research centers began to sprout within the nation's large teaching hospitals. The CCRC at Syracuse, launched in 1963, was one of the first.

Though still a resident, Steinschneider's age and strong personality, his academic accomplishments, and the political advantages of his association with Richmond and Lipton allowed him to assume an unusually prestigious and authoritative role among his peers. Indeed, by this point, Richmond was by now a member of the research team in name only, leaving Steinschneider as Lipton's day-to-day partner. With the federal money that flowed through the CCRC, they pursued their studies in the clock tower atop Crouse-Irving Memorial Hospital, the looming Depression-era brick building that was at the heart of the medical center. Lipton had converted the space into a laboratory with a set of soundproof rooms, and stocked it with the latest innovations in monitoring equipment. What they didn't have, hospital technicians built for them. Steinschneider compensated for his lack of experience with enthusiasm, recruiting a steady stream of babies to the clock tower. His pitch to new parents was an offer they couldn't refuse: an opportunity to see how healthy their newborns were, and a chance to help doctors advance their understanding of how healthy babies differed physiologically from sick ones. No needle pricks. No invasive procedures. No cost. Just a few electrodes on the chest, some measurements on the monitor, and that would be it. The babies would be returned to their cribs in less than an hour.

Steinschneider loved the machines and worked closely with the technicians. He studied how the babies were affected by flickering light, sounds, images, even such basic activities as eating and sleeping. He delighted in poring over bits of data, calculating and analyzing the numbers, writing up the results. By the time he had finished his pediatric residency in 1964, his curriculum vitae included a remarkable twelve publications. In most, he was listed as the second or third author. But that was soon to change.

Earle Lipton was a quiet, sensitive man, with dark, curly hair and an uneven gait, a vestige of childhood polio. A meticulous, serious-minded teacher and researcher, he had grown up and gone to school in Chicago, where, during his internship, he had met and married Thelma Buhrow, a nurse at Cook County Hospital. She was a friendly and levelheaded woman, and she and Earle were a well-liked couple.

When it came to his work, Lipton was a man of high but fundamentally uncomplicated ambition. He wanted to learn, and he wanted to teach what he learned. So when his cousin Cyrus from Chicago hounded him to develop the baby monitors like a good American—"it's new, it's exciting—you'll make a *fortune*!"—Lipton demurred. "If I wanted to make money," he told his cousin, "I wouldn't be teaching in medical school." He was developing the monitor because it was worth doing and it satisfied him, he said, and besides, he worked for the State of New York. Profiting from work he was doing on time and with equipment paid for by the state would be unethical. Some people found their way around these things, but Earle Lipton was not going to be one of them.

At the beginning of the summer of 1965, Lipton fell into a deep, spiraling depression. He had suffered from clinical depression before, and though it was perhaps an effect and not a cause of this episode, his specific complaint now was that pressures were building at work. Steinschneider, who had finished his training and joined the research faculty the previous fall, was pushing to pick up the pace of their research, to publish even more. A symptom of Lipton's depression was a sudden, overwhelming onslaught of professional self-doubt: He felt he had not been able to live up to the model of his mentor, Richmond, nor could he match the energies of his own protégé. By July, he found it almost impossible to make it into the lab. Most days he stayed home.

Lipton went to see a psychiatrist he knew at the hospital. The doctor prescribed antidepressants and continued to see him, but in August, he left on vacation and referred Lipton to a colleague at Upstate, Dr. Thomas Szasz, a maverick Hungarian-born psychiatrist made famous by the controversial antipsychiatry book he had published in 1961, *The Myth of Mental Illness*. Szasz saw Lipton a few times, but he too was going on vacation. Another Upstate psychiatrist, Dr. John Ross, agreed to keep an eye on him.

One day, Thelma heard a strange noise coming from the bathroom. She found her husband trying to hang himself with a towel. She called Ross, who wanted Lipton to be hospitalized. Lipton refused. "I'm not going in there with all those crazy people," he said. But Thelma was relieved when Ross, a child psychiatrist who knew Lipton casually as a pediatric colleague, offered to let her husband stay with him for the night. Caring for their two young children, and tending to her husband's growing despair, she was exhausted as well as worried. She was also eager to have a professional watch him.

The next day, Thelma picked up her husband at Ross's house, but he grew more and more agitated through the day. When he agreed to spend another night with Ross, Thelma called Steinschneider and asked if he would drive them over. She didn't want to drive him alone. Then she called Julius Richmond's wife, Rhee, and asked if she would watch the two young Lipton children. "Tell Julie I'm sorry," Lipton said to Rhee before he left with Thelma and Steinschneider. When he got to Ross's house, Lipton kissed his wife good night and thanked Steinschneider for driving.

Early the next morning, Lipton seemed calm. Ross, judging the situation under control, decided he could safely leave his colleague alone while he went to the hospital to see to his patients. But at the hospital, Ross got a call from Thelma. Earle was supposed to call her at nine, and hadn't. She had phoned Ross's house and gotten no answer. Ross dashed home. He found Lipton in the basement. He had hanged himself with an electrical cord.

Lipton's suicide lingered in the clock tower. Steinschneider was deeply shaken by his mentor's sudden decline and haunting death. "How could I not have seen it coming?" he asked when he related the news to his sister, Toby.

His mentor's death had come at a point, however, when Steinschneider's career was on a swift, upward trajectory, and that fall, he was more driven than ever. He was about to start his second year on the pediatrics faculty, and he had a lot of research work planned. During the summer, as he, Roz, and their two children moved into a new house, the state university opened a new hospital catty-corner to Crouse-Irving Memorial, a mid-rise building at the foot of a steep urban hill whose modern window-and-panel architecture was a stark contrast to the forbidding brick fortress behind it.

The new hospital was designated the State University Hospital, though most people still called it Upstate Medical Center. The CCRC was installed in a corner of the fifth floor, one floor up from the pediatric ward. It was spacious and air-conditioned, had large windows between rooms to maximize observation by nurses and doctors, and had been designed to accommodate Lipton's cumbersome electronic monitoring equipment, which was now in Steinschneider's custody. A small, black, slightly incorrect nameplate appeared on the door of the unit: CHILDREN CLINICAL RESEARCH CENTER.

The new space was open to any member of the pediatrics staff interested in research: Write a proposal, get the protocols approved by the hospital's human experimentation committee, and the okay from Albert J. (Jack) Schneider, the pediatrician who managed the unit, and bring your patients to the corner nursery. There were five beds, a staff of nurses, no bills for patients—and plenty of room. To Jack Schneider's dismay, though, only a few members of the staff took advantage of the research opportunity. The money'll go away if we don't use it, he often warned, though it was also true that he had little regard for much of what *was* being done—"bullshit," as he later described the work of doctors whose research seemed to have no practical goal. (Hearing the disdain flowing from Schneider thirty years later, a visitor was moved to ask if he had considered most of the CCRC's research agenda junk. "As a matter of fact, yes," the retired doctor said with a wry grin. "And I was in charge of it.") Still, he thought at the time that there was no point in discouraging even the most obscure or dubious research. The money was there, at least until the government stopped sending it. Besides, Schneider believed in the general concept of the center. He needed the unit to do his own research.

His work focused on infant metabolic diseases. He used the CCRC to study children with phenylketonuria, or PKU, a congenital disorder that damages the nervous system and leads to severe mental retardation if not detected very early in infancy and corrected with a dietary adjustment. *That,* to Schneider, was research worth doing. He found it frustrating to spend his time trying to drum up research projects that he had no interest in. With many on the pediatrics staff, it was a futile effort. They were more interested in treating children than studying them.

The one exception, everyone knew, was Al Steinschneider. He was turning out a steady stream of papers, giving Lipton his share of the credit as first author until 1967, when his name appeared solo for the first time. It was at the head of a forty-seven-page chapter called "Developmental Psychophysiology" in a textbook on infancy and early childhood. Visiting his academic roots, he ran a psychosomatic clinic, where he would see children with a range of vague medical problems—asthma, headaches, stomach pain—symptoms he felt could have psychological underpinnings. In 1968, four years out of residency, he was promoted to associate professor of pediatrics, and was now a member of a slew of hospital committees: the Research Committee, the

Subcommittee for Respiration, the Advisory Committee on Inhalation Therapy, the Resuscitation Committee. A man who had been crushed by his rejections by medical schools years before was now interviewing applicants to Upstate as a member of the admissions committee. At Crouse-Irving, Steinschneider became director of nurseries and chairman of the perinatal committee. He was also starting to make a name for himself nationally. He was elected president of the medical school's chapter of the American Association of University Professors and was appointed to the editorial board of the prestigious Society for Research in Child Development.

Despite such expansive responsibilities, Steinschneider never lost an ounce of passion for intensive laboratory research, never became restless with the work Earle Lipton had set out for him. Exploring the volatile nervous systems of tiny babies, quantifying and evaluating them, ruminating on the inconsistencies—these were his true loves. The deal he had struck with Richmond when he joined the faculty was that he would teach and work in the lab. His clinical work would be minimal. For the most part, he would only see patients who might contribute something to his research. "Julius B. Richmond, God bless him, I love the man," Steinschneider reflected years later. "He wanted me to do what I wanted to do. That was the environment he created. He built an empire, but not for himself. And I was always one of the pampered ones." Lipton's death, emotionally wrenching though it was, had made Steinschneider a free bird, liberated his energies and ambitions.

He found it easy to become immersed in the kinds of questions Jack Schneider dismissed as absurdly abstract. He would bring a baby to the CCRC, hook the infant up to the monitor, and watch what happened when he gave him a bottle. He would repeat this procedure with dozens of babies until he had observed enough babies to conclude, as he later wrote, "The onset of sucking is associated with an increase in cardiac rate which reaches a peak and then decreases slightly even during the sucking burst." Then he would add the variable of room temperature. The babies would be given bottles with the thermostat set at 75 degrees, and then turned up to a sweltering 90. He would collate the results and painstakingly produce reams of data and endless graphs and charts. The meanings of these recordings would not be clear even to him, but he developed a flair for boldly suggesting plausible hypotheses, then presenting supporting data that he freely admitted were incomplete or inconclusive. The heart rate of a baby sucking on a bottle in a hot room was, he found, not much different from that of a baby feeding in a cooler room. "Thus," he wrote with perhaps a hint of frustration, "once again we find ourselves in the position of not having sufficient data to warrant a definitive conclusion regarding the significance of this observation."

One day late in 1968, Steinschneider got a call from Abe Bergman, who had established himself in his hometown of Seattle in the years since he'd worked with Steinschneider and Lipton during his pediatric research fellowship in Syracuse in the early sixties. Bergman had become involved in crib death, he told Steinschneider, and was putting together an important international conference on the subject. The guest list would be select and serious, and he wanted Steinschneider to come. The knowledge he and Earle had gathered on infant physiology was important work, Bergman told him, and sudden infant death was a compelling and emerging new field. Babies were dying, thousands of them, and a research movement was massing.

Steinschneider was flattered by the invitation, but he also felt somewhat intimidated by Bergman's pitch. Not much had been said about crib death in medical school, and since he was a researcher and not a clinical pediatrician, he had had no direct experience with the problem. In fact, he'd never really thought much about it. But the conference would be a good opportunity. Steinschneider said yes, of course he would come to Orcas Island.

Now he had to come up with something to talk about. He thought of the bottle-sucking tests, and one particular premature baby who had been brought to Upstate because of recurring episodes of apnea at home. It was, of course, a common occurrence in preemies, but Steinschneider had noticed that during one of these brief apneic periods in the lab, the baby had turned blue and his heart rate slowed considerably when he stopped sucking. Steinschneider had become fascinated by the link between breathing and heart rate and began to consider the implications of this clearest manifestation of newborn autonomic instability—apnea. It was during his preparations for the coming conference that he first entertained the possibility that these fluctuations might be connected to death itself. He and Lipton had been unable to get the bottle-test research published (they'd followed it up with a paper on "Problems of Measurement," which did get published), but Steinschneider thought it was good work, and now it seemed to have a purpose. He knew his presumptions were tenuous, but he hoped he could make them work as the centerpiece of his talk on Orcas Island. He agonized about how it—and he—might be received.

It was his own sense of inadequacy that Steinschneider would later remember most vividly about the day he mingled with the crowd of crib death experts and other eminent people on the ferry trip across Puget Sound. "I felt like a novice," he would say. "I didn't really know what I was talking about. Here are people that have been thinking about this big-time and I'm going with nothing to offer. I go because my friend asked me. The big kids are going to kill me. They're going to eat me alive, because I'm silly."

If he was indeed stricken by such deep insecurity, Steinschneider did a superb job of hiding it. Whether he was on familiar or foreign ground, he was invariably a man difficult to ignore—his silvery, resonant voice deepened by the Raleigh cigarettes he inhaled like air, his face accentuated by what one colleague remembered as "big, rectangular glasses reminiscent of a fifty-six Chevy—they magnified his eyes." And by the afternoon of the second day on Orcas Island, his time at the lectern approaching, he felt emboldened. He realized that the big kids really didn't know that much more than he did. They had a sense that babies were more apt to die suddenly if it was winter and if they had colds and they were two or three months old as opposed to one or nine. But all this thinking had not led them to answers. They had no grip on the mechanism of death, and they seemed wide open to new ideas.

He offered his work, his theory, suggested others follow his lead, and began to detect the unmistakable air of *acceptance*. There was one low moment with this doctor named Walcher, and it stayed with him. But the others had listened to him with interest and respect, and some chimed in with their own experiences that tended to bolster his. Steinschneider came home forever changed. He thought it "obscene" that somewhere between 10,000 and 25,000 presumably healthy babies would die that year without explanation, and that little was being done about it.

Steinschneider believed that the term invented at the conference was designed to give parents the feeling that doctors knew more than they did. But he knew that if he turned his attentions to SIDS, he, too, would have to emerge from the lab and move into the real world. SIDS would be a whole new universe—filled not only with epidemiologists, with whom he shared a love of statistics, and with pathologists eager for information about living babies because their sights were so narrowly fixed on the dead ones, but also with grieving parents looking to medicine for answers it did not have. He also knew that unlike the cloister in which he'd spent the decade since medical school, a scientific investigation such as SIDS would be full of politics and money, emotion, ego, and conflict. The obstacles to such an immense scientific investigation would be formidable, but in the distance he could see the chance to achieve something wonderful. He had to close down the psychosomatic clinic and get right to work.

Most of what he knew about SIDS he had just learned. He'd heard the epidemiologists talk about factors of age, season, and infection, and he'd heard one of them, Northern Ireland's Peter Froggatt, say that there might be a familial factor at play. Froggatt had found that 5 of the 148 SIDS cases he reviewed had a sibling who had also died of "documented or presumptive" SIDS. Factoring in all the live-born siblings in the entire sample, and taking the data at face value (without exploring further to rule out all other possible causes), Froggatt's study suggested that the chance of a subsequent sibling dying was between 1 and 2 per 100, a figure much higher than the 2 per 1,000 that would be expected from a random sample. Steinschneider, an avid gambler and frequent visitor to Las Vegas, took significance from these odds. But they said nothing about cause.

Warren Guntheroth talked about cause, and it was striking to Steinschneider how his thoughts complemented his own. Guntheroth suggested that maybe SIDS babies were susceptible to a specific variety of breathing interruption. If SIDS occurred primarily during the first few months of life, it seemed sensible to think that it could be related to the autonomic instability peculiar to those same months. Why did only a few babies die? Maybe there was something about *them,* an abnormality they were born with or developed soon after birth, that predisposed them to such a sudden event. Steinschneider found a remark by Marie Valdes-Dapena especially penetrating: There was virtually no role here for pathologists, she'd observed, if a key part of the definition of SIDS was the absence of findings at autopsy. "If there's nothing wrong with these kids," he heard her voice say in his head, "then what do you need a pathologist for, except to say that there's nothing wrong with them?" Steinschneider took this paradox as a touchstone. Perhaps there *was* something wrong with these babies—maybe they *weren't* perfectly healthy the second before they died. It wasn't obvious at autopsy, not yet anyway, but maybe there was a way to find it in living babies, before the final event. Maybe some babies were congenitally vulnerable to pulmonary or cardiac abnormalities so severe that it made their apneic periods not routine, but hazardous—a warning sign.

Guntheroth thought so. He'd seen babies come into the emergency room requiring resuscitation. They had just stopped breathing and turned a pale shade of blue. They didn't die, but conceivably this was some kind of near-SIDS that could help explain why others did. The near-miss concept was probably the most intriguing idea of the conference. For Steinschneider, a close second was Guntheroth's idea to use some sort of monitoring device to protect babies deemed to be at risk. Steinschneider, of course, came from the cradle of monitors. The connections were clicking into place.

He decided that what he needed to do now was figure out which babies might be at highest risk, bring them into the lab, record their respiration, and see whether any patterns emerged. He set out to find these babies. Nobody had ever done that: actually gone out and sought infants who might be at risk for SIDS. Of course, to test his hunch properly, using the statistical research designs that were the bedrock of his training and experience, would be phenomenally arduous and time-consuming: If the SIDS rate was two deaths per thousand live births, a researcher would need to study thousands of babies and compare the breathing patterns of the normal ones to those who went on to die of SIDS, before he could come to any firm conclusions about the role of respiratory control. Unless he was blessed with perversely good fortune, that could take years.

Unfortunately, deaths were critical. Dwain Walcher had demonstrated the crudity of Steinschneider's proposition by virtually cross-examining him on the question of whether any baby he'd seen with apnea had gone on to die. He could not cite a single death. The moment had made him feel foolish. It also made him think about strategy. "This guy was saying you can only study SIDS if you study dead babies," Steinschneider recalled. "So the problem was how do you study living kids to find out about babies that die? What is the difference between high-risk babies and low-risk babies? Maybe that difference existed in the babies that died."

Where to start? The near-misses. Why did they happen, and what did they mean? Taking Guntheroth's experience a step further, Abe Bergman and Russell Fisher, the Maryland medical examiner, had cited cases of babies rushed to the hospital by their parents—survivors of near-misses who later went on to die of SIDS at home. Was there a connection? Steinschneider thought so. The missing piece was direct clinical observation. Documenting the breathing patterns of babies was exactly his line of work.

And so the hunt for babies began. Steinschneider began putting the word out to pediatricians in Syracuse and in the counties beyond: He was pursuing Sudden Infant Death Syndrome, and he was anxious for subjects. "I told docs that if they had kids who came into the E.R. with these near-miss incidents, I wanted to see them," he recalled. "Each of us might see one baby in two years where we don't know what's going on. So what you do is you say, 'Al, you're it. You get them all. You get to understand these kids and then you teach us how to take care of them.' I told them, 'If you don't know what's going on, let *me* sweat about it.' "

19

Ann Hoyt was furious. She couldn't believe what she was hearing. It was the spring of 1969, barely six months after those mind-bending three weeks in September. Now, here was Waneta standing before her, actually saying yes, it was true—she was pregnant. She would have her fourth child by Christmas. Others in the family shook their heads in disbelief. Ann went right at Waneta. "God, woman," she said, screaming at her, "what the hell are you doing this for? You lost three already!"

"Well," Waneta said, "having babies is what my mother told me I was good for."

"You've got to be out of your goddamned head," Ann continued. She never did take to Mrs. Nixon. "If this is your idea of following in your mother's footsteps . . . well, she's just a goddamned quack, that's all. Why in hell are you having another baby?"

"I want one," Waneta said.

"Good Lord, go out and rent one. Just get away from me. You don't want to hear anything I have to say."

Ann moved on to Tim. "Can't you do something about this?" she asked her brother. "It's obvious she's been out talking to her mother. Damn it, why do you keep doing it? Just fix it." Tim's answer said much about where the power lay in his marriage. "I've tried talking to her, but she won't listen," he said. "I don't want any more kids that I'm gonna lose." He told Ann that even Dr. Kassman, the obstetrician, had advised them to stop having children. Then why have them? Ann shot back. If they wanted a child that much, they could adopt.

In fact, when Waneta had a miscarriage soon after, that's just what she

222

and Tim decided to do. They filled out an application with the Tioga County Department of Social Services, and started the adoption process with letters of recommendation from Dr. Hartnagel and Reverend Kuhns, along with friends such as Natalie and Art Hilliard. "Both seem to have an excellent understanding of children," Natalie wrote to the caseworker, Roberta Hickey. "They get along very well with the neighbor children, of which my five-year-old son is one, and he likes them very much. They were very good to their own children from what I could see."

Hartnagel's recommendation was brief and pro forma; whatever his thoughts about the first three deaths, he kept them to himself. But Kuhns put a good deal of thought into his letter to Hickey. He was glad to see the Hoyts were choosing to adopt rather than conceive another child, but he sensed that Waneta was ambivalent about the decision and felt he should express his concerns candidly in his letter of reference:

> By this stage in the adoption proceedings your department is no doubt aware of the three children they have lost to date through no fault of their own. Anyone going through such tragedy could not help suffering a difficult emotional shake-up. This is especially true in Nita's [sic] case. I have been close to them since coming to Newark Valley and am aware of the anguish they have suffered. It would appear that they need a child and should have one. I am of this opinion but should at least raise the following issues: 1) in my opinion, and it is only my opinion, Tim and Nita have not faced the fact that children born of them is now NOT a wise decision in view of the three deaths. 2) the emotional shake-up for Nita has been understandably great, but an adopted child can be no guarantee of a cure. 3) Tim and Nita are limited intellectually and are limited financially. The road ahead for them is not an easy one. Having raised these issues I reiterate my support of their desire for adoption. The difficulties can be overcome and without question they deserve a child.

Kuhns's impressions were correct. Waneta was not ready to give up on having her own children. A month after filling out the forms, she was pregnant again. The caseworker withdrew the adoption application. Ann, once again, was livid. When she asked Tim, *"Why are you doing this?"* Tim didn't answer. But it was obvious to Ann that he was doing it for Neta. She wanted to keep trying, and he could not bear to say no.

At 9:56 on the night of March 18, 1970, Waneta delivered her fourth child at Tompkins County Hospital. There was little celebration in the family—only intense trepidation. In an act of self-protection, a number of her relatives found themselves retreating. "We wondered how you could lose two," Janet recalled. "We wondered how you could lose three. We wondered why you wanted four if you lost three. And after a while I got to thinking, well, you know, I suppose God's got a way of doing this stuff. I was wondering where Neta's getting the strength to get through this. I'd have been a basket case a long time ago."

Molly Marie Hoyt did not leave the hospital without a good deal of attention from Dr. Perry and the maternity and pediatrics staffs. She was a normal newborn—9 on the Apgar, negative on the PKU test, everything looking fine, just as it had for her three siblings. But, of course, she was not normal. Dr. Perry wrote the words "sudden deaths 3 siblings" on nearly every record he generated in the days after Molly's birth, but he could do little more than check her thoroughly, admit his puzzlement, and hope for the best.

Perry was an easygoing doctor whose wife, a fellow pediatrician, worked in the student health clinic at Cornell. In his decade in Ithaca, he had cultivated a comfortable practice in a pleasant Ivy League town, and his patient rolls included children of Cornell professors as well as those of dairy farmers. He found the tragedy of the Hoyts troubling and frustrating. He had attended both Eric and Julie in the days after their births, and pronounced each healthy and fit for the world outside the hospital, only to learn later that they, and their brother Jimmy, had not survived. He had never been involved in the assessments of their deaths. In fact, he didn't hear about them until weeks afterward, when word filtered up from Newark Valley. Perry learned of Julie's sudden death when Waneta phoned the office. She was calling to cancel her appointment for the baby's two-month checkup.

Now he resolved to do everything he could to make sure Molly was all right; he didn't want to miss something that could turn out to be a fatal omission. After her birth, he ordered a chest X ray, tested her kidney function, and measured her electrolyte and glucose levels. When everything came back normal, he discharged the baby to her parents' care only one day later than usual.

Sixteen days later, Vivian Balzer was coming out of the post office in Newark Valley when she heard the rescue alarms. She dashed around the corner to the firehouse. "We're headed up to the Hoyts'," Hank Robson yelled, and she joined them in the ambulance. The squad raced up to Davis Hollow expecting the worst, but found, for the first time, a living, breathing baby. She was in obvious distress, though, her face still blue when they arrived at the trailer. Robson fit an adult-sized oxygen mask over Molly's tiny face, and after a few minutes her color began to come back. Despite their relief, the squad members did not hesitate to pack the baby and her mother into the ambulance and head for Route 96. By the time they arrived in Ithaca and an emergency room doctor checked her over, Molly seemed fine. But almost nobody felt confident this would be the end of her troubles.

Dr. Perry met Waneta in the emergency room. She told him she had checked the baby after a feeding late in the morning, and found her in her crib not breathing, her color dusky, and making jerking movements with her arms. Perry listened intently, with welling concern. He knew that Molly had had a similar episode the week before. In that case, too, Waneta had been able to normalize the baby's breathing, but as a precaution she had brought the baby to Perry's office in Ithaca, where his partner, Dr. Speno, examined her. By then, any evidence of distress had long since dissipated.

For the first time, Perry felt confronted by the responsibility of trying to figure out what might be wrong with the Hoyt children. He wasn't hearing about a death weeks after the fact. The baby was here before him, and clearly, despite her appearance, she was not well. He admitted the baby for tests: cardiogram, complete blood count, urine, blood chemistry, another chest X ray. He wanted to rule out an allergy to cow's milk, and, mindful of the autopsy finding of her brother, adrenal insufficiency.

Perry found the entire situation vexing. He could see no clear medical pattern, aside from the consistently negative test results. He searched his mind. He opened it a crack to the unthinkable: *Could something awful be going on, something beyond the pale of reason? Could somebody be causing these episodes— these deaths?* The Hoyts seemed to him an ordinary rural couple who cared about their children. He had noticed nothing amiss in their behavior. Still, he decided to ask the hospital's social services department to look into it. The report, like all the medical tests, came back negative. Perry never asked the social services people exactly what they did—whether they had called the authorities in Tioga County, talked to the Hoyts, or what—but he was relieved by their finding. "Investigation by Social Service showed no evidence of foul play," he wrote on Molly's chart the morning he sent her home, "and I would believe this to be true."

What now? After three days of drawing blood, taking X rays, and hooking up the three-week-old baby to the wire leads of an electrocardiograph, Perry was out of ideas. His hunch was that the baby and her siblings had some sort of genetic metabolic disorder, but beyond that, he knew he was out of his depth. There was only one diagnosis he could make with reasonable certainty, and for this he scribbled a prescription of Donnatal—half a teaspoon four times a day. Molly, he could say with confidence, was colicky.

Perry discharged the baby on Friday but he was uneasy. He couldn't get the Hoyts out of his mind, and mulled the situation over through the weekend. He talked about it with his wife and with his partner. Then he had an idea. On Monday morning he called the pediatrics department at Upstate Medical Center and asked for Dr. Steinschneider. It was Perry's understanding that Steinschneider specialized in medical puzzles involving babies.

How skillful he was at solving them, Perry couldn't say. Nor did he know whether Steinschneider would take a case so vague as this. Technically, there was nothing wrong with this baby. So he was pleasantly surprised when Steinschneider accepted the referral with enthusiasm. Yes, Steinschneider said, he would be extremely interested in this case.

Perry called Waneta, and told her he had been thinking about Molly. "I'm concerned that there's something going on here that I don't understand," he said. "I'd like you to bring the baby to Syracuse. There's a doctor at Upstate that I think you ought to see."

Molly was twenty-eight days old when her parents drove an hour and a half to the State University Hospital, the centerpiece of a complex of medical buildings just off Interstate 81 at the edge of downtown Syracuse and adjacent to the campus of Syracuse University. They parked in the big lot across the street, then walked to the hospital's main entrance. Molly's round face, topped by a growth of soft brown hair, poked out of the blanket that shielded her from the crisp early spring air.

The young family ambled into the bustling city hospital, past the coffee shop filled with doctors and nurses and visitors, and the gift shop and newsstand with the day's Syracuse papers, the *Post-Standard* and *Herald American,* chronicling the unfolding adventure of Apollo 13. The drama gripped the world, eclipsing Friday's news that the Beatles were breaking up.

The Hoyts went to the front desk and asked where they could find a Dr. Steinschneider. Five C, they were informed; the pediatric research center. They rode to the fifth floor; the doors parted, and they found their way to the Children's Clinical Research Center. They were ushered into a small office. The doctor would be with them shortly.

A few minutes later, an authoritative-looking man wearing a lab coat and a welcoming smile came into the room. "Hello," he said. "I'm Dr. Steinschneider."

Waneta and Tim gave him the rough outlines of their situation. Their children kept dying, they said, and none of their local doctors could say why. They'd already had two scares with their new baby, and while Dr. Perry could find nothing wrong, he was worried. And so were they. Steinschneider told the Hoyts he would try to help them. He was studying just this problem, and he would do all he could to keep their newborn safe. She was a beautiful baby, with a beautiful name. Molly was his mother's name, too.

The Hoyts did not know just how pleased Steinschneider was to see a baby such as theirs. In the year since he had begun putting the word out about his SIDS studies, he'd gotten a number of referrals from pediatricians around Syracuse, but Molly Hoyt was altogether different. If one were pursuing a theory proposing that a hidden abnormality made some babies predisposed to life-threatening spells of involuntary breath holding, then this four-week-old daughter of parents who had buried their three previous children ought to be a perfect case study. He was being presented with a baby, and a family, that was—from the scientist's point of view—almost too good to be true.

Steinschneider asked a pediatric intern to take a complete history from the Hoyts, after which he would return and go over it with them in more detail. Then he would ask them to leave Molly with him in the research clinic. For how long, Steinschneider couldn't say for sure. A few days, a week, maybe two. Long enough to detect any patterns in her breathing that might offer a clue to what was going on.

Let's start with Molly, said the intern, and began to take down the pertinent information about the two emergencies that had led her here. When Waneta said that in the second instance the baby had stopped breathing for five minutes, he dutifully put it in the record, though he followed the note with an editorial question mark. "I gave her mouth-to-mouth and called for help," Waneta said. "This time they put her in the hospital."

She recounted the deaths of her first three children. Eric, her first, had bled from the nose at his death, and the intern wrote this down. He also noted that the third death had followed the second by only three weeks. Then he asked for a more extensive family history. Were there any infant deaths in Tim's family? No, Tim said, though one of his brothers had "breath-holding spells" as a child. "He's got hay fever now."

He turned to Waneta. "One of my sisters has lost two," she revealed. She wasn't sure of the cause in either case. One was three months old, she said, and the other died shortly after birth. Some kind of breathing problem, she thought.

She gave a detailed description of Molly's current health. She'd had a little runny nose, some diarrhea (as did her mother, Waneta volunteered), and was drinking soybean milk at Dr. Perry's suggestion. The intern took the baby into an examining room and checked her over thoroughly. Listening with his stethoscope, he heard the noiseless air of a clear chest, but when he moved the instrument over to the baby's heart, he detected the rushing sound of a small heart murmur that had not been picked up by the doctors in Ithaca. It was not unusual, however, and murmurs like this often turned out to be inconsequential. To the intern, Molly seemed to be essentially normal: an active, alert one-month-old with a hearty cry.

Steinschneider came back into the room and reviewed the intern's notes.

He asked the Hoyts about Molly's first episode. Waneta said she had found the baby in her crib, blue in the face.

"Was she breathing?" Steinschneider asked.

"I don't think so," Waneta said. "Maybe she was barely breathing. I took her out in the fresh air and her color came back."

The next episode came five days later, Waneta said; it was during a feeding. "She holds her breath a lot when I'm feeding her," she explained. "And then when I take the bottle out, she breathes normal again. This time I had to give her mouth-to-mouth. But Dr. Perry said they couldn't find anything, except she was colicky. So we had her home. And then yesterday, I had to bring her to the emergency room again."

This was news to Steinschneider. What happened? he asked.

"I was feeding her and she gagged. Threw up." She reported the events in a patient, matter-of-fact manner. Tim sat quietly beside her. "She wasn't breathing so I gave her mouth-to-mouth, and then I brought her in to Tompkins County. They couldn't find anything, so they sent me home."

Steinschneider moved on to Molly's siblings.

Eric was their first child, Waneta said. "He had passing-out spells. He would gasp, like he couldn't get his breath."

Was there any pattern to it?

"Usually after I fed him and usually when he was sleeping. And then one day he didn't seem to breathe right, and just died. I remember there was some blood in his mouth."

Waneta had told the intern that Eric had bled from the nose, not the mouth, but Steinschneider didn't note the inconsistency. He asked if there had been an autopsy.

"No," Waneta said. "Dr. Hartnagel thought there were some heart problems."

Julie was next. "She was born on July 19, 1968, and she died on September 5. I was feeding her. She seemed to choke and turn blue, and then she just died."

Steinschneider kept writing.

"And James was born on Memorial Day, that was in '66, and he died on September 26, 1968. He seemed fine. It was right after breakfast. Then he called out to me and collapsed. He called out, 'Mommy,' and died."

Waneta said she saw some blood in Jimmy's nose and mouth, but Steinschneider seemed more intrigued by the timing of the episodes she described. How interesting that they seemed to surround one activity: feeding. In fact, one of the children, Julie, had died during a feeding. It wouldn't be inconsistent with the studies Steinschneider had presented to the SIDS conference the year before.

Family history, of course, was the most provocative aspect of the case of the Hoyt family, and nothing Waneta told Steinschneider, or anything contained in the meager records dispatched by Roger Perry from Ithaca, made it any less an enigma. Waneta's recollections of the babies' lives and deaths were not confirmed by clinical observation, and the one autopsy, for two-year-old Jimmy, left more questions than answers. One other curious familial aspect slipped by without much attention. Waneta had told the intern that her sister had lost two babies. She told Steinschneider the same thing. But it was not true.

Steinschneider laid Molly across the padded examining table. He adjusted his stethoscope, listened to her heart and lungs, and examined her head to toe. He ordered another round of blood work, EKG tracings, X rays, a stool culture, and urinalysis. He consulted with a pediatric cardiologist, Marie Blackman, on the only obvious anomaly, the heart murmur. She thought it was most likely a small patent ductus arteriosus—a failure of a fetal pulmonary vessel to close after birth, a condition that usually corrects itself before long. She told Steinschneider it couldn't be the cause of the distress for which the baby was being hospitalized, though given the family history, she thought it wise to recheck in three months. When a nurse asked Steinschneider what she should type under "Admitting Diagnosis," he said simply, "Apnea."

Steinschneider's plan, he told the Hoyts, was to keep the baby on an apnea monitor, a device frequently used in the Children's Clinical Research Center. Molly would be attached to the monitor whenever she was in her crib, night and day. He and the rest of the research center staff would keep a close eye on her, measure her breathing, and test her under various conditions. If she stopped breathing, either the nurses or the monitor alarm itself would stimulate her. He showed them the autonomic lab, where Molly would be brought several times a week for testing. He would do everything he could, he told Waneta and Tim, to discover their baby's—their family's—problem.

The head nurse of the research clinic, a pleasant woman in her mid-forties, took Molly from her mother's arms. The nurse smiled serenely, an offer of comfort from one mother to another, and Waneta passed Molly over without expression or comment. "Set the monitor at fifteen seconds, Thelma," Steinschneider instructed.

The head nurse was Thelma Schneider—formerly Thelma Lipton. In December 1965, four months following her husband's suicide and with her children in school, she had decided to return to work after several years' absence. Not surprisingly, the job opening she found most appealing was in the children's research clinic of the new University Hospital, a unit that Earle

Lipton hadn't lived long enough to use. Two years later, in 1967, she married the head of the research center, Jack Schneider. Eventually, a head nurse's spot came open, and Thelma, a seasoned RN with a clear, intuitive mind, was regarded within the department as the most qualified, despite the inherent conflict of being married to the boss. They decided they could deal with that, and Julius Richmond signed off on the promotion.

Thelma found the work stimulating. She came to regard caring for burn patients, PKU babies, "failure-to-thrive" infants, and older children who streamed through on the research grants of the pediatrics staff, as important, cutting-edge work. Not only was she taking care of children in medical need, but she felt part of a team trying to develop knowledge and techniques that might help many others. Research nursing was a fairly new concept, though, and Thelma surmised that it wasn't very popular among the sisterhood. "I think the other nurses on the regular pediatric floor thought of it as some kind of cushy job, not real nursing," she later reflected, "because it wasn't heroic—we weren't taking care of meningitis patients and all the 'real' stuff. They thought we were doing esoteric things up there, in our own little world. I remember at one point we had to admit some of our patients down on the regular floor, and it would be like, oh well, here come the research patients. They didn't understand why they had to pay so much attention to detail, even though as a good nurse you'd better darn well pay attention to detail."

In Al Steinschneider's world, Thelma knew, the details were measured in seconds. The vagaries of infant respiration, the pauses and resumptions and the lengths of time between them, were what fixed his attention. He had come home from the meeting out west and begun hunting apnea. In his autonomic lab, he tried to lure it out into the open, and capture it on polygraph paper. See it, measure it, analyze it, implicate it. Exploring whether there was a connection between these gentle, unpredictable rhythms and abrupt death was the work that consumed him now.

Thelma spread a dab of cream on Molly's chest, then attached the wire leads of the monitor as Waneta and Tim looked on. "I had to give her mouth-to-mouth," Waneta volunteered, relating the incident that had brought Molly to Tompkins County the week before. "It took five or ten minutes to get her back." Thelma explained that short periods of apnea were common in young babies, but if Molly failed to breathe for fifteen seconds, the monitor would give off a nice, loud beep and a nurse would come quickly. Sometimes it would mean that the baby was breathing too shallowly for the machine to detect, other times that the leads had come loose. But if she was truly not breathing, the nurse would nudge her, and Molly would resume her respiration. The nurses would check the baby frequently, Thelma assured the Hoyts, and they could always see her clearly from the nursing station.

Jack Schneider had designed the research clinic so that all five patient rooms could be observed from the station. Three rooms went directly back, one behind the other, with large picture windows between them offering the nurses a clear view all the way through to the third room. The other two rooms, and a playroom, were off to the side. Because Molly was considered a baby at risk, she was put in the first room in the series of three, closest to the nurses. She would lie in a "nip-nap," a device that propped her up when she slept. A mobile was attached to the metal bars of the crib, and in a corner of the room there was a rocking chair, one of several in the unit purchased with money from the National Institutes of Health.

Soon after Molly's parents departed for the trip home to Tioga County, Thelma gave the baby a few ounces of formula. She saw that her tiny hands became blue during the feeding, an observation she noted in her first entry in the Nurses' Record, a round-the-clock, hour-by-hour account of how much formula the baby took, the color and consistency of her bowel movements, and, of course, how she was breathing. Details. When Julie Evans, a nurse who was one of the veterans of pediatrics, came on for the three-to-midnight shift, Thelma filled her in on their new patient. They were to pay special attention to any episodes of apnea or cyanosis, Thelma stressed—here was one research patient whose problems were anything but esoteric, even if the solution was. The night nurse fed Molly, and also noted that the baby's hands became blue and her fingers swelled. Both nurses knew that these were not unusual events. Babies this age were always changing color, for all kinds of reasons. But in this case, anything could be significant. By the next day, the rest of the nursing staff had adopted a heightened sense of alertness for a baby whose extraordinary family history carried the implicit threat that, despite her peachy appearance, she might be in mortal danger.

Molly made her first trip across the hall to Steinschneider's autonomic lab the next morning at ten minutes to nine. Jeanne Steivang, a nurse who worked directly for Steinschneider in the research center, picked the baby up from her crib and walked her into the lab, a small, soundproofed two-room arrangement divided by a wall with a large window. She laid Molly down on a mattress and placed a mercury "strain gauge" across her tiny chest, another sensor in front of her nose. On the other side of the window, Mario Cipriani, a technician, sat before a wall-sized collection of knobs and gauges and lights. Next to Cipriani was Steinschneider. He would direct the proceedings.

"Let's do the ninety," Steinschneider said. Cipriani turned the temperature in the lab up to the usual point; it always made Steivang sweat under her hospital gown. Now, Steinschneider leaned into a microphone. "You can feed her now, Jeanne," he instructed the nurse. Hearing his voice through the loudspeaker, she served Molly five ounces of Similac. The equipment on the

other side of the window began recording the changes in the baby's respiration and heart rate as she took the formula. "On her tummy," Steinschneider
said when she'd finished. Jeanne turned the baby over and watched her fall
asleep, the machines recording every breath, every heartbeat. After a while,
Steinschneider directed Cipriani to move on to "noise stimulation." The technician flicked a switch, sending a symphony of white noise through the loudspeaker into the testing chamber. Steinschneider watched the needles of the
gauges as the sounds changed in pitch and intensity.

Molly slept for forty-five minutes, with the results now on paper. She
stopped breathing a number of times during the session. Nine seconds was the
longest pause. Though Steivang was concerned, Steinschneider was not. He
knew that for a one-month-old baby in a ninety-degree room, it was not big
news. Her heart rate never slowed and her face never turned blue. He suspected that it was this kind of normal apneic breathing that had thrown
a scare into Molly's parents and accounted for the trips to the emergency
room, along with the probably unnecessary mouth-to-mouth resuscitation. Of
course, given the fate of their first three children, who could blame them for
overreacting?

During the next few days, a couple of patterns began to emerge. In the lab,
Steinschneider found that Molly had much less sleep apnea when the room
temperature was set at 75 degrees than when it was turned up to 90. It confirmed his experience that heat induced apnea, and his idea that heating the
lab was a way to "tease out" the apnea in order to get a better look at it. Still,
even at the higher temperature none of the episodes approached the fifteen
seconds he believed was the appropriate borderline between "short" and "prolonged" apnea. It was a largely arbitrary choice, since neither he nor anybody
else had ever demonstrated what constituted a baby's normal breathing pattern. In that sense, Steinschneider was charting new territory. In Molly's case,
although the tests in the lab revealed only short, presumably inconsequential
periods of apnea, the fifteen-second line was reached a number of times
during the routine monitoring back in her room in the research unit.

Or was it? Much more often, the alarm sounded and the baby was either
breathing normally or shallowly. There was no denying that the devices,
which were now being commercially manufactured and sold to hospitals by a
Pennsylvania company called Air-Shields, were primitive and unreliable. The
technicians from the Inhalation Therapy department who were responsible
for the equipment were always being called to adjust the sensitivity. And
without the ability to record like an electrocardiograph, not merely to
monitor, the machines could offer only a crude, ambiguous, and possibly misleading picture of what was actually going on. Thus, even if the alarm
sounded and a nurse found the baby not breathing, she had no way to be sure
whether Molly had stopped breathing fifteen seconds before, or ten seconds,

or two seconds—or whether she was merely breathing shallowly during some or all of the sequence. Maybe it was an episode of prolonged apnea, and maybe not. For the record, however, Steinschneider didn't preoccupy himself with this question. When an alarm rang, he counted it.

The usefulness of the monitors was a tricky question for another reason. The machines were designed to help see premature babies through their first tenuous weeks of life, when potentially critical pauses in respiration were not uncommon. In his pursuit of the SIDS mystery, Steinschneider was now using the touchy monitors to document apnea—and to do it with full-term, otherwise healthy newborns who had been referred to him either because of a prior SIDS death in the family, or because the parents had seen something that made them worry that their baby's breathing patterns were perilously irregular. The rub, of course, was that the breathing mechanisms of all newborns needed time to stabilize. What Steinschneider had to do now was to try to figure out how to distinguish meaningless apnea from significant and dangerous apnea—at what point, and under what circumstances, the normal became the abnormal. It was inevitable that the corps of nurses taking care of Molly would become drawn into this elusive question.

One day, Steinschneider asked Thelma, "Did you ever stand over your baby's crib and watch him breathe?"

"Yeah, I did," Thelma said.

An amused expression came over Steinschneider's face. He liked little exercises like that, Thelma thought. Ever since she'd known him, all the way back to when Earle had brought him into his lab as a medical student, Steinschneider saw things from a slightly different angle, and had a way of bringing people to his point of view. She began to notice, record, and worry over every pause in breath Molly took. As unpredictable and temperamental as the machines could be, as normal as she knew infant apnea to be, Steinschneider's research focus and Molly's very real family history convinced her in those first few days that the monitor was the baby's lifeline.

Waneta and Tim came for their first visit on Friday evening, two days after they brought Molly to Syracuse. Julie Evans was working that night. "Would you like to feed her?" she asked Waneta when Molly began to cry. Waneta seemed hesitant. "It's okay," the nurse said, thinking that perhaps the young mother was intimidated by the surroundings. She picked Molly out of her crib and handed her to her mother, who fed the baby a few ounces of formula. A few minutes later, with Molly back on the monitor, the alarm sounded, but she was breathing normally. Then it happened again. The baby was fine, Nurse Evans assured them—these false alarms are not uncommon.

Steinschneider was less sanguine. By the middle of the second week, he was concerned about the frequency of the short apneic periods reported by the nurses on the ward and recorded by Jeanne Steivang in the lab. Brief as the spells were, he told Waneta and Tim that they were too numerous to dismiss—and there had been one instance, just before midnight on the baby's eighth day in the hospital, when one of the nurses heard the alarm, came into the room, and decided she'd better give the baby a gentle nudge. "During past week," Steinschneider wrote in his notes, "amount of apnea, if anything, has increased. Have discussed implications of these observations with parents and would plan on continuing hospitalization until, at least, there is evidence that the frequency of episodes are on the downswing."

By the end of April, when Molly's time in hospitals had surpassed her life at home, Waneta and Tim were becoming familiar faces in the research unit. They came on Saturdays and Sundays and a couple of times during the week, after Tim got home from work and ate a quick supper. On the weekends, they'd pack a lunch, and at some point during the visit go down to the parking lot and sit in the car with their sandwiches and a thermos of soup. One Saturday, Tim brought a camera and he and Waneta took pictures of each other with Molly. Waneta snapped one of Tim, surrounded by the nurses.

They found shuttling the seventy miles between Newark Valley and Syracuse grueling. Tim considered drives to Binghamton and even Owego long trips, and the farmboy in him was uncomfortable being out at night. "We lived like our parents did," he remembered. "You were home when it was dark. That's where you belonged, not out on some stupid highway." Where many parents of babies at Upstate came every day and stayed for long stretches, the Hoyts made it in less frequently. They would sit in Molly's room, Waneta often on Tim's lap, and talk quietly between themselves. Though the nurses were taking care of her baby, Waneta's conversation with them never went beyond the obligatory courtesies.

Thelma Schneider was not a judgmental person, but not long after Molly's admission she was struck by how uneasy she felt around the baby's mother. The young woman's demeanor was flat and she rarely smiled, but that wasn't it. Far more important, she seemed disturbingly remote from her child. Other mothers wanted to stay with their babies, feed them themselves, and do all the usual maternal things despite the clinical setting. This mother wasn't like that. She had to be encouraged to hold Molly, to feed her, and even when she did, it was literally at arm's length. Thelma presumed that it was because Waneta was afraid to become attached to the baby for fear that she would lose her as she had lost the others. Whatever the reason for the coolness, it bothered her.

Back home in Newark Valley, meanwhile, word was that the Hoyts' fourth child was being treated by "some big doctor up to Upstate" who was trying to solve the family's medical mystery. One day, Tim and Waneta went to the post office to pick up their mail and ran into Emma Guhman, who had been a gym teacher when they were in school. "We just came back from Syracuse," Waneta told her forlornly. "The baby's up in the hospital. She's having trouble with her breathing." The retired teacher listened with sympathy, and wished them well. Such a nice, unassuming couple, she thought later. Just as they'd been in school. What troubles they were made to suffer.

By the first week of May, Steinschneider saw enough evidence that Molly's apneic spells were on the decline to start thinking about sending her home. Fitting the pattern for a normal six-week-old baby, the number of short periods had dropped, and Molly hadn't had what Steinschneider regarded as a prolonged episode in more than a week. He planned to send her home on Tuesday, May 5, but when Waneta and Tim arrived that afternoon, he told them he had decided to keep her a little longer. Earlier in the afternoon, Thelma Schneider had noticed that Molly was making a lot of "gagging motions" with her tongue, and a few minutes later the apnea alarm went off. Molly resumed breathing on her own after three beeps, but it was the second apparent episode of prolonged apnea in twelve hours. Let's keep her in another couple of days, Steinschneider told the Hoyts.

There was one other thing delaying Molly's discharge. A couple of days before, Waneta had come to Steinschneider with an idea. She had been watching Molly on the monitor for several weeks now, and saw how it alerted the nurses to the apnea spells. Would it be possible to take Molly home with the monitor? Steinschneider surmised that Waneta had come to see the monitor as a security blanket. This did not make it a bad idea. Wasn't this just the kind of thing Warren Guntheroth had suggested at the SIDS conference? Steinschneider asked Waneta if she thought she could handle it. Could she operate the machine, and stay calm if the alarm went off? Yes, Waneta said, she could. She'd been watching the nurses set the switches and change the leads. "I can do that," she said. She had also demonstrated, Steinschneider thought, that she was capable of resuscitating a baby. The monitor might not only protect the baby and reassure her parents, but if the Hoyts kept an accurate log of apneic episodes, as the nurses did, it would be a way for him to continue observing the baby without keeping her in the hospital.

Steinschneider called the local distributor for Air-Shields. He wanted to send one of his patients home on a monitor, he told the sales rep. Could they get a demo, gratis? The parents didn't have much money. The dealer had never heard of putting a hospital monitor into somebody's home, much less at no charge. But Steinschneider could be very persuasive. The dealer said he would see if he could find a demo. It would take a few days.

Steinschneider also wanted Molly's room at home to be kept at 75 degrees. That might be a problem, Tim told him. The trailer could get pretty hot.

"Do you have an air conditioner?" Steinschneider asked.

"No," Tim said, as if to say "of course not."

"I'd like you to get one," Steinschneider said.

By Friday, Steinschneider considered Molly's breathing sufficiently stable to send her home. The man from Air-Shields called to say he had located a monitor and would bring it to the hospital at the end of the day. Tim, meanwhile, had borrowed the money from his sister and brother-in-law, Marion and Weldon, for a small air conditioner. He and Waneta got to the hospital that night around seven, and the Air-Shields dealer arrived with the monitor a little while later. He taught them how to set the sensitivity and calibrate the timing, and then a nurse conducted a quick course in CPR. Steinschneider instructed the Hoyts to return with Molly in a week. He wanted to see how she did at home, and then he wanted to bring her back into the lab and analyze the changes in her respiratory patterns since this first stay, which had lasted twenty-three days. In the meantime, he wanted to keep a tight rein on the home monitor experiment. Call me immediately if the alarm goes off, he told the Hoyts, or if Molly should develop a cold. On Orcas Island, one of the things Steinschneider had learned from the epidemiologists was that the risk of SIDS seemed to rise with the onset of upper respiratory infections.

Julie Evans carried Molly to the front entrance. Tim swung his car around to the hospital's front driveway, loaded up his wife, his daughter, and the boxy apnea monitor, and headed back to Newark Valley. That night, May 8, 1970, Molly Hoyt became the first baby in the world put to bed while attached to an apnea monitor in her own crib, in her own home.

20

The monitor sat atop a dresser in the living room. It was Molly's room—it had the air conditioner. The wires draped over the drawers, snaking into the crib. Tim's sister Ann came by to see the baby that weekend, and she found the contraption unsettling. "It was just creepy being around her," she remembered. "She wasn't a normal kid." She wondered if the baby was warm enough in just a little tee-shirt. Waneta said it was hard to dress her because of the wires.

When the alarm sounded, Waneta poked the baby's foot, which Ann presumed was what you did when your baby stopped breathing, though she couldn't tell if Molly did or not. "She's all right," Waneta said. "You can pick her up if you're careful." Ann shook her head. "I ain't touching her," she said.

On Sunday night, Waneta called Steinschneider. Molly had done fine on Friday night, Saturday, and most of Sunday, but then she had become cranky and developed a runny nose and a slight cough. And then around supper-time, Waneta said, the alarm kept going off.

How many times? Steinschneider asked. About twenty, Waneta said.

Twenty times? Did she start breathing on her own? Most of the times the alarm made her start breathing again, Waneta said. But sometimes they had to shake her to get her started.

Any change in her color? No. Was she all right now? Waneta thought so.

"All right," Steinschneider said finally. "I think you should bring her in tonight."

The Hoyts arrived at the hospital around 10:30, and Steinschneider met them. He called over the chief resident, Martin Kleiman, reviewed the history,

237

and asked what he thought. The patient had apnea, Kleiman wrote, "documented both by apnea monitor and parental observation," and a slight cold. What would he suggest? The pediatrician-in-training did not want to screw up. With Steinschneider's assent, he admitted Molly to a room on the pediatric floor, sent up an apnea monitor, and ordered some special equipment for her bedside: wall-suction setup, oxygen and a face mask, a laryngoscope and endotracheal tubes. A full complement of resuscitation equipment.

Molly didn't need any of it, but she did seem to have a difficult few days, perhaps exacerbated by her slight upper respiratory infection—and maybe a heightened sense of vigilance on the part of the nurses on the regular pediatrics ward who were unfamiliar with the irascible monitors. A dozen times during the next forty-eight hours, they heard the beeping of the monitor, and in three of those instances, they stimulated Molly with a gentle poke. But the false alarms continued as well. Were the nurses' nudges necessary? Nobody was in a mood to take chances.

At midweek, Steinschneider moved Molly back upstairs. By this point, a month since she was first admitted, Thelma Schneider was beginning to think there was nothing really wrong with Molly. She found herself responding to many more false alarms than real ones, and her early concerns were now giving way to experience and instinct. The baby's mother had said she twice had to give Molly mouth-to-mouth resuscitation during her early time at home, and that the baby had turned blue a number of times. Maybe it was a simple overreaction on the mother's part, but the fact remained that Molly had not had one instant of distress while in the hospital. There was little question in Thelma's mind that she would have no reason to be in the hospital if not for her family history.

Something else had been troubling Thelma. She had been unable to shake her initial discomfort about Molly's mother. In fact, the more she watched her, the more she began to think that something more complicated than grief was at play. Thelma talked about it with some of the other nurses, and it turned out they had been having the same reactions. In fact, one of them, Corrine Dower, had come to Thelma with her worries. As the head nurse, Thelma decided she should talk to Steinschneider about it. On Friday, she came into his office and told him that the apnea alarm had sounded five times during her shift, but that Molly was breathing each time. She thought the monitor's failure to pick up shallow breathing was probably the cause of most of the alarms being reported. But this was just a preamble to what was really on her mind. She thought the baby had a problem, she told Steinschneider, but apnea was not it. "It's the mother," she said.

"What about the mother?" Steinschneider asked.

Well, Thelma said, she doesn't seem to want much to do with the baby when she visits. She never cuddles her. She feeds her, but only when a nurse suggests it. Thelma said she had thought that perhaps Mrs. Hoyt was afraid to get close to Molly because she feared losing her. But now, she believed it was more than that.

Thelma saw that Steinschneider was not quite getting what she was saying. She tried to give him a concrete example. "When you hold a baby you hold her close, like this," she said, cradling her arms into her breast. "Not her. She holds her at arm's length, in a very awkward way. Al, it's very peculiar." Thelma could see everything going on in the baby's room through the picture window above the desk at the nurses' station, and one of the things she saw over and over, she told Steinschneider, was that the baby's father, and not the baby, seemed to be Mrs. Hoyt's focus when she visited. "Today, Daddy was holding the baby, and she came along and took the baby away from him, sat on his lap, and then held the baby out that same way. That's not normal behavior. It's like the attention has to be on *her*."

Steinschneider listened to Thelma impassively, as if at a loss to know what it was she wanted him to do and unable to see what possible relevance it had. They had known each other for years and had come to be good friends. With her first husband and now her second, Thelma socialized with Al and Roz. Their children were about the same age, and sometimes the Steinschneider kids came over for dinner. Like most of the nurses who worked with Steinschneider, Thelma found him an open man with an engaging sense of humor, and their personal relationship made him especially approachable. But Thelma also knew that when it came to his research, Steinschneider could be extraordinarily focused. Whatever he believed, he believed completely. Apnea and SIDS—he was on the case. Maternal instincts? It frustrated her that he seemed to have no idea what she was talking about.

Steinschneider's lack of interest didn't cool the talk, it heightened it. Over the next few days and weeks, the nurses grew still more concerned, especially veterans like Thelma and Corrine Dower who had raised their own babies. They began watching Waneta more closely and talking about what they were seeing. What was left unexpressed, because it was so vague, was the notion of how it related to the family history. Maybe it was simply that she was afraid of becoming attached to the baby. Or was it, as they were beginning to suspect, something more—something unspeakable? Thelma knew that one of the previous children had been well past two when he died, and she kept thinking about a bell curve Steinschneider had showed her when he came back from the SIDS conference the year before. It showed how the incidence of crib death peaked at two or three months, then declined steadily. By the time you got to age two, it was almost unheard of.

One day when the Hoyts were visiting, Corrine watched them with Molly.

"She never once picked up the baby," she told Thelma. She had a gut feeling, she said, that something awful was going on. A younger nurse, Joyce Thomas, remarked that Waneta never asked her about the baby, never seemed concerned, even when the monitor alarm sounded. She could not believe that a woman who had already lost three children could be so indifferent. "She doesn't pay any attention at all to the baby," she told Thelma and Corrine one day. "All she does is sit on her husband's lap."

Hearing such pointed remarks, picking up the suspicious whispers among the other nurses, Jeanne Steivang bristled. "How can you say these things?" she said to Thelma one day. "Get off this poor girl's back. She's lost *three* children. And this one has definite apnea problems."

Jeanne was Steinschneider's champion among the nurses. She was idealistic about research nursing—it was where you could change the world, she believed—and Steinschneider's SIDS studies made her feel part of a great mission. She believed in his nascent apnea theory, and she found him to be one of the most likable men among the doctors she'd encountered. "His purpose was what I would call noble," she would say one day years later. "A lot of them are in it for the money. Al's emotions were right out there." She had worked with Steinschneider since his days as a resident under Earle Lipton, and he had always impressed her as a "clean scientist," an objective investigator with strongly held views, but no particular agenda other than true discovery.

SIDS, though, raised the stakes. Steinschneider's drive to break the code imbued her and the lab technicians with a sense of urgency. "Not everyone bought into SIDS in those days," she remembered. "Some people thought it was due to bad parenting. But we were onto something—there was definitely something wrong with some babies that was not perceptible by looking at them, and Al had this grievous concern that they would be forever lost if we, or somebody, didn't figure it out. He was excited, but it was more that he had this overwhelming worry that we weren't going to get an answer quick enough. It affected all of us in the lab. I know I felt it. We had to keep plugging along because every day we didn't have an answer meant another baby dying somewhere in the world."

Where the other nurses dismissed Molly's apneic periods as insignificant, Jeanne took Steinschneider's view that they might well be the key to SIDS. She dutifully recorded each one, elevating it to the status of an "episode." Where the other nurses saw bad mothering, she saw judgmental nursing. She had done postgraduate work in maternal-child nursing, and from this she had developed an abhorrence for pediatric nurses—and there were more than a few, she felt—who were too hard on mothers. True, she had not yet met Mrs. Hoyt—working weekdays in the lab, she often tested babies without ever seeing their parents—but she was appalled at what she took to be the mean-spiritedness of the talk at the nurses' station. She chastised Thelma, sometimes angrily and at length. "I'm sorry, that's the way I feel," Thelma would reply. *There's no talking to Jeanne,* she thought. *She's young and she knows everything.*

If Steivang felt badly for Waneta, her sympathy paled in comparison to the pity the other nurses felt for Waneta's child. They tried to fill the void. They gave her special attention, rocked her, held her, played with her, talked to her. "TLC given," Joyce Thomas took to writing in the nursing record, an unconventional and telling note amid all the medical acronyms. In pediatrics, it was easy to become attached to the patients, and Joyce was one of several nurses who went home each night worrying about Molly. She became a peculiarly cherished patient. The nurses found themselves doting on a baby who was, by any standard reading, not sick.

On May 19, a Tuesday, Steinschneider decided it was time to send Molly home with the monitor again. He had seen a marked decrease in her apneic spells over the course of her second hospital stay, which had lasted nine days. Barring a recurrence of the longer apneic episodes, Molly was to return to Syracuse in two weeks.

In Newark Valley the next morning, Margaret Horton picked up her dispatcher's phone and heard the plaintive voice of Waneta Hoyt. The baby was breathing, Waneta said, but Dr. Steinschneider, with whom she had just talked, told her to get Molly back to Syracuse in a hurry. The baby had stopped breathing twice that morning, and Tim was at work. Would Margaret send the squad? Right away, said Margaret. It was the second emergency call for Molly in six weeks, but in each case the rescuers were relieved not to find a dead child upon their arrival on Davis Hollow Road. In fact, in both instances they could look at the baby during the ride to the hospital and see a patient in no distress at all. Not that Waneta didn't appreciate their efforts. After the last trip, to Tompkins County, she had enclosed with her usual thank-you note a picture of Molly.

"She was fine last night," Waneta told Steinschneider in the Upstate emergency room. "Then this morning the alarm went off. I came in her room and she wasn't breathing, and she was blue. I started shaking her to get her to breathe, but it took longer than the last time. And then it happened again about an hour later."

Steinschneider had a thought. "How was she sleeping?" he asked. "On her back or her tummy?" On her back, Waneta said.

Molly was examined—she was a "vigorous infant with good color, no respiratory difficulty and strong cry," an intern in the E.R. found—and was taken immediately to the autonomic lab for testing. When Waneta told Thelma Schneider what had happened that morning, Thelma looked at her coolly. "Mother states child was blue all over and limp," she wrote on the chart.

In the lab, Jeanne Steivang fed Molly a couple of ounces of formula, and the baby promptly fell asleep. Despite the reading of the E.R. doctor, it was Jeanne's impression that Molly was listless, and her cry was "even weaker than usual," as she put it in the notes. But her breathing was fine—Jeanne did not detect any pauses of significance during a session that lasted two and a half hours. She returned the baby to her room and gave her to Waneta to feed, crossing paths with Corrine Dower, who noted, with an edge, that Molly seemed "a bit fussy" in her mother's arms.

The next day, Steinschneider invited Tim and Waneta into the lab to watch a session of tests on their daughter. Since the episode at home had happened while Molly was on her back, Steinschneider wanted to see if this meant something. Testing his suspicion, he found she had more respiratory pauses while she was on her back, though none was prolonged or caused her any distress. He told the nurses to put Molly to sleep only on her abdomen.

The nurses scoffed. The circumstances of Molly's readmission to the hospital had ignited their smoldering anxiety. It crossed Thelma's mind that the cause of Molly's return might have been an aborted attempt on her life, but she couldn't bring herself to say it. A mother actually killing her own children? Was this possible? She cornered Steinschneider again. She chose her words carefully. There seemed to be a serious discrepancy, she said, between what the mother was reporting and what the nurses saw day after day. "Don't you want to know what's going on in that home?" she asked suggestively. She hoped he would pick up her signals and start broadening his perspective. She hoped he would at least bring in one of the hospital social workers. Two were assigned to pediatrics. The baby's chest was now red and raw from the monitor leads—was this necessary? Of course it was necessary, Steinschneider said—the baby had apnea. "He so believed in what he was doing," Thelma remembered with high exasperation. "To him this was just a bunch of opinions from nurses."

One day in the lab, another of Steinschneider's research assistants, a young nurse named Polly Fibiger, wondered aloud why Molly seemed to have trouble only at home. Her implication was clear to Jeanne Steivang, who was standing nearby, and Jeanne didn't like it a bit. They were good friends, but on this they disagreed. Jeanne told Polly she was way off base to think there was "something wrong" at home. "Maybe there's a stuffed animal in the crib or something," Polly said to Steinschneider, trying to put an innocent face on her concern. She had an idea: Next time they discharged Molly, why not send a nurse home with her? They could get a look at the home environment, a sense of how the mother handled the baby outside the hospital. Molly keeps coming back, Fibiger said. Maybe they could find out why.

"We've checked out the house," Steinschneider said enigmatically. "There was nothing unusual."

By the first of June, Molly had spent fifty-one of her seventy-five days of life in hospitals. In that time, she had had only one moment of drama. It came during a visit by the Hoyts one Saturday in May, when a nurse's aide named Pearl Dowdell heard the alarm on the apnea monitor and went into Molly's room. She found both parents shaking the baby, mashing her chest. The aide pushed her way in and discovered that the monitor leads had come loose. Molly was fine.

The Hoyts' visits had tailed off by now to once every three or four days. It seemed to Thelma Schneider that the baby was virtually motherless. In recent days she had been paying close attention to what she felt was a continuing divergence between Molly's physical condition and her emotional and mental development. She ate well, slept well, and gained weight on schedule. But her rosy cast was giving way to a certain dullness. Despite all of Joyce Thomas's "gave Enfamil and TLC" notes, Molly, Thelma thought, was responding less to the nurses and her surroundings. She began entering these observations into the record. On Tuesday morning, June 2, she wrote:

8:30   Awake. Weighed, bathed & lotion applied. Inhalation therapy in to check new monitor which isn't working.
9:00   Took formula eagerly. Right eye noted to be tearing again. Child has little or no affect. Looks to the left most of the time. . . . Does not smile at people.

Forty-eight hours later, on Thursday, June 4, Steinschneider scheduled Molly for her third discharge. By now, the nurses were speaking more openly. How many times could Molly come back to the hospital? "I just know something's going to happen," Corrine said to Thelma. "One of these times, she's going to do it." She was not one of the nurses who found Steinschneider charming. She thought he was pompous, and she was scornful of his abilities as a physician. "I'd been around too long," she later reflected. "I didn't think his little jokes were cute. This was serious. If he had any brains at all he would have seen that she didn't want that baby. You can tell in the grocery store if a person cares about their child. We were just disgusted with Steinschneider."

For Thelma, talking to Steinschneider about Molly Hoyt had become nearly routine—and routinely fruitless. On the morning the baby was to be sent home again, Thelma tried once more. Steinschneider listened, said nothing. Under other circumstances, it would be unlike him. She wondered what lay beneath his reticence. She found his behavior paradoxical. Here was a man who seemed dedicated to helping babies, yet he had no clue what it was, on the most basic level, that babies needed. She wondered how a pediatrician who also held a doctorate in psychology could be so unperceptive, so uninterested in the dynamic between mother and child. How could he not notice that there was just something wrong about this woman? If one looked into it even a little bit, it might turn out to have something to do with the deaths of her children. Molly Hoyt's life hung in the balance, Thelma believed, but only Steinschneider had the power to do something to confirm or refute the suspicion. That was the immutable protocol of the hospital.

Shortly after noon, knowing that Molly would be going home in six hours, Thelma sat down at her desk and began to write her thoughts into the nursing record. By convention, the nurses' notes were a dispassionate chronicle of routine hospital minutiae, written on a lined form divided into two columns, so that a page could chronicle twenty-four hours or more of the baby's life. Thelma took nearly an entire column to unburden herself. To the seven weeks of clinical detail that had preceded it, her entry added an incongruous note of frustration and anxiety:

12:15   Took 95 cc formula. Burped. Right eye tearing slightly during feeding. To sleep on abdomen. This baby was able to focus on moving object today and respond to it. I discussed my concern for this baby with Dr. Steinschneider this A.M. At times Molly will not respond to her surroundings at all—her head is turned to the left and she has a glassy stare. At these times the baby totally lacks affect and appears retarded. At other times she has been known to "coo" and watch the mobile. She rarely smiles in response to another person. The interaction between mother and baby is almost nil in my opinion.

                                                              T. Schneider RN

This, meanwhile, was Steinschneider's note for that day:

6/4   Does not appear to have much apnea during sleep and has continued to do well on ward. Will discharge today and plan on readmitting to CCRC in 2 weeks.

                                                              A. Steinschneider

Early in the evening, Corrine Dower dressed Molly in a pink dress that Julie Evans had brought in for her. "She was absolutely adorable," Corrine remembered. "And I was livid." She watched as Waneta used the phone at the nurses' station to talk to Steinschneider before taking the baby home. Waneta nodded as Steinschneider, who had already left the hospital, repeated his instructions about the apnea monitor and room temperature, adding one new assignment. Molly was to sleep only on her stomach.

Joyce Thomas carried Molly onto the elevator, descending the five floors with the baby's mother in silence. She tried hard to keep her composure. So much was unknown, so much unspoken. The mind games confused and terrified her in a way she couldn't articulate—she couldn't bring herself to actually say, as Corrine did, that "something" was going to happen. Coming in for work that afternoon, she'd heard that Molly was going home in the evening. *Oh my God,* she'd thought. Now she was the one carrying her out, putting Molly into her mother's arms.

Tim pulled the car up, and Waneta got in. Joyce placed Molly on her mother's lap, then went back inside the hospital and rode the elevator upstairs. She went over to Corrine at the nurses' station and began to cry. Corrine put her arm around Joyce. "We've done everything we can," she said, the consoling words poisoned by bitterness. "We're just *nurses,*" Corrine said. "We don't know *anything.*"

She scribbled a final note in Molly's nursing record: "No apnea noted."

Later that night, Corrine looked at the clock over the nurses' station. "I wonder if she's still alive," she said to Joyce.

Floyd Angel was the assistant manager of the Owego A&P until he got a promotion to head a corps of traveling inventory auditors. There were eleven of them who roamed New York's Southern Tier and northeastern Pennsylvania, counting every can, box, and bag on every shelf of every store, all 126 of them, in the region. They worked in crews of three, and it could take four or five hours to cover one of the bigger stores before moving on to the next one. It was a job that kept Floyd on the road from Monday night to Thursday or Friday, but the schedule could be irregular, so he always made sure to leave his itinerary with the Tioga County sheriff's department, to let them know when he was available for coroner calls.

Floyd was the coroner in charge of Owego and the southeastern part of Tioga County, but occasionally he found himself up in Newark Valley or one of the other northern villages, where people in the hills sometimes referred to him as "Dr. Angel." Dr. Hartnagel had retired to Cayuga Lake the year before and hadn't been replaced yet as coroner. On this Friday in early June, a call came at midmorning. "Floyd," a sheriff's deputy said, "we've got a report of a small baby that died at the Tim Hoyt residence on the Davis Hollow Road in Newark Valley. There's a request for a coroner. Can you go?"

"I'm on my way," Angel said. Minutes later, Undersheriff Ray Cornwell was heading north on Route 38 as well.

An hour before Angel picked up the phone, Waneta Hoyt had called her mother-in-law and said that her baby daughter had turned blue, and that she couldn't get her to breathe. Ella Hoyt came running to the trailer and found Molly in her crib, lifeless, the apnea monitor disconnected. Waneta called Margaret Horton for help, and the emergency siren wailed once again across Newark Valley. Molly had been home from the hospital barely twelve hours.

Bob Vanek, Art Balzer, and Hank Robson came to the fire station, piled into the ambulance, and a minute later they were screeching around the corner at the gas station on Main Street, where one of them saw Chuck Hoyt at work and hollered that they were headed up to his brother's place. They raced to the door of the trailer they knew as well as any home in Newark Valley. Chuck pulled up right behind them.

He dropped to his knees and held his tiny niece. He thought he detected a faint breath. The squad began trying to bring her back, first with mouth-to-mouth, then with oxygen. Waneta went to the phone to call Upstate. In pediatrics, she reached Polly Fibiger. "Are you giving CPR?" the nurse asked. Waneta said that the squad was working on her. Polly told her Steinschneider would be in any minute. He'd call her right back.

Ann Hoyt ran over to the trailer when she heard what was going on. She had never wanted Waneta and Tim to have this baby in the first place, and she watched in disbelief as the men kept at her.

Robson kept feeling for a pulse. There was none. "She's deceased," he said finally. Molly was two months and eighteen days old.

Silence fell over the gathering. Then Chuck walked over to Waneta, put his arm around her, and asked where Tim was working that day. He got in his car and drove off. Bob Vanek, who had kept his suspicions to himself after the deaths of Julie and Jimmy twenty months before, went home and had a shot of whiskey. Someone else on the squad called the sheriff's department.

Arriving a little while later, Floyd Angel ordered the body removed to the pathology lab at Wilson Memorial Hospital, in Johnson City. "Mrs. Hoyt," he said awkwardly, "we need to conduct an autopsy on this child."

Waneta said she didn't want her baby's body cut into pieces.

Angel had been elected one of the four county coroners in 1961 after many years teaching a first aid course at the Owego firehouse. He retained a physician in Owego to pronounce routine causes of death, and usually sent his autopsy cases to a pathologist named Rudolph Muelling at Wilson Memorial. He wanted Molly's body to be autopsied because that was now the procedure with any unexpected death outside a hospital. He was reluctant to go ahead against the mother's wishes, however. He turned to Ray Cornwell, an easygoing man nicknamed the Silver Fox for his shock of gray hair. The undersheriff pressed her on the need for the postmortem examination, and Waneta relented.

Steinschneider arrived at work fifteen minutes after Waneta's conversation with Polly Fibiger and went right to the phone. Waneta told him that Molly had died. She had bathed and fed her early in the morning, she said, then put her in the crib. "I left the room for a minute to get something," she said. "When I came back, her face was blue and she wasn't breathing. The squad came but they couldn't bring her back."

A few minutes later, a chorus of agony—"Oh no!" "Oh my God!"—erupted at the nurses' station. "I told you she was going to kill her," Corrine Dower told Thelma caustically when she came in later for her shift. She had never been so furious in all her years as a nurse. Thelma was only slightly more circumspect. "There was not a thing wrong with that baby," she said to Steinschneider. "Something's definitely going on here." Again he didn't respond directly. He told her the baby would be autopsied that day. Thelma said she was anxious to hear the results.

Back in Newark Valley, Ray Cornwell commenced an investigation. Later that day, he completed it. After talking to Dr. Perry and a few neighbors, he filed a report:

> Molly Hoyt dob: 3/18/70 daughter of Timothy and Waneta Hoyt had expired. This is the 4th child lost by these parents. There seems to be a gland problem on the mothers side this was verified by the family Doctor. Coroner Angel ordered the body to be taken to Wilson where a post will be performed. At first the mother refused to authorize a post, but later consented. The squad worked over the baby, mouth-to-mouth and oxygen, for approx ¾ of a hour. People in the area spoke very highly of the couple and since the baby had been in the hospital recently for this problem I do not feel a further investigation is necessary other than the post.

Hank Robson carried Molly's body directly into the pathology lab, where Dr. Muelling began the autopsy right after lunch. Muelling saw that Molly's face was still deeply cyanotic, but found nothing else remarkable during his external examination. Nor did he find anything of obvious lethal consequence inside. Examining the aorta, he noted a coarctation, or narrowing, at a point where the great vessel met the ductus arteriosus—the fetal blood vessel that the pediatric cardiologist at Upstate suspected had failed to close after birth, causing Molly's murmur. Muelling saw that the ductus arteriosus had, in fact, closed on schedule. But neither the physical nor microscopic observations revealed any disease process normally associated with death.

Muelling didn't do many autopsies of two-month-old babies. And with little practical experience with Sudden Infant Death Syndrome, the notion of natural death without any disease process was foreign to him. There was the narrowing of the aorta, but that couldn't have caused the death. Meanwhile, he was unsure how to read the slide of lung tissue, and decided to show it to another pathologist. His colleague thought the tissue contained some cells indicating possible pneumonia. In a case like this, you couldn't go wrong with pneumonia. Under "immediate cause" on Molly's death certificate, Muelling wrote "interstitial pneumonitis, acute." He handed it to Floyd Angel, who signed it as coroner.

"How could she get pneumonia that fast?" Thelma Schneider asked Stein-schneider later that day. "I mean, we took her temperature, checked her breathing, the monitor, the whole thing." For an instant she questioned her intuition. Maybe the pathologists saw something the nurses didn't. Nurses weren't supposed to diagnose—that was drummed in from the first day of nursing school. Maybe Molly really did have an infection that killed her without warning. But Thelma also knew intuitively that the diagnosis didn't stand up logically: As far as she knew, fatal pneumonia didn't run in families.

Polly Fibiger also thought the autopsy was nonsense, but she didn't get a chance to talk about it with her partner in the lab, Jeanne Steivang. In an odd bit of timing, just days before, President Nixon had slashed federal support of pediatric research, a direct hit on centers like the CCRC. Jeanne was among those called together and told the research clinic would have to be drastically scaled back and that they were out of jobs. She left instantly, angry and dis-illusioned, worried about the fate of all those babies who would keep dying of SIDS. She spent the summer in the Adirondack Mountains, then moved to California. She never heard about the death of Molly Hoyt.

Steinschneider arranged to receive a copy of Rudolph Muelling's full autopsy report, along with the twelve tissue slides. When they arrived, he showed the microscopics—the "histology" in pathology parlance—to Bedros Markarian, a veteran pathologist at Upstate. Markarian found nothing that could explain the death—he didn't agree that the lungs contained evidence of pneumonia—so Steinschneider decided to call Molly Dapena, the pediatric pathologist and SIDS researcher whom he'd met on Orcas Island, and asked her to take a look. But when she put the slide of Molly Hoyt's lung section under her microscope in Philadelphia, she, like Markarian, saw no evidence of pneumonia, or anything else revealing. The tissue samples looked no different from those of scores of babies Dapena had seen in the last fifteen years.

Each time, Tim Hoyt recalled years later, the road foreman would say, "Tim, there's a problem at home." It was always while he was out on a job site, usually in the middle hours between morning coffee and lunch. The foreman never said what the problem was, but after Julie's death, it was unnecessary. "Anytime anybody came to me with a funny look, I knew something was wrong," he remembered. For years afterward, the wail of a passing ambulance shook him the way the distant pop of a hunting rifle had made his brother Donald jump ever since he got back from Vietnam. When Tim had gotten the call about Jimmy, the foreman told him to wait—he'd get him a police escort—but Tim said, "I ain't waitin'." He took off down the long stretch of unopened road they were building, Route 17 outside Waverly, and by the time he reached the other side of Owego, the speedometer needle was jumping past 100. Again and again, Margaret Horton would see Tim speeding past her house, hanging on to the steering wheel, his eyes ablaze. "I worry about that boy," she once told Ann. "One of these times he's gonna end up in a wreck."

The ambulance was always gone, or just leaving. He would find a small crowd at the house, and Waneta would be in the middle of them, shaking. "She was just standing there . . . just totally broken," Tim remembered. He was thinking of the morning Julie died, but it was always the same. "And she was sobbing and crying and saying, 'I don't know . . . she just quit breathing, she just turned blue, she started gagging. . . .'" And Tim would envelop her with his arms. "I just tried to comfort her, like I've done all my life. Ever since we've been married. Anything tragic happens, it's me that she wants."

Tim's family could see the toll of the children's deaths every time they looked at his face. His big, toothy smile had been replaced by a permanent frown. His family did what it could to lessen the pain. His sister Janet would enter the children's birthdays on her calendar, along with the days of their deaths. "Julie gone today," she would write in the box for September fifth; "Molly gone," she'd enter on June fifth. "Just so that if Tim came around that day I wouldn't screw up and say something to hurt his feelings," she explained. Meanwhile, some among them were baffled by Waneta's sometimes unpredictable reactions to the deaths of her children. The day after Molly's funeral, she bought herself a new dress and decided she and Tim should go out dancing. The next day, she told people what a good time they'd had. One of her relatives asked her if it wasn't a little soon to be having the time of her life. "People deal with grief in different ways," Waneta replied.

When she was with Tim, Waneta tended to deal with it by blaming herself. After Molly died, and Waneta once again said it was her fault—if she hadn't left her for a few seconds, the baby would be alive—Tim told her it was not nearly that simple. Even Dr. Steinschneider could not save Molly.

When Tim asked him why Molly had died despite the intense care he had given her, Steinschneider became philosophical. "We're doctors; we're not God," he said. "We practice medicine—we are not medicine." Molly was Steinschneider's first SIDS case.

Waneta also talked to Steinschneider that summer. She had nothing to live for, she told him despondently. All her children had been taken from her. He became one of those men of authority in her life who gave her compassion and counsel. In Newark Valley, there was Gary Kuhns, the pastor who presided over the funerals of Julie, Jimmy, and Molly. At Sunday church Waneta found herself surrounded by the pity of her community, and for Kuhns, a youthful man with an activist bent, ministering to the Hoyts became a central preoccupation of his life. "Oh God," he remarked years later with an immense sigh, "so much went down between me and that family."

Now Waneta had Steinschneider too. No doctor had ever taken such an interest in the health of her children. Though he was an important man at a big hospital and she had not known him long, she always found him a solicitous presence. Every time she called after taking Molly home, he had listened carefully. Every time Molly was in distress, he acted. Waneta did not lose his sympathetic ear when her baby died. "She talked to him about whatever was bothering her, how she felt about the children's deaths, about life itself," Tim remembered. She left her family with the impression that for her, as her sister-in-law Loretta put it, "the sun rose and set with Dr. Steinschneider." He, however, did not regard it as a special relationship. He did not consider their private life his province. If he had in fact "checked out the house," as he told Polly Fibiger and Jeanne Steivang, he made no record of it, nor did he mention it to Thelma Schneider, the nurse who pressed him most.

Nonetheless, the Hoyts were coming to play a powerful role in his evolving absorption with dying babies. Between mother and doctor, a complex but unacknowledged relationship was unfolding. When Waneta said the deaths of her babies were somehow her fault, Steinschneider replied that it was not so. When she said she had nothing to live for, he countered that all was not lost. She and Tim were still both healthy and young—Waneta was still just twenty-four, Tim twenty-eight—and despite everything, he said, they did not necessarily have to give up on the idea of having a family. Based on what he'd heard from the epidemiologists the year before, Steinschneider thought SIDS could have a *familial* aspect, but that it was probably not genetic. Familial meant that some environmental or social circumstance common to a family—prenatal care, for instance, or smoking—could cause subsequent siblings of SIDS victims to have a higher than normal risk themselves. Steinschneider, though, did not explore the nuances with the Hoyts. What they heard him say was that SIDS was not genetic.

This opinion presented a dilemma for Tim. He had presumed, after the deaths of Julie and Jimmy, that the problem was indeed genetic. Molly's death only strengthened this belief. He had the notion that his father's drinking had somehow infiltrated the family gene pool, poisoning his children. Or perhaps something was running through Waneta's bloodlines. He began pursuing the possibility of serious genetic testing, but his labor union's insurance company refused to pay for such a speculative and expensive procedure. The genetic question baffled both their families for an obvious reason: Waneta's sister Donna was married to Tim's brother Donald, and they had four perfectly healthy children.

As Tim puzzled over genetics, Waneta was thinking ahead. On June 12— four days after Molly was buried alongside her brothers and sister in Highland Cemetery—Waneta went to see their caseworker at Social Services to ask that their adoption application be reactivated. But she changed her mind again after talking with Steinschneider and receiving an official green light to conceive another child. She wasted no time persuading Tim that they should act on the encouragement.

In Syracuse, Steinschneider continued his call for referrals of babies with apnea and near-misses. Though the federal government was no longer picking up the tab for the Children's Clinical Research Center as it had been constituted, the space remained available for research. The center would see outpatients, the autonomic lab was still open for business, and there were plenty of pediatric beds on 4A. The hunt for a cause of Sudden Infant Death Syndrome would continue.

In Newark Valley, two months after Molly's death, Waneta Hoyt became pregnant with her fifth child. She would be due the following May. When she called Steinschneider with the news, he told her that the baby should not go home after its birth. She should bring the newborn straight from the maternity ward of Tompkins County Hospital, right up to the research center on the fifth floor of Upstate Medical Center.

21

MOUNT SINAI SCHOOL OF MEDICINE
of The City University of New York
Fifth Avenue and 100th Street, New York, NY 10029

Department of Psychiatry

May 19, 1971

Alfred Steinschneider, Ph.D., M.D.
Associate Professor
Department of Pediatrics
Upstate Medical Center
Syracuse, New York

Dear Dr. Steinschneider:

I have read with interest your involvement in the Second International Conference on S.I.D. Because of your active work in this area, I have hopes of enlisting your help in a study with which we have been involved at the Mount Sinai Hospital of New York for several years.

Several members of our Department of Psychiatry here have been interested in the phenomenology of Post-Partum Depression. We have been impressed with its variable duration, even up to one year, and of the various phenomenology it may exhibit. Such depressions may only reveal themselves through some unexpected and serious behavior. Attempts at suicide are, of course, our greatest concern, and sometimes may be the first evidence of a hidden post-partum reaction.

However, our group has come to recognize another phenomenon of the post-partum period that has been less well recognized or considered for a variety of reasons. We have found several instances of infanticide, not always associated with suicide, during the months following childbirth (or even adoption; interestingly enough. This curious occurrence can be explained psychiatrically).

As a result we have become very interested in infanticide as a specific manifestation of a depressive reaction to parturition. Our study excludes those cases in which infanticide is committed with full awareness and intent, in order to conceal or remove an unwanted pregnancy. This is a different category of infanticide, and unlike the post-partum reaction cases which apparently occur without the mother's full awareness of her actions.

We are very eager to collect information about cases of infanticide in infants under one year, which you may know about. Since it is possible that some infanticides may be inadvertently hidden in S.I.D. statistics, I have been writing to various workers in the field asking for information. We are very anxious to avoid public dissemination of this study which would be needlessly disturbing to S.I.D. families. My article on this topic, "Crib Deaths: Their Possible Relationship to Post-Partum Depression and Infanticide" (Journal of Mount Sinai Hospital, May–June, 1968), did unfortunately get some unauthorized dissemination and we are anxious to avoid this in the future. Thank you for giving your time to this letter. We would be very grateful for any pertinent data you can send us.

Very truly yours,
Stuart S. Asch, M.D.
Associate Clinical Professor
Unit Chief
Mount Sinai Medical Center

Stuart Asch was a psychiatrist fresh out of residency when he accidentally walked into the morbid fears and fantasies of some young mothers-to-be. In the mid-1960s, he was a newly trained psychoanalyst, pondering the next step in his career at New York's Mount Sinai Hospital, when he asked for a meeting with the hospital's chairman of obstetrics and gynecology, Dr. Alan Guttmacher. He was interested in applying his specialty to obstetrical medicine.

Guttmacher, the first president of Planned Parenthood, thought it was an interesting idea. He gave Asch permission to hang around the obstetrics and gynecology floor. Talk to the women, he told him; see how they feel. When he did, Asch found that some women approached motherhood with deep insecurities about their ability to care for a baby. When he probed further, some of them confided that they were haunted by fears that their babies would die and that it would be their fault. As he accumulated records of these morbid musings, Asch wondered if any of them ever converged with reality. He knew that some women suffered severe postpartum reactions. He also knew that thousands of babies died each year without medical explanation.

When he broached this notion with obstetricians, he was met with great skepticism and a fair amount of anxiety. Not surprisingly, the doctors didn't want to think that some of their patients might actually do harm to their babies. Furthermore, some pointed out, wasn't psychiatry replete with latent wishes never fulfilled? It was a valid point. Asch decided to use his psychoanalytic tools to test his theory. In 1967, he called the legendary chief medical examiner of New York City, Dr. Milton Helpern. He was neither surprised nor displeased to learn that Helpern had himself wondered what might be behind the numbers of babies arriving in the city morgue after dying suddenly and inexplicably. Asch told the medical examiner he wanted to study the question from a psychiatric point of view. And he wanted to do it firsthand.

He proposed sending one or two psychiatric residents to interview mothers and their families after such deaths, right at the scene. They would do it delicately, of course, but perhaps some cases would provide enough psychiatric clues to piece together a homicide, along with a hypothesis. Helpern knew this was extremely tricky business—he was on the board of the local crib-death group—but he also believed that questions needed to be asked when babies died mysteriously.

To do the legwork, Asch recruited the hospital's chief psychiatry resident, David Shapiro, whose wife happened to be pregnant, and another resident, Nathaniel Karush. Helpern arranged for the police to notify the Mount Sinai doctors whenever they responded to an infant death in the city, and deputized them as medical examiners—gave them badges and stickers that would give them access to virtually any death scene. The calls came steadily. Shapiro and Karush studied the scenes like detectives, talking to parents, watching for anything unusual—an affect, a circumstance—that might call into question a diagnosis of crib death. It was difficult work. Karush didn't stay with it long. He decided he didn't believe the premise that mothers could kill their own children. In fact, he found it appalling.

But Shapiro persisted and went out on about forty cases over the course of a year. He found five he thought were probable homicides. One was a young baby found dead by his parents, who were apparently winding down from a night of drinking. It looked like a classic crib death, but Shapiro was skeptical of the death scene: the house in shambles, the parents' breaths a vapor of alcohol. Indeed, when the baby was brought to the medical examiner's office and autopsied, a skull fracture on X ray made what really happened obvious. Asch wrote up his preliminary findings and sent the paper to the *National Law Journal*. Its publication had swift results. Helpern was inundated with calls and letters from parents who had lost children to crib death and thought Asch's assertions cruel and horribly misguided. They called Asch a quack, a charlatan—a mother hater. A congressman from Seattle called Guttmacher's office to complain. Abe Bergman wrote Asch a series of heated letters and so did Mary Dore. ("I was totally hysterical about Dr. Asch," she remembered. "He was somebody you put up on a dartboard.") Even the controversial Helpern found it too hot to handle. He asked for the badges and stickers. But Asch felt he had learned enough to justify pursuing his theory, even if it was the one scientific hypothesis whose validity depended on legal evidence.

Asch was skeptical of SIDS as a true medical entity. If you looked hard enough, he suspected, there would almost always be an explanation— whether it was an undiagnosed medical condition, an inadvertent overlaying or other form of accidental smothering, or, in some cases—he thought the figure could be as high as twenty percent—infanticide. The response to his first paper told him that his medical colleagues were unwilling to confront the darkest side of a dark question, that he was virtually alone in his thinking. But the reactions also chastened him. He realized he had underestimated the sensitivities of parents and their growing power as an interest group. He decided that his theory was perhaps still too speculative, and too incendiary, to disseminate widely. When he wrote his next paper, in 1968, he submitted it to a publication with a small audience—the journal of his own hospital.

Though his first paper had appeared in a legal publication, Asch didn't approach his subject from a criminal justice point of view. He didn't want to prosecute mothers who killed their children during a postpartum psychosis, or, for that matter, during any other kind of infanticidal episode with psychiatric roots. Prison wasn't the place for them, he believed. When the Queens district attorney's office asked him for the names of the women he suspected after his first paper was published, he refused. He was a psychiatrist, and he wanted them to be given treatment. Mostly, he wanted to shed light on the issue—maybe it could save some children. He managed to get his theory listed at the bottom of a table of "Recently Proposed Hypotheses" presented by Marie Valdes-Dapena at the 1969 SIDS conference, but, not surprisingly, he wasn't invited to Orcas Island to speak about it. His theory was reduced on Dapena's table to three words: "Asch—1968—Infanticide." That was the price, Asch supposed, of devoting one's research to such an abhorrent thesis as this: "Some hostile impulses and thoughts toward both the fetus and the newborn infant are quite within the normal range of maternal ambivalence." He believed that the vast majority of women with such feelings managed to repress them, but as he would note ruefully in a later paper, most of his fellow citizens found it impossible even to consider the suggestion that in some cases "mother love might be replaced by murderous impulses."

But the subject continued to preoccupy him, and in 1971, Asch set out to gather another round of data—case studies from around the United States that might demonstrate that infanticide was more common than people dared think—and this time, if the results were solid enough, to publish it in a major psychiatric journal. He began writing to pediatricians and others who dealt with sudden infant death, asking if they were aware of any possible infanticide cases, particularly those initially attributed to the newly popularized medical acronym SIDS. One response came from a doctor who described a mother who was a "cold, unempathic woman" whose "relationships with people were determined by their ability to fulfill her needs." After the birth of her son, she became depressed, withdrawn, and preoccupied with the fear that the baby would die of pneumonia. She took to immersing him in cold water to build up his resistance and pinning a blanket tightly over him in his crib. He was found dead one morning, his face pressed down into the mattress.

Alfred Steinschneider did not respond to Asch's query. His private reactions to the psychiatrist's letter are unknowable. But it is a pertinent question, considering the timing of the correspondence. On the morning that Asch wrote to Steinschneider, ten-day-old Noah Timothy Hoyt was attached to a polygraph machine in the pediatric autonomic lab at Upstate Medical Center. Six days before, Steinschneider had admitted the fifth child of Waneta and Timothy Hoyt to the hospital for observation and study.

The baby was born twenty-one minutes before midnight on Sunday, May 9, 1971—Mother's Day. He was named for Noah Kassman, the obstetrician who had delivered him and all his brothers and sisters. In the maternity ward of Tompkins County Hospital, the routine was the same. For the fifth time in less than seven years, the Hoyts became parents of a "normal newborn," as Dr. Roger Perry put it once again on the birth record. A note jotted in the lower left corner of the nursery record by the delivery room nurse added Molly to the list of dead siblings, trailing off perfunctorily: "1st—died heart, 2nd—thymus, 3rd—choked, 4th—died."

The nurses at Tompkins County noted that Noah had some trouble with feeding his first couple of days, but other than that he seemed fine. "Good baby," a nurse wrote. Shortly after noon on his fourth day of life, she snipped off his hospital ID bracelet, put him in his mother's arms, and sent him into the world. The latest version of the Hoyt family headed straight for Syracuse.

If Waneta and Tim had had their way, they would have had another child as well. Despite Waneta's new pregnancy, they had decided to keep open the adoption application they'd reactivated the week after Molly died. The file contained an updated report from Dr. Kassman. "Patient has had four live births," the obstetrician wrote. "All children have died in infancy, possibly from poorly understood genetic disease. Parents and children have been under study at Upstate Medical Center."

Waneta requested an older child, telling her new caseworker at Social Services that she "needed" a child in her home to help her through the pregnancy. And if her fifth baby followed the fate of the first four, she added, she would still have the adopted child. The application received a cool response from the caseworker, a mother of five herself named Alberta Weisz. She felt uncomfortable with the Hoyts' history of loss and the impulsive way they pursued adoption, and she was especially concerned about Waneta's expressed "need" for a child. She made a point of dragging her feet on the application.

Impatient, the Hoyts applied to a private agency in Tompkins County, Family and Children's Service of Ithaca. In January, Weisz got a call from the Ithaca caseworker, asking what she knew about the Hoyts. Weisz wrote back:

> . . . It would appear that this couple has suffered a great deal of grief. Neither has resolved their emotional need for a natural child. It almost seems like the couple considers the adoption process as a second resource, but not a complete fulfillment. The Hoyts requested an older child. It does not seem a particularly good time to introduce an older child into a home during final months of pregnancy. . . . It seems like an adopted child could be an "insurance policy" for the family. The Hoyts need a child in their home to help them through their fifth pregnancy. They need the child to buffer their grief should the fifth child not survive. The question in mind is whether a child needs them as parents.

Four months later, Noah Hoyt, an only child, was settled into his first home—the pediatric ward of Upstate Medical Center.

His sister's death eleven months before had aroused Steinschneider as a scientist. He saw it not in the context of Stuart Asch's hypothesis, but in terms of his own. Molly's death fit just about everything he had come to believe about SIDS: the near-misses, the recurring apnea, the association with respiratory infection, the final event coming in her third month. There was only one loose end. Most SIDS deaths seemed to occur during sleep. It wasn't clear that Molly was asleep when she died.

A year later, Steinschneider was even more absorbed by the pursuit of his theory. Though Molly was the most dramatic of his subjects—the only one he studied who had gone on to die—she was but one of a number of babies he had recruited for his apnea research in the two years following the 1969 conference. There was, for example, a month-old boy whose mother had rushed him to the emergency room one day when she noticed he was pale and not breathing. Steinschneider admitted the baby to the CCRC, studied him in the lab, and, as with Molly, sent him home with a monitor after three weeks in the hospital. The baby spent the better part of four months shuttling between his home and the hospital. Later, in pursuit of a possible familial link, he studied the baby's sister, with similar results. In all instances but one, the emergency was apparently triggered not by any signs of distress in the baby but by the hyperactive apnea monitor, set to alarm at fifteen seconds.

Steinschneider's consuming fascination with apnea and its possible connection to SIDS had become well known among the pediatrics staff at Upstate. They tended to see him as an intrepid investigator of SIDS whose work was shrouded in a little mystery: the driven scientist, always up in his lab, hooking up babies to monitors, poring over polygraph paper, scribbling calculations. Since Molly's death, he had been trying to refine his sleep studies in an effort to isolate the difference between normal apnea and perilous apnea in advance of the final event. He hadn't been able to do it for Molly, but her death could be viewed as a step in the scientific process. Predicting and preventing death was becoming his obsession.

The work of researchers at UCLA had made him fascinated by the notion of rapid eye movement sleep and its relationship to breathing. In the lab he began labeling each fifteen-second period of his subject's sleep either a "REM epoch" or a "Non REM epoch," and then correlating these with incidence of apnea. He also came up with an elaborate formula he called the Apnea/Duration percentage—A/D% for short—to quantify a baby's apnea, whether brief or prolonged. He calculated a baby's A/D% by adding up the duration of all periods of nonrespiration of two seconds or more (measured in tenths of a second), dividing that number by the duration of the total sleep, and then multiplying that number by 100. It was a kind of apnea scoring system.

Jack Schneider, the head of the research unit, had long found Steinschneider's research a waste of time—"all this nutty monkeying around," as he put it. Now he felt his fixation on measurements and statistics bordered on the ridiculous. "I thought it was a crock of shit myself," Schneider said. "But I'm not into that sort of thing. It's fairy-type stuff. You know, they run off reams and reams of polygraph paper, and what do they have?" Schneider's views had nothing to do with the Hoyt family or with his wife's suspicions about Molly's death. Nor was it the theory he found misguided, so much as the method of research. "It was the whole approach. It's like you take a shovel full of pebbles and you throw them into a large swimming pool and then you measure the wave heights and you try to locate where some particular pebbles fell. You're relying on ten billion pieces of information to try to extract which pebble made that wave. And that never did strike me as a very intelligent way to find things out. He's measuring respiratory rates. What can you measure?

Well, you can measure how often it occurs, right? You get a tracing of it. Somebody's breathing. And you've got a thing that moves when he breathes. But is there anything about the previous ten thousand breaths that tells you that the next one is going to be the last?"

Noah Hoyt's early life was a replay of his sister's. The day of his arrival at Upstate, Steinschneider met the Hoyts in the examining room and arranged for a resident to take a history and examine the baby. She found him healthy, though "suspect for respiratory distress syndrome." He was admitted as a research patient, but because the CCRC was now only an outpatient center, he was placed in the pediatric nursery, a glassed-in room on the main pediatric ward on the fourth floor, a level beneath the research center. It had five cribs holding babies with assorted congenital and neonatal difficulties. Like Noah, some of the babies came from long distances to be treated by the pediatric specialists at Upstate. Unlike Noah, these babies had obvious, sometimes serious problems, everything from hydrocephalus to the more general "failure to thrive."

The closing of the CCRC as an inpatient unit, and the changes in the nursing staff that resulted, meant that only a few of the nurses who had gone through the trauma of Molly the year before would now be taking care of her brother. Joyce Thomas and Corrine Dower were gone, but Thelma Schneider was still there and so was Julie Evans. That was more than enough memory to cause a stir when Noah appeared on the ward just eleven months after his sister's mysterious death. The two senior nurses would have opposite roles in Noah's care. Assigned to the pediatric nursery on the fourth floor, Julie had been with Molly only sporadically. Now Noah would be hers. Thelma was still up in the research clinic, working with outpatients, so she would not have much to do with Noah.

Julie was in her mid-fifties, a grandmother of three. She had worked for Jack Schneider at Crouse-Irving Memorial a decade before, then followed him to the new university hospital when he became the head of the research unit. She was full of energy and efficiency, always scurrying around in care of the babies in her charge. She reminded one of the young nurse's aides who came under her wing of Dorothy's Aunt Em—all business, a mother hen who was much too busy taking care of babies to pay attention to the social scene that was an inevitable backdrop of the nurse's life. Some of the younger, unmarried nurses did their jobs, chatted over coffee, made plans for after work, and kept their eyes open for an eligible doctor. Julie had eyes only for the babies. If something bothered her about a baby's care, she did something about it. She had not been centrally involved in the talk about Molly, but she knew about it. Now, as Thelma had been to Molly, she would be one of Noah's surrogate mothers; his protector.

From the night of the Hoyts' first visit, Julie felt that Waneta was unlike any mother she had encountered as a nurse. "You don't see your baby for a few days," she remarked. "You come in and you want to pick up your baby and hold him and feed him and talk to him. She didn't do any of that."

When they came to visit, Waneta and Tim would ride the elevator to the fourth floor and make their way to the ward. It would be early evening, dusk beginning to settle on a spring night in Syracuse, when this subdued, insular young couple from a distant farming town appeared at the nursery. Two decades later, Julie could still see the scene unfolding in her mind, in sharp detail because the visits were so ritualized, Waneta's behavior so consistently disturbing: *She comes in, looks at the baby, and then she sits down. She doesn't kiss the baby. She doesn't pick him up. She doesn't ask, but I tell her how he's been doing. Then I pick him up and hand him to her, put him in her lap. I bring in a chair for her husband. And she's holding the baby, but I know that she doesn't want to hold the baby. You can tell just by the way she's holding him. I'm afraid she's going to drop him or something. She doesn't have her arms around him. She has one arm around him, and the other is . . . I don't know where the other one is. So I take the baby from her and put him in her husband's lap. And she doesn't like that one bit. She pulls her chair next to him, and she strokes her husband's leg, runs her hand up and down his leg. She's jealous, is my impression. Her husband is more affectionate with the baby. She resents it. You can see it in her face. And then the minute I pick up the baby and put him back in the crib, she's all right.*

Picking up where Thelma had left off with Molly, Julie began bringing her observations to Steinschneider. Like Thelma, she had known him a long time—ever since he was a medical student—and liked him. His wisecracks made her laugh, and his lack of ceremony made him easier to be around than some other doctors. Julie had a bit of the firebrand in her, and with Steinschneider she felt comfortable stepping on, if not actually crossing, the line of authority long established by the hospital caste system.

"I don't like the way the mother is acting," she told him after her first few encounters with the Hoyts. "There's no maternal instinct there. She pulls away from the baby, like she really doesn't want to be bothered. I've never seen a mother act that way."

Steinschneider had heard all this before, but apparently Molly's death had not caused him to reevaluate his stance. When Julie said she'd be afraid to send the baby home, he told her he couldn't keep the baby in the hospital indefinitely, and went back to looking for apnea.

His studies were now a good deal more inventive than those he had conducted with Molly. Several times a week, he brought Noah into the lab and, besides the strain gauge on the baby's chest, he put four electrodes around his left eye—one above and one below and one on each side—to measure his eye movements. He found that Noah had many more brief periods of apnea during REM sleep. Sleep position, though—stomach versus back—made no difference. He had the baby, now three weeks old, injected with drugs such as Ritalin, a brain stimulant whose use on hyperactive children would later become hotly debated. He determined that both Ritalin and another drug, Diamox, seemed to decrease the frequency of Noah's apneic pauses. In fact, they made him breathe *too much*. The nurses documented the pitiful incongruity of a seemingly healthy baby being alternately fed and drugged, the results barely distinguishable in the charts. "Given Ritalin in left buttocks," Thelma Schneider wrote on May 27. "Took 5 oz. Enfamil. Burped well. Developed generalized flush and rapid breathing." It was all part of a day in the life of Noah Hoyt.

Noah's breathing was even less eventful than Molly's. He had far fewer periods of what Steinschneider defined as prolonged apnea, and the ones he put into the record were suspect. When a nurse reported a monitor had buzzed but that she couldn't tell whether Noah had stopped breathing, he counted it. When another nurse wrote during her shift, "2 short 5 sec apnea periods, stimulated self," Steinschneider described both periods in his record as "prolonged." He listed one prolonged episode for May 29. "Having short periods of apnea" was all that was reported by the nurses that day. In none of these instances did a nurse have to take any action to stimulate Noah's breathing. By the time Steinschneider sent him home with an apnea monitor on the afternoon of June 15, after thirty-three days of observation, Noah had gone 813 consecutive hours in the hospital without a moment of respiratory distress. He arrived home for the first time in his life at 4:00 that afternoon.

The next morning, he was rushed back by a Newark Valley ambulance. Waneta told the emergency room doctors she'd called for help after reviving Noah with mouth-to-mouth resuscitation.

It had been an awful morning, she told Steinschneider when he met her in the examining room. "I was in the kitchen when I heard the alarm," she said. "I went in and he wasn't breathing."

Steinschneider asked if the baby had become cyanotic. "He was kind of dusky pale," Waneta said. "I shook him and he perked up. Then fifteen or twenty minutes later, he was asleep in my arms and he turned dark and pasty and he stopped breathing again. I gave him mouth-to-mouth, and he started breathing again. He slept most of the time in the ambulance."

Steinschneider put down his pen and examined Noah. The only thing obvious was that he had a very slight runny nose. He ordered a round of tests—electrocardiogram, urinalysis, blood work, chest X ray. Everything was negative, but Steinschneider readmitted Noah to the ward, instructed the nurses to monitor him around the clock, and made plans to get more of his respiration on paper in the lab. It seemed to him that Noah, the brother of four dead children, had survived a near-miss—maybe two.

The treatment was going to cost the Hoyts a lot of money. A week before Noah's discharge, Steinschneider had been forced to transfer him off "research status." With federal money now in short supply and the reins being tightened, Noah was now just like any other patient. Tim talked about his financial problems with Steinschneider, who told him he would try to keep the baby as a research patient. If the Hoyts allowed him to use Noah in his research, there might be a way to avoid the hospital charges. They signed a consent form permitting Steinschneider to use the voluminous and still growing records of their babies to help Noah qualify as a subject.

Gail Dristle had never had what she considered a serious job before she was accepted into the nurse's aide training program set up by Upstate Medical Center in 1970, soon after her twentieth birthday. She didn't count the job she quit to enroll, working the counter at the Plaid Stamps redemption center on West Onondaga Street. The nurse's aide program she saw advertised on a bulletin board could lead to a career: interesting work, good pay, dependable benefits. She was a single mother with a two-and-a-half-year-old daughter. Maybe she would even go on to become a full-fledged nurse. She was eager to get her life in order.

The training period was a nine-week, 360-hour course beginning with classroom study in a building across the street from the hospital, followed by hands-on clinical training. At graduation, Dristle was asked what area she'd like to work in, and she picked pediatrics. The hospital was careful about assigning new nurse's aides to pediatrics because of the high-level care required and the emotional toll of working with sick children. But she had done well in class, and when nobody else asked for it, she got the assignment. Her first patient was a one-year-old girl with a brain tumor.

Gail found the hospital culture slightly mysterious, and the pecking order of the nursing staff—a hierarchy within a hierarchy—formidable. She watched and listened, tried to learn the nuances of caring for ill children, observed the boundaries between nurses and nurse's aides. Doctors were a whole other level. "M.D. equals Major Deity," one of the nurses told her one day. She watched the interactions, and saw how completely the dynamic was defined by gender. If women knew their place, nurses *really* knew their place. Nurse's aides? Watch yourself. "If a doctor indulged a nurse, treated her nicely, she just lapped it up," she remembered. By the same token, a doctor's authority was supreme. She felt the aura the first hour she was on the ward.

Gail was flattered when one of the senior nurses, an energetic woman who seemed to be one of the unofficial authority figures on the ward, began taking a special interest in her. "Half these nurses weren't trained right," Julie Evans told her. "I'm going to train you right."

Julie brought Gail into the nursery. "These babies have special needs," she said. "The parents can't always be here, so we have to take special care of them." She explained the requirements of each baby and showed her how to document the care in the Nurses' Notes. Gail remembered what she'd been instructed in the classroom. "Just write down the facts. No opinions, no judgments. You never know—these notes could wind up in court. If you have an opinion about something, there are other systems to deal with it."

Julie was a natural mentor, and Gail felt a warmth and a basic goodness that struck an emotional chord. Julie, she thought, was everything her own mother was not. She also appreciated the rebel in her. Julie was not one of those nurses who observed a quiet subservience in the presence of doctors.

When she came in for work each day, Gail got herself a cup of coffee, then walked down the hall to a small room for morning report. The charge nurse from the previous tour would pass along pertinent information about patients to the next shift, then the supervisor for the oncoming staff would assign nurses to patients—eight or ten nurses for twenty or thirty children. It was a gathering of white uniforms that occurred three times a day, not unlike what goes on in a typical police station house between shifts. It was here, a few months into her career as a nurse's aide, that Gail first began hearing about Noah Hoyt.

This was the baby everyone was watching. He was in for observation because of a family history of infant death, Gail understood, and was to be kept on an apnea monitor virtually around the clock. She found it unsettling that a baby so young, so seemingly normal, could be in so much trouble that every one of his breaths had to be accounted for because it might be his last. *Here's one you have to worry about every time he goes to sleep.* It didn't take long for her to figure out that there seemed to be more to it than that.

Gail wasn't assigned to Noah during his first few weeks on the ward, but she couldn't help but pick up on some of the coded gossip about the baby's mother that hung in the air at report, and in the ward generally. She felt uncomfortable with the talk, unqualified to pass judgment. But she was curious. A nurse who'd introduced herself as Dotty seemed especially hung up on the baby's mother. One day, Gail asked her which one Mrs. Hoyt was. Gail hadn't noticed anyone visiting Noah. "She doesn't come much," the nurse said sharply.

A couple of days later, Dotty walked up to her outside the nursery. "Gail," she whispered conspiratorially. "The Hoyts are here. Go in and tell me what you think."

"What?" Gail replied, taken aback. She thought Dotty was a bit too judg-mental, and she was reluctant to feed the gossip.

"Just go in and tell me what you think," Dotty pressed.

Gail looked in through the nursery window, then back at Dotty. The nurse nodded her encouragement. "Okay," Gail said tentatively. *Go in easy,* she told herself. *These people have lost children.*

She went into the nursery, turned toward a corner of the room, and stopped abruptly. There was Noah's mother, standing about eight feet from the crib, near her husband, her arms folded tight. She was glaring. A split second later Gail realized that she was glaring *at the baby.* Gail thought, *What's wrong? What's she going to do?* She was about to ask what the matter was when Waneta broke her concentration, and her eyes met Gail's.

"Uh . . . hi . . ." Gail stammered. "I'm Gail." Neither Waneta nor Tim said anything in response, and Gail tried to exit as quickly and unobtrusively as possible.

She was shaken by the encounter. She was sure the look she had seen was anger—"a very quiet, very powerful anger"—and she felt sure that it was di-rected at the baby. *How could a mother be angry at such a tiny, helpless thing?* she thought. *Maybe she was going through some crazy kind of grief,* Gail told herself. *Maybe she's angry at God for killing her children.*

"Something's wrong here," she said to Dotty. "I don't know what it is, but there's something real wrong here."

"Oh yeah," Dotty said. "Something's wrong all right."

Noah's return in the ambulance on June 16 focused the concern of the nurses in the same way that Molly's cycle of discharge and readmission had intensi-fied the worry of the nurses who were taking care of her. Juxtaposed against Waneta's obvious disregard for her baby in the hospital, the consensus among Noah's nurses was that, at the very least, his mother was emotionally inca-pable of caring for a baby. Like the nurses a year before, they flipped through the possibilities. Perhaps the earlier deaths had scarred her so deeply that she could no longer connect with her child. Whatever the reason, the nurses agreed Waneta's behavior was nothing short of bizarre. They decided they should try to draw her into a relationship with her baby. At afternoon report one day when the Hoyts were expected in that evening, Julie Evans said, "Let's try to get Mrs. Hoyt to bond with the baby today." It became a familiar refrain.

Comments like these struck a raw nerve in Gail Dristle. As a child, she had been the victim of relentless abuse at the hands of her mother, a woman so brutal that Gail often wondered how she and her brother had survived.

Her mother had been confined to a psychiatric hospital for a time after her brother's birth, and Gail spent years looking into her icy gaze, searching for peace that never came. Her mother's abuse had left an indelible mark and made her attuned to the signs. Now she was beginning to realize that there were children passing through the pediatrics ward who were very likely being physically abused at home and that there didn't seem to be a reliable system to protect them. She began to see that the medical mores of the time made it difficult for staff members to take responsibility for what might be going on outside the walls of the hospital. "People saw what they saw," she remembered. "The worst was when you knew they were going back to a bad situation. I remember a five-month-old baby with a skull fracture. There was a social work department. But what they emphasized in training was what *not* to do."

She decided to tell Julie about the incident in the nursery. She wanted to see if it fit with the vibrations she was picking up, and if it did, what they added up to. Julie listened, and nodded empathetically. She acknowledged that there was a problem with Noah's mother, but left it at that.

Gail, though, could not leave it at that. On days when she was assigned to Noah, she would mother him, not merely nurse him. On days that Noah was not among her patients, she made it a point to visit him. *He was such an agreeable, sweet-natured, beautiful baby,* she thought, the kind about whom mothers tended to say later, "He was my best baby." If only his mother could see that. She found it impossible to maintain the delicate emotional balance Julie had instructed her was essential for survival in pediatrics. She saw that Noah began to notice when she came in the room, that he stirred, smiled at her with his sky-blue eyes, as if reaching out for her attention—"like he was just laying there waiting and loving it when somebody walked in the room." She would feed him, then lull him to sleep with a song, the rhythm of the rocking chair keeping time with the lullaby. *"Hush, little baby, don't say a word,"* she would sing, just as she had sung at home to her own daughter, Maria, *"Poppa's gonna buy you a mockingbird. And if that mockingbird don't sing, Poppa's gonna buy you a diamond ring. . . ."*

Gail began listening closely to the whispers that she had made a conscious decision to tune out before. She paid careful attention to what was said about Noah at report. And she began asking questions. How many children had died before Noah was born? How old were they? How did they die? Some of the answers were right in the history at the nurses' station, but she didn't want to seem like a snoop. Julie began opening up, but cautiously. She told her Molly had died after leaving the hospital, but didn't say how soon after. She said there had been other children, but wasn't sure how many, or how they had died. There was confusion among the nurses about the entity Steinschneider was studying. When Gail heard from one of the nurses that one of the Hoyt children was two years old when he died suddenly, she said, *"Two?"* "Well, apparently this can happen at any time," the nurse said. And Gail said again, *"Two?"* She resolved to never allow Waneta to be alone with Noah in the nursery and noticed she wasn't the only one with this self-imposed rule.

By mid-July, Noah had spent virtually his entire two months of life in the hospital. In all this time, Julie could not remember Waneta ever kissing him. What she remembered, couldn't forget, was how she stroked her husband's leg whenever he had Noah in his arms. The father was warmer, she thought, though some of the nurses could be heard ridiculing his seeming obliviousness.

When the Hoyts visited, Julie would accompany them into the nursery and try to lead by example. She would pick up Noah, kiss him, and cuddle him, sometimes with exaggerated enthusiasm. "I would try to get the baby's mother to react," Julie later remembered. "But it was a lost cause. And then when I saw how she'd react, I would tell Dr. Steinschneider right away."

It was an echo of Thelma Schneider's pleadings a year before. Like Molly, Noah had not had a moment of illness more serious than a runny nose. Even by Steinschneider's standards Noah could not be considered a baby with problems. Though he remained committed to his original diagnosis of apnea, Steinschneider had to concede that the machines made it difficult to confirm. "Alarm has sounded," he wrote one day, soon after Noah's readmission. "However I believe this was not because Noah became apneic but rather that the machine was not picking up shallow respiration. Will have machine checked out." A week later, he wrote, "No bona fide prolonged apnea. Awaiting new machine." Another day, Len Weiner, a fellow pediatrician filling in on rounds, looked in on Noah and tried to think of something to write in the Physician's Record. He came up with this: "53-day-old baby followed by Dr. Steinschneider for apnea. Four sibs died of 'crib death.' Essentially the child is here for testing on the polygraph." Noah might have been the healthiest patient in University Hospital, yet those taking care of him sensed disaster if he was allowed to leave.

As Steinschneider got closer to discharging Noah for a second time, Julie Evans began begging him to find an alternative. Cornering him in the hallway one day after a visit by the Hoyts, she decided to tell him her worst fears. "I think she's doing something to those kids," she said. It was the first time anyone had put it so bluntly.

"We have no proof of that," Steinschneider said dismissively. As far as he was concerned, the nurses were making extreme assumptions, thinking the worst without any evidence. As a scientist, Steinschneider believed, he had a more rigorous standard. What counted was what you knew, not what you thought. "I knew that babies were killed—c'mon," he would say one day. "We talked about it at the meeting in 1969. We talked about it in the hallways. I thought about it. And I thought about other things. I thought maybe there was a genetic cardiac anomaly. Maybe there was a genetic endocrine problem. The first baby died of heart disease. The second baby died of choking. The third baby died of congenital adrenal hypoplasia. This is what the experts are telling me. Are they competent? You call them incompetent—I ain't. Then when the fourth baby died, I had just met Molly [Dapena], and I asked her to review the case because I thought maybe these cats are missing something. Because I want to know. I may be dogmatic, but I'm not pretentious. And she came back and said, 'I don't know.' "

Doing something to those kids? Steinschneider considered it a baseless thing to say. Certainly, he had no intention of having a talk with the Hoyts. Nor was he inclined to discuss it with anyone else. Among those he didn't consult was Stuart Asch, the psychiatrist who had written him two months before. He had asked Molly Dapena to look at the tissue slides of Molly Hoyt, but had not broadened his query. Had he asked her, for instance, to look at the autopsy report of the third child, Jimmy, she might well have called the pathologist incompetent, might have told Steinschneider something like: "Where did this man go to medical school? The whole autopsy doesn't make sense. It's totally off the wall." That's the way she would put it years later. In 1971, given what she had come to know about the "Moores," the Philadelphia family mythologized by *Life* magazine, had Steinschneider given her all the circumstances of all the Hoyt children's deaths, Dapena might well have advised him against dismissing too easily what the nurses were telling him.

Julie Evans looked up at Steinschneider with beseeching eyes. "You're going to send Noah home," she said, "and that'll be the end of him."

That afternoon, July 20, Steinschneider did send the baby home. He told the Hoyts to bring him back in a week.

When Steinschneider was working on his Ph.D. at Cornell in the mid-1950s, he became fascinated by a psychological precept called the Yerkes-Dodson law, and made it the centerpiece of his doctoral dissertation. Its essential principle was this: Determination was a good thing but only up to a point; if a task was especially difficult, a puzzle overly complex, too much motivation could be detrimental. Many years later, oblivious to any irony, Steinschneider explained it this way: "If something's very difficult, too much drive can get in the way. Which is not surprising. When people panic because the drive is so strong, they persevere and make errors. People trying to open the door when there's a fire in a closed place, even though there may be two doors, they get stuck on one door and won't go to the other one."

Cognizant of Molly's death a year before, Steinschneider thought about how it might be linked to her brother now in his care; how all of it—the autonomic studies in the clock tower, the puzzling deaths of the first three Hoyt children, the studies of Molly and Noah—might be connected. There were two doors available, but he could see only one. The apnea door.

After sending Noah Hoyt home for the second time, Steinschneider wrote a discharge summary of the baby's month-long stay in the hospital. In this entry, he wrote that Noah had had three spells of prolonged apnea on July 1, three more on July 2, two on July 9, and one each on June 23, June 30, July 3, July 4, July 10, July 15, and July 19. It was a curious way to interpret the observations of the nurses whose carefully documented reports were his source. In fact, ten of those fifteen incidents were either unquestionable false alarms or undocumented instances in which the apnea monitor sounded but Noah was found to be breathing. And on three of those days—June 23, July 10, and July 19—the nurses documented no apnea at all, not even short periods. "No apnea noted," read the nursing notes of each shift. Nor had Steinschneider himself documented any prolonged apnea in the lab on those days. Contrary to the Physician's Record handwritten and signed by Steinschneider, when Noah went home that Wednesday afternoon, he had gone thirty-four days in the hospital with barely a hint of apnea.

The next morning, Steinschneider got a call from the baby's mother. Noah was not doing well. He had slept through the night, Waneta said, but after his morning feeding he started to cough and "turn colors." What colors? Steinschneider asked. "Red, blue, pale," she said. "And then he held his breath. I gagged him, and he spit up."

"He probably aspirated some formula," Steinschneider said. He decided that the baby should come back to the hospital.

Waneta called her brother-in-law. "Can you take me and the baby to Syracuse?" she said to Chuck. "I've gotta get him to Upstate Medical."

Chuck picked up Waneta and the baby, and raced north. Noah seemed basically okay, if a bit listless. "But with the luck she had with the rest of them," Chuck would say later, "I wasn't taking any chances." Howard Horton's question three years before—Was Waneta doing something to the babies?—was now just a distant painful memory. Obviously, these were babies with problems. Chuck made the trip in forty-five minutes.

When word spread among the nurses on the fifth floor that Noah was back yet again, they were at once dumbfounded, relieved, and overwhelmed by the sense that Noah was running out of time. How many times could they go home for the night with Noah discharged, only to find him in the nursery when they came in for work the next day as if he'd never left? Were these emergencies his mother's way of saying she didn't want the baby? Were they aborted attempts on his life? Julie Evans sensed that even Steinschneider seemed to be aware of the absurdity of the pattern. "Noah Hoyt's back," he told her that morning. "I can't find anything wrong with him."

Gail Dristle had said her good-byes to Noah that Wednesday, hoping, as she later put it, that Waneta "didn't have the guts to do what I felt deeply she was capable of doing." When Gail came in to work the next afternoon and found Noah in the nursery, she breathed a sigh of relief. And then, she realized the implications. She overheard two nurses talking. He has no apnea, one was saying. She's making it up. Maybe *we* should be making it up, said the other. Maybe it would be better if we say there *is* apnea, so he doesn't send him home again. They decided to try to enlist the help of one of the pediatric residents.

Gail went into the nursery. She picked Noah up, kissed him, and carried him over to the rocking chair. She fed him, rocked him, and began to fantasize. *I'll take him home with me,* she thought. *I'll just walk out the door. I'm not going to keep him and raise him. I'll just take him home, and wait for them to come after me. And then I'll say, "Do something about this woman."*

Gail wondered where the doctors fit into this. She saw Steinschneider's name on the charts, but never saw him in the nursery. "Is there a doctor aware that Mom's not okay here?" she had asked Julie one day.

"He's aware," Julie had said.

"Well, why isn't anything happening?"

"It's not what he's concerned about."

"What's he concerned about?"

"SIDS. Research."

Rocking Noah now, Gail gazed out the window of the nursery and played out her interior fantasy. She looked down at Noah and began to cry.

Dr. Roger Stanke, the resident, listened to what the nurses had to say about Waneta's failure to bond. He thought it might be a good idea to bring her in for some remedial mothering lessons before sending the baby home again. All she needed, he felt, was some "reassurance and guidance." Steinschneider had no objections. On Sunday, Stanke saw Waneta sitting in the nursery, feeding Noah, with Tim beside her. She was surrounded by a group of nurses who were animatedly trying to teach her how to connect with her baby. The attention had at least one effect. For the first time that any of the nurses could remember, Waneta was smiling. Stanke was pleased with what he saw. He scribbled his note for the day in the Physician's Record. "Parents here taking active part in patient's care," he wrote. "No apnea noted."

Gail, watching the same scene, saw it from a different angle. "She was the center of attention, and she basked in it," she remembered. "It was like you were teaching a five-year-old how to change her doll—and the woman's already had five children. And I'm standing there looking in and saying to myself, 'I don't think it's gonna take.'"

On Tuesday, six days after Noah's last readmission, the mood on 4A was as anxious as on any day since the Hoyt family had first appeared at Upstate fifteen months before. Noah was to be discharged once again that evening, and everyone knew it.

Late in the afternoon, Julie Evans pulled Steinschneider aside. "Why are you sending him home?" she challenged him, her voice rising.

"There's no reason to keep him here," Steinschneider said.

"Here's a nice, normal baby that anybody would give anything for, and it's so obvious his mother doesn't care about him. She doesn't want him. She doesn't give a *damn* about him."

"Look," Steinschneider said, opening his hands. "What can I do about it?"

"She's going to do away with him," Julie said flatly. "I'll bet you she killed the other one."

"But can you prove it?" he challenged her.

"I'll even tell you how she does it. I'll bet she puts a pillow over their heads and suffocates them."

"You can't prove that," he repeated.

Julie had to concede this point. She couldn't prove it. "I'll bet you a quarter that baby is dead by tomorrow," she said finally, exasperated.

Steinschneider chuckled at the notion of such a macabre wager. When she heard this, Julie knew that she had done all she could. She knew who was in charge. She had worked within these protocols of medicine for thirty years, and even a situation as extraordinary as this could not change them. There was no other place to go with this. Julie felt betrayed, as much by medical culture as by Steinschneider, and embittered at her powerlessness.

Gail shuddered when she saw the Hoyts step off the elevator shortly after 6:00 in the evening and make their way onto the ward. In the nursery, Steinschneider examined Noah and pronounced him fit. He wrote that Noah had been fine this last stay, except for one period of prolonged apnea on Friday. ("Alarm went off, pt. breathing," a nurse had written.) Waneta, picking up where she left off on Sunday, fed her baby and played with him as two nurses looked on. Steinschneider gave the Hoyts the usual instructions. "Let's bring him back next Monday," he said. Then Julie, following hospital rules, picked up Noah and carried him toward the elevator, his parents close behind.

They descended to the lobby and walked past the front desk and through the front door. Julie waited with Waneta, while Tim brought the car around and pulled up. Waneta slid in beside him. Julie cradled Noah, kissed him gently, and placed him on his mother's lap. "Good luck with him," she said stoically. She turned back toward the hospital. *That's the end of that poor baby,* she said to herself as she headed back upstairs.

"Dr. Scott?"

"Yes."

"Sheriff's Department calling. We've got a baby in distress up in Newark Valley. The parents haven't been able to get any medical assistance. Can you go up there?"

Dr. John Scott, an osteopath, was one of the Tioga County coroners, but when he got this call just after breakfast on a hot Wednesday morning in July, it was his service as a physician that was being requested. He drove quickly from his home in Apalachin to the sheriff's department in Owego. Then he hopped in a patrol car and took off for Route 38, a deputy at the wheel. *This must be some emergency,* Scott thought, watching the radar in the police car climb all the way up to 108 miles an hour as the signal bounced off trees and parked cars. He held on to the door handle, looked over at the deputy, and prayed nobody got in the way.

They made it to Newark Valley in seven minutes, the sheriff's siren wailing past the dairy farms on a summer morning, and reached Davis Hollow Road just ahead of the local ambulance. "It's the trailer," the deputy said. He pulled to a halt, and he and Scott headed for the front door.

Inside, Scott saw his tiny patient lying on the couch, motionless. The baby's mother stood apart, swaying from side to side, her husband trying to comfort her. Scott saw that there were two electrode receptors with wire leads attached to the baby's chest, the kind he associated with electronic monitoring devices in hospital intensive care units. He'd never seen one in someone's home, or on an infant. He sat on the couch, and leaned into the baby. He detected no breath. He checked for a pulse, then examined the baby's eyes. He looked up at Waneta. "The child is deceased," he said. She was crying quietly. "I'm sorry," Scott said.

"Can you tell me what happened?" he asked. Waneta didn't answer.

"He's had problems," Tim said agitatedly, jumping past the immediate question. He had been summoned home as soon as he arrived for work on a road job. "He's been at Upstate Medical. We just brought him home last night."

"Who's been treating him at Upstate?" Scott asked.

"Dr. Steinschneider."

Scott reached Steinschneider in his office in Syracuse. "This is Dr. Scott in Tioga County," he said. "I'm at the home of Mr. and Mrs. Hoyt here in Newark Valley. I understand you've been treating their infant son."

"Yes, I have," Steinschneider said.

"The baby has passed away this morning."

There was a pause. "I'm sorry," Steinschneider said softly. He asked Scott what had happened. He wasn't entirely sure, Scott said; the baby had apparently died suddenly while asleep. He presumed the death was related to whatever condition required the use of the monitor.

"This is the fifth child in the family that's died," Steinschneider informed him.

"The fifth one?" Scott said.

"He spent most of his life on our pediatric service. I discharged him last night. We treated another child in the family last year, who also died suddenly. There seems to be a problem sustaining life in this family."

"I see."

"We've had this baby on an apnea monitor continuously in the hospital. He's been maintained on one at home."

"Yes, I see that here."

"Are you going to do an autopsy?" Steinschneider asked.

"Certainly," Scott replied. He had arrived as a physician; it had turned into a coroner's call.

"Would you let us do it here in Syracuse?" Steinschneider asked. "I'm very interested in the case."

Fine, said Scott. Just as long as I get the results. Of course, said Steinschneider.

Waneta took the phone, and Steinschneider conveyed his sympathies. He asked her the same question he'd asked her a dozen times before: "What happened?" Waneta said the apnea alarm had gone off while the baby was sleeping and she was in the shower. Tim had just left for work. The baby was blue and not breathing when she got to him. She tried to revive him, but this time, she said, it was too late.

Steinschneider asked Waneta to come up to Syracuse. She and Tim would have to sign a form consenting to an autopsy. "All right," she said.

Steinschneider hung up the phone and went downstairs to the ward. He saw Julie Evans and pulled her aside. "Noah died," he said softly.

Julie stared up at him. "I told you so!" she snapped. "I *told* you so!" She turned on the heels of her white shoes and stomped off, leaving Steinschneider alone in the hallway.

Gail Dristle came to work full of trepidation. She had stirred half the night, then awakened with such overwhelming fear that she considered not going in to work. Now she stepped off the elevator on 4A, and walked to the small room off the nurses' station. She put her lunch in the refrigerator. She poured herself a cup of coffee. She came out into the hall and started walking down for morning report. In the hallway she saw a nurse standing by herself, with a strange look about her. The nurse looked up as Gail approached, and their eyes met. Grim-faced, the nurse shook her head slowly, side to side. "Oh my God!" Gail cried out, collapsing against the wall in tears.

A few minutes later, the nurses gathered for report in stark silence, their heads bowed in shock and anger.

"Noah Hoyt died this morning," the charge nurse announced.

"What was it this time?" somebody asked, her voice dripping with disdain.

"Oh, the monitor went off and she didn't hear it," came the answer, equally sardonic. "She was 'in the shower.'"

"Maybe they'll do something now," Gail said tersely. Nobody responded.

The nurses went about their duties that day in a fog of unreality. They believed they had virtually watched a murder being committed. Gail went home in tears, and didn't come back to work for four days. At night, she sat alone in the dark and got drunk.

Noah arrived at the hospital for the fourth and final time on the morning of his death. He was taken to pathology; his parents rode the elevator to the fifth floor to see Steinschneider.

During Noah's life, as the cycle of hospital admissions became more foreboding, Tim had begun to wonder if Steinschneider was the authority he seemed to be. "I don't think they know what the hell they're doing up there," he told Chuck after his brother had raced Noah back to the emergency room. Now, seeing Tim's frustration after Noah's death, Steinschneider told him that some things in medicine simply could not be explained. SIDS was a great mystery, and that was why he was studying it. "When we go to medical school," he said, "they don't give us a book that says, 'This is all you'll ever need to know; use this and you'll always be right.' There is no such book."

Maybe the autopsy would offer some clues. Tim signed the consent form first, with Steinschneider signing as a witness; then Waneta signed, with Nurse Fran Tomeny as her witness. In his lab on the same floor as the pediatrics ward, Bedros Markarian stood beside pathology resident William Kleis, who began the autopsy at 2:30 that afternoon.

Markarian had consulted on Molly's tissue slides a year before, but didn't connect that passing matter with the body before him now. Steinschneider, though, prepared the pathologist for Noah's autopsy with a brief history of the baby and his four siblings. Whatever the reason for the misunderstanding,

Markarian noted in his report that Noah's brothers and sisters "all died from crib death before one year of age"—notwithstanding the ostensible circumstances of the deaths of Julie and Jimmy, and Jimmy's actual age. But if Markarian was a little fuzzy on the details, the unusual string of deaths did lead him to think it wise to rule out trauma. Before Kleis made the first cut, Noah was given a total body X ray.

Steinschneider made apnea, and his emerging belief about its relationship to sudden infant death, the central theme of his briefing with Markarian. "He was very intense," Markarian remembered. "And he talked a lot about apnea." Steinschneider told Markarian that Noah had been observed on an apnea monitor virtually his entire life, both in the hospital and at home, because family history made him a high risk for sudden death. And the monitors had picked up plenty of potential trouble. The baby's life, he said, was marked by many apneic periods, including episodes at home that were serious enough to require resuscitation and readmittance to the hospital. Markarian did not question the accuracy of what Steinschneider was telling him. He had no reason to. He thought Steinschneider was a good man with a fine reputation. So he did not know, for instance, that the second Discharge Summary, dated eight days before Noah died and documenting fifteen episodes of prolonged apnea in the hospital, was largely a fiction. It camouflaged the fact that every one of Noah's crises had come on the three days he had spent at home with his mother.

Thus briefed, Markarian brought Noah's body into the lab, just down the hall and past a pair of doors from the pediatric nursing station. He supervised as Kleis began the postmortem, narrating as he went. ". . . The eyes are blue in color . . . there is frothy fluid exuding from both nostrils and from the mouth. . . . There is no evidence of trauma . . . a total body X ray performed before the autopsy revealed no evidence of fractures."

Kleis removed Noah's organs, examined them, and found them to be normal, though the lungs contained an unusual amount of fluid. Looking further, the pathologists saw that the right bronchial tree contained a large amount of "frothy, blood-tinged fluid," and that there was some swelling indicating bronchiolitis, an inflammation similar to bronchitis, caused by a respiratory virus. "The left lung is saved for the pulmonary research lab," Kleis dictated. Examining Noah's brain, he found some additional mild swelling. Pending the results of the microscopic examinations, the pathologists reported their provisional diagnoses as bronchiolitis, pulmonary and cerebral edema, and pulmonary atelectasis, a failure of part of the lung to expand at birth, most commonly associated with premature babies. The latter finding could only be confirmed by examining the lung tissue slides.

None of the preliminary diagnoses really explained Noah's death, leaving

Coroner John Scott with a dilemma when he got the results the next day. He was known for his industriousness as a physician. His office hours sometimes ran past midnight. He tried to be equally diligent as an arbiter of death. He knew that all the autopsy findings were "secondary to some causative situation," as he put it in his coroner's report. But under the circumstances, Scott hadn't expected the results to be otherwise. Though he, too, misunderstood the family history Steinschneider gave him on the phone—he thought two of the previous siblings were toddlers, not one—Scott's conversation with the SIDS researcher from Syracuse left him with little doubt that all five children were victims of what he still called crib death. That, he believed, was the unknown "causative situation."

Scott wanted to write the words "sudden unexplained death" on Noah's death certificate. That, he felt, would be the most medically accurate thing he could say. But he believed such an empty finding was frowned upon by the profession, and that the custom of the day was to list instead the factors contributing to death, as best as they could be determined. Hence, he listed Noah's immediate cause of death as "acute bronchiolitis." Where the document asked for "approximate interval between onset and death," Scott wrote, "2 HRS." As a secondary condition, he listed pulmonary atelectasis.

Neither of these findings survived microscopic examination. The lung tissue revealed mild pulmonary congestion, but no virus—no bronchiolitis. The histology examination also failed to show any cells with abnormal growth that would sustain a finding of pulmonary atelectasis. This left only two final diagnoses: pulmonary edema and cerebral edema—death by swelling, as it were. Markarian knew the findings were meaningless.

John Scott never changed the official cause of death to reflect Markarian's final diagnosis. But to him it was a moot point. He wrote his report attributing Noah's death—and the deaths of all the baby's brothers and sisters—to SIDS. Without another word to the sheriff's department, he sent the one-page report to the county clerk's office in Owego for filing.

22

Waneta collapsed at Noah's burial. "I thought we were going to lose her right there," the Reverend Donald Washburn later remarked. A month before, Washburn had replaced Gary Kuhns as the pastor at the United Methodist Church of Newark Valley, becoming the third minister to preside over the funeral of a Hoyt child.

Like the deaths themselves, the aftermaths had by now become numbingly ritualized. A succession of Hoyts and Nixons picked up their phones to hear the painful familiar news. The baby died this morning; the funeral's Sunday. In Richford, Clarence Lacey answered a knock at the front door and found the Hoyts on the porch once more. There would be a service at MacPherson's, Dave Cooley, Neil MacPherson's successor, handling everything for fifty dollars, on credit. The minister would try to get everyone through the service with dignity. Then the procession of cars would follow the hearse up Route 38 into Richford for the burial of another miniature casket—simple pine, or Styrofoam—next to the others. The baby would be delivered to the earth beneath the drooping Norway spruce as the mourners offered their sympathies to the child's mother and father. A little extra pity was reserved for the mother.

Waneta had her own private rituals. With the birth of each child, she added pictures to her photo album, the black-and-white images of Eric, Julie, and Jimmy followed by the square color snapshots of Molly and Noah. Some of the pictures had tiny captions written on their narrow white borders— "Mom, Jimmy, Neta, 6/25/67," "Tim and Molly, March 23, 1970"—but most needed no explaining. It was just Waneta and Tim and the children, the babies appearing and then disappearing one by one. In some, a friend or relative or hospital nurse would make a cameo appearance with one of the babies, their faces often marked by a vague look of concern. There was one photograph of Noah in the hospital with Dr. Steinschneider. It was a sweet moment, the doctor cradling the baby in his left arm, more like a parent than a doctor, gently tickling the infant's tiny chest with his free hand, the inkling of a smile crossing his face as the baby's gaze met his. After Noah died, the album was all Waneta had left of her children.

On the opening page of her Bible, Waneta kept a chronicle of her children's lives and deaths. With each passing, she added the pertinent information, always in the same format: date of birth, date of death, cause of death. For Eric, she wrote, "heart." For Julie, "choked." For Jimmy, "enlarged thymus gland." For Molly and Noah, "crib death or SIDS." Waneta cherished her Bible.

After each of the babies died, she and Tim would go driving. Sometimes, they went for miles and miles without talking. It became their grieving process. After Noah's death, Steinschneider suggested they take a long trip. Get away, he said. Go to Canada. Go somewhere.

They got in the old Pontiac, intending to drive up to Ogdensburg, where Waneta's parents were renting a cabin on a lake near the Canadian border. It was a four-hour drive, but when they got to the lake and saw the Nixons out on the water in a rowboat, Waneta became upset and wanted to leave immediately. It was the water, she said; she had become terrified of water after nearly drowning in a swimming hole while pregnant with Jimmy. She later explained that she had gotten a cramp, and gone under. "A friend of mine had to save her," Tim said. "After that, ever since, she won't even take a shower with water running over her head. She'll stand back and let it run around her. And she *doesn't* want to be in a boat." So Waneta and Tim got right back in the car. They continued north, on a road that hugged the St. Lawrence River, before heading east toward Lake Champlain and the Vermont border. "We just kept driving and driving," Tim remembered. "The road got narrower, the weeds got taller, and we thought, where the hell are we? But there was tire tracks so it didn't bother me any. I kept going. We ended up in Montpelier, Vermont. We got all the way up there and I thought, well, I'll look in my wallet, see how much money we got, maybe we could stay the night. And they wanted sixty-eight dollars. Well, my budget didn't include sixty-eight dollars. So we went to a store and got a little bite to eat and we drove home. We drove all day and all night."

"Well, she killed another one," nineteen-year-old Yvonne Lane said when her cousin Bonnie called that July morning. Yvonne's aunt was Betty Lane, who lived across the street from the Hoyts and had called the ambulance when

Eric died. Now, six years and four babies later, Betty's daughter Bonnie, Yvonne's cousin, was on the phone saying the ambulance had just left with another dead baby. For Yvonne, as with many people in Newark Valley, it was always a case of suspicion weighed against what the doctors said—and the doctors always said it was something other than murder. "We whispered, 'Here comes the baby killer,' " she recalled, "but then it was labeled SIDS and you felt bad for saying that." Not long after Noah's death, Yvonne got a job in Amelia's hair salon and found Waneta sitting in her chair. She became one of her regular customers, and Yvonne didn't know *what* to think. "Once or twice I wondered whether she'd get caught. But you didn't want to be proven wrong. And she was so depressed. You had to feel sorry for her. But everybody suspected—everybody did."

But of course that was not so. Some people looked at the Hoyts and worried not about Waneta, but about their own babies. It sounded like a strange and exotic malady, this SIDS. Was it something contagious? Of course, they couldn't quite comprehend Waneta and Tim's luck, or why they kept tempting fate. In Newark Valley, people could recall only one other family with a crib death. It did not go unnoticed that they went on to have three more children who did just fine. Was it just a bad combination of genes between Waneta and Tim, or something more sinister? It wasn't for people to say, at least not in public. From her perch inside her dress shop on Water Street, Margaret Cornwell kept waiting to hear that the authorities were looking into the matter; she'd been waiting since the second and third deaths that September three years before. But after a while, the bewilderment and unasked questions faded. Still, as Margaret remembered it years later, the unresolved confusion still seemingly fresh in her mind: "You hear the ambulance call—'Where's it going?' 'Down for another baby'—but you don't go pushing because nobody wants to be the bad guy. It's a small town and nobody wants to be the one to put the spotlight on her. Everybody just clammed up and just watched and listened. Now, the sheriff's department was never noted for overinvestigation. It's sort of like they get here when they get here."

It cannot be said that the sheriff's department—or anyone else in Tioga County, for that matter—was given much to go on by the local physicians and coroners who became involved with the Hoyts during those seven years. Hartnagel, Kassman, Perry, Scott—the local medical society was on record about its puzzlement in the matter of the Hoyt family. The presumption of innocence was reinforced by the intense studies Molly and Noah were said to have undergone at Upstate Medical Center: Why would a doctor, a specialist, keep babies in the hospital all those months, endlessly readmitting them, if they were not sick? If they didn't, in fact, have a fatal breathing problem?

The answer, to Tim, was in the outcome: With their last breaths, the babies proved that they had been at the edge of death from the very moment of birth. That was the circular logic that grew out of the Children's Clinical Research Center and wrapped itself around the Hoyt and Nixon families and the hamlet of Newark Valley. Alfred Steinschneider was the unseen authority sanctioning the conceit of the death gene.

Aside from his advice that they take a trip somewhere, Steinschneider had one other recommendation for the Hoyts. "I don't think you should have any more children," he told them not long after Noah's death.

"Oh, don't worry about that," Tim replied sharply. "I've taken care of *that*." After Noah's second hospital admission, a few weeks before he died, Tim had decided enough was enough. Fearing the worst was imminent, he resolved to end the cycle of tragedy the only way he thought he could. He underwent a vasectomy. It was against Waneta's wishes. She wanted more children.

The Hoyts told Steinschneider they would try to adopt, and he told them that was a good idea. A few weeks after Noah's funeral, they went down to the Tioga County Social Services office and asked for a baby. Having been rejected by the Family and Children's Society in Ithaca, they reinstated their original application at the local county agency.

The agency was housed in a century-old stone building on the outskirts of Owego, presided over since the fall of 1952 by Commissioner Russell Rawley. By 1971, Social Services had fifty-one employees. Its thirteen caseworkers were beginning to be burdened by a variety of modern social ills, among them the growing number of child abuse and neglect cases that intruded on the more traditional lines of social work, helping the sick and the poor. As a specialist in child protection, Alberta Weisz's work ran the gamut: foster home care, day care, abuse and neglect investigations, adoptions. She couldn't help but develop instincts about people. It was a crucial part of the job.

As Weisz had implied in her letter to the Ithaca agency back in January, instinct had told her that the Hoyts were not a good bet for adoption. She was now even more convinced there was something wrong, though it was more a general anxiety than firm suspicion. "I didn't believe she had actually *murdered* her kids," Weisz later explained. "I felt she just didn't handle it right." She remembered Waneta's reasons for wanting an older child while pregnant with Noah, and how relentless she found the couple's pursuit of a child: "One kid dies, pregnant again, two kids dead, pregnant again, three kids dead, pregnant again. And in between to the agency: *need a kid, need a kid, need a kid*."

But she had to go through the standard evaluation process, and tried to approach it objectively. Arriving on Davis Hollow Road, Weisz found their home to be warm, clean, and exceptionally orderly. Mr. Hoyt had a steady job. Mrs. Hoyt was articulate. She kept a nice garden. "Although not fancy or ornately landscaped, the yard offers ample opportunity for a child's outdoor play," Weisz wrote in her report.

She sat with Waneta and Tim at their kitchen table and discussed how they had handled the tragedies. Waneta spoke of how "Upstate Medical is studying the case," and how she and Tim had finally concluded that it would be too risky to have another child. At one point, Waneta remarked that she had wanted a child for so long that she found it hard to fathom how a mother could give up her own for adoption. The harsh tone of the comment gave Weisz pause. She thought Waneta was a bit defensive about the deaths of her children. Trying to be charitable, though, she wrote in her notes that perhaps this was because "so much grief and turmoil has made their family the target of much community talk and comment."

But as the conversation moved along, Weisz began to notice a worrisome dynamic between the Hoyts. "As a couple, they were very difficult to interview," she recalled. "She talked too much, he talked too little. If you asked him a question, she answered it. 'How do you make decisions? What becomes of your paycheck?' She had a know-it-all way about her, and he was like a nonperson. Most couples, each person has a niche. She kind of claimed their whole life. She talked a mile a minute—whatever you wanted to know. So then I would turn my back to her and face him. You try all the tricks of the trade. It didn't work. I made a point to interview him alone. I asked him to come to the office without his wife." When he did, she found him nearly as reticent as before—a lot of brief answers to important questions.

Weisz reported her concerns to her supervisor, Roberta Hickey. "See what you can do," said Hickey. A registered nurse, she had been the caseworker on the Hoyts' original application in 1969. "See how the letters are."

The letters were fine. Weisz later wrote in her report: "All the references received have been good, considering the Hoyts as people with an 'excellent understanding of children.'" According to Dr. Kassman, she added, "Waneta seems stable and well-balanced emotionally."

Nevertheless, Weisz told Hickey that the letters didn't ease her qualms. She thought they should reject the application. In November, still less than four months after Noah's death, Hickey told Weisz that she had taken the question to Commissioner Rawley and they had agreed that the Hoyts might have an easier time handling an older baby. There was one available. He was a nine-month-old boy with blond hair, born to an unwed teenager and living with foster parents. The caseworkers had named him Scotty.

"I'm uncomfortable with these people," Weisz protested. "The woman asked for her adoption record to be opened *six days* after the fourth child died. She's trying to replace her children like a dog that got squashed in the road." She said the whole situation made her nervous. "There's too many dead kids," she said.

"But it's nothing concrete," Hickey replied. "You can't deny an adoption based on feelings." There were no problems on record with the sheriff's department, she pointed out, and the doctors all recommended the adoption. It was not as if the Hoyts didn't have indoor plumbing, Hickey said—a problem they could hang their hats on. "I don't think we have a choice," she said. "If there's something wrong, it'll surface. You can have six months supervised before the adoption's final. You can supervise for a year."

Weisz felt cornered. With none of the pleasure she normally brought to such calls, she phoned the Hoyts and told them there was a child for them. The next morning, a Friday, Waneta and Tim came down to Social Services and took Scotty home to Newark Valley with a bag of clothes and toys.

Weisz called the Hoyts first thing Monday to see how the weekend had gone. So far, so good, Waneta told her. Weisz decided she would wait a week before making her first post-placement visit. Four days later, her phone rang at home, an old farmhouse in the rolling hills between Owego and Candor.

"This is Waneta Hoyt," said the voice on the phone. She sounded upset. "My psychiatrist told me to call you." Weisz felt herself tensing. *Psychiatrist?* "Dr. Jafri told me to call you to take the baby. Before I do it harm."

Weisz recoiled in horror, a burst of adrenaline sending her heart into palpitations. She threw on a coat and sped off toward Newark Valley. *I knew it,* she thought as she drove. *I knew something was wrong.* She felt deceived—chagrined to find out that Waneta had been under the care of the county psychiatrist. As she made her way to Newark Valley, the words rang in her head: *"Before I do it harm."*

Tim answered the door, and Weisz marched inside. She found Waneta agitated and apologetic. "I'm sorry, I'm just ... I don't know what to say," Waneta said as Weisz grabbed Scotty. "I'm just confused. I'm so embarrassed." Tim stood back in silence. "I guess he just reminded me of the other children and I just couldn't bear it."

"Of course you know this'll be it," Weisz said sharply. "You're not getting another baby after this."

Waneta averted her eyes and said nothing.

Tioga County Community Psychiatric Services was located on the second floor of a wooden house on Main Street in Owego. It had a staff of three: a psychiatrist who was also the director of the agency, a psychologist, and a social worker. Mokarram Jafri, the psychiatrist, had come to Tioga County a year before from a state hospital in Massachusetts, replacing Waldo Burnett. Of all the county residents who came to see him because they had more problems than money, Jafri could not have had a patient more woeful than Waneta Hoyt.

She had first come to the clinic after that staggering September in 1968, when Burnett suggested church activities. Two more babies had come and gone since then, and Waneta's psychological disarray had only worsened, giving Tim no respite from her already boundless need. As he had since the beginning of their marriage, he spent nearly all his emotional energy trying to soothe and accommodate her. He knew better than to expect reciprocation. "When I needed something of that nature," he said, long after he had given up, "I knew she wasn't capable of giving it to me, so I took it out on something else. I worked myself to death. I worked twenty hours a day."

Tim's industriousness was also a necessary response to the Hoyts' mounting money troubles. The cost of the hospitalizations of Molly and Noah, along with the bills from Waneta's continuous medical attention for maladies real or imagined, was a perpetual strain on their marriage. Twice they refinanced their trailer and the land beneath it. Though their financial troubles and emotional upheavals had lately taken a heavy toll, they managed to present themselves to the adoption authorities as a devoted couple whose misfortune had strengthened their relationship. In fact, they were at an emotional standoff. Tim kept his pain inside. Waneta kept her secrets.

When Alberta Weisz made her first follow-up phone call the Monday after she and Tim took Scotty home, Waneta told her things were going fine. But two days later, at 7:20 on Wednesday morning, the day before Thanksgiving, Tim called the emergency number for the psychiatric clinic. He told Miriam Elkin, the staff psychologist, that his wife was in a terrible state and needed to see someone right away. Elkin instructed Tim to bring Waneta to the clinic.

The woman Elkin saw before her two hours later was a slender brunette in her mid-twenties whose face was pale and full of distress. When Elkin asked her what was wrong, Waneta said it was the baby.

"What about the baby?" Elkin asked.

"I've been having very wicked thoughts," Waneta said softly.

Elkin asked her what she meant.

"I'm afraid I might hurt the baby," Waneta replied.

"What might you do?" Elkin asked warily.

"I feel like I want to wring his neck."

Waneta explained how she and her husband had applied for adoption soon after the death of their last child, thinking it would take a year to get a baby. Instead, they got one within a couple of months. "I think if I had some time I could love the baby," Waneta said, "but I don't think I can take care of somebody else's child right now."

Elkin called Dr. Jafri, who told her he thought Waneta should be admitted to Tioga General, "so she can be relieved of caring for the baby without a stigma," as he later put it. But when Elkin broached this idea, Waneta refused adamantly. Instead, she wanted to go home with medication. When she met with Jafri personally later in the morning, she was equally resolute. "She sat, her face impassive, but her manner definite," Elkin, who sat in on the session, wrote in her notes. "Since Mr. Hoyt will be home over the holiday and the weekend, Dr. Jafri gave in and prescribed medication." Meanwhile, he suggested she return Scotty to Social Services, though he did not feel the need to order her to do so or to call the agency himself.

Waneta thought things over that night and the next day. She told Tim that she felt caught in a terrible dilemma. If they gave Scotty back, it might ruin their chances of ever adopting a child. But she was afraid to go against Dr. Jafri's advice. She believed he would commit her if she wasn't better by the end of the Thanksgiving weekend. Meanwhile, she still felt an impulse to hurt the child. Waneta called Alberta Weisz on Friday morning.

"She couldn't really explain the feelings that came over her, just that the child unnerved her to the point that she couldn't stand his presence," Weisz wrote in her report of the incident. "She feared that she might harm the child in her condition." Years later, the social worker would look back on these moments and see a strong indication of Waneta's presence of mind. "She might have been able to get away with five natural children," she observed, "but she couldn't say, 'Oh, guess what—Scotty stopped breathing.' I felt we had very narrowly averted a tragedy."

Waneta's chilling thoughts, meanwhile, seem to have set Jafri to wondering about the Hoyts' previous children, especially after Waneta's next appointment. "She has been feeling better since returning the adopted child," he wrote that day, "though still she feels she hasn't gotten over the loss of her five children and mostly in some ways feels responsible, as if she has herself killed them."

Jafri asked Waneta to tell him about the deaths of her children: their names, dates of birth and death, what she could remember about the circumstances. He took down the information, jotting some notes as she spoke: "Crib death ... Cyanotic-episodic-apnea ... Dr. Steinschneider ... researcher in crib death." He summed things up in his record of the session: "She cannot understand why and how they died and apparently no reason was found in any case definitely excepting one child. Apparently thymus was found enlarged." He concluded: "She says she has been feeling better, not as depressed, and denies any problem with the husband, except pressure from the family on her [side] as well as his side to adopt children. They are not pressuring now."

The next day, December 7, Jafri wrote to the records department of Tioga General Hospital and Wilson Memorial, and personally to Steinschneider at Upstate, requesting copies of the autopsy reports for Jimmy, Molly, and Noah. "Such information," he wrote, "will greatly help me in assisting Mrs. Hoyt through depression and pathological grief reaction."

The reports came in during the following week, but they didn't clarify much for Jafri. His letter to Steinschneider, however, did lead to a phone conversation between the two doctors in early January. Whatever was said between them, neither physician seemed too interested in pushing the envelope of suspicion; it seems more likely that they helped each other avoid it. After they spoke, Jafri sent a copy of James's autopsy report to Steinschneider. "I felt you might be interested in their finding of adrenal insufficiency," he wrote. His closing comments were suggestive. "We have not uncovered any useful clues," he remarked, "except feelings of guilt of moderate severity, which she seems to be working through adequately. As I told you on the telephone, if I have anything new, I will write to you."

In the research clinic in Syracuse, Steinschneider told Thelma Schneider about the developments with the Hoyts and the baby they had tried to adopt. "My God," Thelma replied. "Well, thank heavens she returned the baby."

She had not talked to Steinschneider about the Hoyts much after Noah's death. In fact, among the nurses there had been no collective consideration of the experience. If the talk before the babies died had been discreet, now it was inaudible. The whole thing had turned Gail Dristle, for one, inside out. But on the ward the nurses behaved as if none of this had happened. "You're lost in your own torment, dealing with the guilt about what you should have done," she reflected years later. "Nobody wants to confront that, so you just keep silent and walk away." But hearing about the baby the Hoyts returned, Thelma Schneider was moved to try one last time to draw from Steinschneider some acknowledgment that the nurses' instincts were right. As Steinschneider told it, Waneta had given up the baby because she was "afraid something would happen to him." Hearing this, Thelma looked at Steinschneider dubiously. "Why would she be afraid of something happening to a foster child?" she asked him. "Al, doesn't it tell you something?" Once again, Steinschneider didn't respond. They never talked about it again.

In Newark Valley, Waneta moved about woefully, a childless mother in a permanent fog of grief. She ignored the people who were suspicious of her, gravitating to those with empathy in their eyes. She encouraged the other young women in the family, her sisters and Tim's, to feel guilty that they had their children, and she didn't have hers. She talked openly, cried easily, when she told people about all the children she had lost to "that crib disease," as she had called it before Dr. Steinschneider taught her that it was SIDS that had taken them from her. At his invitation, she and Tim attended a meeting of a SIDS support group he had started at Upstate. The group met in a basement room next door to the anatomy department. When Waneta came into the meeting and sat with the other SIDS parents, it was as if a kind of celebrity was in their midst, the greatest sufferer among them. The other mothers offered solace against tragedy even they could not imagine. Though it was not Waneta's way to allow her miseries to go unpitied, the setting made her uncomfortable. "I can't handle this," she told one of the regular members toward the end of the meeting, and never went back. She preferred the more intimate visits of Joyce Aman, the county public health nurse who had first come to the trailer three years before. Aman came on a bereavement call after Noah died, and Waneta told her how much she appreciated it. "I hope you'll come back," she told the nurse.

None of this tempered Waneta's continuing preoccupation with the question of having more children. It became a virtual obsession. To her psychiatrist, it was an ongoing puzzle. Soon after she returned Scotty, Waneta told Jafri that she and Tim would not adopt any more children, that they would "do for each other." She complained that she and Tim had never been able to spend enough time together "because of children coming, and their deaths, which has also caused financial difficulties," Jafri wrote. But she vacillated constantly. At one point she discussed the possibility of reversing Tim's vasectomy, or failing that, having artificial insemination; at another she said she was contemplating a hysterectomy. "The only reason that came out seems not as a measure of contraception," Jafri, turning Freudian, wrote of the hysterectomy, "but, in my opinion, in self-mutilation, especially the organ which did not give her what she wanted." At a session on May 9, which would have been Noah's first birthday, Waneta said she was very upset that she could no longer have her own children. She said she was angry at Tim for having the vasectomy, and they fought about it bitterly.

At one of her frequent emergency appointments, she told Jafri that she felt she was falling apart. She was unhappy living in the same house where four of her five children had died. "Everything reminds me of the past," she said. It was an ongoing issue for Waneta, well known within the family. There was some suspicion among them when, the following spring, the trailer was destroyed by fire. Waneta and Tim moved back in with Tim's mother for a while, then into another trailer when the insurance payment came in. But Waneta told Jafri that she was nervous staying alone in the new trailer because she was afraid it might explode.

By the spring of 1973, she seemed to be doing better. She was sleeping well and getting along better with Tim, though she told Jafri she had been thinking lately about other men. The Hoyts settled into an austere life, shadowed by Waneta's occasional penchant for melodrama—the day, for instance, when she told Tim she had been raped. She'd gone to look at some used furniture with one of their neighbors, she said, and he'd forced himself on her. Tim called the police and had the neighbor arrested. But the man said Waneta was lying—that on the way to his mother's house in Broome County to look at the furniture, she'd willingly had sex with him at the roadside. He was in jail for two days before Waneta decided she didn't want to go through with a prosecution, though by then she had made the incident common knowledge among neighbors and relatives, some of whom were skeptical of the story because Waneta was so open about it, and not very upset. A more private episode soon followed. One day she went down to a garage in Newark Valley and asked the owner if she could talk to him in his office. A minute later, the man emerged with a strange look on his face. "Hey, you guys," he said when Waneta left. The mechanics looked up from their work. "You're not gonna believe this. Waneta Hoyt just told me she has dreams about me and wants to 'get to know me better.' I told her thanks but no thanks."

Meantime, the Hoyts were talking again about adoption. They had gone back to Tioga Social Services, but left with the distinct feeling they ought to take their application elsewhere. The people in Tompkins County seemed friendlier. Waneta asked the agency in Ithaca for two children. They didn't have to be babies. But she and Tim resigned themselves to a long wait.

For now, Waneta would visit her children in Highland Cemetery, though her mother advised her not to. She would look through her photo album, though her mother told her not to do that either. She would buy presents for Tim on Father's Day. And she would retreat further into her world. She would take her daily Valium, and sit in a booth and quietly drink Cokes with Tim at Betty's Luncheonette, leaving such a sad and soulless impression on the people who saw her that a quarter-century later Betty, now gray and aging, could drag on a cigarette and effortlessly summon the image of the young Waneta. "She was," Betty remembered, "a lost person."

PART THREE

The Theory

It was a rumination.

—Alfred Steinschneider

23

From the July morning in 1971 when the Tioga County coroner called him from a trailer in the distant hills, Alfred Steinschneider considered the implications of Noah Hoyt's death. Through the end of that summer and into the fall, as the Hoyts were waiting to adopt a baby in Tioga County, Steinschneider was in Syracuse reading, collating, and pondering the research data he had gathered on the deaths of their last two natural children. It had been two years since the 1969 SIDS conference—for Steinschneider, two years of single-minded investigation during which, he imagined, twenty thousand more babies had died in the United States, suddenly and without apparent cause. Now he felt he had something to share.

Steinschneider viewed his data from the cold angles of thesis, measurement, and outcome. The measurements were murky, but that was not the issue as he saw it. The thesis was what counted. The outcome was the evidence. What he saw in Molly and Noah Hoyt were two babies whose deaths suggested a subtle but lethal respiratory abnormality—whose apneic pauses were a precursor to the final event. Each baby, it seemed to him, had experienced the kind of near-miss episodes that had aroused his interest in the first place. Each had gone on to die without medical explanation. In both cases, sudden death had come at a little less than three months of age—Molly's at seventy-nine days, Noah's at eighty—right in the heart of the period of peak incidence of SIDS. Steinschneider had wanted a swift answer. Perhaps, miraculously, he had found one. He dismissed what the nurses on 4A and 5C had told him; he ignored the dark notions of Stuart Asch. His studies of the Hoyt babies, he concluded, were based on sound scientific observation.

Whatever retrospective spin he would give his theory a generation later,

Steinschneider's actions almost from the moment of Noah's last breath suggest a man on a crusade. On August 16, 1971—three weeks after Noah died—Steinschneider went to a meeting in Bethesda, Maryland, headquarters of the National Institute of Child Health and Human Development. Prodded by the parents' movement, the NICHD was contemplating the first serious assault on SIDS, and this meeting was a prelude to what was to become three years of forums aimed at organizing a national research strategy—and at building a case for seeking money from Congress to pay for the battle ahead. At this meeting, Steinschneider reported that while collecting data on colds and apnea, he had studied one baby who was apneic *fifty* percent of the time when he had a cold. The baby had gone on to die of SIDS. He left it at that, but not for long.

In "documenting" prolonged apnea where it didn't exist, Steinschneider created his own reality. Now he was ready to put it out for the consumption of a world ravenous for answers. Over the next few months, he made his calculations and connections, and he made his big decision. His cases were undeniably dramatic, the theory groundbreaking and sure to attract attention. He would submit his first work on SIDS to the American Academy of Pediatrics monthly publication *Pediatrics*. If accepted, it would be his first solo publication in the most prestigious journal in the field. His last submission, a paper he'd written several years before with Earle Lipton, in which they'd described the difficulties some premature babies had coordinating feeding and breathing, had been rejected. This was the presentation he had gone on to make to the 1969 SIDS conference. It was the prologue to his official unveiling of the apnea theory of SIDS.

If there was risk in using Molly and Noah to make the connection between apnea and death, it would not be the first time Steinschneider had decided to put his neck on the line. Still, he would hedge his bets. Though the Hoyt babies were his only research subjects who went on to die, Steinschneider decided to include his observation of several other babies, including the two siblings who had shuttled between home and hospital during their first months of life. They didn't die, but they had, by Steinschneider's calculations, a solid record of prolonged apnea. He started with nearly a dozen cases, and gradually whittled them down to five. He titled his paper: "Prolonged Apnea and the Sudden Infant Death Syndrome: Clinical and Laboratory Observations."

Sitting at his typewriter that fall, Steinschneider introduced his readers to what for many would be unfamiliar ground. "Sudden unexpected, unexplained death in infancy (SIDS) continues to represent a problem of major medical significance," he opened. "It has been estimated that greater than 10,000 *apparently* well infants die each year in the United States suddenly and, in spite of detailed autopsy study, without adequate explanation." He went on to say that on the frontier of SIDS investigation, researchers hadn't been able to agree on how to explore the problem, much less solve it. His study, he wrote at the beginning of the 5,000-word article, was based on a set of beliefs: that SIDS occurred primarily during sleep, that such physiologic functions as heart rate, blood pressure, and respiration are subject to change during sleep, and that sleep apnea was a well-documented entity that seemed particularly relevant to the question at hand. "For the purpose of providing direction to this study it was proposed that SIDS occurs as the result of an exaggeration of the physiologic changes noted to occur during sleep. This report consists of the study of five infants, two of whom died of SIDS."

To preserve their confidentiality, Steinschneider used initials to refer to Molly and Noah and the three other babies in the paper. Waneta Hoyt became Mrs. H.

He wrote that prolonged sleep apnea, in the two babies who had died as well as the three who had not, occurred most often during REM sleep and at times of upper respiratory infection. To illustrate this, he prepared a series of graphs showing each baby's incidence of prolonged apnea, and how it correlated with REM sleep and colds. Some episodes of apnea were accompanied by cyanosis and required "vigorous resuscitative efforts," he reported.

For a research scientist, Steinschneider's concept of documentation was notably broad. In the case of Molly and Noah, he had only measured routine, short periods of apnea on paper in the laboratory. The critical data upon which his thesis rested was based largely on clinical "observation" that was either presumed, embellished, or on occasion apparently fabricated. The discrepancies and ambiguities in what had and had not been observed, however, were masked by Steinschneider's description of his innovative research techniques. He explained how he calculated his formula for measuring apnea, and offered a detailed catalogue of methodology. He described the way the electrodes for the various gauges were attached to the babies in the laboratory, and how he had kept the lab temperature at 90 degrees during testing. He did not point out that the heat tended to induce apnea.

He included a bar graph showing that Molly had thirty-three episodes of prolonged apnea. In truth, it was impossible to know how many actual episodes she had—if any—because of the unreliability of the monitors. Steinschneider did not disclose this problem, or that he had included all the instances when the nurses heard the alarm and found Molly breathing, as well as those when the baby's mother reported episodes at home that were not independently substantiated. He did report that in the laboratory—the only place where apnea was truly documented—the longest episode recorded in all Molly's sessions over those two months was 11.2 seconds, well within normal range. The vast majority were much shorter than that, even in the heat.

The picture of Molly's brother was even more misleading. Steinschneider reported that Noah had twenty-eight episodes of prolonged apnea during his two and a half months of life. In this case, readers could easily be distracted by Steinschneider's intricate analysis of how the episodes occurred more frequently when Noah had a cold: ". . . 12 of the episodes occurred during the 71 days when he was free of disease whereas 16 episodes were observed during the total of 28 days during which he was ill. Furthermore, 10 of the 13 episodes that occurred when free of disease were observed on the days following an A/D%, Apnea %—REM or Apnea %—NREM of greater than 3, 20, and 5, respectively. . . . At its maximum, 52.5% of the REM epochs were associated with the onset of apnea. During the same sleep session, apnea occurred in conjunction with 39.6% of the NREM epochs. On the day prior to his death, apnea occurred during 22.1% and 4.1% of the REM and NREM epochs, respectively."

Buried in these seemingly sophisticated calculations was an error of arithmetic so basic that anyone catching it would have to question the credibility of the researcher. Adding the days of Noah's life—the "71 days when he was free of disease" and the "28 days during which he was ill"—made a total of 99. In fact, as one of Steinschneider's own charts showed, Noah lived only 80 days. But it was only a hint that Steinschneider's entire premise was built on shaky data. His readers would have no way of knowing that the stacks of notes locked away in a hospital records room in Syracuse documented not babies with recurrent prolonged apnea, but babies with occasional colds.

In preparing his hypothesis, Steinschneider paid close attention to the epidemiological construct he had taken home from Orcas Island. Nasopharyngitis—a cold—preoccupied him particularly. SIDS seemed to strike more often when babies had some kind of upper respiratory infection. Steinschneider made much of his finding that his cases fit this pattern. "On the evening of her discharge M.H. appeared to be 'coming down with a cold,' " he wrote. "From 6 A.M. to 8 A.M. the following day she had six prolonged apneic episodes. . . . [S]he had slight rhinorrhea and a rectal temperature of 101F. Mrs. H. placed her in the crib and left the room for 'a minute to get something.' When she returned M.H. was apneic and cyanotic. She was given mouth-to-mouth resuscitation without success."

Did the ostensible circumstances of Molly's death color Steinschneider's reporting of her brother? He wrote that Noah had evidence of infection on twenty-eight days. In fact, this was so on only nineteen days, and in most cases the nurses noted nothing more severe than a sniffle or a single "dry cough." He paired this data with the inflated record of prolonged apnea he had written into the Physician's Record at Noah's second discharge from the hospital. In that instance, he had listed the dates on which he said Noah had

experienced prolonged apnea. Virtually all of the episodes were either unconfirmed—based on one of the nurses' "alarm sounded but patient breathing"
notes—or simply fabricated. Moreover, they tended to coincide with days
when the nurses observed that Noah had some evidence of infection. It was a
matchup that would tend to bolster the hypothesis. The unseen record told
another story. Some examples:

JUNE 30	NURSING NOTES:	"Sounds stuffy. Appears to be getting a cold."
	STEINSCHNEIDER:	1 prolonged apnea
	NURSING NOTES:	"Alarm [went] off, baby breathing"
JULY 1	NURSING NOTES:	"Loose nonproductive cough, nasal discharge"
	STEINSCHNEIDER:	3 prolonged apneas
	NURSING NOTES:	"Apnea monitor went off at 10:55 but child was sleeping and breathing;" "Alarm off 1X, baby was breathing."
JULY 2	NURSING NOTES:	"Has runny nose, coughs at intervals, sounds congested"
	STEINSCHNEIDER:	3 prolonged apneas
	NURSING NOTES:	"Monitor went off numerous times in AM but child breathing;" "Apnea alarm rang X2, no apnea noted."
JULY 10	NURSING NOTES:	"Pt. periodically coughing, sneezing, some drainage from nose."
	STEINSCHNEIDER:	1 prolonged apnea
	NURSING NOTES:	No alarms, no apnea

Readers would also have to look closely to grasp the discrepancies in the
other half of Steinschneider's evidence: the apparent "near-miss" episodes
that he suggested were a predictor of SIDS. "The five patients participating in
the present study demonstrated frequent episodes of apnea while asleep," he
wrote. "Although the majority of these apneic periods were brief and self-
limited, a number were sufficiently prolonged to be associated with cyanosis
and were of sufficient severity to prompt vigorous resuscitative efforts. To this
must be added the fact that two of the five infants ultimately died during a
similar episode. These observations support the basic hypothesis that prolonged apnea, a concomitant of sleep, is part of the final physiologic pathway
culminating in SIDS." Steinschneider assiduously avoided clarifying a key
point: None of the cyanosis and "vigorous resuscitative efforts" had occurred
in the hospital, but only at home, as reported by Mrs. H.

While Steinschneider found a way to make Molly and Noah fit his theory, he still faced the dilemma presented by the strange and inconsistent ways in which their three prior siblings had purportedly died. How did Eric, Julie, and Jimmy fit into the theory that it was prolonged sleep apnea that caused the sudden deaths of Molly and Noah? Steinschneider did not venture into this unclear territory and dispensed with the first three children as inconspicuously as possible. The first baby, he wrote, was a boy who "had been noted to develop recurrent cyanotic spells while asleep and died suddenly at 102 days of age." The second child, he reported, confusing the orders of birth and death, was a baby girl: "At 48 days of age and during a bottle feeding she suddenly 'seemed to choke,' turned blue, and died. No autopsy was performed." And the third child, a boy: "Following breakfast, he called out and died suddenly; he was 28 months old at this time. An autopsy was performed and revealed congestion of the liver, kidneys, and brain. The adrenal glands were considered to be of small size." He offered no thoughts about how these deaths related to the two that followed.

He was also selective in what he noted. When Steinschneider transferred into his paper, almost verbatim, the histories of the first three children given by their mother, he left out the "bleeding" she said she had seen at the deaths of Eric and Jimmy. But in his narratives of the lives and deaths of Molly and Noah, a prosaic recitation of their cycle of hospital admissions, discharges, readmissions, and sudden deaths within a day of their final return home, Steinschneider included, for no apparent reason, an extraneous detail that would serve, two decades later, as the dangling thread that would help unravel a mystery. Following the death of N.H., he wrote, an autopsy was performed at the hospital. Its number was A-71-109.

Steinschneider's paper put in writing what he had suspected ever since the day he had begun thinking about what to talk about on Orcas Island: that sleep apnea and exaggerated autonomic instability were the mysterious culprits that had eluded the world's SIDS investigators. If it were published, he would be the first researcher to formally suggest that the fate of babies who died of SIDS was destined at birth—that they came into the world with a physiological abnormality that turned respiratory pauses which were routine and inconsequential in most babies into a fatal flaw. He did not declare that SIDS could run in families. He didn't have to; the claim was made by implication. And he laid a foundation for his evolving belief that the monitors he had helped develop in Syracuse could save babies from death. He concluded with a radical thought. "It is suggested," he wrote, "that infants at risk might be identified prior to the final tragic event."

Steinschneider showed his paper to two colleagues, Jack Schneider and Mary Voorhess, who offered what he called "numerous constructive suggestions" in his paragraph of acknowledgments. He also thanked several nurses, including Thelma Schneider. But if he heard any inner voices of caution before he pushed the button, he failed to heed them. On January 10, 1972, Dr. Mokarram Jafri wrote his letter to Steinschneider, saying he would let him know if he came up with any "useful clues." Two weeks later, Steinschneider put his SIDS paper in an envelope and mailed it to a pediatrician in Cambridge, Massachusetts.

Pediatrics was published from Chicago, headquarters of its parent organization, the American Academy of Pediatrics, but the real work derived from wherever its editor happened to teach or practice medicine. Founded in 1948 by the country's premier professional organization for pediatricians, the journal was edited and reviewed by working physicians, a far-flung group that included the top editor, an editorial board of twenty, and two thousand specializing pediatricians who made themselves available to evaluate the scores of articles, among the six hundred submitted each year, which the editor judged worthy of peer review. Those accepted were published in a journal mailed each month to the academy's 12,000 dues-paying members.

In early 1972, the editorial helm of the journal was in the process of changing hands. After a seven-year tenure, Harvard's Clement Smith was passing the job on to the chairman of the editorial board, Dr. Jerold Lucey, who at forty-six would be one of the journal's youngest editors. An associate professor of pediatrics at the University of Vermont, Lucey was a leader in the emerging field of neonatology, a new subspecialty devoted to the newborn. He was at the moment establishing one of the first regional neonatal intensive care units in the country. He was also a credible researcher in his own right. A few years before, he had developed and tested the use of fluorescent light on jaundiced babies. He had published his results in *Pediatrics* in 1968, and by 1972, the year he was taking over as editor of the journal, the treatment had become standard procedure in hospital nurseries across the country.

That January, Lucey was traveling weekly from Burlington to Cambridge to learn the nuts and bolts of editing the journal from Smith, who would officially turn over the reins in July. One winter day in his office at Harvard, Smith handed Lucey a paper that had come in from a researcher who thought he had found a possible mechanism of sudden death in babies. Smith thought it was a provocative monograph, and a good one for teaching a new editor how to decide what to publish.

Like most pediatricians, Lucey had seen many theories of sudden infant death come and go, without paying much attention to the nuances. Steinschneider's paper, though, was not particularly nuanced, and Lucey found it fascinating and instantly credible. He knew just enough about the elusive entity—knew that little was known—to conclude that the study could be a real breakthrough. Smith liked the paper, too. He liked, among other things, that it had something to do with the real lives (and deaths, in this case) of children—that it was clinical research with potential practical value, as opposed to the basic science that some people in Chicago thought weighed the journal down. "The clinical doctors at the Academy wanted more clinical articles—they beat down sheep and cat studies," Lucey remembered. "It was the beginning of the boom period for clinical pediatric research." Steinschneider's work struck Lucey and Smith as extraordinarily lucky, clinically speaking. Had this been a formal research study, with protocols and controls, Steinschneider would normally have had to test a thousand babies or more before seeing two deaths, let alone two in the same family. Reading the submission that day in Cambridge, Lucey was struck by the sensation that Steinschneider was blessed by providence—that he'd beaten the odds and perhaps stumbled upon a revelation. "I thought," Lucey would say years later, "that he had been in the right place at the right time."

In that case, so, too, had Steinschneider's Mrs. H. He reported in his paper that both babies turned blue at their sudden deaths, and that their mother had been there when it happened. It would be the first case in the literature of a witnessed SIDS death—two, in fact—and dramatic evidence that SIDS babies didn't merely die silently, without showing outward signs of distress, but that they turned blue, as if deprived of oxygen. It would lend credence to the concept of "near-miss SIDS," and to the notion that the process might be reversible if caught in time.

In their enthusiasm, Smith and Lucey didn't linger over the oddity of both M.H. and N.H. dying within twenty-four hours of their discharge from the hospital. Nor did they question the babies' family history. In his cursory, matter-of-fact description of the lives and deaths of the babies' three siblings, Steinschneider did not say they had died of SIDS, though, of course, this was the clear inference. Elsewhere in the paper, he stated his belief that SIDS occurred primarily during sleep, and that "any reasonable theory of the causation of SIDS must be consistent with the observation that most deaths occur between 4 and 16 weeks of age." These principles were two of the critical underpinnings of his theory. But they were also inconsistent with the implication that the second and third H. children—the one who choked during a feeding and the one who was past two—died of SIDS, raising fundamental flaws of logic and probability. A reader might well ask: If not SIDS, what? Could any family be so cursed as to lose five children in so many different ways?

Lucey recognized that Steinschneider's method was a sort of scientific hybrid: He presented five case reports, five anecdotes, and subjected them to his own quirky research protocols. It was nothing like the controlled research Lucey had conducted on jaundiced babies. But he assumed the data's integrity, stood back, and regarded the big picture. He and Smith concluded that Steinschneider's findings were so striking, his theory potentially so important, that there was no question that the paper should go to the next level of review. Lucey sent it out to two specialists in the field of SIDS.

Back in Syracuse, Steinschneider quietly began using the results of his unpublished apnea studies to try to attract the backing he would need to sustain his work. Between 1969 and 1971, his inquiry into infants at risk had been financed principally by the annual federal grants that Upstate had received for years to operate the Children's Clinical Research Center. But now the money was gone. If he wanted to continue his SIDS research, Steinschneider realized, he would have to go out and get the money himself.

He was a relative novice at research politics. The money had always come reliably, and he'd never paid too much attention to how it got there. But he was a quick study, and Abe Bergman gave him the lay of the land. True, government-funded research had been cut by the Nixon administration, but there was reason to be optimistic about SIDS. By the early part of 1972, it appeared that the first serious research money the field had seen might soon be on its way. Steinschneider began getting to know the right people at the NICHD, the nine-year-old agency that would preside over whatever SIDS program the government eventually undertook.

The positive developments in Washington had just come together in the past year, surmounting what had become some fierce internal rivalries in the SIDS movement. In one corner were Saul and Sylvia Goldberg and their Baltimore-based Guild for Infant Survival, an organization of parents that had begun to run on the fuel of their bitterness toward the federal government's failure to tackle SIDS. In 1971, the government supported only one project targeting the cause of SIDS—it was with Bergman's Seattle group—for a sum total of $46,258. The guild flooded Congress with mail, demanding to know why the government was so callous toward all the dying children. The Goldbergs regularly drove down to Bethesda to harangue the NICHD director, Dr. Gerald LaVeck, who always listened sympathetically.

In another corner was Bergman, who had recently become president of the National Foundation for Sudden Infant Death, the group formerly named for Mark Addison Roe. While he admired the Goldbergs' tireless efforts to help SIDS families—nobody did more to help parents feel better—Bergman chafed at what he deemed their political clumsiness. LaVeck, a pediatrician who had grown up with Bergman in Seattle's Madrona neighborhood, had told him that it would take "a pot of gold" from Congress to get the attention of the nation's medical scientists, whose general reaction to crib death through the sixties had been: If it can't be prevented, why bother? But Bergman worried that when the money came, the political climate the guild was creating would make it hard for the NICHD to resist *any* kind of research with the letters SIDS attached—scientifically sound or not. When he pointed out to the Goldbergs that there were probably 10,000 SIDS deaths a year, not 25,000 as their literature said, they looked at him dismissively.

Ultimately, the two groups formed an uneasy alliance. The Goldbergs always went for pure emotion. For years they had come to congressional sub-committee meetings, SIDS parents in tow, mothers and fathers with jobs in all-night restaurants and plastics factories and on family farms, pitiable people carrying snapshots of their babies to the witness table. Their affecting stories led to articles in newspapers and national magazines. Meanwhile, Bergman went right for the money. Fancying himself a political insider, he negotiated the twists and turns of federal appropriation legislation. But when the big break came—when a Senate subcommittee chaired by Walter Mondale announced it would hold a major hearing on SIDS in January 1972—it was the Goldbergs' intense letter-writing campaign, and not the backstage lobbying of Bergman's SIDS foundation, that had brought it about.

Bergman was not about to look a gift horse in the mouth. Once the hearing was officially on the calendar, he took over the witness list. He realized this was probably the one time the Goldbergs' way might not be such a bad idea. He made sure there would be plenty of emotion, and that plenty of reporters and photographers would be there to record it—a task eased considerably by an impassioned and widely read article on "the sudden death mystery" by the *Washington Post* columnist Colman McCarthy that appeared on the paper's editorial page three weeks before the hearing. This was a moment the SIDS movement had waited a decade to see. A few minutes before dropping the gavel on the morning of the hearing, Mondale looked out across the hearing room and marveled at the crowd, which included crews from all three television networks. Not realizing the TV mikes were live, he turned to Senator Alan Cranston and said, "Look at all those cameras. We'll get a lot more mileage out of this than I expected."

A succession of SIDS parents stepped to the witness table and recounted their heart-wrenching stories. Judie Choate, a former fashion model who was the SIDS foundation's executive director, and Arthur Siegal, the New York ad man whose office housed the foundation's offices, told the senators and the nation what it was like to discover your baby dead in its crib. Frank Hennigan, a meat-packing executive from Chicago, related the poignant aftermath of his son's death: "The cruelest part of this whole nightmare was the inquest. . . . My feeling is that it is a crime to subject loving parents, grieving for their child stricken by crib death, to such treatment."

The senators wanted to know what could be done about SIDS. A lineup of doctors offered a variety of views, their theories so scattershot that when they were finished, the senators could easily have concluded that SIDS was the Wild West of medical research. Anything went, and often did. "It may well be that the common cold virus acts in a strange way on the nervous system of the sleeping baby," Bergman explained when he took his turn at the witness table. He had been preceded by Dr. Merlin K. Duval, assistant secretary of Health, Education, and Welfare, who said that in the majority of cases, "the baby does not have a cold or infection."

Mondale's subcommittee decided the country ought to give these people some help. The senators drew up a resolution, later passed unanimously by the full Senate, directing the NICHD to "designate the search for a cause and prevention of sudden infant death syndrome as one of the top priorities in research efforts." The painfully clear message of the hearing was that nobody had the foggiest notion of why thousands of babies died inexplicably every year, while in some cases parents, outrageously, were being blamed. The resolution didn't come with any money, but it was the clearest sign yet that the mysterious deaths of babies was becoming a hot national cause. The SIDS movement was coming of age, and money might not be far behind.

At the NICHD, the responsibility fell to Eileen Hasselmeyer, the director of the perinatal biology and infant mortality branch. A pediatric nurse with a doctorate in physiology, she would be the czar of the agency's fledgling SIDS program. One of her first moves was to make it known, through full-page ads in journals such as *Pediatric Research* that spring, that money from the agency's general research fund was available for worthy SIDS projects. She also launched a series of seminars for researchers, each session devoted to one aspect of SIDS and followed by the publication of a handsome booklet reporting on what had been said. Most of the scientists she recruited came in knowing almost nothing about the topic, which was more or less the idea. She hoped that they would learn just enough to pull them in. It worked. In the wake of the administration's cutbacks in research funding, the scientists began pitching SIDS grants. But on this frontier of science, putting out an open call for research was something like offering a bounty on a fugitive. In Bergman's view, many of the proposals came from the scientific equivalent of nutty tipsters—uninformed researchers "seeking licenses to chase wild geese." It made the good proposals look even better. And sometimes it made it hard to tell the difference.

The day before the Mondale hearing in Washington, Steinschneider's apnea paper had arrived on the desk of *Pediatrics* editor Clement Smith at Harvard. The dramatic, widely covered testimony was still resonating when Smith and

Jerold Lucey sent the unusual paper out for peer review. If the upshot of the hearing was that the cause of SIDS was anyone's guess, Steinschneider's seemed anything but wild.

Six weeks later, two responses came back. The reviews were mixed. One reader found the science too soft and anecdotal, the conclusions too speculative. He was a hard science man. The second reader was very positive. He also had a certain intrinsic bias. Like Lucey, he believed that whatever the flaws of the study, the findings were too provocative not to share. Unlike him, he knew something about the subject. "I thought it confirmed my theory," Warren Guntheroth would later say. Guntheroth, the University of Washington pediatrician whose thesis had helped launch Steinschneider's quest, his ally in apnea at the 1969 meeting, thought the paper was marvelous. "He had an apnea index," he said, recalling his excitement.

Guntheroth apparently did not carefully scrutinize Steinschneider's methodology. In the abstract at the top of his paper, Steinschneider ended the summary of his findings in the sleep laboratory with this statement: "All infants had a number of prolonged apneic and cyanotic episodes during sleep, some requiring vigorous resuscitative efforts." The unmistakable implication was that these life-threatening events had been recorded on paper, in the lab. It wasn't backed up by the data, but Guntheroth accepted—and would later disseminate—this most fundamental deception, virtually repeating the untrue statement verbatim in his widely read medical reference book, *Crib Death: The Sudden Infant Death Syndrome*. The babies in Steinschneider's study who died, Guntheroth was to write, "were documented polygraphically as having episodes of prolonged sleep apnea with cyanosis, some requiring vigorous resuscitation...." In March 1972, Guntheroth sent a most enthusiastic review across the country from Seattle: Yes, he told Jerold Lucey, certainly publish this paper.

Lucey wanted to publish it, but with split reviews, Smith instructed him to send it out for a third opinion. This reviewer returned an affirmative note. Including Lucey, the vote was three for publication, one against. Smith sent Steinschneider a letter saying that the paper would be published after some routine revisions and cuts. Smith and Steinschneider wrestled over length and language but left the substance essentially undebated. On May 22, four months after it was submitted, the apnea paper was officially accepted for publication. Steinschneider's first solo work in a prestigious journal would appear in the October issue of *Pediatrics*.

A few weeks after getting the good news, Steinschneider traveled to Bethesda for one of Hasselmeyer's research workshops on the campus of NICHD's parent agency, the National Institutes of Health. He'd dropped the first circumspect hints about his theory during the meeting in Bethesda three weeks after Noah Hoyt's death the previous summer. Now, he discussed it publicly for the first time, letting Hasselmeyer in particular know that he was onto something important. Many people talked about many things at these seminars, but few had devoted anything approaching the concentrated time and energy Steinschneider had to SIDS in the last few years. Certainly, none offered a hypothesis with as much conviction. He knew that his proposal of prolonged apnea as "the critical event" in SIDS, and his implication that monitoring might one day be a way to stop it, was interesting, and possibly accurate. He also knew he hadn't come close to proving it. His sample had been way too small. He hadn't used a control group. To prove it, he needed to study a lot of babies—babies with pronounced apnea, babies without—and see how the two groups differed over a few years' times. To study a lot of babies, over a lot of time, he would need a lot of money.

His timing was impeccable. In a few months, the apnea theory of SIDS would be a published hypothesis. For the grant makers, under instructions from the United States Senate to make SIDS research a priority, it would be almost impossible to ignore.

There is a standard way to quickly read an article in a research journal like *Pediatrics*. A doctor interested in SIDS in the fall of 1972, but short on time, could read Steinschneider's abstract summarizing the paper directly under the title, scan the methodology section, pause over the history, and save his full attention for the discussion of the results and implications at the end. For most of the journal's readers, clinical pediatricians with busy practices and little direct experience with SIDS, the news was not just that apnea appeared to play a key role in the cause of SIDS—that was for the researchers to puzzle over—but that it was possible that a machine could detect the abnormality and maybe even prevent death. The other message, that SIDS could run in families, came though even more clearly.

The readers that Steinschneider was most interested in reaching, however, were the people who counted in the nation's small but growing SIDS community, a world that now included a few suddenly influential federal employees. He wanted to stir them, and he did. The paper struck many of those who conducted and financed SIDS research as it had struck the editors and all but one of the peer reviewers. The plausibility of the thesis, not the accuracy of the data, was what gripped them. Steinschneider had made no secret of his soon-to-be-published theory that SIDS babies were not normal prior to death, and when the article arrived in subscribers' mailboxes in the fall, it caused a wave of excitement and a small explosion of immediate follow-up studies. Medical detectives from coast to coast began considering the apnea theory, while at the highest levels of the SIDS research establishment, Steinschneider's paper was warmly greeted as important, if less than conclusive.

In Philadelphia, Molly Dapena, who had consulted with Steinschneider on the autopsy slides of Molly Hoyt, thought his paper must mean something, though exactly what she wasn't quite sure. In Seattle, Abe Bergman and Bruce Beckwith were ambivalent. On one hand, they didn't think the descriptions of two of the earlier deaths fit SIDS. On the other hand, the cases of M.H. and N.H. were not inconsistent with their thoughts about sudden airway obstruction.

Beckwith, though somewhat puzzled, concluded that Steinschneider's paper was a compelling development. Bergman was glad to see that his Orcas Island invitation had led to something productive. But when the two men talked about the paper, there was much they did not dwell on. They acknowledged the oddities, but didn't explore them. Their reticence had less to do with science than with the political philosophy of SIDS they'd held for a decade, and which was now deeply rooted: Don't ever blame the parents.

The excitement had not yet begun to subside when a lone voice of dissent emerged from the hinterlands of American pediatrics. The first hint of doubt about the legitimacy of Steinschneider's paper came from a young pediatrician with a modest practice in Winona, Minnesota, who had no particular expertise in SIDS, but who knew something few of his peers did.

To John Hick, Steinschneider's study just didn't add up. The odds against five deaths occurring in the way Steinschneider described had to be astronomical. Hick found the report of the third death especially unsettling. The child ate something, called out, and died? For Hick, the whole thing brought up uncomfortable memories from his residency days in Chicago. Reading about the babies of Mrs. H., his mind shot back to the mid-1960s, to Children's Memorial Hospital and the woman behind the one-way mirror. It was the reason he was so skeptical.

A young child had been brought to the hospital with ataxia, wild movements of the limbs. The symptoms were episodic, which defied logic; a central nervous system condition would be constant. The child was admitted, and again sporadic symptoms emerged. A disturbing thought came over the doctors. They decided to assign the child to a room with a one-way mirror. The next day they were stunned to see the child's mother take pills from her purse and feed them to her child, triggering the baffling movements. The pills were phenobarbital. More than a decade would pass before such bizarre maternal behavior would be medically recognized and given a name: Munchausen syndrome by proxy.

Few pediatricians could count such a grotesque incident in their catalogue of training experiences, and for Hick it was a revelatory moment. Unlike most of his colleagues, he did not find it "ethically unacceptable," as he later put it, to consider the possibility of child abuse, even murder, in cases that, when all was said and done, did not make sense. Reading Steinschneider's paper, Hick suspected a mother playing out a bizarre and deadly charade and a doctor whose attention reinforced, rather than uncovered, her sickness. Hick believed "Mrs. H." was the key. Perhaps her psychological motivation mutated over time, and in the mystery of SIDS and the theory of a SIDS doctor, she came to recognize what amounted to a blank check. Hick couldn't let the paper go unchallenged:

To the Editor:

In reporting two siblings who succumbed to "sudden infant death syndrome," Steinschneider exposes an unparalleled family chronicle of infant death. Of five children, four died in early infancy and the other died without explanation at age 28 months. Prolonged apnea is proposed as the common denominator in the deaths, yet the author leaves many questions relevant to the fate of these children unanswered.

Apnea of greater than 15 seconds has been well documented for the two siblings studied. This is not a long enough period of apnea to produce cyanosis and the author fails to state whether artificial stimulation was necessary to terminate the episodes. Except for the unsuccessful attempt to resuscitate M.H. (the mother was attending the child at the time and the monitor was temporarily disconnected), neither child apparently required resuscitation during extended periods of hospitalization.

The youngest sibling, N.H., was hospitalized for all but three days of his life. Several attempts to discharge the child to his mother's care met with failure, for symptoms of asphyxia would quickly develop at home. Nasopharyngitis was a recurring problem, as it was for all children monitored as a part of the study. The child eventually died at home within 24 hours of the third hospital discharge, at 2½ months of age.

Despite the circumstantial evidence suggesting a critical role for the mother in the death of her children Steinschneider offers no information about the woman: not her age, marital or socioeconomic status, her feelings about the loss of the children, her observed efforts at mothering, nothing. There is a comparable lack of information about the developmental progress of the hospitalized siblings.

The potential for child abuse inherent in the family history and the danger of hospital-acquired infection are two variables which could have been more adequately controlled in this study, had Steinschneider only chosen a foster home as his laboratory for the investigation of the youngest sibling. Perhaps the outcome would have been different?

John F. Hick, M.D.
Winona, Minnesota

Jerold Lucey was astonished when he read Hick's letter. As intrigued as he had been by Steinschneider's theory of SIDS, he found the suggestion that the mother had murdered her own children darkly provocative. That possibility hadn't occurred to him, not for a second. But was Hick's hypothesis valid? Should he publish the letter? A decade before, Lucey had been one of several pediatricians who responded early to the Battered Child Syndrome alert of the Colorado doctors by testifying before a Vermont legislative committee and urging the state to pass its own child abuse laws. But Lucey's experience was with hard evidence of physical abuse, everything from cigarette burns to broken bones and fractured skulls. What Hick was suggesting was much more subtle, and, to Lucey, much more dangerous territory for physicians. Still, although he believed that enormous care had to be taken when raising such disturbing accusations, he concluded that Hick was making some intriguing points, and that the letter should appear in a future issue. He sent a copy of it to Steinschneider, and asked if he wanted to respond.

Steinschneider was indignant. What evidence did Hick have? What doctor had the right to place a baby in a foster home? The local authorities had concluded there was no reason for suspicion, and the pathologists agreed. Who was he to say otherwise? Steinschneider much preferred to consider the letter Lucey published from a pediatric researcher at Johns Hopkins: "The article on prolonged apnea and SIDS by Steinschneider is very exciting in that it suggests the possibility of identifying infants at risk from SIDS before the final event," wrote Dr. David S. Bachman. Steinschneider got to work on his reply to Hick. It took some time. Months later, having done some research, he sent it in to Lucey, who read it and decided to throw some support his way. Between Hick's reproach and Steinschneider's rejoinder, Lucey inserted a brief Editor's Note: "Dr. Steinschneider comments as follows. We are particularly impressed by his second, third, and fourth sentences."

> The possibility of child abuse should be considered in every case of sudden infant death. However, extreme restraint must be exercised that this diagnosis not become one of exclusion. Failure to define the cause of a sudden death can never be used as support for the diagnosis of child abuse. Humanity as well as logic dictates the need for positive evidence as well as extreme sensitivity into the collection of such information. No such evidence was available in the family Dr. Hicks [sic] refers to.
>
> Mr. and Mrs. H. were 29 and 25 years old, respectively, when their last infant died. They lived in a trailer approximately 1½ hours driving distance from the medical center. Mr. H. was employed as a foreman for a construction company. Subsequent to the death of their third child a referral was made to the County Public Health Nursing service. Following numerous home visits, it was the nurse's impression "that there was a

fairly good relationship between mother and children." It should also be noted that the district supervising nurse, after reviewing the available information, questioned the validity of the clinical diagnosis on the referral form (enlarged thymus) and suggested that it might, more appropriately, be categorized as a sudden infant death.

The relationship between Mr. and Mrs. H. was one of warmth and mutual support. Although they lived some distance from the hospital, they frequently visited and for long periods of time. During these visits both parents often would be found sitting by the crib and had to be urged to make physical contact with the baby. It was my impression that they feared becoming too attached emotionally with either infant because they anticipated a tragic outcome. Mrs. H. expressed, on a number of occasions, considerable guilt over the death of her children, and, because of the inability of physicians to define the cause of death, felt there must have been something she did or failed to do that was responsible. Following the death of the fifth infant Mrs. H. did seek and receive outpatient psychiatric care.

During the periods of hospitalization M.H. and N.H., as well as the other three infants described in the report, were noted by the nursing staff to have periods of apnea and cyanosis. On these occasions vigorous stimulation was required before spontaneous respiration resumed and skin color returned to normal.

Dr. Hick glibly suggests that a foster home might have been a more appropriate "laboratory for the investigation of the youngest sibling." This suggestion, though superficially reasonable, denies the importance of parental wishes and feelings as well as the needs of a developing child. It also assigns to the physician a right he does not have; that of removing a child from its legal parents and placing it in a foster home. Furthermore, it should be made clear that in providing medical care for the infants described in the report, "home" was never conceptualized as a laboratory but rather as a home.

Alfred Steinschneider, M.D., Ph.D.
Syracuse, New York

"He's stonewalling," Hick thought when he read the response—going through contortions to defend his position. But no one reading it could know that Steinschneider's defense was built upon the kind of little white medical lies that marked the paper itself. The Hoyt babies had not been "noted by the nursing staff" to have prolonged periods of apnea and cyanosis requiring "vigorous stimulation."

Hick's voice was ultimately a whisper in the wind. The long national campaign to lift the burden of blame from parents was bearing fruit, and in the same decade when physical child abuse was emerging as a national preoccupation, it was now becoming, to borrow a phrase from the future, politically incorrect to consider child abuse in SIDS cases. This paradox made Stein-schneider's view, not Hick's, the enlightened one. Its most conspicuous bene-ficiary was his theory: At the very first research strategy meeting he had attended at the NICHD three weeks after Noah's death, homicide had been quickly dispatched as a factor in SIDS. "Infanticide," a report of the meeting declared, "is all but discredited."

As Hick's letter retreated to the archives, Steinschneider's theory gathered energy, taking hold just as the money arrived. A year after the Mondale hearing, Congress appropriated $4 million for SIDS research, news that ignited and expanded the SIDS world. Another $9 million would come the following spring, when President Nixon signed an even broader initiative, the Sudden Infant Death Syndrome Act of 1974. It would certify the national commitment, and finance both research and counseling for parents. For the SIDS research community, it was the pot of gold.

24

Exhilarated by the reactions to his paper, burning to do more, Steinschneider was now an unstoppable force in the Syracuse pediatrics department. He believed he was onto something extraordinary and set out to spread the news like an evangelist.

On the eve of his paper's publication, he had submitted his first grant application to the National Institute of Child Health and Human Development. He explained his theory and asked for nearly half a million dollars to continue his studies of babies at risk for SIDS. It was a vast amount of money in the context of the times, and Steinschneider worked hard to craft a strong proposal. "There was a way to write a grant, and a way to write a grant," he later said. "It was always Earle, and he knew how to do it. You had to be careful. A little error can be very costly. Once they pick up lack of integrity, you're dead. You're dead. Because in science we're like vultures."

After the application arrived in Bethesda, a team of NICHD reviewers converged on Syracuse for a site visit. By then, they were no strangers to Steinschneider. The nation's culture of SIDS investigation was just forming, and he had already made himself a member of the inner circle. Eileen Hasselmeyer had already appointed him to her branch's research and training committee. Though they maintained the professional distance required of grantors and grantees, Hasselmeyer and her group couldn't help but to regard an ambitious investigator like Steinschneider as a compatriot. They were pioneers in a stirring new field, each dependent on the other for the success of the conquest. Steinschneider had the ideas. Hasselmeyer's agency had the money. Steinschneider had long ago realized the value of a patron, and the stakes had never been higher.

Hasselmeyer arrived from Bethesda with Jehu Hunter, a research planning director who had joined the child health agency from NIH's Cancer Institute, and an NICHD research statistician named Howard Hoffman. They were joined by Dr. Sydney Segal, a pediatrician from Vancouver who worked closely with the agency as a consultant. Segal had been researching SIDS since 1957, the year he lost his thirteen-week-old daughter, a twin, to crib death. The fifth member of the team was a not-yet-famous Harvard pediatrician named T. Berry Brazelton.

Steinschneider took the group on a tour of the research center and laid out his plans. Over lunch he talked about the babies in his recently published study, and what he thought the deaths of the last two meant. Hasselmeyer, among others, wondered if perhaps a genetic metabolic disorder was the problem running through the H. family, but neither she nor anyone else challenged Steinschneider on the data he had published. "All the scientific journals have strict peer review," Hasselmeyer explained years later. But as Jehu Hunter remembers it, the site visitors weren't shy about raising another possibility. "That family was a big deal," he said. "We had never seen anything like it, so we were questioning him closely. Someone asked him: 'How do you know these infants were not killed?' He said he had no evidence of that. The family seemed to be all right, cooperative, and concerned about the deaths. We accepted that. What else could we do?"

Steinschneider tried to keep the conversation focused on his theory, not on metabolism and surely not on murder. The site visitors listened attentively as he elucidated his ideas about sleep apnea, displaying his apnea-density formula like a wonder drug. Sydney Segal was struck by how skillful he was. "He was quite a promoter; he was selling his idea strongly," Segal recalled. "He was emotional—I don't remember any encounter with Al that wasn't emotional. He is brilliant at seeing situations as he sees them."

If Steinschneider sounded a bit more like P. T. Barnum than Jonas Salk, it was also true that the group was in the market. "We were all hungry for an idea that would give us a lead, and we figured he may be onto something," Segal said. "He thought he had found the mother lode," remembered Howard Hoffman—and who were they to say he had not? The reviewers went home, had a meeting, and wrote up a report. After some negotiation and budget shuffling, Steinschneider was awarded the government's first major grant in the new era of SIDS research: a total of $406,405 over four years. The race to find a "cure" for SIDS was on, and Steinschneider was off to a fast start.

The grant certified Steinschneider's status as a pioneer of SIDS investigation and marked a turning point in the broadest sense. With the arrival of the first check from Bethesda, he officially moved the hunt from the impersonal labs of pathologists, virologists, and epidemiologists to the intimate medical setting of clinical research, where patients became subjects and the distinction between them was sometimes blurred. Less than four months after the publication of his paper, a stream of babies began arriving in Steinschneider's autonomic lab on the fifth floor of Upstate Medical Center. He tried to recruit one normal newborn from maternity every day so that he could compare their breathing patterns with those of the apnea babies who came to him as referrals from local doctors. The NICHD grant would take Steinschneider into the middle of 1977. It would allow him to study a good number of babies. It would also give him a pulpit.

A central tenet of his emerging ideology was his hope for a glorious future for the home apnea monitor. In the three years since he had arranged for Molly Hoyt to become the first baby in the world sent home on a monitor, he had made serious use of her mother's idea. He would later say that a seminal moment was the sudden death of a baby boy who had come to him not long after the last death in the family he had written about. The infant had been tested as a normal subject, but Steinschneider found in the lab that he "had apnea." He sent the baby home, but twenty-three days later—a week before he was to come back for another round of testing—the baby died. Steinschneider decided he must start sending all "vulnerable" babies who came to him back home with Air-Shields monitors, black boxes roughly the size of a tape deck. The parents would be instructed to keep careful logs of any apparent pauses in breathing and be taught cardiopulmonary resuscitation.

Among the first of these babies was a son born to one of the research nurses, Polly Fibiger. She had helped him collect the statistics he used in his paper. She had also been one of the nurses who silently worried that Molly Hoyt had died of something more sinister than apnea. Shortly after the birth of her first child in the fall of 1971, a boy she and her husband named Jamie, Fibiger volunteered the baby as a normal subject. But when she brought Jamie into the lab and hooked him up, Steinschneider told her that he was, in fact, not normal. He had apnea. Polly saw the tracings herself. They were just short periods, but Steinschneider told her they could mean trouble. It was absolutely vital, he said, that the baby be kept on a monitor at home. Polly was twenty-two years old, a first-time mother, and Steinschneider's work had made her hyperconscious of SIDS. She would never forget the call she had taken from Waneta Hoyt the morning Molly had died. Whatever had caused her death, Polly knew one thing: "If I lost a baby, I would never smile again." She didn't need much persuasion to take the monitor home.

She hooked Jamie up and plugged in the machine right next to the yellow crib she'd bought from the hospital for five dollars when the CCRC was shut down. Before long, though, she realized that the problem was not with the baby, but with the monitor: "It beeped all the time," she remembered. "I'd call Al and say his breathing was shallow and the monitor wasn't picking it up. I wanted to take him off the monitor. Al said, 'You have to keep him on.' Finally, after about six months, I told him it was driving me looney. I hadn't enjoyed my baby for six months. Al was adamant. He wanted it on for two years. But I just couldn't deal with it, and my pediatrician said I should stop it."

Steinschneider met less resistance from mothers such as Beverly Whitney, whose baby daughter Debbie had come to him as a normal recruit off the maternity floor. Debbie's first test in the lab, when she was three days old, was normal. But after her second session three weeks later, Steinschneider told her parents that she had apnea. In fact, he was quite agitated about it, especially when they told him they had lost a baby son three years earlier—congenital heart defect, the doctors had said; pneumonia, the medical examiner had written. Steinschneider got a copy of the autopsy report. It was almost certainly SIDS, he told the Whitneys. He let them know that he was worried about their new baby. "Her sleep study set him on his heels," Beverly remembered. "He was so troubled that he admitted Debbie into the hospital. She stayed for three days, then we went home with a monitor. He had sheets made out: How often did the monitor go off, how long was the alarm, what color was she? I filled the sheets up right away. I had a whole stack of them. I had about twenty alarms a day, though her color was normal."

Steinschneider kept Debbie on the home monitor until she was a talkative preschooler, bringing her into the lab periodically for follow-up studies. The home monitor played havoc with the family's peace, but that was all right with Beverly. She believed her daughter would surely die without it, even when she was more than two years past the risk period for SIDS. Debbie, meanwhile, seemed to take it all in stride. "At night," her mother recalled, "she would brush her teeth, get in bed, plug herself in, and turn the machine on. That was her job. She'd say, 'Mommy, I'm all set. Come kiss me good night.' I remember one time Steinschneider put her in for a sleep study and she wouldn't go to sleep without her wires on. She had electrodes on her head and bands on her wrist, but it wasn't what she was used to. She said, 'I can't sleep. I'm not plugged in and turned on.'" The scene disturbed Steinschneider. "He was afraid we were creating a monster."

But to him it was the price of progress. By the spring of 1973, his personal research center was busy with babies referred to him by pediatricians throughout Onondaga County and beyond, babies he tested for apnea, and those deemed at risk of SIDS sent home with monitors and, for their parents, frightening implications. Some were siblings of babies who had died of SIDS. Their parents had heard the monitors could keep it from happening again. Other babies had seemed to stop breathing at home; their pediatricians sent them to Steinschneider for diagnosis and "treatment." The research made him something of a medical celebrity around Syracuse, where he was creating a virtual monitoring culture of parents who passed the coveted machines among themselves with a fervent belief that the black boxes would save their babies from SIDS.

Some in the pediatrics department at Upstate saw Steinschneider as a quixotic figure. They found his devotion admirable, his methods avant-garde, if also vaguely unsettling. "He had the kids connected to all these things," remembered one physician who was a pediatric resident at the time, "like something from a Jules Verne novel." Certain others found him less captivating. "I'd kid him about it every now and then," said Jack Schneider. " 'Who gives a shit whether the slope of the curve is going up this far or that far?' I often wondered if he ever had any other ideas."

By this point, despite his funding and the bustling research center, Steinschneider was without an important ally in the department. Julius Richmond had recently ended his seventeen-year tenure in Syracuse and moved on to chair the department of preventive and social medicine at Harvard, and his departure had both immediate and long-term consequences for Steinschneider. The new pediatrics chairman, Dr. Frank Oski, who had arrived from the University of Pennsylvania in June 1972, did not see the blazing talent that Richmond had nurtured. Oski was chagrined to find Steinschneider a dominating presence in the department.

Arriving at Upstate at the moment of Steinschneider's ascent, Oski's aversion was instantaneous and irreversible. He realized the researcher was considered by some a man of great enterprise and intellect, but what Oski saw was a fast talker who strutted around the pediatrics unit crowing about the babies he was saving, while shrouding his work in an aura of mystery. Oski, a pediatric hematologist, was repelled by what he viewed as shallow science and cleverly packaged self-promotion. It was his opinion that Steinschneider was one of the finest examples of excessive, unjustified self-esteem he had ever encountered. He used two of the powers at his disposal—allocation of lab space and support for academic promotion—to demonstrate his disapproval. Steinschneider would get neither from Frank Oski.

Steinschneider, however, was looking beyond Syracuse. His federal grant had provided him with the wherewithal to capitalize on the prominence of his paper and to push the field in the direction of his theory. By 1974, he was traveling regularly, barnstorming medical meetings with accounts of the two babies in his lab who had died after brief, apnea-plagued lives, and news of the babies who were sleeping with federally funded monitors in Syracuse as he spoke.

One day early in 1974, Steinschneider drove over to the Onondaga County Medical Examiner's Office and told Martin Hilfinger he wanted to examine the county's SIDS statistics for the past few years. He began going through the records, then did some quick arithmetic with the local birth rate. He came up with a striking piece of information. The county's SIDS rate had dropped sharply in the previous two years, he determined: from 2.34 per thousand live births before 1971, to 1.34 per thousand in 1973. Steinschneider couldn't ask for better news. These were the years when he had begun using monitors on babies he considered at risk of SIDS. He knew he could not say he had proved that monitors actually prevented SIDS. He knew the monitors he was using were inadequate. But their potential electrified him. The early machines developed by Earle Lipton and the technicians at Upstate could someday be seen as the Model Ts of infant apnea monitors—the start of a worldwide movement to save babies' lives.

That winter, Steinschneider seemed to be everywhere, talking about sleep apnea, extolling the virtues of apnea monitoring. So convinced was Hasselmeyer that Steinschneider might have hit paydirt that she gave him his own meeting. In February, he went to Bethesda to chair an NICHD-sponsored seminar on "Recognition of Infants at Risk"—the title itself an indication of the impact he was having. The conference would be the final workshop in the three-year series meant to point the nation's scientists in a logical direction and to build a case for funding. In these three years, millions of dollars had been voted by Congress, and the scientists were being pointed in the direction of apnea.

By this time, the legions of babies rolling through his lab were giving Steinschneider the kind of research depth he knew his original study had lacked. It had been two years since he had completed the paper, and the grant had helped him refine his hypothesis. He now believed that it was not just prolonged apnea that people should be concerned about, but patterns of brief pauses. Testing dozens of babies in his lab, Steinschneider had found that he rarely saw apneic periods exceeding fifteen seconds. "Rather," he told his colleagues at the meeting, "I see periods of brief apnea which I believe are a reflection of respiratory instability." He considered a baseline of fifteen seconds, or even twenty, to be somewhat arbitrary, and acknowledged that many babies had apneic spells lasting twenty seconds during sleep without going on to die. This had led him to surmise that perhaps the answer was more subtle than he had first thought.

Discussing his latest work with the panel in Bethesda, a group of seventeen researchers that included Warren Guntheroth, Steinschneider professed that even a two-second pause could be significant if it happened frequently enough. From his chairman's seat, he postulated that babies with these brief

PROLONGED APNEA AND THE SUDDEN INFANT DEATH SYNDROME: CLINICAL AND LABORATORY OBSERVATIONS

Alfred Steinschneider, M.D., Ph.D.

From the Department of Pediatrics, State University Hospital of the Upstate Medical Center, Syracuse, New York

ABSTRACT. Little is known of the final physiologic mechanism(s) resulting in SIDS. Five infants participated in this study, three of whom were referred at about 1 month of age because of cyanotic episodes of undetermined etiology. Respirations and eye movements were recorded during several sleep sessions on each patient. In addition, patients were observed on an apnea monitor and a record was kept of the incidence of prolonged apneic episodes (≥ 15 seconds).

The laboratory sleep studies revealed frequent periods of apnea (≥ 2 seconds) which (1) decreased in amount after a certain age and (2) were most frequent during REM sleep. All infants had a number of prolonged apneic and cyanotic episodes during sleep, some requiring vigorous resuscitative efforts. Prolonged apnea most often occurred in conjunction with an upper-respiratory tract infection or when frequent apnea was noted in the laboratory. Two of the infants subsequently died of SIDS.

These data support the hypothesis that prolonged apnea, a physiological component of sleep, is part of the final pathway resulting in sudden death. It is suggested also, that infants at risk might be identified prior to the final tragic event. *Pediatrics*, **50**,646, 1972, SUDDEN DEATH, INFANTS, APNEA, SLEEP, NASOPHARYNGITIS.

S UDDEN unexpected, unexplained death in infancy (SIDS) continues to represent a problem of major medical significance. It has been estimated that greater than 10,000 *apparently* well infants die each year in the United States suddenly and, in spite of detailed autopsy study, without adequate explanation. For an intensive review of the literature see Valdes-Dapena.[1,2]

The plethora of suggested etiologic mechanisms of SIDS attests to the lack of agreement among investigators of this problem. This disagreement extends as well to the methodologic approaches employed in the search for the cause of SIDS. The approach taken in the present study derives, in part, from the observation that SIDS occurs in most instances while the infant is asleep. Furthermore, considerable sleep research has demonstrated marked alterations in such fundamental physiologic functions as cardiac rate, blood pressure, and respiration.[3-9] Of particular relevance is the observation of periods of apnea in both sleeping adults and infants. For the purpose of providing direction to this study it was proposed that SIDS occurs as the result of an exaggeration of the physiologic changes noted to occur during sleep. This report consists of the study of five infants, two of whom died of SIDS.

SUBJECTS AND METHODS

The five infants participating in this study were from three different families. Patients 1, 3, and 5 were seen initially at 29, 32, and 40 days of age, respectively, because of recurrent cyanotic and apneic episodes. The remaining two patients, 2 and 4,

---

Abbreviations

NREM: Nonrapid eye movement
REM: Rapid eye movement
SIDS: Sudden infant death syndrome

(Received January 24; revision accepted for publication May 22, 1972.)

Supported in part by a grant (RR-229) from the General Clinical Research Centers Program of the Division of Research Resources, National Institutes of Health.

ADDRESS FOR REPRINTS: (A.S.) Department of Pediatrics, State University Hospital of the Upstate Medical Center, 750 E. Adams Street, Syracuse, New York 13210.

PEDIATRICS, Vol. 50, No. 4, October 1972

The first page of Alfred Steinschneider's landmark apnea paper, published in the October 1972 issue of *Pediatrics*.

Dr. Linda Norton. (Pat Stowers)

Stephen Van Der Sluys after his arrest for murder in 1985. (Courtesy of the Rochester *Democrat and Chronicle*)

Bill Fitzpatrick during the Van Der Sluys prosecution in 1986. (Michael Davis, Syracuse *New Times*)

The teenaged Waneta Nixon, in a photo used thirty years later in a flier for her defense fund.

The tenth-grade class of Newark Valley Central School. Waneta is far left, at the end of the middle row.

ABOVE: January 11, 1964: Tim and Waneta on their wedding day in Richford.
RIGHT: Home scene. Waneta is in a favorite position on Tim's lap.

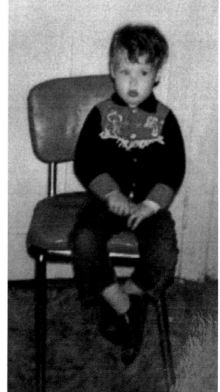

All of these snapshots, taken as evidence, were in the album Waneta brought with her to the state police station in Owego on the morning of March 23, 1994. Waneta's tendency to hold her babies at a distance is clearly visible. Jimmy was the only child to live past infancy. (Courtesy New York State Police)

MOLLY AND NOAH: M.H. AND N.H.

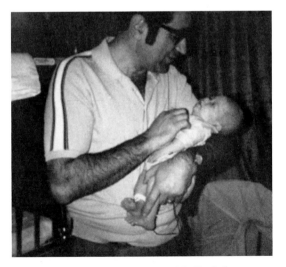

Fearing the worst, Thelma Schneider guardedly wrote her concerns about Molly Hoyt into the nursing record on June 4, 1970, six hours before the baby's discharge from Upstate Medical Center. Molly died the next morning.

Noah Hoyt is shown at Upstate Medical Center a year later, in the arms of Dr. Alfred Steinschneider (left), and with his mother (right).

DIGGING INTO THE PAST

March 23, 1994: Investigator Sue Mulvey and Trooper Bob Bleck lead Waneta Hoyt from the state police station in Owego after taking her confession. (Holly McQueen, *Press & Sun-Bulletin*, Binghamton, N.Y.)

Announcing the arrest: Senior Investigator Bob Courtright (far left) and prosecutors Bill Fitzpatrick (center) and Bob Simpson. (Holly McQueen, *Press & Sun-Bulletin*, Binghamton, N.Y.)

January 1995: With Bob Simpson looking on, Dr. Michael Baden leads the exhumation of the Hoyt children at Highland Cemetery. (Courtesy New York State Police)

Defense attorneys Bob Miller (left) and Ray Urbanski (Chuck Haupt, *Press & Sun-Bulletin*, Binghamton, N.Y.)

Steinschneider testifies for the defense: "I wrote it, therefore it's true." (Michael Okoniewski)

"She held the baby away from her," Thelma Schneider testifies, using her hands to show why she thought the interaction between mother and child was "almost nil." (Chuck Haupt, *Press & Sun-Bulletin*, Binghamton, N.Y.)

Dr. Janice Ophoven, a key prosecution witness, demonstrates for the jury how easily a baby can be smothered. (Chuck Haupt, *Press & Sun-Bulletin*, Binghamton, N.Y.)

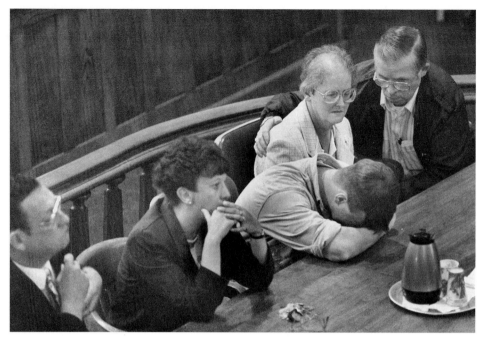

April 21, 1995: Tim Hoyt comforts Waneta and Jay Hoyt drops his head in despair as the jury delivers the first of five guilty verdicts against his mother. (Michael Okoniewski)

Five months later, sheriff's deputies lead Waneta from the courthouse after her sentencing. (Chuck Haupt, *Press & Sun-Bulletin*, Binghamton, N.Y.)

periods were at risk for developing the endless apneic spell he believed was the "final pathway" of SIDS. The babies at risk of sudden death were the ones whose autonomic systems had trouble limiting the short episodes. What he was trying to do now was to come up with a way of identifying those babies. He was inclined to think that the SIDS statistics from Onondaga County were an indication that he had.

Steinschneider's modified theory was even more difficult to prove or disprove than the hypothesis in his paper. The prolonged apnea theory did have the virtue of a certain instinctive logic, its plausibility bolstered by the frightening mental image of a sleeping baby going fifteen or twenty seconds without showing any signs of life. But his new version was trickier, since all babies went a few seconds now and then without breathing, some more frequently than others. Who could know which babies were the ones whose brief apnea was a harbinger of the longer episodes that, according to Steinschneider, triggered SIDS? Once again, this was where the Hoyt babies came in.

Molly and Noah fit Steinschneider's new improved theory as well as they had the original. The two babies in his 1972 report who died, he told his colleagues, had had many prolonged periods of apnea—and plenty of short ones, too. In fact, he had come up with a new formula that showed just how much at risk they had been. He called it the PSA_4 score, for Prolonged Sleep Apnea using four measurements. The score was the statistical concoction that emerged from a recipe of four equations he had devised: relative frequency of apnea during REM and non-REM sleep, average duration of apnea, and his original A/D percentage. Babies with a PSA_4 score of 0.20 or more, he explained, would be at high risk for SIDS. Since coming up with this formula, he had gone back over the data for the two babies from his "SIDS family," as people were calling it, to see whether it showed they had been at high risk. Sure enough, he told the fascinated group, "the two full-term infants who died of SIDS and were studied within the first week of age had the highest PSA_4 value of over eighty comparable babies studied."

Molly had actually been studied beginning at four weeks of age, not one, and Steinschneider had not scientifically documented her apnea, nor that of her brother. But there was something else that might have turned Steinschneider's audience skeptical had they known about it. In all his discussions of REM and non-REM apnea, effects of nasopharyngitis, postnatal age, birthweight, and PSA_4 scores, Steinschneider never disclosed the strong possibility that he might actually have *caused* much of the apnea he was reporting in the babies in his current studies. Though he had disclosed in the 1972 paper that he kept the temperature in his lab at 90 degrees, it was just one more matter the peer reviewers had either overlooked or left unchallenged. Now, when he talked about his theory at the meeting in Bethesda, and at others where spirited discussion was always a part of the agenda, the most important detail of his methodology was the only one he left out.

He had first discovered the heat effect while testing the premature baby he later described at the 1969 meeting. "The baby," he said then, "showed periodic breathing only at the higher temperature." Then, a year later, he read an article in *The New England Journal of Medicine* reporting that premature babies with apnea had more pauses as the temperature in their Isolettes climbed. "I said, 'Hold it,' " Steinschneider later recalled. "The implication is if you *don't* raise the temperature and they're predisposed, you may see the same as with babies that are *not* predisposed. Elevation of the temperature might tease out the difference. So I said, 'I gotta do something—I'll do the ninety.' It's not to see these big episodes. If you see it, you got it made. But the likelihood of that happening is very slight."

He saw, instead, an increase in the number of short pauses. That's how the heated lab had affected Molly Hoyt—it was why he had instructed the Hoyts to buy an air conditioner when they first took her home. In the years since she and her brother had died, Steinschneider had come to conclude that by testing babies in the heat, and then calculating their PSA_4 scores, he might be able to say which babies were at risk of SIDS. But there were some flaws in his logic. He was not only presuming a link between apnea and SIDS that was based on defective data; he was applying an experience with premature babies, who were known to experience more apnea, to general populations of normal, full-term infants. An alternative view would be that the conditions were unnatural and might simply induce apneic pauses in perfectly normal babies.

With his elaborate argument that apnea could be finely quantified, and his distinction as the only researcher in the world who had personally studied victims of SIDS *before* their deaths and come up with a plausible explanation, Steinschneider's pitch for monitors needed no further introduction. He unveiled his smoking gun: In the past two years, he said, he had sent more than fifty babies home on monitors. During this period, according to his calculations, the SIDS rate in Onondaga County had dropped by nearly fifty percent. "The results," he said, "are interpreted as consistent with the hypothesis that the use of apnea monitors lowers the incidence of SIDS." How had he decided which babies were at such great peril that they should be monitored at home? PSA_4 scores. He believed he had written an equation for measuring predisposition to SIDS, and that he had found a way to save the babies who fell into the realm of risk.

There was one problem. Hearing Steinschneider's claims, Dr. Donald Peterson, the epidemiologist from Seattle who had been one of the first researchers recruited into the SIDS battle by Mary Dore a decade before, urged him, and the rest of the group, not to get carried away just yet. SIDS rates had also dropped in his state, Peterson said, without the help of monitors or anything else. In fact, it was part of a national trend, though nobody really knew what was causing it. Steinschneider's data should be viewed with caution, Peterson advised, since he hadn't put them to the most basic scientific test: a comparison of monitored babies to a control group. This was true, Steinschneider conceded. But it did not alter his conviction that his theory was a good one. What was more, he asserted, parents wanted monitors. For elaboration, he called on Lois Henning, a research psychologist who worked with him in pediatrics at Upstate.

Henning was a true believer in Steinschneider and his theory. She thought his PSA$_4$ formula was ingenious; she had even found an application for it in her own work. With her own federal grants, she used it to pursue her idea that babies with a lot of apnea, routinely deprived of oxygen, had developmental problems later on. But Henning's more immediate task had been to help Steinschneider assess the impact of home monitors on families. If he was ultimately going to campaign for the development and widespread use of monitors, he wanted to know how well parents would take to the intrusion. Henning told the group in Bethesda that she'd questioned thirty-one families sent home with monitors and found that most were glad to have them. Yes, there were problems—hypersensitive machines, many false alarms, along with the inevitable arguments that erupted around whether the devices were worth the effort and anxiety—but most families told Henning that they'd adjusted, and decided the stress was a small price to pay. That was the double edge of monitors: They made parents feel at once nervous and secure.

For Steinschneider the chairmanship of the Bethesda seminar marked the moment his theory acquired the imprimatur of the federal government. "A consensus did materialize," the National Institutes of Health said in a report of the meeting distributed in the scientific community, "suggesting that centrally induced apnea is part of the physiologic sequence of events resulting in sudden death." With Hasselmeyer at his side, Steinschneider's studies went essentially unchallenged. His message was clear: Monitor a baby with short but frequent pauses in breathing and you may well save that baby's life. And the message was about to spread. The seminar in Bethesda would be followed by a much more important event: the third International Symposium on Sudden and Unexpected Deaths in Infancy, to be held in Toronto in May. It would be a reunion of the Orcas Island group, and then some.

A few weeks later, Steinschneider found in his mail a letter from a doctor who had only recently read his 1972 paper and had some questions.

MOUNT SINAI SCHOOL OF MEDICINE
of The City University of New York
Fifth Avenue and 100th Street, New York, N.Y. 10029

Department of Psychiatry

April 8, 1974

Alfred Steinschneider, Ph.D., M.D.
Department of Pediatrics
Upstate Medical Center
Syracuse, New York 13210

Dear Dr. Steinschneider:

I enjoyed your article on Apnea and S.I.D. in the October 1972 issue of Pediatrics. I would like to share some ideas of mine with you concerning S.I.D.

As a psychiatrist, I have been investigating attitudes of mothers towards their infants. This has led to my interest in infanticide and child battering. As you know, both of these are much more common phenomena than are usually recognized. I have been investigating the incidence of infanticide by smothering, possibly being hidden within the category of S.I.D. A number of such cases are known to us, but unfortunately not in percentage terms. However there are good psychiatric reasons for suspecting that a sizable percentage of S.I.D.'s are in fact infanticides.

In your case histories you include two infants who died. I was struck by the fact that neither of these infants had serious apneic episodes while under observation in the hospital despite long periods of hospitalization. Serious apneic episodes, and the eventual deaths, all occurred within 24 to 48 hours after discharge and while at home. One can't help wondering why these would occur only at home, and so soon after discharge, and presumably with a clean bill of health. It supports our own contention, shared by Dr. Milton Helpern, the recently retired medical examiner, with whom my team has worked, that no case of S.I.D. in New York has occurred in a hospital and been verified as such by the medical examiner's office.

Your first case is also suspicious in view of the similar deaths of three siblings. In our experience of three families with multiple S.I.D.s, they were all hidden infanticides. . . .

I would appreciate your comments.

Very truly yours,
Stuart S. Asch, M.D.

Asch had been gathering case studies of infanticide for publication in the *American Journal of Psychiatry* when he came across Steinschneider's 1972 paper. His query to him three years before had gotten no reply. This time, he got back a prompt and biting response.

First, Steinschneider replied, he strongly disagreed that many SIDS cases were actually homicides. And there certainly was no reason to believe it was the case here. All the babies in his 1972 study had prolonged apneic and cyanotic episodes *in the hospital,* he wrote—spells severe enough to "precipitate resuscitative procedures by the nursing staff." So, he informed Asch, it was not true that the two babies who died only had problems at home.

Steinschneider spent the balance of his reply heatedly attacking Asch and his infanticide hypothesis. It showed little "intellectual and scientific integrity," he said. Solving the riddle of SIDS required "vigorous efforts to obtain sufficient objective data"—especially, he warned, in the case of a proposition like Asch's, which could have such an adverse emotional impact on families. He cautioned Asch to be very careful about what he published. "My own data and observations fail to support your hypothesis," he closed.

Asch read Steinschneider's response, then reread his paper. He was less concerned with the pediatrician's rhetoric than with his case studies. The central clinical observation supporting the thesis, that Patients M.H. and N.H. had documented, life-threatening apnea before their deaths, still didn't seem consistent with what Steinschneider had published. Asch wanted to pin Steinschneider down on this point, but he could only fish for telltale signs. He had no way of knowing, for instance, that in his letter Steinschneider had inflated the little white medical lie of "vigorous stimulation" that he had written for publication in response to John Hick into an unabashed invention: his statement that the babies had been *resuscitated* by the nurses, in the hospital. But Asch did wonder why, if this were true, Steinschneider had not mentioned it in his paper. "Contrary to your letter," he wrote back, "your article indicates that the two infants who died (siblings), had severe episodes *only* after discharge from the hospital, and those occurred while at home. . . . You make no mention of resuscitative measures being required by the staff."

In reply—his tone leaving no doubt that it would be his final one—Steinschneider ignored the question of why he had omitted such a vital piece of information. He simply repeated his claim that all five babies in his paper had been resuscitated in the hospital.

The thrust and parry with Asch failed to interrupt Steinschneider's momentum. But its timing was consequential. No one can know what intellectual process triggered his statements that the H. babies had been resuscitated by the nurses at Upstate. But these fabrications now became his truth. A week later, he would put it on the record.

A lot had changed in the five years since the meeting on Orcas Island. SIDS had received so much public exposure that it was as if the world had discovered a horrible new disease. New research was being launched in labs populated by scientists of many varieties, backed by the newly endowed overseers at the NICHD.

The Toronto meeting was testament to the explosive growth of the field. The 1969 conference had attracted twenty-seven researchers to a remote island and virtually no public notice. The Toronto gathering, to be held in the ballroom of a large hotel, would be more like a convention. It would bring together 250 physicians and researchers from 42 hospitals and universities on four continents, along with dozens more from government agencies and parents' groups. When Bruce Beckwith arrived at the hotel, he looked out in amazement at the crowd gathered in the ballroom to talk about SIDS. "What a way we've come," he said to Abe Bergman.

Steinschneider, an unknown at the last meeting, was now a star. He would be one of thirty-two presenters during the three-day conference, but he and his theory aroused a flurry of anticipation. Everybody, it seemed, had read his paper; now they would have a chance to hear from its author.

The conference was opened by the Countess of Limerick, a British philanthropist who had taken up SIDS as her cause. A dynamic woman with a gift for extemporaneous public speech, Sylvia Limerick had chaired a SIDS conference organized in Britain a few years before by people trying to jump-start research efforts there. "Having acquired the name I have," she told the convention in Toronto, "perhaps I may be forgiven for trying to sum up our conclusion in a verse of appropriate meter:

> *When theories compete in profusion,*
> *Then the experts conclude, in confusion,*
> *There'll be flaws in all laws*
> *Of this unexplained cause*
> *Till the problem is solved by exclusion."*

With that, the meeting turned its focus to pathology and epidemiology, including a brief but significant report by Marie Valdes-Dapena in which she said that the 10,000-deaths-a-year figure cited at the 1969 conference was probably a bit of an overstatement, though not nearly as exaggerated as the 25,000 figure used at the birth of the movement, in 1963. She reported that the incidence of SIDS had been declining for several years, though why this was so was "at this point, purely speculative."

Although speculation defined the nature of most SIDS research, the first investigator to present his work was anything but equivocal. Dr. Richard Naeye, the chairman of pathology at Penn State University's Milton S. Hershey Medical Center, took the podium and reported that his explorations of the pulmonary tissue of forty SIDS victims indicated they had chronic hypoxemia—low concentrations of oxygen in the blood, the result of inadequate intake of air into the lungs. He had published his findings in one of the world's preeminent medical journals, *The New England Journal of Medicine,* less than a year after Steinschneider had published his in *Pediatrics,* and the work, though not yet confirmed by others, was widely viewed as exciting, early backing for the apnea theory. Naeye too had become an ascendant star in the SIDS world because of these studies, and his presentation was a perfect opening act for Steinschneider. The entire second day of the conference would be devoted to what had emerged as the field's most promising avenue of research: physiological development and SIDS, with an emphasis on apnea. He would be the day's opening speaker.

The next morning, the ballroom was packed. In the audience were all the big names in SIDS: Bergman, Beckwith, Guntheroth, Valdes-Dapena, Naeye, and Eileen Hasselmeyer, who had given the conference's keynote speech. Steinschneider took the podium and looked out across the crowd. He spotted Warren Guntheroth, and thanked him for first suggesting apnea as a possible cause of SIDS. For Steinschneider, there was a certain triumphant symmetry between this moment and the last hours of the 1969 meeting, where he had first offered the rudiments of his theory and Dwain Walcher had challenged him: *Have you observed any infant with apneic spells who subsequently died of the Sudden Infant Death Syndrome?* Now, five years later, Walcher was nowhere in sight, and Steinschneider stood before a group ten times the size, the bearer, it seemed, of a breakthrough.

"Probably the major direction for my thoughts regarding the possible mechanisms of SIDS," he began, "came from the study of five babies. A report on these five infants was published in 1972. These were very, very important babies for me. These babies were referred to me, in part, because my colleagues knew I had been thinking about and had expressed interest in the 'near-miss' infants. One of these babies was the fourth in a family that had three previous sudden unexplained deaths. . . ."

The audience was rapt. ". . . All five babies were noted, in the hospital, to have rather prolonged periods of apnea occurring during sleep. These were not of the obstructive type. The infants merely slept, stopped breathing, and turned blue. They were not struggling. At some period in the hospitalization, the nursing staff felt obligated to initiate resuscitative measures for each of these infants. Two of the babies subsequently died, and the autopsies were compatible with SIDS. Both of these babies were siblings and came from the same family that had lost three previous babies.

"On the basis of these observations there emerged certain firm conclusions. It was clear that prolonged sleep apnea can occur in the postneonatal period. This was something of a surprise to me. . . . I was aware, certainly, that prolonged apnea can occur in premature infants within the first week or so of life. However, I had been taught that these episodes do not occur after infants achieve a certain weight or age. I was surprised. And, to me, that was very, very important. The second conclusive observation was that prolonged sleep apnea can result in SIDS." Steinschneider left no doubt how he felt about his theory: "The fundamental issue is not whether or not prolonged sleep apnea is the mechanism of death in *some* infants who die of SIDS, but rather whether this mechanism is responsible for the majority—or all—of the deaths."

At great length and in complex detail, with the requisite overhead projections of charts and graphs, Steinschneider burrowed into a murky explanation of his theories about REM sleep, his discovery of the significance of brief apnea, and how it all came together with the PSA_4 score, a concept that struck many in the audience as nothing if not original. "These data," he said at one point, "were reanalyzed by employing a multiple linear regression model. All of the eight measures were included in one analysis and a single best-fit equation calculated. The resulting PSA_8 equation, which is the uppermost equation in the table, accounted for seventy-six percent of the variance. This represents a correlation coefficient between zero-point-eight and zero-point-nine. I then calculated the next best equation excluding those laboratory measures that contributed very little to the discrimination." He offered a table titled "Coefficient of determination ($r2$) for sleep measures examined individually and in selected combinations (Apnea>2 sec: N=53)," which included four equations such as this one:

$$PSA8 = -2.552 + 0.004 \, (PERI) - 0.156 \, (A/D\%) + 0.028 \, (APT)$$
$$+ 0.014 \, (APR) + 0.025 \, (APN) + 0.566 \, (AVED)$$
$$+ 0.007 \, (LOND) - 0.002 \, (REM\%): \qquad r2 = .762$$

Wrapping his studies in such esoterica, presenting his theories with a careful mix of salesmanship and sobriety, Steinschneider compelled the attention of his audience, a room packed with physicians and researchers from many fields seeking their own paths in the understanding of SIDS. "He was always a magnetic, tremendously powerful presenter," Bergman remembered, though in this case he found his talk "a little round-the-bend." By concentrating on his more recent laboratory studies, and on the largely impenetrable statistical underpinnings of his theory, Steinschneider managed to steer clear of the discrepancies buried beneath his data. In the SIDS world, the deaths of the H. babies were already part of the mythology. That they had died of SIDS was a given; the researchers were more interested in hearing what could be learned as a result. One Canadian physician, Dr. Harry Bain, asked at the conclusion of the presentation, "Dr. Steinschneider, with regard to your two children who were in hospital and died having had three others at home die, did the other two die at home as well?"

"All five died at home," Steinschneider replied. Bain, the chairman of this international symposium, was chief physician of Toronto's Hospital for Sick Children and head of the Department of Paediatrics of the University of Toronto. He had been involved in a case of infanticide back in the 1940s, and a suspicious thought crossed his mind now. But he decided this was not the time or place to open that door. He followed up on Steinschneider's answer that all five died at home by remarking on the need for "constant vigilance" by parents.

Steinschneider was deft in guiding his colleagues to an acceptance of the principles of his hypothesis. "I never understood his formula, but I didn't try very hard," remembered NICHD consultant Sydney Segal, who introduced him that day. "I just thought he must know what he's talking about." That assumption had easy access in this room populated by people growing impatient with their own ignorance. "He cast his bread upon ready waters," Bruce Beckwith observed. "In 1974, not many people could digest the finer points of sleep apnea. But the world was hungry for answers. All the parent power, where all the energy in SIDS comes from, was directed at the quick answer. To predict and prevent—that was what people wanted."

The next afternoon, Steinschneider gave his second and arguably more influential presentation. He titled it "Living with an Apnea Monitor." Though his enthusiasm for the potential of monitors for saving lives had been growing, he was appropriately cautious with this audience. At this meeting at which Molly Dapena had already reported a national drop in SIDS incidence, he did not cite the lower SIDS figures in Onondaga County as an argument for monitors. In fact, he turned his whole philosophy on its head. He told his colleagues that he had become concerned that there would be a mad dash for monitors before the time was right—before their value had been demonstrated and the machines themselves improved for home use. This was a serious problem in his home county, he said. His research, and his use of monitors, had become so well known that local pediatricians and parents were clamoring for the equipment as a protection against SIDS. "If the infant is viewed by me to be at risk for prolonged apnea, there is the implied assumption that I will employ an apnea monitor as a means of preventing SIDS," he said. "Keep in mind, this occurs even though it has been stated repeatedly that considerably more data will be necessary to determine if, in fact, SIDS can be prevented by the use of apnea monitors. Although this is understood, the pressure continues because families and physicians will pursue any reasonable course of action that might prevent this terrible tragedy."

It was an interesting spin on his continuing work in Syracuse. After putting the blame, in effect, on parents and other doctors for the demand he was creating, Steinschneider offered a candid primer on apnea monitors. Though the models he used, the ones from Air-Shields, were technologically uncomplicated, they were full of problems, he reported with what was evidently long-simmering frustration. "I do not have one here," he said, "nor do I have a picture of one. Part of the reason is I do not particularly like this piece of equipment and I would not want you to go out and buy one. Hopefully, there will be smaller and better machines in the future." The most basic problem, he said, was as simple as the machine itself: the problem of the false alarm. "Consider the following example, which has occurred, unfortunately, innumerable times. The mother is busy in the kitchen doing whatever mothers do, having a cup of tea or whatever, and the alarm goes off. When this occurs, she dies a little, rushes to the baby full of anxiety, finds the baby breathing and in no distress, yet the monitor is indicating that the infant is apneic. She does not have a sick baby, just a sick machine."

Beyond the trauma of false alarms, Steinschneider pointed out that these new gadgets were designed for hospitals, not homes. They were not easily portable and ran only on electrical current so couldn't be used during power outages. "I think it becomes clear what engineers must do," he said. "Develop apnea monitors for use in the home." But even if they did, he conceded, the monitor would continue to wreak havoc with a family's lifestyle. The burden fell most on the mother, who found herself constantly listening for the dreaded beep. "The vacuum cleaner is very noisy, and certainly she cannot take a shower during the day. Shopping poses a problem. The family's social life is severely disrupted. In fact, the family begins to feel extremely isolated. During the day, the mother cannot leave to visit family or friends. How can the mother drive alone with the baby? One of the best descriptions of this concern was given by a mother during a discussion with other families living with a monitor. At first, she would place the baby on the car seat beside her and would have one eye on the road and the other on the baby. This led to many near-accidents. She went on to explain that, at present, she places the baby on the car seat, looks skyward, and says, 'Look, God, I've watched her all day; it's your turn now.' Most of the mothers just stay home. Now, at night, the parents cannot leave. How many baby-sitters can you trust to resuscitate a baby?"

Despite all these problems, Steinschneider made the monitoring concept—the novel idea of putting hospital equipment in people's homes and deputizing parents as medics—the big news at the conference. As he was summing up his talk, the SIDS doctors in the audience were feverishly writing questions on index cards and sending them up to the stage:

"How many babies died at home with the monitors? How many do you think you have saved?"

"Do you think there is any place for monitoring newborns in the nursery before going home, even in low-risk children if there have been previous sudden deaths in the family?"

"Do your babies on monitors and babies who have had forms of apnea have to be monitored on a twenty-four-hour basis or just during the night periods?"

"How long have you got to resuscitate a baby once the alarm has sounded?"

"What is your experience with how the parents cope when the babies actually stop breathing?"

"Dr. Steinschneider, when the monitor goes off and because a parent wasn't there to immediately respond to this, the baby dies. Who is to blame? Have there been any cases of this and were the parents guilt-ridden?"

Pressed for time, the chairman for the afternoon session, Calgary pediatrician Alan Finley, read the questions and asked Steinschneider if he would take a minute to consider them together. "If you have any personal questions," Finley told the audience, "would you corner him afterwards?"

"Let me respond this way," Steinschneider said, addressing the first question a few minutes later. "There were two babies who died while on monitors. One of the babies who died was not actually on the monitor at the time. The baby was taken off the monitor for its bath and was put down in the crib after it was dry. The mother left the room for a minute. When she came back, the baby was dead. In the second case, the mother was in the bathroom when the alarm went off. The door was closed and she didn't hear the alarm when it first sounded. When she did hear it and got to the baby, it was too late. This gets us to the question, what happened to the family? Actually, both babies died in the same family, the same mother. She received psychiatric care. I believe she has recently adopted a baby and the baby is doing fine."

The baby may have been doing fine, but as Steinschneider certainly should have remembered, it was not with Waneta Hoyt. Having left his colleagues with another piece of false information that might tend to deflect suspicion about the mother, as well as questions about his research, Steinschneider moved on to the other queries. He ignored the one asking how many babies he'd saved, and said he didn't know how long parents had to respond to an alarm, though in every case so far they had gotten to the crib in plenty of time to gently stimulate the baby. Would he monitor all babies routinely? "No. I think before we choose this course of action, we have to ask some very significant questions. Are we really dealing with a valid theoretical model? The answer to that question requires more research. I think one has to recognize the possibility—I say it though I don't believe it—that this theoretical model is incorrect."

And finally, to the future development of monitors. "I know there are a number of companies or engineers who have talked about building a better machine. When I see it, I will believe it. I have been told that for years. I think one will be developed because a number of companies now see a large potential market, and when they see a market and smell money, they will develop one."

Listening to all this talk about apnea monitors, moderator Finley found himself wondering about Steinschneider's notion that some babies were born with a vulnerability to SIDS, and his audacious belief that they could actually be picked out and saved. "Dr. Steinschneider," he asked, "would you like to say how you select potentially at-risk babies?"

"I do it by watching them sleep," he answered, "and essentially trying to assess the degree of respiratory irregularity they have during sleep. But this, too, is a research project, and as to what extent we will be successful, only time will tell."

There were some lawyers in the room, and Steinschneider's talk about monitors troubled one of them. In the waning moments of the symposium, Robert Joling added a note of caution to his prepared text on autopsy legislation and other legal aspects of SIDS. A teacher of medical jurisprudence from the University of Arizona, he gave voice to the unspoken fears that had moved Dwain Walcher to challenge Steinschneider when the monitoring idea first came up at the Orcas Island meeting five years before.

"When we talk about Dr. Steinschneider's apnea monitoring devices," Joling said, "I can envision, as a former trial lawyer, the type of case that is going to come down because of the product liability theory of negligence in the United States. If you sell this device, there is going to be an implied warranty that it is fit for the purpose for which it is used. I can see salesmen pounding at the doors of doctors and parents and trying to sell them a bill of goods for no other reason than to line the pocket of the manufacturer. I fear this idea, with all due respect to Dr. Steinschneider, and I am sure he appreciates it. I am fearful that the reliance on these machines may go from being a help to a hindrance."

In the audience, Abe Bergman silently agreed. What he heard coming through Steinschneider's talk was a disturbing implication: *If you don't put babies on monitors, you are letting them die.*

". . . I would like to conclude by just paraphrasing the Countess of Limerick's remarks the other day," Joling was saying now. "She said something about the true mark of a politician is that he continuously goes about with his mouth open. . . . I would hope that the true mark of the artful scientist is that he continually goes about with his *mind* open."

25

In 1967, aerospace engineer Parker H. Petit—everyone called him Pete—had decided it was time to leave Texas and come back home to Georgia. He and his wife, JoAnn, were in their late twenties, the parents of a baby son, and their two years in Fort Worth, where Petit worked for General Dynamics, had been an adventure. Now they were ready to return to Georgia and settle down. Petit went to work for Lockheed and bought a house in the Atlanta suburbs. In the winter of 1970, JoAnn gave birth to their second child, another boy. They named him Brett.

And then the unthinkable happened. Petit had just finished mowing the lawn when he heard his wife's screams. He rushed upstairs and found JoAnn holding their lifeless baby in her arms. They rushed him to the hospital. The emergency doctors brought back Brett's vital signs, but by then the loss of oxygen had caused massive brain damage. After two days, they removed the baby from life support. Brett was six months old. He left no medical clues behind.

Like all SIDS parents, the Petits struggled to understand how their healthy, active baby could just . . . *die*. After they buried Brett, they drove to the North Carolina mountains for a few days of reflection. They talked about whether there was anything they could have done to save their son. It seemed that JoAnn happened to walk in on a SIDS in progress, but she hadn't walked in quite soon enough. Petit couldn't get past that. It occurred to him that there ought to be some sort of device to warn parents if their babies stopped breathing. Maybe it would save the lives of other babies, and save their parents from excruciating torment. Returning from the mountains, Petit called Brett's pediatrician, Dr. Scott James, and asked him what he thought of the idea. The doctor liked it. The only monitor he knew of was the Air-Shields model used on preemies in the hospital. It was notoriously unreliable, and unsuitable for home use. Petit and James made a drawing of a prototype. With three dials and an antenna, it looked like a ham radio.

Petit went back to work at Lockheed, but all he could think about was building a baby monitor. He and his wife joined the local chapter of the SIDS Foundation, and entered a world where parents like themselves were bound by a distinct and painful group psychology. The guilt and confusion could be agonizing. The SIDS diagnosis conceived the year before offered some succor; parents needed to hear that there was nothing they could have done. But Pete Petit was different. The idea that there was nothing he could have done didn't make him feel better. It made him angry.

And it made him think about money. Petit's name was pronounced like the French word for diminutive, which happened in his case to be only partly appropriate. He was a small man with big ideas. He quit Lockheed, and persuaded his friends, neighbors, and a number of local doctors to invest in a company he named Life Systems. He went to night school for an MBA and hired a couple of electrical engineers at Georgia Tech to help him develop an infant monitor, paying them in future stock. The idea he and Scott James had come up with was to use telemetry, radio signals transmitting over short distances. A miniature monitor, held to the baby's chest by a belt, would measure heartbeat and respiration, then transmit the information to a receiver. If there was trouble, the receiver would send a signal to a smaller receiver that could be carried, like a transistor radio, by the baby's caretaker. It looked good on paper, but they couldn't get it off the page. Petit concluded the device was ahead of its time. He also realized that a successful entrepreneur needed something more than a mountain of moxie and a pretty good general idea.

Trying to keep his venture afloat, Petit began developing devices that could protect children. His first product was Scott James's idea: an alarm that attached to a cabinet and sounded when the door was left open too long. He called it the Toddler Alarm, and began selling it to stores. IT CAN HAPPEN, read the retail display. Petit got the gadget into the Sears and J.C. Penney catalogues, and it made just enough money to support further development of the baby monitor. His first major product, meanwhile, was an artificial ventilator system he began selling to hospitals. On one sales call, he noticed the name Life Systems on someone else's equipment. His lawyers had overlooked the trademark. Petit went home, jotted down some alternative names, and settled on Healthdyne. He liked the suffix "dyne," the Greek word for "force." Maybe it would breathe life into the infant monitor concept, his reason for being. The company was almost constantly on the verge of bankruptcy.

Petit dropped telemetry in favor of photoelectricity, and on November 16,

1972, he filed application number 307,091 with the United States Patent and Trademark Office. He called his invention a "respiration monitor." It used a two-piece light sensor to register pauses in a baby's breath. "To summarize the situation," he wrote in his application, "the currently available monitors are so complex that the expense precludes their use in many instances where they are required." His model, he wrote, would be inexpensive, simple to operate, rugged, and more reliable than current models. Although he refrained from saying it in the long technical explanation of the device—the nine official Claims and twelve Drawn Figures of a baby attached to his monitor—Petit envisioned the contraption as a machine that could save babies from SIDS.

One day soon after, Petit was elated to hear that there was a doctor sending babies home with monitors in upstate New York. Alfred Steinschneider's apnea paper had been published in *Pediatrics* just a month before Petit filed his patent application. Petit realized this was the man to see. He flew to Syracuse with his prototype.

Petit wasn't the only engineer hauling homemade equipment up to the fifth floor of Upstate Medical Center. Steinschneider had made it known that he wasn't happy with the monitors he was using, but couldn't get Air-Shields interested in developing one for home use. Every six months or so, a new vice president of marketing would come see him, listen to his complaints, nod his head when Steinschneider said there was a large potential market for home monitors, and leave. One of them finally told him that the company's market surveys consistently showed that there was no future for a home apnea monitor. "Well, what they didn't realize," Steinschneider said years later, "is that there was no need for a CAT scan either. Nor an X ray. This was a new concept." But with his growing reputation for sending babies home with monitors in the wake of his 1972 paper, Steinschneider found himself testing a parade of prototypes from engineers interested in this new market. "They'd say, 'Al, what do you think?' And I'd say, 'Do you want it straight? It's clever but it doesn't work.' "

Pete Petit's design was a photoelectric cell that would be attached to the chest. If the infant's chest failed to move, the light would flash and the flash would trip an alarm. Very clever, Steinschneider said, but it doesn't work. It was too hard to get the cell positioned to stay on the chest. But Steinschneider was intrigued by the brash young engineer. He invited Petit over for dinner. "He told us how many mortgages he had on his house," Steinschneider remembered. Petit went home to Atlanta and tried to keep from going out of business. But he had been equally impressed by Steinschneider. Maybe he didn't have it quite right yet, but the trip to Syracuse only confirmed his belief that a baby monitor would be his salvation.

———

By 1975, Steinschneider's sleep apnea hypothesis was the leading theory of sudden infant death in the world.

There were other theories. In SIDS, there are always other theories. They appeared and disappeared like blips. It was the deaths of the H. babies that made Steinschneider's theory sound right, and the way he marketed them that caused others to follow. His salesmanship was especially effective because, as he demonstrated in Toronto, his charismatic beliefs were always couched in careful, appropriate language that helped him maintain professional credibility. It was his special skill. But if his methods were not always obvious, his intensity surely was. "What you're talking about is medical zealotry," observed Abe Bergman, who knew as well as anyone how vulnerable the SIDS community was to the pull of emotion. "It was messianic, not scientific."

Steinschneider also had the luck of timing. He began propagating his theory just as the pediatric subspecialty of neonatology—the care of newborns—was beginning to flourish. Medical schools across the country were forming neonatology departments, offering research fellowships that attracted droves of freshly minted pediatricians just out of residency. To accommodate them, teaching hospitals were opening intensive care units just for newborns. The apnea theory of SIDS was made for this new field. In the neonatal research lab, it was something to study, and this was now where the grant money was. In the clinic, it was something new to be aware of and perhaps to treat. Steinschneider had made apnea a condition to worry about. The field was becoming obsessed with infant breathing patterns because he had linked them to sudden death.

It went virtually unnoticed that as the attention being paid to apnea made it more familiar, the baseline concern for full-term babies settled on pauses greater than twenty seconds, not fifteen, which was the criterion on which Steinschneider had based his theory. In fact, some thought even spells that long should not be associated with SIDS. The NICHD, responding to the attention on the apnea theory, had commissioned a nearly $3 million contract with a University of Southern California pediatric researcher, Joan Hodgman, to explore cardiorespiratory reflexes in infants, with a specific emphasis on determining what exactly constituted "normal" newborn respiration. Collaborating with a team from UCLA, Hodgman and her group were beginning to find that the patterns varied so widely—babies with a lot of apnea were apparently just as normal as those with not very much—that it probably wasn't a very good tool for identifying babies at risk. Yet, in the unstoppable rush to apnea, it was Hodgman's data, not Steinschneider's, that were viewed skeptically, and in her failure to go along with the new conventional wisdom, she found it difficult to get her work published.

As other lines of thought about SIDS fell by the wayside, scientists from Cleveland to Palo Alto, many with their own government grants, set about trying to advance Steinschneider's hypothesis. The number of federally supported SIDS research projects was climbing fast—it would go from one project in 1971 to forty in the peak year of 1977, with dozens of others addressing SIDS-related matters—and the vast majority of them had to do with sleep apnea. Researchers in Europe joined the hunt, and even lab animals at Yale and Oxford were doing their part. All these studies were the progeny of Steinschneider's paper. When scientists cited their hypothetical bases at the end of their papers on respiration and SIDS in these years, *Steinschneider, A.: Prolonged Apnea and the Sudden Infant Death Syndrome, Pediatrics, 1972*, was invariably at the top of the list. Steinschneider's call for a "concentrated research effort" at the 1969 meeting was being answered beyond even his imagination.

At Stanford University, William Dement and Christian Guilleminault were dividing apnea into three varieties (central, obstructive or upper-airway, and mixed), and finding that the heart rate slowed during all three. In the neuroscience and anatomy labs at the Veterans Administration Hospital in Sepulveda, California, Theodore Baker and Dennis McGinty were putting ninety-three kittens in Plexiglas chambers and depriving them of oxygen to see if it depressed their respiration and heart rates as they slept. Yes, they found, it did. They thought their conclusions offered credibility to Richard Naeye's hypoxia findings, which had emerged, by reputation, as strong character witnesses for Steinschneider's apnea theory.

Of all the SIDS investigators who embraced the theory, none had a grip more powerful or hotly contested than Dick Naeye. His career took a sharp turn upward at the arrival of Steinschneider's paper, and within a couple of years he, too, had become famous, moving into the company of fellow pathologists Molly Dapena and Bruce Beckwith as one of the leading lights of SIDS investigation. In fact, Dapena and Beckwith argued fiercely about whether Naeye's work was worthy of this distinction. It did not escape their notice that both Steinschneider and Naeye seemed to find much of their self-worth in the lavish acclaim heaped upon their discoveries. Only later would it seem that their work, too, had more in common than was obvious to the casual eye.

A slender man with a ready smile that belied a seething personality—"My highs are his lows," a colleague once remarked—Naeye [pronounced Noya] was a devout Christian whose religious fervor, some felt, gave his scientific beliefs an incongruously moralistic tone. In the four years after Steinschneider emerged with his theory, Naeye's discoveries, set forth in a series of celebrated papers on the possible relationship between SIDS and the conditions of oxygen deprivation known as hypoxia and hypoxemia, shook the SIDS research community like a good-sized earthquake and several tremors. The genesis of Naeye's findings was strikingly similar to the events that had given rise to Steinschneider's: a meeting, a revelation, an immediate, stirring dis-covery. In fact, this sequence came at almost exactly the same points in their careers, when each had reached his early forties having devoted years to scien-tific inquiries involving the health of babies, laborious but largely obscure quests that were to take on new and very public meanings when they came upon SIDS.

Since his early years, Naeye had specialized in autopsies of fetuses and stillborn babies. It was a pathologist's way of studying the environment of pregnancy. In the early 1970s, at the invitation of an Ethiopian pediatrician he met at a meeting in Cleveland, Naeye began traveling regularly to Africa to collect data on how dietary deficiencies during pregnancy contributed to the failure of some babies to make it out of the womb alive. "The years in Africa changed me because I encountered human suffering of untold numbers," he remembered. "So many starving, dying people living on the edge of survival." It frustrated him to be unable to do anything about it. By that time, Naeye had also become expert in the lung disease that frequently killed coal miners in the regions of Pennsylvania and West Virginia near where he worked. But he never lost his interest in infants, and he noticed out of the corner of his eye that SIDS had become a growing preoccupation among his brethren.

Though pathologists had naturally been the early investigators of SIDS, for them it was still a wide-open field. Most crib death victims only made it as far as the emergency room, if they got to the hospital at all, and from there often went directly to funeral homes, remaining, as Bruce Beckwith once noted, "relatively insulated from critical scientific minds." More often than not, the presumed futility of the exercise caused coroners and medical exam-iners to dispense with autopsies of babies.

In the winter of 1973, Beckwith was helping Eileen Hasselmeyer organize one of the NICHD's research workshops designed to draw investigators into SIDS research. The meeting would be devoted to pathology, and among those Beckwith invited was Penn State's pathology chairman, Dick Naeye. At this meeting, Naeye heard about the apnea paper for the first time; it had been published a few months before in a journal he didn't regularly read. Naeye quickly concluded that SIDS was a vital, unfolding field, and that the theory made perfect sense. Why couldn't it be, as Steinschneider seemed to think, that a fatal episode of apnea was only the last and most extreme of many spells, the result of a subtle but chronic abnormality? Naeye knew that some adults had recurring slowdowns in their breathing rates during sleep that stopped short of apnea. The result was an oversupply of carbon dioxide in the blood that could produce measurable changes in the size of the small pulmonary vessels. What if infants had similar episodes, and it led to chronic oxygen deprivation in their blood or in their tissues? "If that's the case," Naeye hypothesized to himself, "I should be able to find it at autopsy." He was edgy with anticipation when he stepped up to Beckwith at the end of the meeting. "Bruce, this is very exciting," he said. "I think I can do some positive stuff."

To Naeye, there were followers in science, and there were innovators. "A real creation in science," he observed, "has to do with unreasonable perseverance. Challenge things people believe in, look at things people ignore." He imagined that he and Steinschneider, whom he'd never met, were cut from the same mold—innovators, restless for discovery. Naeye went back to Pennsylvania and immediately called Russell Fisher, the Maryland medical examiner, looking for subjects of his own.

As a medical examiner, Fisher was right in the middle of the fray, and with Saul and Sylvia Goldberg prodding him along, he had become a prominent source of information and raw material. Naeye invited himself down to Baltimore. Take whatever you need, Fisher said when he got there. Naeye pored through the little file drawers in the basement. In the pathologists' world, subjects came in the form of slivers of organ tissue pressed between thin glass slides. Naeye wanted the pulmonary artery. He collected slides from the autopsies of sixty-two SIDS victims, and thirty-nine from babies who would serve as his control group—victims of accidents, homicides, and such natural causes as bacterial meningitis. He put the slides in his briefcase and raced home to Hershey. There he had a second control group—slides of artery tissue from ten babies who had died in Leadville, Colorado, a place whose high altitude, 10,170 feet above sea level, led to low concentrations of oxygen in lung tissue.

The lung and its environs were Naeye's narrow universe—it was where he directed his eyes when he explored both stillborns and coal miners—but nobody had ever found much in the organ that might explain SIDS. In fact, as pathologists tried to explore the tiny, delicate lung-tissue structure, they often inadvertently upset the integrity of the organ. The lung was a likely place to hunt for a clue, but the search could be as precarious an exercise as the detonation of a bomb. It was not the only reason the lung was one of the most enticing and yet most elusive areas of SIDS investigation. Pathologists generally agreed that lung congestion should best be ignored because it was so unspecific—any number of things could cause it. And attempts to determine if the lungs of SIDS babies were physiologically abnormal were difficult undertakings because of the paucity of good controls. Not many babies who died during their first year died of something other than SIDS. Few pathologists had as large a collection of infant tissue as Russell Fisher.

In Pennsylvania, Naeye and his lab assistants began examining the small pulmonary artery, a thin structure that is the pipeline between heart and lungs, to see whether there was anything distinctive in SIDS babies. Given his working hypothesis, size was the obvious place to start—size as determined by how many cells were in the muscle tissue. Other pathologists had been over this general terrain, but Naeye thought the key might be in the detail. Maybe the usual method for calculating cell counts, a technique called planimetry that involved rolling a device around the edges of the slide, was inadequate to the task. Blood in the tissue hid some cells from the search. There was another way, Naeye decided.

The work was tedious. He laid a sliver of artery muscle on a slide with a tiny grid etched into it. Then he peered through his microscope and started counting the cells one by one. Using this method, Naeye began to see that the SIDS babies seemed to have more cells, more artery muscle, than the controls. Under the microscope, these artery cells appeared to be almost swollen, and when he found a similar abnormality in the tissue from the Colorado babies, he detected a possible breakthrough. Put alongside what he knew about the effects of adult apnea, he thought it was early evidence that SIDS babies had hypoxia—a low concentration of oxygen in the tissue—and hypoxemia, low levels of oxygen in the blood. He took this as the first physical evidence of a respiratory abnormality in SIDS babies and evidence of a chronic oxygen deprivation that fit perfectly with the kind of recurring respiratory pauses Steinschneider had reported in his SIDS babies. In less than three months, Naeye believed, he had turned the key. It was these findings that were published in the eminent *New England Journal of Medicine* within a year of Steinschneider's paper. They were a booster rocket for the apnea theory.

Steinschneider and Naeye met for the first time soon after the *NEJM* paper, and it was an explosion of raw energy. They became partners-in-theory, a dynamic if unofficial team pulling the field in the direction of their ideas. Suddenly, out of the heap had come a theory from pediatrics and backup from pathology, each supporting the other in a delicate balance. With his first paper, Naeye became a SIDS researcher of credibility. A second heralded discovery came less than a year later: that "many" SIDS victims seemed to retain an unusually large proportion of fetal "brown fat" cells around their adrenal glands, cells that are normally replaced by white cells soon after birth. Naeye explained that the reason this was significant—and the reason he had looked for it in the first place—was that other pathologists had found that people who had died of respiratory diseases that prevented them from getting enough oxygen seemed to have brown fat cells coating their adrenal glands. Though he found the brown fat in less than a third of the SIDS victims, Naeye thought it was further evidence of hypoxemia—and apnea.

The second round of findings was published in the equally prestigious journal *Science*. Naeye opened this report by citing Steinschneider's two SIDS victims as the basis of his own theory, then wrote that, thus far, he had found two "tissue markers" linking oxygen deprivation with SIDS. Naeye's work had a powerful impact. He was showered with attention and credit, and by the time he preceded Steinschneider to the podium in Toronto, he was sparking an outbreak of pathology research aimed at confirming his dramatic findings. Eileen Hasselmeyer, who had started to put her money on the apnea theory and had a growing stake in its success, invited Naeye to Bethesda to be a distinguished lecturer. "I want to be cautious, but the pieces of the puzzle are beginning to come together," Hasselmeyer declared in a story about Naeye's breakthroughs that ran on the front page of *The National Observer* a month before the Toronto meeting. Even Molly Dapena, the great debunker of SIDS theories, was excited. She thought Naeye was making wonderful discoveries, and set out to replicate the research.

After fifteen years on the SIDS front, Dapena found it exhilarating that one of her fellow pathologists had finally found *something* to distinguish a SIDS victim. She hoped it was true and wanted to be among those to confirm that it was. Naeye's discoveries sold Dapena on the excitement of the apnea theory—and opened her mind to the monitoring concept that was tethered to it like a baby to the machine itself. It led her to think that Steinschneider, with whom she was becoming close friends, might be right when he said that babies who survived seeming near-misses should be put on monitors at home.

Dapena kept her hopes high despite a problem she confronted from the outset: When she looked at tissue slides under her microscope, she didn't see what Naeye saw. When she told him on one occasion that she was having trouble confirming his findings, she was dismayed to find that she had hurt his feelings. Shortly after the article in *Science,* Dapena drove from Philadelphia to Hershey with John Emery, a British pathologist and SIDS researcher who was visiting from London, to see how Naeye read the tissue marker for brown fat. Naeye explained his technique, and Dapena and Emery returned to their labs to resume the task. Emery still couldn't replicate the findings. Dapena could, but barely. She found that SIDS babies over five months old did have more fetal brown fat than the controls, but the difference was not statistically significant. Moreover, she couldn't confirm the findings at all in babies between two and five months—the prime SIDS age. Meanwhile, she strained to keep up with Naeye's furious pace of discovery. By 1976, his count of markers would reach seven, and when they were sure he was done, his colleagues, though unable to replicate many of them, certified the importance of his discoveries by referring to them as Naeye did. They were the Seven Tissue Markers of SIDS.

"He came up with all seven of his markers in three years," Dapena remembers with a skepticism that she didn't have at the time. "It took me three years just to do one." Despite the murkiness of their validity, the Seven Tissue Markers became a milestone in the SIDS hunt, and elegant evidence for the apnea theory. He was hopeful, Naeye told a reporter from *Science,* that his work would help lead to some kind of test that could predict SIDS.

Still, some researchers had serious doubts about the legitimacy of the tissue markers—and about their effects. Most skeptical was the man who had recruited Naeye in the first place, Bruce Beckwith. He was troubled not so much by the emphasis on apnea as a theory to be explored and tested, as by the hastiness with which it was being accepted. "The mistake was that it was being thrust prematurely into the public arena," he later reflected. "With Steinschneider, Naeye, Dapena, and others, I think there was a lot of eagerness to show some results to the NICHD, to the public, to the press, and here they had something that they could get a finger on. The SIDS victim can be identified in advance. We have a way of preventing it. We have pathologic evidence that they have chronic recurring breathing problems. There was an accumulated, no-holds-barred advocacy for it, and people at the NICHD became very enamored of it." He saw how bright, experienced, well-meaning people—Dapena, in particular—became enthralled with the idea that Naeye's research confirmed Steinschneider's. "Molly was completely taken in by Naeye's findings, and she was the reason he got so much credibility. In the pathology community she was a vigorous advocate for the Seven Tissue Markers, and she was a very credible, very authoritative person, and she was very close with the people at NIH. She was doing all these annual reviews of the SIDS science, and it always started out with the exciting observations of Naeye. I was not convinced, and I argued with Molly about it. I think she took her data and wanted them so much to support him that her conclusion was that it did support him, even though she said flat out in her papers that there was not a statistically significant difference [between the tissue of SIDS babies and that of babies who died of other causes]. And so she's falling from scientific objectivity a little bit. But Molly was a powerful force influencing NIH and others to go along with it."

If Naeye's pathology had the most explosive impact on the science of SIDS inspired by Steinschneider, it was a Boston pediatrician named Dorothy Kelly who was beginning to have the greatest consequence on its culture. With her mentor, Harvard clinical researcher Daniel Shannon, she had started modestly, on an independent track, but by 1975 she was Steinschneider's compatriot in monitoring. Ultimately she would help him turn a concept into a movement.

In the spring of 1972, a few months before Steinschneider's paper was published, a doctor in Cambridge had referred a baby to Shannon, then a thirty-seven-year-old pulmonary specialist who had founded the pediatric ICU at Massachusetts General Hospital and taught at Harvard Medical School. The baby had required resuscitation right in the delivery room, the first of many severe apneic spells just after birth. Shannon determined that the baby had been born with an extremely rare condition commonly known as Ondine's Curse, a malady that caused her breathing to slow down or cease every time she slept. Informed of the "curse," the baby's parents, Portuguese immigrants who spoke no English, took to coming to the hospital dressed in black. Shannon put the baby on a mechanical ventilator and renamed the condition congenital central hypoventilation. Then he began calling pediatricians around Boston to see if they had seen cases like it. Shannon, like Steinschneider, had spent several years studying how the brain controlled infant respiration, and now he wondered if the curse of Ondine came in less obvious varieties, and whether SIDS was the result of one of them.

After twenty calls, he got one referral: a baby who had had apneic episodes that frightened his mother, who was a nurse. Shannon put the baby on an Air-Shields monitor in the hospital, and when his mother asked if she could take him home with it, he had no objection. Shannon was happy to see the baby thrive and come off the monitor, but a few months later, when he retrieved the October issue of *Pediatrics* from his mailbox and read Steinschneider's paper about two babies who hadn't been so fortunate, he concluded he was right to think about apnea and SIDS.

Kelly arrived in the ICU as a resident on rotation the following year and became intrigued by these questions preoccupying Shannon and her new field in general. A nurse who had gone on to medical school in Detroit before arriving at Mass General for her internship and staying on for her residency, Kelly was initially puzzled by Steinschneider's report. It didn't seem to fit what little experience she had with SIDS. A college friend had once lost a baby, suddenly and without any prior symptoms, let alone a chronic condition such as the one Steinschneider described. But with Shannon's cases in the foreground, Steinschneider's theory changed Kelly's assumptions about SIDS and, as it did for Shannon, drew her into the mystery.

Kelly was struck by the "near-miss" and familial connections of Steinschneider's paper, and soon came upon a case that she took as evidence that he was on the mark on both counts. A baby came into the Mass General emergency room, "presenting almost dead," Kelly later recounted. "A trach was done, but she didn't make it." It turned out that the baby's older sister had been a patient of Shannon's a year before. He had treated the older child for recurring apnea requiring a number of resuscitations by her mother. She eventually outgrew the problem, but now, with her baby sister's death in the E.R. a year later, Shannon worried about her again. Though she had surpassed the usual age for SIDS, he wanted to put her on a home monitor. He and Kelly paid no particular attention to the mother's odd reaction. She decided to give her surviving child up to foster care. "She was anxious about using the device," Kelly explained.

With this experience, and with Steinschneider's SIDS family as Exhibit A, Shannon and Kelly decided they ought to start looking very carefully at siblings of SIDS victims. "What Al's paper did for me was to make me believe sibs are at greater risk," Kelly said. And they became increasingly enamored of the monitoring idea. Shannon, who taught at the Massachusetts Institute of Technology as well as at Harvard, was intrigued by the concept of bringing medical technology into the home. Kelly was even more excited by the possibilities. Convinced that SIDS could run in families, and that some babies did almost die, she thought home monitoring was a marvelous way to allow parents, with the proper support from professionals, to protect their children outside the hospital, and at far less expense.

She and Shannon sent only ten babies home on monitors in the next couple of years, but by 1975 Kelly had become an apnea apostle. She moved on to a Harvard pediatric pulmonary research fellowship that year, but it could have been more aptly termed an apnea fellowship. Under Shannon's tutelage, she launched her own home-monitoring program and began soliciting referrals from around Boston. Meanwhile, like Steinschneider, they tried to get a handle on what constituted dangerously abnormal respiration, and whether it could be identified in advance of a life-threatening event. Shannon engaged some of his MIT students to build a device that could print out tracings of a baby's respiration recorded on tape over a twelve-hour period. He and Kelly called these recordings "pediatric pneumograms." It was their hope that they could be used to identify infants at risk of SIDS.

To explore their idea, Kelly went looking for normal babies to bring in for overnight testing. Twice a week, she headed to Cambridge Hospital to sell the concept to pediatricians and new mothers, and with their help she began developing an idea of what she thought an abnormal pneumogram looked like—and hence, which babies might be susceptible to sudden death. Within a year, she would have twenty-five babies at a time on home monitors in the Boston area. By her own account, most of Kelly's peers thought she was at the least jumping the gun and very possibly batty. But she was too convinced to care. Of all the doctors in America who took the apnea leap of faith, none leaped higher, more resolutely, or with more consequence, than Dotty Kelly. And nobody appreciated it more than Al Steinschneider. When he visited Shannon and Kelly that year, he was pleased to see his work being taken up at Harvard.

In the summer of 1975, the medical and scientific world's consecration of Steinschneider's theory became all but official. That August, *Science,* the bible of the American research establishment, announced at the head of a 2,500-word report on crib death that the search for a cause had recently made such bold advances, there seemed good reason to hope that the ancient code might soon be cracked. The two SIDS deaths in Steinschneider's 1972 paper had changed everything, said *Science*. "Now there is a growing body of evidence that the victims of crib death are not completely normal—and their deaths not as inexplicable—as was once thought, but rather that these infants have subtle physiological defects, probably in the mechanisms that control breathing. Thus, it may be possible to detect potential crib death victims and prevent them from dying. . . ." Virtually the entire report was about Steinschneider's apnea theory, along with the support it had received from Naeye's rapid-fire breakthroughs in Hershey.

It didn't take long for the popular press to pick up on the hubbub. "What appear to be the most promising leads about SIDS seem to be emerging from research on breathing patterns during sleep," *Newsweek* reported in its first issue of 1976, quoting Steinschneider and several followers.

"As a result of his experiences," said *Parents,* "Dr. Steinschneider has developed a monitoring system for babies whose prolonged periods of apnea have led to what doctors call 'a near-miss.' This happens when a mother finds a baby seemingly lifeless in his crib and rushes him to the hospital emergency room."

"The experiment is now in its third year and the results are indeed exciting," *Today's Health* proclaimed, early in an eight-page article featuring a huge picture of one of Steinschneider's monitors, followed by an even bigger one of "the father of the apnea theory" himself turning the knobs on the wall-size equipment in his lab. "One hundred babies have been home-monitored; 40 are on monitors now; and not a single one of those in the study has been a victim of SIDS."

The costar of the piece in *Today's Health* was an Air-Shields apnea monitor, its wires circling the opening spread before moving down the page to the crib of the child over which it stood sentinel. In the monitor's custody in this story, however, was not an infant but a toddler from a small town forty miles north of Syracuse. There was a picture of her. "She's nearly three and bright as a button," the caption said, "but since her birth, she has had to be wired to a black box each time she sleeps." In this picture, she looked wary and forlorn, clutching her pet kitten. "The Black Box That Guards Debbie Whitney's Life," read the headline. The story opened dramatically:

> Stridently, insistently, the noise shrills through the darkened farmhouse near Pulaski, New York. Beep . . . beep. It is 3 A.M., yet Beverly Whitney awakens immediately, flings back the blankets, and hurries the few steps to her daughter's crib. She touches the tiny two-year-old body, expertly feeling for reassurance that Debbie's chest is rising and falling in respiration—for the alarm in the night sounded a warning: Little Debbie Whitney has paused in her breathing, and adult aid may be necessary to get the rhythm started again. That aid can be as little as a gentle shake or tickle, yet for Debbie it could mean the difference between life and death. For Beverly Whitney, the midnight alarm is a familiar routine. Some nights she is called to her daughter's bedside as often as 25 times. Yet she seldom complains . . .

Debbie, the baby Steinschneider had kept on a monitor so long that she now plugged it in herself, was apple-cheeked and gregarious—"she looks anything but unhealthy." But as the sibling of a SIDS victim, she was being monitored because of "a growing suspicion that SIDS runs in families," said the magazine. "One Syracuse area family has lost five children to SIDS."

Beverly Whitney was one of the mothers Steinschneider was thinking about when he described life with a home monitor at the meeting in Toronto. She and her husband, Michael, did not know that their daughter's breathing was in all likelihood no different than that of any other normal child. They took as their reality what Dr. Steinschneider told them it was. For Beverly in particular, his evangelism had profound effects. She had recently become president of the SIDS group he had organized at Upstate, and among the SIDS mothers she had encountered in the basement meeting room was the anonymous Mrs. H., the woman who had lost all her children. Beverly thought Waneta Hoyt was without a doubt the saddest person she'd ever met. For her and the others in the group, Waneta's grief was an object lesson. It was one reason why Debbie Whitney remained on an infant apnea monitor as she approached her third birthday.

In Seattle, Abe Bergman and Bruce Beckwith were getting extremely worked up. This was not the way to pursue research, they and their partner George Ray agreed—not an "organized search for knowledge" with the checks and balances of sober peer review.

Some might have thought the Seattle group was simply jealous. In a few years, Steinschneider had far surpassed them in prominence, and not many national magazines were writing about the larynx spasm theory of SIDS. But the trio were comfortable with their motives. They were disturbed by what Bergman regarded as "the herd mentality in science" he saw unfolding across the horizon of SIDS research. It was as if the entire SIDS movement was overcome by a virulent strain of credulousness. He noted how Steinschneider and Naeye turned observations into presumptions, and how their status— and, more important, that of their theses—had been elevated by the implicit endorsement of the prestigious medical journals that published their work.

Bergman's views had nothing to do with suspicion. He thought a lot of Steinschneider's work was solid and provocative, and that his 1972 paper was very possibly a piece of the puzzle. "I admit that I tended to accept it uncritically," he would later say. "Had I looked at the ages and circumstances of his cases more critically, I would have been more skeptical." It was years before he acknowledged even to himself why he had not turned his normally discerning scientific eye on Steinschneider's paper: "I was always worried we'd be discredited by cases like this."

For his part, Beckwith had had misgivings about the cases behind Steinschneider's theory from the beginning, and its increasing acceptance rekindled his concerns. But, like Bergman, he felt a deep emotional and political kinship with SIDS parents, so he looked for every way possible to ignore the tiny voice in his head that suggested he explore the cases more rigorously. Beckwith had performed eight hundred autopsies of SIDS babies by this point and talked to the parents of just about all of them. For him, the presumption of innocence was a moral obligation. To look more skeptically at Steinschneider's paper would have been to abandon an ethic, and it wouldn't have stopped with the H. family.

To keep that door closed, Beckwith even tricked himself, in a sense, into inventing a label to accommodate the occasionally bothersome cases of multiple SIDS in families that he felt were not actually consistent with the agreed-upon definition of SIDS. The vagueness of apnea helped. In medical argot it was a "nonspecific symptom," so there were many ways to apply the term. "I said, 'Al's not looking at SIDS, he's looking at Familial Recurrent Apnea,' " Beckwith recalled. "And we had several families in Seattle with multiple SIDS, and it was the same experience, where some of them were awake, some of them were more than two years old, but they died suddenly and unexpectedly. And I leaned over backward. I started with [Belfast epidemiologist Peter] Froggatt, who mentioned that there were reports of cyanotic spells and stuff, then I went to Steinschneider, and then I went to some of our Seattle cases. I would have to say that what I was wanting to call a disease—because I really hate to blame people—probably wasn't, at least in the majority of instances. And I talked about this. I presented at several national meetings an entity, which thank God I never published, called Familial Recurrent Apnea. And I reckon I called up a few moms in Seattle during my twenty years there and said, 'This death was not your fault,' when she actually had done it. But I used to say I would rather miss ten homicides than falsely accuse one mother. I was on a natural disease bandwagon. There was always the possibility of a death from inflicted suffocation. But I had made a decision early on. I'm either going to be suspicious of them all, or not very suspicious."

In the discreet culture of science and medicine, it was also not quite acceptable to raise that particular possibility. Even when Beckwith, a few years later, began hearing about a strange psychiatric disorder called Munchausen syndrome by proxy, and started entertaining the notion that it might have something to do with Steinschneider's paper, he decided there was not much use in making a public spectacle of it. "I became convinced about Munchausen, and basically knew that's what it was, but I didn't figure there was a chance of proving it, and it wouldn't do any good for Bruce Beckwith to start jumping on Al Steinschneider's case."

But that was years in the future. In 1975, it was just a puzzle with missing pieces. "This just didn't smell like SIDS to me," Beckwith said, "but it was exciting and clearly worth exploring." He concluded that whatever the flaws of Steinschneider's case reports or the deficiencies of his conclusions, he could at least be applauded for the soundness of his general line of inquiry, which Beckwith thought was more than could be said for most SIDS theorists. But while he liked the basic theoretical construct—apnea, after all, was just a stop in breathing, so why couldn't it be caused by a sudden spasm of the larynx?—he detested the public response.

It was the monitors that had Beckwith and Bergman in a lather. Stories like the one about Debbie Whitney in *Today's Health* made them cringe: families at the mercy of some electronic baby-sitter relentlessly reminding them of the precariousness of early life—of SIDS. They dreaded the specter of a stampede of hysterical parents and acquiescent pediatricians. There was Steinschneider in Syracuse, and now there was Dorothy Kelly starting a monitoring program at no less a place than Harvard. It seemed absurd to them, and yet entirely predictable, that the monitors could be on the verge of becoming a *craze,* a must-have for SIDS parents, when there was no evidence that they did anything but play havoc with the fragile psyches of vulnerable mothers and fathers.

Several companies had begun responding to Steinschneider's call for a better monitor, and Bergman and Beckwith were already seeing the beginnings of the marketing: SIDS protectors, crib-death alarms—baby savers. "It was the false hope, the commercialization of it," Bergman remembers. "We were getting calls from monitor purveyors," Beckwith adds, "and we were worried that financial interests could harm the science."

Among the pediatricians of America who shared this concern was Jerold Lucey, whose publication of Steinschneider's paper had started it all. Despite his early excitement about Steinschneider's theory, he thought the embryonic home monitor phenomenon might need to be nipped in the bud—or at least slowed down in order to let the science catch up. An editorial commentary by two of the most credible names in SIDS seemed to him the best way to do it.

At first, Bergman and Beckwith were reluctant to go public with their disagreement with Steinschneider, even if it was philosophical and not personal. But Lucey pressed them. Somebody had to do it, he believed.

In character and appearance, Bergman and Beckwith were something of an odd couple. Beckwith was tall, bearded, and mannerly, with an impish smile and speech that was full of whimsical cultivation. Bergman was half a foot shorter, with a boyish face and a mouth that roared. The pugnacious son of a Seattle luggage store owner, his ardor once reminded Steinschneider of Nikita Khrushchev, the way he would pound on the table when he had something important to say.

Bergman and Beckwith wrote the piece for *Pediatrics* together, and struggled to achieve the right tone. They agreed their commentary should come across not as an indictment of a person or even a theory, but of a mentality. George Ray signed on with them, and Lucey ran the commentary on the first page of his July 1975 issue, under the title "The Apnea Monitor Business."

> ... The "crib death theory-of-the-month club" blazons forth with unremitting regularity. This usually takes the form of an "armchair investigator" propounding yet another explanation for SIDS to a naïve wire-service reporter on a dull news day. The resultant banner headlines in newspapers throughout the country regularly produce hundreds of frantic phone calls and letters to the National Foundation for Sudden Infant Death, as well as exhortations to practicing physicians to "do something." ... The Reemstma-Maloney Law should be borne in mind: "The public impact of instant medical reporting is related inversely to the intrinsic merit of the observation."
>
> One practice that threatens to become widespread in the absence of supporting scientific evidence is the use of electronic respiration monitors in the home to "prevent" SIDS. Some electronic manufacturers are already promoting their wares for this purpose, with justified anticipation of boundless profits. It is true that one of the promising areas of SIDS research involves the exploration of the possible relationship of "sleep apnea" to SIDS. The work is only in the beginning stages, however; to date such an association has not been demonstrated.
>
> A related development is use of the term "aborted" or "near-miss" SIDS,

for infants having unexpected apneic episodes. While there must be a reversible point in the pathologic spectrum of SIDS, there is now no way of identifying that point. . . . SIDS is now a definable entity; "near-miss" SIDS still is not. It is much preferable to admit our ignorance rather than to feign wisdom. Our chief concern is that, on the basis of preliminary and inconclusive evidence, the public will be deluged with information indicating that SIDS can be prevented through the use of home monitors. The resultant pressure on parents, pediatricians, and family physicians would be enormous. This pressure should be resisted. . . .

The physician or parent desperate to "do something" to prevent SIDS would do well to recall the harm done in the 1930s by thymic irradiation. This not only failed to prevent SIDS, but resulted in an epidemic of thyroid cancer. Let us wait until the evidence is in before rushing to the apnea monitor as a panacea for SIDS, lest we again risk significant harm to the patients and families we seek to serve.

Beckwith truly hadn't seen the commentary as an attack on Steinschneider—"We were talking about the world's reaction to Al, not Al himself"—but Bergman knew that's just what it was, and that many people would read it that way. In the end, he didn't much care. Bergman had recruited Steinschneider into the movement, had encouraged him, admired him, agreed with him. It was in good part Bergman's politicking in Washington that had brought the money that was financing Steinschneider's work. But he had watched him emerge with his 1972 paper implicitly hawking the pseudoscience of monitors, then declare at a meeting that SIDS rates had dropped in Syracuse because of them, and that was the beginning of their fallout. Bergman had stood up indignantly and said that it wasn't true—that Steinschneider's interpretation violated every principle of epidemiology. And Bergman sat down and thought, *They used to call them snake-oil salesmen.*

Vacationing on Cape Cod, Steinschneider took the latest issue of *Pediatrics* out of his briefcase and found the commentary staring up at him. He was stung by it—angered, he would later say, by its "misleading" tone. He didn't respond; for a while, he stewed. But others did react, their counterattacks sometimes laid between the lines: Were the Seattle doctors actually calling Steinschneider an "armchair investigator"? Were they impugning his highly acclaimed work? Weren't they just jealous of the attention Steinschneider's theory was getting, at the expense of theirs? Warren Guntheroth saw in the commentary everything he had always disdained in his crosstown colleagues' approach to SIDS. "Their party line was that SIDS couldn't be prevented, and Abe was very aggressive about that," Guntheroth said. "His view was, 'Why should parents feel guilty?' But the contradiction was that they were saying,

'Why aren't all you selfish people doing research?' And we'd come in with research and they wouldn't listen. I always thought parents' feelings and support groups were important, but that idea got in the way of progress for children." Guntheroth did not fear home monitors. After all, it was his idea, broached at the seminal moment of the 1969 meeting, though it wasn't until four years later, after Steinschneider's paper, that he sent a baby home with one. The child had been brought to him after an apparent apneic episode at home. "Will it happen again?" the mother had asked. Probably not, Guntheroth said. *Probably* not? responded the mother.

To Steinschneider's rescue they came, none with more venom than Richard Naeye. He focused his wrath on Beckwith, his fellow pathologist and developing nemesis, sending the first of what would turn out to be a long series of letters—"ugly, vulgar, intense, personal letters," Beckwith recalled. "I have a thick file of them. He and others perceived this as a direct attack on Steinschneider. It was my first experience with anger and hostility in the SIDS arena. It had really been a positive experience up until then."

Beckwith did not shy away from the battle. While he was unwilling to challenge the essential data of Steinschneider's theory—the deaths of the H. babies—he saw no reason not to openly protest Naeye's more abstract laboratory observations. In a fundamental if less personal way, Beckwith was to Naeye what Bergman was to Steinschneider. He had introduced his fellow pathologist to SIDS by inviting him to a meeting and now wondered what he had wrought. As he read Naeye's research and watched him at meetings, Beckwith began to suspect why his tissue markers weren't being replicated. He thought Naeye's science suffered from bias, and that it was important to start talking about his doubts because the findings were constantly being cited as evidence for the apnea theory of SIDS—and by extension, for the argument for home monitoring.

"I began saying, hey, are these really facts that are being presented or are they perceptions?" Beckwith said. "And at least they needed to be redone with different methods and by unbiased people with better defined cases and all that sort of thing." Beckwith believed that Naeye's method of counting cells in the pulmonary artery was improper, and that was one reason why the discoveries couldn't be confirmed. "He responded to me that he had first done the study using planimetry"—the accepted way to measure blood vessels—"but didn't mention it in *The New England Journal of Medicine*. He will twist the truth until it fits. He will keep doing the measurements until they fit."

Not surprisingly, no one embraced and promoted Naeye and the tissue markers more passionately than Steinschneider. He hailed Naeye as a genius, one of the great visionaries of SIDS research. "Dick has the ability to take two pieces of a five-hundred-piece puzzle and tell you what the picture looks like," he would say admiringly.

That was precisely Beckwith's point when he took the podium as the keynote speaker at the annual convention of the National SIDS Foundation in New Orleans. "There are many problems with the tissue marker and chronic hypoxia story," he declared, stunning many people in the audience. "The results are so important that they need much more work before they can be accepted. At the moment, I am unconvinced." Eileen Hasselmeyer and Jehu Hunter were in the audience and Beckwith saw a look of distress on their faces. Naeye and Steinschneider stalked out of the room. "That was a very inappropriate talk," Naeye snarled at Beckwith as they passed later in the hall.

Molly Valdes-Dapena, for seventeen years a member of the Tissue Committee of Saint Christopher's Hospital for Children, was nowhere near ready to give up on any of Naeye's seven markers. She listened to Beckwith's speech in New Orleans, then went home to continue trying to replicate Naeye's findings. Again she failed. She called Naeye to inquire about the confusing results. "He said he couldn't prove how he did it," she recalled. "Everything had been taken apart. He didn't have the data anymore. 'What about the technician who did it?' 'Oh, she quit.' " The frustration drove Valdes-Dapena to distraction. Yet, despite the disturbing implications of Naeye's responses to the problems, confirming his discoveries would remain an intense preoccupation for years. "I almost turned my life into an obsession with tissue markers," she would reflect one day.

Steinschneider took nearly a year to respond in print to the Bergman-Beckwith commentary in *Pediatrics* but made up for the delay with volume, submitting a piece that ran nearly three times the length of the original. He deflected the criticism with a shield of intricate SIDSspeak, a notable chunk of which was devoted to a heated attack on what he regarded as the Seattle group's veiled advertisement for its own theory. "They appear to have allowed their personal involvements and commitments to obscure several important conceptual issues," he wrote. He defended the use of monitors, eventually concluding his response in what had become typical fashion: "In SIDS, as well as in other medical problems, we fail in our responsibilities if we prejudge, respond in haste, and allow professional recommendations and utterances to be based on personal need rather than on reason supported by scientifically acquired information."

For their "critical reading of the manuscript and numerous constructive suggestions," Steinschneider thanked Eileen Hasselmeyer, his patron at NICHD, and Sydney Segal, who had helped approve his first big grant. Oddly, he had also asked Syracuse pediatrics chairman Frank Oski for his suggestions.

Averse to him from the start, for four years Oski had watched Steinschneider talk circles around people—parents, colleagues, reporters, bureaucrats from Bethesda—and had grown even more skeptical of his fervor. He concluded that Steinschneider was, as he later put it without even a pause of circumspection, "a charlatan," a man more interested in promoting his apnea theory than in conducting serious research. Under other circumstances, Oski would have been pleased by the prestige brought to the department by a staff member's success and celebrity. But not in this case. He was perplexed by the impact Steinschneider was having outside Syracuse. "The science escaped him," Oski said. "He was a blowhard, an embarrassment. A malignant growth on the department."

Steinschneider was of course conscious of the antipathy and had begun to recognize that his time in Syracuse was coming to an end. He had never made it to full professor, and as long as Oski was in charge, it was unlikely he ever would, no matter how many papers he published. He was tired of fighting for lab space and for his boss's respect. By 1976, feeling on top of the SIDS world but unappreciated in his own department, Steinschneider was talking openly about leaving. Someday, he told Thelma Schneider, he would have his own SIDS institute. And it wouldn't be in Syracuse.

When the producers of *Marcus Welby, M.D.* planned an episode about SIDS, they sent the script to Saul and Sylvia Goldberg for their review. Among the bags of mail the Goldbergs received over the years was a letter of support from Robert Redford's wife, Lola. The Redfords had lost a child to SIDS. By the mid-1970s, the Goldbergs, a dozen years removed from their baby daughter's death, were the last of the original activist parents still consumed by the cause on a daily basis.

In the summer of 1974, a SIDS activist named Rose Fleischman had invited the Goldbergs up to Syracuse. She'd gotten to know Al Steinschneider and wanted to bring them together. Saul and Sylvia were eager, too. At the 1969 meeting, he had been just one of the doctors they heard, and by the time he spoke, the fifteenth of sixteen researchers to present his data, they were bleary. But of course they knew all about him now. Steinschneider, in fact, had seen to that himself. He had called Saul the spring after his paper was published in *Pediatrics* and given him the highlights of his theory—"2 SIDS on monitors . . . test all newborns twice, pick up prolonged apnea, put on machine," Saul jotted on the back of a pink message slip on May 2, 1973—and then sent them a reprint of the paper. Now, a year later, the Goldbergs packed their car and drove from Baltimore to upstate New York. It was not unusual for them to spend their vacations visiting SIDS people.

Steinschneider was not known among his colleagues in SIDS research as a man who was especially good with parents. He could mesmerize mothers and fathers whose babies he was monitoring, pulling them in with his intensity and authority and the fear he imparted; but when parents who were active in the SIDS movement encountered him in the cooler setting of their meetings, they often found him overbearing and unpleasant. Molly Dapena was among those who noticed the dynamic, and it reminded her of the delicate blend of science and sensitivity required of investigators who chose this particular field of medicine. Steinschneider didn't have it, and he didn't much care. He made no secret of his impatience with what he viewed as the parents-first perspective of the SIDS world. He saw the Goldbergs, though, in a different light. They were the original support group, but they also wanted, like him, to *stop SIDS now*.

Over dinner at Rose Fleischman's house, the Goldbergs listened to Steinschneider hold forth on the future of apnea and monitoring, and on his hopes of taking the SIDS battle to higher planes. What was needed was money—not for more counseling programs, but for research and clinical programs to develop ways to prevent SIDS. Despite the recent success in Washington, the money couldn't all come from there. The government was fickle, and sooner or later support for SIDS would yield to the next trendy cause.

The Goldbergs told Steinschneider how much money they had raised over the years. They talked about their long relationship with Russell Fisher. They listened to one another long into the night and found themselves to be simpatico. Saul and Sylvia were disarmed by Steinschneider's emotional energy, a quality for which they themselves were well known. In a few months, Abe Bergman's group would publish its protest of the monitoring idea, but Steinschneider made his theory entirely convincing to the Goldbergs, who had spent more than a decade looking for hope. "It was easy for us to understand," Saul remembered. Some people thought monitoring meant a parent had the power over whether a baby lived or died, a direct contradiction of the SIDS parent's mantra: *There was nothing we could have done*. But when Steinschneider said, "There *is* something you can do," it had resonance for Saul and Sylvia. And the Goldbergs' power with parents, their access to so many charitable hearts, had resonance for Steinschneider. When they invited him to Baltimore to be the guest speaker at the upcoming tenth anniversary dinner of the Guild for Infant Survival, he enthusiastically accepted.

A report of his talk later appeared in the guild's quarterly newsletter: "If we look at our beliefs critically," Dr. Steinschneider explained, "we will grow. Some things can easily become myths if not examined critically.... Much new material on SIDS is coming out in the press and in scientific journals. Some of it is valid, some of it myth."

It was not too long after the beginning of his mutual courtship with the Goldbergs that Steinschneider got a call from Marvin Cornblath, the chairman of pediatrics at their hometown medical school, the University of Maryland in Baltimore.

Cornblath was a specialist in endocrinology and metabolism, but lately he had been thinking about politics and money. He was trying to come up with some creative ways to attract and spend research money in order to build up his department and raise its prestige. The obvious answer, he realized, was SIDS. SIDS was hot, especially in Baltimore. Just a block from the medical school was Russell Fisher. If it was possible for a medical examiner to specialize, Fisher did, and he was eager to collaborate with the medical school on SIDS projects. Forty-five minutes down Interstate 95 was Bethesda, headquarters of the NICHD. By now, the money for SIDS was pretty well gushing; there was absolutely no reason why the closest state university should not get its share. And there were the Goldbergs. Baltimore was the world headquarters of the International Guild for Infant Survival. The political impact of the parents' movement was well demonstrated; being near one of the hubs couldn't hurt.

A smattering of SIDS research was already underway in the Maryland pediatrics department, and a year before, the school had established a SIDS Center, primarily a counseling program for parents. It was Cornblath's ambition to turn these humble beginnings into something grand. He would start, in fact, with a grand rounds. A medical school grand rounds is like a mini-symposium, a gathering of faculty, residents, interns, and students to hear one speaker discuss one subject. It could be something as focused as a blood cell, as broad as an entire disease. At a party one night, Cornblath was talking about his idea with Stanford Friedman, a pediatrician who headed the SIDS Center and would later become president of the National SIDS Foundation. Cornblath was thinking about whom he should get to lead the grand rounds.

"Why not go for broke?" said Friedman. "Get Al Steinschneider. Get Dr. SIDS."

Steinschneider came to Baltimore and delivered his stump speech on SIDS. And then, with Cornblath and a few others, he waxed ambitious about the future. His first grant was winding down, he said, and he was getting ready for the next one. He planned to acquire a very serious sum of money to continue his apnea work, many times the size of the $600,000 already extended him by the NICHD.

Cornblath thought Steinschneider was marvelous at the grand rounds, and even better in the more intimate encounter that followed. It wasn't just the science to which he was drawn, but Steinschneider's extravagant personality and his ambition. It was remarkable, Cornblath thought. Not often did you find such big thinking in a researcher, such certitude. He could imagine Steinschneider holding sway with the people in Bethesda. The Maryland medical school lived in the shadows of Johns Hopkins. Steinschneider seemed like just the sort of guy who could bring in a lot of grant money, and maybe narrow the gap a little. A few days later, Cornblath called him. Was he happy in Syracuse? Would he be interested in bringing his new grant to Baltimore? There was a full professorship in it for him and more: the chance to get in on the ground floor of a major SIDS research center. Cornblath was so taken by Steinschneider that he never even called Frank Oski.

For Steinschneider, Cornblath's offer was more than a way out of Syracuse. Maryland could help give him the true power that he saw as his due. "He believed," remembered Dr. Charlotte Catz, Eileen Hasselmeyer's boss at the NICHD, "that the field was his."

Twenty years after they'd arrived there for medical school, the Steinschneiders packed up everything they owned and left Syracuse. Their children, a son and a daughter, had grown up there, and now they were in college. Steinschneider was forty-eight years old, a star in his field. But as he said his good-byes around the pediatrics department of Upstate Medical Center and departed for Baltimore, he had the unmistakable aura of a man just getting started, a man who saw greatness within his reach.

26

Do it here," Marvin Cornblath had implored Steinschneider. That was how he had put the job offer. Do the big SIDS grant in Baltimore.

"I'll do it here," Steinschneider had answered. "But here are the ground rules: I'm coming to do SIDS. I'm not coming to be a medical professor. I can do that in Syracuse. If I get the grant, you're to leave me alone. If not, you guys have a problem."

Steinschneider bought a house in a prosperous section of Baltimore known as Roland Park and began getting to know his new colleagues in the pediatrics department at the medical school, which occupied a complex of buildings in downtown Baltimore. Among the first people Cornblath introduced him to was J. Tyson Tildon, a biochemist just back from sabbatical who was the head of pediatric research at Maryland. Tildon was in the Netherlands when Cornblath wrote to him saying he had recruited one of the leading names in SIDS research, and the plans were big. SIDS would be Steinschneider's fiefdom—he would be the project director and principal investigator of the grant they planned to pitch to NICHD—but Tildon would be his partner. Steinschneider made it clear who was the senior partner, but this was fine with Tildon. He had plenty of his own work. Metabolism was his area.

Tildon found his new colleague amiable and engaging. Steinschneider tossed off one-liners as he moved through the world. Tildon was affable himself, a serious scientist with a tough edge but a light heart. The first time he visited Steinschneider at his new home in the upscale Roland Park, Tildon, a black man who had cleared many hurdles to reach his position in the science world, brought over a watermelon. Tildon liked to test white colleagues, gauge their racial sensibilities in an unthreatening way. Steinschneider

349

laughed smoothly enough, passing Tildon's test. And in his own way, Tildon let Steinschneider know that he had not arrived at his station in life by rolling over and playing along. He had his points of view.

As the director of pediatric research since 1972, Tildon had been interested in SIDS for several years, but he wasn't a part of the SIDS world and did not regard Steinschneider as a star descending on Baltimore. To Tildon apnea was just a theory, and he found the landmark paper too anecdotal for his taste. His own hunch was that the heart might have something to do with SIDS. On the other hand, Tildon was keenly aware that research directors were judged in good part by the grant money they brought in, and he had no trouble grasping the potential of a project like the one Steinschneider was said to be bringing with him.

They got right down to business. Tildon was the more experienced grant writer, but it was Steinschneider's vision they were putting on paper. Tildon imagined a research project that would look at SIDS broadly. Everything from the brain to the heart would get attention. Steinschneider, he saw immediately, was interested in nothing but apnea. In fact, to Tildon, he seemed especially *un*interested in the heart, as if he saw the heart and lungs as rivals in the struggle for the soul of SIDS research, and he wasn't giving the heart an inch. They spent months jostling for position, horse-trading, arguing science and philosophy, until Tildon figured he'd gotten the apnea piece down to about seventy-five percent of the project. "Al's stubbornness didn't get us into the heart very much," Tildon said, "but we did get into the immunological, the neurological, and the metabolic. He didn't believe any of it, but he knew I wasn't going to play, and I wasn't going to bring in the rest of the people unless this stuff was in there."

Tildon would lead a project that would explore metabolism and chemistry. Other studies would analyze how babies cried and cuddled, and whether any clues to SIDS could be found in the uterine worlds they left behind. Maternity would save the placentas of every baby born, thousands of them, and a pathologist would study those that had sustained the fetal lives of the babies who went on to die of SIDS. But the centerpiece of the grant was Steinschneider's project. He viewed his Syracuse work as a building block. Baltimore would be the place where he would prove his theory.

It took them most of that academic year to hammer out the grant proposal, but when they were done they had before them a blueprint for an investigation of SIDS such as the world had never seen: well over $5 million worth of research that would eventually involve fifty-seven people under the broad title "Biological and Psychological Aspects of SIDS." The grant application, as thick as the Baltimore phone book, proposed a five-year project that would employ a small army of investigators: developmental biologists, biochemists, pathologists, an epidemiologist, a cell biologist, an immunologist, a data coordinator, research fellows, and a corps of research assistants, nurses, electronic technicians, and secretaries. Researchers from Johns Hopkins would be brought in, and Russell Fisher's office would perform autopsies and open its tissue bank.

Steinschneider labeled the apnea study Project A and planned a major renovation in the pediatrics department that would give him the kind of space and equipment he'd coveted in Syracuse. He hoped to test most of the four thousand or so babies expected to be born in University Hospital during the next four years, and he wanted to send several hundred of them home with monitors. Maybe, by the end of the project, there would be some real progress toward achieving his Holy Grail: identifying babies in danger, getting to them in time, and saving them.

Eileen Hasselmeyer and the members of the grant committee at NICHD were unsurprised by the package of documents that arrived in Bethesda. They had come to expect this kind of ambition from Steinschneider, and he had been talking up the grant proposal for months. He had also kept his theory visible in the scholarly journals. Whatever he wrote about apnea made it into print. His most recent work was a series of papers in *Pediatrics* that focused on an aspect of his theory that had preoccupied him from the beginning: the association between colds, apnea, and SIDS.

In Syracuse, Steinschneider had sent Thelma Schneider down to the Onondaga County Medical Examiner's Office to search out every sudden death of a child under two between 1965 and 1971. She came up with 116 cases. He determined that autopsies and clinical records showed that 51 percent of the babies had some degree of nasal infection at their deaths. How many of the 116 had some degree of apnea? There was, of course, no way to know. But, he pointed out, he had demonstrated in a previous study an association between infection and apnea. "These results," he wrote, "are consistent with a prediction derived from the hypothesis that prolonged sleep apnea is part of a pathophysiologic process resulting in SIDS." He sent the research off to *Pediatrics* shortly before his arrival in Baltimore, and it was published in a standing department of the journal reserved for "short communications of factual material." The section was called "Experience and Reason—Briefly Noted" and always started with a quote from Hippocrates on the dangers of careless science: "In medicine one must pay attention not to plausible theorizing, but to experience and reason together. . . . I agree that theorizing is to be approved, provided that it is based on facts, and systematically makes its deductions from what is observed. . . . But conclusions drawn from unaided reason can hardly be serviceable."

By the time he reached Maryland, Steinschneider's plausible theorizing had made him one of the NICHD's chosen few. He had developed a close working relationship with Eileen Hasselmeyer, sometimes talking business over dinner. She was an industrious and serious-minded woman, married only to her job, but Steinschneider enlivened her. "Al played her like a violin," remarked Carolyn Szybist, the executive director of the National SIDS Foundation at the time. "He made her giggle." In the five years since the publication of the 1972 paper, Hasselmeyer had rewarded Steinschneider with public admiration and appointments to committees, including those that judged grant applications from others in the field. And with his theory, he was helping boost Hasselmeyer's status within the federal health bureaucracy high enough to later win her an appointment as an admiral in the Public Health Service. "Hasselmeyer and Steinschneider were very tight," remembered one of her colleagues at the NICHD. "He was one of her boys. And she enjoyed the fact that by her association with Steinschneider she became a well-known figure in SIDS."

Hasselmeyer, of course, was far from the only one enthralled by Steinschneider's theory, though few were as influential. But her affection for him didn't mean he was going to get carte blanche from her agency. In fact, it would not be her decision. As the chief of the infant mortality branch, she was part of the grant review process but had no vote on the application. Grants were approved by separate committees and then managed by administrators like Hasselmeyer. This division of power was a kind of checks-and-balances system to preserve the integrity of the megamillion-dollar process of government-funded research. But it did not eliminate subtle influences. It was within Hasselmeyer's powers to discourage any overly harsh assessments of Steinschneider and his past work, which she had overseen. The Syracuse grant hadn't brought the apnea theory closer to proof, but Steinschneider had done the work he said he would, and that was all the government asked. Hasselmeyer saw her role as encouraging science. It was for peer reviewers and grant committees to scrutinize the scientists.

Steinschneider was a master when it came to making his theory seem worthier than any other, but even Hasselmeyer thought his new grant application was extravagant. The night before she and Sydney Segal came for the site visit, they told him he had to diminish his expectations. "Al, it's just too much money," Segal said. "You have to cut it down." Steinschneider thought this was nonsense. He had the best theory, he had the data and the formulas. But he hadn't proved it yet. How could they hold him back now? As they tussled, Steinschneider grew increasingly agitated. Segal tried to calm him. Even in science, he reminded him, compromises sometimes had to be made.

After the site visit and a few more skirmishes with Steinschneider, the grant committee retired to its deliberations. Each member rated the application on a scale of one to five. "We were enthusiastic about Maryland," Segal said later. "I don't think we thought about what the accomplishments were in Syracuse."

Steinschneider was breathless to know his fate. He called Hasselmeyer constantly.

"Did I get it?" he would ask.

"Al, don't ask me," Hasselmeyer would say.

"Am I going to get it?"

"Al, I can't tell you."

Tildon was optimistic; he had been through this often enough to know when the vibes were good. Steinschneider didn't allow himself such confidence. When he got the letter that said they were in, Steinschneider called Hasselmeyer. "Why didn't you tell me?" he asked gleefully.

"You don't have it till you have it," she said. "Now you have it."

The NICHD agreed to a project that would cost the government $4,682,289—more than a quarter of the entire federal SIDS research budget for the five years it would last. Caught up in the excitement of the times, the NICHD was not only putting its money on Steinschneider but seriously upping the ante, and the news reverberated through the SIDS world. It was the culmination of everything that had made apnea the magic word in SIDS the past five years.

The grant was announced by the NICHD that summer. Interviewed by *Washington Post* science reporter B. D. Colen, Steinschneider assessed his team's chances of cracking the mystery of SIDS in characteristic language. "If we're really crazy lucky," he said, "at the end of five or ten years we may know if we're heading in the right direction."

Throughout the months when he and Tildon were thinking big numbers, Steinschneider knew Project A had one problem: the monitors. There was still nothing on the market that he was enthusiastic about sending into people's homes. Besides a more reliable machine, he wanted one that was compact and could record, not just monitor, both respiration and heart rate. The best idea he'd heard was from an engineer in a small town near Buffalo who said he would jury-rig an Air-Shields apnea monitor, an EKG monitor, and a recorder made by a company called Oxford.

One day, Steinschneider got a call from a businessman in Georgia who'd heard he'd moved to Maryland and was about to start a major apnea research project that involved home monitoring. It was Pete Petit, calling from Marietta.

Steinschneider barely remembered him; it had been nearly four years since

Petit had brought his photoelectric idea up to Syracuse, and he was not very good with names. But Petit had not forgotten Steinschneider. He had been following the developments in SIDS and wanted to come up and talk about where Steinschneider saw things headed.

Petit was now in his late thirties, a man who like Al Steinschneider didn't give up on what he believed in. The infant monitor had never left the top of his list. He had concentrated on selling ventilators to hospitals and raising money to keep his business afloat, but it was all a prelude to the home apnea monitor. Abe Bergman had already persuaded the Federal Trade Commission to prohibit companies from using the words "crib death" in their advertising. He had also gotten the American Academy of Pediatrics to adopt a position statement saying monitors were fine for research projects, but not for general home use. But Petit was undeterred. The SIDS parent in him told him it was right. The businessman in him told him it was smart.

Petit sat with Steinschneider in a tiny conference room in the hospital and heard all about the massive research project being launched in Baltimore. Steinschneider told him his problem. He planned to test thousands of babies with the high hope of proving that SIDS babies just stopped breathing and died because no one got to them soon enough to resuscitate them. He needed a good machine.

Petit went home and crunched his own numbers. The Oxford recorder ran on batteries. That alone would cost thousands of dollars a year. He thought he could do better. He called Steinschneider the next day. "I'm going to get the equipment for your project," he said.

"Fine," Steinschneider told him. "You have six weeks."

A week later, Petit came back with a prototype. It was similar in principle to the Air-Shields monitor, but it would do what Steinschneider wanted and be smaller and less expensive. It would incorporate an Oxford recorder that would run on house current. Steinschneider thought it was clever—and it worked. How much would it cost? Petit said it depended on Oxford. "I have two hundred thousand dollars," Steinschneider told him. "Go out to lunch with the Oxford guy and divvy it up any way you want."

Petit called his new product the 16000 model—for selling purposes, simply the Healthdyne Infant Monitor. Steinschneider ordered several dozen, and Petit produced them in four months. Maternity, meanwhile, began delivering babies to Steinschneider's baking sleep labs. Project A was off the ground. And Pete Petit could finally see success on the horizon. He thought he could produce these monitors on a large scale for a marketplace that Steinschneider, with the aid of the federal government, was helping create.

———

One day Steinschneider heard from a young neonatology research fellow at Washington, D.C.'s Children's Hospital who had just encountered his first SIDS death. Dr. Steven Weinstein was calling for a consultation and wound up with a personal grand rounds. Steinschneider invited him up to Baltimore and Weinstein followed him around the lab, listening to him describe the finer points of apnea. "He was truly the smartest guy I had ever met," Weinstein recalled. "The clarity of thought . . . I had never met anyone like him." Steinschneider liked Weinstein, too, and imagined the value someone like the energetic young research physician could bring to his team. Soon after, Steinschneider offered him a job and a promise: He would have a lot of babies to study and an important place in the massive SIDS research project—right alongside the chief.

Steinschneider kept his promise. By the time the renovation of the hospital's 5D wing was complete, he was presiding over seven high-tech physiological labs, staffed by six nurses and fifteen technicians. The babies arrived as if on a conveyer belt from the maternity ward a floor above. The lab nurses wrapped gauze around the infants' tiny hands to hold down the electrodes that carried three hours of impulses to graph paper for future analysis. "The only entry criteria was that a baby needed to be healthy enough to go from the sixth to the fifth floor," Weinstein remembered. Four weeks later, the babies would be brought back for another round of testing. There were also newborns from other hospitals in the Baltimore area, which allowed the team to study up to seventy babies a week when the project was running at capacity— and to send several a week home with Healthdyne monitors and log books. At one point, Weinstein calculated, he was personally studying one of every hundred babies born in Maryland, along with apparently apneic infants referred by doctors from twenty other states who had heard about the program. Weinstein spent half his day measuring the respiratory functions of babies, and at night, he would go home with Steinschneider and pore over the day's data as Roz served dinner. The two men sat at a small poker table and worked until ten o'clock, three or four nights a week.

Steinschneider's devotion to his thesis was astonishing to Weinstein. The grant was clearly his one big chance to prove his long-simmering hypothesis, and he was going to do it with mountains of polygraph paper and a forest of digits and decimal points. Though Weinstein made sure to spend half his day seeing patients, he saw that his mentor was happy with a stack of paper and a calculator. "Laying hands on a patient? Steinschneider? Never," Weinstein said bemusedly. "I'd drag him to the bedside."

But it was not long before Weinstein, too, found himself consumed by the great experiment. Two years into it, he gave up on general neonatology to work full-time with Steinschneider in the lab.

The apnea projects were by far the most prominent—Project A was prolonged sleep apnea and SIDS, Project B was prenatal factors and prolonged
sleep apnea—but Steinschneider's staff and colleagues were also busy with
the others: the placenta study, the cry study, the biochemistry inquiries supervised by Tildon, as well as research into the "psychobiological" impact of a
SIDS death on the family. Each of the projects had a principal investigator—
a P.I.—and Steinschneider oversaw them all. His ultimate plan was the establishment of a SIDS institute—a world-class center that would be dedicated to
research, diagnosis and prevention, training for medical people, and counseling for parents. People interested in SIDS could come from all over the
world to learn and join the battle.

To his new colleagues in Baltimore, it had become obvious that Steinschneider was not just "one of the nation's leading authorities on what little is
known about SIDS," as the *Washington Post*'s Colen had described him, but a
man on a mission. He operated in some mystery, guarding the specific
progress of Project A, while still managing to infuse people with a sense that
he was well on the way toward proving the apnea theory, and if he only had
more money, the proof would come that much sooner. "We got twenty-eight
percent of all the money the federal government was spending on SIDS last
year," he told one reporter, "and I'm saying we need even more." He took
care to couch his theories in the standard scientific caveats, while at the same
time leaving some of his colleagues with the vague impression that he considered these disclaimers an obligatory annoyance. One of them was Tyson
Tildon. For the first time, Steinschneider had someone looking over his
shoulder. It was someone who didn't like what he saw.

From the very first day they had met, Tildon had realized that Steinschneider was a persuasive advocate of his theory. "He's *smooth,*" he thought.
Tildon wasn't overly troubled by Steinschneider's vanity—he could handle it
and he'd seen worse. But it became something else when he began suspecting
that Steinschneider's dogmatism was infecting the integrity of the project. It
seemed to Tildon that Steinschneider was intent on confirming his theory, no
matter what the data showed.

When the first baby in the project died, and the autopsy confirmed the
SIDS diagnosis, Steinschneider went back to the cardiorespiratory measurements that had been taken at the baby's first and fourth weeks of life. He did
the same thing when a second baby died. When Tildon asked him what he
was finding, Steinschneider said he hadn't collected enough data yet. "I heard
that a lot," Tildon said. "Meanwhile, he's going off to Oregon or someplace
presenting stuff he wouldn't show back here."

After the third death, Tildon tried to pin Steinschneider down: What *were* the data showing? "It shows apnea is related to SIDS," Steinschneider said. Tildon detected that the evidence was less than overwhelming. He asked to see the raw data. Steinschneider showed him the numbers—how much apnea and heart irregularity the SIDS babies had, compared with the results from the babies who had not died—and explained how they provided evidence of his theory.

Tildon studied the numbers. They didn't add up. The babies who died had experienced no more apnea than those who lived. If anything, he thought, the results showed a possible abnormality of the heart, not of respiration. The data so far didn't support the theory that you could predict SIDS by measuring apnea. In fact, you couldn't point to these numbers and say apnea had anything at all to do with SIDS.

Steinschneider was unbothered. You don't appreciate the nuances of apnea, he told Tildon dismissively. And you don't understand statistics. Don't get hung up on the raw numbers; It's all in the PSA formulas. *"There's* the link," he insisted.

"Bullshit," Tildon said. "There's no correlation here."

Steinschneider responded elaborately. It wasn't black and white, he said—apnea was so much more subtle than that. That's why he was always retooling his formulas, always trying to find the one that worked. "Al, this is sophistry," Tildon said finally. "You're trying to con me." There was a saying: If you tortured data long enough, sooner or later they would confess to something. At meetings of the research team, Tildon was disturbed to see how effectively Steinschneider argued his distorted interpretations. Tildon had been around long enough to know that the world was filled with dogmatic scientists. He liked to quantify things whenever possible and figured that 20 percent of the scientists walking the earth were stuck on either their own beliefs or someone else's. But Steinschneider was on the far end of the self-approval scale, and the consequences were disquieting. There were moments when Tildon thought of Werner Erhard. "Remember est?" he said. "It was like that." Steinschneider was in a position to lead a lot of people astray and, Tildon was dismayed to find, that was exactly what he was doing.

In Boston, Daniel Shannon and Dorothy Kelly were digging their own paths at the forefront of the apnea movement, and with no less tenacity than Steinschneider. They didn't have a fat federal grant like he did, but they did have Shannon's authority and Kelly's entrepreneurial spirit—along with the priceless prestige of Harvard and Massachusetts General, the venerable teaching hospital perhaps most famous for its imperial "Ether Dome," an operating-

room-in-the-round at the top of the original building where the use of anes-
thesia was first demonstrated in 1846.

Though she was still only a research fellow, soon after launching her home
apnea monitoring program in 1975, Kelly had told Shannon they ought to
begin charging for the service. They could use the money to finance their
research. Shannon liked the idea and found that his protégée was right. Monitoring fees quickly paid for a sleep lab and a staff. Three years later, Kelly
was still sending babies home with cumbersome contraptions Shannon had
gotten his MIT students to rig out of Air-Shields monitors and Oxford
recorders. But one day in 1978, with the Steinschneider market sewn up, Pete
Petit flew up to Boston to talk to Kelly about her monitoring needs. He listened carefully, wrote everything down, and shipped five new monitors up
from Atlanta a few months later. Kelly sent the machines out into the field
and immediately began getting calls from irate parents. The new model,
slightly different from the one Healthdyne had built for Steinschneider two
years before, was as temperamental as a Boston politician. Petit made an
emergency trip north, and realized there was a design flaw in the electronic
board. He said he'd fix it. Kelly said she'd test it—for a price. For Petit, it was
the beginning of another important doctor-businessman relationship. The
retooled Healthdyne monitor worked much better, and helped Kelly turn her
home-monitoring program into a thriving enterprise.

The Mass General team used a method different from Steinschneider's to
assess a baby's presumed peril. Rather than turning up the heat, recording respiration for two or three hours when the infant was a few days old and again
four weeks later, and then feeding the results into a mysterious formula, Kelly
and Shannon took a more straightforward approach. They kept their lab at
normal room temperature and recorded respiration and heart rates just
once—but continuously for twelve or twenty-four hours. These were the
"pneumograms" that yielded a hard copy tracking the infant's cardiopulmonary pattern for that day. Though like Steinschneider they had not established what constituted normal respiration, the Boston doctors judged those
babies with "abnormal" pneumograms to be at higher risk of SIDS and most
in need of a home monitor.

Meanwhile, Kelly's continued fascination with the familial question made
the Mass General clinic a magnet for SIDS parents worried about losing
another baby. She and Shannon began encountering a few families who lost
two and even three babies. They confirmed their beliefs and joined their statistical database. Kelly let it be known that by her calculations, parents who
had already lost one baby to SIDS had ten times the normal risk of losing
another. When she tested these subsequent siblings, she found a high percentage of them had abnormal pneumograms. It fortified her faith in the

apnea theory and heightened the anxieties of the parents, who needed no persuasion to put their babies on monitors at home.

The monitors didn't come cheap. Kelly's detailed price list ran half a page, with program charges, doctors' fees, hospital charges, and a full array of lab tests. An average baby in the Mass General program spent eight months on a home monitor, by which point the baby's parents (or their health insurance carrier, if they were fortunate to have one so liberal) had paid as much as $4,000. By the time she finished her fellowship and joined the faculty of Harvard in 1979, Kelly had established a lucrative business for Massachusetts General—and a power base for herself and Shannon. They had more than a hundred babies at a time on home monitors.

Kelly's reputation around Boston grew progressively controversial. Many of her colleagues thought she was being taken in by the overreactions of parents and were skeptical of her prognosis about subsequent siblings, but they referred babies to her just the same. They didn't want a malpractice suit on their hands should something unexpected happen. "Most people thought it was ridiculous to put babies on monitors," she acknowledged. "The Boston community thought it was not correct medicine. They referred babies but still talked bad about me. 'Yeah, she always monitors,' they'd say."

Kelly may not have been held in the highest regard among some members of Boston medical society, but there was plenty of interest in her ideas in other quarters, in Massachusetts and well beyond. With Shannon she was now writing papers on SIDS and apnea—and the familial factor in both—and by 1978 doctors from all over the country were referring babies to them. Kelly was also traveling constantly, spreading the gospel of monitoring with the implicit imprimatur of Harvard and Mass General. She gave grand rounds at medical schools and hospitals, often ending up on a neonatal intensive care unit looking at a problem patient, offering advice that nearly always included home monitoring. "I was invited to virtually every state," she said. "People couldn't get enough of me."

Shannon's influence was quieter, but no less potent. By this point he had decided to give up the ICU he had founded, taking over as chief of the pediatric pulmonary department instead. This allowed him to focus his work exclusively on babies with respiratory problems. In essence the pulmonary department became an apnea center—one of the country's first and by far the most prestigious, more clinically oriented than Steinschneider's research project in Baltimore. While his protégée traveled the country, Shannon did his work closer to home. He took on the most serious cases of apparent "near-miss SIDS" reported by parents and referred by pediatricians from throughout the Northeast—cases that often turned into data that they published as evidence of the apnea theory.

Though they shared many of the same ideas and goals, Shannon was put off by Steinschneider's evangelism and kept him at "greater than arm's length," as he later put it. Their otherwise natural alliance was also undermined by an inevitable sense of competition. Shannon considered the apnea theory as much his idea as Steinschneider's—he just hadn't been the first to publicize it or to do so as dramatically. With the monitoring question emerging as the theory's flash point, Shannon was not averse to allowing Kelly to be seen as Steinschneider's most public ally.

The controversy was now moving from the pages of *Pediatrics* into the workaday world of ten thousand pediatricians' offices. Though the Boston and Baltimore programs were drawing referrals from across the country, most pediatricians remained skeptical of the idea of putting hospital equipment in people's homes and expecting parents to perform possibly life-saving measures—and to know when such a thing was required. It wasn't a question even Kelly and Steinschneider could answer. But apnea had taken on a life of its own, a theory had become a cause, and inevitably, their fervent beliefs began to have a grip on the fears of parents and the insecurities—even gullibility—of doctors.

"Steinschneider and Kelly believed they had struck eureka," recalled one of the many doctors who referred cases to Kelly in the early days, a New York neonatologist and SIDS specialist named Andrew Steele. "But nothing was verified scientifically. A lot of people were jumping into believing something was abnormal when it wasn't. Physicians who run clinical programs aren't scientists, and unless you're involved in research or trained to think critically, you can get sucked in, to the point of no return. It's easy to just follow the leader. Before I understood the physiology, I said, 'This sounds good. I'm helping families. These famous people are doing it.' "

In 1978, the Academy of Pediatrics tried to bring some order by appointing a Task Force on Prolonged Apnea. The task force could not be described as disinterested. Among its members were Alfred Steinschneider, Dorothy Kelly, Daniel Shannon, Warren Guntheroth, and Marie Valdes-Dapena. The NICHD's Hasselmeyer was a consultant. Joan Hodgman, the USC researcher heading the $3 million government-sponsored study of infant respiration, was the voice of dissent.

By this point Hodgman had concluded from her extensive studies of normal babies that breathing patterns were so varied during those early months of autonomic instability that it was bad science to describe some arbitrary measurement as a marker of abnormal apnea, and it was no science at all to use it as a predictor of SIDS. But hers remained an unpopular view. "It was not appreciated that normal babies have apnea," she recalled. "It was a dirty thought that babies stop breathing and heart rates drop. In fact, we found that our risk babies had *less* apnea than normal babies. But I was not following the party line." Predictably, Hodgman's argument that home monitoring had no valid basis did not go over well with several of her colleagues on the Academy task force. "How can you withhold this life-saving equipment from these babies?" Shannon asked indignantly at one point during the panel's debate. To which Hodgman replied, "We have now left science and gone somewhere else."

The task force ultimately voted to adopt a statement, published later that year in *Pediatrics,* saying that "it seems likely that some victims of the sudden infant death syndrome have succumbed to unrelieved prolonged apnea," and that "twenty-four hour surveillance is critical to the management of prolonged apnea. Settings for intensive observation and care may include the appropriately staffed and equipped acute care hospital, and the infant's home." *And the infant's home.* These four words would change the SIDS world irrevocably. Soon after, Jerold Lucey published a commentary by a group of doctors titled "Home Monitoring: A Huge Problem." Their main objection was that doctors were sending babies home without much support for their parents, and they urged states to establish monitoring centers.

Pete Petit was on the verge of becoming a very wealthy man. Healthdyne was the only company with the kind of equipment the Academy task force said was "an acceptable alternative" to hospitalization. With more than a little help from the clinical research labs in Baltimore and Boston, and using the Academy statement to persuade insurance companies to approve reimbursements, Petit's company began selling SIDS prevention—$2,500 retail—to the wider world. The first battlefront was the consumer health-equipment industry itself. "These companies were distributing bedpans and wheelchairs," recalled Steve Combs, a Healthdyne executive at the time. "We had to literally persuade dealers to sell these things."

Thus 1978 was a pivotal year. The Academy of Pediatrics gave the green light to the home monitoring concept. Healthdyne moved into a new plant in Marietta and went into full production. Within a year, its annual revenues would pass the million-dollar mark for the first time. And Alfred Steinschneider was at the height of his prestige. That year, he was appointed to the ethics committee of the Society for Research in Child Development.

By the spring of 1980, nearly two thousand babies had come through Steinschneider's apnea project in Baltimore, and though the reams of polygraph paper revealed nothing even remotely conclusive about apnea and SIDS, he was undiscouraged. Later that year, the Sudden Infant Death Syndrome Institute of the University of Maryland would be formally dedicated at a black-tie dinner.

Steinschneider envisioned the fledgling institute as a departure from the customary SIDS organization. "I had begun to see that the SIDS movement had become a bereavement group, and I was participating in it," he later reflected. "I saw pamphlets that said the ultimate victims are the parents. I appreciate the pain but that's like saying heart attack is an issue of the sur-viving widow. When I'm taking care of patients in the hospital I'm not wor-ried about the visitors." Didn't SIDS exist in the unique emotional context of mothers and fathers and babies? "Don't get caught up in it." That was the paradox he saw in SIDS research: To get the money to figure out how to save babies, you had to appeal to people's sympathy for parents. But don't get caught up in it.

The SIDS Institute would run on federal grants and private donations. It would be under the auspices of the medical school, but have its own governing board stocked with major names from Baltimore society who could bring in money. Steinschneider would be at the helm, the executive director and guiding spirit. Tyson Tildon would be in charge of the research unit, essentially the number two job, but he felt as excited about the institute as Steinschneider. Despite his ongoing worries about Steinschneider's scien-tific principles, he saw the institute as a great opportunity for the medical school.

Tildon played a crucial role—he knew where the money was. He recruited the institute's first board chairman, Sigmund Hyman, the president of a Baltimore investment fund. Tildon's brother, Charles, the president of a local community college, also joined the board. The fund-raising committee was chaired by the president of the Sun Life Insurance Company. With Stein-schneider's vision, Tildon's connections, and the grant that gave them an ongoing relationship with the National Institutes of Health, the institute quickly became one of Baltimore's more aggressive and successful charities. The dedication dinner attracted a thousand people to the Hyatt Regency. Howard Cosell, a friend of Sigmund Hyman's, was a big draw as the guest speaker. He made an impassioned speech and a sizable donation.

Saul and Sylvia Goldberg were now part of Steinschneider's world. He would come to their house for dinner and talk about SIDS late into the night. "He saw us as a conduit for fund-raising," Saul would later say. The institute, meanwhile, hired a Baltimore public relations operative named Tom Moran to be its full-time fund-raising coordinator. When Moran recruited the enter-tainer Ben Vereen into the cause, Steinschneider flew out to California with Roz and, over sushi in Encino, pitched SIDS as he'd never pitched it before. Vereen became a devoted supporter of the Maryland SIDS Institute. He was the star attraction at the institute's second annual black-tie dinner, which raised $195,000. Vereen also did a public service television spot for the SIDS Institute, dancing on colorful oversized blocks, and sang its praises during his concert tours. His manager, Pamela Cooper, was swept away by

Steinschneider. She talked about him to another of her clients, Dionne Warwick.

In large part, it was Steinschneider's passion, and the hope he held out, that appealed to idealistic impulses. "He was always on the verge of a major breakthrough," Hyman remarked some years later. And Steinschneider fed off the esteem. When he held his first major scientific conference a year after the institute began operating—a meeting on the management of prolonged apnea—he already had his eyes on something much bigger. It had been seven years since the last international SIDS symposium, in Toronto. It was about time for another one. As "the major world center for interdisciplinary investigation of the causes of SIDS," Steinschneider wrote in a proposal to the board, the SIDS Institute was the logical host. It would be expensive—Steinschneider wanted to fly in sixty panelists from around the world, and put them up at the Baltimore Hyatt Regency—but the institute was not hurting for money.

It came from Baltimore and beyond: small donations from bake sales and baby-photo contests and bigger ones from private foundations and chapters of the Goldbergs' Guild from across the country. It was a true grassroots campaign. Large companies accounted for a small percentage of the donations—with one notable exception. In December 1981, at the close of a year in which his company's revenues reached $10 million, Parker Petit took Healthdyne public. He sold 26 percent of the company in a stock offering that raised $11 million. He had grand visions for the money: He wanted to keep building the infant apnea market, while diversifying into all kinds of health-care products. He did not forget his roots, however. Just before Petit hawked Healthdyne to Wall Street, Al Steinschneider and Sig Hyman flew down to Atlanta to personally receive a gift for the SIDS Institute from the chairman: five thousand shares of Healthdyne stock, worth $90,000, to start the Parker H. Petit Endowment Fund. Petit was feeling confident and generous. Along with Lady Limerick's United Kingdom Foundation, he pledged to help underwrite the international conference Steinschneider was planning for the following June.

"The SIDS Institute is committed to getting the problem solved as fast as humanly possible," Steinschneider told a young woman writing for the University of Maryland's public relations bulletin. "Anything that can get this problem solved sooner, that's what we want to do." But there was another kind of problem, the kind a scientist did not discuss in public, that was continuing to brew in Steinschneider's lab. His theory was not panning out.

By the end of the third year of the NICHD grant, he and his team had collected data on roughly half the nearly five thousand babies born in University

Hospital since they'd started Project A. Using a variety of his Prolonged Sleep Apnea calculations, Steinschneider found that about ten percent of the normal newborns he tested had scores high enough to place them in the category he defined as being "at risk" for prolonged apnea, and hence, SIDS. This worked out to fifty in five hundred. However, the known risk of SIDS was less than *one* in five hundred. Even if one of Steinschneider's fifty "at risk" babies was indeed vulnerable to dying of SIDS—still only an assumption—it didn't explain much about the other forty-nine he picked out. Moreover, these babies were not simply research subjects; they were people's children. Steinschneider and Weinstein informed the parents of babies with high PSA scores that their newborns were candidates for SIDS, news that put some of them in tears. Then they would offer them a chance to save their babies' lives. Take the monitor home. When it beeps, get to your baby as fast as you can. They wouldn't release these babies until their parents had been taught CPR.

One of these babies was a boy named Michael Grimes. Close friends of his parents had lost a baby to SIDS, so when Michael was born at the University of Maryland Hospital in the spring of 1979, they jumped at the chance to have him tested for "symptoms of SIDS," as one reporter later expressed it. "He had very high risk scores," Michael's mother explained. He spent nine months on a home monitor, and every so often his parents would be summoned to his crib. "Once, he was a little pale and that scared me, and another time his heartbeat had dropped," his mother said. A few months after coming off the monitor, healthy and alive, Michael was appointed the SIDS Institute's first Poster Baby. He appeared on bus cards and in television spots, and at the Institute's dedication ceremony—a symbol of survival and hope. "I strongly believe I would not have him now if it were not for the SIDS Institute," said his mother.

What Steinschneider never told parents like the Grimeses was that there was no real evidence that their children had ever been at risk. By this point, five of the babies in the apnea study had died of SIDS, a predictable number for the size of the sample. But Steinschneider's formulas had identified *none* of them in advance. Even with his liberal measurements, taken in the heated lab, none of the five had shown enough apnea to define them as being "at risk." Therefore, none had gone home with a monitor. Conversely, none of the babies who *were* identified as being at risk had died. Had they been saved by monitors? For a scientist who had spent a decade romancing his theory, it was much easier to believe than to prove. Almost 70 percent of his monitor families reported that their babies had a prolonged episode of apnea at home. But the tapes showed that only 38 percent actually had even a single pause that lasted as long as eighteen seconds. It pointed up the self-fulfilling nature of the apnea concept.

Tyson Tildon had gone along with such things as the poster baby idea, and generally tried to keep the peace with Steinschneider, because he believed in the institute. Swept up in the internationally recognized SIDS program he had helped build (and with no authority over Steinschneider anyway), Tildon had found plenty to occupy him outside Steinschneider's labs. "I'm not sure I was paying as much attention to the science as I should have," Tildon said. But as the five-year project was starting to wind down, and he and Steinschneider had to get started on the application for the next five million dollars, Tildon had begun to ask questions again. Even more than before, he was astonished at the lengths Steinschneider went to deny the failure of the data to support his theory.

"He was always trying to put a spin on something," Tildon said. "There would be kids who died of SIDS, and he would not accept that they did not fit his pattern. He would say, 'All these kids had a twenty-second pause,' and I would look at the data and say, 'Number one didn't have that, number three didn't have that, number five didn't have that.' So then he would try to find ways to say that these kids didn't really die of SIDS. He would go down to the medical examiner and argue that they don't really belong in that population. What we had agreed was to let the M.E., an independent person, define what is SIDS. Al would go down there and say, 'Let me see those slides. Did you look for this, did you look for that?' In other words, if it didn't fit his pattern, it wasn't SIDS. That's the point when I really started not believing this guy. We got in these pissing matches. It was always, 'Show me the data.' 'I will tomorrow.' There are people who put five cards in the deck. I don't play poker very well."

Tildon wondered what Steinschneider was going to tell Hasselmeyer and the staff at NICHD. Technically, all he had to show them was that he had performed the studies he said he would. Realistically, however, the United States government was spending a lot of money on the Maryland project and waiting for the payoff—especially from Project A. What Steinschneider presented to Bethesda was a tap dance, agile as any performance by Ben Vereen, on the central issue of whether apnea predicted SIDS.

"We have accomplished most of the objectives established for the current year," he wrote to the NICHD staff in November 1981. By this point, Steinschneider had completed his analysis of the data he had accumulated on 2,515 babies in Maryland and written almost a dozen complex formulas for measuring the risk of SIDS. But he was still using the Hoyt babies to argue his theory, and even managed to employ the Maryland deaths as further evidence that he was right. "An analysis has been completed on nine infants studied physiologically within the first week of life who subsequently died of SIDS," Steinschneider wrote. He was referring to the five in Maryland and four in

Syracuse—Molly and Noah, and two others who died in the five years that followed. (He repeated his incorrect statement about Molly, whom he had not studied until the fourth week of life.) "A statistically significant number of SIDS cases had elevated scores. These results indicate that potential SIDS victims are, as a group, physiologically different from the general population even within the first week of life. They also are consistent with the hypothesis implicating both sleep apnea and laryngeal apnea in the etiology of SIDS."

But then he acknowledged the bottom line: "It is also clear that the sleep apnea or feeding apnea measures when examined individually are inadequate for the routine clinical identification of infants at risk for SIDS because of the relatively large number of infants who would be classified as at risk. The PSA$_4$ scores inadequately identified infants who subsequently died of SIDS." His conclusion was that his theory and the formulas he employed were valid—even if he could not show that they had saved any babies.

Where Steinschneider's science fell short, he compensated with his indefatigable salesmanship. He toured the country, raising money with affecting speeches about the need to stop SIDS. "Al was under pressure of informing the world that we were figuring out SIDS," Steven Weinstein remembered. "He was trying to be as visible as he could." Steinschneider would visit a city and arrange for maximum visibility with the local SIDS group. The advance people let the local newspapers and broadcasters know that the nation's foremost authority on SIDS was headed to town, and the SIDS Institute's newsletter trumpeted his travels. Some of his fellow researchers found all this increasingly pretentious. "Al Steinschneider became a name in lights," remarked Bruce Beckwith. "The white knight with the answer to SIDS. The kindly scientist who's going to help everybody: 'If you just give me enough money, the answer is right around the corner.' His talks had the aura of an Oral Roberts tent meeting."

Steinschneider's appetite for the limelight was apparently voracious. In the fall of 1981, a Maryland biochemistry graduate student named Marco Chacon, working under Tildon, found that babies who died of SIDS appeared to have elevated levels of the thyroid hormone T$_3$ in their blood. Steinschneider scoffed at the research, but Tildon and Chacon published it in the *Journal of Pediatrics,* and Tildon made sure word got out. The discovery, he told the press, was "the largest single breakthrough in SIDS research that has ever been found." Even he was vulnerable to the sort of hyperexcitement that was an occupational hazard in SIDS research. In his case, there was also a hunger for vindication. The finding, he said, meant that SIDS researchers should now direct their attention to the neuroendocrine system.

Steinschneider stewed. When the reporters asked what he thought, he said the research was preliminary and of unclear importance. Producers from

ABC television, though, liked the graduate student angle, and invited Chacon to New York to appear on *Good Morning America*. Steinschneider wasn't particularly interested in the neuroendrocrine system, and he didn't believe in the hormone findings, but he did believe in network television. Without telling Tildon, he called the producers and suggested it would be appropriate for the director of the SIDS Institute to appear with the graduate student. Steinschneider and Chacon rode the train up to New York. Chacon went on and talked about thyroid hormones. And Steinschneider said that yes, it was an interesting finding, but the most important leads in SIDS were coming out of the sleep labs. Tildon watched the show from Baltimore. "His ego got bigger by the week," he said.

With his growing renown, Steinschneider took phone calls all the time from all kinds of people. Pediatricians, philanthropists, pathologists, parents, reporters, fund-raisers, epidemiologists, biochemists, statisticians, businessmen, entertainers, publicists, countesses.

And detectives. One day, he got a call from an investigator from Syracuse, his former hometown. The man had been referred to Steinschneider by the Onondaga County medical examiner, Martin Hilfinger. How is Marty? Steinschneider asked. Well, just fine, said the detective. I've got a case here, and I was wondering if you could help me with it. Steinschneider listened to the details. Yes, he said, three children could certainly die in one family. It was unusual, but it happened. There were a number of cases in the literature. The detective listened to a short discourse on SIDS and apnea. He thanked the doctor for his time. *No help there,* Frank Budzielek thought, hanging up the phone.

27

Nineteen eighty-two brought Steinschneider trouble in Baltimore. In some ways, it was the mirror image of his last year in Syracuse. Marvin Cornblath, who had promised and given him the world, had been replaced as Maryland pediatrics chairman by a professor from Duke University named David Lang. Lang was Frank Oski all over again, and by 1982, he had had enough. "He was demanding, cocksure," Lang remembers. "He thought he was the answer to SIDS."

Meanwhile, the SIDS Institute was running into financial problems. Steinschneider had insisted on overseeing patient accounts for the clinical unit, and he proved a less than skillful bill collector. Expenses were exceeding income by $10,000 a month, and Lang had to take out loans from the dean's office to keep the institute going. The university chancellor wrote to board chairman Sigmund Hyman that this couldn't go on for long.

But it was the least of Steinschneider's troubles. To realize his plans to expand the institute he needed another multimillion-dollar grant from the NICHD when the current one ran its course. With Tyson Tildon looking on warily, he put together a proposal to continue his quest to discover a way to predict and prevent SIDS. But the disappointing results of Project A made it a tough sell, even for him. The grant committee arrived in Baltimore for its site visit in a decidedly different mood from the last time; not even Eileen Hasselmeyer could help him now. Steinschneider knew what was in store—there had already been several heated telephone conversations—and he came armed for battle, his troops behind him. Sydney Segal tried to keep the peace but the room grew as hot as one of Steinschneider's sleep labs. The message from the government was plain: The apnea project was a failure, and we're not here to sign another check. If you want to stay in the game, we're glad to have you. But you'll need to change your direction and start asking some new questions. Otherwise, you're done. "He didn't take it well," Segal remembers. "He threatened to withdraw the whole application." It was a hollow threat. The agency had little to show for its millions of dollars. Steinschneider could resubmit the application or not. It was his choice. The committee went home to Bethesda, and Steinschneider and Weinstein fumed. "They brought in the biggest bunch of Mickey Mouse investigators," Weinstein would later say. "They had no idea what Al was doing, what his vision was."

Steinschneider began thinking about his options. He was not getting what he wanted, the SIDS Institute was in trouble, and his relations with both the university and the government were crumbling. With that as the backdrop, he turned his attention to the event he'd planned for more than a year. He expected it to be the high moment of his career. What he didn't see was that it wasn't only in Baltimore that his fragile construct was beginning to come apart.

Guests of Alfred Steinschneider, Lady Limerick, and Parker H. Petit, fifty-nine of the world's preeminent SIDS researchers began streaming into Baltimore on Sunday night, June 27, 1982, for the International Research Conference on The Sudden Infant Death Syndrome. The experts, along with 250 other scientists and health professionals, came from all over America and twelve other countries and headed for the Hyatt Regency Hotel. Despite all the turmoil in Baltimore, Steinschneider was beaming. This was *his* SIDS conference. He wore his apnea theory like a badge of honor.

For the first time in two decades, Abe Bergman was not in attendance at an international SIDS conference. Steinschneider did not reciprocate the invitation Bergman had made to him back in 1969, and underscored it by personally calling Bergman's colleague Bruce Beckwith to ask him to come. Arriving at the meeting, Beckwith was eyed with barely concealed hostility by the man whose work he'd so openly criticized, Richard Naeye. Both would be on a pathology panel with Russell Fisher, Molly Dapena, and Britain's John Emery, all of whom had spent nearly a decade puzzling over the enigma of Naeye's tissue markers. Another panel would bring together a number of epidemiologists who had spent years pondering the emotionally charged question brought into prominence by Steinschneider's 1972 paper—the question of familial SIDS. Peter Froggatt, the researcher from Northern Ireland who in 1969 had presented the first data indicating SIDS could run in families, would discuss the issue with such newer investigators as Susan Standfast, a SIDS researcher from Albany, New York, who tended to believe SIDS did not recur. A couple of years before, in fact, Standfast had received a visit from a New York State Police investigator who wanted to know the chances of three babies dying in one family. Astronomical, she had told Harvey LaBar.

And in one of the final sessions, Steinschneider would be exploring the concept of "high-risk" babies with a panel, chaired by Sydney Segal, that included Dotty Kelly and a British pediatrician named David Southall, who had undertaken a major test of Steinschneider's apnea theory and was rumored to be arriving from London with the results in his briefcase. Hovering around the entire assembly, meanwhile, was Healthdyne's Pete Petit. Steinschneider paid no attention to the meeting's resemblance to the gathering of a bickering family. The irony was conspicuous. Steinschneider himself had lit the match a decade before. Now he was presiding over the combustion.

He took the podium just after breakfast on Monday morning. "This is, for me, a particularly exciting moment," he said. "I am convinced that in the next few days we will uncover many differences in opinion on how the results obtained are to be interpreted. I would strongly encourage the clear articulation of these points of difference. . . . We must never lose sight of the fact that infants are dying daily. . . ."

Countess Limerick greeted the doctors, thanked Healthdyne, then recited another of her eccentrically astute verses, summing up all that had happened in the increasingly fractious SIDS world in the eight years since Toronto:

> *The journals with paper abounded,*
> *Their contents amazed and astounded,*
> *Is it cause or effect?*
> *Are there clues to protect?*
> *In conclusion, we still feel confounded.*

As the keynote speaker, Belfast's Peter Froggatt offered the most poignant perspective of this turbulent but ever-hopeful group. A man of formidable intellect and a writerly ear, Froggatt was an epidemiologist who had spent many years pondering not merely the logarithms and pie charts of SIDS incidence, but the culture of science that had developed around the mystery in the two decades since "First Seattle," as he called the premier SIDS meeting in 1963. Froggatt had always found it interesting that SIDS was a national preoccupation primarily in those countries—most notably the United States and Britain, and to a lesser degree Canada and Australia—that had experienced the twentieth century's most dramatic declines in infant mortality. "And as this lethal tide receded, so it uncovered this entity of sudden unexpected and unexplained death in infants, which previously had lain unnoticed beneath the waves: personal tragedies but statistically unimportant." But as the attendance at this and other major SIDS meetings indicated, the hunt had widened. Medical researchers from the Netherlands to New Zealand had made the pursuit of SIDS a worldwide scientific venture.

What, then, was the state of the science in 1982, nineteen years after the first gathering? Froggatt wistfully recalled the "unsuppressed euphoria" that had accompanied the earlier generation of SIDS researchers on their ferry trip home from Orcas Island in 1969. A decade of great bustle and blare ensued, but unhappily the 1970s had turned out to be a disappointing decade—despite the work of "many fine minds, the best techniques, and a scientific rectitude and integrity in which we can all feel proud, much of all this by persons here today." In the new decade, prevention of SIDS seemed "increasingly an ever remote goal if not an actual mirage. New trails were undoubtedly blazed . . . but some are proving perhaps false trails."

As he moved past what seemed a veiled reference to the elusiveness of the apnea theory, Froggatt urged his compatriots to press on—and to broaden their views. For if they continued to see SIDS from the perspective of one disease—one cause, he warned, "crib death may remain a disease of theories with virologists seeing a virological cause, respiratory physiologists seeing respiratory problems, immunologists incriminating immunological aberrations, and cardiologists with eyes only for the heart."

For two days and nights, the researchers discussed, debated, and pondered the continuing puzzle of SIDS in so much conceptual depth that it was often impossible to know that it was dying children they were talking about. The doctors took turns offering their latest observations, and occasionally the exchanges took on a personal edge.

The title of Bruce Beckwith's presentation was "Chronic Hypoxemia in the Sudden Infant Death Syndrome: A Critical Review of the Data Base." After nearly ten years of trying, Beckwith declared at the end of an exhaustive review of the literature, Naeye's peers had been unable to confirm the pathologist's conclusions. Naeye glared. "I wish I'd made all the money in my career that Beckwith has made going around trying to debunk my findings," he muttered angrily.

"What money?" Beckwith replied indignantly, back at his seat. He turned to his side when another panelist, Gordon Vawter, the chief of pathology at Boston's Children's Hospital, leaned over to him. "Thank you for doing that," Vawter said privately. "Somebody's been needing to do it." If Beckwith's review qualified as the official discrediting of the Seven Tissue Markers, it was just a hint of what lay ahead. The uncanny symmetry of apnea and hypoxia—of Steinschneider and Naeye, the one-two punch of the 1970s— would become vivid once more.

———

David Southall had come to Baltimore having spent three years with thousands of polygraph tracings of infant respiration in his lab at London's Cardiothoracic Institute. Financed by a host of public and private British foundations and agencies, Southall had conducted a study of the relationship between breathing patterns, heart rate, and SIDS that dwarfed even Steinschneider's. With his own team in London, a group from the department of medical physics at the Royal Hallamshire Hospital in Sheffield, and a researcher at Thames Polytechnic, Southall had tested thousands of babies and tried to view apnea from half a dozen angles. Conspicuously tight-lipped about what he had found, he had chosen Steinschneider's meeting to announce the results. He came into the meeting room that afternoon and took his seat among his fellow pediatric researchers. Dorothy Kelly would give the first presentation of the session. Southall would follow. Steinschneider would go last.

Since she and Dan Shannon had begun monitoring in 1973, Kelly told the audience, they had seen 202 infants whom they had determined to be at risk. The babies were among those who had come into the hospital after reports of prolonged apneic episodes at home, in some cases resulting in mouth-to-mouth resuscitation. Kelly had evaluated these near-miss babies with pneumograms, confirmed there was an apnea problem that put them at risk, and sent them home on monitors for several months. The results were eye-catching: The parents of thirty-four of these babies later said they had needed to resuscitate them at home yet again. Seven of these resuscitations were unsuccessful. Kelly considered her results credible evidence for the apnea theory. Given the seven deaths, however, they seemed an ambiguous argument for monitors as life savers.

Listening from his seat at the panel table, David Southall found Kelly's numbers perplexing. He wondered whether the Boston team's study groups were too small or their measurements inaccurate. Perhaps it was that they were basing their observations too much on the reports of parents. Whatever the reasons, he was confident their conclusions were wrong. He felt this way primarily because they were so at odds with his own. When Kelly completed her presentation, Southall, a tall and slender man with an air of erudition, made his way to the podium.

Southall had always considered a cessation of breathing efforts to be a plausible if partial explanation for SIDS. But he was worried about the growing use of monitors in the absence of evidence confirming the theory. The demand for the machines had crossed the Atlantic, and Southall didn't like this at all. He would have been happy to prove Steinschneider's hypothesis right, but just as his fellow Briton John Emery had been unable to confirm Richard Naeye's tissue markers, Southall hadn't been able to see what Steinschneider or Shannon and Kelly saw. He flashed his first slide, and got right to the news he had been so carefully guarding.

During two years at three major hospitals, he and his team had made twenty-four-hour pneumograms of 9,251 babies. The audience murmured at the numbers. A third of the babies were low birth weight or prematures thought to be at highest risk. All the babies had been followed prospectively, so that when a baby went on to die of SIDS, as twenty-seven did, Southall went back to the child's pneumogram and looked for evidence of apnea. "None of the recordings on the twenty-seven SIDS cases showed prolonged apnea," he said. Only two had unusually frequent periods of short apnea.

A wave of astonishment washed over the audience. "I almost fell out of my seat," Molly Dapena would say later.

Furthermore, Southall continued, there was no evidence that SIDS ran in families. He had tested and followed 204 siblings of SIDS victims. None died. "Our main criticism of previous sibling studies is that relatively small numbers of cases have been used, perhaps none of which were at increased risk of SIDS," he told his colleagues, some of whom were now trying to read Steinschneider's face, as well as Kelly's. ". . . The relatively low incidence of SIDS means that five hundred infants may have to be studied to include one who will subsequently die."

It was a remark that seemed almost directed at the conference's host. As everyone well knew, Steinschneider's famous paper had included two deaths. Two of the first five babies he studied had died.

Southall kept going. He presented case after case, study after study, slide after slide. He had tried to confirm the apnea theory from every perspective imaginable, but always came up with the same findings. "The data do not support the hypothesis that SIDS is frequently related to apnea," he said.

Steinschneider and Kelly steamed silently as Southall presented his data. "All eyes were on this tiger," Bruce Beckwith remembered.

Now, Southall addressed the other half of the apnea theory. "Home apnea monitoring has been advocated by some as a measure of preventing SIDS," he said. "The evidence provided by this present study would not support home monitoring to detect primary apnea in the general population." He had shown that the pneumograms, embraced so completely by Kelly, didn't predict or help prevent SIDS. "We shouldn't waste time on these technologies," he said flatly.

Southall's findings were unequivocal. He had concluded that just about everything the host of the conference believed was wrong. He began to move away from the podium. In the audience, someone began to applaud. People shifted in their seats to see where it was coming from. It was Bruce Beckwith. He was standing, and clapping. Then others joined him. Molly Dapena was among them. "Southall just blew me away," she said. "It was a fantastic thing to do. A necessary thing to do."

Steinschneider kept calm. He had had no clue in planning the event that Southall would detonate a bomb in his own backyard. And he was the next presenter. He rose from his seat, and walked to the podium with an air of studied confidence. The audience was still, waiting for his response.

"The observation," he began, "that certain categories of infants are at increased risk to die of the Sudden Infant Death Syndrome has provided the basis for a flurry of research studies. This is not surprising. . . ."

Steinschneider was on the defensive, just as he had been with the NICHD committee a few months before, but to the surprise of some who knew him well, he managed to remain the courtly host, following Southall's methodical broadside with his own calm recitation of the facts as he saw them, never deserting his own work for a direct attack on Southall's. He put into play a ringing defense of his concept of "high-risk" babies and of the highly charged doctrine of monitoring. He offered every epidemiological study that ever looked at multiple SIDS, arguing that yes, it could run in families—even if he freely conceded that neither he nor anyone else had produced any scientific evidence. "The incidence of subsequent unexplained death among these infants is not well established," he said, "but has been reported as ranging from twenty percent to one hundred percent." He did not add that he had pulled the 100 percent figure—the notion that every baby in a family could die of SIDS—straight from his 1972 paper. "We believe," Steinschneider said, "that to assume otherwise, without supporting evidence to the contrary, leads only to the self-fulfilling prophecy that infants will die."

If Steinschneider's strategy was to convey to the gathering that he considered Southall's findings just another study by another scientist, it worked. He never mentioned his name or addressed his work. He ended his presentation with his customary statement of frustration and optimism—his call for more research and his unwavering belief in his own judgment. As Froggatt had urged, he would press on. Not everyone had applauded Southall—in fact, his antimonitoring stand brought enough sharp looks and hostile remarks outside the room for Southall to later conclude, "It didn't go over well. The view was I shouldn't interfere—let the clinicians do their work." It was a trenchant assessment of the growing mood of the times. Al Steinschneider would most certainly carry on.

But he would do it elsewhere. His relations with both the university and the NICHD broken beyond repair, Steinschneider called a meeting of the board of the SIDS Institute shortly after the conference, and announced that he wanted to go private. The move would liberate the institute from the shackles of the academic bureaucracy, he told the board members. They would raise more money and no one could tell them how to spend it. He had already decided not to resubmit the grant renewal application to NICHD.

Tyson Tildon was furious. He felt the SIDS Institute was as much his baby as Steinschneider's. He had overseen the medical school's SIDS research since it consisted of a single sleep lab in 1973 and felt every bit as responsible for its phenomenal growth as Steinschneider. "Al," Tildon told him, "you're a slimeball." It rolled off Steinschneider's back.

The board was split. Half thought that Steinschneider *was* the institute, and that he was entitled to leave, taking the private money he'd raised with him. The others felt that there was a deep obligation to the university, and that it would be akin to stealing a public institution.

Tildon was nervous. His brother, Charles, one of the board members, told him not to worry, that the vote was pulling toward keeping the institute at the university. But Charles was wrong. Steinschneider was working behind the scenes. He was leaving, he told the board members, and he was taking the money with him. By this he meant the Parker H. Petit Endowment Fund. In one year, the five thousand shares of Healthdyne stock had tripled in value, to $275,000. Petit sided with Steinschneider. He agreed the money should go to a new private operation they were setting up with Tom Moran, the institute's fund-raiser. They would call it the National Center for the Prevention of SIDS. In the end, Steinschneider managed to persuade a swing voter that this was a battle the university could not win. After some negotiation, it was agreed that Steinschneider would go quietly, with half the Healthdyne money.

For Steinschneider, it was a small price to pay for independence. He made the move official that December, and the Baltimore papers put the news on the front page. "Yes, we're rocking the boat," Steinschneider told the *News American,* "because we believe it's the best way to follow the leads that will make a difference in solving the SIDS problem." Steinschneider said he was leaving because he and the university clashed over research philosophy. "I want to go for the shortest route to prevent deaths. This is my commitment, with no apologies. I'm in a hurry."

He summed up the situation more pithily when he talked to old colleagues. "I told them, 'Screw you, I'll have my own institute and get my own money,'" Steinschneider said to Jack Schneider during a brief trip to Syracuse. His recent colleagues in Baltimore had their own spins on the parting. "I got rid of him," is how pediatrics chairman David Lang saw it. In Baltimore, it was the dismantling of an era. The end of the grant meant the end of a purposeful job for many of the dozens of doctors, nurses, and technicians who made up the research project's labor force.

Steinschneider set up his own shop, but closed it down only a few months later and left Baltimore. In the end, he had not been "crazy lucky," as he had hoped he might when he won the biggest SIDS research grant ever awarded. But he was still convinced he was, as he had put it then, "heading in the right direction." Few were surprised to hear that now the direction was south— that Steinschneider was moving his operation to a fully equipped suite of offices just outside Marietta, Georgia.

28

One British pediatrician notwithstanding, it was commonly believed in America by 1982 that apnea monitors saved babies from dying of SIDS. It was a presumption that percolated up from the most basic of sources.

In Baltimore in 1980, Nancy Kercheval gave birth to a boy she and her husband named Nathaniel. He went directly from maternity to Steinschneider's overheated sleep labs, where he spent two hours on a polygraph and, not surprisingly, had some apneic pauses. None exceeded eight seconds, but Kercheval was told that the pauses were too frequent—Nathaniel was a potential SIDS victim. "My reaction was shock," she wrote when he was four months old and connected to a Healthdyne monitor. "I thought Nathaniel was a perfect baby. He had everything going for him when he was born."

Kercheval happened to be a reporter for the Associated Press. Her thankful story of how Alfred Steinschneider and his Healthdyne monitors were making Nathaniel safe blinked onto the computer screens of editors in newsrooms everywhere in America, many of whom pushed the buttons that put it in front of their readers under headlines like "An Electronic Baby-sitter Wards off Crib Death." "Every time I looked at my baby, I thought it might be the last time I would ever see him alive," she wrote. "But now I'm confident things will be OK . . . Nathaniel is among the 10 percent of babies tested at the SIDS Institute who 'flunked' his sleep study test. So at the age of one month, Nathaniel became a bionic baby with brown and green wires dangling from the legs of his tiny outfits."

By the early 1980s, as the monitoring phenomenon hit its stride, stories about mothers like Nancy Kercheval were everywhere, many of them in magazines aimed at women of childbearing age. The articles commonly

noted that the current thinking about SIDS and monitoring had started with
Steinschneider's paper about the two babies with apnea who had died in
upstate New York. (By this point, their three siblings were all but forgotten.)
Few of the stories were burdened by the caution of earlier times. They were
powerful advertisements for the monitoring industry. "I Saved My Baby from
Crib Death" was the headline over an article in *Redbook*. A page-one story in
The Washington Post reported that a monitor prescribed for a SIDS sibling by
a Georgetown University doctor had "saved the baby's life eight times." And
there was this in the *National Enquirer:* "My Baby Died 200 Times." The
monitors' cultural certification seemed complete when Tyne Daly appeared
in an episode of *Quincy* as a mother of newborn twins who lost one of her
babies to SIDS and put the surviving one on a home apnea monitor.

It was the widespread perception that every time a monitor beeped a baby
was at the precipice of death—another near-miss SIDS, or "near-myth
SIDS," as some skeptics preferred—that helped propagate the belief that
sudden death could be predicted by prior events and that monitors could
intervene. Even *The New York Times,* in a "Healthdyne Gains with Crib
Monitor" business story, described babies as showing "warning signs" of SIDS
that parents could recognize. The article was accompanied by a picture of a
baby hooked to a Healthdyne monitor; the caption explained that his mother
had gotten the monitor after noticing that he had "developed symptoms of
Sudden Infant Death Syndrome" following a viral infection.

It was as if the symptoms were contagious. In New England, more than a
few parents reading about the work of the Harvard team in *The Boston Globe*
suddenly realized their babies had apnea and needed monitors. And more
than a few of their pediatricians got the distinct impression from Kelly and
Shannon that they were virtually committing malpractice if they did not refer
these babies to Mass General for complete workups. Two rooms at the end of
the pediatrics ward were reserved for—and nearly always filled with—
"aborted SIDS cases," as staff members referred to them. At the same time,
pediatricians from around the country, confronting their own perplexing
cases of "apnea," were sending pneumogram tapes to Boston for analysis.
Kelly and her staff put them through a $40,000 machine yielding a hard copy
of the tracings, interpreted the results according to their own apnea protocols,
then ruled on whether the baby in question was at risk of SIDS and needed to
be put on a home monitor.

From its conception, the incongruity of the apnea theory was that it was so
simple yet so vague. A decade into it, the near-miss concept further blurred
the boundary of concern. In the climate of these years, whenever a baby
seemed to be in some sort of distress, or maybe just looked "funny," it was apt
to be called apnea and sometimes a near-miss. By extension, the baby became

absorbed into the SIDS world. Shannon and Kelly helped legitimize this assumption with a widely cited two-part paper in *The New England Journal of Medicine* in April 1982 that implicated apnea as the mechanism of some "near-SIDS"—and by inference linking the theoretical and very subjective near-SIDS with the real thing.

The ambiguity was a perpetual preoccupation among doctors. Even Steinschneider had publicly lamented that near-misses were often unreliably defined by a mother's or father's emotional perception that their child was in peril. It was a climate of fear that he himself had a large hand in creating, though he betrayed no evidence that he saw it this way. It would not surprise him, he had told his colleagues at the Baltimore conference, if a lot of babies made it into the near-miss statistics "when in fact no apnea, bradycardia, or life-threatening event had occurred.... It is at best potentially misleading when reporting that parental resuscitative intervention was 'required' when in actuality it was 'received.' "

When he talked to reporters in these years, Steinschneider consistently took credit for revolutionizing SIDS by "discovering" that victims were born with a fatal abnormality. But along with Shannon and Kelly, he had also revolutionized it by leading countless numbers of parents to fear that their babies had this theoretical hidden abnormality. In Syracuse, where it all began, the effects were especially acute and long-term. When Nessa Vercillo sat down at her first meeting of the SIDS group Steinschneider had set up in Syracuse a decade earlier, she had the strange sensation that she had walked into the remnants of some sort of cult. Her baby son had recently died of SIDS, but she quickly realized this set her apart from the others. "I'm looking around, and there are seven women," she remembers. "The most recent death was seven years ago. A couple of them had babies on monitors for two or three years. SIDS is apnea, they said. Like they were the same thing. They said, 'Don't worry, we can lend you a monitor when you have another baby. Do you know it can happen again? Your next baby can die. Dr. Steinschneider says it's familial and the only way to save your baby is an apnea monitor.' "

The demand for monitors soared with the near-miss phenomenon. "The scene was this: The mother would say, 'My baby stopped breathing, turned blue, and looked dead.' But the baby's normal. The mother would get into the SIDS research and come back roaring mad: Why wasn't her baby being monitored?" The speaker is Dr. Jerold Lucey, editor of *Pediatrics*. "It jumped from a decent hypothesis to a religion. You either believed or you didn't." Inevitably, the anxiety spread to parents of perfectly healthy babies with no family history of SIDS or reports of prolonged apnea. They wanted monitors too. Some new mothers refused to leave the maternity ward without one.

Many pediatricians who had resisted home monitoring in the late seventies now found this virtually impossible. It was easier to prescribe a monitor than to talk a parent out of it, especially now that the National SIDS Foundation— with Dorothy Kelly's help—had persuaded Blue Cross–Blue Shield's national medical advisory board to adopt a policy approving reimbursements for "sudden infant death syndrome monitors," as the board referred to them in its statement. "We were backed into using them," said Lucey. "You had salesmen pushing them, you had parents demanding them, you had fear of lawsuits. But there were never any randomized control trials because the believers would say it's immoral to do a randomized trial. Meanwhile, the rates of SIDS didn't go down. It was a tremendous waste of effort."

It was also not necessarily harmless medicine. Putting a baby on a monitor often meant shrouding a house in fear and gloom—a kind of death watch. Inevitably, a subculture formed out of the experience, and a support network formed around the subculture. This tended to reinforce the fear. In 1982, a committee of the SIDS Foundation, under a "grant" from Healthdyne, produced a 79-page handbook "for the parents of infants who are being monitored due to cardio-respiratory abnormalities." With Kelly as its chairman and catalyst, the committee included Saul Goldberg and former SIDS Foundation executive director Carolyn Szybist, along with the president of a monitor dealership, a professor of pediatrics from Stanford, and a nurse who was monitoring her own twins. Healthdyne published and distributed the book with the endorsement of the foundation and an array of eminent doctors who served on a separate advisory panel.

The handbook advised new monitor parents to expect a period of strain, "including a lack of sleep and associated exhaustion, uncommon irritability with your spouse and children . . . constant hovering over the baby, a reluctance to disconnect the monitor at any time, and a growing feeling of terminal cabin fever. Although not pleasant, these reactions are normal and will pass. Studies have shown that home monitoring can either increase family friction or help bring the family closer together." Advice ranged from how to perform CPR to how to arrange a nursery around a monitor. There were monitor baby clothing suggestions, and a section urging monitor parents to help others by volunteering at their local apnea centers, or at "your local monitor parents association." A chapter on how to select a monitor featured two full-page pictures of the latest Healthdyne equipment.

Despite the warnings about inconvenience and stress, parents were urged to view the monitor experience as an obligation. "By assuming this responsibility, you are offering your baby a chance for a long and normal life. Although it will be trying, you are doing all that is possible." With that subtly grim introduction, the book then posed the big question: "Will My Baby

Die?" The answer implied that Steinschneider's theory had been proven: "Since a cure for infant apnea has not yet been found, home monitoring must be defined as a 'tool.' Unfortunately no tool can guarantee success. Although this may seem pessimistic, the facts are encouraging. Survival rates among monitored babies are nearly 95 percent. This is significantly higher than has been experienced by 'at-risk' infants who have not been subject to monitoring." The book never mentioned that there was no valid research to back up this statement. It wasn't until page 70 that it said that SIDS "is presently neither predictable nor preventable."

The book closed with a section of sample form letters that monitor parents could have their doctors sign in order to receive special attention to their plight. Any parent reading these letters would have to assume that tragedy could strike at any moment and that it was up to them to prevent the unpreventable. The letter requesting insurance coverage stated that the equipment—"in particular, a Healthdyne Infant Monitor, prescribed for its proven reliability and simplicity of operation"—was "necessary for treatment of an illness." Another letter could be used to alert the local rescue squad that the baby's parents, although trained in CPR, might be calling for help. "If this occurs, immediate response will be crucial. Please advise your crews and discuss how best you can reach their home in an emergency situation."

Perhaps no family in America symbolized the way the monitoring phenomenon preyed on vulnerable parents more than the Bittners, Donna and Richard, a suburban New York couple whose triplets were born prematurely and lived their first two months in the hospital. They went home healthy and thriving, but a week later their mother thought one of the babies wasn't breathing, and brought her in to be checked. The baby seemed fine, but the family's neonatologist thought it wise to test the baby, and her sisters, for apnea. He ordered pneumograms for all the babies, and sent the tapes to Kelly's lab in Boston for analysis. The news came back: Two of the pneumograms were "abnormal." Monitors were recommended for all three. When the family's insurance company failed to promptly approve the equipment, the babies' great-grandmother decided to take some action. She wrote a letter and sent it straight to the top. A few days later, a man appeared at the Bittners' front door. He said he was from the White House. The President of the United States wanted to help.

That day, the triplets were attached to a trio of monitors at their crib sides, courtesy of Ronald Reagan and the local county government. But the monitors always seemed to be beeping, which was hard on the babies' parents, even if the cause was usually something simple like a loose lead. Seeing the stress, their great-grandmother, who was now convinced that the monitors were keeping the triplets alive, decided to write another letter to the President: "In the event two or three monitors go off at the same time, my granddaughter has to make a life-and-death decision as to which child lives and which dies. A horrible decision for a mother to make. I would be forever grateful for your help in this matter." The White House arranged for the local authorities to send over a housekeeper and a night nurse. It wasn't long before the next knock on the door was from a reporter.

"Constance, Crystal, and Christina were born suffering from Sudden Infant Death Syndrome," a story in their local newspaper explained bleakly, "a condition that causes a potentially fatal lapse in breathing." The reporter called the White House for comment. "The President and First Lady were very concerned," somebody in the press office reported. TV crews from New York soon followed, and stories appeared in *Reader's Digest* and the *National Enquirer,* among others. Somebody sent the Bittners a story about the triplets from an Italian newspaper. Meanwhile, the couple always kept a bag packed, and the local emergency squad tacked a layout of their house to its bulletin board. The triplets remained on the monitors until they were a year old. Their first birthday party was a major media event. Their parents' sigh of relief could have blown out the birthday candles from forty paces.

Stories of people with "apneic" babies and modest means became a staple of local newspapers. "A wealthy businessman read the story about the five-month-old this week," read one in *Newsday,* "and anonymously donated $2,200 to buy the struggling family an electronic monitor that beeps when baby Nicole, afflicted by a mysterious illness, stops breathing." Nicole had been using a monitor on loan from New York's Flushing Hospital, which had set up a bustling apnea program using Mass General as its model. The hospital needed Nicole's monitor back for another baby. While waiting for the donated machine, her mother called 911 in a panic. Nicole had stopped breathing for "nearly a minute," she reported. "I can't take this anymore," she said, head in hand, tears streaming down her face, as the police whisked the baby to the hospital. "Pray to Saint Luke!" the baby's great-grandmother shouted amid the tumult. The baby was fine, breathing on her own. Her mother wanted to help others. She established the Nicole Near-Miss Foundation.

Meanwhile, apnea centers sprouted like 7-Elevens as hospitals across the country scrambled to start up their own programs. "Why? Because you've *got* to have a program," remarked one New York neonatologist who found himself flying to Boston one spring to take Dorothy Kelly's two-day course in how to run an apnea center. He and the twenty-five other doctors and administrators in his class left with a pile of information that included Mass General's detailed pricing guidelines. It was a laundry list of tests and charges—everything from CAT scans to lumbar punctures to barium swallows—that moved him to remark to himself, "Well, now I know how to run an apnea program. It's a billing factory." Some time later, when he asked a clinical researcher who ran a major monitoring program in Philadelphia, "Do you really believe in this stuff?" the doctor shrugged and said, "It pays my way."

From California, Joan Hodgman, Kelly's chief adversary, looked upon the developments with increasing dismay. She found it infuriating that Kelly drew so much of her influence from the mere fact that she was from Harvard. It bestowed inordinate credibility on someone whose work Hodgman and some others judged maddeningly simplistic. "Dorothy is a monitoring nut but she isn't really scientific," Hodgman would say years later, still in the present tense. "She doesn't evaluate what she is doing, and her stuff spawned the whole entrepreneurial thing."

The "entrepreneurial thing" held special appeal to the administrators of some hospitals who defined a good clinical program as a clinical program that turned a profit. American pediatrics, like medicine generally, was finding itself subject to a social and economic agenda, not a medical or scientific one. It was a remarkable turn of events to doctors such as John Kattwinkel, a SIDS specialist at the University of Virginia who was a member of the Academy of Pediatrics task force on prolonged apnea. "Every medical school had some version of an apnea center," he said. "Our state health department was buying these monitors because they felt they had to."

It could not have happened without the salesmen. Just as the lawyer from Arizona had predicted in Toronto in 1974, they were going door to door selling SIDS prevention. "We put our salespeople in front of the customer," Pete Petit explained to *The New York Times* early in 1983, an oblique reference to the doctors whose patronage his company could not do without. "We try to educate people in the field because the monitors are an emerging health-care product."

The strategy paid off. With the help of Kelly, Steinschneider, and a few other prominent apnea adherents, Healthdyne enjoyed remarkable influence in the medical community, and sales climbed as a result. In the package of information Kelly distributed to doctors who came to Mass General for her apnea course was a six-page paper that she and two other prominent doctors—one employed by the National Institutes of Health—developed under another "grant" from Healthdyne: guidelines for physicians encountering babies who might need home monitoring. More information could be obtained by contacting Healthdyne, it noted. "Healthdyne was teaching doctors the risk factors," recalls onetime executive Steve Combs. "Pete himself was spending a lot of time on the road, meeting with pediatricians and neonatologists. He would tell them how SIDS was the leading killer of babies, but there was something that could be done about it."

From Petit, the doctors who were often his ambivalent middlemen also learned a basic lesson of capitalism. "Doctors may use it just to be safe," a neonatologist in Petit's hometown, Saul Adler, observed at the time, conceding with some sheepishness that he was one of those doctors. "That's bad for health-care costs, but good for Healthdyne stockholders." More than a few physicians realized they were helping Healthdyne dig a gold mine. "Other companies sent a free sample or a pen," remembered the New York neonatologist. "Healthdyne sent a prospectus." The doctor respected the ethical constraints on his own stock investments, but advised his friends and relatives: Buy Healthdyne, quick.

It was excellent advice. By the end of 1982—the year Shannon and Kelly validated the concept of near-miss SIDS in *The New England Journal of Medicine* and the eminent doctors and SIDS activists produced the handbooks that were subtle promotions for Healthdyne and the monitoring concept in general—more than ten thousand babies a year were on home monitors in America. Ninety percent of them were Healthdyne monitors. Petit's company was thriving and diversifying; it was now also selling a line of hospital life-support and monitoring equipment, products acquired from other companies with the profits from monitor sales and the proceeds of the first Wall Street offering. Healthdyne stock was still climbing, a red-hot company with a virtual monopoly of a burgeoning field. A few weeks before the international SIDS meeting it helped sponsor in Baltimore, the company completed a two-for-one stock split. Two months later it had its second public offering, and ten months later, a third. The stock, which had opened at $17 a share only eighteen months before, was trading at $41, giving some of Petit's early private investors from the 1970s a 7,000 percent return on their money. Petit came to New York to sell his company to Wall Street. Over lunch, he told analysts how it all started with his grief over the death of his son, how he was realizing his dream of saving babies, and how business was only going to get better. At the close of the third offering, he had $74 million on his desk to play with.

By the end of 1983, just a few months after the stock offerings, Healthdyne had annual sales of $133 million and the title to no fewer than seventeen medical supply companies it had swallowed up during a sixteen-month buying binge. The acquisitions—a company a month—included the takeover of Healthdyne's hapless competitor, Air-Shields, the company Steinschneider had been unable to coax into the home apnea market in the mid-seventies. Petit had started out marketing the apnea monitors through reluctant independent distributors. Now, his company owned many of the distributors, and the apnea monitor business was growing at the rate of 70 percent a year. A few new competitors struggled to get into the market, but they were far behind Healthdyne. In less than a decade, Petit's business had gone from the edge of bankruptcy to twenty-fourth on *Inc.* magazine's list of the country's top one hundred companies. With the company now selling dozens of products made possible by the success of the apnea monitors, Healthdyne's payroll swelled to 2,500 people working in manufacturing plants and home-care service centers throughout the country and in Europe. Petit couldn't see around the corner, but it surely didn't occur to him that once he made the turn he would find anything but a boundless vista of righteous profits.

The paradox, and it would have tumultuous effects, was that the monitor market was exploding just as the infatuation with apnea was beginning to subside in the SIDS research community. Steinschneider's failure in Baltimore, coupled with David Southall's dramatic results in London, marked the turning point. It wasn't that apnea didn't exist, or that monitors were worthless. Premature babies and those few full-term infants with documented, severe apnea could benefit from monitors. But the link between apnea and death had not been confirmed—indeed, it had been discredited. The simplicity of the hypothesis had always been one of its most appealing features. Now, it seemed to an increasing number of people an emperor without clothes.

But it was too late. The idea hatched by Waneta Hoyt one day in 1970 was now a part of life. A decade later, people were clamoring for these electronic boxes, mesmerized by their magical, life-affirming wires. In fact, if one were to draw a graph charting the enthusiasm for the apnea theory of SIDS among medical scientists, and for the rest of the world's devotion to the monitoring idea, this is how it would look: The two lines would climb together steadily from the mid-1970s until about 1982, then split and part company forever, the theory flattening and ultimately going south, the monitors reaching for the stars. Monitoring had come with Steinschneider's hypothesis, but now it seemed as though the theory existed only to justify their use.

In Boston, Dotty Kelly was starting to take personal umbrage with the apnea- and monitor-bashing that was just becoming safe. "As far as I'm concerned, these children have a disease," she said with some annoyance to a reporter from *Newsday* who asked her about the doubts raised by Southall. "And either they can be monitored for less money at home, or in the hospital at a cost of five hundred dollars a day. If the long-term effect is that we decrease SIDS, that's nice." Richard Naeye wondered if Southall's results were different from those in the United States "because they manage pregnancy differently in Britain." For now, he thought there was no question what to do: "We should continue monitoring."

With the apnea theory under siege, its doubters coming out of the bushes, the believers digging trenches, some parents' groups against monitoring and others in favor, pediatricians and veterans of the long struggle against SIDS could see the unfolding specter of civil war. "The science world just went too far with apnea," reflected Bruce Beckwith. "They put all the bucks into that, they put in all this energy, and it was *emotional* energy. You get parent advocacy groups out there, you get Steinschneider's traveling circus, you get big grant money, big neonatal research centers going, a lot of politics and a lot of parents and a lot of money, and it becomes intensely emotional. The whole SIDS scene changed from the rather benevolent, positive approach of the early days to one where it was just a rat's nest of wild-eyed people who were arming themselves in the different camps. It got destructive, and I think it retarded other avenues of SIDS research for a decade."

Thus, the stage was set for battle. And cast across the developing fray was the shadow of Alfred Steinschneider. Confronting the reality that the field was no longer his even as his ideas remained at its core, Steinschneider was making new plans with old notions. Defiantly, and with some start-up money from Healthdyne, he was on his own.

Two-seventy-five Carpenter Avenue was a nondescript office building on the north side of Atlanta, a few miles from Healthdyne's headquarters in Marietta, a world very different from the one Steinschneider had left behind. He relished the fresh start, but brought his sales pitch from Baltimore essentially intact. A breakthrough was just around the corner. Money was the key. He set up the National Sudden Infant Death Syndrome Institute (it would later become the American SIDS Institute) as a private, nonprofit foundation, listing himself as director and president. Steve Weinstein followed him to Atlanta after the "Baltimore fiasco," as he put it, and was also listed as a member of the board when Steinschneider's lawyer drew up the incorporation papers. A third director would be Scott James, the pediatrician who had helped Petit put the first monitor idea on paper back in 1970.

Steinschneider's plan was a version of what he had built in Maryland. The institute would be a SIDS research clinic, focusing on apnea and home monitoring. Money would come, he hoped, from federal grants, private donations, and from the fees he would charge parents for evaluating and monitoring their babies. On the board of directors would be corporate and civic movers who could run the fund-raising machine.

After 1982, Steinschneider wisely realized that no federal agency would fund more of the same kind of research he had conducted in Baltimore. But it did not stop him from thinking big. Only now he was thinking less about the general population of babies and more about a specific segment: subsequent siblings of SIDS victims. Studying them was a way in the back door: He intended to show that subsequent siblings were at increased risk of SIDS because, like their dead brothers and sisters, they were at increased risk of apnea. To fulfill his new research agenda, Steinschneider needed to stir up interest and exposure all over again. Georgia was new territory. Hoping for referrals, he sent letters of introduction to family doctors, pediatricians, and obstetricians throughout the state, enclosing a recent article he'd written with Weinstein—"Prolonged infantile apnea: Diagnostic and therapeutic dilemma"—that had appeared in an issue of the *Journal of Respiratory Disease*.

The title was an apt description of his frustrations. After ten years of trying, he had been unable to make his formulas work. But he intended to pursue the elusive apnea theory the way he always had, even if his two leading allies were now trying to persuade him to reconsider. It was Steinschneider's innovative calculations that had first excited Warren Guntheroth when he peer-reviewed the 1972 paper for *Pediatrics*. But while he still believed in the essence of the theory, Guntheroth told Steinschneider that he ought to take a new approach. "The apnea index didn't turn out to be good," Guntheroth later said, "because short pauses are very common, and when you're in REM sleep you get them, lots of them. Steinschneider used a definition so short that anytime you went into REM sleep you'd have them. The concept that he could predict [death] was not good. The apnea density idea was fallacious. It was too normal. I told him to take it out. It's crucial in science to be able to look at what you've done and say it's wrong. He is not given to second thoughts."

Dotty Kelly also told Steinschneider she thought his methods were flawed. She respected his work, but felt the heated labs skewed his data. She thought it was not the way to understand normal breathing patterns for healthy babies. "I said many times, 'Al, all the work you're doing is great, but I can't do it because you're doing it at ninety degrees. It's not a normal environment.' " She was convinced the pneumogram was the way to go. "He never did publish any normal data."

And he never stopped heating his labs. When he explained why over the years, Steinschneider tended not to give the same answer twice. In 1975, he had told *Today's Health* that he heated the lab in Syracuse to encourage REM sleep, which was a roundabout way of saying he wanted to encourage apnea. He once told Kelly it was because he often tested premature babies who were used to high-temperature Isolettes and he didn't want to jar their delicate systems into hypothermia. This didn't explain why he did it with full-term babies. Still later, during an explanation of his system of "teasing out" apnea in order to compare the normal to the abnormal, he offered the authors this piece of interior logic: "There was an argument for natural conditions. That bothered me. Because babies didn't die under natural conditions. I didn't believe the day they died was the same as the day they didn't die. If I tell you on Monday, Tuesday, and Wednesday the baby's alive, and on Thursday the baby's dead, maybe something was different about Thursday." (Whether it is a mark of how little the data that gave birth to the leading theory of the day were scrutinized, or of how Steinschneider managed to keep his methods obscured, it is also true that many of his most prominent colleagues in SIDS—Marie Valdes-Dapena, Bruce Beckwith, and Abe Bergman among them—never knew that he heated his labs. "He does?" Beckwith said, nearly thirty years after first meeting Steinschneider. "That's amazing. It could have modified his results.")

In fact, using heat to draw out something hidden might be an effective tool of laboratory investigation. The problem, as it had been since the beginning, was that Steinschneider used it clinically—the clinic was his laboratory, and the laboratory his clinic—to come to theoretical conclusions about real babies with nervous parents. Now, he would bring his ideas to the parents of Atlanta. On some, the effects of his obsession would be painful.

Soon after Steinschneider arrived in town, Scott James introduced him to Saul Adler, the neonatologist who ran a small monitoring program at Northside Hospital. Adler welcomed Steinschneider to Atlanta and said he'd be glad to work with him.

"You don't understand," Steinschneider told him. "I'm taking over monitoring in Atlanta. That's why I came here. We are taking over your program."

He was going to do it with Pete Petit's full support. Besides setting up Steinschneider's new suite of offices, Healthdyne allowed Steinschneider virtually free rein of its plant. "They'd give him free monitors and he'd rent them out," recalled Barbara Davis Bokor, a Healthdyne clinical support specialist. Saul Adler remarked to his colleagues: "He's started a 'nonprofit' private practice and people donate money. I guess it's legal."

Steinschneider became the talk of the Atlanta pediatric community. "Al, you know you're very controversial," Bokor told him one day.

"I'd like to call it provocative," he replied.

In Atlanta, as he had been in Baltimore, Steve Weinstein was Steinschneider's aide-de-camp and most tireless apostle. "Nobody understood SIDS like Al," he said. Weinstein began traveling the Southeast, selling monitoring and looking for babies to prove the thesis. "I was plucking from all over Georgia, Tennessee, Alabama. I was looking to get on TV."

Neither Steinschneider nor Weinstein saw their financial relationship with Healthdyne—indeed their dependence on Pete Petit—as a problem. The goal was saving babies. So what if Healthdyne was supporting their efforts? They were not stockholders. In fact, they had discussed that very issue. It would be unethical to have a personal interest in the fortunes of Healthdyne, they had decided.

Others did see a problem: Steinschneider was trying to prove the apnea theory, and Healthdyne was selling apnea monitors. He was trying to prove subsequent siblings were at risk. Selling monitors to their parents could not even be considered selling; it was too easy. People didn't know the precise details—whether he had a personal stake in the sale of monitors, or if it was just a wealthy research patron he saw in Pete Petit—but it almost didn't matter. In science, any alliance between research and commercial enterprise is delicate terrain, and perception can be everything. "He went with a company," Virginia's John Kattwinkel said. "He was selling monitors."

His bias was by now in plain sight. At meetings, fellow researchers heard Steinschneider's performances as a song that kept repeating itself, and veterans came to view questioning him a futile exercise. Ehud Krongrad, a Columbia University pediatric cardiologist who had started monitoring babies after he read Steinschneider's paper in 1972, approached him at a meeting in Baltimore years later to discuss his doubts about apnea. "He got angry and shouted," Krongrad recalled. "You couldn't discuss science in a logical way." After Baltimore, Steinschneider became so routinely furious when others in the field disagreed with him that many stopped bothering to challenge him at meetings. Ultimately, his adamance led them to omit him from meetings entirely. He was such a fanatic about apnea and monitoring, some thought, that he might as well be on the Healthdyne payroll.

His relationship with Healthdyne did not stop Steinschneider from seeking federal grants to continue what he saw as the intellectually honest work he had been conducting for thirty years. With the pipeline from the NICHD dried up, he planned to seek his next grant from the Office of Maternal and Child Health, an arm of the National Institutes of Health that was best known in the SIDS world for running the federal government's multimillion-dollar parent counseling and information programs. As an agency primarily involved in clinical programs, MCH didn't have anywhere near the research budget NICHD did. But what it had, Steinschneider was confident, he could get.

Steinschneider had barely set up shop in Atlanta before he decided to expand his operation into enemy territory, as it were. Monitoring had taken off in the east, but the west was still wide-open territory. As a phenomenon, apnea monitoring was heavily influenced by the eastern roots of its most prominent proponents, while the leading lights of SIDS in the west, Abe Bergman and Bruce Beckwith, had fought publicly against it. Now Steinschneider was about to launch an incursion into their domain. He had found an enthusiastic ally in Portland, Oregon.

Janie Cram was one of the most remarked-upon SIDS parents in the country. A fiery woman, she had lost a baby two decades before but had never stopped grieving. Her Oregon license plate read *SIDS,* and when SIDS parents met her for the first time, they often wondered what had hit them. "When my baby died, she made me feel like I was joining a club," one mother commented. Cram had founded the Oregon SIDS Center, and when she heard that Steinschneider was looking for a second home in the west—that he was now concentrating his research on siblings of SIDS victims—she tried to woo him to Portland.

It wasn't a tough sell. Steinschneider saw in Cram the kind of champion he would need as he tried to establish an outpost in the Pacific Northwest. Oregon would be a challenge, but it was also a fine opportunity. The state had the fourth highest SIDS rate in the country, and no one was doing any serious monitoring of babies. Janie Cram enthusiastically agreed to run the clinic of his new Western SIDS Institute. She quit her job as the Oregon director of the SIDS information and counseling service run by the Office of Maternal and Child Health. Her boss in Bethesda, Geraldine Norris, was not displeased. When she hired Cram, it was obvious to Norris that she had given her the job of her dreams, but she came to believe that Cram was much too personally involved. Instead of objective compassion and administrative skill, Norris felt, Cram brought a torrent of emotion and her own personal views about SIDS, dumping them on her clients. She thought Cram and Steinschneider would make quite a team.

On a spring day in 1984, broadcast crews and newspaper reporters gathered outside Kam House, an historic Victorian home in the center of Portland that Steinschneider had rented for his new operation. An infant attached to a monitor was on hand for the event, and Oregon's Senator Mark Hatfield cut the ribbon. Steinschneider was all over the local news that night: the doctor who would save Portland's babies from SIDS.

To oversee the medical operations of the Portland clinic, Steinschneider recruited a young neonatologist from the University of Michigan named Raul Benagale. Benagale had no particular expertise in SIDS before his move to the Northwest, but Steinschneider described his theories and dictated the protocols for testing subsequent SIDS siblings. There was no federal research support yet, Steinschneider told him, but it would be just a matter of time.

Benagale began testing babies while Cram counseled their parents, but he realized soon that he'd signed on to a shoestring operation. Steinschneider didn't have the proper insurance coverage or a trained support staff. There were weeks when Benagale's paycheck didn't show up. Steinschneider, meanwhile, would arrive in town once every few months and check into the plush Portland Inn, his lodging donated by the hotel, his meals and transportation often picked up by the small staff at the clinic. Benagale quit in less than a year. Steinschneider replaced him with John Schilke, a doctor from Clacka-mas County, a mountainous region southeast of Portland. Schilke agreed to come to Portland once a week to test babies whose siblings had died of SIDS.

By the summer of 1985, Steinschneider was just about back on his feet after Baltimore. Steve Weinstein had decided he was ready for something new and had left to go back to school to learn pediatric neurology, a decision Steinschneider took personally. It caused a rift that would last years. On the other hand, his new fund-raising operations were up and running in Atlanta and Portland, and in August, a grant committee at Maternal and Child Health approved his proposal to study four hundred subsequent siblings of SIDS babies, at a cost of half a million dollars over five years. The risk of babies born into SIDS families was a hotly debated question, and the mem-bers of the grant committee, anxious for some research on it, saw their way past Steinschneider's known scientific bias and his financial dependence on a company with a vested interest in the results. That Steinschneider's goal was to prove that subsequent siblings were at greater risk of death because they were at greater risk of apnea did not preoccupy them either.

Steinschneider hired a publicist to spread word of the grant, which would fund research at the Institute's two "campuses" in Atlanta and Portland, in the words of one press release. A reporter in the Atlanta bureau of the Associ-ated Press asked Steinschneider what he hoped to find with his new grant. He wanted to develop a way of predicting SIDS, Steinschneider told him. In Portland, a lot of people thought he already had done that. "What we have to move in the direction of is a means of identifying babies at low risk who are really at high risk," Steinschneider said enigmatically. "We've got to come up with some sort of test."

In addition to the MCH grant, money flowed in to Steinschneider from some of the old sources. Ben Vereen raised money for the American SIDS Institute, as he had for the institute in Maryland. His agent Pamela Cooper's other major client, Dionne Warwick, also took up Steinschneider's cause. She recorded a touching song, "The Promise of Life," and came to Atlanta to host a fund-raising concert for the institute at the Fox Theatre.

In Atlanta and Portland, as he had in Baltimore, Steinschneider sur-rounded himself with a legion of believers, SIDS parents and civic activists who felt they were on an important mission, led by the "world renowned authority on SIDS," as Steinschneider was described on the institute's promo-tional material. In Portland, there were fund-raising events just about every weekend: golf tournaments, bowl-a-thons, anything that could possibly bring attention and money. One couple sponsored a twenty-four-hour marathon in the name of their daughter, a SIDS victim. Megan's Run brought in $40,000 the first year. There was no question among Steinschneider's staff in Portland that he and Healthdyne had a thriving symbiotic relationship. Petit donated a $25,000 instrument that read monitor tapes, and at a later point when money became short and salaries went unpaid, the paychecks that finally came were from Healthdyne. "Whenever Al was in trouble, Pete was there," said Sherry Alexander, a monitor parent who became the Western SIDS Institute's assistant director.

Because the research emphasis was on subsequent siblings, and because Janie Cram was in charge, Kam House became a kind of haven for SIDS parents, a center of grief, fear, and fund-raising. Parents who had lost a baby to SIDS would have their newborns tested and sent home with a Healthdyne monitor. Cram led the counseling groups, heart-wrenching sessions that Steinschneider, when he was visiting from Atlanta, avoided. Many parents found this strange, though Cram recognized it as a mark of his ultimate interest. "He never intended to be anyone's guru," she remarked. "He is not an advocate for the parents, but for the babies."

Two subsequent siblings tested at the Portland clinic went on to die. The first time, John Schilke immediately called Steinschneider in Atlanta to tell him about it. Was the baby on a monitor? Steinschneider asked frantically. "Yes," Schilke said.

Steinschneider was on the next plane to Portland. Maybe this was it: the first death caught on paper. A subsequent sib. Maybe the tape would tell, for the first time, how and why a baby had died—never mind the question of why the monitor had not saved him. But when Steinschneider got to Portland, Schilke had bad news. Apparently, there had been a malfunction. They could find no recordings. Steinschneider was devastated.

The other death was equally unrevealing—or perhaps not. The baby had not been on a monitor when she died. Later, there came a call from an investigator. Schilke and Steinschneider said it wasn't suspicious, but the authorities disagreed. They suspected the woman had murdered her baby.

29

In the fall of 1985, Steinschneider and Pete Petit flew to Brussels for a SIDS conference sponsored in part by the New York Academy of Sciences. Steinschneider was to run a piece of the meeting. With Healthdyne underwriting the costs, he had organized a panel on the management of infants at risk. He was in high spirits, talking about monitoring to an international gathering, mixing in a little sightseeing with two of his American colleagues. Dorothy Kelly was one of them. The other was a pediatric respiratory specialist from Rochester, New York, named John Brooks.

The head of an apnea program at Rochester's Strong Memorial Hospital, Brooks was an emerging voice in the field that Steinschneider and Kelly had created and cultivated. He was, however, not just another apnea combatant. He had recently been named to a prestigious panel appointed by a conglomerate of federal agencies to come to a consensus about the monitoring question. In essence, Brooks would be helping judge Steinschneider's theory, though he didn't see it in such personal terms. He tended not to regard his peers harshly, and in Steinschneider he saw a dedicated, resourceful physician with an engaging personality.

Brooks was a genial man who was as composed as Steinschneider was volatile. But he had come to Belgium unsettled by a recent experience that intruded on his conception of the notion of "management of infants at risk." Four years earlier, in the spring of 1981, a couple from a small town outside Rochester had come to him, referred by the local SIDS group. The woman was in the late stages of pregnancy and wanted her baby to go right onto an apnea monitor. The child would be a subsequent sibling of not one but two SIDS babies—one of whom had survived an apparent near-miss the week

393

before her death—and a third child who had died suddenly when he choked on a coin at sixteen months of age.

What Brooks found before him was a situation strikingly similar to the one Steinschneider had confronted a decade before, just down the road in Syracuse. Both doctors encountered families that had lost three children mysteriously, including one who was beyond the normal age of SIDS and another who died in an especially strange way. Both families had come to a specialist at the nearest major teaching hospital for help with the fourth. But while Steinschneider was a research doctor and Brooks a clinician, that was not their only difference. Brooks was a cautious man with a measured way of thinking. He perceived something odd about the couple, especially the father, and about the deaths of their three children, but he wasn't sure what to make of it. He was extremely reluctant to cast suspicion on SIDS parents. He decided to put his suspicion on hold and keep an eye on the fourth child. A monitor was probably the safe choice, he concluded—especially since the mother was so insistent on going home with one.

The baby did fine and came off the monitor after nearly a year. The couple's next child stayed on one for six months. The mother was nearing the end of yet another pregnancy when word came, just days before Brooks stepped on the plane for Brussels, that the babies' father had been arrested—charged with murdering two of his earlier children.

Brooks couldn't say that the arrest of Stephen Van Der Sluys had taken him completely by surprise. Not long after the couple had first come to him, he'd told an investigator from the New York State Police that he thought something might be amiss. But he hadn't heard anything more, and found to his relief that the chain of death had been broken. Now, the father's arrest added a new dimension, to say the least, to Brooks's experience. Here he was, a member of a blue-ribbon federal panel looking at apnea, subsequent siblings, and monitoring. Here he was, sightseeing with the apnea theorist himself, along with his most zealous compatriot—champions of monitoring, believers in a heightened risk for babies born into families with previous infant deaths. And here he was, a doctor who had monitored two babies on the presumption that their family history put them at risk of SIDS. Only maybe the first three were murdered. For Brooks, the timing and the circumstances could hardly have been stranger. He could not know how strange the connections really were.

Nor did either of them know how close Steinschneider himself had come to encountering the Van Der Sluys family. Their second child, Heather, died in Syracuse in January 1977, a week after she was rushed to Upstate Medical Center and admitted with an apparent near-miss. Under other circumstances, it would have been Steinschneider's case, and her death, presumably, would have become another piece of dramatic data for the apnea theory. But it came at a time when Steinschneider was closing down his studies in Syracuse and preparing for his big grant project in Baltimore. His departure marked the end of the apnea era in Syracuse. He left behind no followers, and four years later, her family's tragedies became the burden of John Brooks in Rochester.

When he returned home from Europe, Brooks had to make a decision. What if it turned out that the Van Der Sluys babies had not been killed; that their father was one of those tragically unfortunate SIDS parents of the past, hounded by the authorities? The man had been arrested, Brooks told himself, but not yet convicted. What if the first babies did have some undetected abnormality, and his decision to monitor had something to do with their later siblings' survival? It also crossed his mind that perhaps the monitors had acted as a deterrent. "All I knew was that when they started going on monitors, they stopped dying," he observed. Brooks decided he should play it safe. He put the new baby, born as his father sat in the Ontario County Jail, on an apnea monitor. He also prescribed one for the baby's half-sister, born five days before to the teenage girl whose pregnancy first put Van Der Sluys in jail. Then Brooks got back to his reading. The work of the Consensus Development Panel on Infantile Apnea and Home Monitoring was getting into high gear. The NICHD was putting together a reading list. The pertinent scientific articles for the first half of the 1980s alone numbered 471.

For Pete Petit, the Brussels trip came at a time when he might have wondered what had hit him. It was only coincidence, but just as Steinschneider moved to Atlanta, Healthdyne's fortunes had begun to crumble. For a while, Petit hadn't been able to do anything wrong. Now he couldn't do anything right. First, there was his frenzy of acquisition, a breathless campaign to make Healthdyne "a major health care company," as he promised his stockholders in 1983. His ambition was poorly timed. It wasn't just that a package of new federal rules had drastically cut back reimbursements for a number of Healthdyne's newly acquired products, or just that Wall Street had suddenly soured on technology stocks. It was that Petit's grand vision had so distracted the company that nobody seemed to notice that Healthdyne's second-generation infant apnea monitor was the Edsel of its field.

The original Healthdyne monitor that had served the company so well was a bulky piece of equipment that needed a wall outlet. When one of the companies trying to elbow its way into the market, Aequitron, produced the first portable in 1983, Healthdyne scrambled to bring out its own version. The hasty R&D turned out to be the company's first serious misstep in the monitor rush. Petit's portable was a flop; it gave off far too many false alarms on respiration, and on the heart side produced too many cardiac "arti-facts," blips on the tape that looked like episodes of bradycardia—slowed heartbeat—but were not; the baby's heart rate had never wavered. The Healthdyne portable was also extremely heavy. The battery pack alone weighed more than the baby. (And in one case reported to the Food and Drug Administration, the battery burst into flames when a nurse opened its case to demonstrate the monitor to a parent.) In Portland, Steinschneider deflected urgings that he use another brand, telling one meeting of doctors that they shouldn't worry about the weight of the Healthdyne equipment—monitor mothers never went out anyway. But the rest of the marketplace was less for-giving. Petit found himself with a warehouse full of returned SIDS alarms.

With disaster looming but not yet out in the open, Petit brought in an old friend from his General Dynamics days to be president and chief operating officer, retaining for himself the company chairmanship. Jim Ashton had been among Petit's best friends and first backers in 1970; his family had made $800,000 on its initial investment. But despite their personal relationship, Ashton was a decidedly odd choice. He had become something of a corporate whistle-blower in the fifteen years since he and Petit had worked in adjacent offices in Fort Worth. A couple of years before Petit brought him to Health-dyne, Ashton had been fired as a vice president of General Dynamics, the country's largest defense contractor, after he uncovered scandalous cost overruns in the company's Trident nuclear ballistic missile submarine pro-gram. His boss, P. Takis Veliotis, fled to Greece one step ahead of a federal indictment.

Ashton came to Healthdyne in December 1983, believing he was inher-iting a hot company, but found himself in the middle of what one stock ana-lyst called a "corporate personality cult": the Healthdyne staff's passionate loyalty to Petit, a "charismatic but overly zealous entrepreneur," as *The New York Times* once described him. Ashton didn't fit in at Healthdyne, especially a Healthdyne in turmoil. The problems were not yet public, and Petit, Ashton later claimed, neglected to tell him that the bottom was about to fall out. Barely a month after he arrived, the company posted its first quarterly loss. Ashton would later say it quickly became clear to him that Healthdyne's top management had "cooked the books" to disguise its sudden troubles, and that he was isolated when he refused to go along. Petit's view was that his old friend had turned out to be a corporate provocateur. Ashton was fired as president six months after he arrived, then resigned from the board of direc-tors, leaving behind a four-page letter contending that the company had mis-represented its finances to maintain its stock price at a critical time. Among other things, he claimed that Healthdyne's management was well aware of the imminent disaster of the second-generation monitor at the same time it was painting a rosy picture to Wall Street during the third stock offering in June 1983—the one that brought in the last of the $74 million with which it took over all those other companies.

Healthdyne's once-glamorous reputation with investors was severely damaged. As the *Times* observed the week Ashton's firing was announced, Petit's company had lost its status as "a darling of industry analysts" almost as quickly as it had been acquired. Some of the blame was laid squarely at the chairman's feet: "Many analysts say they were misled by Mr. Petit early in 1983 into anticipating earnings of $1 to $1.20 a share for the year, several times the 38 cents a share the company eventually reported." A year later, Healthdyne agreed to a $4 million settlement of a class-action lawsuit filed in behalf of everyone who bought Healthdyne stock in 1983 and 1984.

And after a lengthy investigation prompted in part by Ashton's charges, the Securities and Exchange Commission filed a complaint in federal court accusing Healthdyne (but not Petit or other executives) of violating various antifraud provisions of U.S. securities law. However, no willful fraud was alleged, and to resolve the matter, Healthdyne had only to sign a consent decree with the SEC, a standard agreement in which it neither admitted nor denied wrongdoing but promised to follow the rules in the future.

Life couldn't have been worse for Petit and Healthdyne in those years. Sales dropped eighty percent, the company lost millions, and its stock plummeted to single digits, where it would languish for much of the remainder of the decade. It would take Petit years to climb out of the rubble, but as he had shown, he did not give up on what he believed in.

Nor would apnea believers give up on the cherished product Petit and Steinschneider had given them. Healthdyne redesigned its failed monitor, a few other companies entered the market, and by mid-decade, twenty thousand American babies were being monitored in their homes each year. The numbers kept climbing. Nearly a thousand more babies were going on monitors every month. It made the need for a communal judgment about whether this was right seem ever more pressing to many people in the pediatrics and research establishments. Was apnea related to SIDS or not? Did monitors prevent death or not? The files of the Food and Drug Administration contained a number of reports of babies who died while attached to monitors, some cases followed by the inevitable lawsuits. There were also a few reports of injuries such as burns, and in one case, electrocution: A baby's four-year-old sibling had inserted a loose monitor lead into a wall outlet, instantly killing the baby. But the ultimate question was whether there was evidence, despite such mishaps, that apnea monitors saved babies from SIDS, as the headlines claimed.

Early in 1985, the government announced that the issues would be subjected to the highest form of judgment in American medical research: a Consensus Development Conference convened by the National Institutes of Health.

As all scientists and research physicians knew, a consensus conference was reserved for only the most important and controversial public health debates. The apnea conference, under overall control of NIH, would be sponsored by the NICHD, the Food and Drug Administration, the Office of Maternal and Child Health, and three more federal agencies. The planning committee alone would include fifteen of the biggest names in the federal research establishment. They would draw up the questions to be posed and appoint the panelists. Because of the extraordinary volatility of the subject, they agreed they must bar advocates of every stripe from filling any of the thirteen seats on the panel. The full range of combatants would be invited to speak and to submit their research, but they would not take part in the final judgment. The continuing task forces on prolonged apnea appointed by the American Academy of Pediatrics, which had given the first official backing to home monitoring in 1978, tended to be dominated by advocates. But the NIH consensus conference was going to be truly a jury of peers. In effect, the apnea theory was being put on trial.

When he heard about it, Steinschneider was enraged. It was ridiculous, he told people. Of *course* monitors saved lives—you didn't need a consensus conference to determine that. But if there was going to be a conference, he informed the members of the planning committee, he should be its chairman. It was his theory, after all. To the people organizing the conference, this was absurd—too ludicrous even to discuss. Yet discuss it they did, perforce.

For the duration of their eighteen-month deliberations, the consensus panelists would pick up their phones to hear diatribes by Steinschneider. He considered the attacks on his theory a persecution. He had hundreds of examples of babies who were resuscitated from apneic spells after their parents heard the alarms. Wasn't this evidence enough? One of his special targets was James "Gil" Hill, the NICHD science policy official who was the conference's chief organizer. "Steinschneider made it very clear that he resented that he wasn't the chair," Hill remembered. "I had one telephone conversation with him that went on three hours. He would call and engage me to make him a member of the panel. He is not the typical scientist who sells his work short." Finally, Steinschneider decided that if they wouldn't have him, he wouldn't have them. He informed the people at NICHD that he would not participate at all: wouldn't submit his research, speak to the panel, or attend the public sessions. But it wouldn't be his last word.

Fuming, Steinschneider put on his own version of a consensus conference. He was the chairman. It was a three-day seminar at Georgia's Pine Isle resort, sponsored by his SIDS Institute, in June 1986, four months before the Bethesda panel was due to present its final report. Among those he invited was Geraldine Norris, his current federal supervisor.

Her appearance was more or less obligatory. She was not enamored of Steinschneider the way Eileen Hasselmeyer had been, in part because she became involved with him at a much different time and in part because her primary job—running the vast federal SIDS information and counseling program—gave her a different perspective. She knew that Steinschneider's science could not be separated from the culture it had bred, and she found the impact of his decade of influence disquieting. She had been to the Brussels conference, too, and on the trip home she had sat with John Brooks. They had spent nearly the entire flight talking about the explosion of SIDS groups in these years. It seemed to them as if every time a baby died, a SIDS "foundation" was born. People in every community in America were either giving money to SIDS "research," or asking for it. Nobody really knew where all the money was going. Obviously, Steinschneider alone wasn't responsible for all this, but he had certainly played a leading role in propagating the environment that allowed it to flourish. Before their flight touched down, Norris and Brooks agreed that they should push for the creation of some sort of large umbrella group, an alliance of SIDS groups, to bring some order.

As she sat with Steinschneider's other guests on Pine Isle a year later and listened to people selling apnea and monitors, Norris's problems with him were less conceptual than practical. He had had no trouble putting together the grant proposal for the subsequent sibling study, but it was now a year later, and as was so often the case, he was less than forthcoming about his progress. It was to become an ongoing struggle. "Why can't we get reports out of him?" Norris would say to her colleagues. "It's like pulling teeth." She was about to send Steinschneider a letter demanding he either send in the overdue report or return the money, when he finally responded. (Like Syracuse and Baltimore, the Atlanta-Portland research would ultimately fail to yield evidence for his 1972 hypothesis.) Norris, whose agency was more clinically oriented than the research-based NICHD, was also concerned about how he was going about his work. She felt he didn't staff his labs with qualified people and worried about the effects on all those babies he was bringing in to the clinics in Atlanta and Portland. "I felt he was placing babies under stressful conditions: the test itself, the temperature in the lab, the separation from the parents. He would have babies in for overnight observation, and he was always hiring nurses just out of school who didn't have the kind of experience you needed for this kind of thing."

If he was withholding his work from the federal official to whom he was obliged to reveal it, Steinschneider was even more defiant toward George A. Little, the man who was appointed to the consensus conference chairmanship he wanted. Little, the head of maternal and child health at Dartmouth Medical School, thought it was important to include the research of the founder of the apnea and monitoring camp, so for more than a year, as the panel amassed all the material it could on the issues, he kept trying to persuade Steinschneider to contribute. Certainly, he had the longest history to tell. He hadn't published much lately, but he could present his past research, and offer his opinions at the public hearings. Steinschneider continued to refuse. There was no real debate about monitoring, he insisted. "I'm sorry, Al," Little would reply calmly. "I don't agree with you."

Little was a thoughtful, deliberate man in his mid-forties who was picked as chairman in part because he seemed like the kind of person who could preside dispassionately over this explosive territory. He had observed the apnea world from the sidelines for years and read the literature, but he had never encountered the participants. Now he found himself in the middle of a brawl. "There were people in this who were really *locked in,*" he remembered. "There were people who were saying, 'We know that monitors save lives. It's obvious.' Well, where's the evidence? 'Well, we just know.'" The phone calls with Steinschneider and his allies were so frequent and prolonged that they left Little's ears red. Finally, he bought a speakerphone.

Little's twelve fellow panelists included noted pediatricians and researchers, and one law professor, from all over the country, but they were not experts in apnea or monitoring. Only two of them, in fact, had much first-hand experience with the machines. One was John Brooks. Their primary work was to examine and weigh the literature, then offer some guidance to their thousands of colleagues in the field. But beyond the practical questions at hand, some found themselves intrigued by the larger medical and social landscape that was the backdrop to these issues. As he immersed himself in the events of the past decade, listened to the players, and plumbed their motives, George Little became fascinated by the misshapen outcome their efforts had wrought. He wanted not only to render judgment on the efficacy of infant apnea monitors, but to understand the potent cultural force that had unleashed on the world a highly theoretical and not necessarily benign medical technology. When he dissected it, he realized this was the only way it could have turned out.

"You're dealing with an entity where kids die," he reflected some years later. "Now, when you die, you stop breathing and your heart stops. So there's an intuitive thing that says, Well, if you have a gizmo that tells you how fast you're breathing, or how fast your heart is going, then maybe you can prevent death. With SIDS, you're dealing with parents and their babies. And all you need is to have one event occur, or have your niece or somebody die of SIDS, then somebody comes along and sells you this machine. There is a huge industry here, so you've got a lot of capitalists behind this one. It's an industry that has been entrepreneurial as all hell. They're getting your attention. Now you add this: There are people who don't want to believe the literature. They honestly believe the literature is not what it is, which is that these monitors don't work. There *must* be a black box that can tell us when a baby's going to die. So there's all these things at work here. But let's be fair. Most medical observations start out with a case study."

It was to Steinschneider's fourteen-year-old report about the H. babies that the panel traced its roots. "In 1972, a paper reported that two of five infants with documented prolonged sleep apnea died of SIDS," it was to say in the opening paragraph of its final statement. "A great deal of attention during the 1970s was directed toward the relationship of apnea and SIDS. As the 1970s and 1980s unfolded, the use of monitors in the home environment to detect apnea expanded. Research and clinical programs produced many reports about the merits of this activity, and controversy emerged. In an effort to resolve this controversy, the Consensus Development Program at the National Institutes of Health has now directed its attention to this subject."

With Steinschneider refusing to submit his research, the leading witnesses for the defense were the Harvard team of Daniel Shannon and Dorothy Kelly. The apnea business had only boomed at Massachusetts General since David Southall's acclaimed contradiction of the theory in Baltimore in 1982. Four years later the Boston researchers reported to the NIH panel that forty-one babies who had been through their apnea program since its inception had died—an extraordinary number, which they asserted "confirms the morbid association of infantile apnea and SIDS." The Mass General team found further support for the apnea theory in this statistic: The babies they sent home on monitors because they had "abnormal" pneumograms or because they were siblings of SIDS victims died at ten times the rate of babies who had "normal" pneumograms and weren't monitored.

The numbers reflected the phenomenal growth of the country's leading apnea center. Twenty-two of Mass General's monitor babies had died since 1973, and fifteen of these deaths had come in just the past four years. In a report to the consensus panel, another member of Shannon's pediatric pulmonary lab, Dr. Denise Strieder, said that some of these babies were either not on their monitors at the time of their deaths or their parents did not hear the alarm. In other cases, she wrote, "parents froze and did not intervene."

But nearly a third died despite "compliance with monitoring and CPR directives."

In all, the Shannon-Kelly team had now evaluated 13,401 babies and, like Steinschneider, had fixed on subsequent siblings as the population most at risk. In fact, they had calculated that families that had already lost two infants had an 18 percent chance of losing a third. But the world was a less innocent place than it had been in 1972, and hearing these figures in 1986, some on the panel privately wondered if Kelly and Shannon were ignoring a grim possibility. This wasn't something they said in public.

It was Southall's results, published in 1983 in the *British Medical Journal,* that suggested the Boston group was off the mark. In the years since they had first been unveiled at Steinschneider's 1982 meeting, Southall's data showing no correlation between SIDS and apnea had become renowned throughout the SIDS world. Since then, Southall had traveled back to the United States several times to talk to research doctors who wanted to look more closely at his data, bringing his pneumogram tapes with him. To many people, his numbers added up to an eloquent argument against monitoring, but clearly they had had virtually no practical effect. Now he flew to Washington to personally present his research to the consensus panelists. Weighing Shannon and Kelly against Southall, the panelists believed Southall. (His results seemed so unambiguous that Shannon later decided that he and Kelly should test their interpretations. They flew to London, pored over his pneumogram results, and tried to pick out those of the twenty-seven babies who later died. They couldn't do it. Nor did they stop monitoring babies.)

The cogency of Southall's conclusions had powerful effects on how the panel regarded much of the enigmatic research coming out of Boston. Not only did it tend to discredit the Mass General group's advocacy of monitors and its use of pneumograms to assess a baby's risk of SIDS, but it cast doubt on the doctors' research methods in general. Ultimately it also raised still more uneasy questions about the fate of some of the babies behind the burgeoning Boston numbers. But the panelists embraced Southall's work more than they probed Shannon's and Kelly's.

As the data piled up, the evidence against apnea mounted. Research submitted by Columbia University pediatric cardiologist Ehud Krongrad concluded that monitoring was a misguided exercise. He reported that he had lost six patients to SIDS in twelve years, despite home monitors. The victims had not had high levels of apnea. "We do harm in many ways," Krongrad said later. "Here is a theory that has never been proven, and yet treatment is advocated." Some of the evidence came from one of the panel's own members, Seattle epidemiologist Donald Peterson. When he isolated the numbers of SIDS victims and those with bona fide apnea, he realized the two groups were distinct.

Of all the panelists, Peterson may have been the most skeptical of Kelly's conclusions about subsequent siblings. He had been part of every major SIDS meeting since 1963, and had signed on to the notion that SIDS could run in families. Years before, he had conducted a study in Seattle and found that people who lost one child were at higher risk of losing another. But now he was coming to view the question from the perspective of emerging evidence that fatal child abuse was indeed a factor in multiple SIDS numbers. He thought it could have been tilting epidemiologic conclusions for years.

The consensuses of Consensus Development Conferences are presented at Masur Auditorium, a reverberant hall on the NIH campus in Bethesda. In the case of apnea and home monitoring, a draft of the panel's report was circulated months before its final verdicts were to be rendered, and on September 29 and 30, and October 1, 1986, George Little called for researchers, pediatricians, and parents to step forward with their comments. The panelists had come down hard on apnea.

After fourteen years, this was what they had determined: The mortality rate of babies with serious apnea was somewhere between zero and six percent—the imprecision a function of the inherent vagueness of apnea as a diagnosis. It seemed to the panelists that although premature babies were at highest risk for apnea and for SIDS, the entities were not connected. "There is evidence that apnea of prematurity is not a risk factor for SIDS," they wrote.

The research showed that a very small percentage of SIDS babies had had a previous episode of apnea, or a near-miss, which was a name the panelists declared should finally be retired. They favored Apparent Life Threatening Event, or ALTE, which they defined as "an episode that is frightening to the observer" and is characterized by some combination of apnea, color change, marked change in muscle tone, choking, or gagging. But it was clear to everyone that whatever they were called, these spells remained a highly subjective concept, open to all kinds of parental anxiety, misdiagnosis, and mystery. Half of the episodes were related to regurgitation or seizures; the other half remained unexplained—and questionable. "Maybe we should call them Apparently Apparent Life Threatening Events," one skeptical doctor suggested. "Or a Parent Life Threatening Event," added another. In any case, what seemed most apparent to the panel was that these episodes had little if anything to do with SIDS. This was a conclusion sure to please the National SIDS Foundation, whose leaders had long detested the publicity about "near-miss SIDS" that had led many people to include living babies and dead babies in one big group. The consensus panel agreed: It could not be said that even those very few SIDS babies with previous apnea—or events that were called apnea—were therefore dead because of it.

As bad as the news was for Steinschneider, it was in some ways worse for Kelly and Shannon. Beyond declining to buy their data, in their discussions the panel members had worried aloud about the growing use of pneumograms as a tool to predict SIDS. They decided to say publicly that it was wrong.

The apnea believers were furious. Warren Guntheroth was appalled by what he regarded as the panel's narrow-minded agreement with the anti-monitoring forces. After reading the draft report, he wrote an angry letter accusing the panelists of being biased and not up to the challenge. Their conclusion that SIDS remained a mystery, Guntheroth professed, "should be disturbing to the NICHD after two decades of research funding. . . . For a panel of experts, one would expect at least some best guess as to the final lethal pathway, and to leave it in an entirely agnostic state does little to justify the expense of the panel. Do [you] really believe that SIDS is unknowable and unpreventable?"

As he had promised, Steinschneider boycotted the proceedings for eighteen months. But on the second day of public comment, there came a commotion in the back of the auditorium. Heads turned. Steinschneider's familiar figure marched down to the microphone, trailed by a group of women—monitor mothers. Some had come with their monitors attached to the babies in their arms. Steinschneider took the microphone. He railed about the injustice of the proceedings. This was a biased, uninformed, *improper* group. They didn't know the first thing about monitoring. But he was not here to talk about monitors. He wouldn't even address the findings. He pulled out an NIH brochure and began reading the government's guidelines for consensus development conferences. These were convened not to hear opinions, he asserted, but to assess new data. There were no new data on apnea monitors, so the entire proceeding violated the guidelines. The panelists had heard all this before, but they had no choice but to indulge Steinschneider. "It was the best speech I ever gave," Steinschneider said later. "The place was packed and I was furious. Unless they walked away from this thing, it was going to be adjudicated politically, not scientifically. I didn't personally feel threatened. I'm not committed to any theoretical proposal. But I felt there was an agenda here, a political agenda, a personal agenda, and these guys were idiots. What can I say—bad science is bad science. And I said to myself, they'll never pull me off this, they ain't gonna do it, and I slowed it down, and I was good. And I put my head down, ready to leave, and as I started to walk out, I heard a voice in the crowd: 'Al, you sounded like a Baptist minister.' "

Having said his piece, Steinschneider marched up the aisle and left the auditorium, cheering monitor mothers in tow. The next day, the consensus conference delivered its final report to a packed auditorium. By the nature of the issues, it was indeed a political document, and so on the central question under consideration, the question of monitors, the panelists chose to be cautious. They had debated this issue long and hard for months, knowing that it all came down to science versus fear, and the final arguments, over language rather than substance, had lasted all night long. To keep the drafts straight, they used different-colored paper. They finally quit at seven in the morning and rested a couple of hours before regrouping in the auditorium.

They refrained from a flat declaration that monitors did not save lives. Instead, they said there was no evidence that they did. After all the years, no link between apnea and SIDS had been established. In all the years since monitoring had become common practice, the SIDS rates had remained virtually unchanged. Monitor advocates could say they *believed* babies had been saved, but there was nothing scientific to their assertion. But it could also be said that ultimately, the panel had merely stated that the monitoring question remained open. Faced with an emotional and scientifically murky dilemma— even by the standards of politically intense consensus conferences—it had not been able to put the matter to rest.

And so the apnea business kept rolling. In fact, at Healthdyne they viewed the consensus report's careful language as something of a moral victory. The apnea theory continued to lose scientific credence, but the selling and buying of monitors continued unabated. And the conference only further radicalized Steinschneider. In Portland, he told one couple who had lost a baby to SIDS that if they believed what he believed—that subsequent siblings were at greater risk—it would be "criminal" not to monitor their next baby.

For someone like Gil Hill, who had organized other consensus conferences from his office at NICHD, the continued popularity of monitors was disappointing but not surprising. The panel had prestige but no real authority, and its equivocal stand on monitors was no match for the salesmanship of manufacturers, the anxieties of parents, and the ambitions and beliefs of a few doctors who remained convinced that babies skirted death every day in America, and who could not run their apnea programs without apnea monitors. "That's an awesome political force to deal with," Hill reflected. "And so the sale of monitors went on its merry way, and the insurance reimbursements kept coming."

The best estimates put the number of babies on home monitors at the time of the conference at about 30,000. Four years later, the number would double, and worldwide annual sales would surpass $40 million. The United States accounted for 65 percent of the world market. Healthdyne remained the leading manufacturer, selling nearly half the monitors in use. In 1989, Healthdyne introduced a monitor with a five-channel internal memory which it dubbed the SmartMonitor. It was a major commercial success. But consensus panel chairman George Little never found a reason to believe that any of these electronic enhancements changed the monitors' fundamental inadequacy. "The black box advocates have always said, 'We just need one more level of sophistication.' But it's never enough. Does the black box see something, detect something subtle, that can predict SIDS? And even if it could, if you have something that says SIDS is coming in thirty seconds, can you do anything about it?"

It didn't stop Al Steinschneider from trying to prove he was right. After the consensus conference, Steinschneider, again backed by Healthdyne, called a summit of apnea believers and proposed they go in on a massive study, involving thousands of babies, that they hoped would prove that monitors did save lives. Steinschneider planned to take the idea to NIH, the agency he had just subjected to eighteen months of defiance and a final public tirade. Hoping to surmount the politics, he aligned himself with a dozen reputable people. The study would be even bigger than Southall's because it would involve not merely testing babies in the lab but putting them on monitors at home for months and keeping all their parents with the program. They drafted a proposal to NIH to send ten thousand babies home with Healthdyne event-recording monitors—a virtual nation of monitor babies. The price tag: $20 million. Steinschneider began calling members of Congress for support, but no amount of backstage lobbying could overcome the way the government now viewed him. And for the first time, people were starting to question Healthdyne's role in the science of apnea monitoring.

"We met for two days in Atlanta, met several other times, and went to Washington twice," one of the participants recalled. "But when NIH saw Steinschneider's name and Healthdyne monitors, they rejected the proposal. If you're going to do a research study, you have to minimize the bias. He used money from Healthdyne to bring people down to Atlanta." Bruce Beckwith was a member of the review committee. "I had deep misgivings," he said, "but *all* the scientists had deep misgivings. In those days people weren't as rigorous as they are now about keeping noses clean, about conflict of interest, but this one smelled real bad. One of the logistics review people found there was a strong financial link between Steinschneider and Healthdyne, so it was an easy decision not to fund."

However, the people at NICHD did like the idea of a major monitoring study whose results would be documented by internal event recorders. They sent out their own request for proposals, and later approved the Collaborative Home Infant Monitoring Evaluation, CHIME for short, a five-site, $5 million study that would begin in 1991 and be renewed five years later, the results unavailable until the next century. Dr. Carl Hunt, a monitoring advocate who had recently moved from Northwestern University to the Medical College of Ohio in Toledo, was designated the principal investigator; Steinschneider was excluded. Healthdyne was a finalist as the project's monitor supplier but in the end the government went with a Florida company called Non-Invasive Monitoring Systems. Still, monitoring advocates argued that it would be unethical to monitor half the study's "high-risk" babies and to put the rest in a control group. So even if the CHIME study yielded some new information about how babies live and breathe, and perhaps how they die, it wouldn't prove that monitors saved them from SIDS.

Unlike Steinschneider, Pete Petit hardly missed a beat. The success of the SmartMonitor helped renew Healthdyne's stock price, and Petit, the acquisitive CEO of the early eighties, fought off a hostile takeover of his own company near the end of the decade. Meanwhile, he climbed atop the SIDS world itself. The alliance of advocacy groups that John Brooks and Geraldine Norris had mused about on the flight home from Brussels in 1985 became a reality a few years later. Nearly thirty years after they began, Saul and Sylvia Goldberg's Guild for Infant Survival, along with the National SIDS Foundation once headed by Abe Bergman, and a number of smaller groups merged into a single organization called the Sudden Infant Death Syndrome Alliance. "Experience, Strength, and Hope" became its motto. The Alliance's founding chairman was Parker H. Petit.

Steinschneider's American SIDS Institute, which he had established with Petit and Petit's money, was a founding member of the Alliance. But then Steinschneider, who never felt comfortable with parents' organizations, decided he should remain apart from the crowd. He informed the board of his institute of his decision to pull out of the Alliance while Petit was out of the country. When Petit heard about the betrayal upon his return, he was furious. He withdrew his support from the SIDS Institute, and the two men, collaborators who had helped each other prosper for more than a decade, stopped speaking.

As Petit enlarged his influence in the SIDS world, Steinschneider gravitated to the fringes. He deepened his estrangement from the research mainstream, and his pace of publishing slowed. He would not emerge in print for another five years, and then the subject would have the feel of self-parody: "Effects of Diphtheria-Tetanus-Pertussis immunization on prolonged apnea or bradycardia in siblings of sudden infant death syndrome." He no longer had much to do with the federal people in Bethesda who had once been his patrons, or with the SIDS movement in which he had been a central player. With his old peers largely out of the picture, it was just Steinschneider and the parents, and that had never been a particularly good combination.

———

By 1989, the Portland center had begun to feel like a fly-by-night operation. As had been the case in Baltimore, the institute's fund-raising machinery could not keep up with expenses—especially when the Healthdyne money stopped coming. Nobody but Steinschneider knew the exact situation because he made it clear to the people in Portland that finances were his concern, not theirs. The Western SIDS Institute didn't have so much as a bank account. All the money that came in went directly to Atlanta.

Five years after his ballyhooed arrival, Steinschneider pulled out. Even as his followers were running one more fund-raiser—a celebrity golf tournament featuring Pat Boone and most of the Portland Trailblazers—he and an assistant from Atlanta were at the clinic, going through the inventory. Steinschneider departed without a word, leaving the institute thousands of dollars in debt and its board of directors furious.

Rachel Smith was shattered. A SIDS parent who had been a member of Steinschneider's paid office staff in Portland, her life had been completely wrapped up in Steinschneider's research. She and her husband, Tony, spent a good deal of their time doing volunteer fund-raising work for the institute, and ultimately they took part in the research of subsequent siblings. Two years after her son's death from SIDS, Rachel had given birth to twin girls, Amber and Alexandra, and immediately put them on home monitors. As a paid employee, Rachel was closer to Steinschneider than most of the SIDS parents who floated through the institute. He doted on the twins when he was in town.

A week after he closed the Portland center, Steinschneider called the Smiths. He had read the twins' last monitor tapes. "Alexandra had a bad apnea," he said gravely. "It's serious." He paused. "I'm not there to help her."

Rachel was incensed. It seemed to her that he wanted them to believe that without him there, their four-month-old baby was in mortal danger—that he was the only one who could read the monitor tapes, the only one who could protect her. And he wasn't coming back. Rachel immediately took Alexandra to Dr. Joe Gilhooly, who ran the infant apnea program at the Oregon Health Sciences Center. Gilhooly ran his own test. "I looked at the printouts," he recalls, "and there was nothing." A few days later, the Smiths got a letter from Steinschneider's lawyer demanding they return their Healthdyne monitors. The Smiths refused; their insurance carrier was paying for the monthly rentals. They would return them, they decided, when Amber and Alexandra reached their eight-month birthday.

Sherry Alexander got a letter, too. Another once-grateful parent, she believed so strongly that monitors saved her child—her daughter was one of those rare babies with true apnea and was monitored in a hospital years before Steinschneider came to Portland—that she became the Western SIDS Institute's assistant director and head of fund-raising and donated generously to the cause. A month after the center closed, Steinschneider's lawyer accused her of failing to live up to her "fiduciary responsibility" and demanded $2,500. For her, the letter made it all fit together. "I am a believer in monitors, but Al was an egotist who allowed himself to believe he was God," she said a few years later. "He had no empathy for families. We wore ourselves out. We had one or two events a weekend, but everything went right to Atlanta and most of the time they'd say we didn't make anything. Well, he had expensive tastes. He promised us updates on the research, and nothing ever came. And then when he closed down, we weren't told anything. We had two hours to leave."

When Alexander and the other members of the Portland contingent gathered in the aftermath, they concluded that for five years they had simply been conned. "It would have taken an inordinate amount of energy to stop that man," Terry Shaw, a nurse, reflected. "You fly in, you're met at the airport, you believe you are the authority, you bless it with Dionne Warwick. He gave a sense of illusion to parents, and he wasted a lot of money."

Rachel and Tony Smith took their twin girls off the monitors four months later. They returned the monitors to Healthdyne, and threw out their pictures of Steinschneider holding their babies.

"This is one of our SIDS mommies," an assistant said, introducing Gail and Gene Newby to the president of the American SIDS Institute. The young mother recoiled at the label.

With Portland now history, Steinschneider was refocusing on Atlanta. Finances were a struggle there, too, but as his roots in Georgia deepened, he made the Atlanta center a clinic with a respectable flow of babies and money. On the books, the institute was a nonprofit organization devoted to SIDS research and education. But to some of those who walked through the door of the plush suite of offices, it was a monitoring clinic. They detected an odd air to the place.

Dressed in a white lab coat, Steinschneider stood to greet the Newbys. It had only been weeks since Brian, their second child, had died at three and a half months. Steinschneider listened to their tragic story, one he had heard hundreds of times. Gail expected some words of sympathy and comfort.

"Your son would not have died had he been tested here," Steinschneider said instead.

The Newbys were stunned, speechless. They had come for some answers, but this was not one they expected. Steinschneider told them all about apnea and monitoring. The SIDS Institute, he told them, does research and monitors babies at risk of SIDS—babies like Brian, who might have had breathing abnormalities that could have been picked up shortly after birth.

Their minds reeling, they followed Steinschneider on a grand tour of the institute. He introduced them to the nurses and showed them the sleep labs, still baking at ninety degrees. They met a woman who presented them with a business card embossed with the logo of the institute. She explained that it was parents like them who made the institute possible—who helped raise money for SIDS research. She escorted them back to Steinschneider's office. The young mother found it bizarre that she had come in grief, hoping for solace and information, and found a doctor who wanted her to raise money for him.

"When you have your next baby, you bring the baby to me and I'll make sure it doesn't happen again," Steinschneider said.

"You're telling me you have a cure for SIDS?" she asked.

"Yes."

"Then why did my son die?"

"To be honest with you," Steinschneider said, leaning back into his chair, "there's just not enough money."

Gail Newby was enraged. Had her son been a victim of a preventable condition? Was this the best-kept secret at the pediatrician's office?

"If you have a way to predict who's going to die, why aren't you shouting it from the rooftops?" she said.

Steinschneider, regarding her coolly, didn't answer.

"So you're telling me that our next child will not die from SIDS if you monitor it?" She felt tears coming. "Why did Brian die? If you have these tests, why did my baby die?"

"There's just not enough money," Steinschneider repeated.

30

Wednesday, October 1, 1986, was the afternoon that Dr. John Brooks and his fellow consensus panelists climbed to the stage of Masur Auditorium in Bethesda and rendered their best judgment that there was no proven link between apnea and the sudden deaths of babies, and that the beliefs conceived from the case of Alfred Steinschneider's H. family had not been confirmed.

It was also that afternoon that Chief Assistant District Attorney Bill Fitzpatrick climbed the marble stairway of the Onondaga County Courthouse in Syracuse and opened the verdict envelope in the case of Stephen Van Der Sluys. The defendant was guilty of the murder of his three-month-old daughter, Heather. A few days later, Fitzpatrick would turn his attention to the tantalizing tip he had gotten from his star medical witness.

Brooks heard about the Van Der Sluys verdict on his arrival home in Rochester. He viewed the case as personally unsettling—another strange juxtaposition of events—but of ambiguous relevance to the work he had just finished. He knew that inflicted death was a part of the picture, but surely it was a tiny part. What *was* the truth behind all those multiple deaths within families Dan Shannon and Dotty Kelly had reported in their apnea numbers? It was a loose end of the conference. "The panel felt infanticide was a component of apnea, but they couldn't put their finger on it," remembered conference organizer Gil Hill. He had clipped and distributed two articles on infant homicide from *The New York Times*. "It didn't get discussed very thoroughly because of the extraordinary feeling of SIDS parents. They didn't ever want to let that come out in the open." For his part, Brooks decided that while the Van Der Sluys case intersected with the questions before the panel, it helped answer none of them, and so he left it alone.

That the consensus panel avoided the question was characteristic of the parallel histories of SIDS and infanticide. Murder, the suggestion of it as much as the fact, had always been in the dark periphery of the SIDS world—its nemesis. It sometimes reared its ugly head at meetings—as when some apologetic pathologist brought it up obliquely as an aside—but it was an awkward and impertinent intrusion that was quickly swept back into the shadows of science. SIDS, whatever it turned out to be, was SIDS. Murder was murder. Few dwelled on the reality that it was the SIDS enigma itself that could make the two indistinguishable.

The cat-and-mouse game was most evident in the SIDS movement's uneasy relationship with forensic pathology, a struggle that began with the alliance forged between parents and doctors in Seattle in the 1960s. As the New York forensic pathologist Michael Baden observes, "What the people in Seattle did, with all the best intentions, was to take these cases out of the medical examiner's hands, call them SIDS, and put them in the hands of pediatricians. Because of the emotional aspect of it, babies were separated from every other death. But pediatricians are not investigators. They automatically believe what they're told by parents, who they tend to think of as their patients as much as the kids. So their impulse is to protect parents. This is fine in the great majority of cases, but not for the ones that are suspicious."

From the early days, Maryland medical examiner Russell Fisher was the SIDS movement's model. A medical detective in the usual eccentric mold, Fisher's hobby was collecting miniature reenactments of crime scenes; he had more than sixty. But sudden infant death was the one place he tended not to look for crime. In a wing of his office, built with funds donated by the Guild for Infant Survival, he held sensitivity classes for police officers. While Fisher was the ideal, more probing medical examiners like Milton Helpern, Baden's first boss, were the enemy. In fact, Helpern's retirement in 1973 was a cause for rejoicing among the movement's political leadership and paved the way to a new era in SIDS. By the 1980s, SIDS counselors were working directly out of many medical examiners' offices.

In some ways the pediatric community's denial of infanticide has not been much different from the history of how it once responded to the idea of physical child abuse. There was a time when doctors encountering patterns of broken bones in children drew the conclusion that what they were looking at was a genetic metabolic disorder. It took a radiologist at Columbia University, Dr. John Caffey, to say, in a seminal paper in 1946, that the fractures were the result of trauma, though he, too, lacked the gumption to state the obvious, which was that the injuries in his six case studies were probably the result of inflicted abuse. "The traumatic episodes and the causal mechanisms remain obscure," he wrote. As the doctors from the University of Colorado wrote sixteen years later in their paper on battered-child syndrome in the *Journal of the American Medical Association:* "Physicians have great difficulty both in believing that parents could have attacked their children and in undertaking the essential questioning of parents.... Many physicians attempt to obliterate such suspicions from their minds, even in the face of obvious circumstantial evidence."

Consensus chairman George Little, who had been among those who wished there had been a way to pursue infanticide more vigorously, understood why it had not been. It wasn't just a lack of political fortitude. "We become pediatricians because we love children, and we don't want to believe these things can happen to them," Little reflected. "We resist it. It's not surprising that it took a radiologist to first recognize the signs of battered-child syndrome. And there are parallels with apnea. It's not surprising that the forensic pathologists, the bad news people, were the ones that recognized it first."

Philadelphia's "Moore" family, sympathetically portrayed by *Life* in 1963 and ultimately untouched by prosecutors who felt they couldn't prove what virtually everyone involved thought, may have been the classic example of the human impulse to look away. Among the circumstantial evidence that never became public, according to Molly Dapena, was that the parents had collected insurance on each of their dead children—and that the policies had been taken out in different states. And when Dapena all but told her SIDS colleagues at the 1969 meeting on Orcas Island that it was likely a case of multiple murders, the researchers sat in uncomfortable silence and never brought it up again, at least not in public. The 1969 meeting would set the tone for the next twenty years: It was the discussion of the possible role of respiration raised by newcomer Alfred Steinschneider that many found most intriguing.

It was that same year, however, that the SIDS community had to confront an astonishingly similar case that did come into public view just down the road in Baltimore, the birthplace of the Guild for Infant Survival. But even the landmark arrest of Martha Woods had little impact on the SIDS world, least of all on the local medical examiner, Russell Fisher.

Having been associated with at least one infant death and a recent history of rushing babies to emergency rooms and saying they had stopped breathing, Woods was accused of the murder of her last child, an adopted baby named Paul, in the fall of 1969. By chance, Paul had been born the week of the Orcas Island conference in February of that year—the meeting at which Fisher helped launch the talk of "near-miss" SIDS that would preoccupy the SIDS world for two decades. The baby's body arrived at Fisher's morgue in Baltimore seven months later, at the conclusion of a six-week-long series of reported near-misses. By the time of her murder trial in 1972, Woods, an itinerant Army wife, was linked to the deaths of seven children, stretching back twenty-six years, to 1946. The list of victims included three of her natural children, a niece, a nephew, and a neighbor's child; two others had survived life-threatening episodes apparently induced by Woods. The trial lasted five months and generated nine thousand pages of court transcript. The prosecutor, Charles Bernstein, was dismayed to see in the gallery each day members of a SIDS group who came in support of the defendant. But Russell Fisher supported the prosecution. He told Bernstein that this case had nothing to do with SIDS.

Bernstein's chief medical witness was not Fisher but a young armed forces forensic pathologist named Vincent DiMaio, whose father, Dominick, had once been the chief medical examiner of New York City. The younger DiMaio had started a fellowship in forensic pathology in Fisher's office a few weeks before the body of Paul Woods came into the morgue. DiMaio performed the autopsy and stayed with the case when he moved on to head the Wound Ballistics Section of the Armed Forces Forensic Pathology Branch.

Martha Woods had a profound impact on DiMaio. He realized that the case, both legally unprecedented and medically revealing, offered a mother lode of new knowledge for those in both fields interested in ferreting out cases of infanticide hidden in the SIDS files. He and Bernstein went on to collaborate on a landmark article—"A Case of Infanticide"—in the *Journal of Forensic Sciences*. Published in 1974, it demonstrated how easily a parent could disguise child abuse as both SIDS and near-miss SIDS. But the article went unnoticed by those who attended that year's SIDS conference in Toronto, where the big news was apnea monitors. Two years later, DiMaio moved on to Texas, where his new colleague Linda Norton introduced him to Steinschneider's 1972 paper, a famous monograph in pediatrics but not in forensic pathology. DiMaio didn't have to think twice when he read it. "Oh, yeah," he said. "That's homicide." It was Martha Woods all over again—only in this case, the mother apparently didn't go to the trouble of moving around the country to avoid detection. In fact, it seemed Mrs. H. performed her last two killings while the soon-to-be-famous SIDS doctor looked on—and just as Woods was waiting to go on trial in Baltimore. The trial lasted from February to June 1972—exactly the months when Steinschneider's paper was being peer-reviewed for publication in *Pediatrics*. It would be years before the world medical community would recognize that things were not always what they seemed.

The awakening began quietly in 1977, when a British pediatrician named Roy Meadow came upon evidence that there were some people in the world—

nearly always women—who faked or caused illnesses in their own children to gain attention and sympathy, particularly from the medical establishment. Meadow modified a memorable term that another British physician, Richard Asher, had applied in 1951 to people who invented their own illnesses for the same reason. Recalling the fanciful, fib-telling eighteenth century German baron Karl Friedrich Freiherr von Munchhausen, Asher had coined the name Munchausen syndrome. Roy Meadow added two words and published his observations in the prestigious British journal *The Lancet,* under the title: "Munchausen Syndrome by Proxy: The Hinterland of Child Abuse."

Munchausen by proxy could vary in form and severity. An older child might be poisoned or otherwise made repeatedly sick in a way meant to baffle doctors. In severe cases, children might be forced to undergo years of misguided medical treatment and dozens of unnecessary operations. But with a baby, the ruse was much simpler to pull off. Some mothers might report a fictitious life-threatening incident, others genuinely bring their babies to the brink of death. Still others might actually kill them. It was a description of the behavior of Martha Woods.

In the early 1980s, in the wake of David Southall's London studies, it began occurring to a few pediatric professionals that the apnea theory and the monitoring concept that came with it were a godsend to women playing out this grotesque charade. The concept of pathological apnea had been legitimized by the medical establishment, codified by terms like near-miss SIDS and the acronym ALTE that replaced it. And the monitors could easily be used as devices of deception. *The alarm went off and I gave her mouth-to-mouth.* Or *The alarm went off but by the time I got there it was too late.*

The thought even seems to have crossed Alfred Steinschneider's mind from time to time. As Debbie Fleischmann, one of the nurses who worked in his lab in Baltimore, remembered: "He talked about Munchausen by proxy, that a little flag would go up with repeating incidents. We had a clinical program grow out of the research because so many people were looking to us for help. But if a mother reported repeated episodes but there was never anything going on with their kids, there was suspicion."

It was much more difficult for doctors to prove a Munchausen by proxy case than for mothers to perpetrate it. In 1984, just as the entity was becoming generally known in medical circles in the United States, the chief of psychiatry at Children's Hospital Oakland in California, Dr. Herbert A. Schreier, and a pediatric psychologist at the hospital, Judith A. Libow, encountered several apparent cases that led them to research the topic. In their exploration, which they would later publish as a book, *Hurting for Love,* they heard this from one pediatrician: "As a physician, one of the things you learn early on is to listen to the parents. And what makes Munchausen by proxy syndrome so difficult to deal with is that your ally in the child's health care is really not your ally. I don't want to use the word 'adversary,' but in fact I guess it is an adversarial relationship, because they are playing a game with you, except you don't know you're playing a game. And frankly, I'm not a detective. I'm not Perry Mason and I don't want to be. . . . And I think that makes it even more difficult because when you finally accuse the person, it's a question of, 'Well, can you prove it?' Well, no, I can't prove it. If they are looking for hard evidence, it's not going to be there. . . ."

In the decade following the publication of Roy Meadow's 1977 paper, Munchausen by proxy became a new area of interest in pediatric research. Among those who found the question most compelling was Dr. David Southall.

Having taken notice of his fellow Briton's bizarre discovery, and after spending several years debunking the apnea theory of SIDS, Southall decided to take his research in what he considered a logical direction. He gave his new subject a dignified, medical name—"imposed upper airway obstruction"—but what he was really investigating was child abuse. He wanted to know how commonly Apparent Life Threatening Events, and death itself, were caused by the hand of a parent or caretaker.

In Great Britain, this was even thornier and more ambiguous an issue than in the United States. On the one hand, British law had long been open-minded enough to take into account the possible role of postpartum depression and psychosis in dealing with mothers who killed their children. After a 1927 study by a medical superintendent at the State Criminal Lunatic Asylum at Broadmoor found that nearly half the women there had allegedly killed their babies, the English Parliament changed the official charge in such acts from murder to the noncriminal "infanticide"—provided the victims were no more than a year and a day old—and put the accused in hospitals, not prisons. On the other hand, it was possible that the babies of some of the women in Broadmoor had actually died of cot death. Either way, half a century later Britons were no more interested in thinking of mothers as killers than Americans were. When pediatric pathologist John Emery suggested in 1982 that perhaps ten percent of reported SIDS deaths were what he called "gentle homicides," it caused a national uproar. Emery was the rare SIDS investigator who pursued both natural and unnatural infant death, but for his objective conclusion about infanticide he was pilloried—denounced even on the floor of Parliament. (Perhaps not coincidentally, it was at a time when Lady Limerick and her United Kingdom SIDS foundation were as active in Britain as the forces behind Abe Bergman and the Goldbergs were in America.)

Nevertheless, against the tide on both sides of the Atlantic, Southall took some brave steps away from apnea and in the direction of child abuse. To do this, he and his colleagues would have to become, in effect, a squad of detectives. Monitors and polygraphs had been the tools of Southall's investigation of the apnea theory in the late 1970s. Now, to explore the even more elusive idea of *inflicted* apnea, he realized the only way to know for sure was to use a new piece of equipment: a video camera.

One of his first cases was that of a little boy whose twenty-two months of life had been marked by repeated, mysterious episodes of apnea and cyanosis requiring emergency measures. At twenty months, the child was admitted to London's Brompton Hospital, and attached to a recording monitor. The boy's mother never left his side. The next night, she summoned the nurses, who found him blue and unconscious. They resuscitated him with an oxygen face mask. His mother said she'd heard a "rattling noise" coming from his bed, went to him, and called for help when she found him in trouble. Four weeks later, the child was readmitted and had two similar episodes while asleep and with his mother in the room. When they analyzed the tape from the event recorder, the doctors saw two points in which the tracings indicated sudden body movements, each lasting about a minute. In the second episode, an oxygen monitor lead disconnected five seconds after the beginning of the event and then reconnected just after the end of the body movements. Southall and his colleagues began talking about the mother.

When they examined the hospital records, they confirmed that no episodes had occurred in her absence. Searching further into the child's history, the doctors obtained records showing that the boy had had cyanotic episodes almost weekly during the first year of his life, apparently a more extreme version of his older sister's experience several years before. He had been seen by a number of specialists, and treated with anticonvulsants and other drugs. An apnea monitor had been prescribed. At thirteen months, the family's pediatrician told the mother that the child seemed to be thriving and that further workups would be required only if he had episodes of unconsciousness. A week later, he was rushed to a local hospital, unconscious. "Recovery was protracted," Southall later wrote, "and there was concern that there might be permanent neurological damage. Thereafter most of his episodes included loss of consciousness and convulsions."

A small convention of doctors, nurses, social workers, and hospital administrators met to figure out how to substantiate or exclude the suffocation "hypothesis." That night, the London police arrived at the hospital. They set up video surveillance equipment in the room next to the child's cubicle.

Sixteen hours after they turned on the camera, with the child asleep and only his mother present, this is what they saw: She moved her chair away from the crib and lowered the bars. She put a tee-shirt on the bed, next to the child's face. She walked around the room for a few minutes. Then she put the tee-shirt over her son's mouth and nose and forced his head onto the mattress. He woke up immediately and began to struggle violently. Seeing this, a policewoman alerted the nurses, who dashed into the cubicle. "I was checking his arm," the mother said. "It was twitching."

Now there was a problem. The doctors and detectives had agreed that they would wait until forty seconds into an attack before interceding, a time too short to be life-threatening, but just long enough to get an event recording on paper that matched the previous ones. In the first instance, the policewoman had overreacted, upset at the horrible scene playing on the video monitor.

The surveillance resumed. Half an hour later, the mother repeated the assault. The policewoman cringed as she watched the boy thrash about on the small screen. The nurses went in at forty-two seconds. The child was conscious. "He woke up screaming," said his mother. "I was comforting him."

The mother was arrested, and David Southall's skepticism of the apnea theory had a grim new twist. He published the case in the *British Medical Journal* in 1987, and in the next few years went on to use video surveillance to document thirty-two more cases of "apnea" caused by suffocation. With each case, his views hardened. "One major cause of 'near-miss SIDS' is suffocation," he would say one day in London. "We don't know how many SIDS cases, but it is a third of all near-misses." He took an equally hard line on the notion of multiple deaths within families: "After one, I think they are all Munchausen unless proven otherwise." Eventually it would dawn on him that perhaps the very paper that had launched the apnea theory was just such a case. "I looked at Steinschneider's paper again," Southall said, "and it was obvious to me it was a case of suffocation. It was child abuse. I hadn't been aware in 1972 that parents could do this."

With Southall taking a leading role, the literature on infanticide and Munchausen by proxy began pulling up alongside that of apnea. Even as the consensus conference was doing its work in Bethesda, research on recurrent life-threatening events as a symptom of child abuse was appearing regularly in the world's medical journals, some articles suggesting a merger between *The New England Journal of Medicine* and *Hard Copy*. A group of doctors headed by Carol Lynn Rosen at Houston's Baylor College of Medicine matched Southall's experience with six cases of their own. They became expert in how a small number of mothers used the apnea theory as a weapon of deception, and were the first to report the use of videotaped documentation. When Mary Sheridan asked members of her group, the National Association of Apnea Professionals, if they had seen any cases of infant apnea that they suspected were caused by a parent, the heads of fifty-one apnea programs, forty percent, said they had, though it was a tiny percentage of the total cases. A few years after she founded the apnea organization, Sheridan started an offshoot group: the Munchausen by Proxy Network. She thought parentally induced apnea was common enough to warrant its own designation. She began referring to it as "Munchausen syndrome by proxy—apnea," or MBPA. By the 1990s, a number of the apnea centers begun by hospitals a decade before would install their own video surveillance equipment.

Back in England, meanwhile, Roy Meadow found when he reviewed twenty-seven cases of confirmed suffocation by mothers (resulting in nine deaths and one child left with brain damage) that all but three had had previous episodes, and forty percent had more than ten. Most significantly, eighteen of these children—two-thirds—had siblings who had died suddenly and unexpectedly in early life.

What could lead these mothers to kill their own children remained much more enigmatic. Infanticide is as old as the ages, and the methods, as well as the motivations behind them, are various and complex. The murder of weak, deformed, or unwanted children has been prevalent in many cultures, and anthropologists have argued that infanticide has been used as a method of population control throughout much of human history. In modern times, any number of notorious cases demonstrate there is no limit to the variations and psychological intricacies of fatal child abuse. But serial infanticide—mothers giving birth to babies only to kill them a few months later, repeating the process again and again—is a special sort of perversion.

It is this form of infant murder—as distinguished from the single, perhaps psychotic act—that was coming to be most closely associated with Munchausen syndrome by proxy because of both its repetitive nature and the involuted relationships that often played out between a mother, her baby, and her baby's doctor. It is a different and much more subtle dynamic than that commonly found in cases of classic child abuse. In the view of Oakland's Herbert Schreier, a doctor ensnared in a Munchausen by proxy deception is both the object of the mother's treachery and her unwitting partner. The child is merely a pawn. Schreier's research found that unlike other forms of child homicide, serial infanticide is characterized by cold, premeditated manipulation by a mother whose only goal is to win the sympathy and attention she craves. She has no feeling for her baby, who exists only as an instrument to help her achieve her psychological goal. "I would strongly argue that this is a form of female perversion, and a type of imposturing," he said. "When you see them, they seem very loving and nurturing. But when you videotape them at home, they ignore their kids, don't talk to them. The kids don't matter."

Why they don't matter—*how* they could not matter—is the central enigma. Given an entity that has only relatively recently been recognized and studied, the explanations are more impressionistic than scientific and often influenced by the particular theory a specialist chooses to embrace. Stuart Asch's hypothesis of postpartum psychosis—a rare disorder he has found to be most common in women vulnerable to manic depression—holds that the baby does matter, but as a representation of its mother. She becomes consumed by the idea that the baby is a part of her—the bad part—and that she must destroy it, a form of symbolic suicide that Asch, who has not made a specialty of serial cases, thinks can repeat itself. But this theory, while perhaps valid in some instances, does not fit those that come to involve the elaborate medical con game that characterizes Munchausen by proxy.

In these cases, Schreier thinks, the mother's psychological upheaval is so powerful and all-consuming that she manages to dehumanize the baby in order to achieve her higher goal. To him, the key is in what the doctor represents. He has found that in general, Munchausen by proxy women—whether they kill or only cause illness—have grown up feeling undervalued, unwanted, and powerless. In some cases, physical or sexual abuse in their own childhoods may be a factor, though psychological neglect or abandonment is more common. Often these women have had absent or distant fathers and develop dependent personalities. But a dependent person can also be manipulative and controlling, and this behavior is often facilitated by the weak, deferential men Munchausen women often marry.

Schreier hypothesizes that these women use their own children to form an unreal relationship with a powerful and unattainable person, a doctor, whom they fantasize can fix an earlier trauma. They seize on a baby's birth as an opportunity to control the doctor, inventing or inducing illness that will compel his attention. Some of these women concurrently play out a version of Munchausen syndrome themselves, fabricating their own infirmities for attention. "In so doing," Schreier and his co-author Libow write in *Hurting for Love,* "they try to maintain an intense, yet distant, perverse, and ambivalent relationship with a powerfully loved and powerfully feared paternal representative." Ultimately, the fragility of this complex, obsessive, and illusory relationship may lead to the death of one or more children. But, they add, it may not be until the deception is discovered and the mother perhaps arrested "that the hospital staff pieces together the oddly discontinuous elements of the woman's hospital sojourn: an intense interest in her child's medical procedures coexisting with a surprising absence of parental concern; a response of relief or even excitement when her infant goes under the scalpel for yet another procedure, or teeters near death from an illness she herself has caused; the long hours spent in the hospital during which less attention is paid to the child than to ward clerks and other parents; and finally behavior that puts her at risk of being caught, only to continue her 'pursuit' compulsively as clues to her deception are overlooked."

Munchausen by proxy mothers typically become infatuated not only with doctors but with the whole medical environment—hospitals, procedures, even equipment. "Apnea monitors are a magnet for this type of person," observes Carol Lynn Rosen. (The files of the Food and Drug Administration contain a number of reports of babies whose deaths while on monitors—cases investigated for monitor malfunction—point instead to the possibility of fatal child abuse.) Even the climate of anxiety created by the monitor phenomenon speaks to the motivations of a Munchausen mother. "The moments of greatest medical threat to the baby are the moments when the mother feels most powerful," write Schreier and Libow. If the baby dies as a result, there is no panic—to the contrary—because doctors and others often become even more attentive. It's why this form of homicide is considered one of the few that is recidivistic: The payoff can become addictive. Typically, funerals are elaborately ritualized and marked by the mother's open plays for sympathy. Schreier has found that, despite appearances, there is often "a profound lack of remorse or depression in these mothers, even when their children die. . . . The harm that the mothers do to their infants, at times ghastly and even fatal, takes place as if it were not of their doing."

Though by the mid-1980s it was becoming increasingly apparent that the Munchausen version of child abuse had credence as a small but compelling factor in SIDS—and might be a major element of near-miss SIDS—there remained some prominent holdouts, some more surprising than others. Perhaps the most perplexing skeptic was John Smialek, a highly respected medical examiner who seemed personally insulted by suggestions of infanticide. In 1986 he published a very strange paper in *Pediatrics* in which he cited nine cases from the world literature of infant twins dying simultaneously. He considered this a medical "phenomenon," and seemed bewildered about why people were so suspicious. "It is hoped," he wrote, "that increased awareness of this phenomenon will decrease the profound suspicions of both lay and professional persons that the deaths were due to criminal instrumentality." Smialek later became the chief medical examiner of Maryland, the job once held by Russell Fisher.

Alfred Steinschneider's views on multiple SIDS, recurrent apnea, and infanticide were, of course, immovable and well recognized. When *The New England Journal of Medicine* published an article in 1986 suggesting that many SIDS deaths were actually either inflicted or accidental smothering, Steinschneider was one of many people who rose up in protest. The article's lead author was Dr. Millard Bass, an osteopath specializing in forensic pathology and a controversial advocate of the infanticide theory. With two pediatricians from Brooklyn's Kings County Hospital Center, Bass reported that most of the twenty-six consecutive SIDS cases they reviewed among a poor population in Brooklyn were caused by a variety of identifiable causes, including suffocation and accidental smothering. "They are poor as scientists," Steinschneider told Portland's *Oregonian,* "and the nature of their evidence would not hold up if it were ever brought before a jury."

By this point, Steinschneider no longer had an affiliation with a major university or hospital that gave him access to great numbers of babies for his studies. So it was that the team of Daniel Shannon and Dorothy Kelly emerged as the leading advocates of the concept of familial SIDS and apnea. For years, the Mass General program had attracted referrals of families with previous infant deaths or babies with repeated, unexplained apneic events. In fact, the Boston doctors told the NIH consensus conference that they had treated twenty-eight families with two or more SIDS deaths. Southall's work, and the expanding body of apnea-and-child-abuse literature, failed to persuade Shannon and Kelly that—as some on the consensus panel thought but dared not explore—they might have been unwittingly mixing infanticides into their data.

In September 1987, Kelly and Shannon published a paper in *Pediatrics* from the resolutely unskeptical material they had presented in Bethesda the year before. They called the article, which was prepared from their data by a Harvard pediatric research fellow named Joseph Oren, "Familial Occurrence of Sudden Infant Death Syndrome and Apnea of Infancy." They offered Steinschneider's 1972 paper as the foundation for their premise that SIDS could occur repeatedly within families, then described the deaths of five babies, all of whom had been born into families with two or more previous SIDS cases. "A recent report by Rosen et al, based on a family with three previous SIDS victims, suggests that some cases of SIDS were parentally induced and represent a form of child abuse," they wrote. "Included in the present study are two families who had four SIDS victims and two families who had three SIDS victims; however, we are unable to identify any evidence of child abuse in these families."

The study was one of several by Shannon and Kelly in the mid-1980s that helped reinforce the mythology of Steinschneider's 1972 paper. But times were changing. It also led to futile efforts to point them in the direction of reality. When Carol Rosen read another of their papers, reporting that four of thirteen babies died after they had had two apneic episodes requiring resuscitation—a 31 percent mortality rate, Kelly and Shannon announced—she answered with an article in another journal intended, she wrote, "to show that child abuse may contribute to this high mortality . . . and to review the elements of the clinical history that can be predictive of this possibility." Rosen, who like a number of specialists from around the country had gotten some of her basic apnea training by spending a month with Shannon and Kelly in Boston in the early 1980s, now believed there was no question that recurrent ALTEs were frequently a warning sign of Munchausen-style child abuse.

The *Pediatrics* article also found its way into the hands of Vincent DiMaio. In the fifteen years since the Martha Woods case, he had become one of the country's most outspoken medical examiners on the issue of infanticide. He found the Harvard-Mass General group's naïveté maddening and said so in a letter to *Pediatrics* editor Jerold Lucey, who published it a few months later. All five deaths, DiMaio wrote, were "in all medical probability homicides by smothering." Cases like this usually followed the same pattern, he added: repeated trips to the hospital with reports of life-threatening apneic episodes, nothing found by medical personnel, and finally, death after another purported spell at home. "The perpetrator is virtually always the mother and she will continue this killing unless stopped or until she runs out of children."

DiMaio's final comment (which he would restate in a 1989 textbook, *Forensic Pathology,* co-authored with his father) put a sinister face on the research that Kelly and Shannon had cited as their foundation: "The association of SIDS with apneic episodes as an entity was brought to prominence in an article by Steinschneider," he wrote. "A review of this paper indicates that his two reported cases of sudden infant death associated with prolonged apnea were in siblings and probably victims of homicides, as were prior siblings. This opinion is held by a number of forensic pathologists who have read the paper. The aforementioned opinions elicit savagely antagonistic responses from a number of individuals involved in the sudden infant death syndrome movement. What they have lost sight of is the fact that all that SIDS means is 'I don't know why the child died.' . . . Unfortunately, some cases are homicides by smothering. To deny this is to fall in the same trap that physicians fell into when the original concept of the battered-baby syndrome was put forth. Clinicians denied this entity for years with the explanation: 'They are such nice people. They couldn't have harmed their child.' "

Kelly alone responded to DiMaio. As the central evidence of her defense against the accusation of smothering, she offered the pneumogram, the technique that had been discredited as a tool for predicting SIDS. "Four of these five infants had abnormalities," she wrote. "Also, one of these four infants was prospectively investigated in a study of infant cries, and her cry was distinctly abnormal." She closed with a defense of Steinschneider's case studies that demonstrated how long-surviving the central illusion of his 1972 paper had been: "Although no one except the mother was present at the time of the deaths of these infants, both infants had had multiple episodes of prolonged apnea recorded on polygraph when tested by Dr. Steinschneider. . . ."

The apnea consensus conference did nothing to challenge the mythology. The gathering of pediatricians chose to keep the homicide hypothesis in the shadows, where it had always been, at precisely the same time that both the Marybeth Tinning and Stephen Van Der Sluys cases were playing out in full public view in upstate New York. It was ironic, but not surprising, that they ignored this possibility in yet another case from the same state—the one that was at the core of everything they had come together to discuss. Apnea and infanticide: The two entities kept their secrets and gave each other legitimacy—just as Waneta Hoyt and Alfred Steinschneider had. The strange confluence of events of October 1, 1986, was allegorical: The deaths of her children and the birth of his theory were inseparable.

And it was from that point on—slowly, inexorably, for another eight years—that the truth rose up from the burial grounds.

PART FOUR

Errata

I'm not a mean, depraved Munchausen. I'm a victim of circum-stances, stuck in the middle of a medical and political situation.
—WANETA HOYT

31

March 23, 1994

Waneta Hoyt saw the Owego Town Hall come into view as Trooper Bob Bleck sailed down the road that hugged the south bank of the Susquehanna River. Bleck slowed the unmarked car, turned into the parking lot, and swung around to the back. The state police station was tucked into a rear quadrant of the building. Sue Mulvey alighted from her side of the car, and Bleck opened the other door for Waneta. She climbed out, holding her photograph album like a prayer book. She looked not merely older now, but time-worn. The soft, dark curls that had once covered her head were reduced to scanty colorless strands. At forty-seven, she was a forlorn figure, shapeless in body and soul.

Mulvey and Bleck led Waneta to the door of the police barracks. They walked her through a small reception area and down a narrow hallway. The station seemed empty. Waneta didn't know that the Tioga County district attorney, Bob Simpson, was in a room down another hallway, along with two backup interviewers, two BCI lieutenants, and a court stenographer.

She arrived at the doorway to the tiny interview room, where Bob Court-right stood, trying not to betray the tension that had been building for days. He had barely stopped smoking since the last meeting at the Treadway the day before.

"Waneta, this is Senior Investigator Courtright," Mulvey said. "He's my boss. He's going to be taking some notes, just so we can keep things straight." In his hands, Courtright held five sheets of white paper. At the top of each page, he had condensed the lives and deaths of each of Waneta's children to a few typed lines, a version of the record Waneta kept on the opening page of her Bible: the child's name, dates of birth and death, age at the time of death, and the circumstances originally reported. Courtright didn't want to spook her with a video camera or tape recorder. He would fill the pages as she talked about her children on this day twenty-nine years after they had begun dying mysteriously.

He hadn't planned on Bleck's participation, but when Waneta said, "I'd like Bobby to stay," Courtright said that would be fine. Maybe hearing the Miranda warnings from him would ease the way. It was the next hurdle; another chance for Waneta to decide this conversation was not in her best interest. Mulvey retrieved a chair for Bleck, and Waneta, foiling Courtright's seating plan, sat herself in the corner, at the far end of the six-foot-long table. Bleck sat down next to her. Would you like something to drink? Mulvey asked. Some coffee or soda? Coffee, Waneta said. Black. She put the photo album on the table.

"Trooper Bleck is going to advise you of your rights now," Courtright said, just about holding his breath as Bleck raised his Miranda card to allow Waneta to see the words as he read them. She had the right to remain silent, he said, and the right to a lawyer. Anything she said could be used against her in a court of law. Did she understand these rights? Yes, she said. Did she agree to talk without a lawyer present? Yes.

"This is standard procedure, Waneta," Bleck added, trying to soften the moment. "Whenever somebody comes down here they have to be Mirandized."

Waneta looked unworried, but Mulvey thought it best to move on. "Well, what we'd like to do is start with some general things, some background about you and Tim, that sort of thing." Waneta began recounting her life, how she had grown up in Richford, how she'd quit school to marry Tim, how they'd had their first child in the fall of 1964. Mulvey asked the questions and Courtright took the notes, interjecting now and then to establish a detail. This was Mulvey's interview, and in a subtle way, Bleck's as well. Waneta took his hand soon after he put his Miranda card away and didn't let go. She used her free hand to flip the pages of the photo album, pointing to the faded snapshots as she began to talk about each of her long-gone children. She flipped past a picture of herself with Tim—they were feeding each other wedding cake—to a page of pictures of the child born nine months and one week later.

"That's Eric," Waneta said. "He died early in the morning." He was cold and blue, she remembered, lying on his stomach when she found him. Tim was at work when it happened. "I ran to my neighbors. The Lanes. They called the ambulance." Eric always had problems, Waneta said. "We were up to Mom's one day and he turned blue. She took him out into the fresh air. . . ."

One by one, Waneta summoned images of brief life and sudden death, elliptical reminiscences that the investigators did little to guide. They let her talk, offering occasional words of support, even sympathy, to further the rapport they would need later, when they turned the tables. When Waneta said that Julie just turned blue and died in her crib, they did not point out that twenty-six years before, she said the baby had "choked on rice cereal." The "negative" interview was only a prologue. Get her talking, get her comfortable, that was the plan. Janice Ophoven and Michael Baden, the forensic pathologists, had left them with no doubts about what had become of the five Hoyt children. What they needed was to hear it from their mother.

Not until after they'd driven from the Cornell public safety office to the Ithaca barracks and settled into the senior investigator's office, after Bill Standinger talked about how he used to work construction before he joined the troopers, after they talked about the weather, and the country, and how the country was messed up and why, did Tim Hoyt say, "All right, so why am I here? What do you guys want to talk about?"

Standinger and John Sherman had drawn the assignment of interviewing Waneta Hoyt's husband. They were relieved; they didn't want Waneta. Way too much pressure. "Well, Bob better take her because he's got twenty-five years down," Standinger had joked to Sherman, "so if he screws it up, he can retire." Still, he and Sherman spent a week going over how they'd approach the interview with Tim. It was not out of the question that he was involved, or that he knew something. In fact, they wondered how he could *not* have known. Over beers at Bud's Place, they decided male bonding was the way to go. Tim was working as a guard at the Cornell art museum; Standinger was hoping his Pinkerton uniform made him feel a little like a cop.

"We need to talk to you about your children," Standinger said. "The deaths of your children."

Tim's face tightened. Unlike Waneta, he became instantly upset. "Why are you bringing this up now?" he blurted. "It's been twenty years. We went through this . . ."

"Well, we've been directed by the district attorney to look into this," Standinger said casually, trying to preserve the friendly environment. "We're just doing our job. We've talked to some doctors, and we'd like to hear your version of the deaths."

"This is really gonna hurt my wife," Tim said, growing more agitated by the second. "This'll just break her. We went through all this twenty years ago. Why are you bringing this up now?"

"We know this is hard, but we'd just like you to tell us what you remember. Just take us through each of the children, and tell us whatever you remember."

Reluctantly, Tim unfolded his life story, starting, as Waneta had, with their marriage in 1964. "We were living with my mother," he recounted edgily. "I was working at NCR, or maybe the forging works in Endicott. I can't remember. Maybe Grumman, over in Marathon. You're talking thirty years ago. . . .

"The first baby was born that October. That was Eric. Right away, he had problems. He was what they called a blue baby. We had him to the hospital a bunch of times. . . . The doctors told us he had heart problems. Then it was January 26, 1965. I believe I had left for work that morning and while I was at work someone got ahold of me and told me to go right home. . . ."

"I remember Julie was dainty," Waneta said matter-of-factly. "I think Mom Hoyt found her."

Julie died so close to Jimmy, she said—just three weeks apart—that she had trouble distinguishing the two. Art and Natalie Hilliard helped after the funerals, she remembered. Joyce Aman came from the county to visit. Carla Bonham, a teenager from the neighborhood, used to baby-sit. She lived in Florida now. The sheriff's department brought "Dr. Angel." They did an autopsy.

Courtright, writing everything down, knew Waneta was wrong about many of the details. Jimmy, not Julie, was autopsied; Floyd Angel had responded to Molly's death, not Julie's or Jimmy's. At one point, Courtright asked about the strangely close timing of the deaths of Julie and Jimmy.

"I remember Dr. Hartnagel was suspicious," Waneta said. "He thought I did something to the babies. He was asking people questions." Did anyone else feel this way? "My sister-in-law, Gloria. She criticized me. She died a long time ago."

"Tell us about James," Mulvey said. This was the one Waneta would have the hardest time explaining, Courtright thought. At the top of the third sheet, he had typed: *Number 3. James Hoyt. Born 5/31/66 Died 9/26/68, 2 years 4 months old, came into house from playing and said "Mommy" and bled from nose and mouth and died suddenly.*

"The pregnancy went like a breeze," Waneta said blithely. "It was just one or two hours of labor. He was almost three when he died. He was a healthy, growing baby. Never had any of those turning-blue spells. He was just a per-fectly fine, normal, healthy two-year-old boy." The snapshots confirmed the description. Jimmy was all over the photo album, a vibrant, happy child who seemed older than two. "He died about eight or eight-thirty in the morning," Waneta said.

"Were you home alone?" Courtright asked.

"Yes," Waneta said. "Tim was working construction somewhere in Waverly."

"What happened?"

"Jimmy was in the bedroom. I heard a blood-curdling scream, and he came running down the hall with blood on his nose and mouth and just collapsed in my hands. I knew he was gone. He never said anything."

"What did you do then?"

"I scooped him up and ran outside and flagged down the garbageman."

She had actually brought Jimmy to Natalie Hilliard's house. She had flagged down the garbage man with Julie. But when she got to Molly and Noah, her accounts grew in complexity, the first hint that she might be scratching beneath the surface. She put her finger on a snapshot of Molly, but began talking about herself, not the baby. "I got some help," she said. "I thought I did something wrong. I got help from a doctor. Dr. Jafri. But I didn't like him. He gave me the impression I did something wrong and I quit going. He gave me Valium."

"Did you talk about the children's deaths with Tim?" Courtright asked.

"Not really. We were going through a quiet spell. We were having problems . . . money problems, paying on the funerals, ten dollars or whatever we could give. Marital problems. For a while, we were like strangers."

Tim Hoyt struck Bill Standinger as a middle-aged country boy of uncomplicated intellect, affable enough. With broad shoulders and gray hair as abundant as his wife's was sparse, Tim, now fifty-one, had aged much more gracefully than Waneta. To the investigators, it seemed clear that he didn't know very much about how his children had died. He was always at work when it happened, he told them, but he knew one thing: These babies all had problems, even though Dr. Steinschneider—he was a big expert up in Syracuse—said it wasn't hereditary. They all had breathing problems, all except Eric. Eric had heart trouble. The rest had trouble with their breathing. Dr. Steinschneider said they had apnea. They all died of SIDS. It was all right in the medical records.

Tim remembered what he could about each of the children, tried to recall what Waneta told him each time they died, what the doctors said, where he was when he found out, how Waneta reacted. It was always pretty much the same. "My wife told me she turned blue and died. . . ." he repeated. Waneta was never far from the conversation. "She's got all kinds of medical problems.

She's got heart problems, osteoporosis, hypertension. If we had all the money we spent on doctor bills we could buy a wing on the hospital."

Like Waneta, he had some trouble distinguishing among the children. "We brought Julie to Upstate several times," he said, apparently thinking of Molly. "She stayed there a long time. She had problems with apnea. . . . Jimmy died of apnea, too," he said. "And he had something wrong in his throat."

Tim deflected all the investigator's questions. Was he ever suspicious of the deaths? No—never. Whose idea was it to have children? We both wanted children. Was Waneta under a lot of stress? Well, wouldn't you be? Was he the natural father of all the children? Yes. Were he and Waneta ever separated? Not for one day. At one point, Sherman asked Tim if he had ever thought about other women. "No!" he answered indignantly. "I'm a married man. I love my wife. What are you trying to say?" Sherman had intended the question to be provocative, and he and Standinger thought Tim's reaction was revealing. Incredible as it seemed to them, it appeared entirely possible that Tim never had questioned his wife's stories; never wondered why his children always seemed to die right after he went to work. "He was just a very trusting, devoted type of person," Standinger said later. "If his wife came inside in the middle of summer and said there's snow on the ground, he'd believe it because she said it."

After an hour or so, Sherman asked Tim if he would give a signed statement. "Yeah, all right," Tim said. "I still don't see why you're bringing this up after all these years. This is just gonna destroy my wife. Is she gonna be talked to?"

"Yes," Sherman said, slipping a page into the typewriter. "She probably will be."

"What happened when Molly died?" Mulvey asked Waneta.

"Well, Dr. Steinschneider had her come up to Upstate to check for SIDS. She got better, and he sent her home with an apnea machine. She died maybe three days after she came home. She was in her bassinet. I fed her about nine or nine-thirty. . . . She coughed a couple of times. . . . The machine went off and I called Dr. Steinschneider. Mom Hoyt checked her and said she was lifeless. The squad came and they tried to resuscitate her. . . ."

She flipped to the pictures of Noah. Among them was the one taken with Steinschneider in the hospital. He was holding Noah close, and Noah was looking up into his eyes. "He was born on Mother's Day," Waneta said. "He went right to Upstate. He came home in three weeks and was having episodes on the monitor. A couple of times he quit breathing. He was back to the hospital about four times but Dr. Steinschneider said he was fine and sent him home." What happened when he died? He was in the living room, she thought. The apnea monitor went off. "Usually, I would just give him a nudge, but this time I couldn't get him to breathe."

Was anyone else there? "Mom Hoyt," Waneta said. "She pounded him on the back. He was turning blue. . . ."

"Why don't we take a break," Courtright said after a little more than an hour. "Can we get you anything to eat?" he asked Waneta. No, she said.

Courtright and Mulvey retreated to the room on the other side of the barracks where Simpson and the BCI lieutenants were waiting. Simpson had watched bits of the questioning through a one-way mirror in an adjacent room, but he couldn't hear much. Meanwhile, Bill Fitzpatrick and Pete Tynan had arrived from Syracuse, eager for news. "She says Timothy's mother was with her at two of the deaths, maybe three," Courtright reported as the group crowded around him. For the most part, he said, Waneta was telling them what she'd told everyone else twenty and thirty years before, but the part about her mother-in-law was important. Lieutenant Jackmin decided to dispatch one of the backup investigators to interview Tim Hoyt's mother right away. The other relatives and neighbors could wait, but he wanted an immediate statement from Ella Hoyt before all this broke. If she said she wasn't there when the babies died—which the group strongly suspected—it would establish a key element of the case, no matter how the interview with Waneta turned out.

Sue Mulvey thought things were going just great. She'd gotten Waneta down here, forged that bond with her. Now she was leading her where they had to go. Should they pull the trigger? No, said Courtright, not yet. Waneta was talking freely, without a hint of anxiety. Even her recollections of Dr. Hartnagel's suspicions seemed to come without defensiveness. In fact, Courtright thought, she was amazingly cool under the circumstances—even detached. Hearing her recount her life's tragedies, he looked for real emotion, but couldn't detect any. It didn't seem to bother her that she had trouble keeping the deaths straight. In fact, she seemed almost cheerful, as if, on some level, she was enjoying the encounter.

"Let's keep her talking," Courtright said. He and Mulvey went back in for another round. They touched on Waneta's childhood, looking for a hint of psychological trauma. Nothing there, at least nothing obvious. Waneta talked some more about Steinschneider. "He said we could have more children if we wanted," she said. "It was up to us."

They came out only twenty minutes later. "I think we've covered all we can," Courtright reported.

Fitzpatrick found it impossible to play the silent spectator. "This is it," he said. "She's ready to go. She's gonna give it up. Let's go."

"Yeah," Courtright said, dragging on another cigarette. He was not nearly as confident of the outcome, but he knew there was nothing left to ask but how and why. "We're gonna go in and accuse her now," he said to Simpson. It was the district attorney who would have to live with the result in court. Simpson nodded his assent.

"Sue," Courtright said to Mulvey, "switch places with Bubba." He went over the script one more time. "Don't use the word 'murder.' Don't say 'suffocate.' 'Caused the death of your children.' Let her tell us the rest." Mulvey nodded. She knew the script cold. "Don't waver," Fitzpatrick urged her. Courtright knew there was little chance of that. He could see it in her eyes.

They went back down the hall. Simpson stayed behind, and paced. *This is it,* he thought. *Either she's getting arrested for murder today, or we've got a real tough grind ahead.* Courtright grabbed Bleck and told him the new seating plan. Fitzpatrick and Tynan went into the room with the one-way mirror and saw Waneta Hoyt for the first time. Aside from her startling baldness, she looked much as Fitzpatrick had imagined her, ravaged by time. Tynan, though, was surprised at how pathetic she seemed. He expected to see the face of evil. He wondered if it was guilt that made Waneta Hoyt look so wretched.

They watched Mulvey slip into Bleck's chair. Fitzpatrick's heart raced. He tried to read Waneta's eyes. Did she know what was coming? Would she deny everything? Ask for a lawyer? A ride home? If she did, they'd have to give it to her. He could do nothing but watch through that little one-way mirror. It was all in Sue Mulvey's hands.

Mulvey took Waneta's hand in hers. She laid her other hand on her shoulder. She looked her in the eye and leaned close.

"Waneta," she said, "we know that what you've told us is not the truth. We know that you caused the death of your children."

Fitzpatrick saw the blood rush up through Waneta's neck and redden her face. He strained to hear her response.

"That's not what you said this morning," she said. "You lied to me."

"No, I didn't lie to you," Mulvey said firmly. "I told you we've spoken with doctors and we wanted to know how your children died. Now I'm telling you that these doctors have told us that your children did not die the way you say."

No, Waneta said. They were wrong. Her children died of SIDS. They had breathing problems. Dr. Steinschneider could tell them.

Mulvey shook her head. "The medical evidence shows that you did something to cause the children to die," she said.

Waneta fell silent. She dropped her head. She began to cry softly.

Mulvey remained frozen in her comforting pose. Ever so gently, she rubbed Waneta's shoulder. Sometimes bad things just happen, she said. Maybe you had some problems when you were young. But now it was time to let it out. Waneta extended her right arm across the table to Bleck and grasped his hand. Courtright sat stiffly, waiting for the words to come. In the next room, Fitzpatrick ached for the hammer to drop. Mulvey's words were barely audible. Simpson came in, saw the gripping scene through the mirror. It was good body language. She wasn't demanding a lawyer. Tynan left the room and tried to listen through the crack of the door.

For a while, the only sound was Waneta's soft sobs. Then she fell quiet. "You've carried this burden so many years," Mulvey said. She was inches from Waneta's face. "It's been a long time. It's better to share it, get the truth out. We know it's painful, but we'll help you get through it."

Waneta did not answer. The silence seemed endless. Then, finally, she spoke.

"My husband won't love me anymore," she said. "He'll throw me in the gutter. Everyone will hate me."

"No, that's not true, Waneta," Bleck said.

"From everything you've just told us, I can't see Tim not loving you after all these years," Mulvey said. "Not after all you've been through."

"That's right," Bleck said soothingly. "Nobody's throwing you in the gutter. We'll explain to Tim what's happened."

Waneta seemed to consider this. She was quiet again, no longer crying. Then, she broke her silence.

"I've asked God so many times to forgive me," she said.

This Fitzpatrick heard. Ever so quietly, his heart thumping, he went out into the hall and whispered breathlessly to Tynan, "Did she just say what I think she said?" Tynan was lit up. "Yeah, yeah," he said, "she's going for it. She's going for it."

"Tell us what happened, Waneta," Mulvey said now. "Just pick one of the children, pick any one of them and tell us what happened."

Another long silence enveloped the room. And then Waneta began to speak, her head still lowered.

"They just kept crying and crying," she said. "I just picked up Julie and I put her into my arm, in between my arm and my neck like this"—she demonstrated—"and I just kept squeezing and squeezing and squeezing. . . ."

At this, Courtright felt an instant, enormous release of pressure.

She picked Jimmy next. Her voice was steady now. He was bothering her while she was getting dressed one morning, she said, so she killed him.

One by one, in methodical, emotionless detail, Waneta Hoyt admitted to five acts of murder. Eric. Julie. James. Molly. Noah. "I caused the death of all my five children," she was saying a few minutes later, starting again at the beginning, Mulvey prompting her with questions, writing down Waneta's responses by hand:

I suffocated Eric in the living room of Ella Hoyt's house, where we were living at the time. He was crying at the time and I wanted to stop him. I held a pillow (it might have been a soft throw pillow) over his face while I was sitting on the couch. I don't remember if he struggled or not, but he did bleed from the mouth and nose. After he was dead, I picked him up and went to my neighbor's house. . . .

Julie was the next one to die. She was crying and I wanted her to stop. I held her nose and mouth into my shoulder until she stopped struggling. . . .

The next one was James. I was in the bathroom getting dressed and he wanted to come in. He came in the bathroom and I made him go out. He started crying, "Mommy, mommy." I wanted him to stop crying for me, so I used a bath towel to smother him. We were in the living room when I did this. He got a bloody nose from fighting against the towel. After he was dead, I picked him up and flagged down a garbage truck for help.

The next one was Molly. She was just home from the hospital overnight and was crying in her crib. I used a pillow that was in the crib to smother her. After she was dead, I called Mom Hoyt and Dr. Steinschneider.

Noah was the last child that I killed. He was home from the hospital and was in his crib and crying. I could not stand the crying. It was the thing that caused me to kill them all because I didn't know what to do for them. . . . I held a baby pillow over his face until he was dead. I called for Mom Hoyt and Dr. Steinschneider. I remember it was a hot day in July.

"Waneta," Mulvey said after she'd filled two pages, "I'd like you to read this over, make sure it's correct. Then I'd like you to sign it."

Waneta said she wanted to wait for Tim before she signed anything.

Courtright went across the hall and called Ithaca. "Get him down here," he told John Sherman. Then he went down the hallway to the room where the court stenographer had been waiting since the morning. Follow me, he said. He told Waneta he wanted to discuss the circumstances of each death one more time, for the record. She nodded and said, "Okay." She went through it again as the stenographer pecked on the keys of his machine. Courtright had wanted to get something quick on paper. Now, he had something much better than the statement Mulvey had taken, and Waneta's signature was a little less important. But he wanted still more. More details.

"Which ones do you remember turned blue?" he asked.

All four babies, Waneta said. All the children except Jimmy. "It wasn't totally blue," she said. "They had a blue hue around their lips."

"And that was after they stopped breathing?"

"Yes."

"Of all the five deaths, whom can you remember bleeding from the mouth and nose?"

"James," Waneta said.

"Okay," Courtright said. "What do you think that was caused from?"

"I don't know. I just figure the towel, the pressure from holding it on his face."

"Waneta, how much did James struggle?"

"Not a lot, but he struggled some."

"Was he kicking and flailing his arms?"

"Yes."

"He was?"

"Yes."

"Probably in an attempt to what?" Courtright wanted a clear record of what Waneta did to her little boy. This would be the image nobody connected to this case would ever forget—a two-year-old child fighting for his life, knowing that his mother was killing him.

"To shake me off, I assume," Waneta Hoyt said. "To get me to stop holding him down."

"How do you feel now, Waneta?" Courtright asked a few minutes later. "After carrying that burden for twenty-nine years, do you feel the burden is a little bit lifted?"

"Some."

"You've lived with it for a long time. Has it bothered you?"

"From time to time."

"Do you ever go up to the graves and see your children?"

"Sometimes."

"On a regular basis?"

"No."

"Are you sorry for what you did?"

"Very sorry. I asked God to forgive me over and over and over. I didn't want it to happen."

"Waneta, it's been a few hours since we've been in here. . . . It's been very stressful for you after admitting the truth. What can we do for you to make you more comfortable right now? You tell us."

"Anything?" Bleck asked.

"Just let me know if I can be at home until this is over, be with my family."

"What's going to happen, to give you an idea, to be very truthful with you—I've not lied to you since I've been here. . . . You're going to be arraigned before a judge, okay. It will be up to that judge and the district attorney as to what happens after that arraignment. I'm sure your husband is going to be fully supportive. You two people are married thirty years. That's a long, long time. You have to have something between yourselves. You did something wrong here, which you admit, and we have to do something about it. As police officers we're bound to do that. And at some point you probably will have to pay a penalty, and I hope God forgives you for this."

Courtright asked if she'd like to get some fresh air. "It's a beautiful day," he said. "It might be nice to go outside for a minute."

"That would be nice," Waneta agreed.

She and Mulvey strolled around the parking lot out back, and as they walked, Mulvey tried to clarify a point. Waneta had claimed that she didn't know after the first death, or even after the second or third, that holding a pillow over a baby would kill that baby. Now, Mulvey told her this was hard to believe. "You knew, didn't you, that if you put a pillow or a towel over a baby's face and nose and you waited long enough, the baby would die? By the second or third time, you know that every time you did this, they died."

"Yeah," Waneta said. "I knew that if I didn't release the pillow quick, they'll die." They went back inside, and put it on the record. Minutes later, Waneta was fingerprinted and photographed, and the orchestrated quiet of the barracks gave way to a sudden eruption of activity. Simpson started cranking up the Tioga County criminal justice system. Waneta would need an arraignment in Newark Valley Town Court. She'd need a lawyer. Charges would have to be typed up, and the media alerted. The state police would handle that. After the evidence-tampering scandal, which was not over yet, this would be a proud day for Troop C. And for Bill Fitzpatrick. Exuberant, he went to a phone to call his wife. "She went for it," he told Diane. "She went for all of it." Diane started to cry; she told her husband how proud she was of him. But when he started relating the details of how Jimmy Hoyt had died, all she could say was, "Oh my God . . . oh my God." The Fitzpatricks' children were four, two, and one. "Stop," Diane said, recoiling from the images. "I don't want to hear any more."

Shortly before 3:30, Courtright took Bleck aside. "Go get Jay at school," he said. "I don't want him hearing about this on the news." As he was driving out of the parking lot, Bleck saw Standinger and Sherman arriving. Tim Hoyt was in the backseat.

Tim came into the barracks angry. The investigators' questioning had unsettled him, and the waiting in Ithaca had given him time to think. He knew something was very wrong. They were two decades removed from those years of tragedy, and now, out of nowhere, they were being pulled back into a nightmare. Standinger led Tim down the hall, through the commotion. Courtright met him, introduced himself, and brought him into the interview room. Waneta was in the chair she'd occupied since morning. Bleck had offered to break the news to Tim, but Waneta was adamant. She wanted to tell him. Tim rushed to his wife and took her hand. She looked at him.

"I smothered the babies," she said.

"No!" he exploded.

"No, it's true," she said. "I just told the truth. I couldn't stand their crying."

"I don't believe it. I don't believe it. They were sick. They're making you say this."

"No, it's true," Waneta repeated. "I smothered them."

Courtright sat next to Tim. "I understand you're angry and upset," he said. "But Waneta has told us the truth here today. We have a written statement from her that she would like you to read before she signs it." He put the statement on the table. Tim looked down at the paper and began reading in silence. He had no visible reaction until he finished.

"How could this pass without somebody catching this?" he asked. "We got help. We went to Upstate. Why didn't the doctors catch this? My kids are dead and nobody stopped this."

At 3:43 P.M., Waneta signed her statement. Beneath her signature, Tim signed as a witness. They were left alone in the room, and a few minutes later, Waneta told Mulvey that she wanted to add a third page. She began talking. Mulvey began writing:

After I signed the first 2 pages of my statement, I thought of other things that I would like to add. I sought psychiatric care thru Social Services with Dr. Jaffe [sic] and Dr. Mahoney (he may just have been a counselor) and a lady counselor or psychiatrist. I was seeking their help because I knew that something was wrong with me. I feel that if I got help from them, it would have prevented me from killing the rest of my children. I feel that I am a good person, but I know that I did wrong. I loved my children. I love my son Jay and my husband, I feel the burden I have carried by keeping the secret of my children has been a tremendous punishment. I most definitely feel remorse and regret my actions. I can not go back and undo the wrong that I have done. My husband Tim had no part in any of the children's deaths and I was always alone.

"Do you still love me?" Waneta asked Tim.

"Yes," Tim said. He hugged his wife.

A few minutes later, Bleck drove up to the barracks with Jay in the seat beside him. On the ride down from Newark Valley, Bleck had made only an oblique reference to what had happened in the hours since they had dropped him at school. "Your folks are going to need you," he said when he picked him up. Jay looked puzzled, and they rode the rest of the way in silence. Now Bleck pulled up outside the police station and looked across at Jay. "Listen," he said, "it's very bad what's happened. Your folks are going to need all your support, and I want you to know, if you need anything, don't hesitate to call me." A look of confusion and trepidation crossed Jay's face. He said nothing.

Jay followed Bleck down the hallway and heard his father's angry voice: ". . . I still can't believe it." Tim was signing the last page of the statement when Jay walked into the room.

Waneta looked up at him. She put her hand on the picture album. "You know your brothers and sisters," she said. "I smothered them all."

Jay began to weep. His mother reached across to him. Her child was crying, and she wanted to comfort him.

"Get down to the Owego barracks by 4:30," a state trooper told the news director of WICZ-TV in Binghamton over the phone. Darcy Fauci asked what it was about. "I can't give you any details right now," said the trooper. "All I can tell you is it's an arrest in an old, unsolved murder case." Fauci grabbed a cameraman and headed for Owego. Half an hour later, she was standing outside the barracks with a gathering group of reporters and photographers from the Binghamton stations and the local newspaper, the *Press & Sun-Bulletin*. Most of them were babies and children themselves in the years when the Hoyts were burying theirs in Highland Cemetery. "We were wracking our brains," Fauci said later, "trying to figure out what unsolved murders we knew about." As the cameras waited, Bob Bleck was at the edge of the parking lot. Under instructions from a lieutenant, he was washing a patrol car.

Back inside, Tim Hoyt called his family and told them what was happening. His mother already had a hint that something bad was unfolding. A state police investigator had knocked on her door earlier in the afternoon, she told Tim. The man wanted to know if she had been present at the deaths of any of her grandchildren. No, she said, she hadn't.

In another office, Bob Simpson was calling the maintenance department at Cornell, asking the foreman to leave a message for James Van Nordstrand. A plumber by day, Van Nordstrand was the more senior of the two Newark Valley town justices. "We've got a case that'll need a quick arraignment," Simpson told him when he called back, saying nothing more about it. Now he needed to get Waneta a lawyer. He presumed Waneta qualified for legal aid, so he called one of Tioga County's assistant public defenders, George Awad, whose office was across the street from the courthouse in Owego. "George, we need you for an arraignment up in Newark Valley tonight," he said, as if it were something run-of-the-mill. Awad asked if it could wait until tomorrow. "No, we need you today," Simpson said. "We've got a lady who's just confessed to killing five children. She's gonna need a lawyer."

Jesus, Awad thought.

Simpson suggested he come over to the barracks and see his client before the arraignment. Awad handled mostly small crimes and misdemeanors, a lot of real estate matters and driving infractions. Flustered, he phoned Bob Miller's office in Waverly. Miller was the biggest criminal defense lawyer around, and for the past twenty years served Tioga County part-time as chief public defender. "Bob's in Florida," Miller's paralegal, Annette Gorski, told Awad. "I'll try to reach him."

Awad drove over to the barracks. "The place was buzzing," he said later. "They took me into this small room where she was. I saw her husband in there, and I recognized his face from somewhere. Did I do some legal work for him? Her son was in there, and he was crying. There was a woman holding Waneta's hand. I thought she was a friend, or maybe a social worker." Only later did he realize that this was the police investigator who had extracted Waneta's confession. Awad told the Hoyts he'd be representing Waneta at the arraignment. He told Tim he would meet them in Newark Valley. Tim recognized Awad too. He had sold him a used car years before, to use at law school.

The barracks door opened, and a pitiful-looking woman emerged, escorted by a uniformed trooper and an investigator in a blue suit and a white blouse. The cameras converged, though nobody knew yet who the accused woman was or exactly what she was being charged with doing. This was a photo opportunity, details to come. Coatless, her shirt billowing over a pair of black stretch pants, her downcast face a puzzle of sadness and resignation, she seemed less a suspect than a victim. Bleck and Mulvey held Waneta's hands protectively as they led her to the freshly washed patrol car and the cameras clicked and rolled. There would be a news conference in the town hall meeting room after the woman's arraignment, the reporters were told. Darcy Fauci went on the air at 5:30 and said a major story was breaking here in Owego. Details weren't available yet, but it seemed to be a case of multiple murder. Possibly involving children.

"What's this about?" Town Justice James Van Nordstrand asked George Awad when he arrived in Newark Valley shortly after five o'clock.

"Didn't they tell you?" Awad said. He handed Van Nordstrand ten forms, two for each child, outlining the charges. Van Nordstrand looked stunned. He had handled about as many serious felonies as Awad.

Waneta stood silent and dazed before the justice in the main room of the little town office across the street from the old Newark Valley Central School, the school she'd quit when the principal found out about her marriage plans. Thirty years later, it was a middle school, the lawn in front converted to pavement. Up the street, Betty's Luncheonette was long gone, but the bowling alley once run by Natalie Hilliard's father survived. Still clasping Sue Mulvey's hand, Waneta stood with Awad as the judge read from the stack of pages hastily typed in Owego: ". . . did in fact cause his death by smothering him with a pillow . . . did in fact cause her death by holding the victim's nose and mouth into her shoulder until the victim stopped breathing . . . did in fact cause his death by placing a bath towel over his face and smothering him . . . did in fact cause her death by placing a pillow over her face and smothering her . . . did in fact cause his death by placing a pillow over his face and smothering him." Awad, visibly rattled, pleaded Waneta not guilty, and the judge, equally overwhelmed, consulted with Simpson. There would be a felony hearing a week later, Van Nordstrand announced. Then Bleck and Mulvey returned Waneta to the patrol car and whisked her back down Route 38. She was on her way to the Tioga County Jail.

Courtright, Simpson, Fitzpatrick, and Lieutenants Jackmin and Thomas Kelly headed for the press conference at the Owego Town Hall, just upstairs from the room in which they had taken Waneta's confession. They arranged themselves at a long table normally used by the members of the Owego town board. Word had spread quickly that a major story was breaking, and reporters from Syracuse, Elmira, and a few more from Binghamton converged on Owego to find out what momentous thing was going on in Tioga County. The reporters pored over a press release that began: "Onondaga County District Attorney William J. Fitzpatrick, while preparing for an unrelated child homicide case, began to study available medical literature on SIDS, Munchausen syndrome by proxy, and pediatric breathing disorders. As part of this research, he had occasion to read an article published in the October 1972 issue of *Pediatrics* magazine. The article was written by a Dr. Alfred Steinschneider. . . ." One by one, the reporters started realizing that a local woman had been arrested for the murders of her five children a quarter-century ago.

It was Fitzpatrick's show. "There are a lot of mixed emotions on a day like this," he said, as the reporters scribbled. "We have brought to justice a killer who preyed on her own children." He explained all about Steinschneider's paper, how he'd been tipped by an expert from Texas during the Van Der Sluys case back in 1986, how the whole thing had started with the letter "H." The reporters, tantalized by the mystery, fired questions. How had he identified the family? Fitzpatrick wasn't saying. What did this Steinschneider—how's that spelled?—what did he think at the time? Well, he wrote the deaths up as SIDS. It was a landmark paper. How had they figured out the babies had been murdered? Experts were consulted and a thorough examination was done. "We don't come in here lightly today," Simpson said. What about this Munchausen syndrome? "A person who acts under Munchausen's by proxy is a sympathy junkie," Fitzpatrick explained. "The downside is there are numerous infant deaths that are not suspicious, and this will no doubt cause great pain for those people. You always hate to suggest a mother could do this to her children."

"Turn on the TV, quick!" Art Hilliard's mother told her daughter-in-law over the phone. Natalie hit the power button, and saw Waneta's face flash on the screen. She and Art looked at each other, utterly speechless. Natalie began to cry. Phones were ringing all over Tioga County, like the party line that had once connected Newark Valley. Waneta's sisters Donna and Dorothy, Ruth in Texas, her father in Richford, Tim's brothers and sisters and their wives and husbands—nobody could believe it. Not even Tim's brother George, who had said all those years before, "I think she's killing these kids." It seemed like a lifetime ago.

The reporters descended on Newark Valley that night, grabbing at strands of images of the accused child killer. "You couldn't ask for a nicer girl," a frail, white-haired woman named Martha Nestle told a reporter from the *Press & Sun-Bulletin*. She and Waneta were good friends, she said, like mother and daughter; though they didn't know each other back then, when the babies were dying. "She told me they all died of crib death." The whole thing was just shocking—the charges could not possibly be true. Waneta was a lady who cried when she talked about her lost babies, people said, who cried when she saw other people's children. She visited the graves on Memorial Day. She brought flowers. She couldn't have done what they're saying.

The county jail was a decrepit building across the street from the courthouse in Owego. Waneta sat on a wooden bench in a musty room in the basement, waiting to be booked, crying softly, flanked by her husband and son. A young sheriff's deputy looked on sympathetically from behind the front desk. "Oh, now, jail's not so bad," he said. "It's not like what you see on TV." Wayne Moulton had grown up in Newark Valley and used to bag groceries at the local market. He recognized Waneta when she came in, but his awkward attempt at consolation only made her erupt in sobs.

"I didn't mean to kill them," she told him through tears. "I just wanted them to stop crying. I tried to get help. I went to Social Services."

Later that night, Albert Nixon came to the jail and sat opposite his daughter at a long table with a foot-high divider down the middle. "I hope you're not mad at me," she told her father. "I hope you don't hate me." He was an old man with a hollow look about him, his egg-shaped head topped by a sprinkling of mossy white hair. He was a widower; Waneta's mother had died in a car accident in 1989. He didn't know what to say except no, he wasn't mad at her, he didn't hate her. A few hours later, when a state police investigator came up to Richford to interview him, he signed a written statement: "My family had no idea that this crime was going on. I would like to say that Waneta grieved for each of her children after they died. . . . Waneta was always a nervous person. But to my knowledge she never had a nervous breakdown. To my knowledge Waneta never had any mental problems."

"No, she did *not* confess," Linda Norton said on the phone from Dallas. "You're joking."

"No, really," Fitzpatrick told her. "We have a detailed confession. She went for the whole thing."

"So, what kind of rubber hose did you use?"

"No, no, it's a great confession. She just went for it, and pretty quick. She wanted to wait for her husband to come before she signed it. She told us exactly what she did."

They congratulated each other—it's all because of you; no, no, it's because of *you*—and then went their separate ways to celebrate. Fitzpatrick and Tynan joined the Tioga County contingent for beer and pizza at Bud's Place. Norton, giddy, got off the phone, danced out to her assistant, pumped her fist in the air, and said, *"Yessss!"* But she still couldn't believe that the real-life Mrs. H., this mythological figure of SIDS, the woman whose murdered children gave Alfred Steinschneider his precious, specious theory, had actually admitted the truth all these years later. Norton never knew all that lay beneath Steinschneider's research, but she realized that this meant that everything misguided that had flowed from his paper was about to be exposed. She hoped it would change some perceptions, teach some lessons, and maybe save a few babies. That's what this confession meant to Norton. That's why she was pumping her fist in the air. This wasn't about Waneta Hoyt. To Norton, it never was.

At home after a day of monitoring babies for apnea at his SIDS institute in Atlanta, Alfred Steinschneider picked up his phone and heard the voice of a reporter from upstate New York and then another, and another after that. A woman named Waneta Hoyt has just been arrested for the murder of her five children decades ago, they said, and it was his twenty-two-year-old *Pediatrics* paper that had led the police to her. They wanted to know if he remembered the family. They asked him what he had thought back then and what he thought now. Steinschneider seemed ready for the questions. The reporters heard the voice of a doctor on the defensive, but they detected no shock.

Steinschneider would not acknowledge that Waneta Hoyt was Mrs. H. Patient confidentiality, he explained. What he could tell them was that there was no indication the babies in his paper died of anything but SIDS. What if it turned out that they had been murdered? That would be "rather intriguing," he told one reporter. Why did he attribute the deaths to SIDS? "I don't do autopsies. I accepted the explanations of competent pathologists at the time." Yes, five deaths in a family was "out of the ordinary." But familial SIDS was a recognized phenomenon.

The reporters, who had first heard the word *apnea* only an hour or so before, wondered what the arrest would do to his theory. Steinschneider responded adamantly that it would not affect it at all. It didn't detract from the assumption that babies who died suddenly had a chronic abnormality, or from his theory that apnea was a symptom of SIDS. "The hypothesis generally led to a lot of research," he said. "That's what hypotheses are supposed to do." Other researchers had supported his findings, he noted. In any event, just because Waneta Hoyt was in jail didn't mean she was guilty: It was well known that police interrogators could extract false confessions, especially from grieving, guilt-ridden SIDS parents. He hoped this wouldn't expose thousands of others to unfair suspicion.

Steinschneider had spent twenty years in the combat zone of SIDS that he had done as much as anyone to create. The battles had become intrinsic to his research, and defending himself a way of life. But as he hung up the phone after the last round of questions, he had good reason to know that he was in for the fight of his life. He was sixty-five, and in no mood to start admitting any errors now. The consensus conference of 1986 was not the last word on the apnea theory. Now, he would truly be on trial. For that night, Waneta Hoyt, alone in the shadows of her jail cell, decided she had made a terrible mistake that afternoon. She had not murdered her children. Dr. Steinschneider said it was SIDS. Let them try to prove otherwise.

A quarter-century after their lives had first converged, Waneta Hoyt and Alfred Steinschneider needed each other once again.

32

It had been a wearying two decades for Waneta and Tim Hoyt.

Soon after the turbulent years of their children's deaths, they had sold their second trailer and the land underneath to help with their debts and begun living in a series of rented dwellings around Newark Valley. Waneta's days passed from one to the next. She kept house, watched television, crocheted, worked her crosswords. She wasn't bad with words. Her friend Natalie Hilliard was back teaching nursery school, but Waneta didn't see herself as the working type. Tim put in long days on one construction crew or another, still trying to pay off the medical bills for Molly and Noah, as well as for Waneta's own visits to the specialists in two counties to whom she had brought her vague physical ailments. Their debts ranged from the immense to the trivial. Tim told his brothers that he and Waneta owed $100,000 to various doctors, with Upstate at the top of the list; for a long time he was bringing five dollars a week over to Dave Cooley at MacPherson's funeral parlor, until Cooley said, Tim, forget it.

After their abortive adoption bid in the fall of 1971, the Hoyts' wait for a child lasted five years. They adopted Jay through Family and Children's Services, the private agency in Ithaca, paying the fee with money they borrowed from Tim's brother-in-law Weldon Wait, who never let them forget it. That's my kid, Weldon would joke. But in some quarters of Newark Valley, there was a silent gasp that summer of 1976 when word got around that Waneta Hoyt had a two-month-old baby at home. Hope she has better luck this time, some said. She ought to—this one's not hers. And there were more than a few others who looked on and thought, let's just see what happens this time.

Waneta and Tim fretted over their new baby. They watched him the old-fashioned way. Until he was a few months old, they took turns staying up through the night while he slept beside them. They wouldn't let him sleep in his own room until he was two. He didn't have the death gene, but on this question there was no need for discussion. Tim was taking no chances, and it was Waneta's way to nurture his apprehension.

In 1987, when Jay was eleven, Waneta went to the county mental health clinic for the first time in fifteen years. She answered "yes" to every one of the eighteen questions about her emotional health on a form she was asked to fill out. Yes, she had daily headaches and trouble sleeping, and problems with her temper. Yes, she was almost always lonely and depressed; yes, she felt panic, and yes, she felt guilt. She had recurrent dreams of accidents and fires. She was a housewife with few diversions; she embroidered when she had the money for supplies. Though Jay was not a difficult child, and she was not very busy, she found it impossible to keep up with the demands of raising him. But she seemed even more fixated on her relationship with a dog she and Tim had recently gotten him. "She dislikes the dog and is fearful of losing control of hostile impulses toward the dog," a social worker who interviewed her wrote one day. "She feels quite shaky but her husband is supportive and taking tomorrow off to be with her."

At forty, her physical complaints had also been mounting. She circled "yes" twenty-two times on another form asking her to list her medical history. She said she had both high blood pressure and low blood pressure, a heart murmur, liver disease, stomach ulcers. Did she have chest pain upon exertion? Shortness of breath? Require extra pillows to sleep? Allergies? Hives or skin rash? Fainting spells or seizures? Diabetes? Urinate more than six times a day? Did her ankles swell? Waneta answered yes to them all.

When she talked to a new psychiatrist, Dr. George Primanis, she came back to the dog. She was afraid she "might do something to the dog." She returned four weeks later, and told Primanis that the dog had been killed by a car. She felt guilty, she told him, but also relieved.

For a time, Waneta kept pictures of her babies on the TV set. When one of the Hoyts' landlords, Anna May Kuntzleman, came for the rent each month, she would see the babies staring up at her, and her heart would sink. "They all died of SIDS," Waneta would say. When a new neighbor came over for the first time, Waneta would pull out her photo album. She also knew that she had a certain status in the medical world. Once, when her sister Ruth came up for a visit from Texas, Waneta showed her Steinschneider's article. "This is me," she said proudly. "I'm Mrs. H."

———

When they got themselves in serious legal trouble, some of the poorest people in Tioga County were represented by one of the wealthiest. Bob Miller was decidedly not the archetypal public defender. An ex–Green Beret who marched his commanding figure around a courtroom barking questions at witnesses, he was not given to coddling his clients, especially not those whose defense came courtesy of the taxpayers. He'd agreed to set up the county public defender's office in 1974, figuring he'd pass the chores on to some do-gooder after a couple of years. But two decades later, his private law practice on the bottom floor of a house in the sleepy village of Waverly, entrance around back, was still also the office of the Tioga County Public Defender. It wasn't that Miller was ideologically committed to it. He just found something appealing about the work. It kept things interesting. In the meantime, he had done well enough with (as his business card specified) Serious Personal Injury, Wrongful Death, Products Liability, and Major Criminal Defense Matters, to live in an immense brick house on acres of land in Waverly and to branch out into a business he had come to love, the Greenhills Land and Cattle Company, the thousand-acre ranch he operated with his son just over the border in Chemung County. Not infrequently, Miller and his wife, Rose, got away to their condo on the west coast of Florida.

He was in Fort Myers when he got the harried call from his paralegal, Annette Gorski. *"Thirty years ago?"* Miller said when she reported what George Awad had told her.

"The press is all over the place," Gorski said. "They're calling here. George doesn't know what to do."

By the time Miller reached Awad at home, Waneta had been arraigned and was in jail for the night. "I'll get back as soon as I can," he told Awad. "Don't do anything till you hear from me. Don't talk to the press. Don't do anything. Just lock yourself away till I get there." Then Miller called the jail and talked to his client. "Don't say anything to anyone," he instructed her, well aware that she'd already said plenty. "Okay? Just keep your mouth shut." He called Tim Hoyt and told him the same thing. He called Bob Simpson and asked what the hell was going on. Five children? Thirty years ago? Why now? Miller knew the police had a statement from the defendant, but he wouldn't get a look at it until a felony hearing a week later. With each call, the enormity of this case became more and more apparent. At three in the morning, Miller realized he needed some help and made one more call. In Elmira, an awakened Ray Urbanski picked up the phone and heard his former partner's voice in the darkness. It was Easter week, and Miller was having trouble getting a flight north. He asked Urbanski to stand in for him until he could get home. "Ray, can you go over to the jail and see this lady tomorrow?"

The next day, Miller read about the arrest in the *Miami Herald,* and knew he had his work cut out for him. "It was a medical journal article that sent a prosecutor sleuthing in 1986," the Associated Press story began. When he read Bill Fitzpatrick's comment about a killer "who preyed on her own children" being "brought to justice," Miller was enraged. He and Bob Simpson had been respectful adversaries for twenty years, and neither had to remind the other to fight their cases in court. That was how things worked in Tioga County. This wasn't some big city where half the job, whichever side you were on, was grabbing headlines. Waneta's supposed confession started him at enough of a disadvantage, Miller complained to Urbanski over the phone; he didn't need a poisoned jury pool to go with it. In fact, Miller found the Syracuse prosecutor's entire involvement perplexing and suspicious. Who was this guy anyway? What was he doing down in Tioga County? He wondered if this whole thing was some sort of publicity gimmick.

Bob Courtright launched his long-planned invasion of Newark Valley and northern Tioga County early on the morning after the arrest. That day and those following, Courtright deployed investigators to the front doors of just about everyone who might have known Waneta in the years her children were dying; everyone he knew about. It was the beginning of the reverse investigation. Now that Simpson had the statement he needed from Waneta, it was up to Courtright's team to go out and gather the corroboration. Suddenly, nearly everyone connected to Waneta found themselves taken back twenty and thirty years. What did they remember? How did Waneta act after the deaths? What did she say? What did they think then? The painful past was being dug up, turned over, sifted through.

What came through was a jumble of impressions and images. Little of it fell into the category of corroboration. Waneta was just not capable of killing her children, her younger sister Donna declared. But if she really did it, Donna said, maybe she "just snapped." Donna's husband, Tim's brother Don, agreed that it didn't seem possible. One after another, Waneta's relatives said much the same. "I wondered why she kept havin' kids," her brother Archie said, but he was sure they all died of crib death. Did his sister have any emotional problems growing up? No, he said, no mental problems, she was normal, had a normal childhood. Archie thought Waneta had taken the deaths of the babies in stride, but he seemed to be the only one. Everyone else said it just tore her up, and she never got over it.

Tim's sister Janet Kuenzli offered the investigators her reminiscences of Jimmy. "He was a bubbly kid that liked to go, go, go," she said. "He'd run across the field yelling, 'Grandma, grandma.' I remember he was just learning to tie his shoes when he died." Scrambling to get to people before they fell under a lawyer's gag order, Courtright's investigators weren't always sure whom they were talking to. They'd found Janet's name on Waneta and Tim's marriage certificate, unaware that she was Tim's sister. "Stated she was matron of honor . . ." Courtright wrote, "and has remained in contact with the Hoyts since that time. Mrs. Kuenzli knew all of the Hoyt children and described them all as beautiful children."

The inquisitors fanned out into the far reaches of the county. Dave Cooley, who took over MacPherson's Funeral Home a few weeks after Julie and Jimmy died, and who arranged the services for Molly and Noah, said he'd found no apparent injuries on either baby. He always thought Waneta had some emotional problems, but she seemed to be a nice person. How was she at the funerals? Emotional, Cooley remembered. That would be expected, but this thing called Munchausen, if that's what this was, tended to turn things a little ambiguous. Was she *too* emotional? "This woman you practically carried out of the funeral parlor," Art Hilliard had told one reporter, though when Courtright went to see him, he and Natalie respectfully declined to be interviewed, on the advice of Waneta's lawyer. Like virtually everyone else in Waneta's life, the Hilliards found the charges absolutely impossible to believe.

The hunt for prosecution witnesses was seriously impaired by the passage of time. Dr. Hartnagel had been suspicious, Waneta had said in the interview room, but Courtright already knew he was long dead. The house in which he had lived and worked still bore the doctor's office hours painted on the window of the porch door, but a sign out front read GARY'S GARAGE/WELDING. Also dead were Dr. Noah Kassman, the obstetrician who had delivered all five babies and was the namesake for the last one, and both Howard and Margaret Horton, Newark Valley's police chief and emergency dispatcher. When Standinger and Sherman went to their house, they found the Hortons' son and asked him if he had any of his father's old police records. You're not going to believe this, he said. He had been cleaning out his parents' house, and had burned all his father's records just a few weeks before.

The rescue squad didn't have any records that old, and only a few of the squad members who responded to the Hoyt baby calls were still alive. One of them was Bob Vanek. In September 1968, the back-to-back deaths of Julie and Jimmy made him suspicious, but his wife had urged him to be careful with his thoughts. If anything was wrong, she said, the police would come to him. But they never did, not for twenty-six years. By now, Vanek's memory was a bit fuzzy.

Waneta's change of heart the night of her arrest was swift, certain, and probably not unrelated to the conversations she had in jail with her husband, her son, her father, and her lawyer. The guards watched her carefully throughout the night, considering her a suicide risk, but that was not what was on Waneta's mind. When Ray Urbanski went to see her the next morning, Waneta told him that she was innocent. The police had made her say these things. Now could she go home?

Bob Miller made it home on Friday, and began trying to make some sense of five murder charges stretching back thirty years. He quickly realized he would need Urbanski's help for a while, maybe for the duration, especially if Waneta stuck to her morning-after denials. Not only was the case itself immensely complex as a legal matter, but the bombardment of publicity seemed to be taking on a life of its own. The larger world was fascinated by the story of Waneta Hoyt's arrest and how it came to be. Miller was astounded by the instant notoriety. He had to hire extra office help to handle all the calls—reporters from every medium and assorted countries, producers from network magazines and talk shows, even movie people. The temporary receptionists kept a record of the calls, and within a week of Waneta's arrest, they had logged 537 inquiries. A call every six minutes or so, not counting the contracts people were trying to fax. Everyone wanted Waneta's story. She wasn't giving it.

Miller found the publicity infuriating and blamed Fitzpatrick, who was spending a good deal of his time giving interviews to the national media. The day of the felony hearing, Miller held his own press conference at the county courthouse in Owego. Fitzpatrick was out for publicity, Miller declared: "I'm sure Geraldo and Sally Jesse will want to fit him in between the transvestites who want to marry their mothers." He planned to file an official grievance with the state bar association, accusing Fitzpatrick of making improper and inflammatory remarks that were interfering with his client's right to a fair trial. In Syracuse, Fitzpatrick found the public defender's reaction ludicrous. He couldn't understand why Miller was making him the issue. "Maybe he should concentrate on defending his client," he told reporters.

Miller and Urbanski were about to get their first look at what they were truly up against. To move the case on to a grand jury and trial in the county court, Simpson was required to present a sample of his evidence at the felony hearing James Van Nordstrand would hold in the town court. It would be Newark Valley's most famous hour since the Martian landing of 1964. CNN, among others, had called to ask what time the hearing would be. Van Nordstrand didn't want to mess up. He took several days off from his maintenance job to pore over the criminal procedures laws with the other town justice, Douglas Tiffany, a retired IBM employee whose wife was the court clerk and whose license plate read NV LAW. They also read up on Munchausen syndrome by proxy, in case it came up. Van Nordstrand was relieved he had a courtroom. Until a couple of years before, Newark Valley was run from the various officials' homes, the judge, for instance, holding court on his enclosed front porch. Now there was a modest town office with a makeshift court-room. The judges themselves had built the bench from which they presided, out of plywood.

On March 30, the back of the courtroom was lined with cameras when Waneta Hoyt made her entrance a few minutes after six. The room was filled with reporters, police investigators, lawyers, and a sizable group of her friends and relatives, many of whom were seeing her for the first time since her arrest seven days before. Natalie Hilliard watched Waneta walk through the door and saw the look of confusion on her face. Natalie still couldn't believe what was happening. She asked one of the guards if it would be all right to see Waneta for a moment, and he nodded. She walked up to her and hugged her. "I'll take care of Tim and Jay till you get home," she said. "Thank you," Waneta said. Then Natalie backed away. She was gray-haired now, her chil-dren grown. Dana, the little boy who had palled around with Jimmy Hoyt, was nearly thirty. Natalie reeled her mind back to those years, searching for clarity. In her memory, Waneta was running across the street, Jimmy limp and lifeless in her arms, her shirt unbuttoned. She couldn't match the image to what was going on now.

Tim stood beside Waneta, leaning in close as she sat staring grimly ahead. He dropped to one knee, his arm around her shoulder. He hugged her, gave her a kiss.

"Mr. Simpson, are you ready to proceed?" Van Nordstrand asked, glancing at a script he had prepared. "Mr. Miller and Mr. Urbanski, are you ready to proceed? Mr. Simpson, you may begin."

Sue Mulvey took the witness chair and recounted the events of the Wednesday before. She read Waneta's written statement into evidence. "... Julie was the next one to die. She was crying and I wanted her to stop. . . . It was the thing that made me kill them all. . . ." The television cameras recorded the chilling words. The footage would play on TV screens across the country.

In the audience, Jay sat in dazed silence as the word *smothered* was re-peated again and again; as his mother was accused of "depraved indiffer-ence to human life." He had been crying for days. At school, a posse of friends had formed around him to protect him from cruel remarks and approaches by the press. When he was young, his mother had hovered over him, refus-ing to allow him outside to play with his cousins at family gatherings lest he hurt himself. Now Jay listened to Investigator Susan Mulvey read his mother's statement about all the babies she said she had killed because they cried. "... Jay went through those same crying spells, but Tim was always there for that."

Michael Baden followed Mulvey to the witness chair. Five mysterious deaths, only one person present each time, no evidence of natural death in the medical records—it all pointed, the forensic pathologist testified, to homicide. Miller thought there were huge holes in Baden's reasoning and that he could find his own experts to refute his logic at trial, thereby cutting the legs out from under Simpson's crucial medical corroboration. But for now Mulvey, Baden, and Waneta's statement were more than enough. With great relief, Van Nordstrand sent Waneta back to jail and the case to the County Court judge, Vincent Sgueglia. A few weeks later, Simpson presented the evidence to a grand jury, which quickly indicted her. There were ten counts of second-degree murder, two for each child. One accused her of "creating a grave risk of death" and thereby causing death; the other of intending to kill. (He later had to amend the part of the indictment involving Eric to conform to the statutes in effect in 1965.) Meantime, Miller persuaded Judge Sgueglia (pronounced Squel-ya) to cut Waneta's bond bail to $75,000. Her father and brother pledged their properties to let her go home until her trial.

Money was on a lot of people's minds. A few days after Waneta Hoyt's arrest, the Tioga County Legislature called a special meeting to discuss how much the case was going to cost. "You should be prepared to spend more than you can possibly conceive," Miller told the worried legislators. "This is going to be the most complex, lengthy, and expensive case this county has ever seen, and I plan to defend Waneta Hoyt whatever the expenses involved." Urbanski would have to be paid, and Miller foresaw hiring an investigator and any number of expert witnesses. The legislators ultimately approved $35,000. Miller let them know they should not consider that the end of it.

Waneta began attending Sunday church and found that people didn't hate her at all, most of them at least. They told her they believed in her, that they were sure she would be found innocent, and what could they do to help? They meant it. This baby killer, this monster these big-city types were talking about on the news—this wasn't Waneta. Waneta was gentle and simple and sad, so vulnerable. Those cops could get her to say anything they wanted.

She had become well known around town over the years for her woebegone life. Her list of ailments was familiar to anyone who had occasion to say hello to her. The roster was ever-changing; no two news stories in the weeks after her arrest had the same list. Her family was just as sickly, as if cursed. Two of her sisters, Donna and Dorothy Joan, had cancer. Her brother Archie was also ill. Her mother had been killed in a car wreck. Not long after her arrest, Archie's son was killed in another accident. And one day a tire came flying off a truck axle and smashed through Waneta and Tim's front door.

Why couldn't a woman subjected to this much bad luck also have lost all her children to some mysterious disease?

Some people wanted to get up a petition in her support. Waneta thought this was a great idea, and called Miller daily to find out when he was going to give the go-ahead. Meanwhile, she and Tim went to the library at Cornell to look for information on SIDS that might help her case. Their fifteen-year-old niece Penny, George's daughter, also made a project of it, and pretty soon other people were gathering research too, using the computer down at the church. Helping Waneta fight back became a cause. "They come in every couple of days with material, most of it irrelevant," Miller said one day, half-bemused, half-annoyed.

The minister at the Methodist church, Lisa Jean Hoefner, was part of the cluster of friends and relatives who accompanied Waneta to every court appearance. She had always considered Waneta a pitiable figure. Art Hilliard had first pointed her out: She's the one who lost five kids, he told her soon after her arrival in Newark Valley in 1987. Touched by the tragedies and by the Hoyts' difficult financial circumstances, Reverend Lisa Jean had responded kindly. About once a year since then, she would get a long letter from Waneta, four or five pages detailing her troubles—Tim was out of work, and she wasn't doing too well physically. When the minister visited the Hoyts one winter day, she saw that Jay slept on a cot in the dining room because his parents couldn't afford to heat the upstairs. She thought them a couple with little money but goodly pride. Since coming to "Nerk Valley," Hoefner, who had grown up in a middle-class home on Long Island, had come across families whose surroundings were practically Third World: "Once, I was going to call on someone and somebody at the church said, 'Now, when you get there, the first building that you'll come to, that's the chicken house. Go beyond that and the second one you come to, that's where the people live.' And I was glad they said that because it was very hard to distinguish just from looking at the two shacks which was which." But the Hoyts were not like that. Their home was humble, but neat and comfortable, filled with Waneta's knittings. They were trying their best.

Reverend Lisa Jean was one of the few people allowed to visit Waneta in jail. She had come the day after the arrest, and they had prayed together. The next day was Good Friday. "Jesus knew what it was to be accused," she told Waneta, holding her hand. "He wouldn't have abandoned us in this situation. Even in this pit we can draw on the presence of God." She told Waneta she was here to comfort her, not to judge her. "You don't need to tell me anything," she said. Waneta told her she didn't know why this was happening. Throughout the visit, she fidgeted with one of the snaps on her bright orange jail-issue jumpsuit. It wouldn't close, exposing her underwear. Hoefner found the indignity poignant. She tried to get Waneta to eat some soup.

In the chaos of those first few days and weeks after Waneta's arrest, the minister tried to keep Waneta's family from falling apart. They were numb with confusion, their pain sharpened by the invasion of reporters and photographers looking everywhere for clues to Waneta's past. "Look, this is just a job for them," Lisa Jean told George Hoyt, who was getting a little rough with some of the cameramen outside the courthouse. She reserved her indignation for the prosecutors. "They arrested Waneta and then put her on suicide watch so they could keep her safe and kill her later," she told one reporter. "Nothing is going to bring those kids back now. In the meantime, we destroy Jay and Tim and Waneta. What sense is that?" Like many people, she was confounded by the possibility that Waneta had actually killed her children. "Well, it's just so hard to get your head around it," she said a few months later. "And I just don't think it could have been willful. I can imagine, just trying objectively to imagine, screaming children, or sad little babies, and trying to make a baby stop crying. I can imagine a smothering situation." But five times? "Well, exactly, so I kind of look more toward a, you know, some kind of inheritedness, medical something or other."

Her confusion rang true for many in Newark Valley and the rest of Tioga County. But not for everybody. Maybe they couldn't say it out loud, but some who had known Waneta a long time couldn't stop thinking about this Munchausen syndrome. If it meant a person who thrived on sympathy, who always needed to be the center of attention, it sure sounded a lot like Waneta. And when they first heard the accusations, some people thought: Yes, this was what had happened to these babies.

Nonetheless, it seemed clear that the case of the People versus Waneta Hoyt was not going to be a popular prosecution. The jury pool wasn't poisoned by Fitzpatrick's sound bites, as Bob Miller feared. In Tioga County in 1994, people seemed to take umbrage not at the magnitude of the crime said to have been committed in their midst, but at the length of time between the crime and the punishment. There was less revulsion and vengeance in the air than *Why are they dredging this up now?* Who could prove anything all these years later, and what did it really matter? If she really did it, she must have been sick—"more to be pitied than to be fried," in Reverend Lisa Jean's view. "What is it we want in the name of justice? There's no risk here." Hadn't her guilt punished her enough? some people asked. Others worried about all the money it was going to cost the taxpayers.

Bob Courtright heard these sentiments often in the months after the arrest, and they puzzled him. Was it that people considered babies, in some sense, possessions—that they couldn't visualize them as people? Was it just ancient history? At what point did simple justice cease to be important? Five years after the fact? Ten? Twenty? Courtright refused to get hung up on these questions. Whenever someone gave him a hard time about prosecuting

Waneta Hoyt, he kept his response simple. "I can't give away five free murders," he'd say each time. He hoped Bob Simpson could find twelve citizens who felt the same way.

Simpson, meanwhile, was open to discussions that might keep the case from going that far. He felt a plea bargain would not be the wrong thing to do in the name of the people of Tioga County, so he intimated to Bob Miller that he was available for conversation. The two men had tried cases and made deals for two decades, and the unspoken presumption here was that Waneta could plead guilty to manslaughter and get a relatively modest prison sentence. But Miller knew by now that his client was adamant: She would not agree to anything that would send her to prison. "I didn't do anything," she had declared the one time he mentioned the possibility of a plea bargain. He told Simpson there would be no negotiations in this case. He left Simpson with the impression that he believed she was innocent, and that he planned to prove it at trial.

Miller was posturing. "Manslaughter wouldn't have been a bad deal at all," he later said. "Except that she would be admitting she killed somebody. You have to understand the context of any conversation I ever had with her, or with her husband, or with her relatives, or with her friends. It was always, 'I'm innocent. I've been wrongly accused. I didn't do it.' You don't talk to someone about a plea if they say they're innocent. She was going to have her trial."

And she was going to be acquitted, Waneta was sure. And so was Tim. The police wore her down, manipulated a false confession—surely a jury would understand that's what had happened here. Miller found their confidence inexplicable under the circumstances. "I don't think either one of them grasps the significance of being charged with five counts of murder," he remarked one day to Urbanski. "They're so indignant. They just don't seem to have a conception that they have serious trouble here."

"Well, that's good, from my standpoint," Urbanski replied. "It fortifies me." He was coming to find Waneta's resolve remarkable. "When I first met her, she was sitting in jail, in her jail outfit, just out of it," he said. "But since then, she's gotten so much stronger. She's more articulate than I expected. She's smarter than people think." Only later would he realize that this was not such a good thing for a jury to see.

With their client convinced that they would get her off and people in Newark Valley rallying to her support, the lawyers found themselves caught up in the positive mood. They felt they had a winnable case, despite the confession. There were no eyewitnesses, no physical evidence, and time was on their side: How could Simpson possibly corroborate a confession involving events that went back three decades?

People in Tioga County didn't pay very much attention to the other half of it, but in the universe of medical research, Waneta Hoyt's arrest had a completely different meaning. Alfred Steinschneider found himself a prominent physician conspicuously entangled in a sensational murder case, his reputation dependent on the outcome.

He'd had his own troubles in recent years. He withstood a heart attack in 1989, and went through a period of depression and instability that had worried his wife terribly. Ultimately, it cooled his twenty-year friendship with Molly Dapena. She had always been one of his staunchest supporters, but by the 1990s, she no longer agreed with him scientifically. When he read an article in which Dapena said she had given up on the apnea theory and had changed her mind about the concept of multiple SIDS within families, Steinschneider was furious. Roz called Dapena in Miami in a panic. Al's beside himself, she said. Steinschneider got on the phone and threatened to sue Dapena. Though she flew to Atlanta for the day and calmed him down, it was the beginning of the end of their close friendship.

But Steinschneider was, as always, a survivor, and he remained as dedicated as ever to his ideas about SIDS. He was still measuring apnea in the overheated sleep labs of his SIDS Institute, still sending babies home on monitors, raising money, getting grants, and leading some parents to believe he could prevent SIDS. But with the Hoyt arrest he found himself pulled back to another era—back to the seminal moment of his career. And reporters were calling for appointments. Fitzpatrick was telling the world that Steinschneider should be held accountable, morally if not legally, for the deaths of the babies who had launched his career in sudden infant death. Steinschneider found remarks like these outrageous and hurtful. He considered Fitzpatrick's search of the medical records that had led to Waneta Hoyt's arrest "an abuse of power."

When Barry Bearak of the *Los Angeles Times* came to see Steinschneider a month after Waneta's arrest, he found him to have, as he later wrote in a front-page story, "the affable presence of a country doctor," if one from the heart of Brooklyn. But Steinschneider's smoldering indignation was not far beneath the surface. "What's missing from all this cheap talk, this impugning of motives, this show biz, is that it doesn't save a single baby," Steinschneider told Bearak. "What they ought to be saying is: 'Let's examine the deaths of babies and make better identification of the causes of deaths to help sort things out. . . . If people think there were inadequate autopsies done, then check the autopsies, big shots. If they think these kids were murdered, then show me, because what they are saying now is at variance with what the people who investigated the case said then. If there's criticism I'll accept from the pathologists, it's that I accepted the opinion of other pathologists."

The publicity surrounding the arrest of Waneta Hoyt was also an uncomfortable development for the SIDS community. "When Is Crib Death a Cover for Murder?" asked the headline over *Time*'s report of the case. The story noted that the Hoyt arrest was not an isolated instance: Two other women, Gail Savage of Illinois and Diane Lumbrera of Kansas, had recently been charged with smothering several of their children. The political wing of the SIDS world reacted with a call to arms reminiscent of the early days. When word got around in early June that the CBS program *Eye to Eye with Connie Chung* was about to air a segment on the Hoyt case, Pete Petit's SIDS Alliance went into action. The alliance's national public affairs director, Phipps Cohe, faxed a "Media Action Alert" around the country, urging SIDS parents to help counteract the expected negative effects of the story by sending their protests to the program. "Let them know how coverage such as this perpetuates a longstanding bias against SIDS families," she urged.

Connie Chung and her crew had come to upstate New York weeks before, then moved on to Atlanta, where they spent several hours with Steinschneider. Meanwhile, Chung's segment producer, Patrick Weiland, went on to Chicago to develop an angle of the story suggested to him by Linda Norton in Dallas. It was the provocative case of Deborah Gedzius, who had lost six babies in the late 1970s and early 1980s. Her husband Delos's family was convinced the babies had been murdered by their mother, but it appeared that Steinschneider had unwittingly provided her with an alibi, as he had Waneta Hoyt. After the fifth death in 1980, the Gedzius family's pediatrician, Dr. Eugene Diamond, consulted with Steinschneider, who confirmed that five babies could in fact die of SIDS in one family. Diamond proceeded to write his own paper, adding a new case to the literature. One more child died four years later, as did the babies' father—he was murdered. His wife collected a $100,000 insurance policy and now owned a bar. Prodded by Delos Gedzius's family, a new medical examiner changed the cause of death of the six babies to homicide in 1990, naming their mother as the suspect. But the state's attorney wanted second, third, and fourth opinions. Two of the experts agreed the evidence pointed right at homicide. One of them was Marie Valdes-Dapena. The third consultant said it could very well be murder, but that he could not completely rule out SIDS. This expert was Bruce Beckwith. He based his opinion on Steinschneider's 1972 paper. The state's attorney declined to prosecute.

The *Eye to Eye* segment aired under the title "One by One" and opened with a pastoral view of Highland Cemetery that faded to an aerial shot of Newark Valley. *"For more than twenty years, she was known only as Mrs. H.,"*

Chung narrated, *"a mother who, one by one, buried her babies in this cemetery on the hill. In this valley in upstate New York, the mother's grief was barely noted, nearly forgotten. But in the medical literature, the five H. children are famous— part of a landmark study of Sudden Infant Death Syndrome. The study helped make its author famous as well."* The scene moved to Atlanta, where Steinschneider was seen showing Chung around his SIDS institute. They sat in his office, where he explained his theory and how it revolutionized SIDS research.

"Your paper has been very influential over a twenty-year period," Chung said. The camera zoomed in for a tight shot of Steinschneider.

"No, no, that paper ..." he stammered. *"I'm* influential. *I'm* a big man. Not the paper. The paper was the beginning ..."

It was a handy segue to the story of the Gedzius family, a sample of what the paper had wrought. The scene then moved on to Dallas, and a shot of Linda Norton peering into her microscope as Chung's voice-over explained what the forensic pathologist had to do with the 1972 paper. "It's a scientific error," Norton declared on camera. "It should be purged from the literature." Then on to Syracuse, where Fitzpatrick offered his views of Steinschneider. "His responsibility was to his patients, not to his theory," he said, glaring. "His patients were Molly and Noah. And Molly and Noah are dead."

In Atlanta, Chung asked Steinschneider, "Do you think you could have saved the lives of the two babies from the H. family?"

Here, he said something provocative. "Well, obviously, I've thought about that. I thought about that the day they died. I thought about it the day after they died. And I'm not sure what I could have done in 1972 or I would have done it."

"Your paper has been used as evidence that multiple SIDS deaths do occur in one family," Chung said.

"Those who do, use the paper inappropriately," Steinschneider said.

"They have misinterpreted your paper?" Chung asked.

"Absolutely. They have misinterpreted the literature."

Chung told Steinschneider about the Chicago family. "The grandmother in that case calls the paper a 'license to kill,' " she said.

Steinschneider looked genuinely pained. "I'm sorry to hear that," he said. "I'm truly sorry to hear that."

In both her opening and closing, Chung was careful to say that only rarely were unexplained infant deaths caused by homicide. Rarer still were cases of multiple infanticide. "The overwhelming majority of SIDS cases are tragic, natural deaths that baffle doctors and break the parents' hearts," she said, introducing a report on the latest research showing that babies put to bed on their backs or sides, rather than on their stomachs, ran a smaller risk of SIDS.

The American Academy of Pediatrics, reversing long-held conventional wisdom, had recommended the new sleep position in 1992, after concluding that studies around the world had demonstrated an association between SIDS and the prone position. Preliminary research from Britain and New Zealand, for instance, showed a 50 percent drop in each country's SIDS rate following public campaigns urging parents to put babies to bed on their backs. The research suggested the downward position facilitated a variety of possible airway obstructions.

Two years after the Academy recommendation—and, coincidentally, two months after the arrest of Waneta Hoyt—the SIDS Alliance and the U.S. government, led by a panel of experts that included John Brooks, launched a national campaign they dubbed "Back to Sleep." Steinschneider's SIDS Institute opposed the campaign, saying it was premature. Soon after, he announced that he would be the principal investigator of a new study, involving ten other researchers, looking at the sleep-position question.

He dug in. That October—seven months after the arrest—he and three new followers published a paper in *Pediatric Clinics of North America* in which they noted how Steinschneider had transformed the SIDS world in 1972 by reporting "his observations of five living infants, two of whom subsequently died of SIDS." Indeed, even now the apnea theory's hold on some people was intractable. One mother responded to the reports about Waneta Hoyt's arrest with an indignant letter to *The New York Times*. Her daughter was now thirteen and healthy, she wrote, but she would never forget the morning in 1981 when, at four weeks, "she turned deep blue and became like lead in my arms. I knew she was dying." Oblivious of the apnea mythology to which she had most likely fallen prey, the woman recounted a classic story of new parenthood, circa 1981: how she had rushed her newborn to the nearest emergency room, how the baby had spent three weeks in two hospitals getting "every test in the books," how nothing was found to be wrong. "The diagnosis was near-miss sudden infant death syndrome," and her daughter was sent home on a monitor. "For the next year until [she] was declared out of the woods, I slept with my clothes on, ready to run to the hospital. . . . It was years before I could stop myself from waking several times a night to make sure she was still breathing." Like many other parents who had similar experiences in those years, she still firmly believed that her baby had almost died that day—"and I still don't know why." And so she felt compelled to declare her sympathies for Waneta Hoyt. She had read about her arrest, she said, "with stricken heart, knowing that . . . I could have been in Mrs. Hoyt's shoes—handcuffed and accused of murder."

Steinschneider, meanwhile, sneered at the onslaught of bad press. "I was date-raped by Connie Chung," he said one day in his office. "I invited them

into my living room and I was abused and raped. One shower and I was clean
again. The issues they raised are silly and accusatory. I've been created by the
media. They said I was the most powerful guy, that I wrote a paper in 1972
and nothing happened before or since. It did become important, and
I've thought about why it had an impact. Lots of people have read it—
pediatricians, pathologists, family doctors—and it led to an awful lot of
research. It was heuristic. That's a word I learned in college. The paper led to
a lot of learning. Within a year, a paper gets published by Dick Naeye. Heh,
slow guy, right? Dr. Richard Naeye, one of the best pathologists in the
country. And he said, 'Hell, if this Dr. Steinschneider guy's right, then these
kids must have chronic hypoxia, and I know what chronic hypoxia does to
people. You get scar tissue, you get brown fat, you get thickened pulmonary
vessels.' And he looked at these seven things and said, 'I found it, it's there.'
He broke the whole thing. Mine was a rumination. There was no reason to
believe it. Naeye was the one who broke it open, back in '73. He had a series of
studies, pow, pow, pow, but he's busy working, he's not in show business. He
doesn't go to meetings with a lot of parents, he just goes about his business
and does the greatest stuff imaginable. He was the one who made a rather
weakly based hypothesis into something solid."

Jerold Lucey, among others, had a somewhat different historical perspective. Now in his twenty-third year as editor of *Pediatrics,* he found the arrest
of Waneta Hoyt a stunning development. Soon after the arrest, Lucey
devoted a page to the controversy under the headline "Very Important
Erratum?—20 Years Later." He included excerpts from two stories about
Waneta Hoyt's arrest that appeared in *The New York Times,* along with the
opening paragraph of John Hick's 1973 letter and a succinct Editor's Note:
"This is an incredible story. The whole apnea home monitoring to prevent
SIDS movement began with Steinschneider's original paper." At the bottom
of the page, Lucey printed a single reference, poignant in its isolation all these
years later.

1. Steinschneider, A. Prolonged apnea and the sudden infant death syndrome:
clinical and laboratory observations. *Pediatrics.* 1972; 50:646.

Science, which had anointed the apnea theory in 1975, also took note of
the dramatic development with an unusual news story. The charges against
Waneta Hoyt, the magazine suggested, "may be the final blow to the apnea-
SIDS theory." Steinschneider disagreed. "This is a good paper," he told writer
Ginger Pinholster. To Steinschneider's defense, meanwhile, came the familiar
interests, led by Dr. Carl Hunt, head of the Collaborative Home Infant Monitoring Evaluation, the nationwide study being sponsored by the NICHD. In a

commentary in *Pediatrics,* he bristled at the suggestion that a guilty verdict meant the final invalidation of the apnea theory—and hence, by implication, that the vast CHIME project was irrelevant. Hunt also had a connection to the darker side of this story: He and his colleagues at Chicago's Children's Memorial Hospital had evaluated and sent home on monitors two of the now-dead babies of Delos and Deborah Gedzius. In fact, it was the Chicago doctors' apnea diagnoses that had made Bruce Beckwith unwilling to say, in 1990, that the Gedzius babies could not have died of SIDS.

The news was received elsewhere in the SIDS world with a mixture of astonishment and recognition—and a new round of hand-wringing over what it meant to parents and pediatricians. "Accepting the Unthinkable" was the title of a meditation in *Pediatrics* by Doctors George Little and John Brooks, the chairman and one of the members of the 1986 consensus conference, who were now medical colleagues at Dartmouth. Their discussion of the impact of the "new information" about Steinschneider's H. family brought a response from Vincent DiMaio. That it was murder was "not 'new information' to the forensic pathology community," he wrote with his customary edge of annoyance at his colleagues in pediatrics. "The controversy illustrates the need for better communication between different specialties of medicine." From England, David Southall wrote that pediatricians had to constantly be on guard against the possibility that Apparent Life Threatening Events were acts of child abuse. There was, finally, the value of simple truth. *Better late than never,* Bruce Beckwith thought when he heard about the arrest of Waneta Hoyt. By the early 1990s, he had come to realize that the H. children had almost certainly been murdered—and so, too, had the Gedzius babies.

In Tioga County during these months, Judge Vincent Sgueglia was presiding over the various procedural matters leading up to his first murder trial, a considerably more intricate and explosive case than he might have reasonably expected when he took office. Sgueglia was a man fascinated by the faces of human motivation and saw his new job as a window into the struggle between acts of commission and redemption. One day in May, the judge held a brief hearing on Bob Miller's request to have Ray Urbanski permanently assigned to the Hoyt matter as co–public defender. The case was too complicated for one lawyer, Miller argued, and Sgueglia could not disagree. But the judge also recognized that the prosecution of Waneta Hoyt peeled the cover off a remarkable story that went much deeper than the maneuvers in his courtroom. "What interests me," Sgueglia confided after Waneta and her regular group of supporters had trudged home to Newark Valley, "is Steinschneider." A great, relishing smile crossed the judge's face as he considered a possibility. "Is he going to come and defend his work?"

33

Out to dinner one night in late summer, Bob and Rose Miller and Ray and Linda Urbanski were talking over the reactions to Waneta Hoyt they'd picked up in their travels, and what it meant for the defense. "Everybody I've talked to thinks five babies can't die of SIDS in one family," reported Linda Urbanski, a teacher in the Elmira public schools. "Sometimes lawyers get so wrapped up in the intricacies and they talk to doctors and experts, but when you get to a jury I think you're going to have a real, real hard time."

For an instant, the table was silent. "I think you're right," Miller said then.

"I think you're going to have a real hard time," Linda repeated.

But for Miller and Urbanski, this was the case of their careers, and they were all over it. They had once been partners. They couldn't have imagined a reunion such as this.

Miller was fifty-four years old, a tall, burly man with a manner that was equal parts engaging and brusque. He was one of the relatively few people in Tioga County who came from someplace else, although the town of his birth, Cando, North Dakota, was no bigger than the one that produced Waneta Hoyt. His father, a National Guardsman who also owned a small newspaper, came out of World War II as a colonel in the regular army and decided to make it a career, so Miller spent his youth on the move, from the Philippines to San Francisco, Korea, and Queens, New York. Eventually he made it to Yale, played some football, but left after two years. Hitchhiking across the country in 1960, he met a man who owned the second-largest ranch in Montana. "I punched cows for seven or eight months," Miller reminisced, "then sold insurance in San Francisco." He joined his father's army, and spent four years in Special Forces, doing, among other things, top secret things in South-

463

east Asia. He went back to Yale in 1965, then headed to Cornell for law school. In Ithaca, he clerked for a judge who turned out to be not only his favorite mentor, but Bob Simpson's father.

After graduation Miller went to work for a lawyer in the little town of Waverly, in the southwestern corner of Tioga County, and finally planted some roots. He set up his own office in Elmira soon after, and became an ex–Green Beret who made his living defending draft dodgers. These were assigned-counsel cases from the oldest sitting federal judge in the country, a World War I veteran who thought the government was clogging the courts. "He'd dismiss them in droves," Miller said. "I'd go up to Rochester with three or four cases, get them all dismissed. Made me look like a hero." He had no political feelings about it. It was lawyer's work, and what he liked about being a lawyer was fighting the battles, whatever they happened to be. It was more or less his philosophy when he set up the Tioga County public defender's office.

Miller took on his first murder case two years later, got his first six-figure personal injury verdict shortly after that, and by the mid-seventies had a thriving practice; so thriving that he put up a sign on the bulletin board at Cornell: "Elmira attorney desperately needs law student."

"You're in law school?" he asked Ray Urbanski, the first twenty-four-year-old who walked through the door. "Good, you're hired." Urbanski had gotten his résumé together and put on a suit, all for naught. Miller barely looked up from his desk when he hired him.

Urbanski had grown up in Connecticut, knowing from the seventh grade that he wanted to be a lawyer because it looked so good on TV. "I just always liked the idea of verbal confrontation," he said one day. He practiced a lot on his father, who favored the Vietnam war, at the dinner table, along with most other things that caused fights between fathers and sons in those years. By the time he got to law school, his skills were sharp. He stayed with Miller through graduation, helped with briefs, interviewed witnesses, watched his mentor at trials, and when he passed the bar, became his junior partner.

Neither man was slick in the slick lawyer sense, but they made a good, if somewhat oddly matched team. Urbanski had a thick head of hair, unruly teeth, and a smoky cackle of a laugh. He gave off an exuberant, hard-charging appearance, though he also loved law books—loved trolling for pieces of legal argument he could throw around a courtroom. Miller was much too impatient for legal scholarship. He was more of a bulldog and tended to fly by the seat of his pants. There was no question who was the more intimidating lawyer in the courtroom. They did nicely for a while, but then Miller decided he wanted to go back on his own and war eventually broke out. They called each other sons-of-bitches, and Urbanski wound up suing Miller for his share of a personal injury settlement. They didn't talk for months. But it didn't last.

They had forged a brotherly bond, and there was really no separating them. Eventually they settled the lawsuit, patched up their friendship, if not their partnership, and worked on a few cases together from the safety of their solo practices. And when Miller found himself defending a woman against five murder charges, he did not hesitate to call Urbanski in the middle of the night.

In summer, they decided they needed to hunker down in Miller's condo in Fort Myers and sort out the case before it got away from them. There were half a dozen legal issues to work on, briefs and motions to outline, strategies to mount, facts to study. Miller still didn't have all the children straight in his mind: which one died of what, in what order, what the autopsies and death certificates said and didn't say. His understanding of the medical part of the case was still rudimentary, but he knew one thing, at least. He and Urbanski needed to sit down with the doctor they had heard so much about.

Stopping in Atlanta on their way to Fort Myers, they met Alfred Steinschneider in the law office of one of the SIDS Institute's board members on the Friday after Labor Day. They found him guarded, still brimming with righteous indignation, and clearly no stranger to intellectual combat. In fact, there was something almost lawyerly about him, the way he was simultaneously careful and caustic, the way he framed his defense. "First, I've got to tell you, I never talked about the Hoyts in my paper," Steinschneider said. "Everybody else knows who I'm talking about, but I still have to say Hoyt who? Nobody has authorized me to say anything."

Steinschneider wouldn't say anything about the Hoyts, even to their lawyers, but he was willing to talk about the H. children. Miller asked what he remembered about their parents. They appeared sincere, Steinschneider said. They were concerned. They lived in a trailer. He couldn't remember much else about them. But, of course he remembered their last two children. And he remembered what he saw: a documented history of apnea.

Urbanski asked if there was a reason to believe these babies were victims of homicide. "For all I know," Steinschneider said, "they could have been murdered. I have no way to know that. Who could possibly know that other than her? Could it be homicide? I didn't see any evidence of that, but sure. Could it be some genetic disorder in the family that we simply didn't find? Sure. Could it have been sleep apnea? Sure. And we saw episodes of that in the hospital."

Miller asked about the issue of multiple SIDS. Of course it could happen, Steinschneider said; he'd been saying it for twenty years. But don't take my word for it, he said. He referred them to a doctor who'd written papers about it. Up at Harvard.

For Miller and Urbanski, the meeting was in part a delicate job of salesmanship. They knew Steinschneider would make a less than perfect witness and calling him to testify carried risks, but they needed him nonetheless. If they didn't call him, Miller worried, the jury would wonder why not. And if they didn't put him on, might Simpson? They were careful not to say anything that would discourage Steinschneider from testifying. They had no power to subpoena him and didn't want to give him the impression he was jumping aboard a sinking ship, so they told him what a strong case they had, how weak the prosecution's was. "Sure as hell didn't show him the confession," Miller said later. But he saw that Steinschneider was unmoved. "He didn't want to come up. He wished the whole thing would go away. I didn't think he'd be a great witness because he's got a stake in the case and he's very defensive. Connie Chung sure as hell made him look like an idiot. But we needed him. He took care of two kids, and we needed him to testify about the records and how the monitors were going off and the kids had breathing problems. So we have to get him up here. He has to testify."

On some level, Steinschneider seemed to realize this too. He had to testify, for himself as much as for Waneta Hoyt. He asked if he could just give a deposition. His own lawyer told him no, he'd have to testify in person, if that's what he wanted to do. "Will you pay my plane fare?" Steinschneider asked.

Flying on to Fort Myers later that day, Miller and Urbanski felt reasonably good about Steinschneider. He was willing to testify that these babies had many episodes of apnea that put them at such risk that they spent most of their lives on monitors. At the least, Urbanski thought, Steinschneider might be able to cast doubt on the idea that homicide was the only possibility here. But he also realized his effectiveness as a defense witness depended on how the jury viewed the confession. "You're stuck with the situation that Al has written this article and he will get up there and attempt to validate his position," Urbanski said. "He will consistently indicate that he didn't see any evidence of foul play. But if the jury buys that confession, the more adamant he becomes, the stupider he looks."

In Fort Myers, the lawyers surrounded themselves with their growing files and plotted their course. Their defense had two essential elements: the confession and the medical evidence. There wasn't much they could do with the confession other than attack it with great intensity and imagination. By now, they knew it was worse than they first thought. In addition to the statement handwritten by Sue Mulvey and signed by Waneta, there was also the much more damaging statement taken down by a stenographer. The only way around it was to persuade the jury that Waneta had not voluntarily waived her rights to talk without a lawyer—that she didn't understand the Miranda warnings, and that she was the simplest sort of person, fully capable of being manipulated by those tricky investigators from Troop C. As Waneta told it, the police deceived her—got her to come down to Owego by saying they needed her help with a SIDS "research project," then got her to agree to a false confession by rubbing her shoulders and putting a cop she trusted in the seat next to her.

It was a weak defense, Miller knew. He imagined a jury might be more sympathetic to the suggestion of a mental deficiency, perhaps postpartum depression, as a mitigating factor in the actual deaths of the babies. That would allow him to ask them to consider an appropriately lesser charge and keep her sentence down to a couple of years. But Waneta's unalterable declaration of innocence barred him from taking that approach. It meant that the only place they could use the issue of her mental faculties—*had* to use it—was in the interview room. They would make what happened in there the main battleground of the case.

"We're not going to win by cross-examining Mulvey," Miller said to Urbanski one night. "And Courtright will get on the stand, very smooth." Both from Waverly, Miller and Courtright had known each other for years. "He'll say nothing happened." Miller had a hard time believing Waneta had confessed so easily after a couple of hours of small talk. They had to persuade the jury that there must have been more to it.

Miller was willing to try almost anything to do this. A linguistics expert from California who read about the case called to offer her services; maybe she could show that Waneta had been manipulated by clever language. Miller hired her to explore the possibility. But the expert he was banking on most was a man named Charles Patrick Ewing, a forensic psychologist from Buffalo who also had a law degree from Harvard and was a seasoned expert for the defense. Ewing would interview Waneta and Tim, give her a personality test, and, Miller hoped, form the opinion that her statement to the police couldn't be trusted. In June, Waneta and Tim had driven up to Buffalo to see Ewing, and there would be several more sessions in the coming weeks of fall. Miller told Ewing not to put anything in writing that would have to be given to the prosecution during the discovery process; he thought the only way this could work was to spring Ewing as a surprise at trial, without giving Simpson time to get his own expert. But on the phone, the early reports from Ewing were good. Waneta seemed to like him.

To her lawyers, Waneta's personality—indeed, her whole environment—was becoming a curious backdrop to the case. Miller couldn't remember a client quite so inscrutable, and he found the flock of friends and relatives who attended her distracting. There was a connection. It was from attention that Waneta drew her energy, and there were times at her court appearances when she seemed uplifted by the recognition. Over the years she had developed a keen sense about who was sympathetic to her and who wasn't. To a large degree, it defined her relationships and her life. That she liked going to see Dr. Ewing would come to mean something significant to her defense.

Waneta also liked going to see Ray Urbanski. "She comes to my office often, and often unannounced," Urbanski said one day. "Yeah," Miller added, not displeased, "they like Ray. They don't like me." As Waneta seemed to suspect, Miller didn't feel particularly sorry for her. But he hoped to fill a jury with people who did. You couldn't underestimate the power of emotion in a case like this.

The physical part of the case was more complicated but no less crucial. Waneta couldn't be convicted without her statement being corroborated—without Bob Simpson proving that crimes had, in fact, been committed. The district attorney was starting at the source. Soon after the arrest, Simpson had accepted the arguments of Fitzpatrick and Michael Baden that exhuming the five bodies was unpleasant but necessary. Even if there was a small chance of finding anything conclusive, the prosecutor felt he could not come into trial without having made the effort. The jurors would be looking for this evidence, he believed, and he had to have something to show them. According to Baden, you never knew what you might find. So nineteen days after the arrest, Simpson had made a motion to exhume. Miller had opposed it, though it wasn't an easy choice for him either. He could see how an exhumation could help the defense more than the prosecution. If SIDS couldn't be distinguished from suffocation when it happened, how could Baden possibly find anything a quarter-century later? If they exhumed and found no evidence of homicide, that would be a victory for Waneta. But his client and her family passionately opposed the idea of digging up the bodies, so Miller agreed to object to Simpson's motion, forcing Judge Sgueglia to convene a hearing on the issue in early June.

As the hearing's only witness, Baden had testified why he thought each of the children had been murdered—in the customary phrase, "to a reasonable degree of medical certainty." Then he explained why it was necessary to look for more. Two of the babies had not been autopsied after their deaths, and the other three had been examined by hospital pathologists, not forensic pathologists. "Hospital pathology is essentially concerned with natural diseases," he said. "And that includes ninety-nine percent of the pathologists in this country. And indeed it works out fairly well, because about ninety-two percent of deaths are from natural causes." Simpson's assistant, Peggy Drake, asked Baden what he would look for on re-autopsy. "Bone fractures, which were not systematically looked for at the first two autopsies," he said. ". . . Um, the neck area has to be closely looked at for evidence of injury or hemorrhage, which could be due to compression. . . . The condition of the eyes have to be examined, because sometimes there's hemorrhage in the eyes in this type of death. And the eyes pretty often stay intact. Not always. The eyes are pretty tough." He thought it was possible that fibers from a towel might turn up with Jimmy's remains. For that matter, he told the judge, he could conceivably find evidence of natural disease. Of course, it all depended on the condition of the bodies. He'd found some amazing things on exhumation over the years. When he'd autopsied the corpse of Medgar Evers in 1991, he noted, it appeared as if the slain civil rights leader had been buried the day before. But there were of course no guarantees.

Miller was confident Baden would find nothing. The children were buried inexpensively, he knew. And he thought Baden was just being Baden, with that wizard-of-the-crypt posture he found so irritating. So as the exhumation hearing neared its end, Miller had an impulse. After cross-examining Baden with a great flourish of indignant skepticism, he thought, *Okay, big shot, prove it.* "We join in the prosecution's application in the exhumation of the bodies," he announced, shocking everyone in the courtroom: the judge, the prosecutor, his client—certainly his client—even his partner. "What the hell was that?" Urbanski asked when Miller returned to the defense table. "I don't know, I just figured, fuck it," Miller said. "He won't find anything."

The judge said he'd have his decision in a few days. With the defense dropping its objection, it seemed a foregone conclusion, but Sgueglia was getting a reputation for unpredictability. "I'm not so sure I'm going to go along with it," he confided later that day. That he had held a hearing at all on what is commonly considered a prosecutor's prerogative was an indication of how the judge, a deeply religious man, felt about what was being proposed. A week later, he denied the exhumation request. Simpson, annoyed, got to work on his brief to the appeals court in Albany. Miller didn't care how it turned out. "We're in a no-lose situation," he said. "But it gives us a couple more months."

Aside from Waneta's statement, it was an uncommonly circumstantial case, although how strong it was depended on which side you were on and what it was in your interest to believe. Soon after he got the case, Miller had hired a former New York State trooper, Bill Fischer, hoping to turn up some circumstances helpful to the defense. Fischer had turned out to be an astonishingly enthusiastic investigator. In June, he came up with something the state police hadn't—the only record of a police investigation of the Hoyts from the early years. Even before Waneta was brought in for questioning, the county sheriff's department had looked through its files and nothing had surfaced. But when Fischer filed a freedom-of-information request, the sheriff's department found a misfiled page dated June 5, 1970. It was Undersheriff Ray Cornwell's one-paragraph report of Molly's death: ". . . There seems to be a gland problem on the mother's side. . . ."

By the end of August, Fischer had found several of the rescue squad workers who'd responded to the emergency calls in the sixties and seventies and turned up evidence that one of the babies—it appeared to have been Molly—might have been alive when help arrived. Fischer was excited; he told Miller it was evidence that Waneta didn't kill the baby. Miller was unimpressed. He found that Fischer got excited about a lot of things that didn't necessarily amount to anything helpful for the defense—the sheriff's report, which made the earlier generation of police look inept more than it made Waneta look not guilty, heading the list. Fischer came to believe in Waneta's innocence, but to Miller's disappointment, he produced little that could be used to persuade a jury. Among other things, he could find nothing to refute the prosecution's most compelling piece of circumstantial evidence: Every time a child died in this family, only their mother was present.

One day, Fischer came to Miller and Urbanski with what he considered a huge discovery. He showed them a picture from one of the Hoyts' photo albums from the 1960s. "That's their couch," he said.

"Well, yeah," said Urbanski.

"See any pillows?"

"No."

"That's the case right there, ladies and gentlemen. Where's the pillow?"

"Oh, Jesus Christ," Urbanski said scornfully.

Fischer flipped to another picture that included the corner of a crib. "Where's the pillow?" he asked again, his eyes ablaze.

Urbanski and Miller looked at Fischer as if he were from Venus. It wasn't long before Miller told him his services were no longer required. But Fischer stayed on anyway. He attached himself to the Hoyts.

Miller saw more fertile territory in the conceptual nature of the prosecution's case: "They're saying these are homicides because you can't have five in one family. Well, according to who?" He read the commentary Carl Hunt published in *Pediatrics* in response to Waneta's arrest. Hunt said subsequent siblings *were* at increased risk, Miller observed, as were babies with apnea. "The bottom line is what have they uncovered? The medical records have nothing to do with homicide. Can a jury believe there can be multiple SIDS?" He hoped so. And he hoped he could somehow get the jury around the strongest link in the prosecution's chain, and the defense's weakest: the sudden, inexplicable death of Jimmy Hoyt. "They say you can't have a SIDS death over one year," Miller considered. "Where's the medical evidence? Who drew the line? Why not fourteen months? Why not eighteen months? Why not two years, four months? Their proof is all probability and statistics. That might not raise it to the level of corroboration."

Still, he needed somebody to counter the argument. He started with his old friend, Eleanor McQuillen. She had been an obscure hospital pathologist, and Miller's neighbor, when he pressed her into service in his first murder case twenty years before. On the strength of her testimony—her first appearance in court—he won an acquittal. The jury believed her over the prosecution's expert—Michael Baden. The experience so excited McQuillen that she quit her job, took a forensic pathology residency, and later became Vermont's chief medical examiner and a nationally known member of the forensic fraternity. "I was wondering when you were going to call," she told Miller when he called her in Vermont months after Waneta's arrest. Miller sent her the records, hoping he could count on her, once again, to contradict Mike Baden. But after reviewing the case, McQuillen called Miller and said sorry, forget it: "You're not going to find a forensic pathologist anywhere who will say these are not homicides." About all she could offer were some pointers on how to cross-examine Baden.

Maybe they would do better with a SIDS expert. In their research, the defense lawyers saw that a doctor named Marie Valdes-Dapena seemed to be the classic name. But apparently it was long past the time when she would say anything in Waneta's behalf. "Well, Valdes-Dapena seems to have joined the bandwagon that says, 'Show me two children in the family that have died of SIDS and I will show you murder,' " Urbanski said. "But Steinschneider gave us an article by Doctors Oren, Kelly, and Shannon—Mass General, Harvard Med School. 'Identification of a High Risk Group for Sudden Infant Death Syndrome.' As it turns out," Urbanski said hopefully, "multiple SIDS deaths in families are not so unusual." Steinschneider had told the lawyers that Dorothy Kelly was the country's leading expert on clustering of SIDS deaths. He didn't tell them that she had first gotten her ideas from his 1972 paper about the Hoyt family and had cited it as evidence ever since.

Returning home from their September strategy retreat in Florida, Miller called Kelly in Boston and signed her on to the defense. Waneta's lawyers were right when they concluded that perhaps no doctor in America would argue their case like Kelly. She, too, had a great deal at stake in the case of Waneta Hoyt.

Late in September, just as the defense was sending the Upstate records to Boston, two new members of the state police's Hoyt task force drove up to a small house on a working-class block in Syracuse. They knocked on the door, and a frail woman answered.

"Mrs. Evans?" one of them asked.

"Yes?" the woman replied pleasantly.

"Mrs. Evans, I'm Investigator Gelinger. This is Investigator Conzola. We're with the New York State Police. We wonder if we could talk to you about a family named the Hoyts."

Julie Evans looked up at the investigators framed by her doorway. "Well, it's about time," she said.

She was seventy-nine now, seventeen years retired from her job on the pediatrics ward at Upstate Medical Center. Investigators Gary Gelinger and Jim Conzola had come from the hospital's personnel department, where they'd gotten addresses for some of the nurses and doctors whose names appeared in Molly's and Noah's records. Julie Evans seemed like a good place to start. Her name was all over the nursing notes, and the address on her personnel card matched the one in the current Syracuse phone book. She was now a widow, her gray hair tied back in a bun. She'd lost some of the fire for which she had once been well-known, but not all of it.

"So you remember the Hoyts?" Gelinger asked.

"I'll never forget them," Julie said.

They sat in her living room and Julie told the detectives that yes, she recalled both Molly and Noah, and she certainly remembered their mother. "There was definitely something wrong between her and the babies," she said. "When the babies were put in her arms it looked like she wanted to pull away. Like she didn't want to be bothered. There was no warmth between them. You knew darn well she didn't want them."

Excited by Julie's recollections, Gelinger and Conzola asked her if there had been anything medically wrong with the babies. Was there an apnea problem? "I remember Noah best," Julie said. "He was a perfect little baby. I was on the three-to-midnight shift, and the monitor never went off when I was with him. I knew something would happen to him when he left the hospital. I was positive the mother would kill him." The investigators could hardly believe what they were hearing. Then Julie told them about the wager she'd made with Steinschneider. "I bet him a quarter that Noah would be dead the next day," she said. "I remember how upset and angry I was at him. All I said was, 'I told you so!' It was so obvious what was going on."

Julie gave the investigators a written statement of everything she remembered. "Will I have to come to court?" she asked. Gelinger told her he didn't know, that would be up to the district attorney down in Tioga County. Julie hoped not. She was old, in tenuous health, and though she had been furious with Steinschneider at the time, she did not relish embarrassing him in a courtroom all these years later. For she remembered liking him; she'd known him since he was a medical student. There was also still a remnant of that old, entrenched principle of medical culture that said nurses didn't go over doctors' heads. You couldn't go any higher than a murder trial. Julie didn't know that Steinschneider had written a paper about Molly and Noah that said they had died of SIDS. She didn't know it had made him famous. She had retired right around the time he left Syracuse and lost track of him after that.

When Courtright and Simpson heard what Julie Evans had said, they saw a whole avenue of corroboration opening up. If the first nurse they had found remembered so much and felt so sure that Waneta had killed her children, even had a bet with Steinschneider about it, what might the others say? There was a limit to what Simpson could get into testimony—the bet had little chance, he knew—but their observations of Waneta's lack of maternal instinct could be an important piece of emotional evidence, a first-hand glimpse of those years to go with the detached, retrospective medical opinions of the forensic pathologists. It was also a window into the key moments of this entire affair, the convergence of Waneta Hoyt and Alfred Steinschneider; the first clue that Steinschneider had reason to know more than he had ever told. The nurses had been the silent witnesses; now they could give voice. Gelinger and Conzola went to the next name on the list.

The investigators had been drafted onto the Hoyt task force to pursue the Upstate part of the case. Assistant District Attorney Peggy Drake was their guide. She had gone through the medical records for all five children and painstakingly made cross-referenced lists of every nurse and doctor whose signature she could decipher. They went on for pages. Drake gave the completed lists to Courtright with a note flagging an arresting note a nurse who seemed to be named "J. Schneider" had written in Molly's nursing record on June 4, 1970, the day before the baby died: *I discussed my concern for the baby with Dr. Steinschneider this A.M. . . . . The interaction between mother and baby is almost nil in my opinion.* "She would be the most important nurse to speak to," Drake wrote in her cover memo to Courtright. When they went into the personnel records, the investigators found that "J. Schneider" was probably "T. Schneider."

Thelma and Jack Schneider had retired to a house in Henderson Harbor, a small community tucked into a cove of Lake Ontario, about sixty miles north of Syracuse. It was a life far removed from the one they left behind at Upstate Medical Center. Thelma worked at a community clinic for a while, and got herself elected tax assessor. The Schneiders had a boat, and Jack, the retired pediatric research chief, puttered around the house and commented upon the ways of the world.

They were watching the eleven o'clock news from Syracuse the night of March 23, 1994, and heard about the woman who had been arrested for the murders of her five children decades before. Thelma thought immediately of Waneta Hoyt, but when they showed the suspect being led from the state police barracks, she could not say it was her. The woman looked nothing like the young mother Thelma remembered. Then she heard the name. "Oh, my God," she said to her husband. "How on earth did they come across this after all this time?"

It was six months after the arrest that Gelinger and Conzola came to the

Schneiders' door carrying some of the nursing notes and Waneta's photo album. Like Julie Evans, Thelma told them that she recalled the family vividly. "What I remember most is the bizarre way the mother held the baby," she said. "Not cuddling, but away from her. I remember once she took the baby from her husband, then sat on his lap and held the baby away from her again." Gelinger showed Thelma a snapshot of Waneta and one of the babies. Was this the woman she remembered? Thelma chuckled. "That's what I'm talking about," she said. "That's exactly how she held them." They showed Thelma a copy of her handwritten "interaction is nil" note in Molly's chart. She remembered it well. "We had so many discussions," she recalled, "but then I finally put it in the notes. I said there wasn't any bonding, as they now call it." It was her way of protesting Steinschneider's refusal to consider the possibility that horrendous crimes were being committed, suspicions, she said, that were virtually confirmed the very next day, when word came that Molly was dead.

Thelma gave the investigators the names of two more nurses she thought would be worth tracking down: Corrine Dower, who was now seventy-five and retired in Syracuse, and Joyce Thomas, whom they found in Tacoma, Washington. The picture that was emerging was of a nursing staff connected by whispers and paralyzed by frustration. Waneta Hoyt's arrest forced the nurses to revisit an episode in their careers that had disturbed them deeply, moments they would never forget. They began thinking of each other again, and of the bittersweet bond that had been forged between them. "How is Julie?" Thelma asked during a conversation in her living room a few weeks after the visit from the investigators. "I haven't talked to her in years." One after another, they tried to portray context: The Hoyt babies were Dr. Steinschneider's patients, and in those days nurses knew their place. In the end, how could they prove their suspicions? "Nurses aren't supposed to diagnose," Thelma said, "so we said, all right, maybe. But still you always have that feeling in the back of your mind—no, it's not right. And, of course, today you have hotlines, but even there, what kind of proof do you have if you don't see a mother putting a pillow over a kid's head? Let me put it this way: When it finally came on the news one night, I went, 'Oh my God,' but I was not shocked."

For Thelma, so many thoughts rattled her memory these months, reminders of those early days with Steinschneider, when he was the protégé of her first husband Earle Lipton, and they were all good friends. "He was motivated to have a career, that much I'll say," she said one day, trying to be charitable. She was sitting in a comfortable chair, looking out into the grayness shrouding Lake Ontario on a fall afternoon, her mind's eye journeying back thirty years. "That was the kind of thing that bothered Earle from time to time, because he was very laid back and Al is very pushy. Al had his sights on something better."

Late in November, a letter arrived in the mail at the Onondaga County district attorney's office. Bill Fitzpatrick quickly dispatched it to Simpson:

> Dear Sir or Madam:
> This letter is written out of concern regarding an article on pg 34 in Newsweek Nov 14th issue. In the article is mention of a Waneta Hoyt being charged recently with the deaths of her five children over 23 years ago.
> I, among other staff at State University Hospital in Syracuse, cared for Noah Hoyt in 1971 when I was a nursing aide in the 4A Pediatrics Wing where Noah was a patient. Noah was a beautiful baby app. 4–6 months of age. The reason I remember Noah so long ago is because I lost several nights' sleep over his death, which occurred within 24 hours of his discharge home with an apnea monitor.
> You see, I met his mother once, while I was caring for Noah. I should say I introduced myself to her, and I believe her husband, one day in the nursery and I'll never forget the unsettled feeling I had from that moment on as her mannerism and behavior shown to me was not indicative of a concerned and loving parent. Frankly, I was a bit frightened of her and as weeks went by I became very concerned for Noah's safety as well.
> Other staff members also voiced concern over Noah's mom's behavior as well but I can't definitely say whether written reference to this was made in Noah's chart. You may wish to look into the "nurses' notes" during his stay if you haven't already.
> I simply felt I had to share my thoughts and concern with you, and if there is further information you feel I may have which sheds light on this situation, feel free to contact me. Thank you for your indulgence in this matter.
>
> Gail Pfeiffer (Dristle in 1971)

In the twenty-three years since the death of Noah Hoyt, Gail Dristle had gotten married and divorced, raised three children, moved to a rustic area northeast of Syracuse, and driven a school bus for a dozen years. She was Gail Pfeiffer now, forty-four years old, a student at Mohawk Valley Community College considering social work as a midlife career. Her children were now twenty-six, nineteen, and seventeen. She had salt-and-pepper hair, mostly pepper, clipped short on top, long in the back, a style that gave her a youthful aspect. She and Waneta were only three years apart in age, but looked twenty.

Of all the women who took care of Molly and Noah at Upstate, none had felt sharper, more enduring pain than Gail. What happened to Noah was one of the main reasons she hadn't lasted at Upstate. It killed her ambition to graduate from nurse's aide to nurse. But she had never really left the experience behind. She had thought about Noah often over the years, usually around her birthday because his came three days earlier. She would calculate how old he would have been. People close to her knew about this episode in her life and what it meant to her, almost as if she herself had lost a child. When something triggered the recollection, she would tell what had happened, and then the thoughts would linger in her mind for a day or two.

Because she found so much of what went on in the world painful to know about, Gail didn't read the papers regularly or watch the news on TV, so word of Waneta Hoyt's arrest managed to elude her for nearly eight months. In November, she had a school assignment to review a science article from a magazine and chose that week's issue of *Newsweek,* whose cover line was, by coincidence, "Sins of the Mother." It was a story that gripped America: A young woman named Susan Smith had been accused of drowning her two little boys in a lake in South Carolina. Gail avoided the magazine for days. Then one night in bed, she opened to the cover story. It was followed by a second article headlined "Why Parents Kill." She read this too. Turning the page, she was drawn to a picture of a middle-aged couple walking out of a courtroom. "Waneta Hoyt allegedly confessed to suffocating five babies. . . ." read the caption. Instantly, Gail began to cry. She woke up her fiancé. "Ed, do you know what I'm reading? It's the lady I told you about. They arrested her. Oh, my God."

She thought about little else the next few days. "I have to do something this time," she told a few close friends. "I didn't do enough the last time." The magazine story only briefly summarized the case, mentioning that a "local prosecutor" had discovered the murders while reading an article about SIDS in a medical journal. Gail wrote to the Onondaga County District Attorney's Office in Syracuse. A few days later, she got a call from Bob Courtright down in Owego. His investigators wouldn't have found her on their own. Her name was one of many in the nursing notes made obsolete by marriage. Even at that, there was nothing in what she wrote in her notes to distinguish her as someone to go after.

The Tuesday before Thanksgiving, Gelinger and Conzola drove up to Oneida County and met Gail at a lunch place near where she lived. For the investigators, the recollections were familiar by now, but for Gail they were still mind-bending. "Mrs. Hoyt was very rigid, like she never saw a human child before," she told them. "The father seemed benign, very quiet. But she just spooked me. There was something real wrong here. I don't know anything about the other baby, but I was very close to Noah. And I didn't think he would survive."

"Did the other nurses feel this way?" she was asked.

"The nurses didn't want him to go home, I know that." She seemed to the investigators a thoughtful woman. She strained to find clarity, as much for herself as for them. "There wasn't a lot of open talk about it. Though I was just a nurse's aide. I was just twenty-one years old. So there may have been more that I wasn't privy to." She remembered the day she walked into the nursery and found Waneta glaring at Noah. "I definitely felt she was capable of harming the baby."

It was the first time the investigators had heard someone say they observed behavior other than lack of interest. "Is this helpful?" Gail asked.

"Very helpful," Gelinger said. "This is big stuff here, Gail."

She wondered if she would be called to testify. The thought of seeing Waneta Hoyt again gave her an unsettled feeling.

Reading through the Upstate records one day, Bob Miller was jolted by an unimaginable coincidence. He realized that his son Todd had been in the hospital's pediatric research center at the very same time as Noah Hoyt. Todd Miller, born a few weeks before Noah in 1971, had severe allergies that required his parents to make the long drive to Syracuse each week for tests. Todd stayed overnight several times during the same three months Noah was there; Miller thought it highly possible he and Rose had crossed paths with the Hoyts. "We're thinking of calling Todd as a witness," Miller joked one day. His youngest son was now twenty-four. He had his own black humor. "Glad they didn't switch us," Todd told his father. Miller remembered that Todd's doctor was Jack Schneider. He was unaware Schneider's wife would turn out to be a witness against his client. Miller found it hard to envision a case with more strange twists and odd characters.

Neither could Ray Urbanski. In winter, with an early-spring trial looking likely, he flew to London to see a man named Gisli Gudjonsson. An Icelandic-born psychologist who had once been a police detective in Reykjavik, he was probably the world's leading expert in interrogations and confessions, with a special emphasis on false confessions. Urbanski had read Gudjonsson's book, *The Psychology of Interrogations, Confessions and Testimony.* His most famous credit was the case known in England as the Guildford Four, in which four men wrongly convicted as Irish Republican Army terrorists were released after seventeen years in prison. The story was turned into a popular film, *In the Name of the Father.* Urbanski and Miller hoped Gudjonsson could do the same for Waneta Hoyt.

By this point, Waneta had visited many times with the Buffalo psychologist Charles Ewing, whose relationship with her was coming to transcend that of the standard defendant and expert witness. Waneta and Tim went to see him regularly for months beyond the time arranged for the task at hand. Her lawyers noticed that Ewing seemed to be serving as her therapist, her confidant. Like investigator Bill Fischer, Ewing was becoming emotionally attached to the idea of Waneta's innocence.

As a psychologist who was also a law professor, Ewing planned to testify that, based on what he'd learned during his encounters with Waneta, he believed she didn't understand the Miranda warning when she spoke to the police—that she had not given a "voluntary waiver" of her constitutional rights. Therefore, her confession, true or not—he thought it wasn't—was invalid. He also found that she had several personality disorders that made her especially vulnerable to suggestion. But these were fairly subtle legal concepts for a jury to hang an acquittal on, especially since there seemed no question that her rights had been clearly explained to her, both verbally and in writing, and that she'd said she understood them. Moreover, Judge Sguelgia had already ruled on the issue, finding after a hearing on the defense's motion to suppress the statement that it was valid and admissible. He would leave it to the jury to decide whether it was credible. That's where Gisli Gudjonsson came in. Urbanski and Miller hoped Gudjonsson would go much deeper than Ewing's constitutional psychology. If any man in the world was qualified to say Waneta had confessed to something she didn't do, and to explain how it happened, it was Gudjonsson. All Waneta had to do was convince Gudjonsson.

Urbanski sent off copies of Waneta's statements and other background to Gudjonsson, then went to see him at his office at the Institute of Psychiatry of the University of London. Gudjonsson was world-famous, but his office was tiny, barely big enough for the two of them. "This isn't like the U.S.," Gudjonsson apologized. "This is what you get." They went down to the cafeteria to talk about Waneta Hoyt. Urbanski was disheartened to hear that Gudjonsson hadn't read the materials he'd sent. In fact, he didn't seem particularly interested in the case at all. "Just tell me about it," he said. Urbanski did, conveying the strange story of Waneta Hoyt with all the intrigue and fascination he could muster. The more he told him, the more Gudjonsson became drawn in. They talked for four hours, and when they were done, Gudjonsson was hooked. He agreed to come to America, though he reminded Urbanski he was no gun for hire. "I'm not going to lie for you," he warned.

Gudjonsson arrived a few weeks later and set up shop in the dining room of Miller's house in Waverly. He spent the better part of a week reading documents from the case and talking with Waneta. He administered a test that had come to be known as the Gudjonsson Suggestibility Scales. He read a paragraph about a fictitious robbery, then asked a series of questions about the story, most of which were subtly misleading. Then he told her she'd made a number of mistakes, even if she hadn't, and asked her to be more accurate in the next round of questions. The test was designed to measure a person's vulnerability to suggestion, particularly by police interrogators.

At the end of their second day together, although Gudjonsson didn't tell her the results of the various tests and interviews, Waneta emerged with a worried look on her face. It was not at all the way she appeared when she came out of her sessions with Ewing in Buffalo. Ewing doted on her, told her she was innocent, that she was a victim of police treachery, and she fed on it. But Gudjonsson was altogether different, and Waneta was perceptive enough to discern this. When she left, Gudjonsson told Miller and Urbanski, "I'm afraid I'm not going to be able to help you." The lawyers were crestfallen.

"She's a lot smarter than people think," Gudjonsson told them. "She's manipulating everybody, and if you had me testify, I'd have to say those statements to the police are perfectly reliable." Urbanski and Miller wondered if they could salvage Gudjonsson's rare expertise (for which Tioga County was paying him $7,000) by putting him on the stand and limiting his testimony to the psychology of interrogative techniques, just to plant the possibility that the police had led Waneta to a false confession. Miller in particular hated to pass up the chance to use such a world-renowned expert in the Tioga County Court. But they knew that putting Gudjonsson anywhere near the witness stand could be a fatal mistake. The risk was too great that the judge would allow Simpson to ask Gudjonsson if he had examined the defendant. That, more or less, would end the defense of Waneta Hoyt.

Gudjonsson did agree to meet with Ewing, and perhaps encourage him to keep thinking Waneta was innocent. "We were worried that if Ewing found out that Gudjonsson was here and had an adverse opinion, he might start backing off," Miller said. "We couldn't afford to lose Ewing too." The lawyers soon realized there was little chance of that.

Gudjonsson found it difficult to understand how someone with Ewing's credentials could be so naïve or so easily manipulated, but decided that for the money he was being paid, he could at least help out by imparting the wisdom of his experience. "I'm not going to say the statement's unreliable, but if you want me to help him, I will," Gudjonsson told the lawyers. "If he wants to say it, that's his problem."

The three men drove up to Buffalo to see Ewing. Urbanski marveled at Gudjonsson's diplomacy. "He acted as if he wasn't that good, and Ewing was Sigmund Freud. 'And if I might interject here, a few little things that I've done in my research that might help you. . . .' And Ewing is telling Gisli how he's convinced she's innocent. Gisli handled it well." Getting back in the car, Urbanski asked Gudjonsson what he thought.

The psychologist looked back at the lawyer. "I think," he said, "that Jay Hoyt is one very lucky boy."

Three days before Christmas, the appeals court in Albany overturned Judge Sgueglia's ruling barring the exhumation. In a unanimous decision bearing a certain why-are-you-bothering-us-with-this tone, the five judges said it was a district attorney's right to exhume bodies when he considered it necessary. Bob Simpson, they said, had amply demonstrated that examining the remains of the Hoyt children was a legitimate part of his investigation, even if it came well after their mother was indicted. Simpson, Courtright, and Baden began planning the five exhumations for soon after the turn of the year. It would be a complicated operation.

Meanwhile, Simpson began putting the finishing touches on the rest of his corroboration strategy. He penciled in Dr. Janice Ophoven as his star witness. He remembered how thoroughly persuasive she'd been at the meeting at the Treadway, the day she convinced him he had to prosecute Waneta Hoyt, no matter how the interview with her turned out. A year later, it had become an immensely complicated case requiring a formidable degree of medical sophistication, but ever since that day, the prospect of Ophoven's testimony had given Simpson a visceral feeling of confidence. Baden would back her up with his eminence, a forceful second opinion from the ranks of the celebrity medical examiners. Simpson contemplated bringing in Linda Norton as well. He put her name on the prospective witness list he turned over to the defense, but ultimately concluded that her testimony would be superfluous. He didn't want to overdo it with the expert witnesses. (This was a relief to Norton, who felt her outspokenness about Steinschneider had probably compromised her ability to testify credibly. Assuming Simpson wouldn't be calling her, she had felt no need to refrain from comment, and so for months she freely offered her pithy views to every reporter who called. In an "Eye on America" segment that Dan Rather used to close the *CBS Evening News* one night, Norton called Steinschneider's paper "garbage and nonsense" and said, "Anyone like Mrs. Hoyt who wants to systematically destroy her children and get away with it has an ally in Dr. Steinschneider. Many would consider this trial is not about Waneta Hoyt. It's about his theory.")

For Simpson, the theory was the missing piece in his preparation of the case. While the forensic pathologists would cover most of the important issues at hand, he knew they could not discuss with equal authority the question of infant breathing patterns that was the central theme of the lives and deaths of Molly and Noah. Looking for someone to fill that gap, he found himself on the phone with a pediatrician in New Hampshire who was both a noted figure in SIDS and a specialist in infant respiration: Dr. John Brooks.

After a brief conversation, Simpson sent out the hospital records, and Brooks, who had recently left Rochester to become medical director of the Children's Hospital at Dartmouth, searched them for evidence that the babies had breathed abnormally. Finding none, he agreed to testify for the prosecution, without taking a fee. He did this despite some disquieting personal feelings. Brooks liked and respected Al Steinschneider and was not among those who considered that the doctor was on trial as much as the mother. Based on what he had read and absorbed through the years, Brooks imagined that Steinschneider had been a victim of her deception at a time when much less was known about SIDS, about apnea, and certainly about deceptive mothers. "I think Al Steinschneider is taking an unfair beating," he said at one point. "It's easy to criticize in retrospect." With his own experience with the Van Der Sluys family nearly fifteen years before, he had personal reasons for sympathizing with a doctor in that sort of predicament. Like others in the field, Brooks also worried that the Hoyt case, with all the publicity it had generated, would bring undue suspicion on SIDS parents. But despite these misgivings, he felt that the truth was important to clarify. SIDS needed to be distinguished from infanticide whenever possible, and in an ironic way, this trial was an opportunity to do that.

All set with his expert witnesses, Simpson decided he should talk to one of Miller's. He didn't know if Steinschneider was actually going to testify, since the defense, unlike the prosecution, wasn't required to turn its witness list over to the other side prior to trial. But if he did testify, Steinschneider would be a rare combination of expert and material witness—possibly the key defense witness—and Simpson wanted to get a sense of what he might say on the stand.

"I guess I'm probably the only guy in the world who hasn't talked to you about this Hoyt case," Simpson told Steinschneider when he called, trying to put a friendly face on the overture.

"Oh no, there's a lot of people who haven't talked to me," Steinschneider replied.

"Okay," Simpson said with an indulgent chuckle. He'd decided to tape the call. A transcript would free him from the need to take notes. New York law didn't require him to tell Steinschneider he was being recorded.

"I would venture to say that most people haven't talked to me," Steinschneider said.

"Yeah, well, I'm the prosecutor in the case against Mrs. Hoyt, and I felt that I should really cover the base by giving you a buzz and chat with you for a few minutes if you don't mind."

"I don't mind."

"I want you to understand before I go any farther that I have no ax to grind with you or your diagnosis or your job or anything else. So I don't want you to think that somehow I have any kind of attitude toward you and what you've done."

"May I ask you a question?" Steinschneider said.

"Sure," said Simpson.

"Why do you say that?"

"Because I don't. I think you—"

"Why is it necessary?"

Simpson groped for tactfulness. "I was led to believe by an investigator with the state police that you had some feelings that District Attorney Fitzpatrick in Syracuse might have some feelings . . ."

"I know what I told him and I thought it's an abuse of power. . . . He said I had certain motives in managing the babies when they came to Upstate. Well, since I know what my motives were, I think clearly he was into show business. . . . And to talk about my motives entitles me to talk about his."

Simpson eventually brought Steinschneider around to a discussion of apnea, hoping for a glimpse at his testimony. "Is it a fair statement that most children stop breathing on a regular basis. . . ?"

"Well, everybody stops for three, four, five seconds," Steinschneider said.

"At what point today would you become alarmed by the length of the apnea?"

"I wouldn't be alarmed if the baby stopped breathing for eighteen or twenty seconds."

"Eighteen or twenty?" Simpson asked, aware that Steinschneider's theory, his contention that it was related to the deaths of Molly and Noah, was based on supposed pauses of just fifteen seconds. "What would it have been back twenty-five years ago? Did you have a different standard?"

"Same thing," Steinschneider said.

"Same thing," Simpson repeated, privately pleased.

For the next few minutes, they fenced over the issue of causation, an edge of antipathy creeping into the exchanges as Simpson tried to make his way through Steinschneider's thickly equivocal answers. "I didn't say that," Steinschneider said when Simpson tried to pin him down on a point. "All right, what *would* you say?" Simpson replied with exasperation. "I'm not a doctor. I'm just an idiot. I'm just a lawyer who doesn't know."

"Don't play with me," Steinschneider shot back, although at another point he said, "I'm not angry at you. If I sound annoyed, I'm always annoyed, okay?" He said his argument was with Baden, who had also called him to discuss the case. "I don't think he would get up before a medical group and say that five ignorants equal a certainty." He added, "That's what he believes.

That's what he told me he believes. That if it's five it must be murder. Well, that is pure medical nonsense. 'What I believe' is a religious thing. I don't care about his religion. . . ."

"What you're saying is simply because five children of the same family die as a result of an unknown cause you can't say that therefore it's a homicide," Simpson said.

"Or therefore it's a cardiac anomaly or a neurological anomaly. But you are a D.A. There's only one thing you deal with. It's either that or nothing. And for me it's a whole variety of ideas, and I deal with it every day. And every day I'm faced with the same problem. A woman calls me, she lost a baby, she's worried about the next. I have to worry about all these possibilities. Did she kill the first? It's possible. It's possible. It's just the reality of the situation. You're talking about five. If you want to make the case she killed all five, then the first should have been picked up . . ."

When Simpson brought up the difficulty of distinguishing suffocation from SIDS, Steinschneider said, ". . . We have known that one could in point of fact suffocate an individual . . . put a pillow over a child, kill them, and the medical examiner, given what they knew then could not tell the difference. . . . You didn't have to be a genius to know that some of the babies that were signed out as unexplained were murdered. . . ."

"I think you said that based on what you know about this case she could have suffocated her kids," Simpson said a while later, trying to clarify Steinschneider's thoughts.

"No, I didn't say that," Steinschneider protested.

"Yes, you did," Simpson replied.

"No, I did not."

"Yes, you did. . . . You said she could have or she might not have. You don't know, there's four or five possibilities."

Steinschneider's tone turned indignant. "You're being terribly dishonest. And I would say that in a courtroom and I would say that now. We're through with the conversation. What you've done, you're showing your colors. You are a dishonest human being. I had heard from other people that you're a nice person, but you're a liar."

"Okay, what did you say?" Simpson asked.

"You are a liar. I said that there are many, many possibilities."

"One was homicide."

"That there were other possibilities. . . . There is no evidence for any of them . . . I don't like what you just did. And I think it's disgusting and I now am convinced more than ever that it is your intention to fry somebody even though you believe they're innocent. I truly believe you believe they're innocent. That's my belief, and I will talk to the next CBS . . . whatever they ask me I will tell them that. You called under false pretenses and what you are really doing is searching for what I might have said and pulling it out of context. I'm trying to be honest, and I'm trying to help whoever calls me. . . . But it's clear to me that it's not just Mr. Fitzpatrick. You, too."

"Let me restate it," Simpson tried.

"Sorry. Forget it. I have nothing to say. . . . You want the truth?"

"Yeah."

"I think there is a real possibility that the investigators beat the shit out of her."

On a frigid morning in January 1995, a crowd gathered at the peaceful cemetery on the hill in Richford. Michael Baden, dressed in sneakers and his blue New York State Police jacket, carrying his bag of special archaeological instruments, arrived early for what plainly was the part of his work that challenged and excited him most. Exhumations were exquisite opportunities in forensic pathology, moments when the secrets of the dead were most obscure and only the elite of the field could reveal them. The other people in attendance this morning, trying hard not to be spooked, deferred to his control. Bob Courtright supervised a dozen members of the state police, all clad in jeans and work boots, while Simpson and Peggy Drake, and a pathologist hired by Miller to represent the defense, observed the proceedings. When Tim and Jay Hoyt showed up, Courtright sent them away. "This is a crime scene," he told them soberly. "You won't be able to stay." Tim protested, but Ray Urbanski persuaded him it would be best to leave. There was no reason for them to see this.

Trooper Bob Bleck drove Clarence Lacey, the venerable manager of Highland Cemetery, up to the burial ground and brought him to Baden at the gravesite. Eight hundred men, women, and children had been buried in this patch of high ground in the century since it had been farmed by Waneta Hoyt's ancestors. Lacey had dug about a hundred graves himself, and only he knew where everyone was. On the Hoyt plot, only the graves of Eric and Jimmy were marked by headstones. Lacey presented Baden with a timeworn sketch showing where the others were. He served his function with some reluctance. He found the exhumation a needless invasion, and kept trying to persuade Simpson to call it off. "You're not gonna find anything," he said. "Nothing but bones."

Shortly after 10:00 in the morning, Gary Gelinger and Jim Conzola, the men who had searched out the nurses from Upstate, began the more literal task of digging into the past. Under a green-and-white funeral tent erected for warmth and dignity, they started unearthing the gravesite with shovels.

Bill Standinger, the investigator who had once been a construction worker, joined them. The plan called for the recovered bodies to be driven to Baden's pathology lab in Albany, a three-hour journey. It would not be a simple chore. The frozen earth was unyielding, the remains were buried deep, and Lacey's map turned out to be less than precise.

It was well into the afternoon before the first casket was discovered, a wooden one, though there wasn't much left of it but shards of pine and a pair of metal handles. According to the map, this would be Molly's. Baden decided that the only thing to do was remove the entire section of earth containing her body, and complete the exhumation in the lab. By Lacey's recollection, one other body had been encased in wood and would presumably be in the same condition and require the same strategy. But with darkness descending, this was for tomorrow. At 5:30, they called it a day. Two investigators in a patrol car stood sentinel at the cemetery overnight, protecting the integrity of the cold, dark crime scene until daybreak.

In the morning, a backhoe made its way up the hill and the pace of the exhumation picked up. The two sections of earth containing the decayed wooden caskets were cut out, like cake from a tin, and sheets of plywood forced underneath, allowing the investigators to lift the sections into a station wagon. Exhuming the other three bodies was much simpler. Two were buried in Styrofoam-like material that emerged in perfect condition, and a third came up in a coffin made of a material that Gelinger regarded as concrete.

In Albany, Baden explored the remains, though it could not be said that what he performed were autopsies. To nobody's surprise, Clarence Lacey was more or less right. There was nothing much more than bones. Baden sifted through the mounds of dirt containing all that was left of the two children buried in wood. He pieced together skeletal fragments of the others, like a paleontologist. He found baby hats and bootees. At MacPherson's, the bodies had not been prepared for burial by anyone who thought they might be coming back up someday. Baden cast his findings in the best light he could: He said he could find no evidence of natural disease.

Later in the week, the remains arrived back in Newark Valley. They were placed in new coffins at MacPherson's, and a re-burial service was organized. Waneta composed two poems; she intended to read one herself at the gravesite. She and Tim drove down to the J.C. Penney store at the Oakdale Mall in Johnson City. Jay had given his mother a hundred dollars from his paycheck—after graduation, he had gotten a job in the barns at Cornell—so she could bury the babies the way she wanted. "I wanted a comforter for each one, in a certain color scheme," Waneta explained later. "Pink for the girls, blue for the boys." But the comforters were too expensive, so she settled for receiving blankets. Jay presented his mother with five teddy bears, and the blanket he had used when he was small, the one with the cowboys and Indians, to bury with the vestiges of the brothers and sisters he had never known, and wouldn't have known had they lived.

Waneta took charge of the particulars of the re-burial, in the same way that Baden had been in control of the exhumation. There was a brief service at MacPherson's, where Tim's brother Chuck read one of the poems. "Goodbye My Little Family," Waneta had titled it, and Chuck cried when he read it. Then the group made the once-familiar journey up Route 38 to Highland Cemetery. At the gravesite, Waneta specified how she wanted the blankets placed atop the caskets and how the caskets were to be positioned. She read the second poem herself, and she trembled. The family gathered around her once more—a strange, awkward, painful moment, tears flowing for all kinds of reasons. Waneta, the defendant. Waneta, the victim. Waneta, the center of attention. The family was behind her, a united front, but it occurred to some of them that her behavior seemed to resemble a performance. "That's when it hit me," said one relative. "I'm watching this and she had that deadpan stare. It hit me: She *killed* them. And I lost it, I just cried my heart out. No one knew the real reason I was crying."

Two weeks later, Judge Vincent Sgueglia announced that the trial would commence with jury selection on Monday morning, March 27, one year and four days after Waneta was asked by the state police if she would mind coming down to Owego to talk about her children.

34

With its facade of red brick trimmed in limestone, its tall, narrow windows and gentle arches, and its four towers with pitched roofs rising at the corners, the Tioga County Courthouse was a grand presence in Owego, as much a symbol of reverence as at its opening a century and a quarter earlier. The building, in fact, was reminiscent of a cathedral; the single judge who presided over every matter of law in the county—criminal on Mondays and Fridays, family court midweek, civil and surrogate's cases mixed in—serving as a kind of high priest of civic authority.

On the sunny morning in late March 1995 that eighty-two citizens were summoned to the courthouse to be considered for their fitness for jury service, many of them had already guessed that it was Waneta Hoyt whom those selected would be asked to judge. They converged on the town center, some streaming past the statue of the fireman cradling a baby in its nightclothes.

The prospective jurors filed through the courthouse's south door and climbed a creaky, carpeted, circular stairway to the second floor, where a heavy wooden door opened into the courtroom. It was the most ornate room in Tioga County, dim but airy and encased in oak, its ceiling soaring thirty feet, with glass-and-steel lighting fixtures suspended from above. When the sunlight sliced through the tall strips of windows at certain afternoon angles, it could feel like a place of religious ritual. The men and women of the jury pool filled the dark wooden pews of the gallery facing the carpeted well of the courtroom, with its long tables for the prosecution and defense, the witness stand to the right, the jury box to the far right, the judge's perch positioned majestically above the fray. A pair of narrow balconies looked down upon the proceedings from either side of the courtroom, and behind them were glass-

487

walled rooms filled with law books. On the courtroom's walls hung resolute portraits of all the county judges going back deep into the last century.

Escorted by her regular group of supporters, one hand firmly in her husband's, the other in her son's, Waneta walked up the courthouse steps shortly before nine. Inside, she climbed the circular stairway slowly and entered the courtroom. She stood in the aisle behind the defense table, talking softly with her well-wishers, all eyes upon her. Dressed in a light tan suit and stockings, a white blouse, and black shoes, with a touch of makeup on her face, she looked better than she had at any time since her arrest, though not so well that her lawyers worried she could not engender a jury's pity. But there were moments when her eyes had a certain sparkle, and the corners of her mouth hinted at satisfaction.

It was Bob Miller's misfortune to have to try the case of his life with a severe and painful eye infection, transmitted while giving shots to cattle with pink eye. He would have to go to Rochester for treatment every couple of days, so a good deal of the examination of witnesses would fall to his partner. Waneta took her seat next to her lawyers, and Tim sat beside her and held her hand, as he had at all the pretrial hearings. It was an unusual arrangement, and Simpson had objected to it. He worried about the emotional impact the image of her husband's support might have on a jury. He had even put Tim on his witness list, a ploy to bar him from the courtroom until he testified. But Judge Sgueglia said no: Not only could Tim Hoyt be in the courtroom, he could sit with his wife and hold her hand. Sgueglia's decision signaled that he intended to give Waneta every possible courtesy.

The judge's personality was as informal and quirky as the way he ran his courtroom. He was a handsome, fit man in his fifties, with a disarmingly paternal manner and an engaging smile that he sometimes turned into an abrupt scowl for effect. He dispensed with the traditional "All rise" when he climbed to the bench, and took to personally handing out doughnuts and candy to the reporters and photographers who had pitched camp in his courthouse. Just as the Hoyt case was the challenge of a career for the lawyers, so, too, would it be immensely intricate for the inexperienced judge, who had won election only two years before after a career in general practice. He had never tried a murder case as a lawyer, let alone presided over one as a judge, but he was a man who exuded confidence, and he was not entirely convincing when he claimed in a private moment to be a little worried about how he would do.

"I imagine very few of you are not familiar with this case," Sgueglia told the room full of juror candidates, by way of instructing them that now was the time to forget whatever they'd heard or read, whether they'd gotten their information from radio, television, newspapers, or neighborhood chatter.

"Waneta Hoyt is being charged with the suffocation deaths of five of her children," he announced for the record, then recited the list of official charges, saying the full name and alleged manner of death of each of the five. And then Pete Hoffmann, the court clerk, shook a little box and began pulling out names. "Number one, Linda Ace . . . number two . . ."

"Now wait a minute," Sgueglia cut in, breaking the tension with a gleeful smile. "Number one is named Ace?" The courtroom echoed with chuckles. Even Tim Hoyt smiled; Waneta didn't.

One by one, they came forward from the gallery, filled the jury box and a row of folding chairs in front, and the voir dire of jury selection—inquiry, civics lesson, indoctrination—began. The first task for the lawyers was to pick jurors who didn't know anyone connected to the case, no simple thing in a county of only 51,736 residents, roughly a hundred people per square mile. By the time Sgueglia finished reciting the names of the four lawyers who would be trying the case, along with the handful of part-time assistant prosecutors and public defenders with whom they were associated, he had covered a good percentage of the Tioga County bar. When he added the defendant's family and the list of prospective prosecution witnesses and asked who knew anyone mentioned, fourteen of the first group of twenty-one raised their hands.

For the rest of the day and the two that followed, Simpson and Miller kept their scorecards and consulted with their trial partners—Miller with Urbanski, Simpson with Peggy Drake, an assistant who normally worked part-time and was helping prosecute her first murder case. Alternately standing before the jury box to inquire into the experiences and personal philosophies of the candidates, Miller and Simpson tried to weed out—or keep in—those with biases that might affect the way they viewed the peculiar circumstances of this case. It wasn't a simple matter of here are the bodies, here's the defendant, here's the evidence, did she do it? There were quirks and traps in this case for both sides, and Miller and Simpson each saw benefits in seating the most open-minded jury possible. Miller, though, wasn't leaving it to chance. He hired Phil Jordan, a local psychic, to watch the proceedings and offer his observations when the urge came.

"Anybody here say a mother can't kill her children, no matter what?" Simpson asked. "How about you, Mrs. Adcock?"

"I guess everybody's capable of almost anything," said Mrs. Adcock.

"It's kind of hard to believe," said a man in the front row. "She looks like a nice lady."

"Anybody have any experience with Sudden Infant Death Syndrome, or SIDS?"

"My cousin had a SIDS death," a woman said.

"Anybody else familiar with SIDS? How about apnea? Anybody heard that term?"

"Sleep apnea?" asked a man in the middle row. "I have a brother-in-law who has a case of sleep apnea."

"Can I ask," said another, "what is apnea?"

"That's when you're sleeping and you quit breathing," Simpson explained.

"I have a friend who lost a twenty-two-month-old to SIDS," a man in the back row volunteered. Simultaneously, Miller shot a look at Urbanski, and Tim looked at Waneta. They wanted this man on the jury, but Miller knew he wouldn't get him by Simpson, who put an "X" next to the juror's name.

"Anybody here who feels because young children were exhumed, we did something wrong?" Simpson asked. "How about the lapse of time? Do you think Mrs. Hoyt has suffered enough? Will you disregard the evidence and go with emotion? What do you think, Mr. Michner?"

"I would almost think she has been put through enough."

"Do any of you expect me to prove that these children died of specific diseases or causes?" Miller asked.

"Yes," said a middle-aged man in a flannel shirt. "I do."

"I appreciate your frankness," Miller responded, "but with that I want to point out that I don't have to prove anything. The entire burden is over here"—he tapped Simpson's table with his fingertips, then started back to the defense table. "When you start to move it over here, you may not like it, but that is not how our system works. This will be the first time in your life you will have to come to grips with the concept of presumption of innocence. Similarly, because of the passage of time, you will not say to yourselves, 'Well, if this had happened last year we would have expected a higher standard of proof, and we would want to know this, this, and this. Twenty-five years later, we're not gonna hold 'em to this standard.' It's not her fault she's here twenty-five years later any more than it's his fault he's doing this twenty-five years later. We're all here twenty-five years later simply because this is the way this case happened."

Miller wanted to know how much these people knew. "Anybody heard the name Fitzpatrick?" he asked. "Nobody? Huh. I guarantee you will hear it before this case is over. Nobody at all recognize that name? Well, I must say I'm pleased to see that maybe people don't spend all their waking hours listening to all the trash on television like the travesty in Los Angeles. Anyone see Connie Chung, the just-between-you-and-me lady? Nobody? Huh. Anybody hear about the statements Mrs. Hoyt is alleged to have made to the police?" Now there were some nods of acknowledgment, though many fewer than Miller expected. "Do you believe that in the history of jurisprudence in this country, there's ever been an unreliable statement given by a defendant?"

He cautioned them about the war of doctors that was about to move from the pages of medical journals to this courtroom and take up a good chunk of the trial: "The world is full of 'world's leading experts.' And we'll have a couple of world-class experts too, so I'm not blaming Mr. Simpson for everything. Will you promise me you won't be mesmerized by these experts? Will you, Mr. Ruth? Do you believe that, Mr. Wegman?" They nodded their heads. "I'm not going to prove to you my client's innocent. I'm going to prove to you that the prosecution does not have the evidence to prove beyond a reasonable doubt that she killed five of her children."

Simpson seized on Miller's pledge. "If we prove our case beyond a reasonable doubt," he asked, "could you convict that woman?" This was the kind of question that prompted a number of people to follow the judge's instructions to save for the privacy of his chambers anything they didn't want to say publicly, or which might tend to prejudice the others. At the end of each round, the Hoyts and the lawyers followed the judge into an office off the left side of the courtroom and heard these prospective jurors, one at a time as in a confessional, explain why they could not serve in this case. Some said they did not believe the defendant could be guilty; others were already sure she was. One woman said she could sympathize with a mother overreacting to crying babies. "I had kids and I know there were times they cried when I felt like just"—she looked at the court reporter pecking away—"oh, don't put *that* down." And some, in tears, said they simply could not handle hearing about babies dying, one by one, for the next four weeks. Murdered babies, especially.

Back in the courtroom after the lawyers completed the horse-trading process that followed the voir dire of each group, Pete Hoffmann read the names of those who could go home, swearing in those who remained. Gradually, the jury box filled up and by the end of the third day, the Hoyt jury was seated: seven women, five men, plus two alternates. They were the faces of Tioga County: mothers and fathers and grandparents, median age around fifty. The judge instructed them to keep their minds open, to listen to all the evidence, to refrain from discussing the case, and to avoid newspapers and television. They looked across at the defendant and saw what a puzzle they faced.

Just after 9:00 Thursday morning, Bob Simpson stood, left the jacket of his gray suit unbuttoned, panned the jury box, introduced himself, pointed out his assistant Peggy Drake, and pretended this was a case like any other. He spoke in his native tongue, the monotone of common sense, trying to summarize what the case was and wasn't about, how it all boiled down to correcting five mistakes. "We are not attempting to say SIDS does not exist, and that people who lose children to SIDS are somehow culpable," he told the jury emphatically. "This is the furthest thought from our minds."

Two rows on the defense side of the courtroom were filled with Hoyts,

Nixons, and friends of Waneta. There were two ministers among them: Berkshire's congregationalist pastor Jim Willard, who had known Waneta and Tim for many years, and the new Methodist pastor in Newark Valley, George Goodwin, who'd known them only a few months. Goodwin had replaced Lisa Jean Hoefner, who had moved on to a congregation in Broome County. On the other side of the aisle, half a dozen reporters occupied the first two rows. Several photographers and a pool TV cameraman pointed their lenses from the balcony above them, an awkward position that would give the photographs and videotape of this trial an odd, downward angle. A reporter from the Syracuse *Post-Standard* positioned a tape recorder on the ledge of the balcony; readers of the newspaper could call a special number each night to hear excerpts of the day's testimony.

One person who was not in the courtroom was Bill Fitzpatrick. Simpson had become so skittish about Miller's preoccupation with Fitzpatrick as the interloping prosecutor who must be running for something that he asked the Syracuse D.A. to stay away from the trial as much as possible. Simpson didn't want the distraction. Fitzpatrick agreed, but thought he might come to see some of the key testimony. Certainly, he would come for the verdict.

Simpson had a lot to cover in his opening statement: five lives and deaths, the simplistic, meaningless death certificates, Waneta's deceptions, the answers that finally came when the police sat her down. He introduced the jury to the victims. Eric ... James ... Julie ... Molly ... Noah. These were the children of Waneta Hoyt. How could they have been murdered without anyone realizing it? SIDS and suffocation are indistinguishable. The experts for the prosecution, forensic pathologists who have seen it all before, will tell you about it.

"We'll talk about how genetics had nothing to do with these deaths," Simpson said. "We'll talk about how the deaths all occurred about the same time of day when Mrs. Hoyt was home alone with the kids, all on weekdays. When all is said and done, we're going to ask you to rely on your common sense. We're not here to throw a fastball by you. Common sense tells you five kids don't die in one family the way these kids died." This was Simpson's theme: Don't believe what Waneta Hoyt said in 1965, 1968, 1970, and 1971. Believe what she said in 1994, and not what she's saying in 1995. "These children suffered her wrath because they were crying and she couldn't stand the crying." That was his approach: no Munchausen, no mysterious psychology, no excuses. Just the coldness of the confession. The medical corroboration would be just as cold, he asserted, just as inarguable. Simpson served it straight, pulling no heartstrings. Fitzpatrick might have had a jury crying already, but it wasn't Simpson's style.

Miller sauntered up to the podium. The jurors saw that his right eye was a deep red, swollen almost shut. "There is no denying that Mrs. Hoyt did in fact give an incriminating statement to the police that morning," he said. "But the circumstances will be highly disputed." It was all a setup, he informed the jurors; everything was hatched at a big, secret meeting at the Treadway Inn. His voice boomed, and the jurors were riveted by the suggestion of a police conspiracy. "Mr. Fitzpatrick from Syracuse"—he still hadn't explained who this Fitzpatrick was—"comes to this all-day meeting with the state police at the Treadway. The proof will lead to the undeniable inference that they did not have enough to charge Mrs. Hoyt with anything without an incriminating statement." So what they did was figure out how to get one. "Mrs. Hoyt was confronted at the post office by Bobby Bleck. . . . Bleck is like the local policeman, known by all, respected and loved by all, elevated by this group for a specific reason. He would put her at ease and off guard. Investigator Mulvey was a female, brought in from outside the area. They told Mrs. Hoyt it was a research project. Bleck reads her rights. Waneta says, 'What's that all about?' Bleck says, 'That's just a formality, don't worry about it.' There was no meaningful waiver of those rights."

They didn't videotape the interrogation, he pointed out. "You'll never have the opportunity to know what went on behind those closed doors for that three-and-a-half-hour period," he said, planting the suggestion of a psychological rubber hose. Look at her over there—he said this without saying it—so pathetic, a victim on trial. So when you see the statement taken down by the stenographer, you won't know if it's reliable. And really, how does someone kill five children? There has to be a reason. She couldn't stand the crying? It didn't add up. "Two of the babies were in almost constant medical care. How does that jibe with 'couldn't stand the crying'? And James lived two years and four months. Then, after getting psychiatric care to get over her grief, on the advice of Dr. Steinschneider, she adopted an infant. How do they explain Jay? Tim was home for Jay?"

There will be medical evidence, Miller told the jury. And it will be strongly contested. "It is Dr. Baden's belief that five children cannot die in one family and not be homicide. I think you will be satisfied there is no basis for that belief. There are documented studies done by clinical pediatricians, respected for their research of multiple child deaths in the same family." Miller was so focused on Baden, the superstar expert, that he hadn't thought much about the other forensic pathologist on Bob Simpson's witness list. Dr. Janice Ophoven? Just a backup, Miller presumed. It never occurred to him that it might be the other way around. Nor, for that matter, did it occur to him to worry much about what either of them had to say. "There is no physical evidence whatsoever," he told the jury, his voice draped in confidence, "that Mrs. Hoyt had anything to do with the deaths of her children."

Betty Lane, a round woman with black hair, strode into the courtroom and swore to tell the truth, the whole truth, so help her God—at least what she could remember of it. Simpson's plan was to set the scene, take the jury back in time, start at the edges, and work his way in. He would call up the neighbors, doctors, and nurses to give the jury a sense of the mystery of those years before bringing in the big guns—the state police to present Waneta's self-damning statements, and the forensic pathologists to explain to the jurors why they should believe her words. Betty Lane would be the first witness to turn the clock back thirty years, to the day all this started, January 26, 1965, the morning Eric Hoyt died suddenly. She would set the tone: Waneta, always alone with the babies when they died; Waneta, screaming for help; Waneta, the enigma. "She was hollering something was wrong with the baby," Betty Lane testified under questioning by Peggy Drake. "I heard her from my house and I came out. I followed her into the house and when I got inside the baby appeared to be dead." She remembered putting her mouth on the baby's, hoping to revive him. She noticed "something sticking out of both his mouth and nostrils. I thought it might be thick cereal. It was whitish, with pink streaks."

Drake paused over her legal pad as the last words hung in the air. She was a genial, soft-spoken lawyer who had a four-year-old daughter at home, and though nobody in the courtroom knew it, was two months pregnant. She asked Betty Lane to describe how the young Waneta Hoyt had reacted to the death of her first baby. "Sad. She just stood there." Was she crying? "Not that I can remember."

Miller cross-examined her. Was Waneta in shock? "She could have been." What was the substance in the baby's mouth and nose? Cereal or formula, she believed. Innocent enough. What else did she remember? Not much; she didn't stay long. "I was upset. I had never seen a baby dead before."

Simpson and Drake were trying to unfold a coherent story, but the numbers and circumstances of deaths, the gaps left by the passage of time, and the availability of witnesses made it nearly impossible to present the case in logical order, baby by baby. They hoped the jurors suspended the need for chronology and absorbed the broad picture. They had briefly visited 1965 for a glimpse of the first death. Now they were in 1971, hearing about the last one. Drake was questioning Dr. Bedros Markarian, who had performed the autopsy of Noah Hoyt at Upstate Medical Center.

Of the three pathologists who had done the original autopsies—of Jimmy, Molly, and Noah—Markarian was the only one still alive. He was retired now and had no recollection of the case. When he had first heard about Waneta

Hoyt's arrest, he'd had no idea he was involved. Still, Simpson believed that Markarian had something to offer. Peering in at a copy of the report he left behind in 1971, Markarian confirmed that he'd put down pulmonary edema and cerebral edema—swelling caused by excess fluid in body tissue—as his final diagnoses in the death of Noah Hoyt.

"Are you ruling on a cause of death?" Drake asked.

"No. We're listing changes that vary from normal." Edema would be an effect of death, not a cause.

"Did you conclude what his cause of death was?"

"No."

What might have caused the edema? she asked. Heart failure is a common cause of pulmonary edema, said the pathologist. Lack of oxygen for cerebral edema. Were these findings inconsistent with suffocation? No, he said.

Drake asked Markarian to explain to the jury the difference between a hospital pathologist and a forensic pathologist. "A forensic pathologist deals with violence, unattended deaths, suspicious cases. He or she spends a large amount of effort looking for trauma, toxic substances, et cetera."

"Do you do that as a hospital pathologist?"

"We do not."

Markarian's testimony was subtly revealing. It had less to do with proving homicide than with discrediting the earlier generation of doctors who failed to uncover it. Markarian came off as a perfectly decent hospital pathologist, but not a particularly inquisitive man. There was no evidence that he had taken the family history into account and challenged the likelihood of five children dying in one family in six years. If he was typical of the doctors who were involved at the time, perhaps it wasn't so surprising that these homicides had slipped by. It was a small piece of the big picture, one of the fine distinctions Simpson was prodding the jurors to recognize.

Miller wanted to distract them from any such exercises. He preferred they take the autopsy findings, and Markarian's testimony generally, at face value, without looking for larger meanings. "Are you able to say with a reasonable degree of medical certainty that this child died of suffocation?" Miller asked on cross-examination.

"No," Markarian said.

Could any conclusion at all be drawn from his findings? No again.

The pathologist's testimony was in the ear of the beholder. But if it left neither side with a discernible gain, Simpson's next witness, Dr. John Scott, the coroner to whom Markarian delivered Noah's autopsy report, was about to give the defense an early advantage. In the years after his brief encounter with the Hoyts, Scott had gone on to become president of the Tioga County Medical Society, as well as the county's public health director. He was seventy-three now, with wispy white hair and a self-assured manner that some in the courtroom thought bordered on the haughty. He was here to defend his judgment, and Miller, who had known Scott for years, planned to take full advantage of it.

"Do you remember the morning of July 28, 1971?" Simpson asked Scott.

"Yes, I do," Scott said. "In fact, I'll never forget it." He told the story of how a sheriff's deputy had sped him to the Hoyt trailer on a patient-in-distress call and how he'd come upon a baby lying on a couch with monitoring electrodes attached to his chest. "There were no breathing sounds, his pupils were dilated, he did not respond to pain. There was no livor mortis, no rigor mortis. The child was deceased."

How was the baby's mother reacting? Simpson asked. "She was agitated, her face was distorted. She moved from one foot to the other." Did she say anything? "I attempted to talk to her. She didn't respond. Her husband told me the child had just been discharged from Upstate."

What happened next? "From the trailer home I telephoned Dr. Steinschneider and he explained to me that he was studying SIDS. He wanted the autopsy done up there, and I agreed to it."

"You didn't investigate this as a homicide, did you, Doctor?" Simpson asked.

"I had no reason to investigate it as a homicide," Scott replied.

On Miller's cross-examination, Scott elaborated on what Steinschneider had told him over the phone. "He said [the baby] had spent almost his entire life in the hospital, that he had apnea, that there had been four other SIDS deaths, and they were very interested in the case." What did Steinschneider give him to understand about the apnea? "That it was a very severe problem."

Miller moved the discussion to the question of suffocation. Scott seemed ready for it. He said a baby couldn't be suffocated without his nose being blocked, and it seemed likely it would leave some impression. He hadn't seen any marks on Noah. Miller let this idea sink in, then looked as if an important thought had just occurred to him. How long did you say it was, he asked Scott, between the time of the distress call to the sheriff's department and the time you arrived at the trailer? Scott thought it was about fifteen minutes.

"If this baby had been suffocated with a pillow," Miller said, raising his voice for emphasis, "wouldn't you expect to find within fifteen minutes of its death some evidence on his face?"

"Yes," Scott said firmly, "I would expect to find some indication."

There were murmurings along the press row: *This is a prosecution witness?* Scott now belonged to Miller. Simpson stared blankly, trying not to look annoyed. "Do you have an opinion, with a reasonable degree of medical certainty," Miller asked, "whether this child was homicidally suffocated?"

"Yes," Scott said. "I found no evidence. The circumstances fit a SIDS death very well."

"It was not homicide," Miller said, clarifying for the jury's benefit. "Thank you."

Simpson sprung to his feet for re-direct. In effect, he had to cross-examine his own witness. "Are you certified to perform autopsies?" he challenged Scott, his voice edgy.

"No."

"How many SIDS deaths have you been involved with?"

"Three besides this."

"Do you know the indications of SIDS? Aren't SIDS and suffocation the same?" Simpson's impatience made his question imprecise, and Scott hesitated. "You don't have the answer to the question?" Simpson barked.

"I know the answer to your question. . . . They're not the same."

"Yes, they are," Simpson insisted. He came back to the scene in the trailer. "You did not ask Mrs. Hoyt what had happened."

"She wouldn't talk to me," Scott retorted in mild protest.

"So you did not ascertain any information concerning the circumstances?"

"No. . . . This is not an unattended death. This is a child under the care of a physician. Also, the child has apnea, a life-threatening condition."

Passing between the defense and prosecution tables on his way out, Scott found Miller and Urbanski surrounding him, all smiles, shaking his hand. Simpson watched the scene with irritation. "I knew Scott was going to bite me in the ass, but I had to put him on," he said during a break. "He was at the scene." It was better than letting him testify later as a defense witness; might as well get him in and out early, and move on to the heart of the case. *Weeks from now,* Simpson thought, *the jury won't even remember who John Scott was.*

"Do you remember how angry I was that night?" Corrine Dower asked Thelma Schneider, taking her back twenty-five years. She was thinking of the late hours of June 4, 1970, the night Molly Hoyt went home from Upstate Medical Center for the last time.

The two retired pediatric nurses were reminiscing over dinner at the Owego Treadway, a bittersweet reunion that included Joyce Thomas, Gail Pfeiffer, and Jack Schneider, who had made the three-hour trip down from Henderson Harbor with his wife. Joyce, who had flown in from Tacoma, had been the last prosecution witness of the day, and it was her testimony about June 4 that prompted Corrine's remark. Corrine would get her chance on the stand the next day, as would Thelma and Gail. The only one missing was

Thelma's old friend and Gail's mentor, Julie Evans. Her son, worried about her health, had prevailed on her not to make the trip down from Syracuse to testify. So Gail would be the only member of the nursing staff who could speak, in some sense, for Noah. The others had taken care of Molly.

In her testimony late that afternoon, Joyce Thomas, a youthful-looking woman a year shy of sixty, had described what she remembered about those two months in 1970. She had just come to work at Upstate, and Molly was one of her first patients. The baby was in for apnea spells. "It was an interruption in breathing," she explained. "It was fairly new at that time." Peggy Drake asked her if the baby had any problems in the hospital. The monitor went off a few times, the nurse remembered, but the baby was always breathing.

"Do you recognize Molly's parents?" Drake asked.

Joyce looked across at the Hoyts. "With some physical changes," she said politely.

"Could you describe Mrs. Hoyt's behavior with Molly?"

"I describe it as distant. Not much bonding."

Miller objected to the characterization. The judge agreed. "Please just tell us what you observed," he instructed.

"I observed her not paying much attention to the baby. And when her husband came in, she was sitting on his knees and not looking at the baby."

Drake asked her to recall the night Molly went home. The prosecutors wanted to leave the jury with a vivid impression of these hours, although they knew the subject would be a battleground. So much of it was feelings and worries, so much dark, unspoken speculation—everything that testimony wasn't allowed to be. "I dressed her," Joyce said. "I took her down the elevator to the car. I went back upstairs and cried. I was concerned for Molly—"

"Objection," Miller barked.

Drake paused to consider a different approach. "Was there anything about her health that you were concerned about?" she asked, massaging the implications.

"No," said the nurse.

"Was there any discussion among the nurses on the day you found out Molly died?"

"I object," Miller interrupted. Sustained, said the judge.

Drake tried to sneak back in. "Can you tell us why you cried?"

"Objection."

"Sustained."

Watching the nurse step down, Simpson considered her testimony his first success. He was confident in the jury's powers of deduction. "They know why she cried," he remarked, walking back across Court Street to his office at the end of the day.

No, the nurses agreed during their reunion at the Treadway, they would never forget that night. It was the night Corrine tried to comfort Joyce at the nurses' station after she delivered Molly to her mother's arms; the night they looked at the clock on the wall and wondered if Molly was still alive. "I was so angry that night," Corrine reminded Thelma. "I was so angry at Steinschneider. Remember?" Oh yes, Thelma said. I remember.

The next morning, with Peggy Drake prompting her with questions, Thelma took the jurors on an oral tour of the Children's Clinical Research Center, circa 1970. She spoke clearly, reasonably, a retired head nurse personified. Her husband, once the head of the CCRC, watched with moderate interest from the gallery, a crossword puzzle on his lap.

Having set the scene, Drake handed a copy of Molly's nursing record up to the witness stand and asked Thelma to read selected excerpts for the jury. The important entry, of course, was the note in which she said that the relationship between mother and baby was, for the record, "almost nil." Thelma had written the note at noontime on June 4, right after her last, futile conversation with Steinschneider and just twenty hours before Molly died. At the moment she began to read the poignant passage for the jury—"I discussed my concerns with Dr. Steinschneider today . . ."—a passing ambulance siren wailed outside the courthouse.

What were these concerns you wrote about? Drake asked.

"They were concerns I had about the lack of mother-child interaction, and I felt I had to document it." She paused, then added, "We *all* had concerns about this baby."

"Object to 'we,' " Miller said.

"*I* had concerns," Thelma answered, a little annoyed at the rules of testimony. "What I felt at the time was that she had a rather bizarre way of holding the baby . . ."

"Objection."

"She held the baby away from her." Thelma glanced over at Waneta, and saw that she was dabbing at tears, and that Tim was comforting her. It made Thelma uncomfortable, even made her feel sorry for Waneta. It was the first and last time during her testimony that Thelma looked their way.

"Why was Molly on this unit?" Ray Urbanski asked on cross-examination.

"Our understanding was that they had lost children to SIDS prior to Molly."

Urbanski, too, had Thelma read from the nursing notes, but focused on sections that might hint at medical problems. ". . . Now, at nine-thirty on April 22, 1970"—Urbanski made a point of saying the year often, as if to emphasize the case's ancient history—"you indicate during a feeding, the hands became cyanotic. . . ." In the gallery, Jack Schneider, listening attentively, bristled at the exchanges. *This guy's trying to make a healthy kid a sick kid,* he thought. Urbanski had taken the same approach with Joyce Thomas, with mixed results. At one point, she had read, at his request, "Similac given, burped, loose yellow stool, TLC given." She looked up and explained, "That's tender loving care." By now, the jurors had the unmistakable impression that this was not something that Molly had been getting from her mother.

Urbanski asked Thelma to read the note from the morning of April 22. She peered in at the page. " 'Toward the end of feeding, both hands, particularly the right, became black,' " she read from her own note.

"Black?" Urbanski asked.

"Well, darker than just cyanotic. Positioning, we found, would cause it periodically."

They tussled on notes like this, the lawyer straining to give the jury the idea that they showed Molly wasn't a healthy baby, the nurse struggling to explain that she was. "Every time we come to a problem, an apnea episode, child was cyanotic, where the child's hands are black, you give harmless explanations," Urbanski complained.

"I'm trying to describe why I was writing this stuff," Thelma responded calmly. This was a research center, she explained, so the nurses noted all their observations, without regard to their significance. "The doctor can interpret them," she said.

"Precisely," Urbanski said, delighted to have her help in shifting the credibility from the nurses to Steinschneider, his coming witness. "In other words, it's not a function of the nurses on duty at the time to interpret the notes, but to put down your observations and with regard to the interpretations, leave it to the treating physician. . . ."

"That's correct," Thelma said, confronting the question's double edge. But to Urbanski's obvious exasperation, she continued to downplay the significance of the observations he had her read. Finally, Urbanski asked, with a hint of sarcasm, "Who would be more qualified to interpret the observations—you, or Dr. Steinschneider?" Reflecting her general personality, Thelma had made an agreeable, gently engaging witness; she had controlled herself up to now. But she couldn't bear to answer this question dispassionately.

"Dr. Steinschneider," she said with a perceptible smirk.

Thelma left the witness stand annoyed. "Nurses know a lot more than we're given credit for," she sniffed at the top of the circular stairway outside the courtroom, frustrated that she was still fighting this battle. Though she had been married to two doctors, and though she was too polite to say it quite so pointedly, she thought it was the arrogance of the profession that was in some part responsible for the deaths of Molly and Noah twenty-five years before. She hoped the jury caught the nuance.

Waneta and Tim didn't remember Gail Pfeiffer. They looked on warily— *Who's this now?* they seemed to be thinking—as the former nurse's aide climbed gingerly to the witness box and began talking about their last natural child. It would become part of the lore of this trial that the Upstate nurses had utterly remarkable memories of moments twenty-five years old. It was Gail Pfeiffer's recall that people on both sides would find most startling.

Peggy Drake asked her to describe Noah. "Noah was a beautiful little boy about two months old," she said in a low tone.

After a few questions about Noah's general health, Drake asked Gail if she saw the baby's parents in the courtroom. Yes, she said. She pointed to the Hoyts, first with a finger, then her whole hand, as if trying to bring some dignity to an awkward gesture. Waneta stared straight ahead, making no eye contact.

Drake asked Gail if she remembered meeting Mrs. Hoyt at Upstate Medical Center in 1971. After the state police investigators had interviewed Gail, the prosecutor had gone up to Camden to talk to her, and decided that the answer to this question would be the dramatic high point of her testimony.

"The first time I saw Mrs. Hoyt," she said, "I walked into the nursery where Noah was one afternoon. I saw Mrs. Hoyt off to the left. She was standing about eight feet from the crib. Her husband was with her. She was gripping both her arms with her hands, like this, and she was glaring down at the crib. I realized—"

"Don't tell us what you realized or what you felt," Sgueglia cut in. "Only what you saw. You're a movie camera." He made a movie-camera motion, as in a game of charades.

"I continued to walk toward the crib. I came between her and the crib and saw she was looking at Noah. I observed what appeared to be anger."

At these words, Waneta shook her head in protest, and a doleful expression came over her face. Then she resumed staring straight ahead until Gail described the morning the nursing staff learned Noah had died. At this point, Waneta again wiped away a tear, and whispered in Tim's ear.

The details in Gail's testimony were so specific that they left a powerful but ambiguous image. How could she remember that scene so vividly? How could she be so sure that Waneta was glaring at Noah, that she was "angry" at him? Well, she said later, it was simply something she could never forget. It was the moment she had started fearing for Noah's life. Like Thelma Schneider and Joyce Thomas, she felt frustrated by the legal rules that prevented her from explaining the context of her memories. Still, their testimony, taken together, left the jury with an evolving picture of Waneta as a pathologically cold mother whose disturbing behavior was burnished in their memories. Despite the constraints placed upon their testimony, they did offer emotional context.

Corrine Dower followed Gail to the stand for what turned out to be a brief, emphatic coda to the Upstate segment of the prosecution's case. Rather than feel stymied, this seventy-five-year-old former nurse was glad for the simple chance to finally express her anger. "We're just *nurses,*" she had said bitterly the night of June 4, 1970. "We don't know *anything.*" Now it seemed that she was speaking for all the nurses whose fears Steinschneider had first dismissed, and then perverted. Unbeknownst to them, he had used these women to help market his theory, inventing harrowing scenes of infant resuscitations by them in the hospital. Now, Corrine was reclaiming their integrity.

"Did you ever observe Molly not breathing?"

"Never."

"Did you ever observe her as cyanotic?"

"Never."

"Did you ever need to resuscitate her?"

"Never."

Although it was an invisible subtext to the jury, the nurses' testimony spoke as much to the integrity of Alfred Steinschneider as to the guilt of Waneta Hoyt. For Bob Simpson, it was a portentous prelude to the heart of his case.

35

Each morning, Waneta and Tim drove down from Newark Valley, parked in the lot between the Great American supermarket and the Estey & Munroe Funeral Home, and walked hand-in-hand toward the south entrance of the courthouse. They made their way through the metal detector, nodded their hellos to the sheriff's deputies, and climbed the stairs to the north door of the courtroom, where Waneta often stood for a while to greet the friends and relatives and ministers who came in her support. Sometimes it resembled a receiving line. The group brought along a cooler of food each day and ate lunch in a conference room off the back of the courtroom.

During the proceedings, Waneta and Tim sat close at the defense table, often holding hands, sometimes kissing during breaks. When a piece of testimony upset his wife, Tim put his arm around her and leaned into her comfortingly. The interplay quickly preoccupied the reporters and spectators, whose ranks were beginning to grow. Opening with a tight shot of Waneta's and Tim's clasped hands, Sheryl Nathans, who was covering the case for WIXT-TV in Syracuse, devoted a segment to the question of whether the jury might be affected by such unabashed displays of support. There was no question that her husband's devotion cast Waneta in a more sympathetic light, though its impact lessened as the prosecution's case began to mount. If anything, it made Tim more of a public curiosity, and his relationship with Waneta the subject of a lot of armchair psychology. Their son, meanwhile, wasn't permitted in the courtroom until after he testified. He was on the prosecution's witness list.

As the second week of the trial opened, the Hoyts and their supporters remained secure in their cloud of optimism. They dismissed the recollections of the Upstate nurses as trumped-up distortions that no fair-minded person would confuse with evidence of murder. "That Michelle Pfeiffer," Tim said later, referring, of course, to Gail Pfeiffer, "she was a damn candystriper. She wasn't allowed to write anything in the records. That's by law." He had it on good authority, he reported, that she had been paid off by the prosecution.

Miller and Urbanski weren't terribly worried about the testimony of the nurses. They knew they had bigger problems ahead. This would be the week when Waneta's statements to the police would be presented to the jury. First, though, Miller would get the chance to do something he relished: tear into the testimony of Simpson's forensic experts. A few minutes after 9:00 on Monday morning, he watched Dr. Janice Ophoven make her way to the witness chair. He could hardly wait to get at her.

Just arrived from Minnesota, Ophoven wore a black skirt and jacket with an orange-and-green print blouse, a pair of glasses nestled in her short, thick hair. She had a midwesterner's plainspokenness, the face and manner of authority. Simpson spent the better part of an hour on her credentials and expertise, working in a thorough explanation of what it is that a pediatric forensic pathologist does, and how it was her job to determine the cause and manner of a child's death based on every bit of evidence, whether physical, circumstantial, or historical. Finally, Simpson signaled the real beginning of her testimony, and his case. "Do you know what SIDS is?" he asked.

Simpson wanted the jury to understand that no one dealt more closely with the intersection of SIDS and infanticide than someone in Ophoven's line of work. And no one could speak with more assurance on the specific medical and legal aspects of the unusual case at hand than a forensic pathologist who had once been a practicing pediatrician. First, he wanted to imbue the jurors with the doctrine of SIDS as random occurrence, not given to repeating itself within families. There is no connection between SIDS and genetics, Ophoven explained, setting up one of the basic tenets of the prosecution's case. The chance of one SIDS in a family was remote enough. Two was cause for alarm, and a serious police investigation. "By the time a third event would occur within a family," Ophoven said, "the SIDS diagnosis is no longer a possibility and an alternative explanation must be identified."

Simpson turned immediately to the alternative explanation being proposed. "Do you generally find signs of suffocation?" he asked, alluding to John Scott's testimony. "Fingerprints, bruises, any external or internal sign?" No, Ophoven said, not generally. "A little person doesn't have the capacity to struggle in a coordinated way in that SIDS age group." What if one arrived at the scene fifteen or twenty minutes after a suffocation? "If a hand was used, or if a hard object was used, maybe. But if the object was soft, then I expect I wouldn't. . . . Whether it was fifteen minutes or not, if there's no mark, there's no mark." She demonstrated, spreading her hand to cover her own face. The sound of camera shutters snapping echoed through the courtroom; the front page of the next day's Binghamton *Press & Sun-Bulletin* would be dominated by a large color photo of Ophoven's chilling display.

Simpson was loath to leave the impression that the absence of marks meant the Hoyt children went quietly. Could a two- or three-month-old resist an attempted suffocation? he asked. "Oh, sure," Ophoven said. "Again, those of us who have taken care of little people, if you do something to them they don't like, they let you know instantly. And if it's a big thing they don't like, they arch their back, they get mad right away, they use their muscles, but it's kind of like this whole body reaction, as opposed to a coordinated reaction. But even little, tiny premature infants will struggle if they're uncomfortable or if something's happening that isn't right."

"Would a two-and-a-half-year-old resist differently?" Simpson asked, moving on to the image of Jimmy.

"Oh, Lord, yes. . . . A small boo-boo or a big boo-boo, they turn the whole thing on. For a two-and-a-half-year-old, to draw blood or to start an IV, you may need two or three people to hold these folks down if they don't like what's happening." But regardless of age, it would take several minutes to accomplish a suffocation. A child, like an adult, would lose consciousness after about two minutes without breath. Death would come another two to four minutes later.

Had she had occasion to actually witness the suffocation of an infant? The question startled some of the jurors, as did the answer. "Yes I have," Ophoven said. "In a qualified way." She described two video surveillance tapes she'd seen in the apnea center at the Children's Hospital of St. Paul. In both cases, mothers were observed suffocating their babies. That's how she knew what a baby fighting for his life looked like.

"Just so we're clear on this," Simpson said, "nobody was watching this so that someone should have rushed in and rescued the child." No, Ophoven said, the tapes were viewed later. It was part of the hospital's method of diagnosing apnea. Sometimes, the camera caught a horrific example of "factitious apnea." There are parents out there, she told the jury, who cause or fabricate reports of life-threatening episodes. And sometimes they go all the way. If they do it in the hospital, she implied, imagine what they do at home. She never uttered the term Munchausen syndrome by proxy.

Ophoven's testimony was at once repellent and riveting to the courtroom spectators. Among them was Gail Pfeiffer, who had decided to come back on Monday morning and resume watching the trial. She found she could not stay away—she needed to see this to conclusion. She sat on a chair in the balcony opposite the jury box, peering down, intent on the testimony. People noticed her, jurors included, and began to wonder about her. Some of Waneta's family glared when they encountered her outside the courtroom.

With Ophoven's lecture on suffocation serving as a prologue, Simpson moved on to what it had to do with the children of Waneta Hoyt. He spent the next phase of the testimony introducing twenty-seven exhibits, handing them up to Ophoven and discussing their meaning with her, one by one. They were birth and death certificates of each child, the various records from the hospitals in Ithaca and Syracuse, and eight autopsy reports—the three performed at the deaths of Jimmy, Molly, and Noah, and the five from the exhumations a few months before the trial. Then he moved to the children. His first piece of business was to refute the original causes of death. "I'd like to start with Eric," he said.

In 1965, Dr. Arthur Hartnagel attributed Eric's death to "congenital anomalies of the heart." Ophoven testified there was no clinical record of such a problem, nor could a coroner come to this conclusion without an autopsy. "It is not the kind of thing where you would make the initial diagnosis without any previous information," she said.

They moved on to Jimmy, whose elusive 1968 autopsy report, missing since the beginning of the investigation, had turned up only weeks before the start of the trial. It happened serendipitously. Late in winter, Miller had subpoenaed Waneta's county mental health records. Sgueglia read them first, then distributed them to the defense and prosecution. Flipping through the file when it arrived at the district attorney's office, Simpson's secretary, Pat Gray, came upon a document that tripped a switch. "Which autopsy did you say is missing?" she asked him. James, he said. "Well, here it is." It was part of the record left by Dr. Mokarram Jafri, the psychiatrist who had requested copies of the autopsy reports for Jimmy, Molly, and Noah after the disquieting incident with the adoptive baby named Scotty in 1971.

Jimmy's autopsy was peculiar, full of findings about the thymus and the adrenal glands and congested organs that a jury of lay people might consider descriptive of a sick child. It had had that effect on Waneta's family in 1968. For Ophoven, it made Jimmy's case more difficult than his brother's to clarify on the witness stand. She decided an anatomy lesson was in order. "The endocrine system is like the body's pony express," she said, addressing the jurors directly, "and the brain stem is like the control panel." Revisiting the autopsy performed by Dr. James Mitchell on the morning of September 26, 1968, she took them on a tour of the thymus gland and explained why its size had nothing to do with the child's death. She explained, point by point, why the autopsy described a normal, healthy little boy whose death could not be attributed to any natural cause—not enlarged thymus, not adrenal insufficiency. For the jurors, it was a long and grueling lecture. "Doctor, try and move it along a little bit," Simpson said at one point.

Julie was next. Hers was a simple case. Babies don't choke to death on rice cereal, Ophoven testified. Pieces of hot dog, peanuts, toys—yes. Rice cereal—no.

Now, Molly. Ophoven read from the voluminous hospital records, first from Tompkins County Hospital, then Upstate Medical Center. Here, the jury heard for the first time that the Hoyts, in giving Molly's history, had told the doctors that blood had been present at the deaths of Eric and Jimmy. Ophoven read all the intake notes for Molly's three admissions to Upstate into the record. "Can you point to any life-threatening event in that hospital record?" Simpson asked finally.

"None," said Ophoven. She evaluated the autopsy in the same detail she had devoted to Jimmy's.

". . . And from your review of the records, the autopsy records, and the slides, did it appear that this young lady had interstitial pneumonitis?" Simpson asked.

"No, she didn't."

"Let's just talk about this pneumonitis for a second. And let's assume for a moment that Molly did suffer from that, would that be noticeable to a caregiver?"

"Oh, yes. If someone's dying of interstitial pneumonia, they progressively worsen, worsen, and worsen. It isn't a sudden thing at all. In the most rapid form it would take days. . . . She would have been a critically ill infant who would have been rushed into an intensive-care unit and put on a ventilator and given antibiotics. She would have looked like someone who had pneumonia."

"Anything of concern there for the health and safety of Molly?" Simpson asked at the conclusion of her long review of the autopsy.

"No," Ophoven said. What worried her, she said, was how the purported events at home didn't match up with the hospital experience. "The disconnection is an important factor." She repeated the procedure for Noah, whose life and death mirrored his sister's. "You don't die of cerebral edema," she said. Again, it was the discrepancy between his mother's reports and the "observed medical facts" that was of concern to her.

Late in the afternoon, by which point Ophoven was surrounded by stacks of documents that had accumulated during her testimony, Simpson brought her to the payoff. In dramatic fashion, he asked her whether she believed, based on all the evidence before her, that these children had been suffocated to death.

"Eric Hoyt."

"Yes."

"Julie Hoyt."

"Yes."

"James Hoyt."

"Yes."

"Molly Hoyt."

"Yes."

"Noah Hoyt."

"Yes."

Nothing else could have caused them to die, she stated.

At their corner of the defense table, Waneta and Tim Hoyt held hands, their faces like marble.

Bob Miller stood, walked to the lectern, and asked, "Do you deny there have been forty cases in the last twenty years of multiple, unexplained infant deaths?"

"I know they have been reported," Ophoven replied skeptically.

Miller's first approach was to try to isolate Ophoven's opinion. He called the jury's attention to the traditional wedge between forensic pathologists and SIDS researchers on the question of familial SIDS. Ophoven tried to bring him up to date. "I don't think it's fair to characterize the SIDS people as all believing the genetic theory," she said. "There are a lot of SIDS experts who have the same opinion as the forensic community."

"There's been no medical proof to any degree of certainty regarding that, has there?" Miller challenged her.

"It's just a lot of experience," Ophoven responded.

In arguing the multiple-SIDS idea, Miller was at an interesting disadvantage. Other defense attorneys in his position had had at their disposal the country's most prominent case study: Steinschneider's 1972 paper. Miller, of course, couldn't use it. He decided to go abroad for this line of defense.

"Are you familiar with any of the Norwegian or Australian studies on this very subject?" he asked Ophoven. She said she'd read some of them, but couldn't say she was all that familiar with their case reports or theses. Her tone suggested they weren't worth the effort. Miller let the matter drop, never explaining what the Norwegians or Australians had found.

For the rest of the afternoon, Miller engaged Ophoven in a lengthy debate about the true meanings hidden in the unearthed records of the Hoyt family. He focused on Jimmy. This death was the Achilles' heel of Miller's case—the hardest one to portray innocently—but the autopsy gave him a wide field, and he planned to use every inch of it. Was it plausible, he asked Ophoven, that blood had been present at Jimmy's death, as the prosecution suggested, without its being picked up by the pathologist at autopsy?

"Doesn't surprise me at all," Ophoven said.

"The autopsy examiner is so incompetent in our little county here that he doesn't even make a note of it?" Miller asked, one of several subtly scornful allusions he made during the trial to all the out-of-town experts streaming through the courtroom. "Is that what you're saying?"

"No, that's not what I'm saying. I'm saying I can understand where it would either not be prevalent at the time the autopsy was done . . . or that the injury was inside the mouth and the examination was not done. And it doesn't mean there was an injury."

Miller challenged Ophoven's dismissal of the autopsy findings of congestion of the kidneys, brain, and liver. When she said that none qualified as a cause of death, he asked her what might cause such congestion "in these big, important organs," other than homicide.

"Just about anything," Ophoven replied. "You could have congestion of these organs if you were in a car accident."

"We know that wasn't the case here."

"You could have congestion in these organs if you had a heart attack. You could have congestion in these organs if you had leprosy. . . . You can get this kind of congestion from anything that can kill you. It is not diagnostic of anything."

"Could you have gotten this type of congestion from some source other than internal? Such as a toxicological reason?"

". . . I think I've answered your question. Anything that can kill you could give you congestion in these organs."

"Doctor, I don't mean to either bore you or irritate you. But a woman is on trial here, charged with ten counts of murder."

At another point, Miller brought up Dr. Marie Valdes-Dapena's name. "I believe you called her Molly," he said to Ophoven. "I believe her legal name is Marie Valdes-Dapena."

"Molly Dapena or Molly Valdes-Dapena is how we refer to her."

"All right, one and the same person, is it not?"

"Only one Molly."

"And she was your mentor at one point in time."

"Sure. But not officially. I mean, she's in another part of the United States but back in those days there weren't a whole lot of people who had spent their whole career doing pediatric pathology. So Molly was one of our mentors, at a national level."

"Were you aware of the fact that she reviewed the autopsy of Noah, back in 1971?" (Dapena had actually reviewed the slides of Molly's autopsy, not Noah's.)

"I didn't know which ones. I knew she had received one or both." Miller's implication was that one of the country's preeminent pediatric pathologists had signed off on the case way back in the early seventies; but Ophoven's implication was that all Dapena had done was review a set of tissue slides. It didn't mean they hadn't come from a baby who had been suffocated.

And so it went—Miller scouring the records for reasonable doubt, Ophoven giving no ground. As evening approached, Sgueglia declared the day's end, but Miller wasn't finished. When Ophoven realized she would not be making her 6:30 flight home to Minneapolis, that she'd have to come back in the morning, she groaned. That night, when the courtroom lights were shut, the courthouse locked, the piles of medical records remained stacked in the darkness around the witness stand.

The next morning, Miller had an idea. He wanted Ophoven to list all the factors that went into her judgment that the Hoyt children had been murdered. An easel with a huge pad of paper was brought before the jury, and Miller uncapped a black marking pen, ready to take dictation. Ophoven began talking, and Miller began filling the pages with her reasons, genially asking questions for clarification. Miller intended to use the list to take apart the homicide conclusion with his own witnesses later on, but by the end, he realized he had made a bad mistake. He had unwittingly helped Ophoven demonstrate the depth and logic of her opinion. The jurors saw before them, in the handwriting of the defense attorney, what could have been dubbed Thirteen Reasons Why These Deaths Were Homicides:

1. Noah & Molly—normal babies in hospital
2. No Apparent Life Threatening Event in hospital
3. Autopsies—no natural disease identified as cause of death
4. History of blood from nose or mouth at time of death for two babies
5. Five unexplained, unexpected, sudden deaths in one family and in one environment
6. Inconsistencies over time in family's story
7. No genetic predisposition to recurring SIDS
8. Diagnosis of SIDS cannot be applied to these babies
9. All babies normal at birth
10. All children apparently well & growing & developing normally
11. High risk history (Noah-Molly)
12. Five deaths, no reasonable medical explanation/natural disease for deaths
13. Caretaker's history

What Ophoven meant by the last reason, she explained to Miller and the jury, was Waneta Hoyt's confession to the police. She stepped down from the witness box soon after and headed home to Minnesota.

Simpson was elated. He found that Ophoven's testimony covered the medical case so thoroughly that when Baden took the stand at the close of the prosecution's case later in the week, he appeared as a gray eminence, brought in to underscore the homicide diagnosis. Miller managed to slap him around a bit on cross-examination. "You live in New York City, do you?" he opened, then hammered away with gusto. He ridiculed Baden's contention that the exhumations revealed no natural disease—"How can you say there was no heart disease when you found no heart?"—and Baden's claim to have personally performed twenty thousand autopsies and supervised or assisted in another fifty thousand. At one point, Baden said, "I'm sorry, I'm sorry," apologizing to Sgueglia for interrupting him. "You're not sorry," Miller snapped. "You're a professional. You've done this a thousand times." (In fact, Baden was at the moment also working for the defense in the trial of O.J. Simpson, for whom he would testify three months later.) But none of this was much more than legal sport. Other than his strong second opinion confirming Ophoven's, Baden's main contribution to the prosecution was to give the jury another shade of context to consider. Why had these murders gone undetected all those years ago? Simpson asked. "Doctors don't want to think parents harm children," Baden said. "As happened with the Hoyt babies, doctors wanted to believe the parents and assigned natural causes."

John Brooks flew in from New Hampshire to tell the jury that Molly and Noah breathed like any other babies during their brief lives. As the prosecution's SIDS and infant respiration expert, he conducted a quick course on the history of SIDS, apnea, and apnea monitoring. He explained the apnea theory, elaborated on the meaning of fifteen- or twenty-second pauses, and concluded with David Southall's study of ten thousand babies in England and what had been learned in the years since. "We know a lot more now about the significance or lack of significance of breathing irregularities," he said.

Brooks reported the results of his review of the records of Molly and Noah at Upstate: some apnea alarms in the hospital, but no instances of distress; then, reported life-threatening events within hours of discharge. "Either the family is overreacting or somebody is doing something to the babies," he said. Ultimately, there was the final clue: death the day after discharge. "So many things are atypical of SIDS," he concluded. "It's much more characteristic of child abuse."

Simpson asked Brooks if he'd ever heard of five SIDS deaths in one family. He said he hadn't.

"Ever heard of four?"

"No."

"Three?"

"I'm not aware of any."

"Two?"

"I think so. In fact, I *was* involved in a case of three. Well, I thought it was for a while."

"What happened?"

"There was a conviction. There was infanticide. I didn't come into it until later. I was involved in the fourth, fifth, and sixth children."

"What was the name of that case?"

"Van Der Sluys."

Bob Courtright jangled his keys, nervous as a cat. Simpson wanted him to read Waneta's confession to the jury, an important if not terribly complicated task, and Courtright was all nerves. He had carefully prepared for this moment. He and Simpson had driven to Schenectady to interview the jurors in the Marybeth Tinning case, and each had left the meeting with a piece of advice. Simpson had resolved not to allow any engineers on the jury—the one on the Tinning case was overly analytical, the others felt; an obstacle to common sense. And Courtright made sure not to wear any flashy jewelry to the witness stand.

He was sworn in just after lunch on Tuesday and began describing the events leading up to those critical few hours of March 23, 1994—how the case came to be, the last strategy meeting at the Treadway, the pickup plan for Sue Mulvey and Bob Bleck, the mix-up that put them outside the Berkshire post office at the moment Waneta Hoyt was coming out with her mail. Finally, the interview at the state police station in Owego. "At that point, we all sat down," Courtright said in the clipped, Joe Friday way that he said most things, whether giving testimony in a murder trial or ordering lunch. "I believe at first that we asked Mrs. Hoyt if she wanted any coffee, which she did. We got her coffee. Then we all settled back into the interview room."

With Peggy Drake leading the way, Courtright used a diagram to describe where everyone sat, recalled what was said, how Bleck gave Waneta the Miranda warnings, how courteously she was treated, how cooperative she was throughout—a narration designed to assure the jury that there was nothing sinister behind what came next. Now Drake had Courtright read Waneta's three-page written statement into evidence. "I caused the death of all my five children . . ." he began, but didn't get far before his voice began to choke on the words. It was an unexpected moment, the seemingly unflappable senior investigator caught up in the emotion of a mother admitting to smothering her babies. Some along the press row wondered how genuine it was. It seemed almost too melodramatic to be true. But it was. Courtright had not meant for all the sorrow he had kept in check during the investigation to come out at this moment, but here it was. "... Julie was the next one to die. ..." His voice broke again. "... She was crying and I wanted her to stop. I held her nose and mouth into my shoulder until she stopped struggling. ..." In the jury box, a woman in the back row put her hands to her face; another dabbed at a tear.

Courtright got through the written confession, complete with Waneta's addendum and Tim's signature, but it was only a prologue. Now Drake moved him on to what was perhaps the prosecution's most important document: the statement Courtright had taken from Waneta as a court stenographer sat beside them. Here it was, in her own words, straightforward answers to pointed questions—not in Sue Mulvey's handwriting, but in twenty-five pages of triple-spaced legal transcript. The monotone of Courtright's recitation echoed through the courtroom, giving the confession a ghastly banality.

"... I cradled her to my shoulder until she quit crying," Courtright said, reading Waneta's words about the death of Julie. "When she quit crying, I released her from my shoulder and she wasn't breathing."

Listening in the gallery, George Hoyt, Tim's oldest brother, felt a jolt. Since the arrest, he had kept those years interred, inaccessible. Now, slowly, he began to remember what he'd felt back then.

"When you pulled her away," Courtright said, reciting his own question to Waneta, "did you know that she was dead?" "I suspected that she was," Waneta had replied, her words now bringing quiet gasps from all corners of the courtroom. As much as the cumulative impact of the image of babies being smothered one after another, it was her description of Jimmy's death that cloaked the courtroom in horror:

Q.: Tell us how that death happened.
A.: I was getting dressed in the bathroom, and he wanted to come in, and I didn't want him to. I told him to wait out in the hall until I was done, and he kept yelling, "Mommy, mommy," and screaming. And I took the towel and went out in the living room, and I put the towel over his face to get him to quiet down, and he struggled. And once he finally got quiet, he was gone.
Q.: He was dead?
A.: (Nods head).
Q.: Was he laying on the floor, on the couch when you are smothering him?
A.: On the floor.
Q.: On the floor. Were you on top of him, straddled over him?
A.: No. I was just holding him cradle-type.

Q.: In your arms?

A.: Yes, like a cradle.

Q.: Was he on the floor?

A.: Yes.

Q.: And you were . . .

A.: His head was on my arm here (indicating).

Q.: Were you on the floor on your knees or how were you?

A.: I was on my knees.

Q.: Okay. And you used a towel. Was that a big towel?

A.: A bath towel.

Q.: What happened after James was dead?

A.: Once I realized that he was dead, I scooped him up and ran out of the house, and I flagged down the trashman that was coming by. . . .

Q.: And the reason that you did this to James was because you were upset with him?

A.: Yes. Because he kept bothering me while I was in the bathroom trying to get myself dressed for the day.

The jurors listened as Courtright read them the entire transcript. One of the more memorable passages started with a question he had asked about Jay, a follow-up to Waneta's earlier statement that her adoptive son had survived because Tim was always home when he cried. Courtright had thought this didn't ring true and pressed her on the point.

Q.: Let me ask you this. You adopted Jay, I think you told us, when he was two and a half months old. And after causing the death of five of your children, why didn't this happen to Jay?

A.: I don't know. I just felt maybe I was a sitter to him or something, and he needed a home and somebody to love him, which I was picked out to be that mother.

Q.: Did Jay cry when he was a baby?

A.: Yes.

Q.: Why didn't you do something to him?

A.: I don't know. Honestly, I don't know. It didn't bother me the same way.

Q.: Tell me this: What did you tell Tim about the children's deaths?

A.: I don't recall.

Q.: Did you tell him the truth?

A.: No. He didn't know I did anything.

Q.: Did you tell the doctors the truth how the children died?

A.: No.

Q.: Did you tell anybody in the whole world?

A.: Just God.

With Miller in Rochester getting treatment for his infected eye, the formidable task of attacking Waneta's confession fell to Ray Urbanski. Long before the trial, they had agreed that the only approach was to challenge not so much the words themselves, or whether Waneta had said them, but whether she had said them freely. With Courtright—as well as with Mulvey and Bleck, who would follow him to the witness stand—Urbanski planned to scrutinize the investigators' tactics so relentlessly that when he was done, perhaps one or two people on the jury would have the impression that Waneta had been tricked. He knew it was a mountain he was trying to climb, but Waneta had left her lawyers with no other options.

Urbanski led Courtright through a virtual minute-by-minute account of that day—"Or was she already in the room when you got the coffee?"—but Courtright held firm, giving the defense nothing serious to offer the jury. Wasn't Waneta deceived into coming down to Owego? Urbanski asked. Didn't you tell Mulvey to say it was a "research project?" Why didn't you give it to her straight—tell her she was suspected in the deaths of her children—so she could make an informed and intelligent decision about whether to waive her constitutional rights? Weren't the Miranda warnings downplayed? Didn't Mulvey tell Waneta they were just a formality? Why didn't you videotape the confession? Why didn't you read the Miranda rights again when you began the accusatory phase of the interview? Urbanski devoted fifteen minutes to an inquisition of how Courtright had decided when to bring in the stenographer. He tried to win points with a line of questioning about the advice Courtright had gotten from Joel Dvoskin, the state's chief forensic psychologist, a day before the interview. Courtright said it wasn't anything he didn't know after thirty-two years with the state police.

Urbanski and Simpson played a tug-of-war with each direct, cross, re-direct, and re-cross-examination of the three state police witnesses. They pushed and prodded every nuance of the events surrounding the confession.

"Tell us again what you said to her," Urbanski asked Mulvey.

"That we had first learned of her children through a medical article," Mulvey replied. "That we had been in contact with a doctor from the Midwest, specifically from Minnesota, and that I had been assigned to talk to her to gather information about the lives and deaths of her children."

"Did you tell her this was a research project?"

"No."

"And I think you said earlier today that you indicated to her that you were talking to her to prevent this from happening to other children."

"Yes. I was entirely truthful in saying we wanted to prevent what had happened to her children from happening to other children."

"And how was the purpose of this interview to accomplish that?"

"Well, if we got her to tell us the truth, we could prevent other children from being murdered in the same fashion."

"And how would you know when she was telling you the truth?"

"When what she told us fit the medical facts."

"When what she told you was what you determined had happened, correct?"

"Well, no, because we had no way to know that she had used a pillow to smother the young babies, and we had no way to know that she had used a bath towel or chased little Jimmy down and smothered him in the living room of her trailer."

"But you didn't tell her you believed that she in fact was involved, and that you wanted to question her with regard to this?"

"No, and I'm not required to tell her that."

"You're not required to. That's a police ploy?"

"It's a standard technique. I didn't think we would get very far if we—"

"Ah, that's a standard technique. You didn't think you'd get very far . . . You wouldn't get very far if you were honest?"

"No, that's not what I said."

On re-direct, Simpson tried to turn the jurors' attention away from any notion of police trickery, reminding them of the enormity of the crime and of the coldness of the defendant.

"How long after you had confronted her was it before she started to speak of slaughtering these children?" Simpson asked Mulvey. Later, closing her testimony, he asked her to characterize Waneta's demeanor during the interview. "You indicated that she was crying?"

"No," Mulvey said. "Once she started talking about the children, she wasn't crying anymore. She was matter-of-fact."

On Thursday, Simpson called the two jail officers who heard Waneta admit the murders again while she was being processed the night of her arrest. With that, having brought eighteen witnesses before the jury in little more than a week of testimony, he closed his case for the prosecution. The defense would begin on Monday, the start of the trial's third week.

An hour after Simpson rested, Bob Miller was sitting in his kitchen in Waverly, dragging on a string of cigarettes, catching up on cattle business with his son over the phone. He hung up and rubbed his face. Waneta's confession had deflated him. He had thought he might be able to get around it, but the reality of it had come full force. "I told her it doesn't look good," he said. "It was pretty clear yesterday where she stands. And Ophoven was very good. I couldn't do much with her. I was hoping that list would be a lot shorter. She just kept going on and on." Miller's plan had been to bring the easel back out and have his own medical witnesses, including Steinschneider, cast stones at it. But then he talked about the thirteen factors with another of his medical people, an eighty-year-old neurosurgeon and medical examiner named Arthur King whom he had used on malpractice cases. "Well, I can't disagree with much of it," King told him. "There are too many of them."

It left Miller wishing that Waneta had conceded the veracity of the confession and allowed him to use some sort of diminished-capacity defense that might at least keep her out of prison for the rest of her life. But with everyone around her believing in her, a group psychology feeding on itself, her position had only hardened. "Now the jury will have to draw a distinction in the law about corroboration that may be too much to ask," Miller said. "I mean, they don't need a lot. They could just say, five of them, you know, doesn't make any sense, medically or not. They could say the mother alone with them—that's corroboration. I don't think we've lost them yet. You know when you've lost a jury. I don't think they're gone yet. They're still listening. Only need one or two for a hung jury." The jurors he'd picked flashed through his mind. "You notice during jury selection how the first panel's called in, half of them have an opinion, the next panel, thirty percent, and by the time you get to the last one, only one or two have an opinion? Shit, they all have an opinion." He fantasized about one opinion. " 'Look at her, she looks like a wreck, I'm not gonna pay taxes to put her in prison.' " It might be your best hope, it was suggested. Miller laughed. "Maybe our only hope."

He leaned over the kitchen table. "Confessions are devastating. It's like doing a four-forty dash when the other guy's already gone two hundred yards. Ask F. Lee Bailey how many confession cases he's won. They don't talk about those cases. I would have loved to have tried this without a confession. Really would have given them a run for their money. Why couldn't she just keep her mouth shut? That's what I don't understand. It's not like they tortured her. Probably wouldn't even have been a trial without it. They say they would have kept investigating. Investigating what? They've been investigating right up to the trial, haven't found one single thing."

He felt he had only one card to play: "Maybe they'll buy Ewing's mumbo-jumbo. She didn't understand what was happening when they brought her in, she's got a personality problem where she'll say things to please authority figures, the statement wasn't voluntary, it isn't reliable. That's a shot. He wrote a hell of a report. Oh, there's gonna be an awful fight over that. Simpson will claim it's a psychiatric defense and we're supposed to give him notice. He could demand an adjournment to get her examined by his guy. But we're not talking about the acts themselves. We're talking about the confession. It'll be a hell of a battle. I don't think anyone's tried this before." Of course, the wild card was the testimony of Waneta herself. Miller dreaded it—she hadn't done too well the last time she'd been challenged—but felt there was no way out. "It's an impossible situation. I mean, how else do you, you know, explain your explanation?"

Miller considered some of the more provocative evidence Simpson had put in. The memories of the Upstate nurses puzzled him particularly. He wondered how genuine they really were; perhaps they had been influenced by what they'd read in the newspapers. "Like the glaring. I try to remember traumatic events thirty years ago. I can remember my mother ill with cancer. I can remember caring for her, the details, how traumatic it was. But how could they remember stuff like that?"

They believed Waneta was killing her children, he was told. They never forgot how impotent they'd felt. That was their trauma.

"I'll be damned," Miller said. "That is incredible. Isn't that something, those nurses remember that. So they knew the history of the previous children? Did any of them go to Steinschneider, talk to him, say something's wrong?"

"At least two did."

"What'd he do, just slough it off?"

"Apparently."

"Dumb shit," Miller said. He dragged on a cigarette. "He had a paper to write."

Miller would mount his defense of Waneta Hoyt at 9:00 Monday morning. His first witness would be Dr. Alfred Steinschneider.

36

For the first time in its august 115-year history, *Science,* the journal of the American Association for the Advancement of Science, was covering a murder trial. Among the press corps recording the testimony at the Tioga County Courthouse was Ginger Pinholster, the writer whose first article about the case had appeared in the journal the previous spring.

In the wake of Waneta Hoyt's arrest, Steinschneider had given Pinholster an interview, expecting that *Science* would be the one place he might find sympathy and support. The AAAS was his culture, the magazine its scripture. She was the one reporter he seemed eager to talk to about the Hoyt affair, confident she would tell *his* story. But to his bitter disappointment he had found no ally in the weekly journal. "If the murder charge is upheld," Pinholster's story had observed, "it would demolish Steinschneider's theory that this family's tragedy suggests a link between SIDS and severe apneic episodes caused by an abnormality present at birth. . . . And it would raise a troubling question: Could Steinschneider have prevented the deaths of two of the Hoyt children?"

Pinholster was among those awaiting Steinschneider's appearance on the witness stand as the defense prepared to begin its case. Another was Gail Pfeiffer, who was anxious to lay eyes on the man whose name was all over Noah Hoyt's chart, but whom she never remembered seeing on the ward—the "phantom doctor," as she had called him, ensconced upstairs with his research. Since testifying, she had searched her memory for a fuller picture of the fear on 4A—of what might have been done to prevent Molly and Noah from dying. She remembered the talk had been discreet, but wondered what might have been said that she'd not heard. "That's why I want to call Julie,"

Gail said. "I want to ask her, 'Julie, did we ever dare verbalize it?' " When she heard that Julie Evans had indeed warned Steinschneider, Gail said, "Well, he needs to be in the hot seat then." She decided she would skip school and return to Owego early Monday morning to see it.

On Sunday afternoon, Miller and Urbanski drove to the Elmira airport to meet Steinschneider and his wife. Descending the steps of their plane from Atlanta, the Steinschneiders looked as though they would rather be any-place else.

"You know, I'm just here for him, to hold him together," Roz confided to Urbanski soon after their arrival.

"He looks okay," Urbanski replied.

"Yeah, well, he's putting up a good front."

They struck Urbanski as a remarkably devoted couple, and he was moved by their predicament. "Here's Al, who I'm sure is a decent guy and a dedicated doctor," he said later. "And he writes this article back then. I mean, you can lose the forest for the trees sometimes. You're involved in researching a problem and legitimately trying to find an answer, and if a little bit of fame and glory comes with some breakthrough, that's nice, too. And here's this wonderful opportunity he has where this woman comes in right from his own backyard, and it just never dawns on him that she may be snuffing these kids. You lose peripheral vision. You never had that happen? I have. And now, put yourself in his position. You've got this wild woman Norton down there, saying this isn't a trial of Waneta Hoyt—you're the one who should be standing trial."

Steinschneider wondered if that was just what the prosecutors in New York had in mind. He told Miller and Urbanski about his phone conversation with Simpson a month before. He had cut it off when he realized Simpson was taping the call, he said. He worried that it meant Simpson and Fitz-patrick might be hatching a plan to indict him as some sort of accomplice. The defense lawyers assured Steinschneider he had committed no crime; Simpson was just taping the call to help him prepare his cross-examination. They got Steinschneider checked into the Elmira Holiday Inn, then brought him to Urbanski's office, where they spent the rest of the afternoon getting ready for Monday morning. It was during those hours that Steinschneider read Waneta Hoyt's written confession for the first time. When he finished the third page, he put the paper down and looked up. "Chilling," he said.

The next morning, Urbanski picked up the Steinschneiders and drove them to Owego in his Chevy Suburban, talking about everything but the case as they went. They crossed the river at the Court Street Bridge and parked among the television minivans alongside the courthouse. Steinschneider emerged confidently. He marched briskly up the limestone steps, giving no appearance of a man who wished he were anyplace else. He and Urbanski chatted affably as they made their way up to the courtroom.

They were early for the day's proceedings, so Steinschneider, Roz beside him, took an inconspicuous aisle seat in the gallery's fifth row. He surveyed the baronial courtroom and the spectators and reporters who were milling around, waiting for the first witness for the defense to be called. A few minutes later, Waneta and Tim came down the center aisle, moving toward the rear conference room they used as a lounge. Seeing the Hoyts approach, Steinschneider stood abruptly in awkward deference. It was twenty-four years later, and here they were, once the young mother from the distant hills and the ambitious doctor with an idea, crossing paths one more time. Steinschneider had come to help defend her, but it was also true that none of this would be happening but for the paper he had written. He bowed slightly, and Waneta returned the uneasy gesture with a polite nod, passing without a pause. Not a word was exchanged.

The defense calls Dr. Alfred Steinschneider. He rose and came down the center aisle. The jurors and spectators watched a grandfatherly man in a tweed jacket and tie take the witness's oath and climb to his seat, ready for the chore at hand. It was a climactic moment in the thirty-year history of this case, but nothing about Steinschneider's bearing betrayed a recognition of this. Pulled back to the time and place of his seminal triumph, about to confront the long-overlooked discrepancies and unasked questions of his famous paper, he assumed the role of the innocent bystander.

Asked by Miller to tell the jury about his background, Steinschneider delivered the obligatory details in relaxed and folksy fashion: "... Went on to Cornell University in beautiful Ithaca and got my Ph.D. in 1955 ..." When Sgueglia broke in to ask him to speak up, Steinschneider listened eagerly. "Doctor, you have a beautiful, soothing voice—I'm sure your patients love it," the judge said with a benevolent smile. "But I'm having trouble hearing you in this courtroom. I'd like you to shout it out." Sgueglia pointed to one of the court bailiffs sitting beyond the jury box and asked Steinschneider to direct his voice at her. Steinschneider followed the judge's finger, taking care to be sure he was looking at the right woman, then said, "Okay—you got a deal." It was easy to imagine him as something he had never been, a kindly neighborhood pediatrician surrounded by jars of tongue depressors and lollipops.

Seeking to certify him instead as a world-class SIDS researcher, Miller led Steinschneider on an oral history of his life's work. He started back in his days when he was studying the autonomic nervous system with Earle Lipton, then moved on to the pivotal 1969 meeting near Seattle where SIDS was named and his world changed. "And as a result of that conference," Miller asked, "did you return to Upstate Medical Center and undertake a more directed scheme of research in regard to SIDS?"

"It certainly piqued my interest," Steinschneider replied. "Keep in mind that I'm a teacher, and I was also a researcher. And it always intrigued me that for research to progress, for learning to take place, one had to recognize one's own ignorance, if you will. What intrigued me was the pathologists who were at that meeting who owned up to the fact that they in fact did not know why these babies were dying. . . . And that rather than attribute it to some theory of theirs, what they thought it might be, they said: Wouldn't it be wiser, wouldn't it be smarter, wouldn't it be more honest to say we don't know why they're dying? So part of what intrigued me was the intellectual honesty of the individuals who were there. And the other was that when I spoke, and I felt like a novice at this meeting, my comments were not felt to be totally ridiculous. And so I decided to go back and see what I could find out."

For the moment, Miller skipped past what Steinschneider found out. He asked him to talk about the major SIDS program he had launched at the University of Maryland and to explain what he did as founder and president of the American SIDS Institute. He asked him if he'd been a consultant to the National Institutes of Health; if he'd been given federal grants to study SIDS and apnea, SIDS and race, SIDS and migration, SIDS and subsequent siblings; if he had sixty-eight publications to his credit on "the very issue that we're talking about here this morning—the investigation and academic research involving the subject of how to explain death in children"; asked him if he had been "treating children and babies within the context of his clinical research his entire professional life," right up until this very day. Yes, Steinschneider said—this was all true. He had devoted his life to studying the deaths of babies.

"Dr. Steinschneider," Miller said now, "in 1971, while you were at Upstate Medical Center, you undertook care for two patients, babies, Molly and Noah Hoyt. Is that correct?"

"Yes," Steinschneider said, affirming for the record, for the first time, that Molly and Noah were the H. babies. Molly had come to him first, he said, because of episodes at home in which she had stopped breathing and turned blue.

"Tell me what happened when they were admitted," Miller asked.

"They came in and they were followed in the research unit and we attached an apnea monitor to them. . . . Because of the report that Molly was having these recurring episodes, then medically it was necessary to follow that baby very closely on the ward just in case a similar episode would occur. And then we attempted to determine why the episodes were occurring."

"And were there subsequent occurrences in the hospital?"

"The nurses reported to me and in the chart that Molly had a number of episodes where the alarm would go off, and on occasion they felt the need to stimulate the baby."

"Were there histories of apneic incidents in the hospital in regard to Noah?"

"Yes."

"Of the same nature as you described in Molly?"

"Reported episodes by the nurses."

In the balcony, Gail Pfeiffer pursed her lips.

"There's been another assertion here, by certain witnesses that have testified, that there was never a reported incident of an apneic incident or of difficulty in breathing or of cyanosis, other than by the mother. Does your history and your recollection and your treatment of these children verify that assertion?"

"What I can say is that nurses reported episodes, alarms. They reported that the equipment was functioning, and on occasion they reported that they had to stimulate the baby."

"Is this type of research still done today, using monitors to measure for apnea?"

"Monitors are in common use clinically in the management of babies who are known to be at increased risk to die of SIDS. In the United States today, it's been estimated that there are close to forty thousand babies sent home on alarm systems."

Miller moved into the babies' family history, but only a piece of it. He asked Steinschneider about the circumstances originally attributed to Julie's death. Was it true that babies couldn't die as the result of a feeding? No, said Steinschneider. "We see babies literally every month that get referred to the institute because they have severe episodes, where they become cyanotic, stop breathing, literally pass out. They seem to require resuscitative intervention and this occurs in association with feeding. In fact, that meeting I attended in 1969, one of the few slides I had to present was a slide of a baby who did just that. . . . Babies can overreact. And they literally can die."

Miller steered clear of any discussion of Jimmy. Instead he embarked on a line of questioning about SIDS as the death of an apparently healthy baby, a launching point for Steinschneider to present a lengthy homily on his theory of the "subtle chronic abnormality." Then Miller asked about the recurrence of SIDS. Were there reports in the literature of more than two children dying in one family of unexplained causes? Yes, said Steinschneider.

"Doctor," Miller said, "based on the medical evidence as far as the records of their hospitalization in Syracuse, the treatment that you rendered, the autopsies that were done, and the family histories that were provided . . . is there any medical evidence in this case to your knowledge to corroborate, *independently corroborate,* the statement of Mrs. Hoyt that she smothered these children?"

Steinschneider paused dramatically. "No," he said after a long moment of thought.

"You don't know whether she did or not, do you?" Miller came back, apparently hoping the question would give Steinschneider the appearance of objectivity.

"No."

"But there's no medical evidence to corroborate her saying she did," Miller added hastily.

Sgueglia cut in. "He's already answered that," the judge said, ending Miller's direct examination with a thud.

"I can't believe they brought him all the way up for *that,*" Simpson remarked to Peggy Drake at the break, closing the door to their meeting room behind him. Miller had directed the bulk of Steinschneider's testimony at abstractions and hypotheticals designed to cast doubt on Simpson's medical corroborators, and less at Steinschneider's direct experience with the Hoyt children. But he opened the door to the records of Molly and Noah just wide enough to give Simpson plenty to work with on cross-examination—and to show that as an expert witness, Steinschneider was anything but disinterested. Simpson had come primed for battle. He hadn't forgotten that heated phone call the month before, when Steinschneider accused him of deceit and of knowingly prosecuting an innocent woman. He planned to show which of them was the deceptive one. "Should I ask him about our conversation?" Simpson asked Drake. "Or are they waiting for me to ask and walk into a trap?" *Nothing to be gained there,* Drake thought. "Ask him where he got the family history," she said, figuring it would emphasize that it all came from Waneta. Simpson pondered that a moment. "Do I want to ask him that? I don't want to get into that and let him waffle on it." He had something else in mind.

"Dr. Steinschneider, my name is Bob Simpson, I'm the district attorney here in Tioga County," he was saying a few minutes later, "and you and I have spoken before, is that correct?"

"That's correct," Steinschneider said guardedly, completing the coded exchange that opened Round 2 of their private antipathy.

With an edge the jurors hadn't seen before, Simpson questioned Steinschneider closely, sometimes acerbically, on how he had prepared for this day—whom he had talked to, what documents he had reviewed—before launching an all-out assault on his assertions about his studies of Molly and Noah Hoyt. "Now you have testified that in connection with the incidences of apnea and cyanosis, you relied somewhat on what the nurses at Upstate told you with respect to Molly and Noah. Did you also review the medical records on a daily basis for Molly and Noah when you were up there in your clinic?"

"As best as I can recollect, I reviewed them and I discussed it with the nurses."

"And so, when you come into court today and you testify in front of this jury that you were basing your evidence of apnea on the statements of the nurses, are you referring to their oral statements to you or are you referring to what's in the record?"

"Both," Steinschneider answered blithely.

This was the moment that Bob Simpson, a rural prosecutor who could not say what the letters SIDS stood for until this case, began taking apart the central data of the hypothesis that had gripped the SIDS world for more than two decades. Simpson was the unlikely grand inquisitor of the origins of the apnea theory, and Steinschneider himself had provided the ammunition. Simpson didn't know about Steinschneider's letters to the psychiatrist Stuart Asch, or about his claim, during the 1974 meeting in Toronto, that the nurses had resuscitated the babies in the hospital. But he had in his hand a copy of Steinschneider's response to the 1973 letter to *Pediatrics* from Dr. John Hick.

"Now, prior to coming to court today, were you asked to review the medical records that Mr. Miller and Mr. Urbanski gave you, to find in there the incidences of apnea?" Simpson asked, pacing as he spoke.

"I had gone over it."

"And did you find incidences in the record where there was evidence of prolonged apnea?"

"Yes."

"And did you find incidences in the record where the nurses had to resuscitate the children?"

"Where they stimulated them."

"And tell me the difference between stimulation and resuscitation."

"Well, it's a matter of degree. Very often some people when they talk about resuscitation, talk in terms of mouth-to-mouth resuscitation. Others just stimulation."

"And there is evidence of that, this stimulation, in the record?"

"The alarm sounded ... apparently the baby was stimulated and there's evidence in the record."

"Did the thought ever occur to you, Doctor, as you read the record, perhaps there was a malfunction to the monitor? So it could have been that the monitor went off because the baby quit breathing, or as is set forth many places in the record, it could have been simply that the baby was breathing so softly that the monitor didn't pick it up."

"Correct," said Steinschneider, a significant acknowledgment. He sipped water from a paper cup.

"Were there any evidences in the record of vigorous stimulation of these children to arouse them out of this apnea state?"

"Not that I recollect."

"Yet when you wrote an article in response to Dr. Hick, you specifically mentioned, in your defense, that on two occasions the nurses were required to vigorously stimulate the children."

"If I wrote it, then it happened. But I didn't see it in those notes."

"So which is the truth?"

"The truth is I wrote it, therefore it's true. I wouldn't have written it if it wasn't true."

"So everything you write is true."

"To the best of my knowledge it is, yes."

"Well, do you have a specific recollection in the record, Doctor, of a place where it talks about vigorous stimulation performed by a nurse?"

"No, I do not."

"And wouldn't it be important in your clinic that the nurses put such things down? Isn't that the reason these children were being studied?"

"Would it be important? It would be important."

"And when you questioned the nurses about vigorous stimulation, I presume, based on your testimony, that they related to you orally that they had to vigorously stimulate these infants?"

"That's correct."

"And you recall that as though it were yesterday."

"No, I do not recall it. I recall it because I wrote it."

"Perhaps you wrote it in your letter to the editor in defense of your position as opposed to something that actually happened. Is that a possibility—you fabricated it in defense of your position?"

"No," Steinschneider replied calmly.

"You wouldn't do that?"

"No."

"You wouldn't. All right ... I want to call your attention to the second page of your letter. It says, 'During the periods of hospitalizations, M.H. . . .' Read that paragraph to yourself, Doctor, would you please?" Steinschneider peered down. He had brought some of his own files with him. Hick's letter was among them.

"Did you use the words *vigorous stimulation* with respect to Molly and Noah in that letter?" Simpson demanded. "Did you?"

"The answer is yes, I said on these occasions, 'Vigorous stimulations were required before spontaneous respiration resumed and skin color returned to normal.' "

"And you got that information from where?"

"I got that from my notes, the nurses' notes, and in talking to the nurse."

"Okay. And you will be able on the lunch hour to find your notes and the nurses' notes as to where the term 'vigorous stimulation' comes from?"

"No."

"Why not?"

"The only notes I have are those that apply to the medical record. I've looked for that. I did not see in those particular babies where they said vigorous stimulation."

"So it's not in the medical record."

"There were records I kept following discussions."

"And where are those records?"

"I don't have them."

Simpson continued to pounce, sounding at times more like a prosecutor of scientific malfeasance than of child murder—as if, as Linda Norton said, it really was Steinschneider who was on trial. "And it was those conversations that you're relying on to use the 'vigorous stimulation' that's in that letter."

"It would have to be."

"You don't have any memory of it when you sit here today, do you, Doctor?"

"I have recollections of talking to nurses about their observations."

"I didn't ask you that, Doctor. I asked you if you had a recollection as you sit here today of a nurse advising you of vigorous stimulation."

"No."

"Now let's try this another way and see if we can find someplace else where you put things in a chart that aren't accurate." Simpson contended that the hospital records did not document patterns of prolonged apnea, in part because the inadequacy of the monitors rendered alarms at fifteen-second settings ambiguous at best. "And you went ahead and you wrote an article in 1972. Did you mention in your article that you were basing some of your information on things that were outside the hospital records, i.e., reports that the nurses made to you that aren't documented?"

"Did I say that I used records outside? I did not say where I got the information. I said I got the information from the data I accumulated, that's where I got the information from."

"Excuse me, you got the information from where?"

"I got the information from all—what I would report is the totality of the information without necessarily specifying exactly where I got it from."

"And could you tell us the names of the nurses that made these oral reports?"

"No, I could not."

"You didn't think it was important to put that in the record with the two apparently life-threatening or near-miss SIDS?"

"They were all near-misses."

Simpson pointed out that most of the apneic periods Steinschneider listed in his discharge notes seemed to last only a few seconds. "Are you telling this jury that those were near-miss SIDS?" he asked.

"No."

"Okay, now tell us what a near-miss SIDS is then."

"It would be reported as a prolonged apnea. Fifteen seconds or greater."

"So fifteen seconds or greater is a near-miss SIDS?"

"No, I said it was prolonged apnea."

Simpson asked if there was any evidence in the records that either Molly or Noah had had what was then considered a "near-miss SIDS."

"In the hospital records?" Steinschneider asked. "They stimulated the baby."

"I didn't ask you that. I asked if there was any evidence of near-miss SIDS."

"In the sense in which that term was being used then, I would say at least at those times when they felt the need to stimulate."

"Now, Doctor, over the lunch hour I would like you to go through Exhibits 16 and 17, which are hospital records for Noah and Molly, and I would like you to pick out every incidence where there was stimulation. Can you do that for us?"

"I will try."

Steinschneider stepped from the witness chair, and descended to the defense conference room with a look of concern on his face. He spent the next hour furiously paging through the thick stack of records. What he didn't know was that over lunch, Simpson was deciding to drop the issue. The prosecutors knew that there were a couple of instances when Molly had been stimulated in the days after she had been rushed back to the hospital. Although they felt the stimulation was probably just a precaution by a careful nurse on a heightened sense of alert, Simpson didn't want to give Steinschneider the chance to exaggerate its significance or portray an isolated incident as a vindication. Returning to the witness chair, Steinschneider girded himself for another onslaught. Instead, and to his and the defense lawyers' surprise and relief, Simpson opened the afternoon with a question about his early research work.

Simpson made his way from Steinschneider's long experience with SIDS to the issue of whether he believed the term could be applied to the Hoyt children, and if so, to which ones. It was a provocative historical question since the implication of his 1972 paper had always been that all five fell into the realm of SIDS. Now, in 1995, he said that he wouldn't classify either Eric or Julie as a SIDS victim because neither had been autopsied at their deaths.

Would you consider James a SIDS? Simpson asked. "Me?" Steinschneider said. "No, I would say that James, the best information available, based upon the autopsy done, I would have to go with the pathologist who said that what he saw was a small adrenal, and it was their expert opinion and I have no reason to question it. This baby may have had a small adrenal gland and died of adrenal insufficiency."

Molly and Noah? The autopsies found no known cause of death, Steinschneider said. "This by definition is what we mean by sudden unexplained death in infancy, or the sudden infant death syndrome." He added, "When Noah died, an autopsy was done, presumably a death-scene investigation was done, and the police, the coroner, did what they were supposed to do. Whatever they did."

And shouldn't a complete death-scene investigation be part of any assessment of whether an infant death can be called SIDS? "Should there be?" Steinschneider said. "Of course.... If you're asking me whether or not I think a particular investigator did a thorough job, Lord have mercy, I'm having enough trouble talking about physicians doing appropriate jobs, I'm certainly not going to pass judgment on whether you are doing an appropriate job, or they are, or the judge is. Forgive me, Judge."

"And that's the problem I'm having," Simpson said. "... You come in here and say that Molly and Noah meet the definition of SIDS, yet you haven't taken into account when you make that determination what the death-scene investigation was." Simpson brought up Steinschneider's own recent article in *Pediatric Clinics of North America,* which mentioned the importance of a death-scene investigation.

"I appreciate your reading it," Steinschneider told Simpson. "It was a good article...."

"You're willing to make a SIDS determination in the case of Molly and Noah without knowing what the death-scene determination was, or whether there was one.... You're making a presumption that one was done."

"I would hope that the people are as thorough as I am," Steinschneider said.

"Now, you testified previously at this trial that you're unable to say whether or not the Hoyt children were the subject of a murder, is that correct?" This was the issue that had turned their phone conversation into a conflagration.

"That's correct," Steinschneider said.

"So for all you know, they could have been suffocated."

"For all I know," Steinschneider agreed this time, "they could have been suffocated."

"Did you ever consider that as a possible cause of death of any of the Hoyt children?"

"Yes."

"And did you refer your thought on to any police agency?"

"No."

"Did some of the nurses in Syracuse advise you that they thought these children were dying at the hands of a parent?"

"I could not answer that. I don't recall anybody saying that."

"How about Julie Evans? Nurse Evans. Do you remember her?"

"I remember Julie Evans. I can't give you details, but no I don't—"

"Is it possible that Nurse Evans told you she thought that these children were dying at the hands of a parent?"

"I do not recall—"

"Objection—hearsay," Miller growled.

"Sustained," said Sgueglia, who instructed the jury to disregard the question, though it was, of course, about ten seconds too late for that. Julie Evans hadn't been able to move Steinschneider back then, and demurred from testifying now. But in the end, her voice came through in one last whisper.

After nearly four hours of testimony, Steinschneider left the witness box with an incongruously buoyant smile. In the back of the courtroom during the break, he spotted Ginger Pinholster, and stopped to deliver a heated rebuke for the story she had a written a year before. "You didn't do your homework," he scolded her. He expected more from *Science*. Pinholster thought, *No, you didn't do your homework.* She expected more from a *scientist.* "When I first went to interview him, I thought he was a nice man in the twilight of his career," she remarked to a colleague, her voice flushed with astonishment at the day's events. "But watching him on the stand, all I could think was, *He's just not telling the truth.*"

Steinschneider had been under no legal compulsion to testify. But it would have been out of character for him to decline. Having told his truth, he returned to the defense room to get his coat. A minute later, the Hoyts walked in. This time, Waneta hugged him. Steinschneider wished her luck, then hurriedly left the courthouse with Roz to make their plane home to Atlanta.

Miller called on Dr. Arthur King, the eighty-year-old neurosurgeon-pathologist, to testify that the exhumations had revealed no evidence of anything, least of all homicide. Then he brought up Tim's brother Chuck and sister Ann, and three former emergency squad members—Hank Robson, who came up from his retirement home in North Carolina, and the Balzers, Vivian and Arthur—to offer their recollections of the various death scenes. It turned out to be a blurry, largely incoherent patch of testimony, the old-timers struggling to put names to children, dates to events, memories to truth. The retired rescuers lined up as they once had, mostly on the side of innocence. Though it was nearly impossible to distinguish the substance of their testimony, those who believed Waneta had not killed her children testified for the defense, while only Bob Vanek, the one among them who had been suspicious all those years ago, testified for the prosecution.

It was all so inscrutable that many people in Tioga County reduced the entire trial to pointlessness: *What can they prove now?* It was partly why, despite the power of the confession and the strength of the circumstantial evidence, no one involved considered a guilty verdict anything near a foregone conclusion. As the medical evidence deepened and the defendant's woeful countenance became a fixed part of the setting, a surprising suspensefulness began to envelop the culture of the trial.

On Thursday, April 13, Miller's star medical witness arrived from Texas. In the months since Dorothy Kelly had signed on to the case, she had ended her twenty-year tenure at Harvard and Mass General to join a private operation called the Southwest SIDS Research Institute. She focused, like Steinschneider, on siblings of SIDS victims and babies with apnea whom she sent home on monitors. Shortly before she moved, Miller and Urbanski had gone to Boston to talk about what she had found in the files of the Hoyt babies—the raw materials of Steinschneider's beliefs, and hers. They sat in Kelly's home and heard her say that these were the records of babies who were sick with respiratory disorders. It was tantalizing testimony but for one problem: She could find nothing in the records that might explain Jimmy's untimely death. Miller and Urbanski agreed there was only one strategy for Kelly's testimony. They had to pretend Jimmy didn't exist.

By the time of the trial, there was another problem, and it put Kelly on Miller's growing list of aggravations. A week before she was to testify, Kelly sent the first half of her bill: $8,275 for reviewing the medical records and consulting with the lawyers. She followed up with a message on Miller's answering machine saying she would very much appreciate being paid *before* she came to testify. Miller was annoyed by what he took as an implied threat. Most of the other medical witnesses, on both sides, were taking nominal fees for testifying or none at all. Miller thought Kelly had piled up her $300 hourly fee rather liberally—and he was, for the moment, all out of Tioga County money. But the strength of Simpson's case left him feeling that he needed Kelly more than ever. He sent her a personal check.

Kelly arrived in court a week later, and apparently felt no diffidence about openly demonstrating her fealty to the defense. Waiting for the day's proceedings to begin, she sat down next to Waneta in the well of the courtroom, took her hand, and stroked it. She whispered something into Waneta's ear, and Waneta laughed. Kelly had read the confession, but waved it off. "I'm not here to comment as to whether she killed them or not," she had told the lawyers. "I'm just here to comment on what I see in the records and what my research has shown." Urbanski told her, good—stick with that.

"Dr. Dorothy Kelly," he announced after the judge arrived on his perch, and the jurors saw a woman with curly red hair and glasses rise from her seat at the defense table, the only witness who didn't approach the stand from a neutral place. In this medical debate wrapped in the drama of a murder trial, she was the seventh physician to testify.

Just as she had with Steinschneider's theory in the 1970s, Kelly followed his testimony with an enterprising spin, making a splash of her own. Under direct examination by Urbanski, she offered the jury an alarming new view of the medical records. "Doctor, is there anything in the record of that date that is significant to you?" Urbanski asked repeatedly, rhythmically, stopping Kelly at notation after notation. "Yes, there is," she would respond each time, her forceful Boston brogue reverberating through the courtroom. She would go on to explain that it was not normal for an infant that age to regurgitate that much formula, or for a baby to be cyanotic about the mouth, or to vomit and be cold to the touch, or to have a drop in heart rate in that circumstance, or to go that long without breathing. It was Kelly's theory that what was running through the Hoyt family was a problem with the vagus nerve.

The vagus nerve, one of the dozen cranial nerves that emanate from the brain, plays a role in heart rate and respiration, and Kelly testified that she saw evidence in the records that these children's were overactive. "It means that the parasympathetic part of the autonomic nervous system is overactive," she explained to the jurors. Some had begun to look dazed by the relentless assault of medical testimony, although others seemed to be listening conscientiously for evidence that might attribute the deaths to natural causes.

Kelly used as her critical point of departure a notation in Molly's record by Dr. Roger Perry, her pediatrician at Tompkins County Hospital. On April 10, 1970, three days before he referred the baby to Steinschneider, Perry discharged Molly with a diagnosis of "hyperactive vagus nerve." He came to this conclusion after giving her a simple test: When he pressed on her eyeballs, her heart rate slowed. "The normal response is that the heart rate wouldn't change or it would increase," Kelly said.

"Does that cause a problem?" Urbanski asked.

"That can cause a problem. If the test is positive, that tells me there is overactivity and therefore other things could happen such as not breathing or breathing too slowly or having the heart beat too slowly. So if this were the only sign that I had of a problem with an infant, then I would send that child home on a monitor. And the parents would have to be taught how to help the baby if there is a problem . . . a little stimulation all the way up to CPR. We would have to teach them that."

Kelly said she'd also found something in Eric's record, thin as his file was, that led her to believe he had a similar problem. It was something Steinschneider wrote when he took the family history at Molly's first admission at Upstate five years later. According to his mother, Eric "had recurrent cyanotic 'passing out' spells" during his three months of life. "He would gasp for air 'like he couldn't get his breath.' " Urbanski asked Kelly what that meant to her. "The records from Eric indicate to me that he also probably had a problem with the vagus nerve because of his difficulty getting air in." She added, "I have had many mothers and fathers tell me almost in those same words. 'It's like you can't get air in,' is what they tell me." She felt the description of Julie's death in the same history—"seemed to choke, turn blue and died"—also indicated a vagus nerve problem. "In light of what we see clinically with Molly," Kelly testified, "the histories of both Julie's death and Eric's death are consistent with increased tone of the vagus nerve."

She found a related pattern of problems. Using the nursing notes for Molly and Noah, which provided an unusually detailed chronicle of the babies' daily digestive performance, Kelly offered the jury an ominous analysis of their regurgitations. They spit up more than normal, she said, and with uncommon vigor. "It is unusual for an infant under four weeks of age to actually regurgitate and spit the formula out," she said, though the records didn't actually say they had "spit it out." At this, a look of incredulity crossed the faces of several women on the jury.

"Were you able to determine the number of times during the hospitalization that lasted from April 15 to May 8, 1970 the number of times Molly Hoyt regurgitated?" Urbanski asked.

"The nurses note twenty times when she did regurgitate, and they stated that the amount she regurgitated was between three cc's, which would be half a teaspoon, to a hundred-twenty cc's, which is four ounces. The median amount of her vomiting was forty-five cc's, which is an ounce and a half. . . . To me this is significant because nurses don't usually make note of little bits of spitting-up when they're burping babies."

Now, apnea. She found significance in some of the early nurses' notes from Upstate. "Nurses in general don't note apnea, just like parents don't note apnea, because all babies have periods when they don't breathe, but they're brief and not very frequent. Here is a nurse who says not just apnea but 'many apnea spells.' To me that means the baby stopped breathing many times." At the prosecution table, Peggy Drake, who would do the cross-examination, made a note to ask Kelly a few questions to demonstrate that this was a research setting, and the nurses had been instructed to put everything down, significant or not.

Kelly read a section of Molly's record in which Thelma Schneider had noted, a day after the baby's first admission, that she had breathed periodically. Urbanski asked why this was important. "In the studies that I have done," Kelly said, "I have found an increased amount of periodic breathing in children who have siblings who died of SIDS and in children who have had an apparent life-threatening event and have subsequently died."

"What in your opinion is the clinical picture the child presents to you?" Urbanski asked.

"This is a child who, according to the notes, I would consider having significant problems with apnea, most of it sleep apnea. This baby ought to be tested and treated."

Urbanski led Kelly on a similar review of Noah's records, by the end of which she had portrayed four of the five Hoyt children as abnormal and vaguely unhealthy. All except Jimmy. As he and Miller had decided, throughout the long and painstaking direct examination, Urbanski never mentioned his name, nor did Kelly.

"Now, Doctor," Urbanski said, moving into the climax of Kelly's testimony, "have you been involved in the observation and treatment of families where there have been multiple occurrences of unexpected deaths?"

As part of her preparation for the trial, Kelly had reviewed her files all the way back to the time when she began working under Daniel Shannon as a resident in the pediatric ICU at Mass General. "Since 1974," she told the jury, "I have taken care of twenty-nine families where there have been at least two infants who have died of SIDS. And I have cared for the third infant or the fourth infant and even the fifth infant." Of those twenty-nine babies from families with prior multiple deaths, five went on to die themselves, she said. But even among the babies who did not die, nearly all of them had episodes of apnea.

"To what do you attribute this?" Urbanski asked.

"To an abnormal parasympathetic nervous system, to excess tone of the vagus nerve."

"To what?"

"To excess tone of the vagus nerve or in the parasympathetic nervous system," Kelly repeated. "I can tell you about several families."

The first one she picked had four deaths. "The child was referred to us where two previous siblings had died. His studies in the laboratory showed frequent prolonged apnea. And he was discharged on a monitor, but subsequently had a severe episode, came back into the hospital, and did die as a consequence of that episode. The next child born into that family—they were living in Pennsylvania at that time—was in the backseat of the car, in a car seat in the middle of traffic, the mother looked back and saw her cyanotic, or blue. She stopped the car, jumped out, jumped into the backseat. The consequence was that this infant died. The next infant that was born into the family, the fifth one—they had moved back to the Massachusetts area—was referred to us and he had abnormal studies. He was monitored and he had two episodes during monitoring requiring resuscitation and another two requiring vigorous stimulation. And he survived. . . . I have two other families with similar histories but only having three babies involved. . . ."

"Doctor Kelly," Urbanski said, "there has been testimony as to the odds of unexpected death beyond three children in a family being so phantasmagorical as to be beyond calculation. Do you agree with that?"

"No, I don't agree with that. In general, there are families with one baby that dies of SIDS and none of their other babies have problems at all and don't die. But then we have family clustering, and these are the families I have mentioned where there are two to five children involved. . . ."

"And it is based upon the studies of cases that you yourself have personally dealt with."

"Yes."

"Thank you, Doctor."

Simpson, Drake, and Courtright dashed for their conference room and shut the door. Their medical people hadn't said anything about any vagus nerve. "I'm not worried about the regurgitation," Simpson said. "Anybody who's had a kid knows that's bullshit." But there must be *something* to this vagus nerve—she couldn't be just making it up. Simpson, though, knew they were in no position to mount a safe and intelligent cross-examination. The best course was to leave it alone and bring in a rebuttal witness to deal with it after the defense rested. For now, they'd go after what they did know about.

"Isn't it true, Doctor, that many babies under the age of four weeks old regurgitate?" Drake asked when they resumed.

"That's not true," Kelly said.

"It's not true?"

"I'm—excuse me. They may do small spits with their burps. That's common. But actually to regurgitate an ounce to two ounces is not common under four weeks of age."

"But after four weeks of age it is common?"

"It occurs in children that have gastroesophogeal reflux. It's not the majority of babies, but it may be a third of babies. So in that sense it would be common."

Under Drake's questioning, Kelly also acknowledged that many of her assumptions about the Hoyt babies were based on information that was, under the circumstances, open to question—on what their mother had told Steinschneider. "I assumed it was true," Kelly said.

"Did you at any time question whether or not it was true?"

"I think a physician has to always question whether or not the history is true. The nature of her description made me believe that they were true because the same types of words and phrases were being used that my patients' parents use."

Kelly's allusion to her own patients provided Drake with a perfect segue. "Doctor, I have an article that you wrote with a Dr. Oren and a Dr. Shannon. . . ." The young assistant prosecutor began challenging Kelly's research with Shannon as few had—asking questions that the members of the NIH consensus panel, for instance, had carefully avoided a decade before. The meaning of their provocative data about familial SIDS had always stayed within the bounds of polite scientific discussion, but when the unraveling of Steinschneider's H. case brought their shared theory into the less tactful venue of criminal justice, it was inevitable that the case would cast its long, retrospective shadow upon the Harvard team's families too. The most intriguing were those included in the article that Peggy Drake now held in her hands— the paper Kelly, Shannon, and research fellow Joseph Oren published in 1987 about four families with fourteen SIDS deaths between them.

". . . And as a conclusion of that article," Drake was saying, "you gave a death rate for siblings of SIDS where there were two or more SIDS victims in one family. And the percentage is seventeen-point-nine percent." She asked Kelly how she explained the disparity between that frighteningly high figure and the risk, less than one percent, to babies born into families with only one prior SIDS death.

"It has been my experience that there are families where multiple children have signs of vagus nerve overactivity," Kelly said. "And these children are at risk of death."

"And in fact I think you even made a notation in your article that this small number of families was altering the risk factor, the death rate."

"For the subsequent sibs death rate. I believe that, though I can't prove it."

"And would you agree with me that there is certainly disagreement in the medical community whether or not two subsequent siblings of SIDS raises the risk of death by SIDS?"

"In terms of all the physicians that I am familiar with who actually take care of these infants, the third infant, they are all very careful with them. They all believe the third infant would be at higher risk than a regular first-born child without any family history of SIDS."

"How about forensic pathologists?"

"I'm not in contact with them."

"Doctor, isn't it quite possible that these children are victims of homicide?" Drake asked.

"These children who have symptoms of autonomic nervous system dysfunction have an illness," Kelly insisted. "Any child can be killed, there's no question about it. They're helpless."

"Is it possible that they could be the victims of a homicide?" Drake pressed.

"Any child could be. We're talking about children here who have symptoms of a disease that could lead to death."

Drake asked Kelly about the family whose third child died in the hospital after coming in barely alive, and whose fourth child died in traffic. "In both of these instances you were speaking to the parent about what had happened. Is that correct?"

"That's correct, but don't forget that the third child had been tested and was abnormal. He *had* prolonged apnea."

"I understand that, Doctor, but you were taking her word for what had occurred for both of those episodes and now they died."

"A physician does that with every history that he takes or she takes."

Drake asked if it wasn't important to completely investigate the circumstances of such deaths. Yes, Kelly said. "And is it important also when you're dealing with these multiple deaths in one family, is it important to consider whether the children were in the company of one particular parent when they died? Is that of significance?"

"If you're alluding to Munchausen's by proxy, which is—"

"I'm asking you to answer my particular question," Drake cut in sharply, scrambling to keep the syndrome, and possibly an excuse for acquittal, out of the jury's consciousness. "Is it important to look at it? To look at who is present with the child when the child dies?"

"Yes, it is."

"And is it significant if it is one parent or one person each particular time?"

"It can be significant and you do consider it."

"Are you denying that it is possible that all five of the [Hoyt] children were victims of homicide?"

"No."

"In considering multiple deaths in one family, would you also consider it significant that children die the day after they are released from the hospital?"

"That I would consider significant."

"And why is that significant?"

"Because you would wonder why. With [Noah] I think it was approximately twelve hours after discharge. Noah had such a severe episode that it caused his death. And in the hospital he had not had that. However, on the other side of that, it's the experience of many physicians now across the country of children having significant apneic events in the home. It's recorded and we know it happens."

"We're talking about Molly and Noah. Noah's events were not recorded. Correct?"

"Correct."

Drake asked about the episodes that kept sending Molly and Noah back to Upstate—six admissions and readmissions between them. "Isn't it possible, Dr. Kelly, that these episodes that occurred at home in the presence of the mother were in fact caused by the mother? Isn't that a possibility?"

"That is a possibility."

"Aren't there cases in the literature where the parents will continue to bring their children back to the hospital after life-threatening episodes of apnea and continue to bring them back, and it's later been proven that those episodes were caused by the parent?"

"I haven't done a review on that, a research review, but I think there are only two cases in the literature."

"Two that you are aware of, correct?" By now, the world literature included dozens of cases.

"Yeah," Kelly said, "I haven't done a review on that."

She stepped down and was on her way back to Texas by sundown. A few days later, Miller received the invoice for her day's testimony and its preparation, which included a phone conversation with Steinschneider. The bill came to $7,000, for a total fee of more than $15,000. Miller was outraged. He could only imagine the reaction he would get from the people who ran one of the poorest counties in New York State. "I'm not paying a penny of it," he said. "And I hope she sues me in Tioga County Court."

37

"I look like the village idiot!" Simpson fumed in the middle of the courtroom when he found out about Charles Ewing. Out of the presence of the jury, Judge Sgueglia was holding an impromptu hearing on what he plainly considered a deception by the defense. Well before the trial, Sgueglia had asked Miller if he planned to present a psychiatric case to defend his client; if he did, the defense attorney would have to say so well in advance of the trial to give the prosecution time to have its own expert examine Waneta. Miller had said he had no psychiatric defense in mind. Now, in the middle of the trial, Miller had said, almost as an aside, that he planned to bring in a forensic psychologist to help attack the confession. The judge ordered him to hand over a copy of Ewing's report on Waneta, a blueprint of his testimony. As a result of several personality disorders, Ewing had concluded, "Mrs. Hoyt was particularly vulnerable to, and succumbed to, the interrogative techniques used by the officers who questioned her."

It wasn't a conventional psychiatric defense, Miller contended, because Ewing would not be testifying about Waneta's state of mind during any alleged crimes—only during her police interrogation. His testimony would be restricted to whether she had given her statement "knowingly and voluntarily." Miller turned the floor over to Urbanski, who breathlessly cited a string of case law establishing, he asserted, that no notice was required for the testimony they planned. Ewing would be like any other defense witness. But Miller knew otherwise. He had always felt the Ewing plan could only work if he caught Simpson off guard, denying him the chance to counter the opinion with his own expert. Now, as he had also predicted, Simpson was livid. The prosecutor complained to Sgueglia that he'd been had—Miller had "perpetrated a fraud on me and the court." For a year, they had skirmished over one matter or another that threatened the collegial way they had long done business, but now Simpson was beside himself. "They've had nine months to get an expert; I get nine hours," he told Sgueglia. "I'll have to delay the case and the jury will wonder why the D.A. screwed up." He said there was only one remedy: Bar Ewing from testifying.

Sgueglia was annoyed that Miller had been less than forthright and irritated that he'd been put in this position. But when he made his ruling the next day, the judge seemed unsure about what the law really was on the issue of notice in the case of a psychological defense against a confession. He decided that punishing Miller by excluding Ewing would not be fair to Miller's client. He would allow Ewing to testify, but he would also cancel court for Friday to give Simpson a chance to have Waneta examined by his own expert, who could then be called on rebuttal. And he warned Miller and Urbanski that if Ewing's testimony strayed even an inch beyond the scope of Waneta's state of mind during the confession, he would be all over them. Don't press the boundary, the judge said sternly. The defense lawyers promised they wouldn't. They were ecstatic about the judge's ruling. "We've been planning that for months," Urbanski said gleefully a few minutes later.

Simpson had only a couple of days to prepare his cross-examination of Ewing and to find his own expert, have him review the case and interview Waneta. Even at that, it would seem cursory compared with the twenty hours Ewing had spent with her. The situation only intensified the stress the trial was heaping on Simpson. He had a reputation for not getting overwrought about his job, but by the end of the third week of the trial, he was suffering from stomach pains and relentless headaches. He felt a tremendous burden to bring a conviction. Not only had he come to look upon the case with a good deal of righteousness; he recoiled at the thought that an acquittal might leave the impression that he had prosecuted—persecuted—an innocent woman, and at great expense to the taxpayers. He also recognized that some people perceived that he was merely prosecuting Bill Fitzpatrick's case, so that even a conviction held the possibility that Fitzpatrick, in the end, as he had since the beginning, would have the credit and the glory.

Simpson scrambled back to his office and called Joel Dvoskin, the forensic psychologist who headed the state mental health agency in Albany. Hearing about the situation with Ewing, whom he knew, Dvoskin was surprised that the defense hadn't used him at the suppression hearing. (Miller had concluded that nothing would convince Sgueglia to throw out the confession. He didn't want to sacrifice the surprise strategy in a lost cause.) Simpson faxed a copy of Ewing's report to Dvoskin, who called back with some ideas about cross-examination. "You be Ewing and I'll be you," he told Simpson, then posed several questions he thought would take advantage of Ewing's contention that the police had treated Waneta not too harshly but too gently. "They're trying to portray her as pathetic—don't fight it, embrace it," Dvoskin told Simpson. "Yes, she's a pathetic person, and one of the pathetic things she did was kill her children. You have to get the jury to believe the unbelievable." Dvoskin recommended Simpson send the defendant to a forensic psychiatrist at the University of Rochester named Dr. David John Barry.

On Friday, Miller and Urbanski drove Waneta up to Barry's office. Peggy Drake represented the prosecution. Simpson, meanwhile, spent the day off trying to line up a witness to rebut Dorothy Kelly. He wound up on the phone with John Brooks. Would you mind coming back to talk about the vagus nerve for about five minutes? he asked. Brooks agreed, and Simpson arranged for a state police plane to fly Brooks back from New Hampshire after the defense rested.

Phil Jordan, the psychic from Candor, had become one of Waneta's favorite supporters. After Friday's examination by Dr. Barry, he asked her how it had gone. "There wasn't a dry eye in the house," she said. To those closest to her, the flip remark was not unusual. The Waneta that few people knew had always had a taste for the caustic comment.

She was often in good spirits during the trial, though it was not the face she presented in public. "In the morning before going in, she was always laughing and jolly," her brother-in-law George later observed. "Then the minute she got to the steps of the courthouse, it was like she flipped a switch." As the trial wore on, George came to the conclusion that Waneta was in complete control and that she reveled in the limelight. At one point early on, she asked him to guard her closely as she made her way to and from court. "She said somebody was gonna take a shot at her," he said. For a few days, George dutifully took on the role of Waneta's bodyguard, but he was soon struck by the thought that he was being used. "She'd been in the papers and the TV for a year, and that was getting to be old hat. She was looking for more." On Monday morning, she would have her opportunity. She would take the stand in her own defense. Tim would follow her. And then, Jay.

On Saturday, Tim drove Waneta to Waverly to go over her testimony with Miller and Urbanski. The preparation took several hours, though the strategy wasn't very complicated. Waneta insisted she didn't kill her children; the state police had made it up and persuaded her to agree. "If that's what happened, that's what you tell them," Urbanski said. Miller was more succinct. He told her to just stick to her story: Keep denying it—and cry when you do it. For the lawyers, it had been a long and grueling year, and they were out of ideas.

Waneta was confident the jury would believe her. Most of the people she knew believed her. Their support was her ongoing preoccupation. One day, she hugged her brother-in-law Chuck. He stiffened. She'd never done that before. She kept after Urbanski to make sure he was with her. "You still believe in me, Ray, don't you?" she'd ask.

On Monday morning, an edge of anticipation filled the air of the courthouse as several dozen spectators, the largest crowd of the trial, gathered to hear Waneta Hoyt speak publicly for the first time. It promised to be the dramatic high point of the trial, a rousing counterpoint to the thicket of medical minutiae that had characterized much of the testimony thus far. Here was the mother herself. What might she say about all this? Would she seem as pitiable as she looked, or would another image emerge?

All eyes upon her, Waneta received a larger than usual contingent of well-wishers from her end of the county as she arrived in the courtroom and waited to take the stand. Her teenaged niece Penny presented her with a bouquet of flowers. Aunt Neta was always a favorite of Penny's. Waneta took her usual seat at the defense table, her hand in Tim's. She wore a black dress with little white dots and a cream-colored jacket. Around her neck hung a large crucifix. In the pocket of her jacket she carried an embroidered handkerchief.

"Call Waneta Hoyt to the stand," Urbanski announced shortly after 9:30, and Waneta slowly made her way across the carpeted area in front of the judge. She leaned on the bench as she climbed to the witness seat and took the oath. Urbanski asked her to state her name. "And I'm going to ask you, Waneta, if you can throw your voice out as far as you can so that we can all hear you, okay?" he said. He wanted the jurors to join him in thinking of Waneta as a fragile person.

"Waneta Ethel Hoyt," she said tightly. The jurors gazed at her intently.

Where the medical experts had recited their impressive credentials, Waneta offered the strands of her simple life. Led by Urbanski, the lawyer to whom she gravitated, she revealed the vital statistics of her world in the manner of an uncomfortable, subdued woman. He asked her to point out her husband and her son, and to tell her son's age. He asked her to talk about her health. "Well," she said, "I'm diabetic. And I take medicine for osteoporosis, blood pressure, angina. And I take arthritis medicine. I have Nitrostat, Tenex, colchicine, Toradol." He led her through a detailed recitation of every medical condition she could remember since childhood, from rheumatic fever to the type of glasses she wore.

As she spoke, Bill Fitzpatrick and Pete Tynan walked in the side door and quietly took seats in the middle of the gallery. Simpson's concerns had eased; he'd decided to call Fitzpatrick and invite him to see Waneta's day on the witness stand. Murmurs spread among the press corps.

"... and I have a heart murmur."

Waneta described her family background, her schooling, her close relationship with her mother, how devastated she was when she was killed in a car accident in 1989. "It was just like my life was over," Waneta said through tears that lasted into the next question. "It tore me apart."

Urbanski worked the edges of Charles Ewing's coming testimony. In a sense, he was setting up the psychologist who was the defense's last best hope. When Urbanski asked Waneta if she had involved herself in school activities as a child, she said no. When he asked why not, she said, "I don't like being in crowds." She said she left a job at Endicott Johnson because she "couldn't stand the pressure." But the inconsistencies of her personality sometimes filtered through. After explaining how insecure she'd always been around people, she recalled how she had met Tim on the school bus that day in 1960. "I told him I was going to marry him someday," she said. A certain willfulness began to come through, not at all what many people had expected—or what her lawyers wanted the jury to see.

"Waneta," Urbanski asked, "during those early years of your marriage, and for that matter throughout your marriage, could you describe to us, in your own words, your relationship to your husband?" He wanted the jurors to consider two things about Tim: Waneta's dependence on him—another setup for Ewing—and the presumption that if she had killed their children, surely he would have known about it and wouldn't be at her side now.

"We were very close," Waneta said.

"Would you say he was at that time the closest person to you?"

"Yes."

"Mrs. Hoyt, do you drive a car?"

"I used to drive all the time. I don't drive much anymore."

"Why is that?"

"I just ... my back bothers me a lot. And I just can't stand to drive. And lots of time I fall asleep."

Now Urbanski began asking Waneta about the babies. First, as always, was Eric. "He was sort of blue a lot of the time and we'd take him to the doctor," she said. "And then one time he had a real spell, and we took him in the ambulance to the hospital."

Urbanski asked her to describe Eric's death. "I was feeding him his breakfast, and he started turning blue and gagging," she said. "And I didn't know what was wrong. And I ran out to get the neighbor across the street. And she came over, she said, 'I don't know if I can be of much help, but I'll see what I can do.' And the ambulance people took him, and I don't know what happened after they took him. I was just shocked, I didn't know what was wrong."

James was born next, with "something wrong with his heart," she said. "Because the doctor checked him over and I asked him what was wrong. And he said, well, he didn't think it was anything serious."

"And after James's birth can you tell us what your life was like?" Urbanski asked.

"Well, we were happy. We had a nice little boy."

"Did you attend church back in those days?"

"Yes."

Julie was born in the summer of 1968, Waneta told the jury. She was fine until the day she died just seven weeks later. "Well, she was in her little chair, sitting at the table. I was feeding her cereal. And she just started turning blue around the lips. She started choking. And I ran outside and this garbageman was coming by, and I flagged him down, and I told Jimmy to sit on the couch. So he went over and sat on the couch."

A terrible thought struck some in the courtroom. Jimmy was there. And three weeks later he was dead, too. *He saw something he wasn't supposed to see,* George Hoyt thought.

"And in your own words, Mrs. Hoyt, can you describe for us the circumstances as to how James died?" Urbanski asked.

"Well, I was in the bathroom and I had just gave him his breakfast, and he was sitting at the table. And I was getting dressed and I heard this screaming for Mommy, and I stepped out in the hallway, and he collapsed coming into the hallway to me. And I didn't know what was wrong, so I picked him up, and I went down to my neighbor to get some help. Because I didn't know what was happening.... I think Morris Lyons was there. They started mouth-to-mouth resuscitation on him. And they worked on him for almost an hour. And then, finally Dr. Hartnagel arrived and he told them to stop working because he was gone."

"... And can you tell us how it came about that you and Tim went to see Dr. Steinschneider?" Urbanski asked, moving on to Molly.

"Well, she had a breathing spell in early April, where she would turn all blue. And I called Dr. Perry and told him what was happening." Perry sent them to Syracuse, Waneta remembered, and Steinschneider put the baby into his research.

"How did you feel about her having been admitted?"

"I was terrified, because I didn't know what was wrong. He sent her home on a monitor machine and we couldn't bring her home until we had an air conditioner." She returned Molly to the hospital a few days later, she remembered. "She set the machine off a lot.... She went into one of the deep breathing episodes and I had to resuscitate her. I called the ambulance and they took us to Syracuse."

What were the visits like in the hospital? Urbanski asked. Waneta recounted them in a stoic monotone. "Well, sometimes when we got there, Dr. Steinschneider was in the lab, checking her, so we'd go to the lab and talk with him. Then when he got done, we took her back to the nursery, we talked to her, hung on to her. We'd feed her. Take pictures."

"Did there come a time when Molly was discharged on that second occasion?"

"Yes."

"Do you recall when that was?"

"It was the day before she died. June third or fourth, seventy."

"Can you describe to us, Waneta, in your own words, how it was that Molly died?"

"Well, the machine went off. I don't remember what I was doing. And when I got to her, she was out, bluish-pink color, just real funny looking. And I called Tim's mother, she came over and then I called Dr. Steinschneider, then I started mouth-to-mouth resuscitation, and the ambulance people came, and they took over."

And Noah. "He was born on Mother's Day, May 9, 1971. . . . And we took him right straight to Syracuse, to Dr. Steinschneider." His death twelve weeks later: "Well, he was in his bassinet and the alarm went off on the machine. And I went to him, and he was cyanotic, he was just, like he was lifeless. I immediately picked him up and did mouth-to-mouth resuscitation and I called for the ambulance, and I don't remember who came first. And I remember they called for Dr. Scott and Dr. Scott came."

"What happened then?"

"Dr. Scott said he was gone."

"Waneta, during the period that you described here, after you began taking Molly and Noah to Upstate Medical Center, did you work closely throughout that period with Dr. Steinschneider?"

"Yes."

"After the death of your children, and the contact that you had with Dr. Steinschneider, did you and your husband consider having more children?"

"No. We decided we better not have any, because we felt that it might be hereditary."

"Did you take, or did Tim take any steps to prevent further children from being born?"

"Yes. Had a vasectomy done."

"Did there come a time after this that you and Tim gave consideration to adopting a child?"

"Yes, Dr. Steinschneider suggested that we adopt a child immediately."

Waneta said she and Tim took this advice. "Because we wanted a child," she said when Urbanski asked why. He led her into the story of Scotty, the nine-month-old given to them by the county just before Thanksgiving, 1971.

"Did you ultimately adopt Scotty?" Urbanski asked Waneta.

"No."

"All right. And why was that?"

"We had him, he came, and we just wasn't ready to handle a little baby yet. We couldn't sleep because we were afraid he would go to sleep and not wake up. And we were just terrified. So we called them and told them we just wasn't ready to handle a child right now."

At the prosecution table, Simpson and Drake were discreetly thrilled—and stunned that Urbanski had opened this door, knowing that the records suggested a far less innocent scenario. Like the defense lawyers, the prosecutors had only known about the episode since the mental health records arrived a few weeks before the start of the trial. Simpson had then interviewed Alberta Weisz, the adoption caseworker who was now retired, and planned to bring her in to testify about the morning Waneta, distraught, called her to take the baby back. He came close—he had Weisz come to court one day toward the end of his case—but then Sgueglia ruled that the testimony would be prejudicial. But now it was the defense that was bringing up the Scotty incident. For Simpson, it was a gift he could not have anticipated. Now, he could unearth the damaging records on cross-examination.

Urbanski asked Waneta about the child she eventually did adopt.

"Waneta, was there anything different about the adoption with Jay that made that work, as opposed to the adoption of Scotty?"

"No, we were just ready for the child. He made our life. We felt complete."

Now Urbanski moved on to the heart of the matter: the morning of March 23, 1994, when Bobby Bleck asked her to come down to Owego with Susan Mulvey. For the jurors, the question was simple: Was she telling the truth that day, or was she telling the truth now?

"Were you suspicious in any way?" Urbanski asked.

"No," Waneta said. "Because they said it was a SIDS research project."

She didn't pay much attention to the Miranda warnings. "We all sat down, and Investigator Courtright asked Bobby if he had that little card. And Bobby said, 'Well, I guess I do.' He got his wallet out and he got out this card. I asked him what that was for. And Susan Mulvey spoke up and said, 'Well, that's just procedure for any interviews that we have.' So I didn't think any more about it."

"Had you ever heard of these rights being read to people by police, on television or what-not?"

"No, sir. I don't like to watch those kind of shows."

"And before that day, Mrs. Hoyt, had you ever had any contact with the legal system, with the courts?"

"In 1973."

"And can you tell us how that came about?"

"Do I have to?"

"I prefer you do, yes."

"I was raped."

She'd pressed charges against her neighbor, Waneta said, but ultimately decided to drop them after two or three appearances in court. "I just couldn't handle the questions," she explained. "I couldn't handle the pressures of all you high-society people."

Urbanski brought her back to the interview room in Owego. Waneta said she explained to the investigators how her children had died, just as she had this morning in court. "And then Susan Mulvey and Bobby Bleck switched chairs. . . . And she said now we have to talk. And I said, 'Yeah, what about?' She said, 'Well, we have concrete medical proof that all your babies were suffocated.' And I says, *what*? And she says, 'Yeah, we have this proof, and being you was the only one there, it was you.' And I looked at Bobby Bleck, and I says, 'Bobby, do you believe this?' And he throws his hands in the air and says, 'Who am I?' And I says, 'Well, I couldn't have done anything like that. Who could do anything that horrible?' " Her voice broke on the last word. She dabbed her eyes with the handkerchief, and each time she did this, the stillness of the courtroom was broken by the sound of camera motors.

". . . And she picked out one of the children's names and asked, suggested I used a pillow. She says, did you take a pillow and lay it over [James's] face? And I said no, I didn't do that. That's terrible, who would do such a terrible thing? She went to Eric, I think. And she suggested I used a pillow over Eric and wanted to know if I was on the couch. And I kept saying, 'No. I told you this morning how he died. I was feeding him and he turned all blue.' . . . And then she suggested Julie, she said, 'Did you hold Julie up to your shoulder like this?' and I said, no, I didn't do that. And I kept shaking my head no, no, I didn't. I didn't kill my babies." Her words were riding soft cries now. "She said I must have done it because they have this concrete medical proof, and I said, no, I didn't. I didn't. And she just kept at me for I don't know how long. And I finally says, 'Yeah, I guess I did. If you say I did.' "

"Why did you say that?" Urbanski asked sympathetically.

"Because I couldn't stand the pressure. I just wanted her to leave me alone so I could go home."

"How were you feeling at that point in time?"

"I was in shock. I couldn't . . . I was just in shock. I just couldn't believe they were accusing me of killing my kids after all these years. There was police there back then, they investigated, they went through my house." She said she didn't remember signing the statement. "I don't remember anything at all. I remember Tim walking in. And I told him that they said I killed the kids. And then he started shouting something, he started shouting at them, but I don't know what he said."

"At the time you made these statements to Investigator Mulvey, what were you thinking?"

"I wasn't. I was just . . . gone."

"Why did you make these statements?"

"I don't know."

She said she didn't remember anything about the stenographic statement, either.

"Realizing that you are under oath, Mrs. Hoyt, could I ask you, did you kill any of your children?"

"No, I did not."

"I have no further questions, Your Honor."

Simpson came out swinging. He wanted to show the jury that beneath the veneer of this forlorn-looking woman was coldness and calculation. Against Urbanski's gentle questioning, Simpson's cross-examination seemed especially brusque. His words came at her rapid-fire.

"Define a crowd for me, in terms of pressure, would you, Mrs. Hoyt?"

"A crowd?"

"Yes."

"Too many in here right now."

"You're under enormous pressure right now."

"Yes."

"And how is that reflecting itself? How would we know that you're under enormous pressure?"

"Whether you can see it, I don't know. But I'm uncomfortable."

"You're not having any trouble recalling events."

"I'm trying to remember."

"You're not having any trouble speaking."

"No, sir."

"You're not having any difficulty understanding what I'm saying to you."

"Not yet."

"You didn't have any difficulty understanding what Mr. Urbanski was saying to you."

"Not yet."

"So how does it manifest itself?"

"I don't know. I'm just uncomfortable with a lot of people."

"And what happens when you become uncomfortable with a lot of people?"

"It's time to leave."

"Pardon me?"

"I leave. Except I can't now, obviously."

"Do you lie when there's a lot of people around?"

"Why would I lie?"

Simpson continued asking question after question designed to show that Waneta was sharper, more capable of taking care of herself, and quicker on her feet, than she would have the jury believe. "You're telling me what you think right now," Simpson said. "Are you having any difficulty—"

"Because I have to," she cut in.

"Okay. So you're not having any difficulty telling me what you think."

"Well, you're asking me questions."

"And you don't feel any pressure from me to tell a lie, do you?"

"No, I won't tell a lie."

"And you don't feel any pressure from me to agree with what I say to you, do you?"

"It depends on what you want me to agree to."

"You apparently have enough backbone to tell me if I'm saying something that's untrue."

"Yes, sir."

Simpson asked Waneta to read the Miranda rights aloud from a copy of the card Bleck had used. She read each line, and affirmed that she understood it. Then he asked Waneta a series of questions about her perceptions of what was going on when she encountered the police that day. He especially wanted to correct the idea that she had been asked to help with a SIDS "research project." Yes, she said, she understood Bleck, Mulvey, and Courtright were police officers. Yes, she knew that among the functions of the police was the investigation of crime. "And you at no time were introduced to any SIDS research people who claimed to be doctors or anything like that." No, sir, said Waneta. "So now you're telling us that the police come to your house or the Berkshire post office and want to discuss SIDS research with you and that doesn't kind of trigger an alarm in your head?"

"No, she said it was a project, a doctor was doing research."

". . . Were you ordered to go?"

"No, sir, I was asked to go."

"Isn't it a fact, Mrs. Hoyt, that during the entire period of time you were with the New York State Police, nobody raised their voice to you?"

"No, sir."

"Nobody threatened you in any way."

"No, sir, they wouldn't let me go when I wanted to go."

"Well, we'll get to that in a minute. You can explain that to your heart's content. Don't forget that thought, because I want you to tell us—well, let's do it right now. When did you tell the police you wanted to go?"

"Right after I got through in the morning."

"And it's kind of odd you didn't testify to that, as I recall, when Mr. Urbanski was speaking to you."

"Because I forgot."

Simpson asked her to read her written statement. "You have no recollection of giving that statement," he said.

"No, sir."

"So if you told the police that you in fact suffocated your children, three of them with a pillow, one with a towel, and one up against your chest, you may have told them that?"

"I may have, but I don't remember."

"So rather than Investigator Mulvey making it up, she may have been relying on what you told her, is that a fact?"

"Possibly."

Waneta returned to the stand after the lunch recess with a faraway look about her. She answered Simpson's questions as directly as before, but she was staring straight ahead, as if into a fixed point in space. Yes, she told Simpson, she had read over her transcribed statement to the police. "I didn't say any of this, no," she said.

"You didn't say any of it," Simpson said with a note of incredulity.

"She suggested it," Waneta said.

"Investigator Mulvey suggested it."

"She suggested that's what I did, yes."

"And now, what are we referring to when you say, 'She suggested'?"

"She suggested that I put the pillow over the baby's face."

"Which baby?"

"Eric."

"Okay," Simpson said. "What else did she suggest?"

"That I held Julie into my shoulder."

"Okay. What else?"

"That I used a pillow on Molly and Noah."

"All right. And what else did Investigator Mulvey suggest?"

"That I took the bath towel and suffocated James."

"Explain to us how she did this."

"She just kept asking me, and I kept telling her no. And she kept suggesting that's what I did. . . . She said, 'You took the towel and laid it over his face.' And I said, no, I did not." It was the same for the others. "I kept saying no, I didn't do such a horrible thing."

Simpson asked Waneta who was present at her children's deaths. "Was anyone ever present other than Mrs. Waneta Hoyt?"

Yes, Waneta said. Her mother-in-law was there for Molly. Tim was there for Julie. Dr. Scott for Noah. Floyd Angel for Molly. . . .

"He's the coroner who pronounced your child dead," Simpson snapped, interrupting for clarification.

"Dr. Hartnagel," Waneta said, continuing the list.

"Dr. Hartnagel arrived and pronounced more than one of your children dead. I'm asking who was present when these children had their apparent life-threatening events. When they turned blue and cyanotic, when you had to give them mouth-to-mouth, who was present?"

"Well, I was, but I was trying to save them."

"Who else?"

"The child."

"Who else?"

"I don't remember anyone else."

"So you were the only one that was ever present. . . ."

"Well, my husband worked so he couldn't, obviously, couldn't be there."

"Now, you talked about adopting a child, a child by the name of Scotty." For most of the year since Waneta's arrest, the incident had remained buried in the files at the county mental health office. Indeed, only a handful of people ever knew about it—the Hoyts, Alberta Weisz, the psychiatrist Mokarram Jafri and psychologist Miriam Elkin, and Alfred Steinschneider. But Waneta's lawyers had inadvertently made the episode part of her trial.

"If I told you that Scotty was placed in your home on November 15, 1971, would you dispute that?" Simpson asked.

"I don't know, because I don't remember the time," Waneta replied.

"If I told you that your psychiatrist told you to get the child out of your house on November 25, 1971, would you dispute that?"

"I don't know."

Peggy Drake looked toward the defense table, waiting for an objection.

"If I told you that you told your psychiatrist that you were going to do harm to this child, would you dispute that?" Simpson asked.

A wave of whispers crossed the courtroom. Still no objection from Urbanski.

"I don't know," Waneta said.

"Did you tell your psychiatrist and your mental health worker to get the child out of your house before you wrang its neck?"

Oh my God, a woman in the second row whispered.

"I don't know," Waneta said.

"Is it possible you did?"

"No."

"Did you call Alberta Weisz of the Tioga County Department of Social Services on the weekend and tell her to get that child out of your house before you did it harm?" Simpson asked, his questions coming fast now. Urbanski seemed paralyzed.

"No."

"You deny that?" Simpson barked.

"I don't deny calling her."

"You deny saying that?"

"I deny . . . I didn't say that, no."

"What *did* you say?"

"I called her and told her that we weren't ready to handle the child yet. It was too soon after Noah dying."

"Didn't you tell her that you might harm the child?" Simpson pressed.

"No, I didn't."

"Did you tell Dr. Jafri that you had evil thoughts, and that you were going to wring the child's neck?"

"No."

"So if the mental health records say otherwise, you would dispute that, is that correct?"

"I don't remember saying anything like that."

With this powerful incident hanging in the air, Simpson mounted his final assault. For this, he came back to Jimmy. Simpson wanted to press this particular death. "And you indicated," he said, ". . . that you placed a towel over the face of James, and that he thrashed around and tried to save his own life. You had him down, you were on your knees, holding him. Do you remember reading that in your statement?"

"I read it there, yes."

"You were holding him, he fought for his life. Do you remember that?"

"No," Waneta said, "because I carried him to the neighbor's."

"You told the police that, did you not?"

"I don't recall."

"Are you saying Mrs. Mulvey made that up?"

"She suggested that's what I did."

"She suggested you were down on your knees cradling Jimmy and holding the towel to his face until he quit struggling and died?"

"Yes."

"And you were in there in front of stenographer Callahan, within a half hour of that, and you repeated word for word what Investigator Mulvey had said."

"I don't remember."

"Well, you may not remember, but isn't that the implication of what you're saying?"

"I said I don't remember."

"So, for all you know, it could have been somebody else that made that statement in your absence and these people typed it up and this is all a fabrication. Is that what you're telling us?"

"I said I don't know."

"You just don't have any idea."

"No," Waneta said, whimpering now.

"Isn't it a fact that you love attention, Mrs. Hoyt?" Simpson said, startling many people in the courtroom.

"No," Waneta replied calmly.

"Don't you love attention, you have to be the center of attention at all times?"

"No."

"Isn't it a fact that you couldn't stand to have these children around crying because you were no longer the center of your husband's universe?"

"They didn't cry all the time."

"You said in your statement they cried all the time, and that's why you killed them." Simpson was firing the questions at her now.

"I didn't kill them."

"You said in your statement they cried all the time, and that's why you killed them," he repeated.

"I didn't kill them."

"Don't you enjoy the attention you've gotten in connection with this trial, Mrs. Hoyt?"

"No, *sir*!"

"You haven't enjoyed it at all."

"No, sir."

"You're under intense pressure being here today."

"Yes, sir."

"You wish you were someplace else."

"Yes, sir."

"You're nervous."

"Yes."

"Well, you've handled it very well. That's all the questions I have."

Waneta stepped down, and slowly made her way back to her husband. She looked shell-shocked, defeated. But Simpson had succeeded in exposing her resolve. It was the observation of many in the courtroom that the better she handled the onslaught, the worse it was for her. Waneta had revealed herself to be a stronger woman than her physical appearance had led anyone to expect—and a craftier one.

If Waneta was an enigma, in his own way her husband was equally baffling to those who had followed the case. Now, he stepped to the stand in his wife's defense, the first of a string of witnesses who would buffer the impact of Waneta's testimony on the jury. Tim wore a plaid sportcoat for the occasion, instead of his usual black windbreaker. Answering Bob Miller's questions, he presented himself as a man who simply believed in his wife—always had, always would. With his solid bearing and downcast face, testifying in tones alternately indignant and clueless, he appeared as someone who had no trouble imagining a police conspiracy.

Miller asked Tim to tell the jury what happened when he was brought to the Owego barracks from Ithaca that day the previous spring. "I come over to my wife, and she was sobbing, very upset, and she said, 'They told me I killed my children.' And I said, 'Bull!' I confronted her with the situation because she was crying and she said to me, 'I did *not* do this thing. I did *not* do this.' "

Why did you sign the statement? Miller asked. "I was, excuse me, mad as hell. I was terribly upset, and when I was asked to sign it, I said, 'I sign in protest, damn it!' " He pounded his fist for emphasis. "But I didn't write, 'Damn it' or 'In protest' on it. I just made that statement."

Listening to the testimony on a television monitor behind the glass walls of the balcony, Bob Courtright and Bill Standinger shook their heads in denial. Down in the gallery, Bill Fitzpatrick muttered, "I'd indict him for perjury."

"What was your wife doing all this time?" Miller asked.

"She wasn't herself," Tim said. "I've known her for thirty-one years, and we've went through a lot. And Neta was not Neta. She was just out of it."

As he said this, some of the jurors looked over at Waneta and saw that she was staring straight ahead, as if in a trance. She certainly seemed out of it now.

Miller tried to use Tim as an antidote to some of Waneta's testimony: She and Tim had requested Jimmy's autopsy, Tim said—"after the other two died, we wanted to know *why*." They had returned Scotty because, despite Dr. Steinschneider's advice to adopt, it was too soon. "We didn't have time to get over losing the children. It just tore us up so much that we couldn't handle the fear that we were going to have something go wrong." Later, on Jay's adoption: "We did a lot of soul-searching about whether we wanted to go on with this idea, and we decided we did. . . . After three or four years—I'm not good at dates at all, I'm just terrible—they came up with a baby boy that was healthy, there was nothing wrong with him, and they told us to come on and take a look at him. And we fell in love with him."

Miller asked Tim if his wife was an attention seeker. "No, she's not an attention seeker," he said. "Whenever we go anywhere, we go, just us. Very rarely will she go by herself. As a rule, we do everything together. If we happen to go to a restaurant, and there's a lot of people there, we don't go in, she's not comfortable. I respect that, she just won't go."

Simpson, on cross-examination, questioned Tim hard on his wife's confession. "Mr. Hoyt, is that the kind of thing a mother is going to fabricate—'I suffocated my five children'?"

"She didn't do it, sir."

"Well that's unfortunately, or fortunately, a decision you're not going to have to make. You were not home when these children died, were you?"

"Most of them."

"You were not home when *any* of them died."

"I was there at the last one when the ambulance was there. Now whether they were dead or not, I don't know."

"You don't know how they died, do you," Simpson bellowed.

"No," Tim said, his voice rising in protest. "I can't tell you that. I'm not a doctor."

Jay Hoyt followed his father to the stand. A nice-looking young man with a polite manner, was the consensus of the women in the gallery. He testified that he'd graduated from high school the previous spring, now worked at Cornell feeding cows, that he lived with his parents. He recalled the events of the day his mother was arrested. "I've seen my mom crying before, but not like she was that night," he said. Jay's testimony had only one real point, as far as Miller was concerned. He wanted the jurors to have a look at the baby who grew up—who was here today. When he was through, Jay stopped at the defense table to hug his mother and father.

The long day of defense concluded with this image. In the late afternoon, Waneta and Tim ambled across the street to their car at the far end of the parking lot. They walked alone and apart, a foot or two and silence between them. In the morning, the defense would call its last witness: the forensic psychologist who thought Waneta Hoyt was innocent.

Charles Patrick Ewing had impeccable credentials: a doctorate in psychology from Cornell, along with a Harvard law degree. He was board-certified in forensic psychology, a tenured law professor, co-editor of the journal *Behav-*

ioral Sciences in the Law, author of five books, frequent courtroom expert, recipient of the 1993 Distinguished Contributions to Forensic Psychology Award. A few months before, *Time* magazine's cover story on the Susan Smith case in South Carolina quoted Ewing as a leading authority on child and infant murder. "Far more common than the sensational murders in Union County are the smaller deceptions practiced by mothers who claim that abused or neglected children died of SIDS or accidents," said *Time.* "They are also more perfect crimes. Charles Ewing, a law and psychology professor at the State University of New York at Buffalo, estimates that only half the country's abuse deaths are uncovered."

Ewing's defense of Waneta Hoyt would be the final curiosity of her trial.

At one of their sessions in Buffalo, Waneta had told Ewing something that he believed. "All the years I felt guilty, like I should've done something more, something to keep them alive," he quoted her as saying. "Like I should've got trained more, more medical training or something, CPR or something, something I could have done. We did things but we still felt we should've done more." Though Waneta's own testimony had cast her in a very different light, Ewing intended to portray her to the jury as a woman of such minute competence that she might well have been manipulated into falsely admitting that she had slain her five children. Though he believed that this was what had actually happened, he knew he wouldn't be permitted to say so to the jury. He was here to talk about the defendant's rights.

Ewing had a boyish face and a friendly, energetic air. He strode into the courtroom, reaching up to shake Judge Sgueglia's hand before entering the witness box. It was familiar territory for him. He told the jury he had testified four hundred times before. But it would soon become evident that he was more than a hired gun, that he had developed an emotional attachment to Waneta and to his findings that she was the victim here.

Ewing had seen her nine times, he told the jury, for a total of twenty-one hours. He had administered the 567 questions of the Minnesota Multiphasic Personality Inventory II test. "I read each and every question," he said. "And I recorded each and every answer." Over Simpson's objections, Ewing testified that his analysis showed that Waneta had "responded to these tests in an honest, straightforward fashion."

He spent a while describing the Waneta that he saw—his professional interpretations of what the jury had absorbed the day before. The adjectives flowed freely: She was conforming, passive, submissive, unassertive, anxious, fearful, somewhat confused. "She had what she described as a 'minimal' life, particularly in the wintertime," he said. "But even in the summertime, she had a lot of difficulty breathing and spent most of her time with a heating pad, trying to relieve the pain. She said even to go out to the grocery store she had to bundle up, sometimes wear an afghan to try to stay warm. And she described to me a situation at home where she pretty much stays home, is unable to walk more than a hundred yards at a time without some difficulty. . . .

"She also related a history to me of being dependent on her husband, Tim. And that whenever he's not working, he's with her. . . . And that since 1983, she's had times when she felt like she just couldn't leave the house. She avoids crowded places because, she says, 'People just start to run over you in stores and malls.'" Waneta had told Ewing she looked forward to their visits because it gave her a chance to talk to someone other than her husband. "She clearly has difficulty relating to other people," Ewing said, though he and Waneta had developed a good rapport. He thought her dependent personality "had been fostered by Tim's willingness to allow his wife to depend on him so heavily." As Ewing continued his doleful description in her defense, Tim Hoyt looked down despondently.

Ewing summarized Waneta's psychiatric and medical history as she had related it to him: She told him about the various antidepressants the county psychiatrists had given her over the years. "She said she didn't get anything out of going to see the doctors and she felt that the medications just made her, she said, 'mean and ugly.' And so she flushed them down the toilet." During one visit with him, he said, Waneta had complained about facial pain. He'd referred her to her doctor. "She told me she feels uncomfortable with doctors. And that she avoids going to the doctors as much as possible."

Urbanski asked what all this meant. Ewing said it meant a lot. For one thing, Waneta had a "dependent personality disorder—this is the pervasive and excessive need to be taken care of. And it leads to submissive, clinging, dependent kind of behavior. People who have this disorder have difficulty making everyday decisions for themselves. They need excessive reassurance, advice from other people."

She also had "avoidant personality disorder," Ewing explained. "Again, it's a pervasive pattern of social interaction, something that has been with her throughout her life. She had feelings of inadequacy, hypersensitivity to negative evaluation. . . . Sees herself as socially inept. Feeling inferior to other people." Ewing also diagnosed a long-standing depression.

As Ewing testified, Simpson objected. He complained repeatedly that his opinions were based on observations that were not in the trial record. "I hate to be a pain . . ." he interrupted at one point, arguing that Ewing was essentially telling the jury what to think. But Sgueglia gave the lawyer-psychologist a wide berth. He told Simpson he could rebut the testimony with his own expert, Dr. Barry.

Ewing related Waneta's version of the events of March 23, from the introductions at the Berkshire post office to the interview at the Owego barracks. "Mrs. Hoyt told me that they kept saying to her that she killed her babies. And she kept saying, 'No, I didn't.'" When he asked Waneta why she had made the admissions, she told him, "I don't know, I just wanted them to leave me alone. I just said, 'If you said I killed them all, I must've killed them. I don't remember doing it.' They told me all I had to do was say yes and then I was going home." She told Ewing that Mulvey had rubbed her shoulders to coax her admissions. His written report quoted her as telling him, "I felt like a zombie, like a little kid, like you're mom and dad, the boss, and I do whatever you say, that's just what I did."

Urbanski asked Ewing to add it all up. How did her personality disorders play into the techniques the police had used? "She would be very vulnerable to manipulation, very vulnerable to demands placed on her by authority figures," he said. "She was particularly vulnerable to the use of a man she thought was her friend, Officer Bleck, to induce her cooperation to begin with. She was vulnerable to the misrepresentation to her about the true nature of the interview, that this was a SIDS interview rather than a police interrogation, that giving this interview would somehow be helpful to research on SIDS." An edge of righteous indignation grew in Ewing's voice as he continued. "She was vulnerable to the lying to her about the purpose of the Miranda warning, having been told that this was routine in these kinds of situations. I believe she was especially vulnerable to the use of a female investigator, accompanied by two male authority figures. I also believe that she was extremely vulnerable to the touching and the rubbing of her body, and that this lowered her resistance and induced greater cooperation. I also think that she was extremely vulnerable to the repeated verbal demands, the insistence that she actually did kill her children when she said she didn't. She was also vulnerable to her own feelings of guilt about not having done more over the years somehow to have helped her children live. And finally, I think she was perhaps most vulnerable of all to the fact that she was isolated from her husband, the person upon whom she was totally dependent."

Urbanski asked what the effect of all this had been on her constitutional rights. "It's my conclusion," he said, "that her statement to the police on that day was not made knowingly and it was not made voluntarily."

Simpson was so annoyed by Ewing's testimony—by his very presence—that his cross-examination took on a tone of personal indignation. He felt the psychologist believed everything Waneta Hoyt had told him, especially about the encounter with the police, with barely a moment of professional skepticism.

"Did it ever occur to you," he asked Ewing, "that it might be a good idea to go out and check with other members of the family, other members of the community, and see if in fact the diagnosis that you had reached is accurate?"

"Did it occur to me to do that?" Ewing replied. "No."

"And wouldn't it have been good scientific technique to investigate and talk to people who have no ax to grind or any reason to lie?"

"Well, it's not the general practice to do that," Ewing said. "I see your point. They may have given me additional information, sure." He added, "Had I not believed Mrs. Hoyt, then I would have felt compelled to do that."

"And the reason you believe Mrs. Hoyt was because you were being paid a hundred-fifty dollars an hour?"

"No, the reason I believed her is because I spent twenty-one hours interviewing her and I came to know her well."

Simpson asked Ewing why he had not checked Waneta's version of the police interview against that of the police—why, for instance, he hadn't read a transcript of the suppression hearing nearly a year before, during which Courtright, Mulvey, and Bleck had recounted the events of that day. Ewing said it was because he believed Waneta. Simpson asked why he hadn't looked at the thick file of mental-health records from the early 1970s. "I felt sufficiently confident in the diagnosis that I didn't feel the need to go back and look at records that were eighteen or twenty years old," Ewing said.

"You relied in determining the truthfulness of Mrs. Hoyt totally on Mrs. Hoyt, plus her husband, plus her son," Simpson said.

"Plus the testing, plus the papers I reviewed," Ewing replied.

"Well, you know as well as I that those tests are subject to fabrication."

"This particular test measures for fabrication. And there was no fabrication."

It was a duel in some ways akin to the cross-examinations of Steinschneider and Kelly. This time, Simpson was challenging the competence of one of the nation's prominent forensic psychologists. All experts come to court with opinions favoring whichever side is paying them, but Ewing's conclusions seemed to Simpson absurdly naïve. He became so fixated on this that he took the testimony exactly where Sgueglia had said the defense could not: to the question of whether Waneta had been coaxed into giving a false confession.

"You're coming in here now, asserting to us that Mrs. Hoyt is a truthful person," Simpson said.

"To me," Ewing said. "In my view, yes. She is."

"And she would not lie."

"She didn't lie to *me*."

"Okay. She didn't lie to you. Do you know whether she lied to the jury?"

"I don't know. I didn't hear her testimony."

"Do you know whether she lied to the state police?"

"I don't know."

"What she told the state police could have been true?"

"I don't think so."

"I didn't ask you that. What she told the state police could have been true?"

"In my opinion? No, it couldn't have been."

"It couldn't be true! So she had to lie on one—she either lied to the state police when she gave the statement that was taken down by a stenographer, or she lied to you. And that indicates to me that she's a liar. Now what does it indicate to you?"

"It indicates to me that she was coerced into making a false statement to the police." There was a stirring at the defense table. Waneta had an advocate in the witness chair, not just another expert, and he'd said the magic words—on cross-examination.

Simpson realized where he was. He also realized the only way out was to keep going. "So you're saying, I take it, Doctor, Exhibit number thirty-six is a fabrication."

"Largely."

"And would you go from there and tell us what portions of it are fabricated."

"The portions in which the defendant said that she killed the children."

"Go ahead and read them," Simpson thundered, furious now. "The fabricated parts. Take your time, I got all day."

"You want me to read the entire statement?"

"I want you to read to this jury the fabricated parts."

"I believe that any part where she said that she killed her children is false."

"Read 'em to us, it's right there. I want you to read the truthful parts and then I want you to read the fabricated parts."

"I don't know what is truthful. I do know, in my opinion, which is what you're asking, that the defendant told me she did not kill her children."

"That makes it true?"

"In my estimation, yes."

It went on in that vein until Simpson challenged Ewing to say what the police had done wrong—how they had managed to induce this false confession—and at this point Ewing seemed to shed the guise of the disinterested psychologist. "If you want me to, I'll give my opinion—"

Simpson tried to cut him off, but Urbanski knew another good moment when he saw one coming. He asked Sgueglia to let Ewing finish, and the judge obliged. Ewing's tone turned contentious, as if he felt he'd been unleashed against Simpson's hostility: "The police in this case used somebody who was known to Mrs. Hoyt, who Mrs. Hoyt trusted, Mrs. Hoyt thought of as a friend, to deceive her, to guile her into consenting to what she thought was going to be a research interview, an interview that would help other people regarding Sudden Infant Death Syndrome. Then the police brought in a woman who was not portrayed to her as a police officer—"

"Aha!" Simpson exclaimed—Waneta had testified that Bleck had, in fact, introduced Sue Mulvey as a police investigator. Simpson mocked Ewing's scenario of deception. "You certainly aren't accusing the state police of doing anything wrong for not recognizing she had a dependent personality syndrome or whatever."

"I'm not accusing the state police of anything," Ewing shot back.

Simpson asked how one might recognize such a disorder in a person.

"Extreme dependence on, in this case, her husband and other family members," Ewing said. "I think you've probably seen it in the courtroom."

"Oh, I've seen it, all right," Simpson retorted. "You can bet your money on *that*."

Ewing departed the stand triumphant. "I think he shot himself in the foot," he said to a reporter in the hallway. "Asking about the police tricking her—I wouldn't have been able to get into that." For the first time in the trial, the defense camp could see some sunlight. Gisli Gudjonsson was back in England, but the jury, after all, had heard from a man with impressive credentials who not only thought that Waneta had been duped, but that she was actually innocent. With that unexpected development, the defense rested.

In Albany, when Joel Dvoskin heard how far Ewing had gone, he was stunned. Dvoskin knew Ewing as a civil libertarian with strong opinions favoring defendants, but saw him as an honorable man. Which meant that Ewing had to actually believe Waneta Hoyt was innocent. Dvoskin could only shake his head in wonderment. "It says terrible things about his judgment," he would remark one day after the trial, his voice tinged with disappointment. Sadly, murderous mothers were coming to be conspicuous in the annals of modern crime, and Ewing was a leader in this field whose challenge was to negotiate the deceptions. "It's another fascinating subplot of this case," Dvoskin observed. "My hypothesis? Her manipulation and his biases against the police kind of came together. He's always been incredibly passionate. And denial is a son-of-a-bitch."

The state police flew Dr. John Brooks in from New Hampshire that afternoon. He returned to the stand, said there was no significance to Dorothy Kelly's testimony about the vagus nerve and the regurgitations of the Hoyt babies, then flew back home.

With the enthusiasm of someone calling a plumber, Simpson the next morning brought in Dr. David John Barry, his obligatory rebuttal witness. Dvoskin had recommended Barry because of his levelheadedness. "With all the passion flying around," he told Simpson, "it's important to get someone who tells you what they know, what they don't know, sits down, and shuts up."

Simpson found Barry dispassionate indeed. The psychiatrist matched Ewing's portrayal of Waneta's life as pitiful—even surpassed it, to Simpson's irritation—but his conclusions were different. The prosecutor never wanted psychology to become part of the case—certainly not *his* case. But he had been forced into taking part in an exploration of the mind of Waneta Hoyt. In methodical fashion, Barry related everything that Waneta had told him during their two-hour interview five days before. "She was pleasant, soft-spoken, well-groomed, and made good eye contact," he said. "I found no signs of major mental illness." He concluded that she had neither a dependent nor avoidant personality disorder. "Dependent personality disorder would leave a trail of broken relationships," he said, oblivious to one dark connotation of this comment. "Even if she had those disorders she would be no different from the rest of us in understanding her rights. It's self-preservation." He had asked Waneta about her state of mind the day she went to the Owego barracks. "I didn't think I would get myself in trouble," she told him. At another point in their session, Waneta said of her children, "I didn't want them to die." At the end of the session, Barry reported, Waneta asked him what he thought. To him, it was a demonstration of assertiveness. "It's not often that the examinee says, 'Whaddya think, Doc?'"

On cross-examination, Miller pressed the defense's contention that the police had deceived Waneta to the point that her rights had been denied. In response, Barry told him that Waneta seemed neither gullible nor stupid.

But Miller had made his point. He'd managed to use both psychologists to drive home an issue the jury would feel compelled to consider. No matter how strong the prosecution's case, he wanted the jurors to think long and hard about how the case had come to be. Maybe this would add to—as well as draw its strength from—the sympathy factor that Miller considered so important. Maybe they would feel sorry enough for her to move them from finding her guilty of murder and toward a conviction for manslaughter. If they did that, Miller thought, it would mean her freedom.

Though they had barely discussed it with Waneta because they knew she wanted and expected nothing less than a complete acquittal, this had been her lawyers' backup plan since before the trial. The defense had the right to ask that the jury be allowed to consider both the stated charge and—if the proof also fit—a "lesser included offense." If they thought Waneta had killed her children but did not mean to do it, for instance, they could find her guilty of manslaughter. And Waneta could then go home, because the conviction would be nullified by the statute of limitations. While there was no deadline for a murder prosecution, the statute of limitations for manslaughter had elapsed nearly nineteen years before—on July 28, 1976, five years after Noah Hoyt's death.

The lawyers thought this was Waneta's out. It was their understanding that she could be convicted and not go to prison. But just to be sure, Urbanski decided to ask the state public defenders' association in Albany to research the matter. The answer came back on the last day of testimony: No, Waneta would not go free if she were convicted of manslaughter. If the defense asked the jury to consider the lesser offense, it would have to waive the statute of limitations. Urbanski rechecked it himself with the lawbooks in the courthouse.

Though the bad news from Albany meant that the lawyers could no longer offer Waneta the prospect of freedom as an inducement to go for manslaughter, they remained convinced it was still her safest course. But they also knew that anything involving a possible conviction would be a hard sell. At the break, they sat with the Hoyts and told them the harsh reality of the situation. Waneta had a decision to make, and the judge wanted it after lunch.

Miller explained the significance of the two second-degree murder counts she faced on each child. The first count accused Waneta of *intentionally* causing the child's death. Miller thought Waneta's own statements to the police were a good defense against these counts. He was confident the jury would believe her stated contention that she hadn't set out to kill the children. But the second counts were trouble. These alleged that she had "wrongfully, feloniously, and under circumstances evincing a depraved indifference to human life, recklessly engaged in conduct that created a grave risk of death to another person, and thereby caused the death of another person." It meant in this case that she knew that holding pillows and towels and a shoulder against her babies' faces might kill them, but that she had recklessly proceeded to do just that. Miller told Waneta that there was no way around those five counts. "They're not going to acquit you completely," he said. "They're going to convict you of something." He tried to sell the manslaughter option. A sympathetic jury would surely jump at the chance for a compromise verdict, and a lenient sentence could put her in prison for as little as two years. But if she went for all or nothing—murder or acquittal—and lost, she would almost certainly go away for the rest of her life.

When Miller laid out the alternatives, Waneta protested. "But I didn't do it," she said. "Don't you believe I'm innocent?" Miller told her that this was no longer the issue. Tim couldn't believe the jury would convict her of murder. And he saw no difference between a long prison term and a short one. "Either way," he said, "she'll die in jail."

Waneta and Tim walked outside to weigh the options. Miller's explanation left little doubt that if they gave the jury the manslaughter option, the jury would take it. Waneta would be convicted of killing her children. She would go to prison. There was not much more to discuss.

They came back inside and Tim told Miller what they'd decided. Miller sighed heavily and shook his head.

A few minutes later, the lawyers, the prosecutors, and the Hoyts gathered in the judge's chambers. Miller announced his client's decision to go for all or nothing, and then Sgueglia turned to Waneta. He asked her if she understood that a guilty verdict for negligent manslaughter would expose her to a far less severe sentence than a murder conviction. Yes, she said, she understood that. He asked her if she understood that she was going against her lawyers' advice.

"Yes, I understand," Waneta said. "I only want the murder charge."

38

Waneta's decision to go for broke determined Miller's final words to the jury. He could no longer argue her innocence while nudging the jurors from murder to manslaughter in case it didn't work. Instead, he could only argue her innocence, and this was something he did not relish. Now he stood before them and tried to render a closing statement that would portray Waneta as a pitiful woman dragged into court by the "vast power" of the government, deceived into self-incrimination, possibly false, by a task force of shrewd police investigators.

"I guess the American people know more about their rights than anybody in the world," he said. "But you know, there are people in this world of ours, in this country of ours, that are not as sophisticated, not as intelligent, perhaps not as worldly, perhaps not as well-rounded as others of us would like to think we are. Mrs. Hoyt is what she is. She's no better. And they isolated her from her husband, and they gave her rights that to her were meaningless." After a last, long recitation of Waneta's version of the events of March 23, Miller urged the jury to seriously consider the law: "If you find that there is reasonable doubt that Mrs. Hoyt that morning voluntarily gave up her constitutional, legal right to remain silent, and gave up her right to incriminate herself by a statement that she signed later on that day . . . then you must completely disregard the statement."

He moved on to his next problem. "Now I don't know about you," he said, "but I'll be happy if I don't see another expert for quite a while. There's an expert on everything. And it's amazing to me how experts, depending on what they are setting out to show, can differ so widely on simple facts. You heard Dr. Baden and Dr. Ophoven both say that the possibility of more than one child dying in the same family of an unexplained cause was simply astro-nomical. . . . And here comes Dorothy Kelly, she's a researcher, she's done her own studies, she comes in and explains that that's just absurd. She says there is an absolutely recognized phenomenon of clusters. So a bedrock of their opinion is all of a sudden highly suspect. Just the first study in Boston. Who knows what happened in Houston, Atlanta, and San Francisco and Los Angeles or anywhere else? How many families have more than two or three deaths?"

Miller preached to the jurors about the prosecution's lack of physical evi-dence, hoping they might find some reasonable doubt in the futility of the exhumations, exaggerating their importance to the prosecution in order to tear them down. "How on earth can you rule out natural disease when there's no tissue? How can you find homicide from bones that have been buried for thirty years?"

Miller's voice resounded through the courtroom as he moved deeper into the law. He told the jurors that even if they rejected everything else he said—even if they accepted the confession—it didn't add up to a murder conviction. "Mrs. Hoyt stated to the police, according to them, according to the version they wrote down, 'I didn't mean to kill the children . . . I wanted to stop them from crying.' That, ladies and gentlemen, is not murder in the second degree." He told them they would have to understand the legal definitions of murder in their deliberations. "She may be guilty of something, but not that," he said.

At this, the courtroom stirred. Had the defense attorney actually said his client may be guilty? At the defense table, Tim Hoyt looked perplexed and angry. Miller was hoping that the jury, looking for a way out, would hang an acquittal on a legal technicality they didn't quite understand. Now, all he had left was a last appeal to emotion. He concluded his hour-long summation with an allusion to Waneta as the victim of a witch hunt. "Whenever society begins to fall apart, or when a totalitarian system starts to take over, the first thing that happens is that they start to adjust the court system. . . ." he said. "You are the only people between the incredible power of the government and the common person who is charged with a crime."

Bob Simpson arrived at this critical moment determined to win five murder convictions. He had also been under the assumption that a manslaughter con-viction would be nullified by the statute of limitations, and he had prepared for the possibility of guilt without penalty. "A conviction, whether for murder or manslaughter, would vindicate the investigation and the prosecution, and it would say that she did commit these crimes," Simpson said later.

"Manslaughter would have bothered me, particularly in the case of Jimmy, and I still would have argued for murder, but I was willing to live with manslaughter." But the law books and Waneta's decision to roll the dice had removed the ambiguity. Either she was going to be convicted and sent away for a long time, or she was going home, exonerated. Simpson collected himself for the argument of his life.

In his deliberate way, Simpson had come far in the three years since Bill Fitzpatrick had first called him with his suspicions about the Hoyt family. After a slow start, he had come to believe in the case. But while Fitzpatrick had been on national television, Simpson's acclaim never got much beyond the picture of him and the other members of the prosecution team answering questions at the news conference the night of Waneta's arrest. He kept a framed eight-by-ten print on the window ledge that served as his desk. And while some of the Syracuse reporters had mused during the trial how Fitz-patrick might have tried the case differently, many people who knew Simpson a long time, including Bob Miller, felt that he had risen to the occa-sion. In his understated way, he had mastered a mountain of complexity and built and presented a strong case. Now, he was set to deliver the last word. He would do it in the same reasonable tone with which he had approached the rest of the case.

He was like them, Simpson told the jury. He knew nothing about SIDS or apnea before this case, and he'd learned something from each of the expert witnesses who had streamed through the witness box. But logic, he thought, would dictate the verdict. "They know things that we don't know—that's why they were here," he said of the various experts. "But when they come in and they define terms for us and they go through the records in this case, we don't need them to tell us what ultimately happened here."

At the moment Simpson began talking about the Hoyt children by name, sunlight splashed through the courtroom windows. Judge Sgueglia looked up and smiled. For the last time, the prosecutor reviewed their lives and deaths—how Eric and Julie and Jimmy died suddenly, mysteriously, and inconsis-tently; how Molly and Noah spent most of their lives at Upstate Medical Center and died the day after they went home. He made a thinly veiled reference to the credibility of his Upstate witnesses versus the defense's—Steinschneider. "We brought in four nurses to testify in this case. And we did that for a reason. We did it, obviously, so that you would have a chance to listen to people who have no ax to grind in this particular case, who have no reason to fabricate, who have no reason to make up a story, who don't have a research project that they conducted in connection with it, have no reason to justify any prior findings. Just four honest, hardworking women to testify what kind of children these were."

Don't check your common sense at the door to the jury room, Simpson implored the jurors. There was no genetic explanation for the deaths of the Hoyt children, and the SIDS diagnosis wasn't even applicable here because of the absence of either autopsies or death-scene investigations, or both. The children's father never saw anything—not the deaths themselves, not the reported life-threatening episodes. "Mr. Timothy Hoyt, who lives with his children," Simpson said. "Makes you wonder."

He left his legal pad at the lectern, and paced in front of the jury. "You can take some of these things away, and you wouldn't be suspicious," he said. "If the children had these life-threatening problems in the hospital, we wouldn't be here today. If we had some sickness we could see for these children, if we had some hospital record that showed them other than normal, healthy children, we wouldn't be here today. But the coincidences mount and mount and mount, so that we don't have coincidences anymore."

Now, Simpson added the confession. He scoffed at the defense's claims of treachery and coercion. He refused to make apologies for the way the police had gained her cooperation. "It's what police work is all about," he said. "And the day the police in the State of New York can't try and gain the trust of somebody that they're taking a statement from is the day that statements are no longer taken in the State of New York. It's good police procedure, it was done in this case, and it will be done again and again and again in other cases."

Did Waneta make a knowing and voluntary waiver of her rights? "She wasn't under arrest, she wasn't manacled, she wasn't handcuffed, she wasn't restrained, she wasn't yelled at, abused, or threatened. If Mrs. Hoyt decided that she was going to get up and walk out that door, she would have been given a ride home. The only thing is, Mrs. Hoyt knew one thing that nobody else in that room knew. . . . And that one thing was that she had murdered her five kids. She knew that. When the police read her her rights, she knew."

Simpson set aside the array of evidence and changed his tone. "The events that happened to these five children took place a long time ago, and it would be easy, I think, to minimize the impact because they are twenty-five or thirty years old. But these kids didn't ask to be brought into this world. Mrs. Hoyt made a conscious decision to have five children. And when she made that decision, she had an obligation to protect these children, she had an obligation to keep them safe. She had an obligation to listen to their crying, she had an obligation to put up with all the things that parents have to put up with. And she was lucky that this went unnoticed for twenty-five years because she got to live twenty-five years of her life. . . .

"But five people, five young people, aren't here today because of her. Today they would have ranged in age, I think, from twenty-four to thirty-one, if they were all still alive. They would have families, they would do all the things that you and I have enjoyed doing during the course of our lives. They don't get that opportunity. And they don't get that opportunity because their mother couldn't stand their crying. That's not a good enough reason. Kids cry. These kids have rights. And one of the rights that they have is to have somebody look at their case and see whether they were murdered. And it doesn't make any difference whether the murder is twenty-five years ago, or the murder was yesterday."

Simpson's words enveloped the courtroom. At the defense table, Waneta sobbed openly.

"And Mr. Miller talked about, well, this isn't murder, this is something else," Simpson continued. "Well, there's been testimony in this case that it takes two or three minutes to render an infant or a human unconscious by suffocation. And it takes a couple more minutes to kill a child after the child's been rendered unconscious. These children had two minutes of suffocation before they were rendered unconscious. And we have youngsters two or three months. They can't do anything about it. The person they would normally look to protect them and take care of them is the one that's ending their lives. We have a little boy, Jimmy. Jimmy was two and a half. And it's not very difficult to visualize what happened to Jimmy because his mother talks about him. His mother talks about his struggles and his flailing to save his own life as she held a towel over his face. And she had to hold that towel over his face a long time to get him to stop. She certainly had to hold the towel over his face for a space of two minutes or more as he thrashed around, trying to get air."

Simpson walked over to the exhibit table and picked up a snapshot of Jimmy in a cowboy shirt taken shortly before his death. "We didn't intend to introduce a lot of pictures in this trial, but we did introduce one. And this is the guy, Jimmy, who struggled for his life"—his voice broke as he held up the picture for the jury—"two and a half minutes of agony, that boy had to undergo before he died at two and a half years of age. And this woman should pay for that, because she intended to kill him. That's all she could have ever intended to do, whatever her motive, whatever was bothering her. That could have been her only intent, to kill that youngster.

"Now, Mr. Miller talked about the incredible power of the government. And we do have power. But in this particular case the incredible power of the government is nothing compared to the incredible power of Mrs. Hoyt to be able to murder five children. Mrs. Hoyt has a defense, she has defense lawyers, she has to have us prove that she's done something wrong. Well, Eric, Julie, Jimmy, Molly, Noah—they didn't have that. They didn't have anybody to defend them. You talk about power. The power of the towel and the power of the shoulder—*that's* incredible power. She killed her kids. And she should be convicted for murder."

For a few seconds after Simpson sat down, the courtroom was still. It was a powerful summation, and there were tears in people's eyes—jurors, spectators, reporters. The defense attorneys were stunned. Bob Miller had tried two dozen cases against Simpson over the years, and he'd always thought of the district attorney's closing arguments as his weakness. But this, Miller decided, was probably the best one by any prosecutor he'd ever heard. "I was proud of him," he'd say later.

Judge Sgueglia spent an hour the next morning instructing the jurors on the nuances of the law. He explained how they were to weigh the evidence; how to apply their findings to each count of the indictment. Then, he dispatched them to the jury room. For four weeks, over lunch and during breaks, these twelve people had followed his instructions and talked about everything but what they were hearing from the witness stand. About the closest they'd come to discussing the case was a comment one of them, Lynne Rocha, had made to some of the other women on the jury. She'd looked up at the balcony one day and seen Gail Pfeiffer. "There she is again," she told them. By the end of the trial, the jurors were known in the courtroom by descriptive monikers: the old man, the pretty one, the scraggly beard, the coffee drinker, the sleeper. Now they gathered around a table in a room behind the jury box and got down to the business of judging Waneta Hoyt—and with it, though this was not something they recognized, giving the final word on the medical thesis that had led them here.

Unleashed, the jurors immediately began throwing out comments, talking all at once. Aaron Gowan, a lanky man in his thirties, suggested a quick informal vote. Too early for that, some of the others said, but Gowan persuaded them it would be a good starting point. Only three jurors felt that Waneta was definitely guilty. Gowan was among them. Three felt she was innocent—or at least that thus far, they were not convinced she was guilty. The other six were undecided. There was work ahead.

They decided to start with the confession, the linchpin. If they didn't accept the confession, they all might as well go home—there was no debate on that. It was instantly clear that Miller and Urbanski had done a masterful job of making it a serious issue. Several of the jurors had real trouble with the way the state police had induced Waneta to talk to them, and with how they seemed to downplay the Miranda warning, perhaps lulling her into a false sense of security. Of course, what had actually taken place was in some dispute—had Sue Mulvey "rubbed" Waneta's shoulder, for instance, or merely placed her hand on it?—and the crucial question of what the effect had been on this woman depended on one's view of her. But a few of the jurors seemed willing to throw out the confession because they thought she had been tricked into giving it. It was a sticking point for two jurors in particular, middle-aged men who thought the police should have told her exactly what was on their minds when they first approached her. Whether the confession was true or not, it was important to these two men that the police had obtained it properly, and they didn't allow the police wide latitude.

Aaron Gowan couldn't understand why they seemed so stuck on something he considered no issue at all. He later thought of the federal building in Oklahoma that had been blown up the day before the jury began deliberating in Owego. There were people out there who were excessively angry at government authority, and Gowan felt strains of it in the jury room. Miller's allusion to the "vast power" of the government seemed to resonate for some of these jurors, and so, it seemed, did the image of pity he had assiduously created around his client.

Gowan argued for the confession. He considered nothing the police had done improper, certainly not illegal. Gowan was among the best-educated people on the jury, and apparently the most affluent. He ran his family's business, a chain of three stores selling home-improvement products. Though he'd entered the jury room persuaded the confession was valid, the straw vote showed he was in the minority. It was his impression that a number of jurors, perhaps the majority, simply did not want to believe Waneta was guilty and were looking for a way not to convict her. He judged that it was not so much sympathy for her as it was an inability to come to terms with the enormity of her crimes.

Janice Jacobs sided with Gowan. She was sixty years old and had worked as a bookkeeper until her employer fell prey to the Tioga County economy. As much as anything else, it was Waneta's own testimony that convinced her the confession was legitimate and that she was guilty. "She amazed me," she told the others. "That she could get up there and be in such control. She didn't cry at all during the defense examination, and when Simpson started on her she was like steel. She's a lot tougher woman than people think." And smarter. Jacobs detected intelligence in Waneta's language. "She likes words. She was at the post office to 'retrieve' her mail. She likes 'cyanotic.'"

Lynne Rocha had started the morning as one of the three jurors who voted not guilty. Gowan thought she was one of those looking for a way to acquit. But for Rocha, it was more complicated than that. It was a posture she had felt compelled to take. She was trying to be a good citizen and a dedicated juror. She had spent the entire trial telling herself Waneta was innocent. That was the American way of justice. Now, she would let her mind follow the proof. She agreed that the police hadn't been completely honest with Waneta. "But on the other hand," she told the others, answering her own concern, "what were they going to do? Grab her off the street and say, 'We know you killed your kids, now tell us you did'?"

Another juror, Dan Hogan, suggested they take apart the day of the confession, piece by piece, and decide whether the police had done anything improper at each moment. Early in the afternoon, they went back into the courtroom for a readback of some of the police testimony. They wanted to hear again exactly what had taken place when Mulvey and Bleck first confronted Waneta in Berkshire. It would be a turning point in the deliberations. When they returned to the jury room, Rocha declared she'd heard something of great significance—something that made her think that Waneta had indeed given a "knowing and voluntary" waiver of her rights. Bleck had testified that when Mulvey asked Waneta to come down to Owego, "Mrs. Hoyt said that would be fine, but she was a little nervous and she grabbed my hand and said as long as I could go with them." Rocha told the others: "She took his hand. She knew something was wrong."

The debate over the confession lasted through the day. The jurors analyzed Waneta's handwriting on the addendum on the third page of the written statement, where she wrote that she wanted to wait for her husband before signing anything. "If she was so distraught, if she was a zombie, she wouldn't have been able to write that," Jacobs said. Nor did Tim's neat signature suggest to them a man signing under protest. They wondered about the relationship between the Hoyts. "Ewing's theory is that she's so dependent on him," Jacobs said. "I don't buy that at all. I think she says, 'Jump,' he says, 'How high, honey?' It's like it is with drug and alcohol addiction, where you have these enabling personalities." She, like the others, found it impossible to understand how Tim had never questioned the deaths, especially when they studied the death certificates and realized for the first time that Julie and Jimmy had died within three weeks of each other. Simpson had recited all the dates, but hadn't pointed out this ominous oddity.

The more they talked about the confession, the more it seemed to them that the words on these pages had much greater weight than a lawyer's notion of police deception. Late in the afternoon there came a moment when the jurors knew they had cleared the highest hurdle facing them. Whatever their misgivings about the approach of the police, all agreed that Waneta Hoyt had given a valid, legal confession. They recognized the inexorable course they were now on. They asked the judge if they could go outside for a break.

At 5:00, they walked downstairs and stood on the south lawn of the courthouse, forming an almost perfect circle as spectators and reporters looked on. It was a curious scene, the jurors smoking cigarettes, laughing and smiling and chatting with expressions that suggested comfort and relief. Reading the signs, it was the view of many of the observers that a barrier had been crossed:

Perhaps a verdict had been decided and this was a deep breath before delivery. It was true that a barrier had been crossed, but a verdict was not imminent. There was still more work ahead. The jurors went back upstairs after dinner and moved on to the question of whether the prosecutors had corroborated the confession.

They went witness by witness, deciding who was credible and who was not, an approach that demonstrated how few of the experts had come without an agenda. They gave no credence to anything they heard from Steinschneider, whose motives became obvious to them during Simpson's cross-examination. "He was there to defend himself," Gowan later said. "I didn't think he cared one iota about those babies, nor did he care about Waneta Hoyt. They were meaningless to him. The only reason he was on that stand was to improve his position." Nor, for that matter, did Gowan put too much stock in what the Upstate nurses had to say. Though others disagreed, he felt their obvious emotional attachment to the babies diminished their ability to render an unbiased picture of those months. Dorothy Kelly gave the jurors something to think about, but her contention that young babies don't throw up struck several mothers on the jury as incredible, and a few jurors wondered if Peggy Drake wasn't right when she implied during the cross-examination that Kelly didn't know serial homicide when she saw it.

It was Janice Ophoven who was, by acclamation, the best single witness for either side. She had no discernible interest, the jurors decided, other than the truth, and she came with plenty to back up her views. It was like that day at the Treadway fifteen months before. When Ophoven explained why homicide was the only logical conclusion, the jurors believed her.

As dusk fell, the ritual of jury-sitting took hold outside the deliberation room. Throughout the courthouse, people talked in little groups, and somehow the atmosphere loosened even as it intensified. Waneta joked quietly with the people around her, and every once in a while, she would emerge from her room in back of the courtroom and walk the corridor with confidence. The longer the jury was out, Miller told her, the better.

Bob Simpson strolled around the building, and at one point, Loretta Hoyt walked up to him and complimented him. "You asked a lot of the questions I've wanted to ask," she said. Simpson thanked her; he wondered where she stood in this. Bill Fitzpatrick and Pete Tynan had arrived from Syracuse earlier in the day, and they were waiting out the verdict with the prosecution crew in the room downstairs. The room contained boxes of Tioga County grand jury transcripts from 1909. They began reading about rural turn-of-the-century crime to pass the time.

Simpson encountered Miller in the main corridor on the first floor, and they sat on a bench and reminisced about old cases. At one point, Simpson motioned toward the room in the corner. "You know, your buddy's in there," he said. "Why don't you go in there and bury the hatchet?"

Months before, the state bar association had dismissed Miller's complaint about Fitzpatrick's pretrial remarks. Miller decided now was as good a time as any to end their feud. It seemed strange that they'd never met. He stood up and went inside the prosecution room. He recognized Fitzpatrick from his TV appearances.

"Mr. Fitzpatrick, I'm Bob Miller," he said, extending his hand. "You had one hell of a hunch. You made us earn our salaries around here."

"You did a hell of a job, too," Fitzpatrick said.

A while later, Fitzpatrick was lounging with Tynan and a few reporters in the back of the otherwise empty courtroom when Sgueglia called the jurors back in to see how they were progressing. It was 8:30, and darkness had descended on the courthouse. If they were close to a verdict, he would let them keep going. If not, he'd send them to the Treadway for the night. The jurors looked at each other. "We're close," said one, "but not that close." Sgueglia had asked them to bring overnight bags that morning. He sent them off to the hotel. "We'll see you in the morning," he said paternally.

After they departed, the judge climbed out of his robes, pulled a bag of miniature Snickers bars out from behind the bench, and began throwing them to the reporters. He hadn't noticed that Waneta was still in the courtroom. She looked up, bewildered. "Hey, what about over here?" someone on the Hoyt side of the aisle yelled, and Sgueglia threw some candies in that direction. Seeing the candy bars flying overhead, Waneta walked alone to the back room to get her things. Jay glared at the judge and left the courtroom in a huff. Sgueglia was playing with the reporters, a tension breaker as the courtroom began to empty. But it was an odd, uneasy moment, and he realized instantly it had been a mistake. The next day, he called the Hoyts up to the bench to apologize.

At 11:15 the next morning, Friday, April 21, the jury sent a note out to the judge. Could he explain the difference between the two counts of murder?

Every lawyer and most of the spectators knew what this meant. "She's done," thought Fitzpatrick, who had returned to Owego with Tynan for the day of judgment. Waneta began to cry—she knew, too. The jurors filed back into the jury box and Sgueglia explained it to them: The first count accused the defendant of *intentionally* causing the child's death. If they found her guilty of this count, they were to skip the second count and go on to the first count for the next child. But if they found her *not* guilty of intent, they were to consider the second count, which accused her of *recklessly* causing the death. This was the count that contained the words "depraved indifference to human life."

The jury departed once again. At the front of the courtroom, a group of Waneta's friends and relatives joined their hands in prayer.

In the deliberation room, the jury had indeed reached the decision those outside had guessed. They had gone through the last of the witnesses, read the confessions and the death certificates, and determined that Waneta Hoyt was guilty of five murders. Now they began considering, a child at a time, whether she had intentionally or recklessly killed them. The overwhelming feeling among them was that she had not set out to kill them. If they were going to accept Waneta's confession, the jurors felt, they had to accept the whole thing. That meant taking at face value her explanation that it was the crying that she couldn't stand, and that she hadn't meant for them to die. It seemed a last, desperate reach for a semblance of goodness in Waneta, an unwillingness even now to fully accept what they had decided was the truth. Yes, she had done it. But no, she could not have done it deliberately. As Waneta herself had said, who could do such a horrible thing?

The majority held this view firmly. Their intransigence became clear when they got to Jimmy. By this point, Lynne Rocha had done a complete turnaround. She had come into the deliberations unconvinced Waneta was even guilty. Now, she was arguing passionately for the first count on Jimmy. She agreed with Simpson: That child had struggled and flailed and fought for his life. His mother could have only meant to kill him. No, said the others. She couldn't have meant to do it, even with Jimmy.

Rocha brought a pillow with her to the trial each day to ease the strain on her back. It was, as it happened, a baby pillow. Now, she stood up, pillow in hand, and walked around to Shawn Conway, the jury foreman. "The others may have been accidental or not premeditated," she said, "but not Jimmy." She asked Dan Hogan to look at his watch. "It takes at least two minutes to make someone unconscious. Time it." With that, she put the pillow over Conway's face, allowing him just enough room to breathe. The other jurors looked on uneasily. "You're telling me she doesn't know what she's doing?" Rocha asked, the seconds ticking off. It seemed endless—two minutes was a lot longer than they thought. "This isn't just putting a pillow over a helpless little baby's head. This child is two and a half, and he's struggling. She's got to be thinking about what she's doing. She has plenty of time to think, 'No, don't do it.' And Shawn isn't even wriggling."

The others asked her to stop the morbid demonstration well short of two minutes. They got her point. But they were not persuaded. They had not seen any hard evidence proving intent. Some thought Waneta was an emotionally disturbed woman who really didn't know what she was doing—maybe the crying just made her snap. Simpson had labored to make this a case of fatal child abuse, and nothing else. But some on the jury yearned to know more about the psychological element, as if a part of them was still looking for a way out of convicting Waneta of murder and sending her to live her remaining years in prison. If they had been given the option of sending her to a mental hospital instead, they might well have done that. But they realized they'd been left no choice, and when a last vote was taken and it was unanimous, a somber sense of finality settled over them.

"I'll send a note out to the judge," Conway said quietly, and the room, as Janice Jacobs would later remember, "got quieter and quieter, and then it got silent." Then Lynne Rocha began to sob. Mel Schrader tried to comfort her, but she was disconsolate, and he, too, began to cry. The others looked down, trying to avoid eye contact with each other, but the emotion was too powerful, and more tears began to flow. A few minutes later, the jurors agreed they were ready. Conway sent the note.

It was 12:15 in the afternoon when word made its way around the courthouse. Reporters and photographers and spectators scrambled backupstairs. In the prosecution room, Fitzpatrick and Simpson stood, shook hands solemnly, and began marching up the circular stairway to the courtroom, Simpson returning to his spot at the prosecution table, Fitzpatrick to the fourth row of the gallery. Miller met Waneta and Tim at the defense table for the last time. Now Jay sat with them.

Murmurs filled the room as the judge returned to the bench. The courtroom squirmed to order. "Ladies and gentlemen, I'm told we have a verdict," Sgueglia announced. Eyes fixed on the door to the left of the jury box. They watched Libby Rhodes, the jury attendant, go inside with a box of tissues. "I want to caution everyone here that there are to be no outbreaks in either event," Sgueglia said. "I ask you please to control your emotions."

The judge nodded to Rhodes, and she knocked three times on the door to the jury room. Seconds later, the jurors filed out in the same orderly way they had dozens of times over the last four weeks. This time, though, their faces were reddened with emotion.

At the defense table, Waneta and Tim held hands tightly. The lawyers on both sides stared ahead. In the left corner of the jury box, Shawn Conway stood nervously, holding a stack of verdict sheets in his hands. Pete Hoffmann, the court clerk, addressed him.

"In this case of the People versus Waneta Hoyt, Indictment number ninety-four-dash-forty-one, what's your verdict concerning the first count of the indictment, murder in the second degree?"

"Not guilty," said Conway.

Jay Hoyt bolted upright in his seat, grinned, looked at his mother, and then at his father. But neither of them moved, and a perplexed look crossed Jay's face.

"What's your verdict concerning the second count of the indictment, murder in the second degree?" Hoffmann asked.

"Guilty," said Conway.

Waneta shook her head, her face etched with a look of stunned despair. Jay dropped his head onto the table, collapsed in tears, his shoulders trembling. Tim stayed composed as always. He assumed his familiar position, leaning into Waneta, rubbing her back, his head bowed. She was sobbing now. On the prosecution side, Simpson squeezed Peggy Drake's arm.

The clerk and the foreman continued their litany. What is your verdict concerning the third count, murder in the second degree? Not guilty. What is your verdict concerning the fourth count, murder in the second degree? Guilty ... And so it went for all the children. Not guilty. Guilty. Not guilty. Guilty. Not guilty. Guilty. Five times, the jury affirmed, Waneta Hoyt had displayed not an intent to kill but a "depraved indifference to human life." The nuance vanished as soon as it appeared, and by the time all the verdicts were read, Waneta was heaving, leaning on Jay's shoulder. Tim reached across to his son. In the gallery, Waneta's friends and relatives shook their heads and joined the crying. Her niece Penny cried out, then fell into the lap of one of her aunts. Now Tim pulled Waneta close, their foreheads touching.

As this emotional tableau played out before him, Judge Sgueglia looked toward the jurors to thank them. "Many of you are crying," he said, tears forming in his own eyes. "It's an indication of how difficult—" His voice broke, and it triggered more weeping from the jury. Sgueglia gathered himself together, and said he couldn't adequately express his thanks for the way they had risen to this wrenching challenge. The jurors filed back through the door from which they had emerged.

Waneta, wailing, was led toward the judge's chambers, the quickest way out. Tim and Jay trailed her. In the chambers, sheriff's deputies surrounded her. They handcuffed her. "Why are you doing this?" she asked over and over again. "I didn't kill my babies." The deputies led her downstairs, then out the side door toward the county jail across the street. Tim and Jay walked with her, and she protested her innocence all the way. TV cameramen converged around her, and Jay went after one of them. Waneta implored him to forget about them, stay with her. *Please, Jay.* A few seconds later, she disappeared behind the door of the dilapidated old jail building.

Back in the courtroom, her relatives crowded around Miller, leaning in close to hear what he was saying. There will be an appeal, he assured them.

For now, just stay calm. Downstairs, he told the reporters, "It's an American tragedy. I hope justice was done." As he spoke, Natalie Hilliard walked by in a daze.

There was no sense of joy among the police and the prosecutors. Bob Courtright was headed out the door, stone-faced as ever, in no mood to talk, when Sheryl Nathans, the Syracuse TV reporter, came after him. "Can I get a quick bite?" she called. Reluctantly, Courtright stopped. Nathans asked about the tears he'd shed when he testified. "I fought back tears," he corrected her. The jurors had done their job, and he was proud of them. Justice had been served, but there was no call to celebrate. There were five dead kids, an eighteen-year-old sentenced to terrible despair, a woman going to prison, probably forever. Courtright couldn't have looked less happy if Waneta had been acquitted.

Fitzpatrick and Simpson received the press in the prosecution room. There was no formality to it, just a lot of standing around and trying to put things in perspective, the prosecutors repeating themselves each time another person happened by with a microphone or notepad. It was a muted proceeding. The reporters asked their questions quietly, and the responses came back the same way. Fitzpatrick said he hoped some of the tears shed this day had been shed for the children of Waneta Hoyt. He gave tribute to Simpson, the man he once thought would never bring the case to this conclusion. "What Bob Simpson has done today will encourage prosecutors across the country to look at these kinds of cases," he said. Then he added, "This will put an end, I hope once and for all, to the chicanery of Dr. Steinschneider's paper, which has resulted in a number of killers not being brought to justice over the last several decades."

Outside, a county maintenance man lowered to half-mast the five American flags at the war memorial. It was in recognition of all those who had died in Oklahoma City two days before. But people who had witnessed the events inside the Tioga County Courthouse could be forgiven for thinking the five flags flapped at mid-staff in memory of Eric, Julie, Jimmy, Molly, and Noah Hoyt.

39

One night a few weeks after her convictions, Waneta Hoyt received a group of reporters in the cramped visiting room at the Tioga County Jail. She sat across a narrow table from Tim, their hands clasped above a foot-high wooden divider, the reporters leaning over him, straining to catch her words above the din of Tuesday-night visiting. "I *said,* I didn't kill my babies," she repeated.

She wanted the world to know the truth—she'd go on TV if the sheriff allowed the cameras inside. "I've even got a letter from a German station. I'll talk to CNN if I have to. I'm not the cold, vulgar person that people say I am." The previous weekend had been tough. Saturday was her birthday, and then Sunday was Mother's Day. "It was hell," she said, "because I'm a mother."

Had she gotten any hate mail? someone asked. Waneta nodded at all the notes being scribbled as she spoke. "I guess I will now," she said pungently. But really, she asked, how could people think she could have killed her children and gotten away with it for so long? "They must think I'm the cleverest person." She announced her intention to sue Dr. Steinschneider.

Waneta spent a lot of her time these weeks writing letters. Letters to the judge, asserting her innocence, insisting it was her lawyers' fault that she'd been convicted. Letters to newspaper and television people, asking for attention to her cause. Letters to friends and relatives, complaining about the treatment she was receiving in jail. She wrote to her sister Donna, who was wheelchair-bound with a spreading cancer, berating her for failing to visit more. Waneta remarked to another relative, "I guess I'd get some attention if *I* had cancer." When her devoted niece Penny came to visit, Waneta chastised her for not doing more to help. George Hoyt was enraged. He went to the jail and told the officer at the desk not to allow his daughter in to see Waneta again.

Waneta complained constantly to Tim. "Why aren't you getting me out of here?" she pressed him. After visiting her one day, he released a torrent of guilt-laden frustration to an acquaintance on the sidewalk outside before going home. "You should see what they're doing in there. This whole system—my lawyers, they did nothing. I know these babies had problems. If they weren't sick, what were they doing in the hospital all that time? She did not do this. And her medicine. They changed her medicine in there. They gave her Motrin so all last night she was up complaining about her stomach. She's allergic to these generic drugs, and this dumb county doctor doesn't know what he's doing. I gotta get her out of there. I'll tear the place down if I have to. And we'd leave this county. Leave the whole damn state. All night there's a man in there calling her 'baby killer, baby killer.' And I've got an eighteen-year-old son at home I gotta keep together."

Waneta wrote a long letter to Michelle York, who had covered the trial for the Binghamton *Press & Sun-Bulletin,* closing with an invitation to the jail for a personal interview. The reporter took her up on the offer the following Tuesday night and found Waneta positively chipper throughout their hour-long encounter—until the moment Jim Willard, the Berkshire minister who was one of Waneta's most loyal patrons, entered the visiting room. Spotting him, she became instantly forlorn. When he asked how she was doing, she sighed and said not too good. Later that week, the *Press & Sun-Bulletin* published the letter from Waneta. It read in part:

. . . They rolled me through the dirt, my family, these accusers are the ones with these problems. I am not uncaring, depraved, mad or anything else. I just would like to have my chance to really tell the truth. I been falsely accused and unjustly convicted of killing five human beings 24-30 years ago. No physical evidence, no collaboration. Just bought-off people being paid to lie. They did a good job, didn't they? I would like to ask these 12 jurors if they are able to live with themselves for what they have done in 12 hours to destroy my family, me, son, husband. I'm proud to know they can take 12 hours to ruin 31 years of marriage, two devoted people that loved their children with all their heart and tried to save their lives and seek help when they were sick.

I was convicted on a coerced statement. I can tell a lot more than that attorney allowed me to say. I sure was wrong listening to him. For we know nothing of judicial system and look what has happened to us. We are as human as anyone else. Because we are poor of money and rich on "love" the judicial system just railroaded us for they said they are poor, no one will miss her. Her family will get over it, we can (lawyers, etc.,

D.A.) be rich, and famed into glory like the O.J. case. And that is exactly what has happened. Can you please help or know of someone that would be interested in talking to me? Forgive me if I am a little sloppy. It is difficult in here. I never ever had trouble until these people did this to us. What can I do when I can't find someone to listen?

In fact, many people were listening. Charles Ewing called regularly, offering his continued support, warning Waneta away from journalists who believed she was guilty—these are not your friends, he counseled. Bill Fischer, the investigator who had been officially released from the case more than six months before, told Waneta's friends that she'd been wrongly convicted. The defense had failed to call all the witnesses he'd found, he complained—witnesses who could have helped exonerate her. The people who still needed to believe in Waneta believed Fischer. They started a Hoyt Legal Defense Fund to help pay for an appeal, and Fischer produced a flier that hung in stores in northern Tioga County. It featured a photograph of Waneta as a teenager, and a plea for justice: "Abnormal breathing patterns, vagus nerve irregularities, and heart problems were well documented by attending physicians and pediatric experts. Coroners and police were called to investigate the deaths twenty years ago. Autopsies were conducted, with no indication of homicide. *This is your opportunity to right a wrong and stand up against injustice. It happened to her. It can happen to you!*"

In her kitchen a few days after the verdict, Natalie Hilliard remarked, "If I was on that jury, I would have found her guilty too." The truth, she said, was in what the jury had not heard. She pulled out a memo Fischer had drawn up for the Hoyts and their supporters, outlining his views of the case. It seemed Natalie's last hope.

Privately and collectively, the people in Waneta's life spent the spring trying to come to terms with everything that had happened. But a season was not nearly long enough. As they had from the beginning, Waneta's family—her father, her sisters and brothers—kept themselves apart from the public drama. Albert Nixon alone had appeared at the trial, but only now and then and not on the day of the verdict. Neither he nor his sons and daughters would say anything about it. That had always been the Nixons' way.

Tim's family was in much more open turmoil. One night, his sisters Ann and Janet, his brothers George and Chuck, and Chuck's wife, Loretta, gathered around a dining room table and spent several hours talking about Waneta and Tim, about the babies, about what they remembered and what they'd long forgotten—about what they thought then, what they thought now. Janet ultimately left in tears. Ann seemed alternately knowing and angry, but unwilling to verbalize her final judgment. They all felt terrible for their brother and their brother's son. But Tim's response to the verdict divided them. His brothers were deeply frustrated that he was still operating under Waneta's influence—"She's got some awesome power over him," said George—but his sisters sympathized with his loyalty. It was clear that this remained a family with secrets. The split among them would deepen as time passed.

In the end, the saddest undercurrent for those who accepted the verdict, the sense of remorse that nobody could easily put into words, was the question of responsibility. Could anything have been done to save those children? Three decades later, it was easy to pick out any number of moments when the course of events could have been altered. The trial had cast harsh new light on old perceptions. Ella Hoyt, Tim's aging mother, seemed to be edging toward a different reality when she announced a revelation one day in late spring. She had passed out when she saw the ambulance that had come for her beloved grandson Jimmy that day in 1968. She had always believed he had collapsed and died of a mysterious disease, but now, she told her children, she realized that this was what Waneta *told* her had happened. Still, she wasn't sure what she believed now. All she knew was that she couldn't talk about it.

Could these children have been saved? It was easy to say now, but it was also easy to see how powerful Waneta's deception had been, and how perfectly it combined with the simplemindedness and inaction of some people in authority, the blindness of others, and the reluctance of people in general to face an intolerable possibility.

One day, George came by to talk to Chuck. He had been remembering things, he told his brother. The verdict made it safe to share them. They went out into the barn behind Chuck's house. It was Jimmy who was most on George's mind. He remembered his first wife, Gloria, telling him when he came through the door, one day in 1968, "She lost another one." This time it wasn't a baby. Now George was convinced that Waneta had murdered Jimmy because the little boy had seen her smother Julie three weeks before. He recalled a remark by Gloria when Jay was adopted in 1976: "I hope she doesn't kill this one too."

Chuck told his older brother, "She robbed Tim of his children. She robbed us of our nieces and nephews. Our kids lost their cousins." The words echoed in George's head for days. He went camping with his wife and took off by himself to sit in the woods and write poems and streams of thought on a tiny notepad. One after another, they poured out: verses and simple, disconnected sentences about Waneta's crimes, her continuing deceit, the pain he believed she was still inflicting on the family with her relentless plays for sympathy.

———

In June, days before she was due to be sentenced, Waneta got herself a new lawyer. Bill Sullivan came from Ithaca with a reputation as a rabid defense attorney who had an affection for publicity and an abhorrence of the state police, though he had once been a prosecutor. Among his clients had been the main victim of the Troop C evidence-tampering scandal, and Sullivan wore this like a badge of honor. He had a way of working it into almost any conversation, as did his private investigator on the case, Bill Fischer. The Hoyts had no money to pay Sullivan, but here he was, the lawyer from whom Peggy Drake had once received a two-inch-thick brief on a speeding ticket.

On the day Waneta was to learn her fate, Sullivan emerged triumphant from Judge Sgueglia's chambers. He had persuaded him to adjourn the sentencing for three months to give him time to catch up on the case. Sgueglia rescheduled it for September, and Sullivan held court on the south lawn. "It appears an innocent woman has been convicted of crimes she didn't commit—of crimes that didn't happen," the white-haired lawyer declared to the cameras and notepads. He pledged to work tirelessly on her appeal. Among the legal arguments he planned was that too much time had elapsed between the alleged crimes and the commencement of an investigation.

With Sullivan joining Charles Ewing and Bill Fischer, Waneta's unofficial team of professional supporters was complete. What they seemed to share was a sometimes overwrought mistrust of police, and found in Waneta Hoyt a paradigm of persecution. It was symbolic of the emotional politics that had long set the mysteries of sudden infant death against the sacredness of motherhood. (Waneta had one more sympathizer in Syracuse—Lois [Henning] Black, the clinical psychologist who worked with Steinschneider at Upstate in the early days of the monitoring movement and who remained a member of the pediatrics department's clinical faculty twenty years later. "We must stop pouring resources of the state into the prosecution of cases in which there is no hard evidence of crime," she wrote to the Syracuse *Post-Standard* a few weeks after the trial. "The relentless stalking of a mother whose confused utterances suggest that she must still feel that she somehow caused all of the babies she bore to die may be legal, but it is morally repugnant. Nor is a courtroom the arena in which to judge the quality of our science or the character of our scientists.") This was a case in which some people seemed to have trouble distinguishing the good side from the bad, a difficulty little clarified by the outcome.

The reporters slowly fell away from Sullivan, and then Michelle York spotted Lynne Rocha descending the courthouse steps and went over to talk to her. Others followed, and suddenly Juror Number Five found herself surrounded. Why had she come? they asked. "I just wanted it settled in my mind," Rocha explained. "It was very hard, what we all did, and I haven't stopped thinking about it. We were trying right to the very end not to convict her. But she's guilty. I'm disappointed she's not being sentenced today. I just want her out of my head. And I want justice for her children."

She got her wish three months later. On September 11, Peggy Drake, seven months pregnant, stood before Judge Sgueglia and asked him to sentence Waneta Hoyt to the maximum penalty of five consecutive terms of twenty-five years to life for the murders of her children. "Waneta Hoyt," she said, "does not deserve anything other than to spend the rest of her life in state prison."

Bill Sullivan argued a long, disparate series of motions aimed at further forestalling the sentencing. He raised the Troop C scandals and tried to impugn the integrity of Bob Courtright, who had recently retired amid allegations that he had threatened a man during a personal off-duty confrontation. Finally, taking up his client's battle cry, Sullivan declared that Waneta would die in jail, no matter the length of the sentence. "And probably the prosecutors will stand up and cheer at that point."

It had been nearly five months since the verdict, and Sgueglia had no intention of putting off Waneta's sentencing any longer. He had thought about her punishment through the spring and then the summer. Now he asked the defendant if she wished to address the court.

Waneta stepped forward with her Bible in her hands. "I don't mean any disrespect to no one, but I tried very hard to save my children," she said, her voice barely more than a whisper. Sgueglia asked her to come closer. "I did the best I could," she continued. "Why this story has come out like this, I don't know. I loved all my kids and I'll love them till the day I die. All I can say is God forgive all of you who done this to me. He knows I didn't do anything. I'm an innocent woman. I didn't kill my kids."

Sgueglia looked at her squarely. There was a note of regret in his manner. He had weighed all the factors, he said, but in the end, the verdict left him with little choice. He told Waneta that he was sentencing her to the minimum sentence for each child: fifteen years to life. But she would have to serve the prison terms consecutively, so that the total sentence would be seventy-five years to life.

In the front row of the gallery, Jay Hoyt wept as the sentence was pronounced, and Art Hilliard, sitting beside him, rubbed his shoulders. Sgueglia looked in Jay's direction. For months, the judge had thought about him, and the verdict had intensified his pity. One afternoon soon after the trial, he had sat in his chambers and contemplated this hopeless family. "Jay," he said. "The sixth victim—smothered by his mother in a lie. He's doomed for life." Sgueglia distinguished sharply between the two men Waneta was leaving behind. Tim was an adult. He had lived those years with her. He could confront the truth—his wife's guilt and his own blindness and inaction—or he could run from it. He had a choice, and he was making it. But it was Sgueglia's judgment that Jay had no such choice. This woman was his mother. He had to believe her.

The judge leaned forward, looked into Waneta's eyes. "I have only one other thing to say to you," he told her. "And that is to consider your surviving son. Whatever you tell anybody in this life—whatever you tell your husband, whatever you tell your lawyer, whatever you tell me, whatever you tell God— you owe something to that boy. You owe it to him to tell him the truth."

Sgueglia's remark stunned everyone, fixing the courtroom in one last moment of poignance as all eyes fixed upon Jay. Then, silently, clutching her Bible, Waneta was led away.

"We still love you," a friend yelled as Waneta left the courthouse. "We love you, Waneta!"

"Waneta, anything to say?" a television reporter asked during the short walk across Court Street back to the jail.

"I love my family," she said.

In the aftermath, those who believed the validity of the verdict were left to ponder its meaning. The trial had established how the children of Waneta Hoyt died, but in many ways that was the easy part. Why they died was much harder to say.

Was it the aberrant impulses of Munchausen syndrome by proxy that drove Waneta to kill them? There were reasons to believe that her well-established addiction to sympathy was an element. It didn't work as a rational explanation, but Munchausen behavior is by definition not rational, and these were clearly not rational crimes. Her case does seem to fit this central feature of Munchausen by proxy: The children are only pawns in an intricate psychological game. In the words of Dr. Herbert Schreier, the Munchausen expert in California: "The kids don't matter."

Was it connected to some neglect or trauma in her own childhood, another common factor in Munchausen and child abuse generally? Maybe there was an answer in Waneta's relationship with her mother—seemingly, at once intensely close and painfully distant—or with her aloof father. Of course, not many children of less than perfect parents go on to murder their own offspring, one after another.

Was there a postpartum factor? And if so, was justice done? All the children, including Jimmy, who died three weeks after his seven-week-old sister Julie, were killed within a few months of the end of a pregnancy. If she had lived in Britain, Waneta would not even have been charged with murder (though two-year-old Jimmy's death would have presented an interesting dilemma). Had she allowed her lawyers to concede the confession and raise a psychiatric defense—or even asked the jury to consider manslaughter—she very likely would have spared herself a life sentence. The British view has long been shared by New York psychiatrist Stuart Asch. "It is wrong for American courts to imprison mothers who kill their babies. They suffer from mental illness," he wrote to *Time* after the Marybeth Tinning case. He has testified successfully for the defense in other infanticide cases; given the Owego jury's posture, he might have made an effective witness for Waneta Hoyt.

Grope as they might, those close to Waneta as well as those looking on from the background found no satisfying answers to these questions. While some authorities believe the smothering of a single baby is a more prevalent occurrence than is generally thought, serial infanticide cases are a breed apart, less common and even less understood. The few that have been uncovered, from Martha Woods to Marybeth Tinning, have revealed much about method but little about motive. Along with Waneta Hoyt and any number of mothers videotaped looking over their shoulders before trying to suffocate their babies in the hospital, they have demonstrated that such grotesque repetitive acts are more calculated than impulsive, and clearly a reaction to something more complicated than a baby's incessant crying.

Serial infanticide may be one version of Munchausen by proxy, which itself is one version of child abuse. It may be that mothers who repeatedly murder their babies share some essential sociopathy with mothers who kill only once. In 1994, when the members of the U.S. Advisory Board on Child Abuse and Neglect visited the Bedford Hills Correctional Facility, New York State's maximum security prison for women, they heard a number of women imprisoned for abusing or killing their children describe the abuses they had suffered themselves in childhood. But because such serial infant killers as Hoyt and Tinning have ultimately claimed innocence, it has been difficult to arrive at a real understanding of their lives and crimes. Neither has opened herself to an exploration of the truth, so the question remains: Why? Rarely is the answer as cold as greed, apparently the motivation of Stephen Van Der Sluys, whose gender also stood him apart. But his case, like theirs, does demonstrate how long it usually takes the authorities to catch on, and how many children can die in the meantime.

Ultimately, though it defies a tidy textbook psychology, Waneta Hoyt's case does have a perversely redemptive value. The record of her conviction stands as a landmark itself for all that it finally exposed: not only the deeds of Mrs. H. and the fallaciousness of the 1972 paper that brought familial SIDS, near-misses, and apnea monitors into prominence, but the misguided science that has arguably shielded uncounted other infanticides. The possibility does exist that deaths in some rare cases attributed to familial SIDS are actually not

SIDS but the result of an undetected genetic metabolic or cardiac disorder. And statistically, it is certainly possible for a tiny number of families to suffer two legitimate SIDS deaths. But the national experience suggests that child abuse is a more common cause, particularly when there are three or more in the same family.

Steinschneider himself may have overlooked a second case in Syracuse in the early seventies. In one of his responses to Stuart Asch's correspondence in 1974, he said that he had recently studied the fourth baby of a family that had three previous SIDS deaths. Also potentially questionable are the two deaths of babies enrolled in his study of subsequent siblings in Portland in the late 1980s. As the second babies in their families to die, both warranted careful examination.

The medical and legal landscape is dotted with cases of reported familial SIDS that are more than likely misdiagnosed murders, many of which took Steinschneider's 1972 paper as their precedent. In 1988, the *Journal of the Oklahoma State Medical Association* published an article by five physicians— two pediatricians, two pathologists, and an epidemiologist with the Centers for Disease Control—reporting a case of four SIDS deaths in one family. Homicide was explored but discounted, the authors wrote, when "no evidence of child abuse was found by local authorities or medical examiners." Contacted several years later, however, the lead author, Dr. John Harkess, said he had since come to believe it likely that he and his colleagues had inadvertently added a case of serial infanticide to the literature of familial SIDS.

In Seattle, there are several cases that Bruce Beckwith now suspects were probably multiple murders. In Chicago, there is the Gedzius family—and maybe others. Dr. Carl Hunt, the head of the ongoing federal monitoring study who had a hand in the treatment of two of the Gedzius babies while he was at Children's Memorial Hospital, says he has been involved with perhaps ten families with more than one SIDS death; in most, he has personally evaluated subsequent siblings of SIDS victims who went on to die themselves. "That is the nature of my practice," says Hunt, who moved from Chicago to Toledo in 1988. "That issue [of infanticide] is out there and needs to be considered. But there are physiological events out there also." He found none of his cases suggestive of child abuse.

Hunt's view prevails among the leading apnea and monitoring believers, who tend to say child abuse should be considered but who rarely view their own cases with suspicion. To some of their colleagues, it is a naïve attitude born of the medical and emotional dogmatism that has always gripped the apnea world: To consider a parent's hand in repeated Apparent Life Threatening Events and familial deaths is to undermine the legitimacy of a concept on which more than a few research careers have been built and continue to depend. In contrast, the two most venerable SIDS investigators, pathologists

Beckwith and Marie Valdes-Dapena, and many pediatric researchers as well, now believe that, like the family that started it all, familial cases are less suggestive of some phantom cause that has never been proven—and is usually based largely on the unverified reports of a parent—than of suffocation.

"They're alleging they have families with these prior events," Beckwith argues. "But I think that for them to prove the fatal events are not homicide, they should be required to meet a simple and very specific standard: Have any significant life-threatening episodes been medically observed and documented? A parent's report is not enough and a blip on a monitor tape is not enough. They should be backed into a corner. And if it's a lethal disorder that's affecting every sibling, it would pretty well have to be a dominant genetic condition and that means a parent had it—so why didn't they die? For a long time, I and others said to those who said it's murder—and I still say this—you had better be damned sure. But now we have unequivocal evidence that Munchausen by proxy not only exists but is disturbingly common. And I think the burden of proof is now on the person who would say it's *not* Munchausen when you have a familial situation."

Beckwith finds it significant that many of these familial deaths fall outside the epidemiology of classic SIDS. For instance, whereas ninety-five percent of SIDS deaths occur between one and six months of age—with the overwhelming majority coming at two to four months—a disproportionate number of supposed familial SIDS babies are older than six months, and some are much older. Some are also reported to die suddenly while awake. Moreover, studies have found subsequent SIDS deaths within a family to be so rare that even most apnea believers discount a genetic factor, raising yet more questions about those that do occur. There is reason to believe that even the infinitesimal incidence of familial SIDS reported in the literature is skewed by infanticides. But statistical conclusions remain intangible.

The anecdotal evidence may be more revealing. Nearly forty years after Molly Dapena first encountered the "Moores," the Philadelphia couple made famous by *Life,* there is ample indication that serial infant abuse—fatal or not—is an ongoing hidden problem in America. Medical examiners and child protection workers throughout the country, as well as doctors in emergency rooms and in some of the large apnea centers that grew out of Steinschneider's theory, have confronted cases highly suggestive of Munchausen by proxy—many of which are strikingly similar to the circumstances of a good number of the thirty-one infant deaths associated with Waneta Hoyt, Marybeth Tinning, Martha Woods, and "Martha Moore." It has come full circle: They also match the description of the SIDS cases preceded by "near-misses" that were reported during the embryonic moments of the apnea theory at the 1969 Orcas Island conference.

The consequences vary by the case. One recognized scenario is that of the mother who repeatedly suffocates her newborns in sequence before one actually dies. In these instances one baby can be saved by the birth of another. But hard evidence rarely presents itself even when several deaths are involved, and these cases commonly go unresolved or even unpursued—especially if the abuses occur in different jurisdictions, camouflaging the pattern.

The "Moores" never left Philadelphia. They can be found living out their lives there. They have no grandchildren.

Finally, there is Boston. The truth about what has been going on at Massachusetts General Hospital the past twenty-five years has never been revealed, but the prosecution of Waneta Hoyt has helped clarify some long-standing suspicions. As she made clear in her testimony in Tioga County, the Hoyt case did not cause Dorothy Kelly to see her own experience in a new light. But just like Steinschneider's 1972 paper, her influential work with Daniel Shannon, including their 1987 *Pediatrics* report about four families with fourteen reported SIDS deaths among them, is riddled with implications of child abuse and infanticide that were never reported to outside authorities and which repeatedly cleared the process of scientific peer review. As some people have long suspected—among them Bill Fitzpatrick, who sent a copy of the paper to the Boston district attorney but got no response—evidence of this may be found in the files in the basement of Massachusetts General.

When we asked Kelly, months after the Hoyt verdict, if she and Shannon had encountered any suspicious SIDS deaths in the quarter century they had been evaluating and monitoring babies, she said they had not seen even one. But her response astonished Joseph Oren, the former Harvard research fellow who was their co-author on the 1987 paper. "I don't know how she can say that," he said. He had prepared the article from the files Kelly gave him and remembers discussing the possibility of inflicted suffocation with her. He never met the families himself, but the records made him suspicious. "When we reviewed the charts, I had my own questions," he said. But Kelly dismissed the idea, and the data were published as evidence that SIDS could recur repeatedly within families.

A decade later, Kelly remains resolute. In March of 1994—the same month Waneta Hoyt was arrested in upstate New York—she treated a baby at Mass General whose three prior siblings had all died within two months of their births. Autopsies had ruled out a genetic metabolic disorder. The new baby was monitored for a time and survived, though Kelly says she eventually lost track of the infant. "I know SIDS runs in families," she declared, despite the best evidence to the contrary.

Daniel Shannon's perceptions are more ambiguous than Kelly's, and as always, considerably less public. But whatever his true thoughts as he pursued the apnea theory of SIDS, one thing seems clear. It took an inquisitive and doggedly righteous young physician to force Shannon, in 1996, to confront his and Kelly's failure to intervene in what appears to have been the abuse, and in some instances the murders, of babies who had been placed in their care over a twenty-five-year period. The story of Dr. Thomas Truman, reported here for the first time, may tie up one of the last loose ends of the long history of the apnea wars. It also sets forth the possibility that two of the most prominent clinical researchers in American pediatrics have acted with extraordinary negligence.

Tom Truman was a twenty-nine-year-old father of two when he arrived in Boston from Tampa, Florida, in the summer of 1993. Having just finished his residency in pediatrics, he was set to begin a three-year Harvard research fellowship in pediatric critical care at Massachusetts General. Walking into the intensive-care unit and the pediatric pulmonary department that was its adjunct, Truman found a realm pervaded by the authority of Shannon, who had influenced not only Kelly but many others who had come through as residents, research fellows, or attending physicians during the past two decades. If Steinschneider had been the father of the apnea theory, Shannon and Kelly had made Harvard and Mass General the motherland—*the* place to send SIDS siblings and babies with reported near-miss events or who were otherwise thought to be "at risk" for SIDS. It was a place governed by twenty-year-old gospel well into the 1990s. But Truman arrived with a streak of independence and the perspective of his times: He knew that when babies came into the hospital with reports of relentless but unverified near-death events, a diagnosis of child abuse had to be seriously considered. He would discover that this perspective attacked an almost sacred principle at Massachusetts General.

The summer after the first year of his fellowship, Truman encountered the case of an eighteen-month-old boy who had been having apparent life-threatening events that seemed to strike only in the presence of his mother. Some of the episodes were marked by abrupt drops in heart rate—bradycardia—that occurred even as an event recorder showed movement of the chest wall indicating continuous attempts to breathe. The toddler was being followed by an attending physician who worked under Shannon in the pulmonary department, whose response to the events had been to have a pacemaker installed in the child's chest. A cardiologist had pronounced his heart sound, so the pulmonary pediatricians presumed that the problem might be in the connection with the brain. They thought the pacemaker could act as a safety mechanism against future episodes. But now the child was back. Despite the pacemaker, he had experienced another reported life-threatening event at home.

The attending physician was Dr. Denise Strieder, a pediatric pulmonary specialist who had worked closely with Shannon for years. A tiny woman in her mid-sixties, she had followed his lead into the apnea theory, and in 1986 had the honor of presenting the Mass General team's research to the NIH apnea consensus conference. Now, eight years later, they had a patient like so many others they had seen through the years. With his latest ALTE episode, the eighteen-month-old was readmitted to the ICU. Strieder wanted to check for "pacemaker malfunction."

Hearing about the child from one of the residents who worked under him, Truman wondered what the mystery was. Repeated unexplained near-death episodes, all in the presence of the mother and nobody else? She's doing it, he told the resident. He found the use of a pacemaker dismaying—just the kind of unnecessary and invasive medical procedure typical of Munchausen by proxy cases. He told Strieder what he thought. He wanted to call it in to the state child protection authorities. "She came up into my face, pointing her finger—'How dare you?'" Truman recounted. "And all about autonomic insufficiency and vagal storm, how they had documented the bradycardia, how the nurses had witnessed events without the mom there. When I heard that, I said whoops, sorry, and backed off. I was new, a Florida boy up at the big hospital. Well, the pacemaker checks out and the baby goes home. And the next week he comes into the E.R. He had coded at home with another 'severe episode.' This time it left him in a persistent vegetative state."

Appalled—and filled with regret that he had retreated—Truman went into the baby's file, looking for evidence. Examining the tracings taken from the hospital's event-recording monitor, he found only one episode of bradycardia. It had been directly preceded by a spell of tachycardia—*increased* heart rate—accompanied by erratic breathing. "So just before the bad thing happened," Truman explained, "something was going on in this child's body that was making his heart rate go up and his breathing [efforts] become fast." Truman talked to the mother and established that she was alone with her son at the time of the event. "She said, 'I was in the room, I was watching him, he was sleeping comfortably, he wasn't shaking or doing anything. And then his heart rate went down.' But that documented event and that report are not consistent, so someone's lying, something's wrong." Now Truman checked with the nurses to see if what Strieder had said was true. Had they witnessed any life-threatening events outside the presence of the mother? "They said absolutely not. They said the only event was that one incident when the mom was in the room by herself. She took him off the monitor and ran out to the nurses' station, and he was blue and limp in her arms. That's when they first saw it. They never saw it start. And they were suspicious." Truman felt he had been deceived, and the consequences sickened him. "If [Strieder] hadn't given me that information, then I would have gone beyond her at that point and called in my suspicions, and then at least my conscience would have been clear that I had done all I could to have protected this kid."

It turned out that Truman was not the first doctor to have his suspicions about this case turned aside by Shannon's pulmonary department. "It happened to me too," a resident told him that day. The year before, at the time the pacemaker was put in the child, the resident had expressed the same concerns. But he was pressured to suppress these concerns, and no report was made. "I was squashed like a bug," he told Truman. The case's tragic outcome led to a tense meeting of pediatric residents and the heads of several involved departments to put an end to the suppression of residents' judgments—whether about child abuse or anything else. But Truman found that the problem was more complicated than that when both he and an attending physician in the critical care unit did report the case to the Massachusetts social services authorities. It was August 1994. One state to the west, Waneta Hoyt had been arrested and was awaiting trial, news that was still reverberating through much of the pediatrics world. But at Massachusetts General, a state child protection investigator found the pediatric pulmonary doctors adamant: This little boy was definitely not a victim of child abuse. He had a documented cardiopulmonary problem. Truman was indignant but powerless. He knew who he was up against. "Our hands are tied," the investigator told him. But this case paled in comparison to what came just four months later.

One night in mid-December, Truman got a call at home from another worried resident. "We've got a baby in here that I'm concerned about," the resident told him. "Could you come up here and see what you think? It sounds a lot like that other case."*

Truman headed up to the third floor, where he found a one-year-old girl named Emily with a history of resuscitations by her mother. Shannon had admitted the baby for surgery to install a pacemaker.

"This is crazy," Truman thought after he spent forty-five minutes with the child's parents. Her mother told him that between Emily and an older brother, she had performed about eighty resuscitations at home. Truman questioned her delicately but closely, eliciting a telling detail: The episodes with the other child stopped two weeks after his sister was born—when hers began. Truman turned to the woman's husband. "How many times have you

---

*We have examined the details of the following case apart from the information we received from Truman. Holding to his obligation of patient confidentiality, he referred to the case anonymously, disclosing neither a name nor other identifying details. We obtained this information independently and verified the various aspects of the case with the central participants. We are not naming these sources in order to honor our promise not to disclose the family's name or its hometown.

had to resuscitate them?" he asked. "None," the man said. "I've never been there when it happens." Then he asked about the children's grandparents: How many times had they had to do it? "None," the man repeated. "It's only been with my wife."

"I'm waiting for the lightbulb to go off," Truman said later. "No lightbulb." More important, the circumstances had no effect on Shannon—even given how the previous case had turned out. He deflected Truman's urgings to hold off on the pacemaker, at least until they could explore the meaning of the history.

Emily's family was from a rural area in northern New York State just south of the Canadian border. Truman called the referring pediatrician, and learned that he was not alone in his suspicions: Emily's older brother had been seen by a specialist in Burlington, Vermont, who suspected the mother had either caused or fabricated his life-threatening episodes. When the referring pediatrician wanted to send Emily to the same specialist, her mother refused. But the suspicion did not lead to any official action. Instead, a series of referrals eventually brought Emily, now ten months old and having Apparent Life Threatening Events several times a month, to the pediatric pulmonary unit of Massachusetts General. The local doctor, hoping for clarification, heard the results of the hospital's evaluation from Denise Strieder on October 7, 1994: The baby had a seizure disorder that put her at risk of sudden death. The pediatrician felt he had no choice but to put his concerns aside and defer to "the fancy Boston doctors," as he later put it. Two months later, Emily was brought back to Mass General, and the pacemaker was implanted in her chest.

With the baby about to be sent home after surgery, Truman told Shannon he intended to call the authorities in her family's home county. Shannon tried to talk him out of it—"Think about the implications of a false accusation," he said—but Truman was resolute. "I'm just doing what the law says I have to do," he replied, and Shannon, perhaps with the recent meeting in mind, retreated—at least for the record. "I want you to do what you feel you have to do," he said. And then Shannon did what he apparently felt he had to do: He placed a phone call to a public health nurse in the family's home county, whose name he had found in the file. The nurse remembers the call. "You will probably be hearing from another physician here who believes this child is the victim of abuse," she says Shannon told her. "I want you to know that I don't think this is the case." Truman did call the nurse later in the day, and she referred him to the county's child abuse hotline. "I called it in," Truman said, "but it was the same as before. They basically ignored me because there was this world-famous physician saying this child has a medical diagnosis."

Truman, stewing, kept track of Emily long-distance after her discharge.

He stayed in contact with the county nurse, who began developing her own suspicions. She gave him distressing news on a regular basis. Despite the pacemaker, Emily continued to have events at home—always when she was alone with her mother—ending in visits to the emergency room, where the doctors could find nothing wrong. The nurse called Truman in a panic one day. While a county social worker was in the family's house, the mother had taken Emily into the bathroom and closed the door. A few minutes later, she came charging out with the child in her arms, limp and blue. "We're all worried here—we know she's doing it," the nurse told Truman. "And you're worried. But I talk to the investigators and they can't do anything because of what Dr. Shannon tells them."

The two cases left Truman with a bitter taste, along with a queasy feeling about the underlying moral culture of his prestigious new home. But the incidents also puzzled him. *Who is this guy Shannon?* he wondered. *Why is he putting pacemakers in child abuse victims and protecting their mothers?* Truman was in grade school in Ohio when Shannon and Kelly were helping launch the apnea world. Kelly had left Mass General by this point, and Truman knew little about Shannon other than that he was a famous man—a full professor of medicine at both Harvard and MIT, a doctor eminent for his research into apnea and SIDS. But Truman found his distinguished image incongruous with the kind of judgment he was seeing now.

Curious, Truman went to the Harvard medical library and began pulling old journals. *Oh, wow,* he thought when he read Shannon's work with Kelly in places like *The New England Journal of Medicine* and *Pediatrics. They had a lot of these cases.* He also started reading the research of David Southall and others on the relationship between apnea and Munchausen by proxy. He was struck by a thought. One of the main requirements of his fellowship was that he pursue a piece of research leading to the publication of a paper of which he was first author. He hadn't come up with a topic that compelled his interest during his first year. But the two recent cases, the juxtaposition of Shannon's published research against Southall's, and the unfolding Hoyt case gave Truman the germ of an idea. His interest was piqued further when he began talking to some of the doctors and nurses who had been around since the seventies. "Oh, we used to have these near-SIDS kids in here all the time," one nurse told him. "We had a couple of rooms reserved for them." He talked to an attending physician who had been a resident during the boom days of the eighties. The doctor told Truman that he, among others within Mass General, had always been skeptical of the pulmonary department's apnea diagnoses. Truman asked him about the name he kept seeing attached to Shannon's. "Who's this Dorothy Kelly?" he asked. The physician looked at him and chuckled. "Sit down," he said.

By the spring of 1995, Truman was seething with frustration over what he was convinced was the continuing abuse of the little girl from New York State, and Shannon's refusal to recognize what was going on—or even to see the need to investigate the possibility. But he was now coming to understand the historical context, and it occurred to him that maybe Shannon was simply in too deep—that he couldn't suddenly start seeing child abuse in the kinds of cases he had been diagnosing as apnea for twenty years. Shannon's denial pushed Truman into a decision. He now knew what the subject of his fellowship research would be. With Waneta Hoyt's conviction in the news and on his mind, he decided he would go back in time himself. He would try to learn how many other cases of apparent child abuse—and possible infanticide— doctors at Mass General might have overlooked or ignored over the years. A decade before, another research fellow, Joseph Oren, had been quietly suspicious. In the end, he had gone along. Truman, though, had moved beyond suspicion, and went the next step.

With the help of a hospital research specialist, Truman plugged the phrases SIDS, near-SIDS, aborted SIDS, near-miss SIDS, subsequent SIDS sibling, and Apparent Life Threatening Event into the Mass General database. He wanted to identify every case involving repeated unexplained near-miss events of babies admitted to the hospital all the way back to 1972. More than a thousand names emerged, and Truman went through them all, painstakingly eliminating patients who did not meet the criteria until he had pared the list down to 155 babies. Thirty of them had at least two admissions, and a few had a half a dozen or more. Of the thousands and thousands of babies who had come through the Mass General apnea program through the years, these were the most serious cases—the ones that helped establish the concept of near-miss SIDS and sell the monitoring industry.

Notepaper and data sheets in hand, Truman descended to the records department in the basement. He filled out the forms promising patient confidentiality, signed out the first batch of files, then went into a reading room to begin sifting through stacks of medical records, some nearly a quarter-century old. Discreetly—he knew Shannon had the power to quash his research if he found out about it—he spent the next six months studying the files of these babies who provided the data for much of the apnea research Shannon and Kelly had published in prominent journals and presented to such forums as the New York Academy of Sciences and the 1986 Consensus Conference convened by the National Institutes of Health. Whenever he had time, he headed for the basement, pulled a few files at a time, then sequestered himself in the reading room and watched the data pile up. By the end of the year, the records yielded what Truman considered strong circumstantial evidence suggestive of Munchausen by proxy in over one-third of the 155 cases. Many of the rest of the babies, he suspected, suffered from nothing more serious than nervous parents caught up in the hysteria of the times.

He describes a classic case from the suspicious pile. Though it did not end in death, the circumstances were remarkable for their resemblence to the lives of Molly and Noah Hoyt: "A baby is hospitalized for a month, has no events in the hospital, and then on the day he arrives home, he has four or five events. He comes back in the hospital, has a pacemaker implanted, and does fine. He goes home and has multiple events. Now the patient is made a 'resident' of the hospital—not this one but a local one—for a year. The kid goes six months without having an episode except on the one day he goes home on a leave of absence for three hours and he's alone with mom, when he has an event."

Other cases were nearly as suspicious. Truman found one in which a baby had a life-threatening event in the hospital parking lot just minutes after discharge. In each of the fifty-six cases he considered suggestive of Munchausen by proxy, only one person seemed to be present at the onset of all the life-threatening episodes. Some case files alluded to events allegedly witnessed by a third person, but, says Truman, "when you read the other people's accounts, they witnessed the child blue and not breathing or gasping, but that was *after* something happened earlier that they didn't see. There's this leap, this big void in what happened before that. Admittedly, that's a limitation of my study. That's why it should have been investigated at the time. But those are the ones that scare me: the ones nobody else ever saw but the parent. About half of them gave me a terrible feeling in my stomach, when it was just grossly suggestive."

Truman's ultimate purpose was to study the response of the doctors, and here his findings were unequivocal. There was no indication that any of these cases was ever reported, or even investigated internally. Instead, home apnea monitors—and in some cases pacemakers or antiseizure drugs—were prescribed. According to Truman, "They would write that the home monitoring showed something serious—this 'data' they collected when the patient was two hundred miles away. But if you've got something that happens ten times in one day at home and then when you're admitted to the hospital you don't have an event for a week, and then on the day you're discharged you have five more, it doesn't take a rocket scientist to realize something's wrong. In medical school you're taught that 80 percent of the time you can make a diagnosis on history alone. Yet they go totally against common sense, they ignore all the history and put all their money on this one abnormal event recording that was done so unscientifically it's not funny."

Truman found only two instances when the pulmonary doctors even addressed the possibility of child abuse. In one case, they were considering the various potential diagnoses of a child's repeated events and wrote, "Munchausen by proxy—definitely not." There was nothing indicating how this possibility had been ruled out. The other case came from a referring physician who wanted the Mass General doctors to figure out if his patient's ALTE episodes were being caused by her mother. "The outside physician wrote, 'I've got numerous people that think this could be Munchausen by proxy.' The response was, 'This might be Munchausen by proxy, but we can't prove it.' Well, that's flawed logic. Nobody can prove it; it's not our job. You suspect it, you report it. Now, I definitely don't want the pendulum to swing the other way. Leaping to conclusions would be as bad as what I'm saying they're doing. But those were the only two records showing they even thought about it. The rest—nothing. In all the records I reviewed, I found no case in which they filed a 51-A"—a report Massachusetts law requires medical personnel to make in cases where they suspect child abuse—"for a suspected Munchausen by proxy case by suffocation."

A subtext emerged from the files: a sense of the influence Shannon exerted on the judgments of other doctors. The records showed that his colleagues—whether they were attending physicians or consulting specialists from neurology, cardiology, and gastroenterology—deferred to Shannon's invariable finding of autonomic abnormality over maternal dysfunction. "The pediatric pulmonary diagnosis was like a tattoo," Truman observed. "The baby had it for life, no matter what happened. Whoever saw that patient saw it in the context of, oh, this patient has this problem."

This applied to cases that were not suspicious as well as to those that were. In that way, the files offered a glimpse of the high anxiety of the apnea world of the early 1980s. "A baby spits up and now he's on an apnea monitor for six months," Truman recounts. "Or you had siblings of bona fide SIDS babies—the parents are anxious, it's the eighties, the new baby looks fine but he's admitted and goes home with a monitor which costs his family a couple of thousand dollars." He found some of the artifacts of the monitoring movement: a copy of a letter signed by one of the doctors, asking for special attention for a monitor family from a utility company—a form letter from the guidebook Kelly produced with Healthdyne's money; pneumogram tracings showing nothing but short apneas, as routine as breath itself, for babies who then spent months on home monitors.

As he plowed deeper into the files, Truman found himself continually referring back to the Shannon-Kelly team's published research to see if it clarified the records. He found one influential paper particularly illuminating. Like Steinschneider, the authors had used the initials of some of their subjects. Truman plugged the initials into the database and found that the subjects were already part of his study group. And all four were among the fifty-six that suggested to him Munchausen by proxy—and in one instance, what he viewed as an astonishing case of scientific dishonesty. "They leave out that the child and a sibling had multiple near-death events until they were taken out of the custody of the mother and put in foster medical care. Then they mysteriously stop having events. When I first saw this file, I thought,

Okay, great, here's one they recognized and got the kids out. But the reason they
got the kids out was because they were worried she's not going to be able to
resuscitate them. They even admitted [in the records] that the mom was
having psychiatric problems, but they didn't take it the next step and say, 'She
has a psychiatric problem, my God, maybe she's doing this.' What they say is,
'We're going to take the kids away because we're afraid she won't be able to
take care of these gravely ill children.' In all their publications, I didn't see a
single social history documented. They wrote reams and reams about how
inborn errors of metabolism were ruled out, seizures were ruled out, congenital heart defects were ruled out. Not once did they say, 'And of course we also
did a full psychosocial evaluation and episodes occurred in front of numerous
caregivers and in front of nurses.' It was all bullshit, but no one questions you
if you're from Harvard. Everything flies once you attach the big H."

Truman's search of the documents obviously stopped short of hard proof.
To gain access to the records, he had signed a standard research statement
affirming that he was only pursuing a retrospective chart review and that he
would not attempt to contact any of the patients or their families. Nor was it
his purpose to do police work. But the files—and his own personal experience
in two cases—gave him what he considered abundant evidence that the
Harvard–Mass General apnea program had a long and sad history of
ignoring suggestions of child abuse, some of it fatal. "I am convinced they
were worried about their research and grants and they kept their blinders
on," he said. "They were going to get the answer to SIDS and along with that
a Nobel Prize. But to do that you need data, and to get data you need patients.
If a pediatrician refers a family and we suspect abuse, the parents get angry
and no more referrals."

Through these months, Truman kept his work between himself and his
research advisors. But as he neared the end of his fellowship in the early
winter of 1996, he decided to take an audacious step. He arranged to report
his findings at a grand rounds for the pediatrics staff. He planned to title his
talk "Considering the 'Unthinkable' in the Evaluation of Children Experi-
encing Recurrent Apparent Life Threatening Events, SIDS and Their Siblings." Truman did not seek Shannon out to tell him what he had found, but
word of the upcoming presentation spread in whispers. Truman and Shannon were on a collision course. It might have had something to do with an
encounter Shannon initiated one day in the pediatric ICU, two weeks before
the grand rounds.

"Remember that baby girl we put the pacemaker in?" he asked
Truman.

"I do," Truman replied curtly. It had been a year since then, and Emily—
now two years old—had continued to show up in the emergency room at the
local hospital.

"Well, you know what?" Shannon said. "I got a letter from a doctor up there who said she's been doing just fine."

"That's fascinating," Truman responded. "Because I get a call about every month about how concerned everybody is that her mom's been suffocating her. She's been to the E.R. no less than four or five times."

"Oh," Shannon said with a look of bewilderment. "That's interesting. I hadn't heard anything about that."

"Well, maybe you should consider following up this patient you put a pacemaker in."

One week later, Truman heard the news he had feared all along. Emily was dead.

She had stopped breathing at home. The local rescue squad had been summoned to a familiar address. They had rushed her to the emergency room, where she was barely resuscitated. Then she was airlifted to the nearest major hospital—the Fletcher Allen Health Care Center in Burlington, Vermont, home of *Pediatrics* editor Jerold Lucey. She died there four days later. The final episode prompted her pediatrician to call the New York State Police.

It was true that the doctor had written to Shannon a few weeks before, saying Emily was "doing better." But it was a relative assessment. What Shannon didn't tell Truman was that the doctor had also written that despite the pacemaker, Emily had continued to have life-threatening events—it was simply that they were no longer coming every few days—and that he remained suspicious about their cause. "I CANNOT RULE OUT that they are being induced," he wrote to Shannon, hoping the uppercase letters would emphasize his worries. For more than a year, the pediatrician had deferred to Shannon's expertise, despite Truman's beliefs and his own suspicions. It wasn't until he found himself in the emergency room with a virtually dead child and a mother who seemed not very upset that he concluded that Truman had probably been right all along.

Questioned by the state police four days later, Emily's mother denied killing her, but did admit she had previously pressed the toddler's face against her chest. She evaded questions about why she had done this. She said that on the day of the fatal episode, she left the room for a moment as Emily played happily. When she returned, she was "having one of her spells," which did not respond to her usual resuscitative efforts. She agreed to take a polygraph, and the investigators found her early answers suggestive of guilt. But when the questions became more pointed, she "became wild and vicious," one of the investigators recounted. "She screamed and cursed, then just got up and left." He became yet another detective digging into the Munchausen by proxy literature. "My position is she is definitely guilty of the homicide of her daughter," he said. "I've read cases and cases and cases in the medical literature and she fits the profile to a T."

An autopsy performed by the office of Vermont's chief medical examiner listed Emily's cause of death as "hypoxic ischemic encephalopathy"—lack of oxygen and inadequate flow of blood to the brain—due to an Apparent Life Threatening Event. The real question, however, was not so much the cause but the "manner" of death. The medical examiner listed this as "undetermined." But then the New York investigator called Michael Baden at the state police forensic sciences lab in Albany. Baden reviewed the autopsy report, considered the child's age, got the history from Truman, and examined the circumstances surrounding the fatal event. He found the mother's account inconsistent with Emily's body temperature when she was brought into the E.R. It indicated to him that the "spell" had occurred much earlier than she said. He also tested the pacemaker; it was working fine. Baden thought the case was highly suggestive of homicide.

But it was not enough for the district attorney. Though Emily was long past the SIDS age, and the state police investigator argued long and heatedly that there was a circumstantial case to be made, the prosecutor concluded that he would be unable to win a conviction. The major reason: Dr. Daniel Shannon. Getting the subtleties of Munchausen by proxy across to a rural jury would be difficult enough, he felt; with someone of Shannon's stature testifying for the defense, it would be nearly impossible. "I'm stymied," the prosecutor would say nearly a year after Emily's death. "You have an older, more established doctor that has never acknowledged this to be a Munchausen case. You have a younger doctor who has always believed it. So you have a conflict of medical opinion. Secondly, there is the appearance from the medical records of problems from birth. They installed a pacemaker and did a variety of treatments. I've seen pictures of this mother holding the baby and the baby's all hooked up to these machines. The jury's not going to want to believe a mother would do this. They see those pictures—and they would—and they really won't believe it. So from an evidentiary perspective, it's almost impossible to prove unless you have a parent that's admitted it. The circumstances remain very suspicious, and I haven't dropped it, but right now I'm not going anywhere with it because I can't win. I can't get beyond Shannon. If we could knock him out of the box we'd have a whole new ballgame." Would he proceed if not for the specter of Shannon's testimony for the defense? "Probably."

The medical and social workers in New York made clear to Truman how they viewed Shannon's role. "They were up in arms like you would not believe," he said. "Their view was here we are, this small community, and we have this system set up to protect kids and we think we're pretty good at doing that. And somebody screwed with our system and we've got a dead kid because of it."

To Truman, there was no doubt that both babies who had received pace-makers for supposed "autonomic insufficiency" during his fellowship had been repeatedly assaulted by their mothers. One was now dead, the other hopelessly damaged. As far as Truman was concerned, Shannon had done nothing in either case to intercede—in fact, he had actively suppressed investigations, thereby facilitating the continuing abuse and, ultimately, the horrible outcomes. It was 1996. There was no excuse.

Bringing such a stunning message to a grand rounds was a courageous move. But as angry as Truman was, he had to be careful. A young, obscure research fellow was about to challenge the entire career of one of the most important men in his field, and this man would be in the audience. He resolved to give his presentation the measured, objective thrust of serious research. To deflect any appearance that he was mounting a direct personal attack on Shannon, he decided, in fact, not even to mention the freshest and most glaring cases in point. Focusing on the data he had compiled from the older files might make his talk slightly less confrontational. Nevertheless, the sixty people who packed into the miniature auditorium had no trouble quickly discerning the import of his investigation. Truman opened dramatically, showing a videotape of a mother suffocating her baby in the apnea center of a San Diego hospital. It was presumably not lost on those gathered that a video camera was not a piece of equipment used in their department, the home of the world's leading apnea center. The video made several people cry.

The tension in the room grew as Truman discussed the Hoyt case, then laid out what he'd found in the Mass General files. Nobody left. Nobody said a word. Finally, he opened the floor to questions. Shannon stood up.

"I would expect that we cared for a majority of these patients," he said. "And I would say that these data are misleading. You are not correct in suggesting we have ignored child abuse. We did consider it."

"Well, it wasn't documented," Truman responded.

Shannon countered that suspicions were sometimes noted, though not in the official hospital record but rather in the private files of the pulmonary lab.

A friend of Truman's stood. "Dr. Truman, did you find any notations in any of the hospital files indicating the existence of another file?" None, said Truman. But he'd be interested in any new information and would adjust his conclusions if warranted. Afterward, doctors began coming up to Truman and asking why he had refused to look at the private files. *What?* he asked. He was astounded to hear that Shannon was telling people he had offered Truman the files months before, but that Truman would not look at them.

Over the next few months, the question of Shannon's "private files" was left hanging in the air of the pediatrics department. Meanwhile, it was understood that Truman planned to publish these results as the paper required of his Harvard research fellowship, which was due to end in June. Soon after, he got a letter from Shannon asking him not to publish his research. Shannon asserted that many parents would be harmed by what he termed Truman's erroneous conclusions, and repeated his contention that he had considered child abuse in a number of cases and that there was documentation of this in the private files. But regardless of Shannon's contentions, such an attempt to squelch the publication of research is considered classically improper in the scientific world. It led to a showdown between the two men with the Harvard pediatrics chairman, along with the heads of human studies and critical care, the latter of whom was both Truman's mentor and an old friend of Shannon's. Truman left the meeting relieved. There was no disagreement among the department chiefs that despite the potentially explosive consequences, Truman should seek to publish his work. Meanwhile, Shannon was urged to share his private files with Truman.

Afterward, Truman says, Shannon said to him privately, "Why are you so hell-bent on finding me at fault?" Truman immediately brought up the case he had omitted from his grand rounds. "Because I think you were wrong about that little girl," he said. Then he described case after suspicious case and asked, "How many 51-As have you filed?" Shannon said he didn't know; he'd have to look at the records. "I've read the records," Truman said. "None." When he pressed him on the private files, Shannon was noncommittal. He told Truman he was reluctant to let him see them because he was worried about patient confidentiality. More than one of Truman's colleagues asked, with a mixture of admiration and concern, if he planned to practice in Massachusetts after his fellowship. No, he told them, he would return home to Florida. Good idea, they said.

Truman's discovery of so many unreported suspicious cases—including many that came after the Munchausen pattern was well-known in the field—put Shannon in an almost untenable position. If he and Kelly had in fact gone to the trouble of documenting their concerns, then why hadn't they reported them, as the law in Massachusetts and most other states has required since the 1970s? The other choice—that they'd had no concerns, or too few to report—suggested in some cases incompetence or negligence. This seemed especially likely in a case such as Emily, who ultimately died in the face of blatant implications of child abuse by her mother and persistent efforts to save her by Truman and others. As it was for Steinschneider, the ultimate issue for both Shannon and Kelly was what they chose to see and not to see, and what they might have known or suspected and kept to themselves. Shannon in particular had a great deal at stake in the fallout from the Hoyt case. Steinschneider's and Kelly's reputations within the field had long since been diminished by their zealotry and their conspicuous associations with the monitoring industry. Shannon, however, had maintained an image of aloof high-mindedness—"His focus was too narrow, not questioning enough, it made me uneasy," he said of Steinschneider—but ultimately he could not escape the same questions of basic medical responsibility as those posed to Steinschneider by the exposure of the Hoyt case.

As this drama was playing out within Mass General, Shannon considered his official posture. It was by coincidence that we interviewed him in the midst of these events—but months before we became aware of them. So as we questioned Shannon about his twenty years of research on SIDS and apnea, and about the possible role of child abuse in that research, we had no way to know the actual context of what seemed to be his remarkable candor. Told that Kelly had disavowed any knowledge of suspicious cases, Shannon seemed eager to distance himself from his longtime protégée and partner. He freely acknowledged—publicly for the first time—that they may well have been dealing on a number of occasions with Munchausen infanticides that were never reported.

"Even before '77 [when such behavior was first identified and named], we had a family that raised Munchausen," Shannon said. "It was one of the first babies we saw. He came from a family where there had been [prior] SIDS cases in the family. The question was what to do about the next baby. We had that baby transferred down here from New Hampshire, and I talked about the possibility of factitious illness with the physician. If we ever had evidence, we would intervene." But they did not intervene in this case, and the baby later became the fourth in his family to die. "It was a naval family and they got transferred to Philadelphia. The baby in question came in DOA there. The mother was going to the naval base and she got stuck in traffic and the baby died in the car."

With some slight variation of detail, that was one of the cases Kelly had cited as evidence of "family clustering" of SIDS when she testified for Waneta Hoyt. Shannon acknowledged it was not a unique case. "There were several others that we suspected," he continued. "One was a third baby after two SIDS deaths, and the question arose. It was a case from Maine. We were suspicious because we couldn't find anything wrong with the baby. The mother took the baby back home alone. She brought him into a small hospital on the coast, DOA. I asked her to come down to talk, and I remember the chill that came through me. I asked the mom how she felt. She said, 'I think God put me in the world to make angels.' The physician in Maine didn't want to report it."

It seems likely that Shannon, faced with Truman's accusations, was anxious to publicly establish his awareness of child abuse. But he also appeared to recognize the problem this raised for him: his failure to act in the cases he himself was now calling suspicious. In the case of the baby from Maine, he passed the responsibility on to the referring physician. But apparently neither these cases nor the landmark work of such colleagues as David Southall and Carol Lynn Rosen influenced Shannon's thinking about the most recent death. In our interview—just weeks after Emily died but eight months before we learned of it—he said: "I have seen a number of kids with a rare seizure disorder that affects the breathing muscles. By the time I see them they've been through a round of doctors. Three got cardiac pacemakers. Three were put on anticonvulsants. Of the three on pacemakers, one had a SIDS death."

In retrospect, it appears that Shannon was alluding to Emily—that he believed she died of a "rare seizure disorder," despite the implantation of a pacemaker that was found to be working and despite considerable circumstantial evidence of fatal child abuse. It also seems he considered the two-year-old's death to be due to SIDS, even though since 1991 the federal government has applied the term only to children under one year of age whose deaths remain unexplained after thorough autopsies, death-scene investigations, and examination of the clinical history. We tried to clarify his view of this case as well as other issues raised by Truman's experience, but Shannon didn't respond to half a dozen requests for a follow-up interview, and we were left to consider something he had said in the earlier conversation. He had mentioned that his own daughter died suddenly and without explanation at twenty-nine, and that his wife died abruptly of a stroke. "I think there are mechanisms of sudden death that we just don't understand," he said. "I don't know if it's the heart, the lungs, the brain—or all of them. I think that anything is possible."

The Truman files and Shannon's belated if equivocal acknowledgments shed new light on why the Harvard research of the 1970s and 1980s (and some that Kelly has published with other doctors in the 1990s) often seemed to raise more questions than it answered. Most notable is the 1986 presentation to the NIH consensus conference. In this report, prepared by Denise Strieder, the Mass General doctors said that because forty-one babies had died after being evaluated by their internationally recognized apnea program since 1973—yielding a death rate of 3.2 per thousand babies, twice the national SIDS rate at the time—it confirmed an association between apnea and SIDS. But the new discoveries and the weight of modern experience—including the illuminating case of Waneta Hoyt—suggest there may have been other reasons why the Mass General program witnessed so much death.

There is now this maxim in forensic pathology: One unexplained infant death in a family is SIDS. Two is very suspicious. Three is homicide. But at Mass General, the maxim has been: One death is SIDS. Two deaths is SIDS. Three deaths is SIDS—apparently ad infinitum.

The 1986 report included twenty-eight families that had two or more deaths attributed to SIDS between 1973 and 1986—another huge number that Kelly in particular uses to argue that SIDS runs in families. Her well-known posture is one reason Mass General drew so many referrals over the years from pediatricians in the Northeast encountering families with previous infant deaths. According to the paper she and Shannon published with Joseph Oren in *Pediatrics* the following year, two of these twenty-eight families went on to have a third death; two others had a third *and* a fourth. (In addition, six parents said they had had to either resuscitate or vigorously stimulate their third child.) Out of this experience came the Shannon-Kelly team's widely quoted calculation that babies born into families with two previous deaths had an 18 percent chance of dying themselves. In fact, they had this high risk, but perhaps not for the reasons the Harvard doctors thought. Totaling all these deaths (including those of all the prior siblings who died before their families were referred to Mass General) yields the staggering possibility that these doctors may have been dealing with families in which there were as many as sixty-two infanticides among them—all before 1986. "Siblings of two or more SIDS infants form an extremely high-risk group," their report to the NIH said with unintended acuity. They "require extraordinary care.... These infants should be studied with all available medical resources...."

A decade later, Kelly still considers these cases compelling evidence of familial SIDS. Shannon, however, now acknowledges it is possible that the fourteen babies in the 1987 paper were victims of murder rather than SIDS. "You'd have to ask if any are infanticide," he said. "We just didn't know."

Massachusetts General emerges as a particularly vivid textbook case of the predicament that confronts pediatricians and other doctors who come face to face with suggestions of hidden child abuse and murder. It appears that Kelly and Shannon and their colleagues have faced it more often than most because they unwittingly have made their prestigious program a lure to the kind of child abusers who feed on the apnea and familial SIDS theories that are its bedrock. In the Shannon-Kelly team, some mothers have found the allies they needed. In their babies, the doctors have found the data they needed. Locked in this symbiosis, Massachusetts General appears to have become a Munchausen haven, while contaminating the research of SIDS with highly dubious data.

Six months after finishing his Harvard fellowship and taking up the practice of pediatric critical care in Tallahassee, Florida, Thomas Truman returned to Boston in one final effort to examine Daniel Shannon's private files. Shannon did turn over some files from the pulmonary lab at that point, but they consisted of innocuous cases. Several months later, in mid-1997, Truman finished his research paper and submitted it for publication in *Pediatrics*.

———

A few days after she was sentenced by Judge Vincent Sgueglia, Waneta Hoyt was moved from the Tioga County Jail to live out her life as an inmate of the Bedford Hills Correctional Facility, situated nearly two hundred miles away, in the suburbs north of New York City. Her husband, Tim, visited her each weekend, and at home he accepted thousands of dollars' worth of collect calls that he could not afford to pay for. Her son Jay also visited, though less frequently. Those around him saw that he was in obvious torment, but they felt helpless to alleviate his pain. As best as could be determined, his mother did not heed Judge Sgueglia's parting words to her.

In a conversation at Bedford Hills three months after her arrival, Waneta said her health was not good, and Tim complained that the authorities had ignored her problems until Charles Ewing intervened in her behalf. Asked if the state facility was more comfortable than the jail in Owego, Waneta replied, "Owego sucks." Had she encountered her fellow inmate Marybeth Tinning? A few times, she said, but she was not friendly. "She keeps to herself mostly," Waneta said. "She's . . . different." Waneta continued to claim her innocence, but in a way that seemed obligatory. There was about her a vague air of blitheness; she did not seem all that unhappy in prison.

But a final postscript began to unfold fifteen months later. In March of 1997, Waneta's physical complaints brought her to the Westchester division of New York Hospital. There, tests revealed that this time she was indeed ill— and gravely so. She had an advanced case of pancreatic cancer. To those who had known her through the years, as well as those who knew her only in the end, it seemed a last twist of fate in the unhappy saga of her life.

In another New York State prison hundreds of miles away, Stephen Van Der Sluys remained many years from parole and still in the peripheral consciousness of his ex-wife and three surviving children, who lived modestly in a small apartment in Mechanicville. The children, ranging in age from nine to thirteen at the time the Hoyt case pulled their father back into the news, thought about him now and then. They referred to him as Steve, and never visited him. Their mother, who had not remarried, did not lie to them about why he was in prison. She showed them pictures of Heath, Heather, and Vickie. But the first of the Van Der Sluys children to survive, Shane, who was five when his father was convicted of killing two of his siblings, was showing the first sign that he might want to see him someday. Shane's sister Jennifer didn't remember her father, and Corey, born after he was arrested, had never met him. They were amazed to think that their oldest brother would have been almost twenty.

The Hoyt case reopened painful wounds for Jane Bowers and her parents.

Jane seemed in some ways still closely connected to those three years when she lost her first three children. She recalled the details almost matter-of-factly one day in her parents' kitchen, but then broke into tears when the conversation turned to her thoughts at the time. "Why didn't I listen to you?" she cried to her father, falling onto his shoulder. Jim Bowers hugged his daughter. "It's okay, Janey, it's okay," he said, his voice breaking. "You did the best you could." It had been eighteen years since the first death, sixteen since the last. This was the first time they had had this conversation.

Life in Tioga County returned to the routines of the anonymous American community it had been before Waneta Hoyt drew the attention of the outside world.

Bob Miller and Ray Urbanski retreated to their solo law practices. Miller tried to let his ill-fated defense of Waneta Hoyt slip into memory and spent as much time as possible on his cattle ranch in Chemung County.

Bob Simpson went back to prosecuting the rural crimes that arrived on his desk and covering his share of the little village courts around Owego. "Let's go out here and talk about this," he said to a defendant one day soon after he'd won five murder convictions that got on the front page of *The New York Times*. He guided the young man out of the Owego village courtroom to talk about that little speeding situation. The routineness of it seemed comforting to him. But Simpson also knew he'd just experienced the highlight of his career. He said as much when he presided over Bob Courtright's retirement party a few months later. When he talked about the Hoyt case to a couple of hundred of Courtright's friends and colleagues at the Owego VFW hall, there was a touch of wistfulness in his voice. The case would stand alone for both of them. (Nor was it bad for Sue Mulvey's career. With Courtright's retirement, she was promoted to senior investigator, overseeing investigations in Tioga County.) But for Simpson, the case lived on, after a fashion. During the trial, he had caught the eye of a reporter for *People* magazine, an effervescent young woman named Maria Eftimiades, and the feeling was mutual. So now the country prosecutor was driving his old brown Honda down to New York City on the weekends.

Bill Fitzpatrick came down from Syracuse with Pete Tynan for Courtright's retirement party and stepped up to the dais to present him with a plaque bearing the names of the five Hoyt children. It would be Fitzpatrick's last visit to Tioga County, this place he'd found on a map the day three years before when he realized he could not be the one prosecuting Waneta Hoyt. For Fitzpatrick, though, there was a piece of poetic justice. Shortly before the Hoyt trial, a young man in Syracuse had seen him on a network news segment about the case and decided to approach him with a story of his own. Leonard Hare had long believed that his mother had murdered his two brothers—a baby in 1964, and a three-year-old in 1967, the year Hare was born. Fitzpatrick wasted no time exhuming the bodies; a new autopsy revealed that the baby had a fractured skull. A week before Waneta Hoyt went on trial, Fitzpatrick's investigators confronted the children's mother, Dorothy Mae King, and she confessed to beating the baby to death and choking the toddler. But Fitzpatrick found his case to be legally weaker than the one Simpson had against Waneta Hoyt, and he eventually accepted an unusually lenient plea bargain: two counts of manslaughter; six years at Bedford Hills. Meanwhile, and to the expressed concern of local SIDS activists, the new Onondaga County medical examiner, Dr. Sigmund Menchel, announced that he would begin a review of the records of every death involving a child in the county since the 1960s.

In Alfred Steinschneider's part of the world, as in Waneta Hoyt's, the fallout of the guilty verdict was interwoven with layers of regret, recrimination, and ambiguity. There were many among his colleagues who wished they had seen in 1972 what they saw now. One of them judged that Steinschneider had set the field back ten years. Twenty, thought another. "He will take apnea to his grave," said yet another.

There were, however, those who believed the crimes of Waneta Hoyt had nothing to do with the value of the theory. Researchers continue to pursue a variety of respiratory theories, exploring such ideas as the effect of overheating and whether some SIDS babies have been forced to rebreathe air from a pocket formed by soft bedding. Meanwhile, tapes of some babies who have died while on event-recording monitors indicate that their hearts stopped before their breathing ceased, implying to some researchers an underlying and perhaps developmental cardiac defect that may account for a percentage of SIDS deaths. The only thing that can be said for certain is that the ultimate mechanisms of SIDS remain as elusive as ever. There still is no test for SIDS, no way to use apnea or anything else to predict or prevent death. In the end, as in the beginning, the lives and deaths of the H. babies had nothing to do with SIDS. By the time of their mother's murder convictions, the latest research showed that parents should concern themselves not with apnea, but with something much simpler.

In June 1996, the National Institute of Child Health and Human Development announced that in the four years since American pediatricians had begun instructing parents to put their newborns to sleep on their backs or sides rather than on their stomachs—and two years into the national "Back to Sleep" campaign—the SIDS rate had plummeted 30 percent. It was the first significant decrease ever recorded and represented 1,500 saved lives a year. By the 1990s, epidemiologists had fixed the number of annual SIDS deaths at between 5,000 and 6,000. With the drop that followed the sleep position campaign, the number was down to fewer than 4,000. The data's clear implication was that the medical community had finally come upon a method of preventing at least some SIDS—the closest thing to the breakthrough the SIDS world had sought since its inception. Meanwhile, mounting evidence suggested an important role for cigarette smoking. A baby's exposure to smoke could double or even triple the risk of SIDS.

Still, a tinge of regret shadows the back-to-sleep idea's success. Though researchers had suggested it as far back as the 1960s, the idea had not been able to rise above the clamor over the apnea theory. Reports from the Netherlands in the 1970s, for instance, had noted a rise in SIDS that followed an increased popularity in putting babies to bed on their stomachs in that country. But not until the mid-1980s, as apnea fell out of favor, did the back-to-sleep idea begin to spread, and it didn't reach American shores for another few years. The lag suggests another unfortunate consequence of the SIDS world's preoccupation with the apnea theory, and for a generation of SIDS parents, a tragic one.

Moreover, Steinschneider's impact, and that of physicians such as Shannon and Kelly, continues to be powerful deep into the 1990s. Many thousands of babies still sleep with monitors as a defense against SIDS—no small number of them siblings of SIDS victims whose parents worry that it can happen again. The fear instilled in 1972 runs deep. The newer monitors are more sophisticated; they can record large amounts of cardiorespiratory information. But there is no evidence to suggest that they are any more capable of saving lives than the monitor Steinschneider sent home with Molly Hoyt on the night of May 8, 1970.

In 1995, Healthdyne celebrated its twenty-fifth anniversary. Its chairman, Parker Petit, remained in charge of the SIDS Alliance. A history of Healthdyne commissioned by the company for its silver anniversary noted that the company had sponsored an annual conference of prematurity researchers, and that Petit had been instrumental in drawing federal funds to SIDS research. In 1985, he personally gave a million dollars to endow a chair in biomedical engineering at the Georgia Institute of Technology. "Healthdyne is driven by the goal to reduce suffering and improve patients' quality of life," the corporate history said. "Growth in revenues and profits are the means to that end."

Ultimately, for some people, the entire apnea affair was a long lesson in epistemology—how we know what we know. When Janice Ophoven first became involved in the Hoyt case in 1993, she gave the Upstate records of Molly and Noah to her pediatric colleague at the Children's Hospital of Saint Paul, Dr. Stephen Boros. He was one of the country's apnea specialists who had found it useful to also become expert in Munchausen syndrome by proxy. He had written and lectured extensively on the subject. After reviewing the records, Boros assured Ophoven that these babies had no problems with apnea and agreed all indications pointed to murder. Then, with a degree of professional outrage, he made the case an object lesson. Handing out Steinschneider's paper, he urged his medical students at the University of Minnesota not to believe everything written in the stacks of professional journals they would see during their careers. Scrutinize the data, he lectured. Question the conclusions. Be careful out there.

Steinschneider himself remained indefatigable. He continued the work of his American SIDS Institute as if nothing had changed. His glossy quarterly bulletin, a direct-mail appeal to many thousands of potential donors across the country, contained news of his perennial fight against SIDS, and of the gala dinners and celebrity endorsements financing it. Members of the Atlanta Braves and corporations such as Coca-Cola were reliable benefactors. Meanwhile, the SIDS Institute received regular referrals from the clinical faculty of the Emory University pediatrics department, whose residents rotated through the center as part of their training. "All of our residents go down one afternoon a week to interview families and learn about monitoring," explained faculty member Gary Freed, a Steinschneider supporter. At the same time, however, Steinschneider remained the adversary of other physicians and SIDS professionals who bristled at the reports that surfaced among them periodically that he was still telling parents that he could prevent SIDS. "What he says and what he puts in writing are two different things," says one of his longtime foes, Denise Brooks, an influential Georgia SIDS educator. "When I challenged him, he said, 'It's all in the marketing.'"

But sometimes he does put it in writing, after a fashion. Since 1995, Steinschneider has produced and distributed a brochure that includes the erroneous statement, "We now know that the majority of babies who die of SIDS are not normal before birth." It says that some babies exhibit "symptoms" of SIDS that can be used to save them, that siblings of SIDS victims are among those at increased risk, and that home monitors have lowered the SIDS rate in such "high-risk" infants. The brochure—the American SIDS Institute's main piece of literature, titled "SIDS: Toward Prevention and Improved Infant Health"—contains not a single mention of sleep position. Half a million pamphlets have been sent to pediatricians' waiting rooms across the country and to anyone who calls the SIDS Institute for information.

Though the arrest of Waneta Hoyt forced Steinschneider to defend himself as never before, nobody who knew him was surprised to see that it had not induced any public self-doubt. But his intellectual processes remained elusive. "When you do research, you can easily be seduced into believing what you want to," he said one day in his office, without a trace of irony or recognition. He made it clear he was not talking about himself. "You can go up and down like a yo-yo. I had already done my yo-yo bit before I wrote that paper." Though his scientific quest had long resembled a ministry, he scoffed at how so much of the SIDS world remained locked in the faith of one unproven belief or another: "He believes, she believes—I don't care about anyone's religion." As for Waneta Hoyt: "I can't deny that twelve people found her guilty. But what's her guilt got to do with me?"

During the preparation of this book, Steinschneider was interviewed at length three times. The final encounter, nine months after Waneta Hoyt was convicted, lasted six hours, and Steinschneider's motivations grew more inscrutable as he talked—and yet in some ways more transparent: "Look, don't change history. A paper was written. Did I think it was important at the time I wrote it? No, I didn't. Quite the contrary. I didn't like it. Why? There were no data. I can remember thinking, 'Why am I writing this?' In fact, I wasn't even going to publish it because it can be misleading. I spoke to a colleague and his comment was, 'Al, you've got to publish it.' I said it's weak, and his comment was, 'You've got to share that.' I can't remember his name, but I can remember being in his office, someone on the faculty. Who made it an important paper? I didn't. If someone had said 'Al, this is silly,' I would have dropped it like a shot."

His manner was alternately contentious and avuncular. "Dr. Al," as he was known at the SIDS Institute, was looking ahead. The institute had gone through some rough times financially after Pete Petit pulled Healthdyne's direct support, but now it seemed to be on solid ground, and he had big plans. He envisioned satellite SIDS Institutes sprouting across the country, all of them raising money for the holy war against the elusive baby killer. At sixty-seven, he remained a man of high ambition and energy. He could look back, but what would be the sense of that? "Everybody sees history in a very different light and they're all real and they're all of value," he said. "They're *our* histories. It depends on who you are."

Some people thought the history of SIDS needed a footnote. Soon after Waneta Hoyt's conviction, Jerold Lucey asked Steinschneider to comment upon the outcome for publication in *Pediatrics*. It was Lucey's view that Tioga County had corrected one error. He hoped Steinschneider would correct the other one. He asked if he would write an erratum to his 1972 paper.

Steinschneider declined. He believed he had nothing to correct. These were babies at risk. And they had died. He could not change history.

Afterword

Social perception is always evolutionary. According to the Centers for Disease Control and Prevention, the homicide rate for children less than a year old climbed steadily from 1979 to 1991—from 4.86 to 9.24 per 100,000 babies. More than a growth in incidence, the statistics suggest heightened awareness and better medical and criminal investigation. They also mean that by the start of this decade, a baby a day was being murdered in America. But those were only the ones that were being uncovered.

If, as researchers such as David Southall and Roy Meadow have surmised from their studies, some five to ten percent of deaths attributed to SIDS are actually homicides, there may be several hundred undetected murders of babies each year in the United States. But which ones are they? SIDS can claim any baby, regardless of the social, racial, or economic circumstances into which that baby is born.

Therein lies the conspicuous ethical challenge that we faced in the research and writing of this book. Almost from the moment we first learned of Waneta Hoyt on the day of her arrest in March 1994, we heard pleas from many we met in the SIDS world—physicians and social workers from across the country, as well as SIDS parents themselves—that we take care to avoid casting suspicion on the thousands of unfortunate parents who have lost babies to SIDS. This issue was an enduring backdrop to our reporting. We agree that this much is clear: Though some babies who die suddenly and without explanation are the victims of homicide, they are a minority—and most probably a very small one. After decades of research by dedicated scientific investigators, several thousand babies still die mysteriously each year and legitimately fall into the category of Sudden Infant Death Syndrome. Their parents are utterly blameless. Though the central theme of this book is the emotionally charged intersection of SIDS and infanticide, and how the former has sometimes masked the latter, it is essential to bear this in mind.

Likewise, we hope that parents of SIDS babies, and others in the field, will recognize the value of bringing into view the cases and consequences examined here. It is a balancing act for the writers and readers both. Our new friend Carrie Sheehan, who lost her baby to crib death forty-two years ago in Seattle and has since worked professionally with younger SIDS parents, discerns two levels of pain that someone like Waneta Hoyt, a mother of healthy children, inflicts on parents who have not been so blessed. "To use SIDS to rationalize infanticide can turn the clock back to ignorance and isolation," she wrote to us. "But to a SIDS parent any form of child abuse is unspeakable. The act spreads like a poison, mocking the innocence of all families of newborns."

Ultimately, legal as well as medical authorities must take care to avoid the kind of cruel and reckless suspicion that marked earlier eras—while still thoroughly investigating reported cases of multiple SIDS and those presenting conspicuous circumstantial evidence of Munchausen by proxy. This is not the standard response now. In June 1996, the federal government issued guidelines intended, in part, to help pathologists, medical examiners, and coroners detect child abuse as well as other causes when dealing with deaths customarily attributed to SIDS. But the rigorous death-scene investigations the government recommended are still not routinely performed in most jurisdictions. Even when they are, and even when the circumstances are suspicious, cases are commonly left unresolved because everyone involved knows how hard it can be to prove parental abuse in court. As the Texas detective once told medical examiner Linda Norton: "I'm not wasting my time. The D.A. doesn't do child abuse." Another bias goes to the core of our expectations: "Our society has an endless need to see mothers as good," a Munchausen expert in Alabama, Dr. Marc Feldman, pointed out. This attitude becomes easy to adopt when there is no one speaking for the children—when the person who would normally press for action is the accused herself. Ultimately, of course, what is needed most is not prosecution so much as intervention. The patterns are now known. Murder may be one of the most preventable forms of sudden infant death.

The SIDS movement has brought one valuable moral obligation to the proceedings. No one should lose sight of the fact that the vast majority of SIDS deaths are not suspicious. But this fact also makes it easier for some other babies to slip away, victims of the perfect crime. That is the conundrum that has not changed in the thirty-five-year history of the SIDS movement—indeed, in the centuries since King Solomon brandished his sword the morning after the first recorded crib death.

Sources

This account is based primarily on interviews with more than three hundred people, on our own personal observations, and on several thousand pages of medical records, trial testimony, police files, private correspondence, and government documents. We also drew upon a wealth of professional research articles and books, publications by government agencies and private organizations, and newspaper and magazine articles going back to the 1940s. To the best of our knowledge, everything in the book is true. We have used unnamed sources very sparingly, and changed the names of only two people—the sixteen-year-old girl, referred to as Paula Byron, who became pregnant by Stephen Van Der Sluys in 1985, and the two-year-old we call Emily who died under suspicious circumstances in 1996.

We have tried to adhere rigorously to the standards of documentary journalism, while doing justice to the many compelling personal stories of those involved. At times, this meant reconstructing dialogue based on the memories of the participants; in other cases, we used records. The exchanges between Alfred Steinschneider and Waneta Hoyt in 1970 and 1971, for example, are based primarily on Molly's and Noah's Upstate hospital records, in which Steinschneider handwrote the information Hoyt gave him upon the babies' admissions and readmissions to the hospital. These notes were highly detailed, and in many cases included Hoyt's exact language. They were contained in the medical files that became part of the trial record after they were subpoenaed by investigators in 1992. These documents formed the cornerstone of everything we have written about the medical aspects of the Hoyt case and their relationship to the paper Steinschneider published in *Pediatrics*.

The descriptions of the deaths of the Hoyt children were pieced together from interviews and court testimony of surviving witnesses, including Waneta Hoyt herself. The conversation that occurred when Tioga County Coroner Arthur Hartnagel and Newark Valley Police Chief Howard Horton came to the Hoyts' trailer following Jimmy Hoyt's death in September 1968 is based on Tim Hoyt's recollection. In no case did we reconstruct a scene, an event, or a passage of dialogue without either the recollection of at least one person involved or a written record.

Our portrayal of the SIDS and apnea worlds was aided considerably by both a voluminous published record and the recollections of dozens of participants. The statements attributed to Steinschneider and other researchers at medical meetings are drawn from detailed records of those meetings. Specifically, the crucial quotations of Steinschneider at the 1969 SIDS conference on Orcas Island and the 1974 symposium in Toronto are reported verbatim from transcripts later published by the organizers. The correspondence between Steinschneider and Dr. Stuart Asch in 1971 and 1974 was obtained from Asch, and his letters are reproduced with his permission.

The chapters covering Steinschneider's post-1972 career and the evolution of the apnea theory and the monitoring phenomenon were developed primarily through original interviews but were enhanced by archival material from newspapers, magazines, and research journals, many of which are cited by name in the text. In addition, we used an array of documents given to us by those who participated in these events and public records obtained through Freedom of Information Act requests to the federal government. These included tax and incorporation records for the American SIDS Institute, Food and Drug Administration files on reports of apnea monitor malfunctions, and records of research grants received by Steinschneider.

With few exceptions, we interviewed every important figure in the book, in most cases several times and at length. As noted, we conducted three extended, tape-recorded interviews with Steinschneider. Two of these took place in his office at the American SIDS Institute in Atlanta, in September 1994 and January 1996; the third was conducted by telephone later in September 1994. We had two brief conversations with Waneta Hoyt at the Tioga County Jail during the months following her conviction in April 1995, and Richard Firstman spent two hours with her at the Bedford Hills Correctional Facility in December 1995. The ground rules were that this was to be simply a "visit"—to occur while her husband was also present, and without the conversation being tape-recorded. However, the visit was not off the record, and it yielded material that helped fill out various points in the narrative. (In Tioga County several months earlier, Tim Hoyt was interviewed alone for three hours and on tape.) Stephen Van Der Sluys did not respond to two letters sent to him at the state prison in Auburn, New York. The only important figure in the book who declined to be interviewed was Healthdyne Chairman Parker Petit. We sent our first letter to him in the fall of 1994 and our last in January of 1996, with numerous phone calls to his office in between. Ultimately his only response was to send us a copy of Healthdyne's corporate history, which we found useful.

Among the many published materials we drew upon for background and source material, two were particularly valuable. Abraham B. Bergman's political history of the SIDS movement, *The "Discovery" of Sudden Infant Death Syndrome: Lessons in the Practice of Political Medicine* (Praeger, 1986), provided us with a crucial understanding of the drive for federal support of SIDS research between 1971 and 1974, and hence, of the context of the wide acceptance of Steinschneider's paper in the years after it was published. *Hurting for Love,* by Herbert A. Schreier and Judith A. Libow (Guilford Press, 1993), was a valuable source about Munchausen syndrome by proxy. Also helpful were articles from the Syracuse *Post-Standard* and *Herald-Journal* and the Rochester *Democrat and Chronicle,* from which we derived background about Bill Fitzpatrick and the Van Der Sluys case; coverage of the Hoyt case by the Binghamton *Press & Sun-Bulletin, The New York Times,* the Syracuse *Post-Standard,* and WIXT-Channel 9 in Syracuse; and *Seasons of Change,* a local history of Tioga County, in particular a chapter about Richford written by local historian and Highland Cemetery caretaker Clarence Lacey.

Following is a selected list of additional published sources and references on the subjects of Sudden Infant Death Syndrome, the apnea theory, Munchausen syndrome by proxy, and infanticide:

BOOKS

Bergman, Abraham B., J. Bruce Beckwith, and C. George Ray, eds. *Sudden Infant Death Syndrome: Proceedings of the Second International Conference on Causes of Sudden Death in Infants.* Seattle: University of Washington Press, 1970.

DiMaio, Dominick J., and Vincent J. M. DiMaio. *Forensic Pathology.* Boca Raton: CRC Press, 1989.

Egginton, Joyce. *From Cradle to Grave.* New York: William Morrow, 1989.

Gudjonsson, Gisli. *The Psychology of Interrogations, Confessions and Testimony.* Chichester, England: John Wiley & Sons, 1992.

Guntheroth, Warren G. *Crib Death: The Sudden Infant Death Syndrome,* 2nd rev. ed. Mount Kisco, N.Y.: Futura Publishing Company, 1989.

Hausfater, Glenn, and Sarah Blaffer Hardy, eds. *Infanticide: Comparative and Evolutionary Perspectives.* New York: Aldine Publishing Company, 1984.

Levin, Alex V., and Mary S. Sheridan, eds. *Munchausen Syndrome by Proxy: Issues in Diagnosis and Treatment.* New York: Lexington Books, 1995.

Reece, Robert M. *Child Abuse: Medical Diagnosis and Management.* Philadelphia: Lea & Febiger, 1994.

Robinson, Robert R., ed. *SIDS 1974: Proceedings of the Francis E. Camps International Symposium on Sudden and Unexpected Deaths in Infancy.* Toronto: Canadian Foundation for the Study of Infant Deaths, 1974.

Schwartz, Peter J., David P. Southall, and Marie Valdes-Dapena, eds. *The Sudden Infant Death Syndrome: Cardiac and Respiratory Mechanisms and Interventions.* Annals of The New York Academy of Sciences, vol. 533, May 24–27, 1987, meeting. New York: New York Academy of Sciences, 1988.

Wedgwood, Ralph J., and Earl P. Benditt, eds. *Sudden Death in Infants: Proceedings of the Conference on Causes of Sudden Death in Infants—Seattle, September 1963.* Bethesda, Md.: U.S. Public Health Service, National Institutes of Health.

RESEARCH PUBLICATIONS

Adelson, Lester. "Slaughter of the Innocents: A Study of Forty-Six Homicides in Which the Victims Were Children." *The New England Journal of Medicine* 264, no. 26 (June 29, 1961).

Asch, Stuart S. "Crib Deaths: Their Possible Relationship to Post-Partum Depression and Infanticide." *Journal of the Mount Sinai Hospital* 35, no. 3 (May–June 1968).

Asch, Stuart S., and Lowell J. Rubin. "Postpartum Reactions: Some Unrecognized Variations." *American Journal of Psychiatry* 131, no. 8 (August 1974).

Bass, Millard, et al. "Death-Scene Investigation in Sudden Infant Death." *The New England Journal of Medicine* 315, no. 2 (July 10, 1986).

Berger, David. "Child Abuse Simulating 'Near-Miss' Sudden Infant Death Syndrome." *The Journal of Pediatrics* 95, no. 4 (October 1979).

Bergman, Abraham, J. Bruce Beckwith, and C. George Ray. "The Apnea Monitor Business." *Pediatrics* 56, no. 1 (July 1975).

Boros, Stephen J., and Larry C. Brubaker. "Munchausen Syndrome by Proxy: Case Accounts." *FBI Law Enforcement Bulletin* (June 1992).

Brooks, John. "Apnea of Infancy and Sudden Infant Death Syndrome." *American Journal of Diseases of Children* 136, no. 11 (November 1982).

DiMaio, Vincent J. M., and Charles G. Bernstein. "A Case of Infanticide." *Journal of Forensic Sciences* 19, no. 4 (October 1974).

Emery, John L. "Families in Which Two or More Cot Deaths Have Occurred." *The Lancet,* no. 8476 (February 8, 1986).

Emery, John L., Enid Gilbert, and Frederick Zugibe. "Three Crib Deaths, a Baby-Minder and Probable Infanticide." *Medicine, Science and the Law* 28, no. 3 (July 1988).

Foreman, D.M., and C. Farsides. "Ethical Use of Covert Videoing Techniques in

Detecting Munchausen Syndrome by Proxy." *British Medical Journal* 307, no. 6904 (September 4, 1993).

Guilleminault, Christian, et al. "Apneas During Sleep in Infants: Possible Relationship with Sudden Infant Death Syndrome." *Science* 190, no. 4215 (November 1975).

Harkess, J. R., et al. "Sudden Infant Death Syndrome: Four Deaths in One Family." *Journal of the Oklahoma State Medical Association* 81 (May 1988).

Henning, Lois, L. Hersher, and Alfred Steinschneider. "Impact of the Apnea Monitor on Family Life." *Report of NICHD Research Planning Workshop, Recognition of Infants at Risk for Sudden Infant Death: An Approach to Prevention.* Bethesda, Md.: Department of Health, Education, and Welfare, 1974. Publication no. (NIH) 76-1013.

Hopwood, J. Stanley. "Child Murder and Insanity." *The Journal of Mental Science* 73 (January 1927).

Hunt, Carl A. "Sudden Infant Death Syndrome and Subsequent Siblings." *Pediatrics* 95, no. 3 (March 1995).

Kelly, Dorothy H., Daniel C. Shannon, and C. O'Connell. "The Care of Infants with Near-Miss Sudden Infant Death Syndrome." *Pediatrics* 61, no. 4 (April 1978).

Kempe, Henry C., et al. "The Battered-Child Syndrome." *The Journal of the American Medical Association* 181, no. 1 (July 7, 1962).

Krugman, Richard D., et al. Committee on Child Abuse and Neglect. "Distinguishing Sudden Infant Death Syndrome from Child Abuse Fatalities." *Pediatrics* 94, no. 1 (July 1994).

Light, Michael J., and Mary S. Sheridan. "Munchausen by Proxy and Apnea (MBPA)." *Clinical Pediatrics* 29, no. 3 (March 1990).

Limerick, Sylvia R. "Sudden Infant Death in Historical Perspective." *Journal of Clinical Pathology* 45, no. 11 (November 1992).

Lipton, Earle L., Alfred Steinschneider, Julius Richmond. "The Autonomic Nervous System in Early Life." *The New England Journal of Medicine* 273, no. 3 (July 15, 1965).

Little, George A., et al. *Infantile Apnea and Home Monitoring.* Full report of Consensus Development Conference on Infantile Apnea and Home Monitoring. Bethesda, Md.: National Institutes of Health, 1986.

Market Intelligence. "World Fetal, Neonatal, and Infant Monitor Markets." Mountainview, Calif.: Market Intelligence Research Corporation, 1992.

Meadow, Roy. "Munchausen Syndrome by Proxy—The Hinterland of Child Abuse." *The Lancet,* no. 8033 (August 13, 1977).

———. "Suffocation, Recurrent Apnea, and Sudden Infant Death." *The Journal of Pediatrics* 117, no. 3 (September 1990).

Moseley, Kathryn L. "The History of Infanticide in Western Society." *Issues in Law & Medicine* 1, no. 5 (1986).

Myers, Steven A. "The Child Slayer." *Archives of General Psychiatry* 17 (August 1967).

Naeye, Richard L. "Pulmonary Arterial Abnormalities in the Sudden Infant Death Syndrome." *The New England Journal of Medicine* 289, no. 22 (November 29, 1973).

———. "Hypoxemia and the Sudden Infant Death Syndrome." *Science* 186, no. 4166 (November 29, 1974).

Norton, Linda. "Child Abuse." *Clinics in Laboratory Medicine—Symposium on Forensic Pathology* 3, no. 2 (June 1983).

Oren, Joseph, Dorothy H. Kelly, and Daniel C. Shannon. "Identification of a High-Risk Group for Sudden Infant Death Syndrome Among Infants Who Were Resuscitated for Sleep Apnea." *Pediatrics* 77, no. 4 (April 1986).

———. "Familial Occurrence of Sudden Infant Death Syndrome and Apnea of Infancy." *Pediatrics* 80, no. 3 (September 1987).

Peterson, Donald R., et al. "The Sudden Infant Death Syndrome: Repetition in Families." *The Journal of Pediatrics* 97, no. 2 (August 1980).

Resnick, Phillip. "Murder of the Newborn: A Psychiatric Review of Neonaticide." *American Journal of Psychiatry* 126, no. 10 (April 1970).

Rosen, Carol Lynn, et al. "Two Siblings with Recurrent Cardio-Respiratory Arrest: Munchausen Syndrome by Proxy or Child Abuse?" *Pediatrics* 71, no. 5 (May 1983).

———. "Child Abuse and Recurrent Infant Apnea." *The Journal of Pediatrics* 109, no. 6 (December 1986).

Savitt, Todd L. "The Social and Medical History of Crib Death." *Journal of the Florida Medical Association* 66, no. 8 (August 1979).

Schechtman, Vicki L., et al. "Sleep Apnea in Infants Who Succumb to the Sudden Infant Death Syndrome." *Pediatrics* 87, no. 6 (June 1991).

Shannon, Daniel C., and Dorothy H. Kelly. "SIDS and Near-SIDS" (two parts). *The New England Journal of Medicine* 306, nos. 16 and 17 (April 22 and 29, 1982).

Sheridan, Mary S., ed. *The NAAP Handbook of Infant Apnea and Home Monitoring.* Waianae, Hawaii: National Association of Apnea Professionals, 1992.

Southall, David P., et al. "Apnoeic Episodes Induced by Smothering: Two Cases Identified by Covert Video Surveillance." *British Medical Journal* 294 (June 27, 1987).

Steinschneider, Alfred. "Prolonged Apnea and the Sudden Infant Death Syndrome: Clinical and Laboratory Observations." *Pediatrics* 50, no. 4 (October 1972).

———. "Sleep Apnea and the Sudden Infant Death Syndrome: An Overview of a Research Program." *Report of NICHD Research Planning Workshop, Recognition of Infants at Risk for Sudden Infant Death: An Approach to Prevention.* Bethesda, Md.: Department of Health, Education, and Welfare, 1974. Publication no. (NIH) 76-1013.

———. "Nasopharyngitis and Prolonged Sleep Apnea." *Pediatrics* 56, no. 6 (December 1975).

———. "Nasopharyngitis and the Sudden Infant Death Syndrome." *Pediatrics* 60, no. 4 (October 1977).

———, Steven L. Weinstein, and Earl Diamond. "The Sudden Infant Death Syndrome and Apnea/Obstruction During Neonatal Sleep and Feeding." *Pediatrics* 70, no. 6 (December 1982).

Valdes-Dapena, Marie. "The Pathologist and the Sudden Infant Death Syndrome." *American Journal of Pathology* 106, no. 1 (January 1982).

Willinger, Marian, et al. "Infant Sleep Position and Risk for Sudden Infant Death Syndrome: Report of Meeting Held January 13 and 14, 1994, National Institutes of Health." *Pediatrics* 93, no. 5 (May 1994).

MAGAZINE AND NEWSPAPER ARTICLES

Bearak, Barry. "A Mother Who Lost Five Babies." *Los Angeles Times,* 22 May 1994.

Brandon, M. H. "A Crib Monitor for Mary Melinda." *The Saturday Evening Post,* October 1982.

Cadwalader, Mary H. "One after Another." *Life,* 12 July 1963.

Clark, Matt. "Crib Death." *Newsweek,* 5 January 1976.

Goldstein, Marilyn. "The Fight Against SIDS." *Parents,* May 1982.

"Healthdyne Gains with Crib Monitor." *The New York Times,* 5 March 1983.

"Integrity." *Iowa Engineer,* Fall 1994.

Johnson, Joyce. "Death Runs in the Family." *New York,* 10 April 1995.

Keister, Edwin Jr. "The Black Box That Guards Debbie Whitney's Life." *Today's Health,* October 1974.

Klemesrud, Judy. "Tragedy With an Aftermath of Guilt." *The New York Times,* 19 June 1972.

LeBlanc, Rena Dictor. "Somebody Help My Baby!" *Good Housekeeping,* July 1972.

Marx, Jean L. "Crib Death: Some Promising Leads but No Solution Yet." *Science,* August 1975.

Nieves, Evelyn. "In Prison, a Mother Proclaims Innocence in Babies' Deaths." *The New York Times,* 18 May 1995.

Palmeri, Christopher. "Born Again." *Forbes,* 23 December 1991.

Pousner, Michael. "Healthdyne Moved Off Critical List." *Atlanta Business Chronicle,* 20 January 1986.

Rodgers, Joann. "UM Loses Scientist Probing Crib Death." Baltimore *News American,* 5 December 1982.

Seide, Diane. "Unlocking the Mystery of Crib Death." *Parents,* November 1974.

"The Tenth Child." *Newsweek,* 15 January 1968.

Toufexis, Anastasia. "When Is Crib Death a Cover for Murder?" *Time,* 11 April 1994.

"Trouble at Top of Healthdyne." *The New York Times,* 6 July 1984.

Van Biema, David. "Parents Who Kill." *Newsweek*, 14 November 1994.

Weinstock, Cheryl Pintzman. "Monitoring and Sudden Infant Death." *Newsday*, 5 December 1983.

York, Michelle. " 'I'm a Victim of Circumstance,' Hoyt Says in Jail Interview." Binghamton *Press & Sun-Bulletin*, 12 May 1995.

Young, Patrick. "Research Stalks a Baby Killer." *The National Observer*, 20 April 1974.

Acknowledgments

We owe a great debt of gratitude to the many people whose contributions, large and small, made this book possible. A number of them became something more than sources during the three years we worked on the project, and they have our appreciation and affection.

Obviously, the book would not exist if not for what Linda Norton saw that others didn't and for what Bill Fitzpatrick and Bob Simpson did about it. We thank all for their lucid accounts of the experience; each devoted many hours to the task. The cooperation of defense lawyers Bob Miller and Ray Urbanski was also vital to our portrait of the case. They made our work easier in many ways. Thanks are also owed to Bob Courtright, and to the members of the New York State Police who worked under him on the Hoyt case in Tioga County. Peter Tynan, meanwhile, was always a friendly face and a helpful hand in Syracuse.

Loretta, Chuck, and George Hoyt have our deepest thanks both for their memories and their kindnesses, as well as our admiration for the strength of character they demonstrated throughout a painful ordeal. Thanks also to Arthur and Natalie Hilliard, who were good to us under extremely difficult circumstances. Likewise, we extend our appreciation to Jane Bowers and her parents, James and Anita, who spent many hours talking about someone they would sooner forget, Jane's former husband Stephen Van Der Sluys.

Among the former members of Upstate Medical Center's pediatric nursing staff, our special thanks go to Thelma Schneider and Gail Pfeiffer for the time, energy, and support they gave us. Their memories brought the chapters about Molly and Noah to life, and Thelma and her husband, Dr. Jack Schneider, were of invaluable help in the chapters covering Alfred Steinschneider's Syracuse years. In Baltimore, Dr. J. Tyson Tildon was generous with his time, his perceptions, and his files. In Washington, Jehu Hunter and Gil Hill provided us with valuable historical background. In Atlanta, Denise Brooks helped fill out the picture. And in Seattle, we thank Carrie Sheehan for both her perspective and her moral support.

This book would have been much diminished without the candid and trenchant recollections of three admirable physicians who play key roles in the events we describe: J. Bruce Beckwith, Jerold Lucey, and Marie Valdes-Dapena. We could not have made our way through the thicket of medical and political complexities of the SIDS world without them, and we benefited from their intelligence and integrity throughout the project. We also owe a great debt of gratitude to Dr. Andrew Steele, head of the infant apnea program at Long Island Jewish Medical Center, who became our friend, confidant, and apnea adviser. The deeper into the book we got, the more we came to depend on him for reality checks. Along with Bruce Beckwith and Jerry Lucey, he also helped us immeasurably by reading and commenting on large portions of the manuscript.

We didn't find our way to Dr. Tom Truman until four months after we had delivered the first draft of the manuscript, but he turned out to be, for us, one of the real heroes of this story. Not only did he have the strength of his convictions to pursue his remarkable and vital research at Massachusetts General, but with a good measure of his reputation at stake, he entrusted his story to us. We hope it has the effect he desires: to educate his peers and ultimately, perhaps, to save a few children.

For their various contributions and courtesies we also thank Harvey LaBar, Frank Budzielek, Julie Evans, Clarence Lacey, Patti Myers, Violet Metikulus, Judge Vincent Sgueglia, Pete Hoffmann, John Sherman, Jessica Mooney, Deborah Cosher, Michelle York, Sheryl Nathans, John Falitico, Saul Goldberg, Mary Dore, Andy Hanson, Ed Nizalowski, Alberta Weisz, Janice Jacobs, Lynne Rocha, Aaron Gowan, John Graham, and Drs. Michael Baden, Janice Ophoven, Vincent DiMaio, Abraham Bergman, George Little, and Stuart Asch. We thank, also, the many people of Tioga County who made us feel welcome in their community.

Closer to home, Paul Levitt was a sounding board from the beginning, and we repaid him for his always incisive counsel by asking him to read the entire first draft. He gamely did so, and the final product is better for his comments. Thanks, as well, to all our good friends and colleagues, including many at *Newsday,* whose encouragement carried us farther than they knew. We continually drew on the infinite reservoir of faith of our families, and in this we mean to include our most ardent cheering section, our children Allison, Amanda, and Jordan, whose patience with frequently distracted parents (who for a long time refused to tell them what the book was about) was amazing. Thanks to our agent, Jane Dystel, who was always in our corner. At Bantam Books, Lauren Field was the source of astute and meticulous counsel. Saralyn Smith provided another set of careful eyes. Finally, this book could not have had a more dedicated or skillful editor than Ann Harris, who was unflagging in her belief in us and the book we envisioned and whose intelligence and good judgment are reflected on every page.

Index